The Oxford Handbook of Hope

OXFORD LIBRARY OF PSYCHOLOGY

The Oxford Handbook of Hope

Edited by

Matthew W. Gallagher

Shane J. Lopez

OXFORD
UNIVERSITY PRESS

OXFORD

UNIVERSITY PRESS

Oxford University Press is a department of the University of Oxford. It furthers
the University's objective of excellence in research, scholarship, and education
by publishing worldwide. Oxford is a registered trade mark of Oxford University
Press in the UK and certain other countries.

Published in the United States of America by Oxford University Press
198 Madison Avenue, New York, NY 10016, United States of America.

Library of Congress Cataloging-in-Publication Data
Names: Gallagher, Matthew W., editor. | Lopez, Shane J., editor.
Title: The Oxford handbook of hope / edited by Matthew W. Gallagher, Shane J. Lopez.
Description: New York : Oxford University Press, [2018] | Series: Oxford library of psychology
Identifiers: LCCN 2017002545 | ISBN 9780199399314 (jacketed hardcover : alk. paper)
Subjects: LCSH: Positive psychology. | Hope.
Classification: LCC BF204.6 .O934 2017 | DDC 152.4—dc23
LC record available at https://lccn.loc.gov/2017002545

9 8 7 6 5 4 3 2 1

Printed by Sheridan Books, Inc., United States of America

CONTENTS

ABOUT THE EDITORS

Matthew W. Gallagher

Matthew W. Gallagher is an assistant professor in the Department of Psychology at the University of Houston. He received his doctorate in clinical and quantitative psychology from the University of Kansas in 2011 and was previously a staff psychologist in the Behavioral Science Division of the National Center for PTSD and Assistant Professor of Psychiatry at Boston University School of Medicine. His research focuses on the role of hope in promoting resilience to and recovery from emotional disorders, the development of novel treatments for PTSD and anxiety disorders, and the predictors and benefits of positive aspects of mental health. He is the author of over 80 articles, chapters and books and is a licensed psychologist.

Shane J. Lopez

Shane J. Lopez was a Gallup Senior Scientist and Research Director of the Clifton Strengths Institute. He received his doctorate in counseling psychology from the University of Kansas in 1998 and was previously faculty in the Counseling Psychology Program at the University of Kansas. He was a fellow of the American Psychological Association and the International Positive Psychology Association. His research focused on developing and disseminating hope and strengths promotion programs in schools, examining the impact of hope on engagement and well-being across the lifespan, and refining a model and measures of psychological courage. He published more than 100 articles and chapters, more than a dozen books, including *Making Hope Happen, The Oxford Handbook of Positive Psychology, Positive Psychological Assessment: A Handbook of Models and Measures*, and *Positive Psychology: The Scientific and Practical Explorations of Human Strengths*, and was a licensed psychologist.

CONTRIBUTORS

Michal Al-Yagon
School of Education
Tel Aviv University
Tel Aviv, Israel

Craig Anderson
Department of Counseling Psychology
Santa Clara University
Santa Clara, CA

Randolph C. Arnau
Department of Psychology
University of Southern Mississippi
Hattiesburg, MS

Meenakshi Balaraman
Department of Counseling Psychology
Santa Clara University
Santa Clara, CA

Steve Bisgaier
Institute for Graduate Clinical Psychology
Widener University
Chester, PA

Kristina Schmid Callina
Institute for Applied Research in Youth
Development
Tufts University
Boston, MA

Jennifer S. Cheavens
Department of Psychology
The Ohio State University
Columbus, OH

Malin Patricia Chromik
Department of Psychology
University of Hamburg
Hamburg, Germany

Brian P. Cole
Department of Psychology
University of Kansas
Lawrence, KS

Paul Davis
School of Life Sciences
Northumbria University
Newcastle upon Tyne, UK

Saarang Deshpande
Department of Science and Technology
Studies
Cornell University
Ithaca, NY

Lisa M. Edwards
Department of Counselor Education and
Counseling Psychology
Marquette University
Milwaukee, WI

David B. Feldman
Department of Counseling Psychology
Santa Clara University
Santa Clara, CA

Chris Feudtner
The Pediatric Advanced Care Team
The Children's Hospital of Philadelphia
Philadelphia, PA

Ron Freche
Clinical Psychology Program
University of Kansas
Lawrence, KS

Matthew W. Gallagher
Department of Psychology
Texas Institute for Measurement,
Evaluation, and Statistics
University of Houston
Houston, TX

Amber M. Gum
Department of Mental Health Law
and Policy
Louis de la Parte Florida Mental Health
Institute
University of South Florida
Tampa, FL

Henrik Gustafsson
Faculty of Health, Science and
Technology
Karlstad University
Karlstad, Sweden

Madison M. Guter
Department of Psychology
The Ohio State University
Columbus, OH

Douglas L. Hill
The Pediatric Advanced Care Team
The Children's Hospital of Philadelphia
Philadelphia, PA

E. Scott Huebner
Department of Psychology
University of South Carolina
Columbia, SC

Xi Jiang
Department of Psychology
University of Memphis
Memphis, TN

Todd B. Kashdan
Department of Psychology
George Mason University
Fairfax, VA

Jenny Y. Lee
Department of Psychology
University of Tulsa
Tulsa, OK

Laura J. Long
Department of Psychology
University of Houston
Houston, TX

Shane J. Lopez
Clifton Strengths Institute
School of Business
University of Kansas
Lawrence, KS

Malka Margalit
School of Education
Tel Aviv University
Tel Aviv, Israel;
School of Behavioral Sciences
Peres Academic Center
Rehovot, Israel

Susana C. Marques
Faculty of Psychology and Educational
Sciences
University of Porto
Porto, Portugal

Jessica B. McClintock
San Francisco, CA

Monica N. Montijo
LiveInFlow Consulting
Orange County, CA

Angela R. Mouton
LiveInFlow Consulting
Orange County, CA

Elise D. Murray
Institute for Applied Research in Youth
Development
Tufts University
Boston, MA

Kristin Koetting O'Byrne
School of Organizational Leadership
Abilene Christian University
Abilene, TX

Gabriele Oettingen
Department of Psychology
New York University
New York, NY;
Department of Psychology
University of Hamburg
Hamburg, Germany

Anthony D. Ong
Department of Human Development
Cornell University
Ithaca, NY

Kristin L. Otis
University of South Carolina
Columbia, SC

Jennifer Teramoto Pedrotti
Associate Dean for Diversity and
Curriculum
College of Liberal Arts
California Polytechnic State University
San Luis Obispo, CA

Leslie Podlog
Department of Health, Kinesiology and
Recreation
University of Utah
Salt Lake City, UT

Kevin L. Rand
Department of Psychology
Indiana University—Purdue University
Indianapolis
Indianapolis, IN

Michael Rapoff
Department of Pediatrics
University of Kansas Medical Center
Kansas City, KS

Heather N. Rasmussen
Department of Educational Psychology
University of Kansas
Lawrence, KS

Lorie A. Ritschel
Department of Psychiatry
University of North Carolina at Chapel
Hill School of Medicine
Chapel Hill, NC

Sage Rose
School of Health Sciences and Human
Service
Hofstra University
Hempstead, NY

Christopher S. Sheppard
Department of Psychology
University of North Carolina at
Chapel Hill
Chapel Hill, NC

Karrie A. Shogren
Department of Special Education
University of Kansas
Lawrence, KS

Hal S. Shorey
Institute for Graduate Clinical
Psychology
Widener University
Chester, PA

Nicole Sieben
School of Education
SUNY College at Old Westbury
Old Westbury, NY

David R. Sigmon
Hutchinson, KS

Nancy Snow
Institute for the Study of Human
Flourishing
University of Oklahoma
Norman, OK

C. R. Snyder
Department of Psychology
University of Kansas
Lawrence, KS

Taylor Standiford
Department of Human Development
Cornell University
Ithaca, NY

Scott R. Thien
Institute for Graduate Clinical
Psychology
Widener University
Chester, PA

Marcy Vandament
University of Kansas
Lawrence, KS

Marco Weber
Department of Psychology
Technical University Darmstadt
Darmstadt, Germany

Michael L. Wehmeyer
Beach Center on Disability
Department of Special Education
University of Kansas
Lawrence, KS

TABLE OF CONTENTS

HOPE: INFLUENCING THE LARGEST TERRAIN OF HEALTH AND WELL-BEING FOR THE GREATEST NUMBER OF PEOPLE

Todd B. Kashdan

I had no early talents for science. I had public speaking anxiety throughout my young adult years. I did not want to be a psychologist. My childhood role models were athletes (Don Mattingly), musicians (Fugazi), and mavericks such as Phillip K. Dick and Arnold Schwarzenegger. Following my family's financial world tradition, my first adult job was working on the floor of the New York Stock Exchange. And yet, here I am, with a clinical psychology PhD in 2004, in love with conducting research to understand the link between emotional disorders and well-being, improving the measurement of both, and refining naturalistic interventions where there can be therapy without therapists. And much of my time is spent giving presentations to large groups about science around the world. I offer this brief set of autobiographical details as a typical serpentine road across a 20-year time span. How can we best predict what leads people to uncover what matters most to them? How can we best predict who will overcome adversity to become stronger and clearer in their mission? How can we enable children, teenagers, and adults to stay on task, doing what matters most to them, while encouraging sufficient flexibility to switch courses when beneficial outcomes are best found elsewhere? Hope, as defined and operationalized by Dr. Rick Snyder, surpasses nearly every individual difference to capture psychological variability in healthy life trajectories.

People differ from one another on virtually any psychological dimension that can be imagined. As of this writing, there is a cultural push to increase mindfulness, be gritty, steer toward an ultimate purpose in life, support emotional intelligence trainings in the workplace, and create more opportunities for introverts. Each of these individual differences distinguishes how someone generally feels, thinks, and behaves. With hundreds of individual difference variables, scientists and practitioners can be paralyzed about what to measure and, more importantly, what to invest in as a strategy for improving vitality, social connections, meaningful contributions, and long-term happiness and well-being.

If we are interested in knowing which military recruits are likely to complete basic training, which college men are less likely to engage in high-risk sex, which adults are going to start and sustain a practice of physical exercise, and what best predicts superior academic, athletic, and work performance, turn to a nearly 30-year old body of research on hope. Hope research was spearheaded by the late Dr. Rick Snyder and expanded in new directions by one of his disciples, the late Dr. Shane Lopez (among dozens of other scientists). I had the fortune of having long-standing friendships with both of them, inspiring me to join the crusade of studying and enhancing hope in the world.

Hope is about energetically pursuing one's goals and being able to generate multiple strategies to devote effort and make progress. Essentially, Rick Snyder created an elegant formula:

Hope = Agency Thoughts × Pathways Thoughts

Having the motivation to pursue a well-defined goal, known as agency, is a starting point. For that energy to be dedicated to a goal, one must be able to formulate pragmatic routes to reach them and produce alternative courses in case there are obstacles or blockage. When a goal is ascribed particular personal meaning or centrality, such as alignment with core values or a purpose in life, this generates more intense and powerful agency and pathway thoughts.

The reason this formula is elegant is that such a small number of hope-related concepts are needed to capture a complex psychological phenomena that is implicit or explicit in nearly every facet of well-being—whether it is satisfying the basic need for belonging, competence, or autonomy, happiness, meaning and purpose in life, self-acceptance, personal growth, positive relations with others, or mental and physical health. Using experimental, longitudinal, experience-sampling, and intervention approaches, researchers have found hope to be a robust predictor of well-being, in all its forms.

Rick Snyder was, and is, the exemplar of hope. In 2004, my first talk as a psychologist was part of a symposium at the American Psychological Association titled *Gratitude and Hope: Emotional Pillars of Positive Psychology*. Rick Snyder spoke on hope as social commerce: how agency and pathway thinking pulls us toward other people, as allies to support goals and whose goals we can support. I spoke after him, nervously flipping through Powerpoint slides that were heavily laden with 10 bullet points of information. When I thanked the audience and returned to my seat next to Rick, he put an arm around me and whispered: "Nobody is going to know who is the professor and who is the graduate student; welcome to the club." In that moment, Rick enveloped me in his hope. He transferred hope to me. Many readers never met Rick. He is an unsung hero. Not just because of the profound research he conducted but because of his humility and generativity. Some of his mentorship was direct, such as Shane Lopez, who became the leading thinker of hope in the 21st century—creating interventions for children and older adults. Much of his mentorship was indirect, including consumers of his seminal articles and books. These consumers followed his blueprint for predicting and instilling healthy life trajectories in counseling clients, patients in hospitals, athletes in training, children in schools, workers in organizations, and human beings navigating the shoals of everyday life.

Hope should be receiving significantly more attention from scientists, practitioners, and policymakers. Let me offer a few explanations why this is not the case. The word *hope* might have been poorly chosen. Open the Oxford English Dictionary and *hope* is a synonym for *optimism*. But Rick Snyder's theory of hope is far more comprehensive than the layperson's usage. Optimism is about outcome expectancies. Someone believes that desirable goal-related outcomes are highly probable. An optimistic person believes positive events that occur can be attributed to internal, stable, and global forces. Choose either of these definitions of optimism. Neither definition captures the psychological flexibility of the highly hopeful person who regardless of his or her expectations is ready and willing to find a way to work around internal and external obstructions.

Another reason that hope is not being given sufficient attention is an unfortunate bias toward the new. Hope continues to outperform against cognitive, physical, emotional, and environmental factors in predicting success and fulfillment. But researchers have fallen in love with newer terms coined by psychologists. Take *grit*, which is operationalized as the passion and perseverance for long-term goals. If this appears to be a piece of the hope construct, that's because it is. Recent research has found that only the perseverance dimension of grit predicts performance and well-being, whereas the more unique dimension of *long-term consistency of interests* has nearly zero predictive power. What is effective (agency and pathways) is not new, and what is new (consistency of interests) is not effective. Take *distress tolerance*, which is operationalized as the ability to endure uncomfortable thoughts and feelings in order for problem-solving skills and goal-related pursuits to take place. If this appears to be a piece of the hope construct, that's because it is. To me, these new strands of research only provide further evidence for the longevity of hope theory. I find it unfortunate that this new work is artificially divorcing itself from 30 years of research. It is hard enough to keep abreast of recent scientific findings. When different terms are used for the same phenomena, the burden is placed on those of us who can benefit from this science.

With this new volume of 27 chapters, the theory, measurement, and cultivation of hope should return to a deserved place of prominence. We should never abandon rich psychological constructs that can predict a large amount of variance in a wide array of domains, settings, and populations. It is my hope that the current and next generation of thinkers pay careful attention to a body of evidence that is too compelling to ignore. Rick Snyder and Shane Lopez laid the groundwork for great potential discoveries. Let us continue to build on the strongest, hopeful shoulders of the past.

MEMORIAM: REMEMBERING SHANE J. LOPEZ: A LEGACY OF SPREADING HOPE

Matthew W. Gallagher

Shane J. Lopez passed away on July 23, 2016. He was born on April 4, 1970, in New Iberia, Louisiana, and was proud of his Cajun heritage. Shane is survived by his wife, Alli Rose Lopez, and their beloved son, Parrish. He is also survived by his sister, Crystal Gaudin Lopez, his brother Harry Lopez Jr., his father Harry Lopez Sr., many other family members, and numerous friends and colleagues who were fortunate to have known Shane. I was fortunate to have known Shane as a mentor, colleague, and friend. Shane passed away a few months before we finalized *The Oxford Handbook of Hope*, but his contributions were crucial and this handbook is just one of his many legacies of helping to share the science and practice of hope.

After earning a bachelor's degree in psychology from the University of Southwestern Louisiana, Shane attended the University of Kansas for his master's and doctoral degrees in counseling psychology. Shane's strengths as a scientist were quickly recognized at KU. He received numerous awards as a graduate student including the Brooks-Cole Award, given to the outstanding doctoral student in counseling psychology, and KU offered him a faculty position before he finished his internship to make sure that he remained at KU. Rick Snyder, the preeminent expert on the topic of hope at the time, mentored Shane in his early years at KU, and Rick and Shane went on to develop a remarkably productive and collaborative working relationship and a deeply meaningful friendship. Shane continued to flourish at KU, quickly rising to the rank of tenured full professor and making invaluable contributions to the KU counseling program and the education and training of his own advisees and many other students. Shane had a passion for mentoring and advised many students who have gone on to have successful careers as faculty and clinicians. Shane valued relationships, was great at developing and nurturing them, and was a wonderful role model for demonstrating the benefits and importance of helping others rather than just focusing on personal accomplishments. Shane was also an excellent teacher and won numerous awards for his teaching while at KU.

After a successful decade at the University of Kansas, Shane's ongoing collaborations with Donald Clifton and others at the Gallup organization ultimately led to Shane leaving academia to accept a position as Gallup's Senior Scientist in Residence and Research Director for the Clifton Strengths Institute. At Gallup, Shane collaborated with his dear friend Connie Rath and was able to apply his passion for helping individuals of all backgrounds, and particularly students, better understand their strengths and recognize how hope could help them accomplish their goals and dreams. One of his most impressive accomplishments was in guiding the development and execution of the Gallup Student Poll, which has now been used to measure and promote the hope, engagement, and well-being of more than 4 million students. While working at Gallup, Shane also published *Making Hope Happen* (Lopez, 2013), which represents his magnum opus in many ways and synthesized nearly two decades of creative and rigorous scholarship that Shane had done to best understand how to spread ripples of hope.

By every metric of professional success for academics, Shane was exceptional. He published more than 100 articles and chapters and more than a dozen books. These publications, many in collaboration with his dear friend Rick Snyder, included many of the most crucial publications in the field of positive psychology in the past two decades: including *The Handbook of Positive Psychology, The Encyclopedia of Positive Psychology, Positive Psychological Assessment,* and one of the first positive psychology textbooks for undergraduates. He was an award-winning teacher and mentor and was a fellow of the American Psychological Association and the International Positive Psychology Association. Shane was also a remarkable leader for the field of positive psychology and helped to organize many of the early conferences in the field of positive psychology, was on the board of directors of the International Positive Psychology Association, and served in many other leadership roles that helped to build the field of positive psychology.

Shane was also passionate about ensuring that the findings of educational and positive psychology were spread beyond academia and were used to actually improve the lives and education of youth. He was passionate about conducting applied research to bring the science of hope outside of the laboratory and into the classroom. He spoke regularly to teachers and educators throughout the United States and around the world and had a remarkable gift for distilling the essence of recent scientific findings so that they could best be applied to help others. Shane delivered multiple TEDx talks and other presentations in which he used his unique gifts to spread the findings of hope and positive psychology more broadly. Through all of these efforts, Shane was able to make sure that his scientific studies were brought to life and had an important impact on promoting hope, particularly in students.

Shane's professional accomplishments were just one aspect of his life and alone do not do justice to the positive impact he had. Shane led a rich life full of friendship and was a devoted husband and father. Meeting with Shane at La Prima Tazza or one of his other favorite coffee shops in Lawrence, Kansas, was always an interesting experience, as nearly every time we'd gather to chat about work we'd end up running into one of Shane's many friends who clearly cared deeply for him and appreciated having him in their life. My relationship with Shane began a decade ago at the University of Kansas. Rick Snyder was my graduate advisor and Shane's mentor, colleague, and friend, and after Rick unexpectedly passed away in January 2006, I reached out to Shane for guidance. Shane was not in my department, but he never hesitated in providing help, and I know that he played a similarly important role in supporting and promoting the careers of many others. Although Shane left academia for his position at Gallup shortly after we began working together, he remained an important mentor, and I was fortunate to be able to consider him a friend and to collaborate with him on variety of projects over the past decade. Despite his immense success, his kindness and generosity never wavered, and Shane continued to provide guidance and mentorship to colleagues and students worldwide.

Unbeknownst to many, Shane achieved his professional and personal success despite experiencing a series of debilitating health conditions. While in graduate school, Shane developed mononucleosis that led to chronic fatigue syndrome, which he struggled with for two years. In 2003, Shane was then diagnosed with West Nile virus. The effects of this virus and the subsequent complications that arose were debilitating and continued to impact him for years. For the last few years of his life Shane also struggled with severe depression. Throughout it all, Shane persevered with Alli by his side and with the support of numerous colleagues and friends such as Tom Krieshok. Shane's resilience was inspirational, and he continued to spread ripples of hope even while battling the series of illnesses.

As news of Shane's passing spread last July, the outpouring of messages from family, friends, and colleagues across the country and the world spoke to the remarkable impact that Shane had on many people's lives. Celebrations of Shane's legacy and impact were organized for the annual conventions of the American Psychological Association and the International Positive Psychology Association, and memorial services were held in Lawrence and in his hometown of New Iberia, Louisiana. At the service in New Iberia, held in the same church in which he married his dearly beloved wife Alli, family, friends, and colleagues gathered to celebrate his life. When asked during an interview Shane did a few years prior to his passing how he would like to be remembered, he said that "I would love for people to smile while telling stories of me at my funeral." That is exactly what took place. Childhood friends, beloved colleagues at KU and Gallup, and cherished former graduate students all shared stories of a life well lived and how Shane improved the lives of those around him.

Like Rick Snyder before him, Shane was a remarkable man who we lost too soon. Shane was fond of speaking about the importance of spreading ripples of hope. The many scientists, practitioners, and students he inspired to have the passion and skills to study and spread hope are just one of the many ways in which Shane leaves a legacy of spreading ripples of hope to bolster the hope and well-being of those around him. My last conversation with Shane was shortly before his passing. We spoke briefly about some remaining decisions regarding how best to finalize and finish this handbook but also spoke about Alli and Parrish. Shane was still struggling with depression at that time, but he never lost his passion for spreading hope, and his love for Alli and Parrish was always clear. Two things that were apparent then and that I will always remember about Shane are how much his face would light up when we spoke about Alli and Parrish and how passionate, generous, and effective he was in spreading ripples of hope. Shane was an inspirational mentor, colleague, and friend, and he is dearly missed.

Matthew W. Gallagher
Houston, Texas

The Oxford Handbook of Hope

PART I

Defining Hope

Introduction to the Science of Hope

Matthew W. Gallagher

Abstract

Hope has long been a topic of interest both within and outside of psychology. Although historical perspectives on hope were mixed, decades of research have now demonstrated that hope can be reliably measured, that hope is malleable, that hope promotes resilience, and that hope is beneficial across contexts and the lifespan. Rick Snyder developed the dominant model of hope that emphasizes agency and pathways thinking as the two core components of hope, and this model has provided the foundation for the scientific study of hope. The two most prominent scientists in the field of hope have now passed away, but hope remains a robust area of positive psychology that is being examined by scientists worldwide. This chapter introduces the goals of this handbook: to review what has been learned about the theory, measurement, promotion, and benefits of hope and to highlight important future directions in the science of hope.

Key Words: hope, agency, pathways, positive psychology, resilience

Hope is a concept that has long been a topic that has fascinated philosophers, scientists, and the general public. Although hope is now recognized as a robust source of resilience with many benefits, historical perspectives on hope were more mixed. One of the earliest discussions of the idea and potential benefits of hope was the myth of Pandora, in which hope represented the one potential source of strength that remained after Pandora opened the jar and unwittingly unleashed all of the evils upon humanity. Various religious and spiritual traditions have also identified hope as a virtue to be cherished and cultivated. Other historical perspectives framed hope as more of a naïve delusion that could be harmful. For example, Benjamin Franklin famously said that "he who lives upon hope will die fasting." Similarly, philosophers such as Plato, Sophocles, and Nietzsche described hope as a fault or weakness that only brought about negative outcomes.

Within psychology and psychiatry, perspectives on hope were also mixed until recent decades. In *The Future of an Illusion*, Freud (1928) made the

case that positive expectations for the future may be common but are a delusion that is inspired by religious traditions and can represent a disconnect from the reality of the human condition. As with other positive psychology constructs, hope was largely ignored as a topic of study for much of the 20th century in favor of focusing on more negative personality dimensions and characteristics such as pessimism and hopelessness that confer a vulnerability to various forms of mental illness. Psychiatrists then began to shift in the mid-20th century to consider that hope was not only worthy of study but could have a positive influence on human functioning. One of the key developments in this shift was *The Academic Lecture* on hope delivered by Karl Menninger (1959) at the annual convention of the American Psychiatric Association. Menninger argued that hope was a crucial yet understudied factor in the efforts of mental health professionals to help individuals recover from mental illness to live more pleasurable and productive lives. This idea was then echoed by Jerome Frank

(1968, 1973), who argued that hope was perhaps one of the most consistent and powerful forces in psychotherapy that played a vital role in promoting recovery, and Lionel Tiger (1979), who argued that a positive belief about the future was a defining feature of humanity and represented a remarkable cognitive resource that may have helped spur human evolution.

Hope subsequently began to be increasingly examined within psychology, with theoretical perspectives and empirical evidence rapidly shifting to frame hope as a positive resource that was worthy of study and something to be promoted. Early theories of hope that helped to advance the idea that hope was an adaptive strength included the theories of Mowrer (1960) and Stotland (1969). Other conceptualizations of hope developed within related fields such as nursing but shared the perspective that hope was a positive resource that helped individuals attain their goals (e.g., Herth, 1991). What these early theories all shared was the premise that hope represented a positive expectation about achieving goals.

Snyder's Hope Theory

Snyder's (1994) theory of hope also emphasizes the pursuit of goals as the organizing principle of human behavior and that positive expectations related to the pursuit of goals are the essence of hope. Snyder's theory and model of hope was initially developed as on offshoot of work examining how individuals make excuses and engage in the process of reality negotiation (Snyder, 1988; Snyder & Higgins, 1988). Whereas excuses represent thoughts or beliefs that can be used in an attempt to distance oneself from negative outcomes, hope represents thoughts or beliefs that can be used in an attempt to bring about positive outcomes. An early definition of hope provided by Snyder was that hope is "a cognitive set that is composed of a reciprocally derived sense of successful (1) agency (goal-directed determination) and (2) pathways (planning of ways to meet goals)" (Snyder et al., 1991, p. 570). This early definition of hope has proven to be a remarkably robust and useful conceptualization of hope and has provided the basis for decades of hope research within and beyond psychology. The core principles and predictions of hope theory are explained in detail in subsequent chapters, but the fundamental premise is that hope is the combination of both agency and pathways thinking and that hope not only helps individuals to identify goals but that hope is strong source of

resilience and determinant of positive outcomes in most circumstances and that individuals of all backgrounds can and do benefit from hope.

Snyder's theory of hope quickly became the dominant approach to conceptualizing and studying hope and continues to be the primary way in which hope is understood, studied, and promoted within psychology. The major influence of this model is demonstrated by the thousands of citations of Snyder's early publications on hope, the breadth of research that continues to be published on an annual basis demonstrating the many benefits of hope, and the scientists worldwide that are actively studying how best to understand and promote hope. What we have learned so far about hope is that it can be reliably measured and promoted and that hope is a powerful predictor of psychological, educational, professional, interpersonal, and health outcomes. The development of the science of hope coincided with work examining the benefits of related constructs such as self-efficacy (Bandura, 1977) and optimism (Scheier & Carver, 1985) as well as more general evidence that positive expectations for the future represent an adaptive resource rather than a delusional deficit (Taylor, 1989; Taylor & Brown, 1988). As articulated later in this handbook, hope represents a conceptually and empirically distinct construct from optimism and self-efficacy, and there is now decades of research demonstrating that hope uniquely and independently predicts many outcomes above and beyond these related constructs.

In addition to developing the core tenets of hope theory, Snyder was also instrumental in developing measures that could be used to assess hope. The first measure of hope that Snyder developed was the Adult Hope Scale (Snyder et al., 1991), which consists of 12 items: four items that measure pathways thinking, four items that measure agency thinking, and four filler items. The Adult Hope Scale remains the most widely used assessment tool for quantifying hope, and extensive psychometric work has now been conducted that demonstrates that the Adult Hope Scale is a reliable and valid measure of hope and that it assesses a latent construct that is distinct from related constructs such as optimism and self-efficacy. Snyder and colleagues (1996) subsequently developed the State Hope Scale to provide an alternative measure, which is more sensitive to changes in hope, and the Children's Hope Scale (Snyder et al., 1997), which is more developmentally appropriate for examinations of hope in youth. Other strategies of measuring hope such as domain-specific measures continue to be developed, but the three measures developed by Snyder and colleagues continue to be the most widely used and empirically supported tools for measuring hope.

The Legacy of C. R. Snyder and Shane J. Lopez

Unfortunately, the field has now lost the two individuals who have been most responsible for developing and promoting the science of hope: Charles Richard "Rick" Snyder and Shane Lopez. Rick Snyder was the primary developer of hope theory and spearheaded much of the seminal work on hope in the first 15 years after his model was developed and was a pioneer in the field of positive psychology. He was a prolific scientist who published more than 20 edited volumes and books and more than 250 articles and chapters, a gifted teacher who received dozens of awards for teaching, and an inspiring and award-winning mentor. He was the director of the clinical psychology doctoral training program at the University of Kansas for more than 25 years and supervised dozens of students' dissertations, many of whom are now successful researchers, clinicians, and educators. In addition to being an extremely hard-working and creative scientist, Rick was also very gifted at sharing the science of hope and positive psychology more broadly. A great example of this is when Rick appeared on the television show *Good Morning America* and conducted a live experiment with the cast members to describe the theory of hope and to demonstrate how hope was linked to pain tolerance. In addition to publishing the foundational literature on hope, Rick was a key figure in the development of the field of positive psychology and also published extensively on many other areas including forgiveness and coping with pain. Unfortunately, Rick had a very personal understanding of how hope influenced coping with pain as he experienced chronic and intense chest and abdominal pain for the last fifteen years of his life. Despite his personal experiences with pain, Rick always remained a beacon of hope both personally and professionally. He was also extraordinarily generous and was an exemplar of humility even after decades of impressive professional success and awards. Rick was fond of saying that "If you can't laugh at yourself, you have missed the biggest joke of all" and taught many people not only how to study hope but how to spread hope. Rick passed away in January of 2006 after developing transitional cell carcinoma.

After Rick's passing, Shane Lopez picked up Rick's mantle as the world's leading expert on the science of hope. Shane and Rick were good friends and frequent collaborators, and Shane had a similar passion and gift for building and spreading the science of hope. Like Rick, Shane was an award-winning teacher and researcher and was remarkably productive. He published over 100 articles and chapters and more than 10 edited volumes and books, many of which were in collaboration with Rick and represent seminal contributions to the field such as the *Handbook of Positive Psychology* (Snyder & Lopez, 2002). Shane was a fellow Jayhawk and professor at the University of Kansas. After more than a decade at KU, he transitioned from academia to industry and left KU to accept a position as Gallup Senior Scientist in Residence and Research Director for the Clifton Strengths Institute, where he was able to apply his passion for helping individuals of all backgrounds, and particularly students, better understand their strengths and recognize how hope could help them accomplish their goals and dreams. While working at Gallup, Shane also published *Making Hope Happen* (Lopez, 2013), which represents his magnum opus in many ways and synthesized nearly two decades of creative and rigorous scholarship that Shane had done to best understand how to spread ripples of hope. One of his most impressive accomplishments was in guiding the development and execution of the Gallup Student Poll, which has now been used to measure and promote the hope, engagement, and well-being of more than 4 million students. In addition to being a gifted teacher and scientist, Shane was also a remarkable leader for the field of positive psychology and helped to organize many of the early conferences in the field of positive psychology, was on the board of directors of and a fellow of the International Positive Psychology Association, and served in many other leadership roles that helped to build the field of positive psychology.

Shane had a unique gift for inspiring and fostering collaborations among people from various backgrounds and organizations with the mission of helping people better understand and capitalize on their hopes and strengths. He was a valued mentor, collaborator, and friend of many researchers in the field and internationally and was always generous with his time in helping others to flourish. After many years of fighting a series of health conditions, Shane passed away in July of 2016 as we were in the process of finalizing this handbook, but his legacy lives on through the many scientists, practitioners, and students who he inspired to have the passion and skills to study and spread hope.

Shane and Rick were extraordinary scientists and exemplars of hope and are dearly missed.

Overview of the Handbook

In planning this handbook, the goal was to carry on Rick Snyder's legacy, to synthesize current knowledge about hope, and to help promote further work into the science and practice of hope. With Shane's passing, the handbook now also serves as a tribute to his legacy of studying and spreading hope. The first attempt to synthesize what was known about the science and practice of hope was the *Handbook of Hope: Theory, Measures, and Applications* (Snyder, 2000) that Rick Snyder edited. Hope has remained a vibrant area of research and practice in recent years, and our understanding of the characteristics and consequences of hope has continued to progress. The present handbook represents a comprehensive update on the science and practice of hope research. In addition to summarizing the past research that has now accumulated from over 25 years of study, contributors to the volume were asked to highlight some of the key questions and topics that may represent the next 25 years of hope. Chapters primarily focus on theory and empirical findings related to Snyder's model of hope, as it represents the model that by far has been the most widely studied, although alternative conceptualizations and measures of hope are also discussed in some chapters when relevant.

The handbook is organized into seven sections. The first section focuses on defining hope and includes a chapter written by Rick Snyder that provides an overview of his hope model, a chapter reviewing historical perspectives on hope, and chapters that highlight the similarities and differences between hope and related theories such as self-efficacy and self-determination and how hope generally influences the pursuit of goals. The second section focuses on the measurement of hope and includes a chapter that reviews current methods of assessing hope and a chapter that discusses the importance of considering how culture may influence how we measure and influence hope. The third section focuses on strategies and interventions for promoting hope in multiple contexts, including promoting hope in children in academic settings and other contexts, in psychotherapy, and among older adults.

The fourth section focuses on the links between hope and physical health and includes chapters reviewing the literature on the influence of hope on health in both adults and children, the benefits of hope in athletics, and how hope may be protective in the context of terminal illnesses. The fifth section focuses on how hope promotes resilience to and recovery from various forms of mental illness, including anxiety disorders, depression, learning disorders, posttraumatic stress disorder, and stress resilience more broadly. The sixth section focuses on how hope influences positive functioning across diverse contexts, including the benefits of hope on positive aspects of mental health in adults and adolescents, how hope promotes positive relationships, the benefits of hope in professional settings, and how hope helps individuals seek and maintain meaning in life. Finally, the handbook concludes with a collaborative perspective on the future of the science of hope written by a team of experts in the field who were also former colleagues, students, and friends of Rick and Shane.

We were fortunate to have had so many distinguished hope researchers contribute to this handbook and believe the quality and breadth of these chapters exemplifies the robust nature of the scientific study of hope. With the passing of both Rick and Shane, the scientific study of hope is now being conducted by a second generation of researchers. I believe they would be pleased to know that tremendous progress has been and continues to be made in demystifying what it means to be hopeful, why hope is so crucial for achieving positive outcomes across context and the lifespan, and how hope can be promoted for individuals of all backgrounds. I hope that this volume will not only help researchers and practitioners understand what is currently known about hope but serve to spark the next decade of hope research.

References

Bandura, A. (1977). Self-efficacy: Toward a unifying theory of behavioral change. *Psychological Review, 84*(2), 191–215.

Frank, J. D. (1968). The role of hope in psychotherapy. *International Journal of Psychiatry, 5,* 383–395.

Frank, J. D. (1973). *Persuasion and healing* (rev. ed.). Baltimore: Johns Hopkins University Press.

Freud, S. (1928). *The future of an illusion.* London: Hogarth.

Herth, K. (1991). Development and refinement of an instrument to measure hope. *Scholarly Inquiry for Nursing Practice, 5,* 39–51.

Lopez, S. J. (2013). *Making hope happen: Create the future you want for yourself and others.* New York: Simon & Schuster.

Menninger, K. (1959). The academic lecture: Hope. *American Journal of Psychiatry, 116*(6), 481–491.

Mowrer, O. H. (1960). *The psychology of hope.* San Francisco, CA: Jossey-Bass.

Scheier, M. F., & Carver, C. S. (1985). Optimism, coping, and health: Assessment and implications of generalized outcome expectancies. *Health Psychology, 4*, 219–247.

Snyder, C. R. (1988). Reality negotiation: From excuses to hope and beyond. *Journal of Social and Clinical Psychology, 8*, 130–157.

Snyder, C. R. (1994). *The psychology of hope: You can get there from here*. New York: Free Press.

Snyder, C. R. (Ed.). (2000). *Handbook of hope: Theory, measures, and applications*. San Diego, CA: Academic Press.

Snyder, C. R. (2002). Hope theory: Rainbows in the mind. *Psychological Inquiry, 13*(4), 249–275.

Snyder, C. R., Harris, C., Anderson, J. R., Holleran, S. A., Irving, L. M., Sigmon, S. T., . . . Harney, P. (1991). The will and the ways: Development and validation of an individual-differences measure of hope. *Journal of Personality and Social Psychology, 60*(4), 570–585.

Snyder, C. R., & Higgins, R. L. (1988). Excuses: Their effective role in the negotiation of reality. *Psychological Bulletin, 104*(1), 23–35.

Snyder, C. R., Hoza, B., Pelham, W. E., Rapoff, M., Ware, L., Danovsky, M., . . . Stahl, K. J. (1997). The development and validation of the Children's Hope Scale. *Journal of Pediatric Psychology, 22*(3), 399–421.

Snyder, C. R., & Lopez, S. J. (Eds.). (2002). *Handbook of positive psychology*. New York: Oxford University Press.

Snyder, C. R., Sympson, S. C., Ybasco, F. C., Borders, T. F., Babyak, M. A., & Higgins, R. L. (1996). Development and validation of the State Hope Scale. *Journal of Personality and Social Psychology, 70*, 321–335.

Stotland, E. (1969). *The psychology of hope*. San Francisco, CA: Jossey-Bass.

Taylor, S. E. (1989). *Positive illusions*. New York: Basic Books.

Taylor, S. E., & Brown, J. D. (1988). Illusion and well-being: A social psychological perspective on mental health. *Psychological Bulletin, 103*, 193–210.

Tiger, L. (1979). *Optimism: The biology of hope*. New York: Simon & Schuster.

The History of Philosophical and Psychological Perspectives on Hope: Toward Defining Hope for the Science of Positive Human Development

Kristina Schmid Callina, Nancy Snow, *and* Elise D. Murray

Abstract

This chapter presents ideas from philosophers and psychologists throughout history about why scholars should study hope and how it should be defined in the science of positive human development. It uses the relational developmental systems metatheory as a framework for these ideas. Drawing from historical and contemporary philosophy and psychology, several key ingredients necessary for hope are presented: positive future expectations, agency, and trust. The chapter presents evidence from historical and philosophical perspectives on hope, including perspectives from modern and contemporary philosophy, as well as perspectives from the more recent history of hope within the psychology. The chapter then looks beyond the most common conceptions of hope. Drawing on a range of sources, but especially nursing science studies of hope in terminally ill patients, it also suggests that people can have hope not only in the present for the future but also in the present for the present.

Key Words: hope, relational developmental systems, positive future expectations, agency, trust, positive development

To the extent that the course or outcomes of human development are uncertain, it is nevertheless a hopeful endeavor. Neither faulty genetics, nor environmental constraints or affordances, nor any other causal processes or "mechanisms" are fully deterministic of our futures. Across the first few decades of life, the individual may pursue different pathways from infancy to childhood and adolescence to future adult roles and take any number of routes toward his or her goals. In addition, although starting at different points in infancy and childhood, whether those starting points relate to socioeconomic status, cognitive abilities, or macro-level constraints or affordances, such as civil rights, individuals may end up attaining similar goals during adulthood (Lerner, 2002; Overton, 2010). Developmental pathways are characterized by

fusion of multiple levels of the individual's ecology and relative plasticity across the life span, which allow for multidirectionality, equipotentiality, and equifinality of those pathways. Thus humans have the capacity to hope for a nearly infinite number of possibilities.

In this chapter, we address three key questions. First, *why* study hope? We believe that hope is fundamental for understanding human flourishing. As we have hinted already and will describe in greater detail later, the ontology of human development justifies an optimistic stance for the life chances of any individual. This is the contemporary paradigm for the study of human development: ideas and methodologies characterized by process-relational and relational developmental systems theories (Overton, 2015). When a parent encourages his child to have hope, implicit in that message is that the chain of events of her life—caused by the mutually influential relations between a growing individual and the institutions, natural environment, socio-political landscape, and relationships with parents, teachers, and peers that shape her developmental trajectory—are unknown and therefore open to myriad opportunities. Relational developmental systems theories provide a framework for elucidating how a range of outcomes may be possible over the course of the life span. Such theories shed light on why and how an individual might hope for the future and are therefore useful for understanding the critical role of hope in positive human development.

Next we address the question, *what* is hope? Scholars throughout the ages have argued that hope may be a human strength, which allows people to optimize resources in their environments and place themselves on positive pathways of development (Schmid & Lopez, 2011). Yet, varied and sometimes contradictory definitions of hope exist across diverse fields of study. Scientists, in particular, are left with questions of what exactly hope is and how we can recognize it, in order to better understand its role in positive human functioning. Drawing from historical and contemporary philosophy and psychology, we present several key ingredients necessary for hope. Specifically, we define hope as having three necessary ingredients: positive future expectations, agency, and trust. To provide support for this conception, we present evidence from historical and philosophical perspectives on hope, including perspectives from modern and contemporary philosophy, as well as perspectives from the more recent history of hope within the psychology and nursing literatures.

Finally, we pose the question: in addition to the components we have already identified, *what else* is hope? Again using evidence from philosophy and psychology, we examine two areas where hope transcends positive future expectations, agency, and trust. These two areas are *radical hope* and *hope for the present*. Concepts from process-relational and relational-developmental systems theories of human development are again useful to help us understand these two promising directions for future research on hope. We turn now to these ideas as a frame for understanding why hope is so important for the study of positive human development.

Why Study Hope?

A defining feature of contemporary developmental science is a focus on the nature and influence of individual and contextual characteristics on the attainment of developmental outcomes (e.g., Lerner, 2006). Historically, philosophical foundations for the study of human development were based on a Cartesian split conception, that development could be reduced to direct influences of either the environment or biology. However, the contemporary study of human development is predicated on a relational scientific worldview, which holds that all levels of organization within an individual's ecology, from the biological to the sociocultural and historical levels, are fused (Lerner, 2002; Overton, 2010). Theories within this relational paradigm are therefore often modeled in a relational developmental systems framework (e.g., Bronfenbrenner & Morris, 2006; Ford & Lerner, 1992; Magnusson & Stattin, 2006; Overton, 2010). We propose that this framework and its associated concepts is useful for understanding the importance of studying hope and its role in positive human development.

The relational developmental systems theoretical perspective purports that debates of "nature versus nurture" (and other split conceptions, such as continuity–discontinuity) of human development are inherently counterfactual (Lerner & Overton, 2008). Relational developmental systems theories (Overton, 2010, 2011; Overton & Müller, 2012) emphasize that the basic process of development involves mutually influential relations between individuals and contexts: particular developmental paths are shaped by characteristics of the individual (e.g., aspirations, values, cognitive and behavioral skills, etc.) and by the specific features of his or her family, school, peer group, and neighborhood or community, as well as by the vicissitudes of the historical era within which he or she is embedded (Elder & Shanahan, 2006). Relational developmental systems theories focus on process (systematic changes in the developmental system), becoming (moving from potential to actuality; a developmental process as having a past, present, and future; Whitehead, 1929, 1978), and holism (the meanings of entities and events derive from the context in which they are embedded). According to Lerner and Callina (2014), this perspective particularly emphasizes the importance of the relationship between the individual and other individuals in the development of character virtues, including hope.

The potential for systematic change constitutes a potential for (at least relative) plasticity across the life span. As explained by Lerner (1984, 2002), the concept of plasticity has been emphasized by developmental scientists who are interested in countering the idea of fixity in human development. This idea that developmental pathways are fixed, such as by genetic inheritance or neuronal "hard wiring," is a primary example of reductionist views that contemporary developmental science seeks to counter. Accordingly, the idea of plasticity arose to communicate the capacity in human development for systematic and relatively continuous changes across the life span. Such systematic change can arise through individual-context relations that are either ontogenetically or historically normative or from nonnormative life or historical events (Baltes et al., 2006).

A recent empirical example of the importance of the distinction between plasticity in development versus developmental fixity comes from the study of epigenetic changes (e.g., Misteli, 2013). This scholarship illustrates that the genes received at conception (i.e., the genotype) are not a fixed blueprint for development. Genes are constantly turned on and off across the life span, and these epigenetic changes may be due to a host of factors including exercise and nutrition (e.g., Lindholm et al., 2014), the quality and perception of social relationships (Slavich & Cole, 2013), and other physiological, psychological, and social influences (Meaney, 2010). Most of this epigenetic activity is stochastic and short-term (and of largely unknown origin; Misteli, 2013). However, epigenetic changes are enduring, systematic, and even cross-generational (Meaney, 2010, 2014; Misteli, 2013; Slavich & Cole, 2013). The notion of plasticity therefore rationalizes a certain optimism that individual developmental pathways can change, and change for the better. We believe that it is important to study hope because it orients scholars and practitioners toward openness to possibilities inherent in the relatively malleable, relational developmental system.

Relational developmental systems theories hold that development—for example, involving the physiological, somatic, cognitive, emotional, behavioral, and social processes that comprise ontogeny—results from dynamic interaction between the individual and his or her context. Because of the integration of the levels of organization within the individual's ecology, such theories emphasize that the individual and context are fused and thus mutually influence one another (Lerner, 2004; Overton, 2006). These fused person–context relations regulate the course of development. To the extent that the fusions between individual and context are mutually *beneficial*, that is, individuals are positively engaging with and contributing to their environments, which in turn are supporting the healthy and productive development of the individuals living within them (e.g., Brandstädter, 2006; Lerner & Overton, 2008), there are *adaptive developmental regulations* between individuals and contexts.

Here again, a relational developmental systems perspective justifies a hopeful orientation to human development. Adaptive developmental regulations occur when the strengths of the individual and the strengths of the context are optimally aligned. Moreover, individuals have agency in directing their relations with the context. We propose that hope is a unique character strength, or virtue, that allows individuals to direct the adaptive developmental regulations that promote human flourishing (Lerner & Callina, 2014; Schmid & Lopez, 2011). Later, we describe in greater detail the links between hope and agency.

In sum, a relational developmental systems perspective, as a philosophical approach to the study of human development, rationalizes an optimistic stance that all individuals have the capacity for thriving across the life span. As such, this perspective elevates the study of hope in positive human development and provides some useful concepts for understanding hope, including plasticity, adaptive developmental regulations, and embeddedness. Yet despite its importance for human development, psychologists' definitions of hope have been found lacking and have yet to be reconciled with historical and philosophical perspectives of hope. In the following sections, we explore the question, *what is hope?* Drawing on perspectives from philosophy and psychology, we propose a conception of hope that will be useful for the study of positive human development.

What Is Hope?

In Greek mythology, when Pandora released all of the evils upon man, Hope (*elpis*) did not escape but remained in the jar. The tale is recounted in Hesiod's *Works and Days* (c. 700 BCE), although he leaves the mystery of hope to our interpretation. According to Verdenius (1985), modern explanations for why *elpis* remains in Pandora's jar fall into two camps based on whether the interpreter believes that the jar was meant to safeguard hope *for* humans or to keep hope *from* humans. The former interpretation gives hope a positive connotation: hope was precious and must be preserved. The latter interpretation assumes that hope is the worst evil and must be imprisoned in the jar. The ancient Greeks, therefore, either saw the role of hope "to comfort man in his misery and a stimulus rousing his activity" or as "the idle hope in which the lazy man indulges when he should be working honestly for his living" (Verdenius, 1985, p. 66).

To say that throughout the course of human history there has been a discrepancy about the conception of hope is an understatement. Perhaps the Greeks, much like philosophers, poets, and theologians throughout the ages, understood hope as both good and evil. Four hundred years BCE, Euripides called hope *man's curse*; according to the Greeks, fate was unchangeable, and therefore hope was an illusion. The Old Testament, however, tells us that those who "hope in the Lord will renew their strength" (Isaiah 40:31).

Such adages illustrate the range of ideas about hope that have been forwarded across the millennia. Martin Luther gave hope sweeping powers, particularly as it relates to faith in God, claiming that "Everything that is done in this world is done by hope" (Luther, 1569/2004, p. 198). Benjamin Franklin is credited with warning us that "He that lives upon hope will die fasting." In the American Enlightenment during the mid- to late-19th century, many thinkers found hope antithetical to rational thought.

Much more recently, scientists have weighed in on the meaning of hope and its role in positive human development. Although fairly nascent relative to the attention given to the topic by philosophers, psychologists have been disseminating their ideas about the role of hope in human behavior and life-span development since at least the 1950s. This branch of thought has largely considered hope to be a positive attribute. Early references to hope in the psychological literature include Karl Menninger (1960), who called upon scientists to speak up about the "ancient but rediscovered truth" about the "validity of Hope in human development" (p. 11). Ezra Stotland (1969) referred to hope as "a necessary condition" for the therapeutic process. Erik Erikson (1959) noted that hope is the first of the "psychosocial strengths" that emerge from resolving conflicts of developmental stages. An empirical body of research has also developed from these conceptualizations about hope, as researchers attempted to apply definitions of hope to the measurement of psychological processes. Snyder's (2002) Hope Theory, which we describe in greater detail later, is certainly the most widely cited conception of hope in the psychology literature. However, critiques of Snyder's hope measure (e.g., Tennen, Affleck, & Tennen, 2002) point to a need to more fully integrate ideas about hope from other scholars and from other disciplines, particularly philosophy. In the following sections, we present ideas of modern and contemporary philosophers and evidence from psychology about the necessary ingredients for studying hope and its role in positive human development. The following sections are organized by philosophical and psychological perspectives for the sake of clarity, although it should be noted that these fields are intertwined, particularly as they pertain to defining hope.

Positive Future Expectations

Scholars widely agree that hope involves positive expectations for the future. We refer to this as the "bare-bones" conception of hope, as it seems to be a minimum requirement for defining hope. However, we later challenge this part of the definition, when we discuss hope in the present, for the present.

MODERN AND CONTEMPORARY PHILOSOPHICAL PERSPECTIVES

The term "modern philosophy" refers to philosophical writing done in the 17th and 18th centuries and includes figures such as Thomas Hobbes, Rene Descartes, Baruch Spinoza, John Locke, David Hume, and Immanuel Kant. Each of these philosophers wrote on hope. Hobbes, Descartes, Spinoza, Locke, and Hume adopt the aforementioned bare-bones conception of hope, while Kant famously asks the question, "For What May I Hope?" The bare-bones conception is that hope is a desire for an end perceived to be good and the belief that the end is possible. In this sense, hope is a complex mental state that has an intentional object. That is, to hope is to hope *for* something of which we are not assured—a good biopsy outcome, fine weather for the picnic, an end to the drought (our hopes can also be expressed in propositional form: we hope that certain desired states of affairs obtain, for example, that I have a good biopsy outcome, that there is fine weather for the picnic, and so on). Hope occupies a conceptual space between certainty and impossibility. In other words, the hoped-for end is a possibility. Hobbes (1968; see also Mittleman 2009, pp. 27–28) asserts that "Appetite with an opinion of attaining, is called hope. ... The same, without such an opinion, despaire" (p. 123). In *The Passions of the Soul*, Descartes writes that a high probability of obtaining that which we desire excites hope in us, whereas low probability elicits fear (see Mittleman 2009, p. 27, n. 9). Thus, despair and fear have been considered opposites of hope. Locke similarly contends that hope is a pleasurable internal sensation brought about by the thought of "a probable future enjoyment of a thing" (Mittleman 2009, p. 28, n. 12).

Though modern philosophers adopt the bare-bones conception, they amplify it in various ways, mainly by regarding it as a passion and situating it within a nexus of other passions. What this means is that modern philosophers think hope is an emotion that is related to other emotions, either through similarity or contrast. Spinoza and Hume, for example, have complex views of hope as a passion, according to which hope is intertwined with fear. Both philosophers explain hope in terms of joy and fear, in terms of sorrow or grief (on Spinoza, see Mittleman 2009, pp. 94–96). Spinoza claims that "*Hope* is a joy not constant, arising from the idea of something future or past, about the issue of which we sometimes doubt" and makes parallel claims about fear as "a sorrow not constant, arising from the idea of something future or past, about the issue of which we sometimes doubt" (Wild, 1958, p. 270; italics in original). He writes that hope and fear are inextricably linked, both having their roots in doubt about what the future holds (Wild 1958).

Hume's analysis is similar in some ways to Spinoza's: both philosophers acknowledge roles for doubt, fear, probability, and certainty in their analyses of hope. According to Hume (1978, pp. 439–448), both hope and fear are primarily explained by reference to joy and grief on the one hand and the probability of an event occurring on the other. He writes: "'Tis evident that the very same event, which by its certainty wou'd produce grief or joy, gives always rise to fear or hope, when only probable and uncertain" (pp. 439–440). Probability can be either objective, when the event is uncertain as a matter of fact, or subjective, when it is certain as a matter of fact but uncertain according to the agent's judgment (Hume 1978, p. 444). Both kinds of probabilities cause fear and hope due to the "uncertainty and fluctuation they bestow on the imagination" (Hume, 1978, p. 444).

Spinoza and Hume anticipate themes taken up by contemporary philosophers, that is, those writing in the 20th and 21st centuries. (Contemporary philosophers whose work is not discussed in this chapter include Godfrey [1987], Steinbock [2006], Meirav [2009], Govier [2011], and van Hooft [2011], whose views are largely consistent with the central themes of those presented here, and Ratcliffe [2008, 2010, 2011], who advances a very different view of hope according to which hope, hopelessness,

and other states such as deep depression and guilt are preintentional orientations.) Pettit (2004), for example, echoes Spinoza's belief that hope's value lies in its ability to check other emotions, though his concern is with the effects of negative affect, not excesses of joy. Hume's comments on the imagination also prefigure Bovens (1999), who stresses mental imaging, and Martin (2011, 2014), who defends the importance of fantasy for hoping.

A good place to start in reviewing the work of contemporary philosophers is with those whose views do not go far beyond the bare-bones conception. J. M. O. Wheatley (1958), for example, endorses the bare-bones view and clarifies the nature of possibility at stake in hoping that an end is possible by contrasting hoping with wishing. He maintains that a central difference between the two is that "hoping, unlike wishing, entails 'belief in possibility'" (p. 126). What kind of possibility—physical or logical? According to Wheatley, "I hope that he went" is consistent with my not knowing whether he went or not but not with my knowing that he had not gone. By contrast, "I wish he had gone" is consistent with my knowing that he had not gone. "I hope that he went" entails my belief that his going is physically possible. This is not true of "I wish he had gone," which entails only my not believing that his going is logically impossible. Hoping, then, must be accompanied by the belief that the hoped-for end is both physically and logically possible.[1]

J. P. Day (1969), by his own admission bucking the predominant trend in the history of philosophy, clings to a theoretically parsimonious version of the bare-bones account, arguing that hope involves desiring and estimating a probability: "'A hopes that P' is true if and only if 'A wishes that P, and A thinks that P has some degree of probability, however small' is true" (p. 89). Other contemporary philosophers move well beyond the bare-bones account and contend that it is a more complex cognitive-affective state. Margaret Walker (2006, pp. 47–48), for example, criticizes Day (1969) for failing to explain the motivational force of hope, as well as for neglecting a panoply of what she calls "hope phenomena": desires, perceptions, and forms of attention, expression, feeling, and activity, that are characteristic of hope or associated with hope. Luc Bovens (1999) enriches the bare-bones account by adding the element of mental imaging, which goes beyond simply imagining a future state of affairs to include behaviors that demonstrate a person's anticipation of an event, such as checking the clock when one is hoping for someone to arrive at one's house.

Philip Pettit (2004) also moves beyond the bare-bones conception of hope but in a different direction from Bovens (1999). Pettit (2004, pp. 155–157) offers a conception of what he calls "substantial hope" and defends its pragmatic rationality by noting its parallels with the rationality of precaution. As with the bare-bones conception, substantial hope consists in the agent's desiring that something obtain and believing that it might or might not obtain. However, substantial hope occurs when the agent's belief in attaining the desired prospect is at a low level of confidence. In other words, substantial hope bolsters those who would otherwise be low-hopers. It consists in the agent's acting as if the desired outcome will obtain or has a good chance of obtaining and buffers him or her against losing heart and, as a consequence, effective agency, in the face of fluctuations in evidence (Pettit, 2004, pp. 157–158). We discuss the role of agency in hope in greater detail in a later section. First, however, we turn to psychologists' perspectives on positive future expectations as the bare-bones conception of hope.

PSYCHOLOGICAL PERSPECTIVES

Psychology itself is a relatively new science, and the study of hope within psychology is only about 50 years old. One of the first explicit mentions of hope in the psychological literature was by Karl Menninger, in a 1959 address to the American Psychiatric Association. Menninger (1960) challenged his colleagues to consider hope to be a viable line of scientific inquiry: "If we dare to hope, should we not dare to look at ourselves hoping?" (p. 12). The focus on hope in Menninger's address reflected the zeitgeist in the field: with the end of World War II, psychologists were looking to more positive constructs, such as hope, faith, and love, to make sense of traumatic events. Since Menninger's address, each generation of psychologists has attempted to capture the meaning of hope for positive human functioning. (We also note that interesting philosophical work on hope was also done in the wake of World War II; see Pieper [1994, 1997], Marcel [1978], and Bloch [1986]).

In the main, psychologists have studied hope as a key variable in the therapeutic process. About a decade after Menninger's address, Ezra Stotland (1969) wrote *The Psychology of Hope*, in which he defined hope as "expectations of the attainment of goals" (p. 4) and proposed that hope is "a necessary condition for action" (p. 14). Stotland's theory

of hope proposed that hope links action with perceived probability of success. Furthermore, Stotland argued that greater probability of goal attainment, combined with greater importance of the goal, leads to increases in positive affect. Staats and Stassen (1985) likewise regarded hope as consisting of a cognitive element of expectation and an affective element of feeling good about expected pleasant events or outcomes.

Psychologist C. R. Snyder has more recently presented a detailed theory, the agency-pathways theory of hope, stressing hope's roles in effective agency. Snyder's model has been the most commonly studied approach to hope within psychology since the early 1990s, and we discuss some of the key findings of his model in greater detail later. For Snyder, hope is a positive cognitive-motivational state characterized by strong agency and pathways thinking that provides high-hopers with the motivational determination and cognitive tools to successfully pursue their goals. Snyder contends that high-hopers are flexible in their pathways thinking and can generate multiple means to goal achievement. They are able to identify barriers to goals and to invent new means to achieve goals that can circumvent such impediments. According to Snyder (2002), high-hopers are less likely than low-hopers to view impediments as sources of stress, approach their goals with more positive emotions and energy and experience positive emotions upon reaching their goals, whereas low-hopers experience negative affect when they do not attain their goals. For Snyder, hope is not an emotion, but rather it is a motivational process with secondary affective responses.

Throughout the history of hope within psychology, hope has been intertwined with other constructs, most notably *optimism*. In fact, several authors have used "optimism" and "hope" interchangeably: Gottschalk (1974) defined hope as "A measure of optimism that a favorable outcome is likely to occur, not only in one's personal earthly activities but also in cosmic phenomena and even in spiritual or imaginary events" (p. 779; see Snyder, Rand, & Sigmon, [2002] and Rand [this volume] for discussion of the distinction between optimism and hope). However, the recent emergence of the field of positive psychology—the beginning of which may be marked by Martin Seligman's 1998 presidential address to the American Psychological Association—has brought new attention to strengths and virtues and a new call for clarification in an often ambiguous literature. For instance, hope is featured in Peterson and Seligman's (2004) comprehensive taxonomy of character virtues, but in that volume it is synonymous with optimism, future-mindedness, and future orientation.

Carver and Scheier (2002a, 2002b; Scheier & Carver, 1985; Scheier, Carver, & Bridges, 1994) have arguably conducted the most extensive work on the psychology of optimism. This body of work conceptualizes optimism as a stable personality characteristic that generally orients the individual to perceive experiences, particularly adverse or difficult ones, with the expectation that the outcome will be positive. According to Carver and Scheier (2002b), optimists are more likely to react to difficult events with emotions that are ultimately positive, resulting in more adaptive coping strategies and greater well-being.

Clearly, hope and optimism are closely related. This point may create some confusion for readers who are familiar with Snyder's hope theory, which is certainly the most influential model of hope in psychology (and, indeed, the one that informs most of the chapters in the present volume). Snyder and others have debated the distinction between hope, optimism, and other similar constructs (e.g., Aspinwall & Leaf, 2002; Shorey, Snyder, Rand, Hockemeyer, & Feldman, 2002; see also Rand, this volume). At the heart of this debate, however, lie distinctions in how one conceptualizes hope. Some have argued that Snyder's model is more reflective of goal pursuit tenacity or perseverance (e.g., Aspinwall & Leaf, 2002; Callina et al., 2015) and does not fully capture the essence of hope as articulated by philosophers and other social scientists. We agree. Thus we propose that optimism, as an indicator of positive future expectations, is a key ingredient of hope.

According to Carver and Scheier (2002a), the conceptual difference between optimism and hope lies primarily in the element of control that exists in hope with respect to the individual's ability to attain his or her goals. Optimism refers to confidence that a positive outcome will occur but not necessarily to the individual's ability (or perceived ability) to realize a goal (Carver & Scheier, 2002a). Later, we return to this issue of efficacy in goal attainment when we describe the role of agency in hope. Evidence supports our claim that positive future expectations, which may be measured by optimism, are one key ingredient of hope but that hope and optimism are not overlapping constructs. For example, Shorey, Little, Snyder, Kluck, and Robitschek (2007) found that hope produces unique variance (beyond optimism) in the prediction of positive

developmental outcomes such as "personal growth initiative."

Agency and Trust

The bare-bones definition of hope described previously—hope as positive expectations for a desired future goal—may leave the reader with some unanswered questions about the role of hope in positive human development. Is hope the intangible strength that helps us get through our darkest hours? Or is hope to blame for our naïve delusions, leading us to wish for instead of work for what we want in life? Finally—because human development necessitates social relationships, as emphasized in the relational developmental systems perspective earlier—what role do other people play in supporting or inhibiting an individual's hope?

Hope is often present when individuals have both high expectations for success in meeting goals as well as motivation to pursue future goals. As we have already noted, hope is one way in which individuals may contribute to adaptive developmental regulations necessary for positive development (Little et al., 2006). This conceptualization of hope as an agentic process follows from philosophical perspectives about whether hope is rational and realistic, as well as psychological perspectives, such as Ezra Stotland's (1969) assertion that hope is necessary for action, and Snyder's (1994) theory that hope self-beliefs arise from a learned history of cause and effect and from the individual's role in causing chain events leading to goal attainment. In the recent history of hope, philosophers and psychologists have also explored the relationships in an individual's life that make hope possible, with particular attention to trust (Callina, Johnson, Buckingham, & Lerner, 2014). To address these issues, we describe theories of psychology and philosophy that extend beyond the bare-bones definition of hope as positive future expectations, linking hope to agency and trust.

CONTEMPORARY PSYCHOLOGICAL PERSPECTIVES

In addition to focusing on positive future expectations, Ezra Stotland (1969) recognized that hope is derived from the organism's agency in working toward its goals, by selectively attending to aspects of the environment that would help in goal attainment. Stotland's theory also emphasized that the organism's actions toward a goal would be proportionate to the perceived probability of goal attainment. Thus Stotland embedded hope in previous theories about motivation (e.g., French, 1952;

Lewin, 1951) and set the stage for future work on expectancy-values theories (e.g., Wigfield & Eccles, 1992), as well as action theoretical accounts of intentional self-regulation in childhood, adolescence, and adult and aged years (Brandtstädter, 2006; Geldhof, Little, & Colombo, 2010; Gestsdóttir & Lerner, 2008; Heckhausen, 2000; McClelland, Ponitz, Messersmith, & Tominey, 2010).

In contrast to his contemporaries, Erik Erikson (1959) conceptualized hope as far more foundational to human development. Erikson articulated a theory of life stages—a schema of how people develop throughout the course of the life span. He links ego development, that is, the emergence of the self at various life-span stages—childhood, including infancy, adolescence, and adulthood—with a schedule of virtues, understood broadly as "strengths" (Erikson, 1964, pp. 111–157; see also Erikson, 1997). Hope is integral to the ongoing process of healthy ego maturation and development. He offers this understanding of hope: "*Hope is the enduring belief in the attainability of fervent wishes, in spite of the dark urges and rages which mark the beginning of existence*" (Erikson, 1964, p. 118; italics in original).

Erikson writes of the infant as having "hope" (1964, 1997). Clearly, though, the infant is not capable of having an "enduring belief in the attainability of fervent wishes." Given hope's belief-desire structure, it is better to conceptualize the infant's experience as a form of "proto-hope" that is capable of developing into fully fledged hope as the baby matures. The growing infant has "urges," "rages," and impulses to explore the new reality into which she has entered. Erikson (1964) writes that "Hope relies for its beginnings on the new being's first encounter with *trustworthy maternal persons*" (p. 116; italics in original). The first hurdle in life, the most elemental paradox we encounter, in his view, is that between trust and mistrust. Hope develops when the infant is able to trust her caretakers—that they will satisfy her wants, afford her pleasurable experiences, protect her from harm and pain, and enable her to successfully achieve the inchoate ends at which she aims. Hope is essential for the development of other childhood strengths of will, purpose, and competence. Erikson (1964) contends that "Hope is both the earliest and the most indispensable virtue inherent in the state of being alive" and notes that others have called this virtue "confidence" (p. 115). Yet he believes that hope is more basic than both confidence and trust, writing that "if life is to be sustained hope must

remain, even where confidence is wounded, trust impaired" (Erikson, 1964, p. 115).

Erikson makes four important observations about hope. The first is to distinguish between the disposition of hope, which he calls "hopefulness," and specific hopes. Specific hopes will pass or be superseded by new sets of hopes as "The gradual widening of the infant's horizon of active experience provides, at each step, verifications so rewarding that they inspire new hopefulness" (1964, p. 117). The infant's successful explorations of the world around her—aided and abetted by caring, trustworthy adults—nurtures her ability to hope.

Erikson's second observation is that, as infants progress in their abilities, they are able to renounce ends they cannot attain and to redirect their expectations to more reasonable prospects. Hope is thus connected with what has been called "reality surveillance" (this term comes from nursing science scholarship on hope; see Miller, 1985). Good hopers monitor their circumstances for information about what they can and cannot achieve and revise goals accordingly. Connected with this point is his third: "maturing hope not only maintains itself in the face of changed facts—it proves itself able to change facts" (Erikson, 1964, p. 117). Maturing hope, informed by accurate monitoring of the individual's circumstances, is what we might call a "game-changer." Hope allows individuals to see what can and cannot be changed in their circumstances. If the hoped-for end is of enough value to them, hopers can take effective action to change their circumstances or even aspects of themselves in their efforts to attain it. Finally, Erikson (1964, p. 117) maintains that, from an evolutionary standpoint, hope helps humans to approximate the instincts that help other animals survive in their natural environments.

Erikson's points about realistic hopes and the individual's efficacy in directing his or her goals mesh well with more recent theories and research on hope and effective agency. The most commonly used theory and measure of hope in psychology comes from research done by C. R. Snyder, a clinician and researcher who renewed psychologists' interest in hope in the 1990s and coincided with the burgeoning field of positive psychology. As we noted earlier, Snyder offers two definitions of hope, each reflecting his view that hope is essentially a matter of taking effective means to achieving one's goals. According to the first, hope is "a positive motivational state that is based on an interactively derived sense of successful (a) agency (goal-directed energy) and (b) pathways (planning to meet goals)" (Snyder, Irving, & Anderson 1991, p. 287). The second describes hope as "a cognitive set that is based on a reciprocally derived sense of successful agency (goal-directed determination) and pathways (planning to meet goals) (Snyder, Harris, et. al. 1991, p. 571).

Research by Snyder and his colleagues (e.g., Snyder, Harris, et. al. 1991) and others (Lopez, Rose, Robinson, Marques, & Pais-Ribeiro, 2009) have demonstrated the power of scores on his Hope Scale to predict positive outcomes (indeed, as we noted earlier, the majority of research discussed in the present volume is based on Snyder's model). Research derived from Snyder's hope theory and using the measure he and colleagues developed to index one's confidence and competence to set and achieve goals has demonstrated covariation between high levels of hope and physical health (e.g., involving knowledge about health-related issues and intentions to follow health-supported regimens), coping with disease and injury, and mental health and adjustment (see Rand & Cheavens, 2009, for a review). Among children and adolescents, pathways and agency thinking also has been linked to more positive goals for the future, psychosocial well-being, academic achievement, and athletic achievement (Lopez, Rose, Robinson, Margues, & Pais-Ribeiro, 2009).

Despite the potential utility of Snyder's hope measure to predict positive outcomes, there are some criticisms about whether it accurately depicts hope. For instance, Tennen, Affleck, and Tennen (2002), referencing Erikson's original ideas about the antecedents of hope, noted that the virtue of trust is absent from both theory and measurement in the contemporary hope literature. Aspinwall and Leaf (2002) noted that a critical element missing from Snyder's treatment of hope is an explicit focus on future orientation, that is, the content of one's future goals and beliefs regarding future prospects. Finally, Carver and Scheier (2002a) argued that the items in Snyder's measure that purportedly assess agency more accurately measure whether individuals have prior success in attaining goals (or at least, according to the authors, the items greatly confound agency with prior success; however, cf. Shorey et al. [2002] for response to these criticisms). Thus critiques of Snyder's hope theory point to the need for psychologists, in particular, to return to the historical annals of hope scholarship and bring the ingredients of positive future expectations and trust back into theory and assessment of hope.

CONTEMPORARY PHILOSOPHICAL PERSPECTIVES

Victoria McGeer (2004, 2008) continues broadly Eriksonian themes in her work on hope's roles in the development of agency vis-à-vis trust.[2] She argues that hope is "a unifying and grounding force of human agency" and claims that "[t]o live a life devoid of hope is simply not to live a human life; it is not to function—or tragically, it is to cease to function—as a human being" (2004, p. 101). In her view, the ability to hope is both a precondition of and a constitutive element in our abilities to function as effective agents. It not only underwrites our actual capacities as agents but also provides us with the imaginative vision, resolve, and practical wherewithal to project our agential capacities into the future (she cites Snyder's hope theory approvingly in this regard; see McGeer, 2004, p. 103). She writes: "human agency is about imaginatively exploring our own powers, as much as it is about using them. Hence, it is about imaginatively exploring what we can and cannot do in the world" (McGeer, 2004, p. 104). This is where hope comes in: "For, no matter what the circumstance, hoping is a matter, not only of recognizing but also of actively engaging with our current limitations in affecting the future we want to inhabit" (McGeer, 2004, p. 104). Good hope is not wishful thinking or flights of imaginative fancy but clear-headed engagement with our capacities as they are, geared to bringing those capacities to where we want them to be. Thus hope grounds effective human agency. Even in the limited case in which circumstance or our limitations prevent us from affecting the world we inhabit, hope enables us to orient our energies toward the future, in thought if not in deed (McGeer, 2004, p. 104). Hope, as a forward-looking ground and unifying force of human agency, is a complex dynamic of many things: attitude, emotion, activity, and disposition (Mc Geer, 2004, p. 101). To hope well, McGeer (2004) claims, is not just to formulate and pursue desired ends; it is to "take a reflective and developmental stance toward our own capacities as agents—hence, it is to experience ourselves as agents of potential as well as agents in fact" (p. 115).[3]

Drawing on psychologist Jerome Bruner's (1983) theory of parental scaffolding, McGeer (2004) provides a backstory to our abilities to hope. Parental scaffolding—the kinds of support and encouragement parents provide their children—enables children to learn how to be effective agents. Echoing Eriksonian themes, McGeer notes that good parents encourage children to explore their own agency, to experience and overcome agential limitations. Good parental scaffolding allows children to deal with these limits in constructive ways—to experience frustration and other negative emotions, to be sure—but to learn from such episodes how to do better next time. Good parental scaffolding also teaches children the cognitive skills needed for effective agency, such as how to choose their ends well and take effective means to their ends. Children thereby learn to have confidence in their agency and to be resilient in the face of failure. Developing these and other qualities are part of the process of becoming effective agents, as well as good hopers. One important lesson of this backstory is that hope is deeply social (McGeer, 2004). Though we eventually become independent agents, or "self-scaffolders," in McGeer's (2004, p. 108) terms, we never completely lose the need for supportive others in maintaining our agency and our hope.

The social dimensions of hoping are apparent in McGeer's (2004) descriptions of three forms of hoping: responsive hoping, which is good, and wishful and willful hoping, which are bad. In short, wishful hopers are deficient in two ways: their desires are fanciful and impractical, and their capacity for effective agency in realizing their desires has been impaired by too much dependency on the agency of others. Willful hoping is "the hope of fear," being intimately bound with unreflective dread and ego anxiety. By contrast with wishful hopers, who seem inept in both desire formulation and their practical abilities to realize their hopes, willful hopers, whose hope is motivated by "self-protective dread or fear" seem neurotically driven to achieve their ends, blind to the passions that animate them, and impervious to the devastation the pursuit of their plans might cause (McGeer, 2004, p. 116). Unsurprisingly, according to this model, both wishful and willful hopers can be created by defective parental scaffolding.

Now for good hope. Responsive hoping, "the hope of care," has both intrapersonal and interpersonal dimensions (McGeer, 2004). Intrapersonal features of good hoping—for example, clearsighted, yet imaginative engagement with reality, resilience, flexibility, and the willingness to stretch one's agential capacities—are noted by McGeer (2004). What McGeer calls "peer scaffolding" is paramount for the interpersonal aspects of good hoping. Peer scaffolding is a form of interpersonal support for one's hoping that supplants the structures of parental scaffolding. It is made possible by being part of a community of self-scaffolding hopers—sympathetic, caring others who support one in one's hopes by helping one to formulate and pursue hopes in a positive way (see also Callina, Mueller, Buckingham, & Gutierrez, 2015). Peer scaffolding helps to keep one on the "straight and narrow" and away from the pitfalls of wishful and willful hoping, as well as to cope with the debilitating emotions that can result when hopes are not realized. Perhaps most importantly, creating a community of responsive hopers fosters clarity—clarity about the limits of our own agency and those of others.

Hope makes possible what McGeer (2008) calls "substantial trust." Substantial trust is characterized by two features: "(1) it involves making or maintaining judgments about others, or about what our behavior should be towards them, that go beyond what the evidence supports; and (2) it renounces the very process of weighing whatever evidence there is in a cool, disengaged, and purportedly objective way" (p. 240). Hope, according to McGeer, not only underwrites substantial trust but also allows us to understand the sense in which it can be rational.

How does hope support substantial trust? It does this through peer scaffolding. McGeer (2008) affirms: "by way of such hopeful scaffolding, we also give trusted others something substantial in return—namely, a motivationally energizing vision of what they can do or be" (p. 249). Through hopeful scaffolding, we express to others a vision they themselves might not have but trust that they can attain that vision, that they have the agential power to reconstruct themselves as we see them and as we hope they will come to see themselves.

Let us briefly recap the main points of this section, which has focused on agency, goal pursuit, and trust as key ingredients for hope. Erik Erikson offers a developmental account of the life span in which hope has crucial parts to play in ego maturation. Integral to this account is the role of caregivers in providing a trusting environment in which children are encouraged in their explorations and goal pursuit. Snyder takes up the notion that hope is a form of goal pursuit and offers an elaborate account of this in his agency-pathways theory of hope. Themes of hopeful agency and the development of hope are pursued by the philosopher Victoria McGeer. Her account underscores how hope aids the development of agency, how hope is cultivated in children and sustained in adults, and how modes of hoping can be both good and bad. She also relates hope to trust, reinforcing themes found in the work of philosopher Margaret Walker.

The foregoing philosophical and psychological accounts highlight hope's connections with positive expectations for the future, agency, and trust. Other approaches take a broader purview. These conceptions invite the question: *What else is hope?*

What Else Is Hope?

Church fathers, such as St. Augustine (1961) and St. Thomas Aquinas (Aquinas & Perry, 2008), viewed hope as moving us beyond the earthly realm toward the divine. For them, hope is, ultimately, hope for unification with God in the afterlife. We discuss contemporary variants of this view from the work of philosophers Patrick Shade (2001) and Jonathan Lear (2006). Drawing on a range of sources, but especially nursing science studies of hope in terminally ill patients, we also suggest that we can have hope not only in the present for the future but also in the present for the present. In conditions of extremity, such hope can be life-sustaining.

Radical Hope

Hope is not only an occurrent mental state; it can also be a general orientation or global attitude of positivity and openness toward life. As such, a hopeful orientation seems to be a *sine qua non* for meaningful human life and effective agency. The distinction between state and "trait" hope and the antecedents and consequences of each for positive human functioning are empirical questions for psychologists (e.g., Snyder, 2002). Nevertheless, researchers may draw from theoretical models of philosophers to help guide this area of inquiry.

To distinguish among different types of hoping, the philosopher Patrick Shade (2001) offers what he calls "a pragmatic theory" of hope. Drawing on the views of the philosophical pragmatists Charles S. Pierce, William James, and John Dewey, he presents a theory of hope as consisting of three main elements: the particular ends of hope; habits of hope, which he identifies as persistence, resourcefulness, and courage; and the enduring disposition of hopefulness. Shade (2001) examines hope's roles in the formation of self and the growth of agency as well as its social nature. He defines "hopefulness" as an energetic openness to possibilities—"an attitude or general orientation toward the future which defines how we respond to life's trials" (p. 136). Hopefulness is a general, enduring character state or global disposition—the deepest level at which hope can take root in the human psyche and personality. In addition, Shade argues that hope can be a form of "conditioned transcendence." By this he means that hope is conditioned by our situations and abilities yet allows us to transcend these limits by "stretching" our agency, prompting us to grow as agents through intelligence, adaptability, and a creative openness to new possibilities. He contrasts hope as conditioned transcendence with hope as unconditioned transcendence, or "hoping against hope" (Martin [2014], too, attempts to parse the meaning of the phrase "hoping against hope," not by adverting to factors beyond human agency but by arguing that hopers may take a "licensing stance" toward the probability of a hoped-for outcome). When we hope against hope, we draw upon the resources of an unconditionally transcendent being, such as God (Shade, 2001). The difference between hope as conditioned and unconditioned transcendence is this: when we hope in the sense of conditioned transcendence, we trust in our own agency, intelligence, adaptability, and creativity, as well as that of others, to move us toward our hoped-for ends. When we hope in the sense of unconditioned transcendence, we realize that what we hope for outstrips human capabilities. Consequently, we look to that which lies beyond our powers; we place our hopes in the will of the divine.

Similar to unconditioned hope is what Jonathan Lear (2006) calls "radical hope." Lear hypothesizes that the Crow nation had this form of hope at a crucial historical juncture—when they were faced with the destruction of traditional tribal ways of life by White domination. He writes:

> What makes this hope *radical* is that it is directed toward a future goodness that transcends the current ability to understand what it is. Radical hope anticipates a good for which those who have the hope as yet lack the appropriate concepts with which to understand it. (Lear 2006, p. 103; italics in original)

He develops this fascinating concept through an examination of the end of the Crow civilization with the advance of Whites across the Great Plains. Unlike other tribes, the Crow were able to survive the demise of their culture, keep some of their land, and create new forms of flourishing in a White world that was radically different from the ways of life they had known. Lear attributes their success to the ability of their chief, Plenty Coups, to have radical hope. He hypothesizes that Plenty Coups led his people through the demise of their civilization guided, in large part, by the imaginative possibilities suggested to him by dreams that reflected tribal anxieties at the incursions of Whites into tribal ways of life (Lear, 2006). To understand these dreams and their significance for the Crow, some background is necessary.

Plenty Coups had a series of prophetic dreams that prepared him to lead his tribe through the demise of their civilization. In one such dream, he sees a great forest in which the trees are inhabited by many tribes of bird-people (Lear, 2006). A great storm destroys all of the trees in the forest except one—that of the Chickadee-Person. Tribal elders interpreted the Chickadee lodge to represent the Crow tribe; the message of the dream was that the Crow should use the wisdom of the chickadee to survive (Lear, 2006). The wisdom of the chickadee was simply to listen and learn. The dream was content-poor in the sense that it did not give the Crow substantive advice on how to cope with the coming of White civilization. It gave them a procedure in barest outline—listen, learn, and do the best you can to live—to hold onto Crow lands and sustain Crow culture. Enigmatic though that was, it was the most that the imagination of the Crow was equipped to deliver. This is because they did not have the concepts in terms of which future ways of life would be comprehensible. They did not have, for example, the concept of individual property ownership and, consequently, did not have the notion of land parceled out to individual farmers. These notions would become parts of their conceptual repertoire in life under Whites and would frame the terms in which their lives would subsequently unfold. Thus their hope for a future good—for future flourishing—was radical in the sense that it outstripped the concepts available to them at the time of Plenty Coups' dream.

In sum, modern and contemporary philosophy offer a wide range of perspectives on hope, from the bare-bones conception according to which hope is the desire for an expected positive benefit and the belief that it is probable, or at least, possible, to the notions of hope as including mental imaging and a panoply of emotions and associated behaviors, to conceptions of hope as unconditioned transcendence, or as radical. Both of the latter conceptions entail that the positive expectations for which one hopes outstrip one's conceptual or imaginative abilities. Thus if philosophers such as Shade and Lear are correct, it seems we are able to hope for that which we cannot conceptualize or imagine.

Hope in the Present for the Present

In this chapter, we propose that key ingredients for hope include agency, trust, and positive future expectations. But burgeoning ideas about hope from different fields of inquiry identify it as something greater than the sum of its parts. Concepts from relational developmental systems theories—especially *holism*, which refers to the idea that the meanings of entities and events derive from the context in which they are embedded—help us understand hope in a different way. In other words, hope is not just a psychological process or personality characteristic of the individual implying activity, or *becoming*; hope is also a way of *being*, of both interacting with and receiving feedback from the ecology (Kylmä & Vehviläinen-Julkunen, 1997). We refer to this notion as *hope in the present for the present*. This conceptualization of hope is consistent with the individual-context relations of focal concern in relational developmental systems theories.

This type of present-oriented hope is especially salient when there are constraints on one's future. Viktor Frankl (1959), a psychotherapist and Jewish holocaust survivor, wrote extensively on the search for meaning and the importance of optimism in the context of hopelessness and suffering. He proposed that, "When we are no longer able to change a situation . . . we are challenged to change ourselves" (p. 116). Thus there may be instances where the focus of one's relationship with his or her context is not some macro-level layer of the ecology or the arrow of time but rather a more immediate focus on the present. Within the past 20 years or so, nursing science studies of palliative care patients find a phenomenon that challenges our view of hope as exclusively future-oriented: the dying can have hope in the present for the present (Herth & Cutcliffe, 2002; Nekolaichuk & Bruera, 1998; Parker-Oliver, 2002).

Nekolaichuk and Bruera (1998) seek to provide a framework for instilling hope in terminally ill patients. To do this, they devise strategies to shift patients' focus away from future-oriented hopes to hopes centered on the construction of meaning in the present. For example, they stress the cultivation in the dying of "the hoping self." This is an "inner self" that focuses more on being than on doing. As the patient's capacities for agency contract, hope can be maintained, they believe, by focusing on the patient as a "be-er" rather than a "do-er." Even as the patient loses physical functionality, he or she can maintain a hopeful presence in the world through connection with past memories. The hoping self imbues the present situation with meaning. The meaningfulness of the present for the dying person, then, is constructed by reaching back into the past. Hope arises from the meanings the terminally ill patient constructs for and ascribes to his or her present situation. These meanings should involve neither a false hope for a cure, nor for a physical life that is not possible in the circumstances. Perhaps more controversially, the authors argue that hope in the present can also be ignited by encouraging the patient to think about immortality in expansive ways that go beyond the notion of immortality as avoidance of physical death. This point, though interesting, does not challenge the notion that hope is not exclusively future-oriented. This is because conceptions of immortality always seems to point toward some form of continuation of the self in the future, for example, in life after death, or through a legacy left in this world.

Nevertheless, Herth and Cutcliffe (2002) reinforce the point that hope need not include an emphasis on future-oriented agency. They define hope in palliative care contexts as "an inner power directed towards enrichment of 'being'" (Herth 1990, cited in Herth & Cutcliffe, 2002, p. 979). Drawing on a study by Benzein, Norberg, and Saveman (2001) of 11 terminally ill cancer patients experiencing palliative home care in Sweden, Herth and Cutcliffe (2002) note a tension between "hoping for something" and "living in hope" in the terminally ill. The lived experience of hope in these patients included the hope of living as normally as possible and having supportive relationships.

The present orientation of the hope of the dying is seemingly at odds with the typical view of hope as future-oriented. We believe, however, that the present orientation of hope is consistent with our everyday experiences. In other words, a case can be made that we hope in and for the present and not only in the present for the future. Without such hope in and for the present, our lives would be largely bereft of meaning and certainly lacking in joy and zest.

Conclusions

This chapter deals with the history of philosophical and psychological perspectives about hope. We examined three questions about hope: *why* is hope important; *what* is hope; and finally, *what else* is hope? To address the first question, we presented concepts from relational developmental systems theories, which are the contemporary paradigm for the study of human development. This perspective justifies a hopeful orientation toward human development. Moreover, it emphasizes plasticity, agency, and the mutually influential relations between individuals and their contexts, and these ideas provide a useful framework for defining hope and understanding why it is a necessary variable for the science of positive human development.

To address the second question, we drew perspectives from modern and contemporary philosophy and psychology to provide evidence for three key ingredients for hope: positive future expectations, agency, and trust. These are the aspects of psychosocial development that scientists should attend to if they are to understand hope and its role in positive development (Callina et al., 2015).

Finally, we explored other areas that go beyond these three key ingredients. Radical hope and *hope in the present for the present* are two promising avenues for future scholarship. The latter view may be especially salient for work that seeks to promote hope in contexts that are especially constrained, such as terminal illness. According to this view, hopeful people have positive attitudes toward and expectations of their present experiences as well as of those in the future. Their hopeful attitude in and for the present is carried forward into the future. The hope that we have in and for the present is what motivates us to get out of bed in the morning, to look forward to the day ahead, to attend to our chores, and to lead our lives—doing all of the mundane, happy, sad, exciting, multifarious things we usually do as we go through our day. Moreover, our hope in the present is similar to that which caregivers find and seek to cultivate in the terminally ill, insofar as it is intimately connected with the meanings we find in and give to life events. Their telling phrase for this is "living in hope." We submit that many of us "live in hope" in our experiences of the present. Living in hope is precisely what the depressed, apathetic, and resigned cannot do, or do only in truncated, withered ways. Both, in different ways, find their lives bereft of meaning and cannot, in Tennen, Affleck, and Tennen's (2002) phrase, muster "a sense of trust that the world makes sense" (p. 312).

These observations lead us back to the point that hope is a *sine qua non* of meaningful human life and agency. Meaning and hope are intertwined—joined at the hip, so to speak. If, as in the case of the dying, hope responds to context and imbues life events with meaning, a way of destroying hope is to render the context so unintelligible and beyond the hoper's control that he or she cannot make it meaningful. Thus captors try to destroy hope in their prisoners by rendering their lives unintelligible—subjecting them to unpredictable, senseless routines, or compelling them to undertake meaningless tasks, such as digging deep holes and filling them up again.

Creating unintelligibility in a life is a way of making it seem meaningless to its possessor, of destroying the sense of rational control or purpose that a captive has in life. Destroying meaning, the sense of control, and the sense of purpose are ways of depriving people of hope. Yet, if there is some meaning that can be found or constructed around life events, hope can take root.

If we are correct in our view that we can hope in and for the present, we need an error theory to explain why we so seldom notice that fact. Why have so many theorists assumed that hope is mainly, if not exclusively, future-oriented? We conjecture that the present orientation of hope is missed because of its very ubiquity in our lives. Hope, inculcated in our lives from our earliest childhood experiences, as Erikson and McGeer maintain, is as natural to us as water is to fish. Its present orientation comes to the fore only when we consider the plight of those who are without hope, who have sunk into despair, apathetically float along, or resignedly endure a life bereft of happiness. But, as Stephen Hawking observed, "Where there's life, there is hope." When we live in hope, we live with an interest in how our lives will go; we care about how events unfold and how our projects and plans will turn out. When we lose hope, we become disinterested. Chronic apathy, despair, and the sense that life is meaningless or absurd are the most serious symptoms of the loss of hope (Farran, Herth, & Popovich, 1995). Less serious manifestations are boredom, or the frenzied quest for continual amusement, which fills the void of meaninglessness in lives lacking hope.[4]

In short, hope enhances our agency, helping us to achieve our goals and cope with obstacles and challenges. It orients us positively toward the possibilities inherent in the future and also gives meaning and zest to our experiences in the present. People whose lives lack hope are impaired; those with hope are able to engage more fully with their environment. Consistent with relational developmental systems theories, our abilities to hope develop in community with other hopers. We hope well or badly, if we do hope, in the company of others. Thus developing positive "ecologies of hoping" is essential for healthy development and meaningful human lives.

Future Directions

- What is the relationship between psychological and philosophical theories of hope?
- What empirical studies can or could be done to test the empirical validity of philosophical conceptions of hope?
- What kind of empirical studies could be conducted to ascertain the extent to which hope is in the present for the present, as opposed to in the present for the future?
- What relationship does unconditional hope have to belief in God or the afterlife, or to belief in some transcendent being?
- How do philosophical and psychological conceptions of hope relate to theological or theistic conceptions of hope?
- What is false hope, and how does it relate to pathological hope or hope that is positive?

Acknowledgments

This chapter was supported in part by grants from the Templeton Religion Trust and the John Templeton Foundation's "Science of Virtues" project.

Notes

1. From Wheatley's (1958, p. 126) example, it seems that wishing need only be consistent with logical and not physical possibility. But surely we can have wishes that are not consistent with what is logically possible. I might wish to be the one who squares the circle, but since it is logically impossible to square the circle, my wish is inconsistent with what is logically possible. Wheatley's (1958, p. 124, n. 2; see also p. 124) analysis of this kind of case is to deny that such wish-tokens really express wishes: "Many a seeming wish-token, of course, is other than it seems." We see no reason to accept this. My wish to square the circle is still a wish; it does not lose its character as a wish because of the logical impossibility of its object.

2. Victoria McGeer (2004) and Margaret Walker (2006) have been said to hold "agential investment" theories of hope (see Martin, 2014). McGeer and Walker have similar positions about hope and agency, but McGeer goes beyond Walker in her treatment of developmental aspects of hope, so we focus on McGeer.

3. A caveat to this is in order. Though McGeer stresses the importance of good hoping for effective agency, her account, as we understand it, does not preclude the possibility that we can hope for something for someone else (see McGeer, 2004). In other words, hope is not always self-centered, nor need it always involve the hoper's agency. I might hope, for example, that a loved one overcomes a personal problem or achieves a desired goal, though I am powerless to effect this though my own agency. We are grateful to Lucy Randall for calling this point to our attention.

4. Commenting on the work of the philosopher and theologian St. Thomas Aquinas, the Thomist philosopher Josef Pieper (1997) defines *acedia* as the "sorrow according to the world" that "produces death" (p. 119). Pieper (1997, p. 120) claims that *acedia* is the root of despair. In addition to despair, *acedia* gives rise to a number of interesting

phenomena. They include an uneasy mental restlessness that Aquinas calls *evagatio mentis* (1997, p. 120–121). *Evagatio mentis* is manifested in excessive talkativeness and curiosity, irreverent urges, interior restlessness, and instability of place or purpose (Aquinas, 1997, p. 121). Interestingly, a similar phenomenon has been identified in people lacking hope by nursing science researchers (see Farran, Herth, & Popovich, 1995, p. 32). They describe it as a sort of busyness that is an avoidance of the real issues that a person must face in order to overcome hopelessness and restore effective agency.

References

Aquinas, T., & Perry, J. (2008). *Commentaries on St. Paul's epistles to Timothy, Titus, and Philemon*. South Bend, IN: St. Augustines Press.

Aspinwall, L. G., & Leaf, S.L. (2002). In search of the unique aspects of hope: Pinning our hopes on positive emotions, future-oriented thinking, hard times, and other people. *Psychological Inquiry, 13*(4), 276–321. doi:10.1207/S15327965PLI1304_02

Baltes, P. B., Lindenberger, U., & Staudinger, U. M. (2006). Life span theory in developmental psychology. In W. Damon (Series Ed.) & R. M. Lerner (Vol. Ed.), *Handbook of child psychology: Vol 1. Theoretical models of human development*. (6th ed., pp. 569–664). Hoboken, NJ: Wiley. doi:10.1002/9780470147658.chpsy0111

Benzein, E., Norberg, A., & Saveman, B. (2001). The meaning of the lived experience of hope in patients with cancer in palliative home care. *Palliative Medicine, 15*(2), 117–126. doi:10.1191/026921601675617254

Bloch, E. (1986). *The principle of hope*. 3 vols. Translated by N. Plaice, S. Plaice, & Paul Knight. Oxford: Blackwell.

Bovens, L. (1999). The value of hope. *Philosophy and Phenomenological Research, 59*(3), 667–682. doi:10.2307/2653787

Brandstädter, J. (2006). Action perspectives on human development. In W. Damon (Series Ed.) & R. M. Lerner (Vol. Ed.), *Handbook of child psychology: Vol. 1. Theoretical models of human development* (6th ed., pp. 516–568). New York: Wiley. doi:10.1002/9780470147658

Bronfenbrenner, U., & Morris, P. A. (2006). The bioecological model of human development. In W. Damon (Vol. Ed.) & R. M. Lerner (Series Ed.), *Handbook of child psychology: Vol. 1. Theoretical models of human development* (6th ed., pp. 793–828). New York: Wiley. doi:10.1002/9780470147658

Bruner, J. (1983). *Children's talk: Learning to use language*. New York: Norton.

Callina, K. S., Johnson, S. K., Buckingham, M. B., & Lerner, R. M. (2014). Hope in context: Developmental profiles of trust, hopeful future expectations, and civic engagement across adolescence. *Journal of Youth and Adolescence, 43*(6), 869–883. doi:10.1007/s10964-014-0096-9

Callina, K. S., Mueller, M. K., Buckingham, M. H., & Gutierrez, A. S. (2015). Building hope for positive development: Research, practice, and policy. In E. P. Bowers, G. J., Geldhof, S. K. Johnson, L. J. Hilliard, R. M. Hershberg, J. V. Lerner, & R. M. Lerner (Eds.), *Promoting positive youth development: Lessons learned from the 4-H study* (pp. 71–94). New York: Springer. doi:10.1007/978-3-319-17166-1_5

Carver, C. S., & Scheier, M. F. (2002a). The hopeful optimist. *Psychological Inquiry, 13*(4), 288-290.

Carver, C. S. & Scheier, M. F. (2002b). Optimism. In C. R. Snyder & Shane J. Lopez (Eds.), *Handbook of positive psychology* (pp. 231–243). New York: Oxford University Press.

Day, J. P. (1969). Hope. *American Philosophical Quarterly, 6*(2), 89–102.

Elder, G. H. Jr., & Shanahan, M. J. (2006). The life course and human development. In W. Damon (Series Ed.) & R. M. Lerner (Vol. Ed.), *Handbook of child psychology: Vol. 1. Theoretical models of human development* (6th ed., pp. 665–715). New York: Wiley. doi:10.1002/9780470147658

Erikson, E. H. (1959). *Identity and the life cycle: Selected papers*. New York: International Universities Press.

Erikson, E. H. (1964). *Insight and responsibility: Lectures on the ethical implications of psychoanalytic insight*. New York: Norton.

Erikson, E. H. (1997). *The life cycle completed: Extended version with new chapters on the ninth stage of development by Joan M. Erikson*. New York: Norton.

Farran, C. J., Herth, K. A., & Popovich, J. M. (1995). *Hope and hopelessness: Critical clinical constructs*. Thousand Oaks, CA: SAGE.

Ford, D. H., & Lerner, R. M. (1992). *Developmental systems theory: An integrative approach*. Newbury Park, CA: SAGE.

Frankl, V. E. (1959). *Man's search for meaning*. Boston, MA: Beacon Press.

French, T. M. (1952). *The integration of behavior*. Chicago: University of Chicago Press.

Geldhof, G. J., Little, T. D., & Colombo, J. (2010). Self-regulation across the life span. In R. M. Lerner (Ed.), *The handbook of life-span development: Vol. 2. Social and emotional development* (pp. 116–157). Hoboken, NJ: Wiley. doi:10.1002/9780470880166.hlsd002005

Gestsdóttir, S., & Lerner, R. M. (2008). Positive development in adolescence: The development and role of intentional self-regulation. *Human Development, 51*, 202–224. doi:10.1159/000135757

Gottschalk, L. A. (1974). A hope scale applicable to verbal samples. *Archives of General Psychiatry, 30*, 779–785. doi:10.1001/archpsyc.1974.01760120041007

Godfrey, J. J. (1987). *A philosophy of human hope*. Dordrecht, The Netherlands: Martinus Nijhoff. doi:10.1007/978-94-009-3499-3

Govier, T. (2011). Hope and its opposites. *Journal of Social Philosophy, 42*(3), 239–253. doi:10.1111/j.1467-9833.2011.01532.x

Heckhausen, J. (2000). Developmental regulation across the life span: An action-phase model of engagement and disengagement with developmental goals. In J. Heckhausen (Ed.), *Motivational psychology of human development: Developing motivation and motivating development* (pp. 213–231). New York: Elsevier Science.

Herth, K. (1990). Fostering hope in terminally ill people. *Journal of Advanced Nursing, 15*, 1250–1259. doi:10.1111/j.1365-2648.1990.tb01740.x

Herth, K., & Cutcliffe, J.R. (2002). The concept of hope in nursing 3: Hope and palliative care nursing. *British Journal of Nursing, 11*(14), 977–983. doi:10.12968/bjon.2002.11.14.10470

Hobbes, T. (1968). *Leviathan*. Edited by C. B. MacPherson. Harmondsworth, UK: Penguin Books.

Hume, D. (1978). *A treatise of human nature*. Edited by P. H. Nidditch. Oxford: Clarendon Press.

Kylmä, J., & Vehviläinen-Julkunen, K. (1997). Hope in nursing research: A meta-analysis of the ontological and epistemological foundations of research on hope. *Journal of Advanced Nursing, 25*(2), 364–371. doi:10.1046/j.1365-2648.1997.1997025364.x

Lear, J. (2006). *Radical hope: Ethics in the face of cultural devastation.* Cambridge, MA: Harvard University Press.

Lerner, R. M. (1984). *On the nature of human plasticity.* Cambridge, UK: Cambridge University Press. doi:10.1017/CBO9780511666988

Lerner, R. M. (2002). *Concepts and theories of human development.* Mahwah, NJ: Lawrence Erlbaum.

Lerner, R. M. (2004). *Liberty: Thriving and civic engagement among American youth.* Thousand Oaks, CA: SAGE.

Lerner, R. M. (2006). Developmental science, developmental systems, and contemporary theories of human development. In W. Damon (Series Ed.) & R. M. Lerner (Vol. Ed.), *Handbook of child psychology: Vol. 1. Theoretical models of human development* (6th ed., pp. 1–17). New York: Wiley. doi:10.1002/9780470147658

Lerner, R. M., & Callina, K. S. (2014). Relational developmental systems theories and the ecological validity of experimental designs. *Human Development, 56*(6), 372–380. doi:10.1159/000357179

Lerner, R. M., & Overton, W. F. (2008). Exemplifying the integrations of the relational developmental system: Synthesizing theory, research, and application to promote positive development and social justice. *Journal of Adolescent Research, 23,* 245–255. doi:10.1177/0743558408314385

Lewin, K. (1951). *Field theory in social science; selected theoretical papers.* Edited by D. Cartwright. New York: Harper & Row.

Lindholm, M. E., Marabita, F., Gomez-Cabrero, D., Rundqvist, H., Ekström, T. J., Tegnér, J., & Sundberg, C. J. (2014). An integrative analysis reveals coordinated reprogramming of the epigenome and the transcriptome in human skeletal muscle after training. *Epigenetics, 9*(12), 1557–1569. doi:10.4161/15592294.2014.982445.

Little, T. D., Snyder, R., & Wehmeyer, M. L. (2006). The agentic self: On the nature and origins of personal agency across the lifespan. In D. Mroczek & T. D. Little (Eds.), *The handbook of personality development* (pp. 61–79). Mahwah, NJ: Lawrence Erlbaum.

Lopez, S. J., Rose, S., Robinson, C., Marques, S. C., & Pais-Ribeiro, J. L. (2009). Measuring and promoting hope in school children. In R. Gilman, E. S. Huebner, & M. J. Furlong (Eds.), *Handbook of positive psychology in the schools* (pp. 37–51). Mahwah, NJ: Lawrence Erlbaum.

Luther, M. (2004). *Table talk.* Translated by W. Hazlitt. Granville, FL: Bridge-Logos. (Original work published 1569)

Marcel, G. (1978). Homo viator introduction to a metaphysic of hope. *Philpapers.*

Magnusson, D., & Stattin, H. (2006). The person in context: A holistic–interactionistic approach. In W. Damon & R. M. Lerner (Eds.), *Handbook of child psychology: Vol. 3. Social, emotional, and personality development* (6th ed., pp. 400–464). New York: Wiley. doi:10.1002/9780470147658.chpsy0108

Martin, A. (2011). Hopes and dreams. *Philosophy and Phenomenological Research LXXXIII*(1), 148–173. doi:10.1111/j.1933-1592.2010.00422.x

Martin, A. (2014). *How we hope: A moral psychology.* Princeton, NJ: Princeton University Press.

McClelland, M. M., Ponitz, C. C., Messersmith, E. E., & Tominey, S. (2010). Self-regulation: The integration of cognition and emotion. In W. Damon (Series Ed.) & R. M. Lerner (Vol. Ed.), *The handbook of life-span development: Vol. 1. Cognition, biology, and methods* (pp. 509–553). Hoboken, NJ: Wiley. doi:10.1002/9780470880166.hlsd002005

McGeer, V. (2004). The art of good hope. *Annals of the American Academy of Political and Social Science, 592,* 100–127. doi:10.1177/000271620326178

McGeer, V. (2008). Trust, hope, and empowerment. *Australasian Journal of Philosophy, 86*(2), 237–254. doi:10.1080/00048400801886413

Meaney, M. J. (2010). Epigenetics and the biological definition of gene × environment interactions. *Child Development, 81*(1), 41–79. doi:10.1111/j.1467-8624.2009.01381.x

Meaney, S. (2014). Epigenetic regulation of cholesterol homeostasis. *Frontiers in Genetics, 5*(311), 1–10. doi:10.3389/fgene.2014.00311

Meirav, A. (2009). The nature of hope. *Ratio (New Series), XXII*(2), 216–233.doi:10.1111/j.1467-9329.2009.00427.x

Menninger, K. (1960). Hope. *Pastoral Psychology, 11*(3), 11–24. doi:10.1007/BF01759243

Miller, J. F. (1985). Inspiring hope. *American Journal of Nursing, 85*(1), 22–25.

Misteli, T. (2013). The cell biology of genomes: Bringing the double helix to life. *Cell, 152*(6), 1209–1212. doi:10.1016/j.cell.2013.02.048

Mittleman, A. (2009). *Hope in a democratic age: Philosophy, religion, and political theory.* New York: Oxford University Press.

Nekolaichuk, C. L., & Bruera, E. (1998). On the nature of hope in palliative care. *Journal of Palliative Care, 14*(1), 36–42.

Overton, W. F. (2006). Developmental psychology: Philosophy, concepts, methodology. In W. Damon (Series Ed.) & R. M. Lerner (Vol. Ed.), *Handbook of child psychology: Vol. 1. Theoretical models of human development* (6th ed., pp. 18–88). Hoboken, NJ: Wiley. doi:10.1002/9780470147658.chpsy0102

Overton, W. F. (2010). Life-span development: Concepts and issues. In W. Damon (Series Ed.) & R. M. Lerner (Ed.), *The handbook of life-span development: Vol. 1. Cognition, biology, and methods* (pp. 1–29). New York: Wiley. doi:10.1002/9780470880166.hlsd002005

Overton, W. F. (2011). Relational developmental systems and quantitative behavior genetics: alternative or parallel methodologies? *Research in Human Development, 8*(3–4), 258–263. doi:10.1080/15427609.2011.634289

Overton, W. F. (2015). Processes, relations, and relational-developmental-systems. In R. M. Lerner, W. F. Overton, & P. C. M. Molenaar (Eds.), *Handbook of child psychology and developmental science: Vol. 1. Theory and method* (7th ed., pp. 12–62). New York: Wiley. doi:10.1002/9781118963418.childpsy102

Overton, W. F., & Müller, U. (2012). Meta-theories, theories, and concepts in the study of development. In R. M. Lerner, M. A. Easterbrooks, & J. Mistry (Eds.), & I. B. Weiner (Editor-in-Chief). *Comprehensive handbook of psychology: Vol. 6. Developmental psychology* (2nd ed., pp. 19–58). New York: Wiley.

Parker-Oliver, D. (2002). Redefining hope for the terminally ill. *American Journal of Hospice and Palliative Medicine, 19*(2), 115–120. doi:10.1177/104990910201900210

Peterson, C., & Seligman, M. E. (2004). *Character strengths and virtues: A handbook and classification.* New York: Oxford University Press.

Pettit, P. (2004). Hope and its place in mind. *Annals of the American Academy of Political and Social Science, 592*, 152–165. doi:10.1177/0002716203261798

Pieper, J. (1994). *Hope and history: Five Salzburg lectures.* Translated by D. Kipp. San Francisco, CA: Ignatius Press.

Pieper, J. (1997). *Faith, hope, love.* San Francisco, CA: Ignatius Press.

Rand, K. L., & Cheavens, J. S. (2009). Hope theory. In S. Lopez & C. R. Snyder (Eds.), *Oxford handbook of positive psychology* (2nd ed., pp. 323–333). New York: Oxford University Press.

Ratcliffe, M. (2008). *Feelings of being: Phenomenology, psychiatry, and the sense of reality.* Oxford: Oxford University Press.

Ratcliffe, M. (2010). Depression, guilt and emotional depth. *Inquiry, 53*(6), 602–626. doi:10.1080/0020174X.2010.526324

Ratcliffe, M. (2011). What is it to lose hope? *Phenomenology and Cognitive Science, 12*(4), 597–614. doi:10.1007/s11097-011-9215-1

Scheier, M. F., & Carver, C. S. (1985). Optimism, coping, and health: Assessment and implications of generalized outcome expectancies. *Health Psychology, 4*, 219–247. doi:10.1037/0278-6133.4.3.219

Scheier, M. F., Carver, C. S., & Bridges, M. W. (1994). Distinguishing optimism from neuroticism (and trait anxiety, self-mastery, and self-esteem): A reevaluation of the life orientation test. *Journal of Personality and Social Psychology, 67*(6), 1063–1078. doi:10.1037/0022-3514.67.6.1063

Schmid, K. L., & Lopez, S. (2011). Positive pathways to adulthood: The roles of hope in adolescents' constructions of their futures. In R. M. Lerner, J. V. Lerner, & J. B. Benson (Eds.), *Positive youth development: Advances in child development and behavior* (Vol. 41, pp. 72–89). New York: Academic Press. doi:10.1016/B978-0-12-386492-5.00004-X

Seligman, M. E. (1998). What is the good life? *APA monitor, 29*(10), 2.

Shade, P. (2001). *Habits of hope: A pragmatic theory.* Nashville, TN: Vanderbilt University Press.

Shorey, H. S., Little, T. D., Snyder, C. R., Kluck, B., & Robitschek, C. (2007). Hope and personal growth initiative: A comparison of positive, future-oriented constructs. *Personality and Individual Differences, 43*, 1917–1926.

Shorey, H. S., Snyder, C. R., Rand, K. L., Hockemeyer, J. R., & Feldman, D. B. (2002). Somewhere over the rainbow: Hope theory weathers its first decade. *Psychological Inquiry, 13*(4), 322–331. doi:10.1207/S15327965PLI1304_03

Slavich, G. M., & Cole, S. W. (2013). The emerging field of human social genomics. *Clinical Psychological Science, 1*(3), 1–18. doi:10.1177/2167702613478594

Snyder, C. R. (1994). *The psychology of hope: You can get there from here.* NewYork: Free Press.

Snyder, C. R. (2002). Hope theory: Rainbows in the mind. *Psychological Inquiry, 13*(4), 249–275. doi:10.1207/S15327965PLI1304_01

Snyder, C. R., Harris, C., Anderson, J. R., Holleran, S. A., Irving, L. M., Sigmon, S. T, . . . Harney, P. (1991). The will and the ways: Development and validation of an individual-differences measure of hope. *Journal of Personality and Social Psychology, 60*, 57–585. doi:10.1037/0022-3514.60.4.570

Snyder, C. R., Irving, L., & Anderson, J.R. (1991). Hope and health: Measuring the will and the ways. In C. R. Snyder & D. R. Forsyth (Eds.), *Handbook of social and clinical psychology: The health perspective* (pp. 285–305). Elmsford, NY: Pergamon Press.

Snyder, C. R., Rand, K. L., & Sigmon, D. R. (2002). Hope theory: A member of the positive psychology family. In C. R. Snyder & S. J. Lopez (Eds.), *Handbook of positive psychology* (pp. 231–243). New York: Oxford University Press.

St. Augustine. (1961). Confessions. Translated by R. S. Pine-Coffin. New York: Penguin.

Staats, S. R., & Stassen, M. A. (1985). Hope: An affective cognition. *Social Indicators Research, 17*, 235–242. doi:10.1007/BF00319312

Steinbock, A. J. (2006). Time, otherness, & possibility in the experience of hope. In P. Vandevelde (Ed.), *Issues in interpretation theory* (pp. 271–289). Milwaukee, WI: Marquette University Press.

Stotland, E. (1969). *The psychology of hope: An integration of experimental, clinical, and social approaches.* San Francisco, CA: Jossey-Bass.

Tennen, H., Affleck, G., & Tennen, R. (2002). Clipped feathers: The theory and measurement of hope. *Psychological Inquiry, 13*(4), 311–317.

Van Hooft, S. (2011). *Hope.* Durham, UK: Acumen Publishing.

Verdenius, W. J. (1985). *A commentary on Hesiod: Works and days.* Leiden: E. J. Brill.

Walker, M. U. (2006). *Moral repair: Reconstructing moral relations after wrongdoing.* New York: Cambridge University Press. doi:10.2277/0521810884

Wheatley, J. (1958). Wishing and hoping. *Analysis, 18*(6), 121–131. doi:10.1093/analys/18.6.121

Whitehead, A. N. (1929). *The function of reason.* Princeton, NJ: Princeton University Press.

Whitehead, A. N. (1978). *Process and reality* (corrected edition). Edited by D. R. Griffin & D. W. Sherburne. New York: Free Press.

Wigfield, A., & Eccles, J. S. (1992). The development of achievement task values: A theoretical analysis. *Developmental Review, 12*, 265–310. doi:10.1016/0273-2297(92)90011-P

Wild, J. (1958). *Spinoza selections.* New York: Charles Scribner's Sons.

Hope Theory: A Member of the Positive Psychology Family

C. R. Snyder, Kevin L. Rand, *and* David R. Sigmon

Abstract

This chapter provides a conceptual introduction to and overview of Snyder's hope theory. Hope is defined as "a positive motivational state that is based on an interactively derived sense of successful (a) agency (goal-directed energy) and (b) pathways (planning to meet goals)". The interactions among the goals, agency, and pathways components of hope theory are identified as well as the role of emotions in hope theory and how hope motivates behavior in the face of obstacles. A brief overview of the two most widely used measures of hope (the trait hope scale and the state hope scale) is provided. The conceptual differences between hope theory and related positive psychology theories such as optimism and self-efficacy are identified. Finally, the role of hope in promoting positive functioning in academics, coping with stress, psychotherapy, and other life contexts is reviewed.

Key Words: hope, agency, pathways, goals, trait hope scale, state hope scale

An Introduction to Hope Theory
The Birth of a Theory

A new theory typically begins with the proponents offering a model that supposedly is more heuristic than the prevailing, older view. Our development of hope theory began in this manner. So, what was the accepted scholarly view of hope that we sought to alter? The perception that one's goals can be attained was a common thread in the scholarly work that defined hope in the 1950s through 1960s (Cantril, 1964; Farber, 1968; Frank, 1975; Frankl, 1992; Melges & Bowlby, 1969; Menninger, 1959; Schachtel, 1959). Our hypothesis was that this view, although shared by many previous scholars, did not fully capture that which is involved in hopeful goal-directed thought. At this beginning stage, we sought a definition of hope that was at once more inclusive and relatively parsimonious. Although we sensed that this new view of hope was possible and necessary, we were not sure what that model would be. Our breakthrough came when we

followed a suggestion made by a former colleague, Fritz Heider, that we ask people to talk about their goal-directed thoughts. After participating in informal interviews about their goal-directed thought processes, people repeatedly mentioned the pathways to reach their goals *and* their motivation to use those pathways. Recall the previous view of hope as "the perception that one can reach desired goals"; it was as if people were suggesting that this overall process involved two components of goal-directed thought—pathways and agency. With some listening on our part, a new theory was born. Simply put, hopeful thought reflects the belief that one can find pathways to desired goals and become motivated to use those pathways. We also proposed that hope, so defined, serves to drive the emotions and well-being of people. Having given this very brief history of that which has come to be called hope theory, in the remainder of this section we will describe the various aspects of this theory in detail.

Goals

We begin with the assumption that human actions are goal directed. Accordingly, goals are the targets of mental action sequences, and they provide the cognitive component that anchors hope theory (Snyder, 1994a, 1994c, 1998b; Snyder, Cheavens, & Sympson, 1997; Snyder, Sympson, Michael, & Cheavens, 2000; Stotland, 1969). Goals may be short- or long-term, but they need to be of sufficient value to occupy conscious thought. Likewise, goals must be attainable, but they also typically contain some degree of uncertainty. On this latter point, when people have been interviewed, they report that hope flourishes under probabilities of intermediate goal attainment (Averill, Catlin, & Chon, 1990).

Pathways Thinking

In order to reach their goals, people must view themselves as being capable of generating workable routes to those goals.[1] This process, which we call *pathways thinking*, signifies one's perceived capabilities at generating workable routes to desired goals. Likewise, we have found that this pathways thinking is typified by affirming internal messages that are similar to the appellation "I'll find a way to get this done!" (Snyder, Lapointe, Crowson, & Early, 1998).

Pathways thinking in any given instantiation involves thoughts of being able to generate at least one, and often more, usable route to a desired goal. The production of several pathways is important when encountering impediments, and high-hope persons perceive that they are facile at finding such alternate routes; moreover, high-hope people actually are very effective at producing alternative routes (Irving, Snyder, & Crowson, 1998; Snyder, Harris, et al., 1991).

Agency Thinking

The motivational component in hope theory is agency—the perceived capacity to use one's pathways so as to reach desired goals. Agentic thinking reflects the self-referential thoughts about both starting to move along a pathway and continuing to progress along that pathway. We have found that high-hope people embrace such self-talk agentic phrases as "I can do this" and "I am not going to be stopped" (Snyder et al., 1998). Agentic thinking is important in all goal-directed thought, but it takes on special significance when people encounter impediments. During such instances of blockage, agency helps the person to apply the requisite

motivation to the best alternate pathway (Snyder, 1994c).

Adding Pathways and Agentic Thinking

It is important to emphasize that hopeful thinking necessitates *both* the perceived capacity to envision workable routes *and* goal-directed energy. Thus, hope is "a positive motivational state that is based on an interactively derived sense of successful (1) agency (goal-directed energy) and (2) pathways (planning to meet goals)" (Snyder, Irving, & Anderson, 1991, p. 287). In the progression of hopeful thinking in the goal-pursuit sequence, we hypothesize that pathways thinking increases agency thinking, which, in turn, yields further pathways thinking, and so on. Overall, therefore, pathway and agency thoughts are iterative as well as additive over the course of a given sequence of goal-directed cognitions (see Snyder, Harris, et al., 1991).

Hope, Impediments, and Emotion

Although most other views have characterized hope as an emotion (Farina, Hearth, & Popovich, 1995), we have emphasized the thinking processes in hope theory. Specifically, we posit that positive emotions should flow from perceptions of successful goal pursuit. Perception of successful goal pursuit may result from unimpeded movement toward desired goals, or it may reflect instances in which the protagonist has effectively overcome any problems or blockages. Negative emotions, on the other hand, are the product of unsuccessful goal pursuits. The perceptions of unsuccessful goal pursuit can stem from insufficient agentic and/or pathway thinking or the inability to overcome a thwarting circumstance. We thus are proposing that *goal-pursuit cognitions cause emotions*.

Related to these points, through both correlational and causal methodologies, we have found that persons confronted with insurmountable goal blockages experience negative emotions, whereas successful, unimpeded goal pursuit or successful goal pursuit after overcoming impediments yields positive emotions (Snyder et al., 1996). These findings parallel those from other laboratories, where people who encounter severe difficulties in pursuit of important goals report lessened well-being (Diener, 1984; Emmons, 1986; Little, 1983; Omodei & Wearing, 1990; Palys & Little, 1983; Ruehlman & Wolchik, 1988). Furthermore, the growing consensus is that the perceived lack of progress toward major goals is the cause of reductions in well-being, rather than vice versa (Brunstein, 1993; Little, 1989).

Full Hope Model

Moving from left to right in Figure 3.1, one can see the proposed temporal order of the goal-directed thought sequence in hope theory. The etiology of the pathways and agency thoughts appears at the far left. Newborns undertake pathways thinking immediately after birth in order to obtain a sense of "what goes with what" (i.e., what events seem to be correlated in time with each other; Schulman, 1991). Over the course of childhood, these lessons eventually become refined so that the child understands the process of causation (i.e., events are not just related in time, but one event elicits another event). Additionally, at approximately 1 year of age, the baby realizes that she or he is separate from other entities (including the caregiver). This process, called *psychological birth,* portends another important insight for the very young child—that he or she can cause such chains of events to happen. That is to say, the self is perceived as a causal instigator. These psychological birth and instigator "lessons" contribute to a sense of personal agency.

In summary, the acquisition of goal-directed hopeful thought is absolutely crucial for the child's survival and thriving. As such, parents, caregivers, teachers, and members of society in general are invested in teaching this hopeful thinking. For the reader who is interested in detailed descriptions of the developmental antecedents of the hope process, we would suggest previous writings on this topic (e.g., McDermott & Snyder, 2000, pp. 5–18; Snyder, 1994c, pp. 75–114; Snyder, 2000a, pp. 21–37; Snyder, McDermott, Cook, & Rapoff 1997, pp. 1–32).

As shown in Figure 3.1, "outcome value" becomes important in the pre-event analysis phase. If the imagined outcomes have sufficiently high importance so as to demand continued mental attention, then the person moves to the event sequence analysis phase wherein the pathways and agency thoughts iterate. Sometimes, however, the iterative process of pathways and agency thinking may cycle back in order to assure that the outcome remains of sufficient importance to warrant continued goal-directed processing. In turn, pathways and agency thoughts (as shown in the bidirectional arrows) continue to alternate and aggregate (summate) throughout the event sequence so as to influence the subsequent level of success in any given goal pursuit. The left-to-right broad-lined arrows of Figure 3.1 reflect the overall feed-*forward* flow of hopeful goal-directed thinking.

If a particular goal pursuit has been completed, the person's goal attainment (or nonattainment)

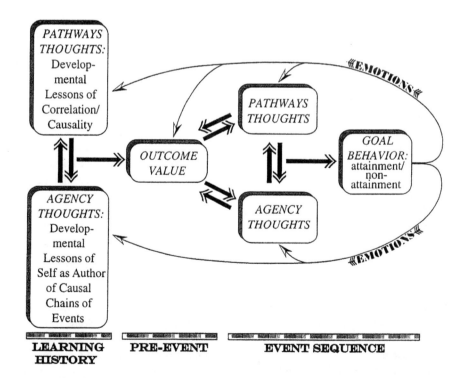

Fig. 3.1. Schematic of feed-forward and feed-back functions involving agency and pathways goal-directed thoughts in hope theory.

thoughts and the resultant success-derived positive (or failure-derived negative) emotions should cycle back to influence subsequent perceived pathways and agentic capabilities in that situation and in general, as well as to impact the outcome value. As shown in the narrow-lined, right-to-left arrows in Figure 3.1, the feedback process is composed of the particular emotions that result from perceived successful or unsuccessful goal attainment. It is important to note, therefore, that hope theory involves an interrelated system of goal-directed thinking that is responsive to feedback at various points in the temporal sequence.

Individual-Differences Scales Derived From Hope Theory

One important step in the evolution of a new psychological theory is the development of individual-differences measures that accurately reflect the structure of the construct and are reliable and valid. Individual-differences measures allow for tests of a theory, and they facilitate the application of a given construct to research and applied settings. We report next on the development of three such instruments for measuring hope.[2]

Trait Hope Scale

The adult Trait Hope Scale (Snyder, Harris, et al., 1991) consists of four agency, four pathways, and four distracter items. In completing the items, respondents are asked to imagine themselves across time and situational contexts. This instrument demonstrates (a) both internal and temporal reliability, with two separate yet related agency and pathways factors, as well as an overarching hope factor (Babyak, Snyder, & Yoshinobu, 1993); and (b) extensive convergent and discriminant validational support (Cheavens, Gum, & Snyder, 2000; Snyder, Harris, et al., 1991). The Trait Hope Scale is shown in Appendix A.

State Hope Scale

The State Hope Scale (Snyder et al., 1996) has three agency and three pathways items in which respondents describe themselves in terms of how they are "right now." Numerous studies support the internal reliability and factor structure, as well as the convergent and discriminant validity of this scale (Feldman & Snyder, 2000; Snyder et al., 1996). The State Hope Scale is shown in Appendix B.

Children's Hope Scale

The Children's Hope Scale (for ages 8 to 16) (Snyder, Hoza, et al., 1997) comprises three agency and three pathways items. The internal and test-retest reliabilities of this scale have been documented, as has its two-factor structure. Relevant studies also support its convergent and discriminant validities (Moon & Snyder, 2000; Snyder, Hoza, et al., 1997). The Children's Hope Scale is shown in Appendix C.

Similarities Between Hope Theory and Other Positive Psychology Theories

We now turn to the relationships that hope theory has with five other related theories in the positive psychology family. Fortunately for the process of making comparison with hope theory, in addition to thorough theoretical expositions, each of these five other theories has an individual-differences scale. Our premise is that hope theory should manifest some relationship similarities to these other constructs so as to support its being part of the positive psychology group (i.e., convergent validity), and yet it should have sufficient differences so as not to be a proxy for an already existing theory (i.e., discriminant validity). We have prepared Table 3.1 to highlight the shared and not-shared components of the theories, as well as the relative emphases in each theory.[3]

Optimism: Seligman

Abramson, Seligman, and Teasdale (1978) emphasized attributions that people made for important negative life events in their reformulated helplessness model. In a subsequent evolution of those ideas, Seligman (1991) uses the attribution process as the basis for his theory of optimism (see Table 3.1). In this regard, the optimistic attributional style is the pattern of external, variable, and specific attributions for failures instead of internal, stable, and global attributes that were the focus in the earlier helplessness model.[4] Implicit in this theory is the importance placed on negative outcomes, and there is a goal-related quality in that optimistic people are attempting to distance themselves from negative outcomes. In hope theory, however, the focus is on reaching desired future positive goal-related outcomes, with explicit emphases on the agency and pathways thoughts about the desired goal. In both theories, the outcome must be of high importance, although this is emphasized more in hope theory. Unlike the Seligman optimism theory, hope theory also explicitly addresses the etiology of positive and negative emotions.

Optimism: Scheier and Carver

Scheier and Carver (1985) emphasize generalized outcome expectancies in their theory and

Table 3.1. Implicit and Explicit Operative Processes and Their Respective Emphases in Hope Theory as Compared with Selected Positive Psychology Theories

Theory						
Operative Process	Hope	Optimism: Seligman	Optimism: Scheier & Carver	Self-efficacy	Self-esteem	Problem-Solving
Attributions		+++				
Outcome Value	++	+	++	++	+	+
Goal-Related Thinking	+++	+	++	+++	+	+++
Perceived Capacities for Agency-Related Thinking	+++		+++	+++		
Perceived Capacities for Pathways-Related Thinking	+++		+	++		+++

+ Operative process is implicit part of model.

++ Operative process is explicit part of model.

+++ Operative process is explicit and emphasized in model.

Thus, interpret more plus signs (none to + to ++ to +++) as signifying greater emphasis attached to the given operative process within a particular theory.

assume that optimism is a goal-based approach that occurs when an outcome has substantial value. In this optimism model, people perceive themselves as being able to move toward desirable goals and away from undesirable goals (antigoals; Carver & Scheier, 2000a). Although pathways-like thoughts and agency-involved thoughts are implicit in their model, the outcome expectancies (similar to agency) are seen as the prime elicitors of goal-directed behaviors (Scheier & Carver, 1985, 1987). Thus, Scheier and Carver emphasize agency-like thought, whereas equal and constantly iterative emphases are given to pathways and agent thoughts in hope theory (see Table 3.1).[5] Both hope theory and optimism theory are cognitive and explain behavior across situations (Snyder, 1995); moreover, measures of the two constructs correlate in the .50 range (Snyder, Harris, et al., 1991). It should be noted, however, that hope has produced unique variance beyond optimism in the prediction of several variables, and that the factor structures of these two constructs differ (Magaletta & Oliver, 1999). Finally, these two theories differ in that hope theory describes the etiology of emotions (positive and negative), whereas Scheier and Carver are largely silent on this issue.

Self-Efficacy: Bandura

According to Bandura (1982, 1997), for self-efficacy to be activated, a goal-related outcome must be important enough to capture attention. This premise is similar to that held in hope theory. Although others have devised a trait measure of self-efficacy,[6] Bandura has steadfastly held that the cognitive processing in self-efficacy theory must focus on situation-specific goals. This goal emphasis parallels hope theory, but it differs in that for hope theory there may be enduring, cross-situational, and situational goal-directed thoughts. Within self-efficacy theory, the person is posited to analyze the relevant contingencies in a given goal attainment situation (called *outcome expectancies*, somewhat similar to pathways thought). Relative to the outcome expectancies wherein the focus is on the given contingencies, pathways thinking reflects the self-analysis of one's capabilities to produce initial routes to goals, as well as additional routes should the first become impeded. Thereafter, the person is hypothesized to evaluate her capacity to carry out the actions inherent in the outcome expectancies (called *efficacy expectancies*, with some similarity to agency thought). Whereas the efficacy expectancy emphasizes the personal perception about how a person *can* perform the requisite activities in a given situational context, hope theory emphasizes the person's self-referential belief that she or he will initiate (and continue) the requisite actions. A key difference is between the words *can* and *will*, with the former pertaining to the capacity to act and the latter tapping intentionality to act. Bandura posits that the situational self-efficacy (agency) thoughts are the last and most important cognitive step before initiating goal-directed action (see Table 3.1), whereas both agency and pathways thoughts are emphasized prior to and during the goal-pursuit sequence in hope theory. Ma galetta and Oliver (1999) report that hope provides unique variance independent of self-efficacy in predicting well-being, and that the factor structures of the two constructs vary. One final difference is worthy of note. Namely, Bandura's self-efficacy theory does not address the issue of emotions per se, whereas hope theory gives an explicit hypothesis about emotions being the result of goal-directed thoughts.

Self-Esteem

Hewitt (1998) concludes that self-esteem reflects the emotions flowing from persons' appraisals of their overall effectiveness in the conduct of their lives.[7] In the words of Coopersmith (1967), "Self-esteem is the personal judgment of worthiness" (p. 7). Additionally, self-esteem models are implicitly built on goal-directed thoughts (Hewitt, 1998; see Table 19.1), and they assume that an activity must be valued to implicate self-esteem. These latter two characteristics also apply in hope theory, but the emphasis in hope theory is on the analysis of the goal-pursuit process that elicits emotion or esteem. Self-esteem and hope correlate in the .45 range (Snyder, Harris, et al., 1991), but there is research support for the theoretical assumption that goal-pursuit thoughts (i.e., hope) influence esteem and not vice versa. It also has been reported that hope enhances the prediction of several positive outcomes beyond self-esteem (Curry, Snyder, Cook, Ruby, & Rehm, 1997; Snyder, Cheavens, & Michael, 1999).

Problem Solving

In problem-solving theory, the person's identification of a desired goal (a problem solution) is explicitly noted, and it is assumed implicitly that an important goal is involved (see Table 3.1; Heppner & Hillerbrand, 1991). Another major explicit emphasis, similar to that in hope theory, is on finding a pathway that is the basis for a problem-solving solution (D'Zurilla, 1986). Relative to problem-solving theories, the agentic thinking in hope theory is posited to provide the motivation to activate pathways thoughts (problem solving), and agency is thus explicit and emphasized. Significant positive correlations (*r*s of .40 to .50) have been found between hope and problem solving (Snyder, Harris, et al., 1991). Problem-solving theory does

not touch upon the topic of emotions, whereas in hope theory the emotions are posited to result from the perceived success in goal pursuits.

Summary of Shared Processes in Theories

Although there are differences relative to hope theory to be discerned in our discussion of these five theories, one can see considerable overlap (with varying emphases) in the plus signs of hope theory and the plus signs of the other positive psychology constructs (see Table 3.1). Also, these theory-based similarities are buttressed by modest correlations between hope measures and the scales derived from each of the other theories. Finally, as a point that we believe is of considerable importance, hope and the other theories share in providing psychological and physical benefits to people, and they all are members of the positive psychology family.

Hope and Looking Through a Positive Psychology Lens

Elsewhere, we have written that the positive psychology lens "reflects the viewpoint that the most favorable of human functioning capabilities can be studied scientifically, and that . . . we should not be minuscule in our focus, but rather positive psychology should embrace many foci—a wide lens that is suitable for a big topic" (Snyder & McCullough, 2000, pp. 151–152). By adding hope theory, we have yet another research framework for understanding and enhancing adaptive ways of functioning that are the foci in positive psychology. In this section, we report on the various topics that have been looked at through the frame of hope theory.

Academics

Learning and performing well in educational settings are important avenues for thriving in American society. By applying hopeful thinking, students should enhance their perceived capabilities of finding multiple pathways to desired educational goals, along with the motivations to pursue those goals. Also, through hopeful thinking, students should be able to stay "on task" and not be blocked by interfering self-deprecatory thoughts and negative emotions (Snyder, 1999a).

Based on presently available research with grade school, high school, and college students, it appears that hope bears a substantial relationship with academic achievement (Snyder, Cheavens, & Michael, 1999). Hope relates to higher achievement test scores (grade school children; Snyder, Hoza, et al., 1997) and higher semester grade point averages (college students; Curry et al., 1997). In a 6-year longitudinal study, Hope Scale scores taken at the beginning of students' very first semester in college predicted higher cumulative grade point average[8] and graduation rate, as well as lower attrition (as tapped by dropout rate; Snyder, Wiklund, & Cheavens, 1999).[9] Imagine the negative ripples—lost opportunities, unfulfilled talents, and sense of failure—that may flow over a lifetime for some students who drop out of high school or college. Hope may offer a potential antidote.

Given the predictive power of the Hope Scale for academics, perhaps it also could be used to identify academically at-risk low-hope students who would especially profit by interventions to raise their hopeful thinking. Or such hope interventions may be targeted toward all students irrespective of their initial levels of hope. There are many opportunities to apply hope to the benefit of students. Indeed, interventions for schools already are being developed. For example, a college class aimed at teaching hopeful thinking could help students to improve their levels of hope and academic performances and, in turn, self-esteem. This is what has been found in an ongoing 6-year project at the University of Wyoming (Curry, Maniar, Sondag, & Sandstedt, 1999). Yet another approach that we are testing involves the beneficial effects of hope training for new college students during their first orientation week. Likewise, Lopez and his colleagues (Lopez, Bouwkamp, Edwards, & Teramoto Pedrotti, 2000) have had promising early results in a program for promoting hope in junior high students. Starting even earlier with students, perhaps we should explore how to maximize hopeful learning environments of children in grade schools.[10]

Athletics

Two athletes may have similar natural talents, and yet the more hopeful one should be more successful, especially during stressful points in their competitions (see Curry & Snyder, 2000). This follows because high-hope thinking enables an athlete to find the best routes to the goal in a given sport, as well as the motivation to use those routes. In support of these predictions, we (Curry, Snyder, et al., 1997) have found that Division I college track athletes with high as compared with low hope perform significantly better in their events (even when removing the variance related to natural athletic ability as rated by their coaches). In another study by Curry et al. (1997), athletes' trait and state hope together accounted for 56% of the variance related to their actual track performances.

Sports psychologists and coaches can use hope theory in working with individual athletes and teams. Actual courses to impart hope also should prove beneficial. In this regard, a college class titled "Principles of Optimal Performance" has been operating for several years, with resulting significant improvements in athletes' confidence in their performances (these benefits have been maintained at a 1-year follow-up; see Curry & Snyder, 2000).

Physical Health

In health psychology, the focus is on promoting and maintaining good health and preventing, detecting, and treating illness (Matarazzo, 1982). Based on our research, hope has been positively implicated in each of these areas (Irving et al., 1998; Snyder, 1996, 1998a; Snyder, Irving, & Anderson, 1991). Snyder, Feldman, Taylor, Schroeder, and Adams (2000) have described the powers of hope in terms of primary and secondary prevention. Primary prevention involves thoughts or actions that are intended to reduce or eliminate the chances that subsequent health problems (either physical [Kaplan, 2000] or psychological [Heller, Wyman, & Allen, 2000]) will occur in the future. Secondary prevention involves thoughts or actions that are directed at eliminating, reducing, or containing a problem once it has occurred (Snyder, Feldman, et al., 2000).

At the individual level, hope and the primary prevention of physical illness have begun to receive some attention. People with higher levels of hope seem to use information about physical illness to their advantage (Snyder, Feldman, et al., 2000). High-hope persons use information about the etiology of illness to do more of what helps and less of what hurts. Within the frame work of hope theory, knowledge is used as a pathway for prevention. Related to this point, women with higher as compared with lower hope have performed better on a cancer facts test, even when controlling for their academic performances and their contacts with other persons who have had cancer (Irving et al., 1998). In addition, higher hope women reported higher intentions to engage in cancer prevention activities than their lower hope counterparts. Additionally, people with high hope report engaging in more preventative behaviors (i.e., physical exercise) than those with low hope (Snyder, Harris, et al., 1991). Therefore, the scant available research does suggest that hopeful thinking is related to activities that help to prevent physical illness.

Beyond the individual level of primary prevention, hope theory can be applied at the societal level in order to prevent physical illness. Societal primary prevention involves thinking that reduces risks and inoculates entire segments of society against disease (Snyder, Feldman, et al., 2000). Societal primary prevention includes increasing desired behaviors and decreasing targeted bad behaviors through the use of advertisements, laws, and shared social values. Likewise, in the degree to which a society implements open and fair systems for obtaining the rewards, the negative repercussions of mass frustration should be quelled. For example, if established laws are perceived as fairly allowing all (or a maximal number of) people to pursue goal-directed activities, then citizens are less likely to become frustrated and act aggressively (Snyder, 1993, 1994b; Snyder & Feldman, 2000). This would result in fewer physical injuries in society. Related to this latter point, Krauss and Krauss (1968) found that the lack of profound goal blockages in countries across the world was associated subsequently with fewer deaths from suicide.

Once a physical illness develops, hope still plays an important role, but it does so in the context of secondary prevention. For example, hope should facilitate one's coping with the pain, disability, and other concomitant stressors of a physical illness. Consistent with this hypothesis, hope has been related to better adjustment in conditions involving chronic illness, severe injury, and handicaps. More specifically, higher hope has related to benefits in dealing with burn injuries (Barnum, Snyder, Rapoff, Mani, & Thompson, 1998), spinal cord injuries (Elliott, Witty, Herrick, & Hoffman, 1991), severe arthritis (Laird, 1992), fibromylagia (Affleck & Tennen, 1996; Tennen & Affleck, 1999), and blindness (Jackson, Taylor, Palmatier, Elliott, & Elliott, 1998).

Once ill, people with high versus low hope also appear to remain appropriately energized and focused on what they need to do in order to recuperate. This is in stark contrast to the counterproductive self-focus and self-pity (Hamilton & Ingram, 2001) that can overtake people with low hope. This self-focus in low-hope people increases anxiety and compromises the healing process. Furthermore, the higher anxiety in low-hope people may result in avoidance coping, which often can be quite unhealthy (Snyder & Pulvers, 2001).

An increasingly common problem involves people who are experiencing profound (and perhaps chronic) pain. Pain represents a difficult challenge for researchers and practitioners alike. We believe that persons with higher hope should be able to lessen their pain through enlisting more strategies (pathways) and having a higher likelihood of using those strategies (agency). Related to this point, in two studies using a cold pressor task (a pain tolerance measure), high-hope people experienced less pain and tolerated the pain almost twice as long as did the low-hope persons (Snyder, Odle, & Hackman, 1999).

Moving to the societal level, secondary prevention also may be influenced by hope. For example, successful television advertisements that are intended to promote health may work by giving people clear goals (e.g., "I definitely need to get help!") and pathways (e.g., referrals to local resources). These TV spots also influence agency by motivating people to get the help that they need. When people realize that their problem is not an isolated incident (i.e., it has high consensus), they tend to seek help. In support of this latter point, Snyder and Ingram (1983) found that people with targeted problems responded to high-consensus information so as to seek help. Overall, whether it is at the societal or the individual level, we foresee useful applications of hope theory in regard to prevention,[11] detection, and effective coping with illnesses.[12]

Psychological Adjustment

There are many ways in which we can use hope theory to foster better understanding of adjustment, as well as the best approaches for facilitating it. One way in which psychological adjustment is influenced by hope is through the belief in one's self, and this supposition is consistently supported in our research (e.g., Snyder, Hoza, et al., 1997). As posited earlier, hope should bear strong relationships with affectivity, and we have found that hope is related positively with positive affect and negatively with negative affect (correlations in .55 range). Moreover, manipulations to increase levels of hope have resulted in increases in positive affects and decreases in negative affects. Likewise, in tracking research participants over 28 days, higher hope was related to the report of more positive and fewer negative thoughts each day (Snyder et al., 1996). Furthermore, high-hope as compared with low-hope college students have reported feeling more inspired, energized, confident, and challenged by their goals (Snyder, Harris, et al., 1991), along with having elevated feelings of self-worth and low levels of depression (Snyder, Hoza, et al., 1997; Snyder et al., 1996).

In order to understand the stressor concept in the context of coping, we begin with a definition of coping. In this regard, coping is the ability to effectively respond to a stressor so as to reduce psychological (and physical) pain (Houston, 1988). Within hope theory, the stressor represents that which is interfering with one's normal ongoing goal of being happy. When confronting a stressor, therefore, one must find alternative paths to attain the "normalcy" goal, as well as become mobilized to use those paths. When confronted with a stressor, higher as compared with lower hope people produce more strategies for dealing with the stressor (pathways) and express a greater likelihood of using those strategies (agency; Snyder, 1994c, 2000d; Snyder, Harris, et al., 1991); moreover, higher hope persons are more likely to find benefits in their ongoing dealings with stressors (Affleck & Tennen, 1996; Tennen & Affleck, 1999). Relative to low-hope people, high-hope individuals also are less likely to use avoidance, a coping style that is linked to distress and decreased psychological adjustment when used over the long term (Suls & Fletcher, 1985).[13]

As is the case with physical health, hope also is crucial for psychological health. Hopeful thought entails assets such as the ability to establish clear goals, imagine workable pathways, and motivate oneself to work toward goals (Snyder, 2000a, 2000b, 2000c). For example, higher versus lower hope yields more successful goal pursuits in a variety of performance arenas (e.g., athletics, academics, coping; see, for review, Snyder, Cheavens, & Michael, 1999). Furthermore, this successful pursuit of goals is associated with elevated self-esteem and well-being (Snyder, Feldman, et al., 2000).

Psychological health is related to people's routine anticipation of their future well-being. In this regard, those with higher levels of hope should anticipate more positive levels of psychological health than persons with lower hope. These positive expectations also will yield higher confidence (Snyder, Feldman, et al., 2000), and high-hope people perceive that their hopeful thinking will protect them against future stressors (Snyder, 2000d). In addition, higher hope seems to moderate the relationship between unforeseen stressors and successful coping (see Snyder & Pulvers, 2001). Thus, in contrast to people with low levels of hope, who tend to catastrophize about the future, those with high levels of hope are able to think effectively about the future, with the knowledge that they, at times, will need to face major life stressors.

In a manner similar to that occurring for physical health, secondary prevention in psychological health involves thoughts or actions that eliminate, reduce, or contain a problem once it has appeared (Snyder, Feldman, et al., 2000). Hope also plays a role in this process. For example, when people with high hope encounter an immutable goal blockage, they are flexible enough to find alternative goals. In contrast, people with low hope tend to ruminate unproductively about being stuck (Michael, 2000; Snyder, 1999a, 1999b); moreover, their low-hope ruminations often involve fantasies about "magically" escaping their entrapments. This is tantamount to avoidance and disengaged coping behaviors, which generally have unhealthy consequences (Bolger, 1990; Carver et al., 1993; Litt, Tennen, Affleck, & Klock, 1992; Stanton & Snider, 1993). Furthermore, by coping through avoidance, the low-hope persons do not learn from past experiences (Snyder, Feldman, et al., 2000), and they become "passive pawns" in the game of life.

People with high hope also are likely to have friends with whom they share a strong sense of mutuality. In stressful circumstances, high-hope people can call on these friends for support (Crothers & Schraw, 1999; Sarason, Sarason, & Pierce, 1990). People with low hope, on the other hand, tend to be lonely and lack friends with whom they can talk. This seems to stem from their fear of interpersonal closeness (Crothers & Schraw, 1999). Likewise, even if low-hope people do have friends, those friends also are likely to have low hope (Cheavens, Taylor, Kahle, & Snyder, 2000). Unfortunately, a dyad of low-hope persons may be prone to "pity parties," in which the unending topic is how bad things are for them.

Human Connection

We have theorized that hope is inculcated in children through interactions with their caretakers, peers, and teachers (Snyder, Cheavens, & Sympson, 1997). As such, the goal of "connecting" with other people is fundamental, because the seeking of one's goals almost always occurs within the context of social commerce. Related to this point, it is the high-hope as compared with low-hope individuals who are especially invested in making contact with other people (Snyder, Hoza, et al., 1997). One measure of the motivation to be connected to others is the degree to which an individual is concerned with the perceptions that others form of him. In this vein, the increasing consensus is that a tendency to present oneself in a slightly positive light is an adaptive coping style (Taylor, 1989). Hope Scale scores have correlated slightly and positively with measures of social desirability and positive self-presentation (Snyder, Harris, et al., 1991; Snyder, Hoza, et al., 1997), suggesting an adaptive concern by high-hope people about impressions they make.

Researchers also have found that higher levels of hope are related to more perceived social support (Barnum et al., 1998), more social competence (Snyder, Hoza, et al., 1997), and less loneliness (Sympson, 1999). Furthermore, high-hope individuals have an enhanced ability to take the perspectives of others (Rieger, 1993). They appear to truly enjoy their interactions with others (Snyder, Hoza, et al., 1997), and they are interested in their goals and the goals of others around them (Snyder, 1994b, 1994c; Snyder, Cheavens, & Sympson, 1997).

Psychotherapy

From the 1960s through the 1980s, Jerome Frank (1968, 1973, 1975) pioneered a view that hope was a common process across differing psychotherapy approaches. We have continued his line of thought using hope theory as a framework for understanding the shared processes by which people are helped in psychotherapy (Snyder, Ilardi, Cheavens, et al., 2000; Snyder, Ilardi, Michael, & Cheavens, 2000; Snyder, Michael, & Cheavens, 1999; Snyder & Taylor, 2000). Whatever the particular system of psychotherapy, we believe that the beneficial changes occur because clients are learning more effective agentic and pathways goal-directed thinking. In particular, the agency component is reflected in the placebo effect (i.e., the natural mental energies for change that clients bring to psychotherapy). The particular psychotherapy approaches that are used to provide the client with a route or process for moving forward to attain positive therapeutic goals reflect the pathways component. By applying hope theory to several psychotherapies, a potential benefit would be increased cooperation among the proponents of varying camps (Snyder & Ingram, 2000).

Beyond the application of hope theory principles to psychotherapies in general, hope theory has been used to develop successful individual (Lopez, Floyd, Ulven, & Snyder, 2000; for related example, see Worthington et al., 1997) and group interventions (Klausner et al., 1998; Klausner, Snyder, & Cheavens, 2000). There also are two books (McDermott & Snyder, 2000; Snyder, McDermott,

et al., 1997) and a chapter (McDermott & Hastings, 2000) in which hope theory has been applied specifically to aid parents and teachers in helping children, as well as a book based on hope theory that is targeted to benefit adults (McDermott & Snyder, 1999). Furthermore, a pretreatment therapy preparation program based on hope theory has yielded benefits for clients (Irving et al., 1997). In our estimation, however, we have only begun to explore the applications of hope theory for psychotherapies.

Meaning in Life

Viktor Frankl (1965, 1992) has provided an eloquent voice on the "What is the nature of meaning?" question. To answer this query, he advanced the concept of the "existential vacuum"—the perception that there is no meaning or purpose in the universe. The experience of this existential vacuum supposedly can be remedied to the extent that persons actualize "values." Frankl (1965, 1966) reasoned that meaning resulted from the choice to bring three major classes of values into one's life: (a) creative (instantiations include writing a paper, giving birth to a child, etc.); (b) experiential (seeing, touching, or any way of experiencing); and (c) attitudinal (the stances people take toward their plights of suffering). The Purpose in Life test (Crumbaugh & Maholick, 1964; Crumbaugh & Maholick, 1981) was developed to reflect Frankl's notion. There also are two other widely used measures of general life-meaning— the Life Regard Index (Battista & Almond, 1973) and the Sense of Coherence scale (Antonovsky & Sagy, 1986).

We posited that hope should relate strongly to meaning because it is through our self-reflections about the goals that one has selected and the perceived progress in the journey toward those goals that a person constructs meaning in his or her life (Snyder, 1994c). In support of this hypothesis, we (Feldman & Snyder, 1999) found that Hope Scale scores evidenced correlations in the .70 to .76 range with the aforementioned three meaning measures. Thus, we believe that hope theory offers a new angle for looking at the nature of meaning.

For Another Time and Place

In this section, we provide brief glimpses of additional arenas where hope may play an important role (for a review of various future applications of hope theory, see Snyder [2000e]). We have made a case for how hope theory can be used to understand depression (Snyder, 1994c; Cheavens, 2000) and have examined the inner hope-related self-talk of depressed persons (Snyder, Lapointe, et al., 1998).[14] Another topic is attentional focus, with the premise being that on-task rather than off-task focus is facilitated by hopeful thinking (Snyder, 1999a, 1999b). We also offer some insights into self-actualization by using hope theory. Although widely discussed, Maslow's (1970) hierarchy of needs has received little recent research attention. Perhaps by using hope theory, with its emphasis on goals, we could enhance our understanding of this hierarchy. The capstone of Maslow's hierarchy is self-actualization, and such an idea is very timely within the positive psychology perspective. On this point, the strongest correlation of any scale with the Hope Scale was obtained with a measure of self-actualization (r = .79; Sumerlin, 1997).

Using hope theory, we also may garner insights into major group differences. In this regard, in over 40 studies (with adults and children), there never has been a significant sex difference in hope. Why? We also need to expand our knowledge of how differing ethnic groups manifest hope (Lopez, Gariglietti, et al., 2000). Likewise, do older persons exhibit differing hope from younger persons, and if so, why (Cheavens & Gum, 2000)? Whether a relationship be of intimate partners, students and teachers, managers and employees, or physicians and patients, the effectiveness and satisfaction flowing from the interactions may be understood and improved via hope theory (Snyder, 1994c, chap. 7). We would emphasize that the topics in this section, as well as those described earlier, represent only a portion of the positive psychology issues that we can examine through the lens of hope theory.

Hope for the Many Rather Than the Few

Our last point, and one that is central to our view of positive psychology, is that the uses and benefits of hope should be made available to as many people as possible (Snyder & Feldman, 2000). Although we have remained at the level of individuals in making our various points in this chapter, we would hasten to add that hope theory also is applicable to people in the context of larger units. In this regard, hope theory could be applied to help build environments where people can work together to meet shared goals. Whether it is a business, city council, state legislature, or national or international organization, there is enormous potential in working together in the spirit of hope. Earlier in this chapter, we described hope theory as a lens for seeing the strengths in people. We would hasten to add, however, that hope is but one pane in the larger window of positive psychology. Through this window, looking across different lands and people, we envision a positive psychology for the many. This is a vision of hope.

Acknowledgments

This chapter was originally published in *The Oxford Handbook of Positive Psychology*, 1st edition (New York: Oxford University Press, 2002).

Notes

1. In Craig's (1943) *The Nature of Explanation*, which is a classic in the evolution of the cognitive psychology movement, he persuasively reasons that the purpose of the brain is to comprehend and anticipate causal sequences. Pinker (1997) makes a similar argument in his award-winning *How the Mind Works*. Additional volumes that were particularly helpful in forming our view about the importance of pathways thought in pursuing goals were Miller, Galanter, and Pribram's (1960) *Plans and the Structure of Behavior*, Newell and Simon's (1972) *Human Problem Solving*, and Anderson's (1983) *The Architecture of Cognition*.

2. We also have developed hope measures that are (a) for children aged 4 to 7; (b) aimed at tapping hope in particular life domains; (c) based on observing either children or adults; and (d) derived from written or spoken narratives. Contact the senior author for further information on these measures.

3. For the reader who is interested in more detailed comparisons of various other theories to hope theory, please refer to the following sources: Snyder (1994a); Snyder (1998b); Snyder (2000b, 2000d, 2000e); Snyder, Ilardi, Cheavens, et al. (2000); Snyder, Ilardi, Michael, and Cheavens (2000); Snyder, Irving, and Anderson (1991); and Snyder, Sympson, Michael, and Cheavens (2000).

4. The instrument used to measure attributional style in adults is called the Attributional Style Questionnaire (Peterson et al., 1982); the instrument used for children is called the Children's Attributional Style Questionnaire (Seligman et al., 1984).

5. There are indications, however, that optimists do use such planful thought (e.g., Carver & Scheier, 2000b; Scheier & Carver, 1985). For example, optimists have elevated problem-focused coping (Scheier, Weintraub, & Carver, 1986; Strutton & Lumpkin, 1992) and planfulness (Fontaine, Manstead, & Wagner, 1993; Friedman et al., 1992). Therefore, the positive goal-directed expectancies (in responses to the LOT and LOT-R) implicitly may tap pathways-related thinking. Related to this issue, Magaletta and Oliver (1999) have found the pathways component of the Hope Scale to be orthogonal to items on the LOT in a factor analysis. The original instrument tapping optimism was called the Life Orientation Test (Scheier & Carver, 1985), and the revised instrument is called the Life Orientation Test-Revised (Scheier, Carver, & Bridges, 1994).

6. Nevertheless, a dispositional measure of self-efficacy has been developed by other researchers (see Sherer et al., 1982).

7. For related reviews, see Wells and Marwell (1976) and Wylie (1974, 1979).

8. The grade point averages of the high- and low-hope students were 2.85 and 2.43, respectively.

9. In the aforementioned studies, the predictive power of hope was not diminished when controlling for intelligence (children's studies), previous grades (cross-sectional college student studies), and entrance exam scores (longitudinal college study).

10. Such hope education also should be available to parents (McDermott & Snyder, 1999, 2000).

11. Based on prospective correlational research, using indices of hope other than the ones derived from hope theory, the absence of hope (i.e., hopelessness) appears to relate to morbidity and mortality. For example, Schmale and Iker (1966, 1971) found that hopelessness predicted later development of cervical cancer among healthy women at high risk for cervical cancer. More recently, Everson and colleagues (1996, 1997) found that hopelessness predicted later cardiovascular disease and cancer among middle-aged men (even beyond number of biological and behavioral risk factors). Although this is correlational research, these findings support the hypothesis that hope plays a role in the prevention of some life-threatening physical illnesses.

12. As an example of this latter point, the role of hope in maintaining adherence to a medicine regime in juvenile and adult diabetes patients is being examined in ongoing research in our laboratory. Results reveal that hope, particularly the agency component, predicts adherence, and that it does so beyond variances related to demographic or quality-of-life variables (Moon, 2000).

13. We refer the reader to the following sources for in-depth coverage of the role that hope plays in facilitating successful coping process: Mc-Dermott and Snyder, 1999; Snyder, 1994c; Snyder, Cheavens, and Michael, 1999; and Snyder, Mc-Dermott, et al., 1997.

14. Anxiety also can be understood within hope theory (Michael, 2000; Snyder, 1994c).

References

Abramson, L. Y., Seligman, M. E. P., & Teasdale, J. D. (1978). Learned helplessness in humans: Critique and reformulation. *Journal of Abnormal Psychology, 87,* 49–74.

Affleck, G., & Tennen, H. (1996). Construing benefits from adversity: Adaptational significance and dispositional underpinnings. *Journal of Personality, 64,* 899–922.

Anderson, J. R. (1983). *The architecture of cognition.* Cambridge, MA: Harvard University Press.

Antonovsky, H., & Sagy, S. (1986). The development of a sense of coherence and its impact on responses to stress situations. *Journal of Social Psychology, 126,* 213–225.

Averill, J. R., Catlin, G., & Chon, K. K. (1990). *Rules of hope.* New York: Springer-Verlag.

Babyak, M. A., Snyder, C. R., & Yashinobu, L. (1993). Psychometric properties of the Hope Scale: A confirmatory factor analysis. *Journal of Research in Personality, 27,* 154–169.

Bandura, A. (1982). Self-efficacy mechanism in human agency. *American Psychologist, 37,* 122–147.

Bandura, A. (1997). *Self-efficacy: The exercise of control.* New York: Freeman.

Barnum, D. D., Snyder, C. R., Rapoff, M. A., Mani, M. M., & Thompson, R. (1998). Hope and social support in the psychological adjustment of pediatric burn survivors and matched controls. *Children's Health Care, 27,* 15–30.

Battista, J., & Almond, R. (1973). The development of meaning in life. *Psychiatry, 36,* 409–427.

Bolger, N. (1990). Coping as a personality process: A prospective study. *Journal of Personality and Social Psychology, 59,* 525–537.

Brunstein, J. C. (1993). Personal goals and subjective well-being: A longitudinal study. *Journal of Personality and Social Psychology, 65,* 1061–1070.

Cantril, H. (1964). The human design. *Journal of Individual Psychology, 20,* 129–136.

Carver, C. S., Pozo, C., Harris, S. D., Noriega, V., Scheier, M. F., Robinson, D. S., Ketcham, A. S., Mofat, F. L., Jr., & Clark, K. C. (1993). How coping mediates the effect of optimism on distress: A study of women with early stage breast cancer. *Journal of Personality and Social Psychology, 65,* 375–390.

Carver, C. S., & Scheier, M. F. (2000a). Optimism, pessimism, and self-regulation. In E. C. Chang (Ed.), *Optimism and pessimism* (pp. 31–52). Washington, DC: American Psychological Association.

Carver, C. S., & Scheier, M. F. (2000b). Optimism. In C. R. Snyder (Ed.), *Coping: The psychology of what works* (pp. 182–204). New York: Oxford University Press.

Cheavens, J. (2000). Light through the shadows: Depression and hope. In C. R. Snyder (Ed.), *Handbook of hope: Theory, measures, and applications* (pp. 326–354). San Diego, CA: Academic Press.

Cheavens, J., & Gum, A. (2000). Gray Power: Hope for the ages. In C. R. Snyder (Ed.), *Handbook of hope: Theory, measures, and applications* (pp. 201–222). San Diego, CA: Academic Press.

Cheavens, J., Gum, A., & Snyder, C. R. (2000). The Hope Scale. In J. Maltby, C. A. Lewis, & A. Hill (Eds.), *A handbook of psychological tests* (pp. 248–258). Lampeter, Wales, UK: Edwin Mellen Press.

Cheavens, J., Taylor, J. D., Kahle, K., & Snyder, C. R. (2000). *Interactions of high- and low-hope individuals.* Unpublished manuscript, Psychology Department, University of Kansas, Lawrence.

Coopersmith, S. (1967). *The antecedents of self-esteem.* San Francisco: Freeman.

Craig, K. J. W. (1943). *The nature of explanation.* Cambridge, England: Cambridge University Press.

Crothers, M., & Schraw, G. (1999, August). *Validation of the Mutuality Assessment Questionnaire.* Presented at the annual meeting of the American Psychological Association, Boston.

Crumbaugh, J. C., & Maholick, L. T. (1964). An experimental study in existentialism: The psychometric approach to Frankl's concept of noogenic neurosis. *Journal of Clinical Psychology, 20,* 200–207.

Crumbaugh, J. C., & Maholick, L. T. (1981). *Manual of instructions for the Purpose in Life Test.* Murfeesboro, TN: Psychometric Affiliates.

Curry, L. A., Maniar, S. D., Sondag, K. A., & Sandstedt, S. (1999). *An optimal performance academic course for university students and student-athletes.* Unpublished manuscript, University of Montana, Missoula.

Curry, L. A., & Snyder, C. R. (2000). Hope takes the field: Mind matters in athletic performances. In C. R. Snyder (Ed.), *Handbook of hope: Theory, measures, and applications* (pp. 243–260). San Diego, CA: Academic Press.

Curry, L. A., Snyder, C. R., Cook, D. L., Ruby, B. C., & Rehm, M. (1997). The role of hope in student-athlete academic and sport achievement. *Journal of Personality and Social Psychology, 73,* 1257–1267.

Diener, E. (1984). Subjective well-being. *Psychological Bulletin, 95*, 542–575.

D'Zurilla, T. J. (1986). *Problem-solving therapy: A social competence approach to clinical intervention.* New York: Springer.

Elliott, T. R., Witty, T. E., Herrick, S., & Hoffman, J. T. (1991). Negotiating reality after physical loss: Hope, depression, and disability. *Journal of Personality and Social Psychology, 61*, 608–613.

Emmons, R. A. (1986). Personal strivings: An approach to personality and subjective well-being. *Journal of Personality and Social Psychology, 51*, 1058–1068.

Everson, S. A., Goldberg, D. E., Kaplan, G. A., Cohen, R. D., Pukkala, E., Tuomilehto, J., & Salonen, J. T. (1996). Hopelessness and risk of mortality and incidence of myocardial infarction and cancer. *Psychosomatic Medicine, 58*, 113–121.

Everson, S. A., Kaplan, G. A., Goldberg, D. E., Salonen, R., & Salonen, J. T. (1997). Hopelessness and 4-year progression of carotid artherosclerosis: The Kuopio ischemic heart disease risk factor study. *Arteriosclerosis Thrombosis Vascular Biology, 17*, 1490–1495.

Farber, M. L. (1968). *Theory of suicide.* New York: Funk and Wagnall's.

Farina, C. J., Hearth, A. K., & Popovich, J. M. (1995). *Hope and hopelessness: Critical clinical constructs.* Thousand Oaks, CA: Sage.

Feldman, D. B., & Snyder, C. R. (1999). *Natural companions: Hope and meaning.* Unpublished manuscript, University of Kansas, Lawrence.

Feldman, D. B., & Snyder, C. R. (2000). The State Hope Scale. In J. Maltby, C. A. Lewis, and A. Hill (Eds.), *A handbook of psychological tests* (pp. 240–245). Lampeter, Wales, UK: Edwin Mellen Press.

Fontaine, K. R., Manstead, A. S. R., & Wagner, H. (1993). Optimism, perceived control over stress, and coping. *European Journal of Personality, 7*, 267–281.

Frank, J. D. (1968). The role of hope in psychotherapy. *International Journal of Psychiatry, 5*, 383–395.

Frank, J. D. (1973). *Persuasion and healing* (Rev. ed.). Baltimore: Johns Hopkins University Press.

Frank, J. D. (1975). The faith that heals. *Johns Hopkins Medical Journal, 137*, 127–131.

Frankl, V. (1965). *The doctor and the soul: From psychotherapy to logotherapy* (R. Winston & C. Winston, Trans.). New York: Knopf.

Frankl, V. (1966). What is meant by meaning? *Journal of Existentialism, 7*, 21–28.

Frankl, V. (1992). *Man's search for meaning: An introduction to logotherapy* (I. Lasch, Trans.). Boston: Beacon.

Friedman, L. C., Nelson, D. V., Baer, P. E., Lane, M., Smith, F. E., & Dworkin, R. J. (1992). The relationship of dispositional optimism, daily life stress, and domestic environment to coping methods used by cancer patients. *Journal of Behavioral Medicine, 15*, 127–141.

Hamilton, N. A., & Ingram, R. E. (2001). Self-focused attention and coping: Attending to the right things. In C. R. Snyder (Ed.), *Coping with stress: Effective people and processes* (pp. 178–195). New York: Oxford University Press.

Heller, K., Wyman, M. F., & Allen, S. M. (2000). Future directions for prevention science: From research to adoption. In C. R. Snyder & R. E. Ingram (Eds.), *Handbook of psychological change: Psychotherapy process and practices for the 21st century* (pp. 660–680). New York: Wiley.

Heppner, P. P., & Hillerbrand, E. T. (1991). Problem-solving training implications for remedial and preventive training.

In C. R. Snyder & D. R. Forsyth (Eds.), *Handbook of social and clinical psychology: The health perspective* (pp. 681–698). Elmsford, NY: Pergamon.

Hewitt, J. P. (1998). *The myth of self-esteem: Finding happiness and solving problems in America.* New York: St. Martin's Press.

Houston, B. K. (1988). Stress and coping. In C. R. Snyder & C. E. Ford (Eds.), *Coping with negative life events: Clinical and social psychological perspectives* (pp. 373–399). New York: Plenum.

Irving, L. M., Snyder, C. R., & Crowson, J. J. Jr. (1998). Hope and the negotiation of cancer facts by college women. *Journal of Personality, 66*, 195–214.

Irving, L., Snyder, C. R., Gravel, L., Hanke, J., Hilberg, P., & Nelson, N. (1997, April). *Hope and effectiveness of a pretherapy orientation group for community mental health center clients.* Paper presented at the annual meeting of the Western Psychological Association Convention, Seattle, WA.

Jackson, W. T., Taylor, R. E., Palmatier, A. D., Elliott, T. R., & Elliott, J. L. (1998). Negotiating the reality of visual impairment: Hope, coping, and functional ability. *Journal of Clinical Psychology in Medical Settings, 5*, 173–185.

Kaplan, R. M. (2000). Two pathways to prevention. *American Psychologist, 55*, 382–396.

Klausner, E. J., Clarkin, J. F., Spielman, L., Pupo, C., Abrams, R., & Alexopoulas, G. S. (1998). Late-life depression and functional disability: The role of goal-focused group psychotherapy. *International Journal of Geriatric Psychiatry, 13*, 707–716.

Klausner, E. J., Snyder, C. R., & Cheavens, J. (2000). Teaching hope to a population of older, depressed adults. In G. Williamson (Ed.), *Advances in aging theory and research* (pp. 295–310). New York: Plenum.

Krauss, H. H., & Krauss, B. J. (1968). Cross-cultural study of the thwarting-disorientation theory of suicide. *Journal of Abnormal Psychology, 73*, 352–357.

Laird, S. (1992). *A preliminary investigation into prayer as a coping technique for adult patients with arthritis.* Unpublished doctoral dissertation, University of Kansas, Lawrence.

Litt, M. D., Tennen, H., Affleck, G., & Klock, S. (1992). Coping and cognitive factors in adaptation to in vitro fertilization failure. *Journal of Behavioral Medicine, 15*, 171–187.

Little, B. R. (1983). Personal projects: A rationale and method for investigation. *Environment and Behavior, 15*, 273–309.

Little, B. R. (1989). Personal projects analysis: Trivial pursuits, magnificent obsessions, and the search for coherence. In D. M. Buss & N. Cantor (Eds.), *Personality psychology: Recent trends and emerging directions* (pp. 15–31). New York: Springer-Verlag.

Lopez, S. J., Bouwkamp, J., Edwards, L. M., & Teramoto Pedrotti, J. (2000, October). *Making hope happen via brief interventions.* Paper presented at the second Positive Psychology Summit, Washington, DC.

Lopez, S. J., Floyd, R. K., Ulven, J. C., & Snyder, C. R. (2000). Hope therapy: Helping clients build a house of hope. In C. R. Snyder (Ed.), *Handbook of hope: Theory, measures, and applications* (pp. 123–150). San Diego, CA: Academic Press.

Lopez, S. J., Gariglietti, K. P., McDermott, D., Sherwin, E. D., Floyd, K. R., Rand, K., & Snyder, C. R. (2000). Hope for the evolution of diversity: On leveling the field of dreams. In C. R. Snyder (Ed.), *Handbook of hope: Theory, measures, and applications* (pp. 223–242). San Diego, CA: Academic Press.

Magaletta, P. R., & Oliver, J. M. (1999). The hope construct, will and ways: Their relative relations with self-efficacy, optimism, and general well-being. *Journal of Clinical Psychology, 55,* 539–551.

Maslow, A. H. (1970). *Motivation and personality* (2nd ed.). New York: Harper and Row.

Matarazzo, J. D. (1982). Behavioral health's challenge to academic, scientific, and professional psychology. *American Psychologist, 37,* 1–14.

McDermott, D., & Hastings, S. (2000). Children: Raising future hopes. In C. R. Snyder (Ed.), *Handbook of hope: Theory, measures, and applications* (pp. 185–199). San Diego, CA: Academic Press.

McDermott, D., & Snyder, C. R. (1999). *Making hope happen.* Oakland, CA: New Harbinger Publications.

McDermott, D., & Snyder, C. R. (2000). *The great big book of hope: Help your children achieve their dreams.* Oakland, CA: New Harbinger Publications.

Melges, R., & Bowlby, J. (1969). Types of hopelessness in psychopathological processes. *Archives of General Psychiatry, 20,* 690–699.

Menninger, K. (1959). The academic lecture on hope. *American Journal of Psychiatry, 109,* 481–491.

Michael, S. T. (2000). Hope conquers fear: Overcoming anxiety and panic attacks. In C. R. Snyder (Ed.), *Handbook of hope: Theory, measures, and applications* (pp. 355–378). San Diego, CA: Academic Press.

Miller, G. A., Galanter, E., & Pribram, K. H. (1960). *Plans and the structure of behavior.* New York: Holt, Rinehart, and Winston.

Moon, C. (2000). *The relationship of hope to children's asthma treatment adherence.* Unpublished master's thesis, University of Kansas, Lawrence.

Moon, C., & Snyder, C. R. (2000). Children's Hope Scale. In J. Maltby, C. A. Lewis, and A. Hill (Eds.), *A handbook of psychological tests* (pp. 160–166). Lampeter, Wales, UK: Edwin Mellen Press.

Newell, A., & Simon, H. A. (1972). *Human problem solving.* Englewood Cliffs, NJ: Prentice-Hall.

Omodei, M. M., & Wearing, A. J. (1990). Need satisfaction and involvement in personal projects: Toward an integrative model of subjective well-being. *Journal of Personality and Social Psychology, 59,* 762–769.

Palys, T. S., & Little, B. R. (1983). Perceived life satisfaction and organization of personal projects systems. *Journal of Personality and Social Psychology, 44,* 1221–1230.

Peterson, C., Semmel, A., von Baeyer, C., Abramson, L. Y., Metalsky, G. I., & Seligman, M. E. P. (1982). The Attributional Style Questionnaire. *Cognitive Therapy and Research, 6,* 287–299.

Pinker, S. (1997). *How the mind works.* New York: Norton.

Rieger, E. (1993). *Correlates of adult hope, including high- and low-hope adults' recollection of parents.* Unpublished psychology honors thesis, University of Kansas, Lawrence.

Ruehlman, L. S., & Wolchik, S. A. (1988). Personal goals and interpersonal support and hindrance as factors in psychological distress and well-being. *Journal of Personality and Social Psychology, 55,* 293–301.

Sarason, B. R., Sarason, I. G., & Pierce, G. R. (Eds.). (1990). *Social support: An interactional view.* New York: Wiley.

Schachtel, E. (1959). *Metamorphosis.* New York: Basic Books.

Scheier, M. F., & Carver, C. S. (1985). Optimism, coping, and health: Assessment and implications of generalized outcome expectancies. *Health Psychology, 4,* 219–247.

Scheier, M. F., & Carver, C. S. (1987). Dispositional optimism and physical well-being: The influence of generalized outcome expectancies on health. *Journal of Personality, 55,* 169–210.

Scheier, M. F., Carver, C. S., & Bridges, M. W. (1994). Distinguishing optimism from neuroticism (and trait anxiety, self mastery, and self-esteem): A reevaluation of the Life Orientation Test. *Journal of Personality and Social Psychology, 67,* 1063–1078.

Scheier, M. F., Weintraub, J. K., & Carver, C. S. (1986). Coping with stress: Divergent strategies of optimists and pessimists. *Journal of Personality and Social Psychology, 51,* 1257–1264.

Schmale, A. H., & Iker, H. (1966). The affect of hopelessness and the development of cancer: Identification of uterine cervical cancer in women with atypical cytology. *Psychosomatic Medicine, 28,* 714–721.

Schmale, A. H., & Iker, H. (1971). Hopelessness as a predictor of cervical cancer. *Social Science and Medicine, 5,* 95–100.

Schulman, M. (1991). *The passionate mind.* New York: Free Press.

Seligman, M. E. P. (1991). *Learned optimism.* New York: Knopf.

Seligman, M. E. P., Kaslow, N. J., Alloy, L. B., Peterson, C., Tanenbaum, R., & Abramson, L. Y. (1984). Attributional style and depressive symptoms among children. *Journal of Abnormal Psychology, 93,* 235–238.

Sherer, M., Maddux, J. E., Mercandante, B., Prentice-Dunn, S., Jacobs, B., & Rogers, R. (1982). The self-efficacy scale: Construction and validation. *Psychological Reports, 51,* 663–671.

Snyder, C. R. (1993). Hope for the journey. In A. P. Turnball, J. M. Patterson, S. K. Behr, D. L. Murphy, J. G. Marquis, & M. J. Blue-Banning (Eds.), *Cognitive coping, families and disability* (pp. 271–286). Baltimore: Brookes.

Snyder, C. R. (1994a). Hope and optimism. In V. S. Ramachandren (Ed.), *Encyclopedia of human behavior* (Vol. 2, pp. 535–542). San Diego, CA: Academic Press.

Snyder, C. R. (1994b, August). *Hope for the many vs. hope for the few.* Paper presented at the annual meeting of the American Psychological Association, Los Angeles.

Snyder, C. R. (1994c). *The psychology of hope: You can get there from here.* New York: Free Press.

Snyder, C. R. (1995). Conceptualizing, measuring, and nurturing hope. *Journal of Counseling and Development, 73,* 355–360.

Snyder, C. R. (1996). To hope, to lose, and hope again. *Journal of Personal and Interpersonal Loss, 1,* 3–16.

Snyder, C. R. (1998a). A case for hope in pain, loss, and suffering. In J. H. Harvey, J. Omarzu, & E. Miller (Eds.), *Perspectives on loss: A sourcebook* (pp. 63–79). Washington, DC: Taylor and Francis.

Snyder, C. R. (1998b). Hope. In H. S. Friedman (Ed.), *Encyclopedia of mental health* (pp. 421–431). San Diego, CA: Academic Press.

Snyder, C. R. (1999a). Hope, goal blocking thoughts, and test-related anxieties. *Psychological Reports, 84,* 206–208.

Snyder, C. R. (1999b, June). *A psychological look at people who do not reach their goals: The low-hope blues.* Paper presented at the annual meeting of the American Psychological Society, Denver, CO.

Snyder, C. R. (2000a). Genesis: Birth and growth of hope. In C. R. Snyder (Ed.), *Handbook of hope: Theory, measures, and applications* (pp. 25–57). San Diego, CA: Academic Press.

Snyder, C. R. (2000b, March). Hope: *The beneficent octopus.* Presentation at the annual meeting of the Eastern Psychological Association, Baltimore, MD.

Snyder, C. R. (2000c, August). *Hope theory: Pursuing positive ties that bind.* Paper presented at the meeting of the American Psychological Association, Washington, DC.

Snyder, C. R. (2000d). Hypothesis: There is hope. In C. R. Snyder (Ed.), *Handbook of hope: Theory, measures, and applications* (pp. 3–21). San Diego, CA: Academic Press.

Snyder, C. R. (2000e). The past and future of hope. *Journal of Social and Clinical Psychology, 19,* 11–28.

Snyder, C. R., Cheavens, J., & Michael, S. T. (1999). Hoping. In C. R. Snyder (Ed.), *Coping: The psychology of what works* (pp. 205–231). New York: Oxford University Press.

Snyder, C. R., Cheavens, J., & Sympson, S. C. (1997). Hope: An individual motive for social commerce. *Group Dynamics: Theory, Research, and Practice, 1,* 107–118.

Snyder, C. R., & Feldman, D. B. (2000). Hope for the many: An empowering social agenda. In C. R. Snyder (Ed.), *Handbook of hope: Theory, measures, and applications* (pp. 402–415). San Diego, CA: Academic Press.

Snyder, C. R., Feldman, D. B., Taylor, J. D., Schroeder, L. L., & Adams V., III. (2000). The roles of hopeful thinking in preventing problems and enhancing strengths. *Applied and Preventive Psychology, 15,* 262–295.

Snyder, C. R., Harris, C., Anderson, J. R., Holleran, S. A., Irving, L. M., Sigmon, S. T., Yoshinobu, L., Gibb, J., Langelle, C., & Harney, P. (1991). The will and the ways: Development and validation of an individual-differences measure of hope. *Journal of Personality and Social Psychology, 60,* 570–585.

Snyder, C. R., Hoza, B., Pelham, W. E., Rapoff, M., Ware, L., Danovsky, M., Highberger, L., Rubinstein, H., & Stahl, K. J. (1997). The development and validation of the Children's Hope Scale. *Journal of Pediatric Psychology, 22,* 399–421.

Snyder, C. R., Ilardi, S. S., Cheavens, J., Michael, S. T., Yamhure, L., & Sympson, S. (2000). The role of hope in cognitive behavior therapies. *Cognitive Therapy and Research, 24,* 747–762.

Snyder, C. R., Ilardi, S., Michael, S., & Cheavens, J. (2000). Hope theory: Updating a common process for psychological change. In C. R. Snyder & R. E. Ingram (Eds.), *Handbook of psychological change: Psychotherapy processes and practices for the 21st century* (pp. 128–153). New York: Wiley.

Snyder, C. R., & Ingram, R. E. (1983). The impact of consensus information on help-seeking for psychological problems. *Journal of Personality and Social Psychology, 45,* 1118–1126.

Snyder, C. R., & Ingram, R. E. (2000). Psychotherapy: Questions for an evolving field. In C. R. Snyder & R. E. Ingram (Eds.), *Handbook of psychological change: Psychotherapy processes and practices for the 21st century* (pp. 707–726). New York: Wiley.

Snyder, C. R., Irving, L., & Anderson, J. R. (1991). Hope and health: Measuring the will and the ways. In C. R. Snyder & D. R. Forsyth (Eds.), *Handbook of social and clinical psychology: The health perspective* (pp. 285–305). Elmsford, NY: Pergamon.

Snyder, C. R., Lapointe, A. B., Crowson, J. J., Jr., & Early, S. (1998). Preferences of high- and low-hope people for self-referential input. *Cognition and Emotion, 12,* 807–823.

Snyder, C. R., & McCullough, M. (2000). A positive psychology field of dreams: "If you build it, they will come. . . ." *Journal of Social and Clinical Psychology, 19,* 151–160.

Snyder, C. R., McDermott, D., Cook, W., & Rapoff, M. (1997). *Hope for the journey: Helping children through the good times and the bad.* Boulder, CO: Westview; San Francisco: HarperCollins.

Snyder, C. R., Michael, S., & Cheavens, J. (1999). Hope as a psychotherapeutic foundation for nonspecific factors, placebos, and expectancies. In M. A. Huble, B. Duncan, & S. Miller (Eds.), *Heart and soul of change* (pp. 179–200). Washington, DC: American Psychological Association.

Snyder, C. R., Odle, C., & Hackman, J. (1999, August). *Hope as related to perceived severity and tolerance of physical pain.* Paper presented at the annual meeting of the American Psychological Association, Boston.

Snyder, C. R., & Pulvers, K. (2001). Dr. Seuss, the coping machine, and "Oh, the places you will go." In C. R. Snyder (Ed.), *Coping with stress: Effective people and processes* (pp. 3–19). New York: Oxford University Press.

Snyder, C. R., Sympson, S. C., Michael, S. T., & Cheavens, J. (2000). The optimism and hope constructs: Variants on a positive expectancy theme. In E. C. Chang (Ed.), *Optimism and pessimism* (pp. 103–124). Washington, DC: American Psychological Association.

Snyder, C. R., Sympson, S. C., Ybasco, F. C., Borders, T. F., Babyak, M. A., & Higgins, R. L. (1996). Development and validation of the State Hope Scale. *Journal of Personality and Social Psychology, 70,* 321–335.

Snyder, C. R., & Taylor, J. D. (2000). Hope as a common factor across psychotherapy approaches: A lesson from the Dodo's Verdict. In C. R. Snyder (Ed.), *Handbook of hope: Theory, measures, and applications* (pp. 89–108). San Diego, CA: Academic Press.

Snyder, C. R., Wiklund, C., & Cheavens, J. (1999, August). *Hope and success in college.* Paper presented at the annual meeting of the American Psychological Association, Boston.

Stanton, A. L., & Snider, P. R. (1993). Coping with a breast cancer diagnosis: A prospective study. *Health Psychology, 12,* 16–23.

Stotland, E. (1969). *The psychology of hope.* San Francisco: Jossey-Bass.

Strutton, D., & Lumpkin, J. (1992). Relationship between optimism and coping strategies in the work environment. *Psychological Reports, 71,* 1179–1186.

Suls, J., & Fletcher, B. (1985). The relative efficacy of avoidant and nonavoidant coping strategies: A meta-analysis. *Health Psychology, 4,* 249–288.

Sumerlin, J. (1997). Self-actualization and hope. *Journal of Social Behavior and Personality, 12,* 1101–1110.

Sympson, S. (1999). *Validation of the Domain Specific Hope Scale.* Unpublished doctoral dissertation, University of Kansas, Lawrence.

Taylor, S. E. (1989). *Positive illusions: Creative self-deception and the healthy mind.* New York: Basic Books.

Tennen, H., & Affleck, G. (1999). Finding benefits in adversity. In C. R. Snyder (Ed.), *Coping: The psychology of what works* (pp. 279–304). New York: Oxford University Press.

Wells, L. E., & Marwell, G. (1976). *Self-esteem: Its conceptualization and measurement.* Beverly Hills, CA: Sage.

Worthington, E. L., Jr., Hight, T. L., Ripley, J. S., Perrone, K. M., Kurusu, T. A., & Jones, D. R. (1997). Strategic hope-focused relation ship-enrichment counseling with individuals. *Journal of Counseling Psychology, 44,* 381–389.

Wylie, R. C. (1974). *The self-concept: A review of methodological and measuring instruments* (Vol. 1, rev. ed.). Lincoln: University of Nebraska Press.

Wylie, R. C. (1979). *The self-concept: Theory and research on selected topics* (Vol. 2, rev. ed.). Lincoln: University of Nebraska Press.

Appendix 3A
The Trait Hope Scale

Directions: Read each item carefully. Using the scale shown below, please select the number that best describes YOU and put that number in the blank provided.

1 Definitely false
2 Mostly false
3 Somewhat false
4 Slightly false
5 Slightly true
6 Somewhat true
7 Mostly true
8 Definitely true

_____ 1. I can think of many ways to get out of a jam.
_____ 2. I energetically pursue my goals.
_____ 3. I feel tired most of the time.
_____ 4. There are lots of ways around any problem.
_____ 5. I am easily downed in an argument.
_____ 6. I can think of many ways to get the things in life that are important to me.
_____ 7. I worry about my health.
_____ 8. Even when others get discouraged, I know I can find a way to solve the problem.
_____ 9. My past experiences have prepared me well for my future.
_____ 10. I've been pretty successful in life.
_____ 11. I usually find myself worrying about something.
_____ 12. I meet the goals that I set for myself.

Notes: When administering the scale, it is called The Future Scale. The Agency subscale score is derived by summing items # 2, 9, 10, and 12; the Pathway subscale score is derived by adding items # 1, 4, 6, and 8. The total Hope Scale score is derived by summing the four Agency and the four Pathway items. From C. R. Snyder, C. Harris, et al., The will and the ways: Development and validation of an individual differences measure of hope, *Journal of Personality and Social Psychology* © (1991), Vol. 60, p. 585. Reprinted with the permission of the American Psychological Association and the senior author.

Appendix 3B
The State Hope Scale

Directions: Read each item carefully. Using the scale shown below, please select the number that best describes *how you think about yourself right now* and put that number in the blank before each sentence. Please take a few moments to focus on yourself and what is going on in *your life at this moment*. Once you have this "here and now" set, go ahead and answer each item according to the following scale:

1 Definitely false
2 Mostly false
3 Somewhat false
4 Slightly false
5 Slightly true
6 Somewhat true
7 Mostly true
8 Definitely true

_____ 1. If I should find myself in a jam, I could think of many ways to get out of it.
_____ 2. At the present time, I am energetically pursuing my goals.
_____ 3. There are lots of ways around any problem that I am facing now.
_____ 4. Right now, I see myself as being pretty successful.
_____ 5. I can think of many ways to reach my current goals.
_____ 6. At this time, I am meeting the goals that I have set for myself.

Notes: The Agency subscale score is derived by summing the three even-numbered items; the Pathways subscale score is derived by adding the three odd-numbered items. The total State Hope Scale score is derived by summing the three Agency and the three Pathways items. Scores can range from a low of 6 to a high of 48. When administering the State Hope Scale, it is labeled as the "Goals Scale for the Present." From C. R. Snyder, S. C. Sympson, et al., Development and validation of the State Hope Scale, *Journal of Personality and Social Psychology* © (1996), Vol. 70, p. 335. Reprinted with the permission of the American Psychological Association and the senior author.

Appendix 3C
The Children's Hope Scale

Directions: The six sentences below describe how children think about themselves and how they do things in general. Read each sentence carefully. For each sentence, please think about how you are in most situations. Place a check inside the circle that describes YOU the best. For example, place a check (✓) in the circle (O) beside "None of the time," if this describes you. Or, if you are this way "All of the time," check this circle. Please answer every question by putting a check in one of the circles. There are no right or wrong answers.

1. I think I am doing pretty well.

   O *None of the time*
   O *A little of the time*
   O *Some of the time*
   O *A lot of the time*
   O *Most of the time*
   O *All of the time*

2. I can think of many ways to get the things in life that are most important to me.

   O *None of the time*
   O *A little of the time*
   O *Some of the time*
   O *A lot of the time*
   O *Most of the time*
   O *All of the time*

3. I am doing just as well as other kids my age.

   O *None of the time*
   O *A little of the time*
   O *Some of the time*
   O *A lot of the time*
   O *Most of the time*
   O *All of the time*

4. When I have a problem, I can come up with lots of ways to solve it.

   O *None of the time*
   O *A little of the time*
   O *Some of the time*
   O *A lot of the time*
   O *Most of the time*
   O *All of the time*

5. I think the things I have done in the past will help me in the future.

   O *None of the time*
   O *A little of the time*
   O *Some of the time*
   O *A lot of the time*
   O *Most of the time*
   O *All of the time*

6. Even when others want to quit, I know that I can find ways to solve the problem.

   O *None of the time*
   O *A little of the time*
   O *Some of the time*
   O *A lot of the time*
   O *Most of the time*
   O *All of the time*

Notes: When administered to children, this scale is not labeled "The Children's Hope Scale," but is called "Questions About Your Goals." To calculate the total Children's Hope Scale score, add the responses to all six items, with "None of the time" = 1; "A little of the time" = 2; "Some of the time" = 3; "A lot of the time" = 4; "Most of the time" = 5; and, "All of the time" = 6. The three odd-numbered items tap agency, and the three even-numbered items tap pathways. From C. R. Snyder, B. Hoza, et al., The development and validation of the Children's Hope Scale, *Journal of Pediatric Psychology* © (1997), Vol. 22(3), p. 421. Reprinted with the permission of the journal and the senior author.

Hope, Self-Efficacy, and Optimism: Conceptual and Empirical Differences

Kevin L. Rand

Abstract

This chapter reviews the conceptual similarities and differences among Snyder's (1994) hope, Carver and Scheier's optimism, and Bandura's self-efficacy. Unlike optimism, hope is focused on beliefs about the self. Unlike self-efficacy, hope is a generalized belief and involves the determination to achieve one's goals. This chapter also reviews the existing empirical literature, which shows that hope, optimism, and self-efficacy are structurally distinct and differentially related to important life outcomes, including psychological adjustment, coping, and goal-directed performance. The chapter concludes with a discussion of further research needed to clarify the causal relationships among hope, optimism, and self-efficacy and to differentiate hope from other positive psychology constructs.

Key Words: hope, optimism, self-efficacy, factor structure, psychological adjustment, coping, goal-directed performance

At this point, it is worth summarizing some key conceptual characteristics of hope. Hope is the trait belief that one will achieve one's goals, arising from two reciprocal thought processes: generation of strategies to reach goals (pathways) and determination to use those strategies (agency). There are several noteworthy characteristics of this conceptualization. First, hope is goal-directed. Hopeful thinking centers on an imagined target that has some value for the goal-setter. This value varies, with less important goals being easily discarded and others being so important as to define and give meaning to the life of the goal-setter (Feldman & Snyder, 1999). Second, hope is future-oriented, focusing on goals that have yet to be achieved. Third, trait hope is a generalized belief that is relevant across different goals and situations. This is particularly important in new goal pursuits, when there may be little specific information available and the goal pursuer must infer expectations about the best course of action and likely outcomes (Rand, 2009).

Fourth, hope theory emphasizes thought processes rather than emotions. Emotions are involved in goal pursuits, but they function primarily as feedback (Snyder, 2002). Positive emotions indicate progress; negative emotions indicate failure. Fifth, hope is self-focused. That is, it centers on what the individual can do to make achieving a goal more likely. Although external factors are considered, hope focuses on what is *controllable*. Specifically related to this characteristic, hopeful thinking involves perceptions of one's goal-related abilities (pathways) and determination to achieve goals (agency). These characteristics of hope are summarized in Table 4.1.

Several corollaries follow from these characteristics. Hope should predict coping behaviors. Higher hope should correlate with greater use of active, problem-focused, and approach coping styles centering on individuals working to achieve their goals. In contrast, lower hope should correlate with greater use of avoidance and withdrawal coping, where individuals reduces effort toward a

Table 4.1. Characteristics of Hope, Optimism, and Self-Efficacy Theories

Characteristic	Hope	Optimism	Self-Efficacy
Goal-directed	Yes	Yes	Yes
Future-oriented	Yes	Yes	Yes
Generalized	Yes	Yes	Maybe
Cognitive	Yes	Yes	Yes
Self-focused	Yes	No	Yes
Perceived ability	Yes	No	Yes
Perceived intention	Yes	No	No

goal because they do not believe they can achieve it. Following from this relationship with coping, hope should predict goal-directed performance and goal attainment. People with higher hope should achieve more of their goals and perform better in goal-directed areas, including athletics and academics. Finally, because so many aspects of our physical and psychological health are determined by how we cope and whether we achieve our goals, hope should predict psychological adjustment across multiple indicators.

As has been reviewed in other chapters of this book, research on hope has generally supported these corollaries. Higher hope predicts greater use of active and approach coping and less use of avoidance and withdrawal (Roesch, Duangado, Vaughn, Aldridge, & Villodas, 2010; Suls & Fletcher, 1985). Hope predicts better academic and athletic performance (Chang, 1998; Curry, Snyder, Cook, Ruby, & Rehm, 1997; Snyder et al., 1991) and more successful goal attainment (Feldman, Rand, & Kahle-Wrobleski, 2009). Greater hope is associated with better physical and psychological health, including less depression and anxiety (Arnau, Rosen, Finch, Rhudy, & Fortunato, 2007; Thimm, Holte, Brennen, & Wang, 2013), greater life meaning and satisfaction (Wrobleski & Snyder, 2005), and better recovery from illness and injury (Barnum, Snyder, Rapoff, Mani, & Thompson, 1998; Elliott, Witty, Herrick, & Hoffman, 1991; Madan & Pakenham, 2014).

Despite the burgeoning empirical literature supporting hope theory, however, scholars have criticized it as being conceptually indistinct from other psychological constructs and lacking discriminant validity in predicting similar outcomes (Aspinwall

& Leaf, 2002; Tennen, Affleck, & Tennen, 2002). Aspinwall and Leaf noted that agency and pathways thinking bear conceptual similarities to other control beliefs, particularly Bandura's (1977) self-efficacy. In addition, they noted that almost all the findings attributed to hope have also been attributed to Scheier and Carver's (1985) optimism. Moreover, research has shown that hope correlates strongly with measures optimism and self-efficacy (Feldman & Kubota, 2015; Snyder et al., 1991), suggesting substantial overlap among the constructs. Indeed, some scholars have chosen simply to conflate hope and optimism into a single construct (e.g., Peterson & Seligman, 2004). Hence, there currently is confusion regarding the distinctions among hope, optimism, and self-efficacy, and delineating their conceptual and empirical differences would help advance our understanding of positive psychology. In the following sections, I briefly define optimism and self-efficacy, highlight their conceptual similarities and differences with hope, and review the empirical evidence of hope's distinctiveness from optimism and self-efficacy.

Optimism

Scheier and Carver (1985) defined optimism as a generalized expectancy that good as opposed to bad things will happen. Their theory is based on an expectancy-value model of motivation (Carver & Scheier, 1998). Like Snyder's (1994) hope model, expectancy-value models begin with the assumption that human behavior is organized around the pursuit of goals or desired states. Hence, optimism is a goal-focused trait. Like hope, optimism is future-oriented and generalized. That is, optimists expect good things to happen to them in the future across a variety of situations. Similar to hope, optimism emphasizes thoughts, with emotions arising in reaction to cognitive expectations (Carver & Scheier, 1998).

The key conceptual distinction between hope and optimism is that optimism is not self-focused (see Table 4.1). Optimism is conceptualized more broadly than hope, and it is purposefully nonspecific about whether the expectation of good outcomes is based on the perceived influence of the individual (Carver & Scheier, 2002). In other words, optimism is the belief that good things will happen, but it does not focus on one's personal control in realizing those outcomes (Aspinwall & Brunhart, 2000). For example, one could be optimistic based primarily on beliefs that external forces (e.g., luck, God, fate, family) will bring about desired outcomes.

This difference is reflected in the instruments used to assess hope and optimism. The Adult Hope Scale (AHS; Snyder et al., 1991) directly assesses the individual's beliefs about the self as a goal-seeker, including perceived ability (e.g., "I can think of many ways to get out of jam") and determination (e.g., "I meet the goals that I set for myself"). In contrast, the primary measure of optimism, the Life Orientation Test–Revised (Scheier, Carver, & Bridges, 1994), measures beliefs about the respondent's more passive role in the world (e.g., "I rarely count on good things happening *to me*" [emphasis added]).

Given their conceptual overlap, optimism should be associated with many of the same outcomes as hope, and research generally shows that optimism is similar to hope in terms of its association with coping, goal attainment, and indicators of well-being. Optimists are more likely to use active, problem-focused coping and less likely to use avoidance and goal disengagement (Aspinwall & Taylor, 1992; Carver, Scheier, & Weintraub, 1989; Scheier, Weintraub, & Carver, 1986). Because of these coping differences, optimism is associated with better goal-related performance, including better academic evaluations (Chemers, Hu, & Garcia, 2001), and greater well-being, especially during adversity (Carver & Gaines, 1987; Carver et al., 1993; Cozzarelli, 1993; Scheier et al., 1989; Zeidner & Hammer, 1992).

Self-Efficacy

Self-efficacy is the belief in one's ability to perform a set of behaviors (Bandura, 1982). It is an aspect of Bandura's (1977) social cognitive theory, which is based on the agentic perspective (Bandura, 2012). According to the agentic perspective, individuals actively influence their functioning and the course of their lives through their behaviors. Like hope, self-efficacy is goal-directed and future-oriented. That is, self-efficacy is a part of the process of how individuals select goals and organize their behaviors to see those goals come to fruition. Also similar to hope, self-efficacy is cognitive in nature and focused on the self (see Table 4.1).

There are two main conceptual distinctions between Bandura's (1977) self-efficacy and Snyder's (1994) hope. First, unlike hope, self-efficacy does not include the intention to perform a behavior, whereas hope includes one's determination (willpower) to achieve one's goals. Self-efficacy is the belief that one *can* do something (Bandura, 2012),

not that one *will* do something (Snyder, 1994). It is one thing to believe that one is capable of running 5 miles; it is quite another to muster the willpower to do it.

Second, in contrast to hope's trait-like nature, the original conceptualization of self-efficacy is more situation-specific. Bandura (2012) argued that people's beliefs about their abilities to perform actions are anchored in specific contexts. Bandura was not opposed to the idea that people develop generalized expectancies based on multiple outcomes. Indeed, he stated that people's behaviors were not governed by the immediate consequences of each situation but by "aggregate consequences" (Bandura, 1977, p. 192) and that success experiences "instill a more generalized sense of efficacy" (p. 194). Bandura was concerned, however, that global expectancies were a mix of several different constructs, including hope, wishful thinking, and belief in the power of the situation (Bandura, 1977). In addition, Bandura (2012) was dubious of global measures of self-efficacy that "decontextualized" the construct from specific goal domains or behaviors, arguing that such constructs were less influential than domain-linked efficacy beliefs. Hence, his research focused on domain-specific and situational expectancies, including beliefs about the ability to interact with a fear-inducing stimulus, such as a snake.

Bandura's reservations about conceptualizing self-efficacy as a general trait have not stopped other scholars from doing so. Several measures of general self-efficacy have been developed (e.g., Chen, Gully, & Eden, 2001; Jerusalem & Schwarzer, 1992; Sherer et al., 1982). Research using these measures has found general self-efficacy to be associated with better psychological well-being. Specifically, greater general self-efficacy is associated with less negative affect, depression, and anxiety and greater positive affect and life satisfaction (Luszczynska, Gutiérrez-Doña, & Schwarzer, 2005; Luszczynska, Scholz, & Schwarzer, 2005). Additionally, general self-efficacy is linked with more adaptive, problem-focused coping (Kumar & Kadhiravan, 2009) and less use of avoidance coping in both healthy (Luszczynska, Scholz, et al., 2005; Schwarzer, Boehmer, Luszczynska, Mohamed, & Knoll, 2005) and ill populations (Brown & Nicassio, 1987). The evidence for general self-efficacy as a predictor of goal-directed performance is more mixed. For example, greater general self-efficacy has been linked to better job performance (Raub & Liao, 2012). In addition, some studies have found a positive association between general self-efficacy and academic performance (Fenning & May, 2013; Luszczynska, Gutiérrez-Doña, et al., 2005). However, other studies have failed to detect a link between general self-efficacy and performance (Choi, 2005; Ferrari & Parker, 1992).

Empirical Distinctions

Although it is helpful to review conceptual differences among hope, optimism, and self-efficacy, to truly test their distinctiveness we must study them concurrently. In the next section, I review the existing empirical evidence regarding the structural independence of hope from optimism and self-efficacy, and then I review their differential relationships with psychological well-being, coping, and goal-directed performance.

Structure of Hope, Optimism, and Self-Efficacy

A fundamental issue in understanding the distinctions between hope, optimism, and self-efficacy is whether these constructs are structurally distinct when measured together. Unfortunately, there is a paucity of research examining the structure of all three constructs together. Magaletta and Oliver (1999) examined the structure of hope, optimism, and general self-efficacy in a sample of university students. They conducted an exploratory factors analysis of the AHS, the Self-Efficacy Scale (Sherer et al., 1982), and the original Life Orientation Test (LOT) measure of optimism (Scheier & Carver, 1985). The results showed that although all three constructs were moderately correlated ($r = .45–.60$), they were structurally distinct. In addition, they found that items from the three measures clustered in ways consistent with the conceptual similarities among hope, optimism, and self-efficacy. Specifically, the agency items of the AHS cohered with items from the Self-Efficacy Scale. This is consistent with these constructs sharing an emphasis on persistence. The items from the pathways subscale of the AHS correlated more strongly with the optimism measure, consistent with a conceptual emphasis on outcome expectancies.

The only other study examining the structure of hope, optimism, and self-efficacy concurrently was conducted by Carifio and Rhodes (2002). Comparing academically at-risk university students to normal students, they examined the structure of the AHS, LOT, and a measure of academic self-efficacy using principle components factor analysis.

Their results showed that the observed factor structures of the hope and optimism measures were consistent with theory in both groups. In contrast, the academic self-efficacy measure was found to be surprisingly complex, consisting of 10 factors. The correlations among the factors were moderate but not large enough to suggest they are redundant constructs. Indeed, agency and pathways subscales only correlated .35 and .08 with academic self-efficacy, respectively. Agency and pathways correlated .52 and .13 with the optimism factor.

The rest of the existing research literature has focused on the structural distinction between hope and optimism. Bryant and Cvengros (2004) used confirmatory factor analysis to demonstrate that hope and optimism, as measured by the AHS and LOT, respectively, could be conceptualized as separate, second-order latent factors that were strongly correlated ($r = .80$). Similarly, Gallagher and Lopez (2009) used confirmatory factor analysis to examine the distinctions between hope and optimism in a sample of nearly 600 college students. They found that hope and optimism were best modeled as separate constructs.

In a sample of 361 Dutch patients undergoing total hip or knee arthroplasty, Haanstra and colleagues (2015) examined the factor structure of hope, optimism, pessimism, treatment credibility, and treatment expectancy using confirmatory factor analysis. Examining the fit of several theory-driven models, they found that the model with all constructs differentiated as separate factors best fit the data. Indeed, post hoc attempts to model hope and optimism as a single factor resulted in a significantly worse-fitting model.

Rand (2009) went a step further and hypothesized a specific conceptual relationship between hope and optimism. In a longitudinal study of 345 undergraduate students taking a psychology course, Rand used confirmatory factor analysis to show that hope and optimism could be conceptualized as distinct facets of an overarching goal attitude construct. This conceptualization acknowledged the empirical fact that hope and optimism have a large amount of shared variance. According to Rand, this shared variance represents a global attitude that the act of pursuing goals is worthwhile. This global attitude arises from beliefs about two different domains: the self (hope) and the world (optimism). Rand found that this hypothesized model showed good fit to the data.

Finally, in a meta-analysis of hope and optimism, Alarcon and colleagues (2013) found that hope and optimism were moderately and positively correlated across several studies (mean correlation = .67). They concluded, however, that the size of this relationship suggested that hope and optimism are not redundant constructs (Kline, 2011).

Unique and Differential Associations with Psychological Adjustment

Studied individually, hope, optimism, and self-efficacy are all associated with better psychological adjustment. Again, to truly understand their unique and differential influences, however, we must study them concurrently. Several studies have compared their relative influences in predicting psychological well-being and distress. These studies suggest that they each maintain some unique influence on psychological adjustment, even when accounting for the presence of each other. However, they also demonstrate differential influences on different aspects of psychological adjustment.

PSYCHOLOGICAL WELL-BEING

In Magaletta and Oliver's (1999) examination of hope, optimism, and general self-efficacy, they conducted a hierarchical regression predicting general well-being (i.e., positive mental and physical health). They found that all three constructs remained significant predictors of general well-being even in the presence of each other. This suggests that hope, optimism, and general self-efficacy each separately influence general psychological well-being, potentially via different mechanisms. This is not to say that the effects of hope, optimism, and self-efficacy are invariable, however, as research has also shown them to exhibit divergent influences across different aspects of psychological adjustment.

Hope and optimism consistently show unique influences in predicting general life satisfaction. In a study of first-year law students, Rand and colleagues (2011) found that both hope and optimism, measured at the start of the semester, separately predicted greater life satisfaction during finals week. Similarly, hope and optimism have been shown to uniquely predict overall life satisfaction among adolescents in Singapore (Wong & Lim, 2009), American university students, and community-dwelling adults (Bailey, Eng, Frisch, & Snyder, 2007).

In contrast, self-efficacy does not predict overall life satisfaction when studied in the presence of hope or optimism. For example, O'Sullivan (2011) found that hope predicted life satisfaction in a sample of undergraduate students, whereas academic self-efficacy did not. Instead, self-efficacy appears

to only influence specific aspects of well-being. For example, self-efficacy predicted job satisfaction among correctional employees, even after accounting for the influence of hope (Law & Guo, 2016).

Unfortunately, there is little research comparing the differential influences of hope and self-efficacy on psychological well-being. As was the case with factor structure, most of the extant research has focused on comparing hope and optimism. To date the most thorough investigation of the differential influences of hope and optimism on dimensions of psychological well-being was conducted by Gallagher and Lopez (2009). They examined the unique contributions of hope and optimism in predicting 14 different facets of psychological well-being across three domains (i.e., hedonic well-being, eudaimonic well-being, and social well-being; see Gallagher, Lopez, & Preacher, 2009). They found that both hope and optimism maintained unique relationships with most of the outcomes, even in the presence of the other construct. In other words, even when studied together, both hope and optimism exerted independent predictive contributions to most facets of psychological well-being. Hope was not a significant predictor of negative affect and social coherence in the presence of optimism. Conversely, optimism was not a significant predictor of autonomy and personal growth in the presence of hope. Examination of the effect sizes revealed that optimism was more influential than hope on hedonic well-being (i.e., greater pleasure and less pain) and social well-being. In contrast, hope was more strongly associated with the facets of eudaimonic well-being, including autonomy, mastery, growth, and purpose.

In contrast to hedonic well-being, eudaimonic well-being centers on meaning and self-actualization (Ryan & Deci, 2001). Therefore, the findings of Gallagher and Lopez (2009) suggest that hope is specifically linked to the creation and pursuit of meaningful goals, whereas optimism is more consistently linked to a diffuse sense of well-being, indicated by life satisfaction and mood. In addition, optimism is more strongly linked to a sense of social well-being than hope. These results are consistent with the conceptual distinctions between the hope and optimism. Hope emphasizes personal goal pursuits, which are the mechanisms by which people give meaning to their lives (Feldman & Snyder, 1999). In contrast, optimism is a more generalized belief about the positivity of life that can incorporate the impact of other people.

Of course, the differential influences of hope and optimism on well-being may change across the lifespan. In a study of older adults (age 60 or older), hope significantly predicted overall physical and psychological health, whereas optimism did not (Barnett, 2014). Consistent with the results of Gallagher and Lopez (2009), this study also found that optimism had a stronger association with the size of the participant's social network than did hope.

PSYCHOLOGICAL DISTRESS

In addition to being positive indicators of psychological well-being, hope, optimism, and self-efficacy are inversely related to markers of psychological distress, including aspects of depression and anxiety. These associations have been found in both healthy and clinical populations. Among a sample of healthy adolescents in Singapore, both hope and optimism separately predicted fewer depressive symptoms (Wong & Lim, 2009). In a sample of American Indian and Native Alaskan college students, both hope and optimism separately predicted less suicidality (O'Keefe & Wingate, 2013). Similarly, both hope and optimism uniquely predicted depressive symptoms among a sample of primary care patients, even after controlling for the influences of age, sex, race, marital status, and education (Chang, Yu, & Hirsch, 2013). Moreover, both hope and optimism had a large effect size in predicting depressive symptoms, which is consistent with the meta-analytic finding of Alarcon and colleagues (2013), who found that hope and optimism had equal effect sizes in predicting depression.

These influences are also found among people experiencing illness or injury. For example, Peleg and colleagues (2009) found that both hope and optimism separately predicted fewer depressive symptoms among people who had sustained a traumatic brain injury, with hope having a slightly larger effect size than optimism. In a sample of Chinese patients with cervical cancer, Yang and colleagues (2014) found that hope, optimism, and general self-efficacy each uniquely predicted depressive symptoms, whereas only hope and optimism uniquely predicted anxiety. Similarly, in a study of hope and rehabilitation-specific self-efficacy among patients undergoing joint replacement surgery, hope was found to predict presurgical depression, whereas rehabilitation-specific self-efficacy uniquely predicted postsurgical depression, even after controlling for hope and presurgical depression (Hartley, Vance, Elliott, Cuckler, & Berry, 2008). Among patients experiencing intractable muscoskeletal pain, optimism, but not hope, predicted less psychological

distress (Wright et al., 2011). This finding is consistent with the hypothesis that optimism may be more influential on well-being in situations marked by little or no control (see Rand, 2009).

Hope, optimism, and self-efficacy retain their influence on psychological distress even in populations being treated for psychological disorders. In a sample of adults receiving psychotherapy for anxiety and depression, optimism predicted less burdensomeness and thwarted belonging whereas hope did not (Davidson & Wingate, 2013). This is consistent with the findings of Gallagher and Lopez (2009), who found that optimism was a stronger predictor of social well-being than hope. In a longitudinal study of people enrolled in a substance abuse recovery program, both hope and abstinence-specific self-efficacy predicted less anxiety and depression over time (May, Hunter, Ferrari, Noel, & Jason, 2015).

There is also evidence of more complex causal relationships among hope, optimism, and psychological distress. For example, in the aforementioned study of primary care patients (Chang et al., 2013), there was a significant interaction between hope and optimism in predicting depressive symptoms. Specifically, hope had a stronger effect in reducing depressive symptoms among pessimists. Indeed, high-hope pessimists had depression levels similar to those of optimists. This suggests that hope can mitigate the detrimental effects of pessimism on psychological distress. Similarly, in a study of college students, both hope and optimism were found to serve a protective function by weakening the associations between rumination and suicidal ideation (Tucker et al., 2013).

Coping

One possible mechanism for the differential effects of hope, optimism, and self-efficacy on well-being is that they predict different coping strategies. Given their conceptualization specific to goal-directed behaviors, hope and self-efficacy should be stronger predictors of problem-focused and approach coping strategies (i.e., assimilative coping; Brandtstädter & Renner, 1990) than optimism. In contrast, optimism, linked to how one views the world, should be more strongly associated with acceptance and positive reappraisal strategies (i.e., accommodative coping; Brandtstädter & Renner, 1990) than either hope or self-efficacy.

Several studies have linked hope to greater ability to engage in active coping behaviors, even in the presence of self-efficacy or optimism. For example, hope has been shown to predict problem-focused coping beyond the influence of optimism, whereas optimism was not shown to predict problem-focused coping in the presence of hope (Bryant & Cvengros, 2004; Snyder et al., 1991).

In a laboratory study using the cold pressor task, Snyder and colleagues (2005) found hope predicted greater pain tolerance, independent of optimism and self-efficacy. Moreover, among the male participants, hope predicted delayed onset of pain recognition. This finding suggests that greater hope may allow people to remain engaged in goal-directed efforts, even when doing so becomes aversive. This ability to tolerate unpleasantness should predict more sustained coping efforts and ultimately better success.

Similarly, in a study of career development among at-risk adolescents and college students in Switzerland, hope predicted active career exploration independent of general self-efficacy (Hirschi, Abessolo, & Froidevaux, 2015). Similarly, hope was shown to influence proactive career development behaviors among samples of university students and working professionals (Hirschi, 2014). Specifically, greater hope predicted more active career planning, which led to greater life and career satisfaction.

As with psychological distress, hope may influence the relationships among other variables related to coping. For example, in a study of college students, hope was found to influence the relationship between optimism and coping, such that pessimists who were higher in hope were less likely to engage in passive coping behaviors (Lopes & Cunha, 2008).

Goal-Directed Performance

Because hope is likely more predictive of goal-directed efforts (e.g., problem-focused coping) than either optimism or self-efficacy, hope should be a stronger predictor of performance and achievement. The discriminant utility of hope has been demonstrated repeatedly with regard to predicting academic performance. Early on, Snyder and colleagues (2002) showed that hope predicts academic achievement among college students, including grades and graduation rates, even when controlling for intelligence and previous academic performance. Research has also shown that hope predicts subsequent academic performance independent of intelligence, previous performance, and other personality traits (Day, Hanson, Maltby, Proctor, & Wood, 2010). Of interest here is the extent to which hope differentially predicts academic performance in the presence of either optimism or self-efficacy.

To date there have been several studies examining the differential predictive ability of hope in the presence of optimism or self-efficacy across levels of education. A study of 10th-grade students in Israel examined hope, domain-specific self-efficacy (i.e., academic, social, emotional), and specific grade expectancies as predictors of academic performance (Levi, Einav, Ziv, Raskind, & Margalit, 2014). The results showed that hope had an indirect influence on grades through grade expectancies. That is, higher hope predicted higher grade expectations, which in turn predicted better academic performance. In contrast, none of the domain-specific self-efficacy constructs predicted grades, although academic self-efficacy did predict effort.

In a study of college students, Feldman and Kubota (2015) examined hope, optimism, and general self-efficacy as predictors of college grades. In addition, they incorporated domain-specific measures of academic hope and academic self-efficacy. The results showed that academic hope and academic self-efficacy directly predicted college grade point average. Trait hope was an indirect predictor of grades through both academic hope and academic self-efficacy. In contrast, neither optimism nor general self-efficacy exhibited direct or indirect influence on grades. Somewhat surprisingly, general self-efficacy did not even predict academic self-efficacy. Instead, only trait hope predicted academic-specific expectancies.

In a study of a large college psychology class, Rand (2009) examined the differential ability of hope and optimism to predict the final course grade. He found that the shared variance between hope and optimism directly predicted the final grade, even after controlling for cumulative grade point average. In addition, the unique aspects of hope indirectly predicted the final course grade through specific grade expectancy. The unique aspects of optimism, on the other hand, offered no predictive utility in terms of academic performance.

In a study examining the effects of an intervention to increase hope among first-year university students, researchers found that students whose hope increased after the intervention received higher grades the subsequent semester, even after controlling for previous grades and initial levels of hope (Feldman, Davidson, & Margalit, 2014). Moreover, hope was more consistently linked with better student grades over time than either optimism or general self-efficacy. This suggests that, when studied together, hope is more of an influence on performance than either optimism or self-efficacy.

Even as academic rigors increase at the graduate level, hope remains an important predictor of academic performance. In a study of first-year law students, hope, measured at the start of the semester, predicted law school grades above and beyond undergraduate grade point average and standardized test scores (Rand et al., 2011). In contrast, optimism did not predict law school grades. Rand and colleagues concluded that this differential influence may stem from hope's influence over goal-directed actions (e.g., studying) that increase the likelihood that goals will be achieved, provided they are actually within one's sphere of influence.

Unfortunately, there is little research examining the relative influences of hope, optimism, and self-efficacy on goal-directed performance in other life domains, such as work. One study found that both hope and self-efficacy separately predicted supervisor ratings of creativity among retail employees (Rego, Sousa, Marques, & Cunha, 2012). Conversely, a study of Chinese factory workers found that neither hope nor optimism predicted supervisor ratings of job performance, whereas resilience did (Luthans, Avolio, Walumbwa, & Li, 2005). However, when all three constructs were combined into a single construct they called psychological capital, the amalgam construct predicted supervisor-rated performance and merit-based salary. Subsequent research combining hope, optimism, self-efficacy, and resilience into the composite construct of psychological capital has shown that it predicts both self-rated and supervisor-rated job performance (Luthans, Avolio, Avey, & Norman, 2007; Peterson, Luthans, Avolio, Walumbwa, & Zhang, 2011).

Functional Relationships Among Hope, Optimism, and Self-Efficacy

Given the evidence for the correlated but distinct structures and differential associations of hope, optimism, and self-efficacy with various outcomes, it is natural to wonder about the functional relationships among them. In other words, how do hope, optimism, and self-efficacy influence each other? Although the extant evidence is sparse, at least two provocative hypotheses are possible. It is worth noting that these hypotheses are not mutually exclusive.

First, all three constructs could represent facets of an overarching trait expectancy. In other words, hope, optimism, and self-efficacy may represent specific manifestations of an overall positive expectation about the future. This is consistent with Rand's (2009) synthesized model of hope and optimism

representing facets of a general goal attitude. Several pieces of evidence support this overarching trait conceptualization. Researchers have been successful at modeling hope, optimism, and self-efficacy as facets of an overarching trait. For example, in a sample of South African college students, Jackson, van de Vijver, and Fouché (2014) found that modeling hope and self-efficacy as facets of an overarching personal resources construct showed good fit to the data. Haanstra and colleagues (2015) found that optimism, pessimism, hope, treatment credibility, and treatment expectancy could be modeled as first-order facets of a second-order general future outlook in patients undergoing knee or hip surgery. This hierarchical model is also consistent with the psychological capital construct created by Luthans and colleagues (Luthans et al., 2007; Luthans et al., 2005). The psychological capital construct not only shows good fit to the data but also predicts job performance.

Changes in the overarching trait expectancy would lead to parallel changes to all three constructs. There is some evidence to support this parallel causation among hope, optimism, and self-efficacy. For example, hope and self-efficacy show the same developmental trajectory during adolescence (Phan, 2013), with both constructs decreasing during the teenage years. This lockstep movement over time is consistent with both constructs being driven by an overarching trait. In addition, interventions aimed at increasing hope have been shown to also increase optimism and self-efficacy. For example, a workshop designed to increase hope in first-year college students resulted in increases not only in hope but also in optimism and self-efficacy (Feldman et al., 2014; see also Davidson, Feldman, & Margalit, 2012). This finding was replicated in another study where a workshop to increase hope among first-year college students resulted in increased in optimism as well (Rosenstreich, Feldman, Davidson, Maza, & Margalit, 2015).

Similarly, stressors have been shown to have similar detrimental effects on both hope and self-efficacy. For example, in a study comparing hope and self-efficacy of adolescents with learning disabilities to those without (matched for level of previous academic performance and gender), Lackaye and colleagues (2006) found that learning-disabled students reported lower levels of hope, academic self-efficacy, and social self-efficacy. This can be interpreted as showing that the experience of a particular stressor can have similar effects on both hope and self-efficacy.

A second possibility is that there is a particular causal sequence among hope, optimism, and self-efficacy. In other words, there may be a specific order to how these constructs develop during childhood and change in response to interventions or stressors. Snyder (1994, 2000) hypothesized a specific developmental sequence for hope and optimism. He argued that general optimistic expectations would emerge first in childhood, as children begin to more fully understand that there are desirable and undesirable outcomes in the world. This conceptualization of the world as having good and bad qualities would map on to optimism as a set of beliefs about the world (Rand, 2009). Similarly, interactions with important others, particularly caregivers, would shape generalized social expectancies (e.g., attachment style; see Shorey, Snyder, Yang, & Lewin, 2003).

Later, when the sense of self begins to develop (i.e., psychological birth), Snyder (1994) argued hopeful thinking begins to emerge, as children learn they can influence the future. In other words, personal agency would emerge later in childhood, after a general sense of positive or negative expectancies about the world and people in it. Following Snyder's theory, we would expect to see that optimism appears first, in response to beliefs about the world, and drives the development of hope later, or that a general sense of goal expectancies develops first, with cognitive differentiation between thoughts about the world and the self developing later.

There is some initial evidence to support this sequential causation hypothesis. In a study of Chinese adolescents, researchers found support for a mediational model where social support predicted greater optimism, which in turn predicted greater hope (Ling et al., 2015). This finding is consistent with hypothesis that relationships with others early in life influence one's view of the world, which then later influences the view of the self (Shorey et al., 2003). However, this was a cross-sectional study, so it could not explicitly test the hypothesized causal sequence.

Self-efficacy may then emerge as a specific manifestation of hope. Self-efficacy measured at the general level resembles hope a great deal. It is when measured at the domain- or behavior-specific level that self-efficacy becomes a more powerful predictor of outcomes. There is some evidence to support this hypothesis. For example, Feldman and Kubota (2015) found that trait hope predicted both academic hope and academic self-efficacy. In contrast, general self-efficacy was not predictive of academic self-efficacy or hope. Similarly, a study of primary school teachers in Turkey found that hope and academic optimism predicted perceived success, which in turn predicted teaching self-efficacy (Sezgin & Erdogan, 2015). In samples of college students and working adults, hope predicted greater career planning, which then predicted greater self-efficacy and life and job satisfaction (Hirschi, 2014). Also, Bryant and Cvengros (2004) found that hope exhibited a stronger influence on self-efficacy than did optimism. It should be noted, however, that these studies were cross-sectional and cannot determine causation or direction.

The influences among hope, optimism, and self-efficacy could be reciprocal. Indeed, some studies have found support for the opposite causal sequence, with self-efficacy predicting hope. In a study of high school students, Levi and colleagues (2014) found evidence that emotional self-efficacy and sense of coherence predicted hope, which in turn predicted grade expectancy and academic performance. This is consistent with Bandura's (2012) argument that specific experiences of mastery can lead to more global expectancies. Clearly, longitudinal studies are needed to tease apart the causal direction between hope and self-efficacy.

The sequential causation hypothesis suggested by Snyder (1994, 2000) may also help make sense of any cultural differences in hope, optimism, and self-efficacy. Collectivistic cultures that emphasize community over the individual may cause the development of individuals with relatively higher levels of optimism but relatively lower levels of hope. In contrast, individualistic cultures that emphasize the person over the community may produce people who are higher in hope than optimism. Consistent with this idea, Hutz and colleagues (2014) compared Americans and Brazilians on measures of hope, optimism, self-esteem, and life satisfaction. They found that Americans had higher levels of constructs pertaining to a sense of self (i.e., hope, positive affect, and life satisfaction). In contrast, Brazilians were more optimistic and had greater negative affect.

Conclusion

Although there are similarities among hope, optimism, and self-efficacy, this review has highlighted important conceptual and empirical differences. The distinction between hope and optimism is clearest and has received the most scholarly attention. Optimism is a broad expectancy (Carver & Scheier, 1998), with no specific focus on the controllability of desired outcomes. In contrast, hope is a more focused expectancy anchored in an individual's ability and intention to bring goals to fruition. Optimism may emerge from core beliefs about the world and others, whereas hope may emerge from core beliefs about the self (Rand, 2009).

Research generally supports this conceptual distinction. Optimism is more consistently related to social and hedonic well-being (e.g., Gallagher et al., 2009) and accommodative coping strategies anchored in how the world is perceived (e.g., Alarcon et al., 2013). Hope is more consistently associated with eudaimonic well-being (Gallagher et al., 2009), goal-directed coping (e.g., Snyder et al., 2005), and goal-related performance (e.g., Rand et al., 2011). Both constructs appear equally influential on general psychological well-being (e.g., life satisfaction) and psychological distress (e.g., depressive symptoms), reflecting the reality that remaining well adjusted in a world replete with both controllable and uncontrollable factors requires both active and passive beliefs. To strive for a better life, one has to believe both that the world is hospitable and that one has the requisites skills to achieve one's goals.

The distinction between hope and self-efficacy is less clear. Conceptually, there are two main differences. First, as originally conceptualized by Bandura (1977), self-efficacy is a domain- or situation-specific expectancy. In contrast, hope is a trait belief that generalizes across situations and goal pursuits. That said, researchers have found empirical support that self-efficacy can be measured at the general level and that it predicts important life outcomes (Chen et al., 2001).

The second conceptual difference between hope and self-efficacy is that hope involves the intention to strive for goals (i.e., agency), whereas self-efficacy is a belief about one's ability only. The difference is between what one *can* do versus what one *will* do. The available research shows that this distinction is more than mere semantics. When studied concurrently, hope tends to be a stronger predictor than general self-efficacy of performance and psychological well-being (e.g., Feldman & Kubota, 2015; Yang et al., 2014).

Three areas of scholarship are needed to further clarify the distinctiveness of hope: (a) resolving measurement issues, (b) conducting longitudinal research, and (c) differentiating hope from other constructs. There are two specific measurement issues related to hope. First, although Snyder (1994) articulated several hypotheses about hope

being anchored in how goals are conceptualized, goal characteristics are not assessed by the AHS. Therefore, the development of a measure that assesses goal characteristics in addition to pathways and agency would allow researchers to more fully test hope theory and better differentiate hope from similar constructs (Shorey, Little, Rand, Snyder, Monsson, & Gallagher, 2009).

Second, there is substantial conceptual overlap between the AHS and measures of general self-efficacy. For example, the Self-Efficacy Scale (Sherer et al., 1982) contains items that appear to measure determination (or the lack thereof: e.g., "I give up easily"), making it more conceptually similar to hope. Scholars must decide if determination is a part of the general self-efficacy construct. If so, then there is little conceptual distinction between hope and general self-efficacy, and the two constructs may be redundant. If self-efficacy is defined to include only beliefs about one's abilities, then research can clarify the respective influences of perceived abilities and determination in achieving important outcomes. With apologies to Plato, it is up to us to decide where the joints are between psychological constructs.

There is a need for more longitudinal research, particularly during childhood, to better understand the development of hope in relation similar constructs, such as optimism and self-esteem. Studying the prospective development of hope and optimism in young children would clarify the nature of their functional relationships. Does optimism develop first, followed by hope, as Snyder hypothesized? Similarly, more longitudinal research is needed to clarify the differential contributions of hope, optimism, and self-efficacy to well-being across the lifespan. For example, one hypothesis is that optimism may become a stronger influence on psychological adjustment later in life, when aging reduces our ability to engage in active, goal-directed coping (Lang, Weiss, Gerstorf, & Wagner, 2013). As such, we might predict that optimism will become a greater determinant of well-being as coping switches from being predominantly assimilative to predominantly accommodative (Brandtstädter & Renner, 1990).

Finally, several other constructs have conceptual and empirical similarities to hope, and more work is needed to delineate their distinctions from hope. For example, Gillham, Shatté, Reivich, and Seligman (2001) have developed a conceptualization of optimism different from that of Scheier and Carver (1985), which involves the style with which one explains past events. In addition, constructs such as hopelessness (Beck, Weissman, Lester, & Trexler, 1974), self-esteem (Hewitt, 1998), and social problem-solving (D'Zurilla & Nezu, 1990) have conceptual overlap with hope. Although Snyder (2002) outlined some of the conceptual differences between the constructs and hope, more empirical work is needed. To date, theory and research have demonstrated that hope is a useful construct that is not redundant with optimism or self-efficacy. Further work is needed to clarify hope's unique place in positive psychology.

Future Directions

• When measured at the trait level, what are the important distinctions between hope and self-efficacy?

• Are hope, optimism, and self-efficacy facets of the same overarching construct?

• What are the causal relationships among hope, optimism, and self-efficacy?

• How do hope, optimism, and self-efficacy develop during childhood?

• What are the conceptual and empirical differences between hope and other positive psychology constructs?

References

Alarcon, G. M., Bowling, N. A., & Khazon, S. (2013). Great expectations: A meta-analytic examination of optimism and hope. *Personality and Individual Differences*, 54(7), 821–827. doi:10.1016/j.paid.2012.12.004

Arnau, R. C., Rosen, D. H., Finch, J. F., Rhudy, J. L., & Fortunato, V. J. (2007). Longitudinal effects of hope on depression and anxiety: A latent variable analysis. *Journal of Personality*, 75(1), 43–63. doi:10.1111/j.1467-6494.2006.00432.x

Aspinwall, L. G., & Brunhart, S. M. (2000). What I do know won't hurt me: Optimism, attention to negative information, coping, and health. In J. E. Gillham & J. E. Gillham (Eds.), *The science of optimism and hope: Research essays in honor of Martin E. P. Seligman* (pp. 163–200). West Conshohocken, PA: Templeton Foundation Press.

Aspinwall, L. G., & Leaf, S. L. (2002). In search of the unique aspects of hope: Pinning our hopes on positive emotions, future oriented thinking hard times, and other people. *Psychological Inquiry*, 13(4), 276–288. doi:10.1207/S15327965PLI1304_02

Aspinwall, L. G., & Taylor, S. E. (1992). Modeling cognitive adaptation: A longitudinal investigation of the impact of individual differences and coping on college adjustment and performance. *Journal of Personality and Social Psychology*, 63(6), 989–1003. doi:10.1037/0022-3514.63.6.989

Bailey, T. C., Eng, W., Frisch, M. B., & Snyder, C. R. (2007). Hope and optimism as related to life satisfaction. *The Journal of Positive Psychology*, 2(3), 168–175. doi:10.1080/17439760701409546

Bandura, A. (1977). Self-efficacy: Toward a unifying theory of behavioral change. *Psychological Review*, 84(2), 191–215. doi:10.1037/0033-295X.84.2.191

Bandura, A. (1982). Self-efficacy mechanism in human agency. *American Psychologist*, 37(2), 122–147. doi:10.1037/0003-066X.37.2.122

Bandura, A. (2012). On the functional properties of perceived self-efficacy revisited. *Journal of Management*, 38(1), 9–44. doi:10.1177/0149206311410606

Barnett, M. D. (2014). Future orientation and health among older adults: The importance of hope. *Educational Gerontology*, 40(10), 745–755. doi:10.1080/03601277.2014.898496

Barnum, D. D., Snyder, C. R., Rapoff, M. A., Mani, M. M., & Thompson, R. (1998). Hope and social support in the psychological adjustment of children who have survived burn injuries and their matched controls. *Children's Health Care*, 27(1), 15–30.

Beck, A. T., Weissman, A., Lester, D., & Trexler, L. (1974). The measurement of pessimism: The Hopelessness Scale. *Journal of Consulting and Clinical Psychology*, 42(6), 861–865. doi:10.1037/h0037562

Brandtstädter, J., & Renner, G. (1990). Tenacious goal pursuit and flexible goal adjustment: Explication and age-related analysis of assimilative and accommodative strategies of coping. *Psychology and Aging*, 5(1), 58–67. doi:10.1037/0882-7974.5.1.58

Brown, G. K., & Nicassio, P. M. (1987). Development of a questionnaire for the assessment of active and passive coping strategies in chronic pain patients. *Pain*, 31(1), 53–64. doi:10.1016/0304-3959(87)90006-6

Bryant, F. B., & Cvengros, J. A. (2004). Distinguishing hope and optimism: Two sides of a coin, or two separate coins? *Journal of Social & Clinical Psychology*, 23(2), 273–302.

Carifio, J., & Rhodes, L. (2002). Construct validities and the empirical relationships between optimism, hope, self-efficacy, and locus of control. *Work: Journal of Prevention, Assessment & Rehabilitation*, 19(2), 125–136.

Carver, C. S., & Gaines, J. G. (1987). Optimism, pessimism, and postpartum depression. *Cognitive Therapy and Research*, 11(4), 449–462. doi:10.1007/BF01175355

Carver, C. S., Pozo, C., Harris, S. D., Noriega, V., Scheier, M. F., Robinson, D. S., . . . Clark, K. C. (1993). How coping mediates the effect of optimism on distress: A study of women with early stage breast cancer. *Journal of Personality and Social Psychology*, 65(2), 375–390. doi:10.1037/0022-3514.65.2.375

Carver, C. S., & Scheier, M. F. (1998). *On the self-regulation of behavior*. New York: Cambridge University Press.

Carver, C. S., & Scheier, M. F. (2002). The hopeful optimist. *Psychological Inquiry*, 13(4), 288–290.

Carver, C. S., Scheier, M. F., & Weintraub, J. K. (1989). Assessing coping strategies: A theoretically based approach. *Journal of Personality and Social Psychology*, 56(2), 267–283. doi:10.1037/0022-3514.56.2.267

Chang, E. C. (1998). Hope, problem-solving ability, and coping in a college student population: Some implications for theory and practice. *Journal of Clinical Psychology*, 54(7), 953–962. doi:10.1002/(SICI)1097-4679(199811)54:7<953:AID-JCLP9>3.0.CO;2-F

Chang, E. C., Yu, E. A., & Hirsch, J. K. (2013). On the confluence of optimism and hope on depressive symptoms in primary care patients: Does doubling up on bonum futurun proffer any added benefits? *The Journal of Positive Psychology*, 8(5), 404–411. doi:10.1080/17439760.2013.818163

Chemers, M. M., Hu, L.-T., & Garcia, B. F. (2001). Academic self-efficacy and first year college student performance and adjustment. *Journal of Educational Psychology, 93*(1), 55–64. doi:10.1037/0022-0663.93.1.55

Chen, G., Gully, S. M., & Eden, D. (2001). Validation of a new general self-efficacy scale. *Organizational Research Methods, 4*(1), 62–83. doi:10.1177/109442810141004

Choi, N. (2005). Self-Efficacy and self-concept as predictors of college students' academic performance. *Psychology in the Schools, 42*(2), 197–205. doi:10.1002/pits.20048

Cozzarelli, C. (1993). Personality and self-efficacy as predictors of coping with abortion. *Journal of Personality and Social Psychology, 65*(6), 1224–1236. doi:10.1037/0022-3514.65.6.1224

Curry, L. A., Snyder, C. R., Cook, D. L., Ruby, B. C., & Rehm, M. (1997). Role of hope in academic and sport achievement. *Journal of Personality and Social Psychology, 73*(6), 1257–1267.

D'Zurilla, T. J., & Nezu, A. M. (1990). Development and preliminary evaluation of the Social Problem-Solving Inventory. *Psychological Assessment: A Journal of Consulting and Clinical Psychology, 2*(2), 156–163. doi:10.1037/1040-3590.2.2.156

Davidson, C. L., & Wingate, L. R. (2013). The glass half-full or a hopeful outlook: Which explains more variance in interpersonal suicide risk in a psychotherapy clinic sample? *The Journal of Positive Psychology, 8*(3), 263–272. doi:10.1080/17439760.2013.787446

Davidson, O. B., Feldman, D. B., & Margalit, M. (2012). A focused intervention for 1st-year college students: Promoting hope, sense of coherence, and self-efficacy. *The Journal of Psychology: Interdisciplinary and Applied, 146*(3), 333–352. doi:10.1080/00223980.2011.634862

Day, L., Hanson, K., Maltby, J., Proctor, C., & Wood, A. (2010). Hope uniquely predicts objective academic achievement above intelligence, personality, and previous academic achievement. *Journal of Research in Personality, 44*(4), 550–553. doi:10.1016/j.jrp.2010.05.009

Elliott, T. R., Witty, T. E., Herrick, S. M., & Hoffman, J. T. (1991). Negotiating reality after physical loss: Hope, depression, and disability. *Journal of Personality and Social Psychology, 61*(4), 608–613.

Feldman, D. B., Davidson, O. B., & Margalit, M. (2014). Personal resources, hope, and achievement among college students: The conservation of resources perspective. *Journal of Happiness Studies, 16*(3), 543–560. doi:10.1007/s10902-014-9508-5

Feldman, D. B., & Kubota, M. (2015). Hope, self-efficacy, optimism, and academic achievement: Distinguishing constructs and levels of specificity in predicting college grade-point average. *Learning and Individual Differences, 37*, 210–216. doi:10.1016/j.lindif.2014.11.022

Feldman, D. B., Rand, K. L., & Kahle-Wrobleski, K. (2009). Hope and goal attainment: Testing a basic prediction of hope theory. *Journal of Social and Clinical Psychology, 28*(4), 479–497. doi:10.1521/jscp.2009.28.4.479

Feldman, D. B., & Snyder, C. R. (1999). *Natural comparisons: Hope and meaning*. Unpublished manuscript. University of Kansas, Lawrence.

Fenning, B. E., & May, L. N. (2013). "Where there is a will, there is an A": Examining the roles of self-efficacy and self-concept in college students' current educational attainment and career planning. *Social Psychology of Education, 16*(4), 635–650. doi:10.1007/s11218-013-9228-4

Ferrari, J. R., & Parker, J. T. (1992). High school achievement, self-efficacy, and locus of control as predictors of freshman academic performance. *Psychological Reports, 71*(2), 515–518. doi:10.2466/PR0.71.6.515-518

Gallagher, M. W., & Lopez, S. J. (2009). Positive expectancies and mental health: Identifying the unique contributions of hope and optimism. *The Journal of Positive Psychology, 4*(6), 548–556. doi:10.1080/17439760903157166

Gallagher, M. W., Lopez, S. J., & Preacher, K. J. (2009). The hierarchical structure of well-being. *Journal of Personality, 77*(4), 1025–1050. doi:10.1111/j.1467-6494.2009.00573.x

Gillham, J. E., Shatté, A. J., Reivich, K. J., & Seligman, M. E. P. (2001). Optimism, pessimism, and explanatory style. In E. C. Chang & E. C. Chang (Eds.), *Optimism & pessimism: Implications for theory, research, and practice.* (pp. 53–75). Washington, DC: American Psychological Association.

Haanstra, T. M., Tilbury, C., Kamper, S. J., Tordoir, R. L., Vliet Vlieland, T. P. M., Nelissen, R. G. H. H., . . . Ostelo, R. W. (2015). Can optimism, pessimism, hope, treatment credibility and treatment expectancy be distinguished in patients undergoing total hip and total knee arthroplasty? *PLoS ONE, 10*(7). https://doi.org/10.1371/journal.pone.0133730

Hartley, S. M., Vance, D. E., Elliott, T. R., Cuckler, J. M., & Berry, J. W. (2008). Hope, self-efficacy, and functional recovery after knee and hip replacement surgery. *Rehabilitation Psychology, 53*(4), 521–529. doi:10.1037/a0013121

Hewitt, J. P. (1998). *The myth of self-esteem: Finding happiness and solving problems in America.* New York: St Martin's Press.

Hirschi, A. (2014). Hope as a resource for self-directed career management: Investigating mediating effects on proactive career behaviors and life and job satisfaction. *Journal of Happiness Studies, 15*(6), 1495–1512. doi:10.1007/s10902-013-9488-x

Hirschi, A., Abessolo, M., & Froidevaux, A. (2015). Hope as a resource for career exploration: Examining incremental and cross-lagged effects. *Journal of Vocational Behavior, 86*, 38–47. doi:10.1016/j.jvb.2014.10.006

Hutz, C. S., Midgett, A., Pacico, J. C., Bastianello, M. R., & Zanon, C. (2014). The relationship of hope, optimism, self-esteem, subjective well-being, and personality in Brazilians and Americans. *Psychology, 5*(6), 514–522. doi:10.4236/psych.2014.56061

Jackson, L. T. B., van de Vijver, F. J. R., & Fouché, R. (2014). Psychological strengths and subjective well-being in South African white students. *Journal of Psychology in Africa, 24*(4), 299–307.

Jerusalem, M., & Schwarzer, R. (1992). Self-efficacy as a resource factor in stress appraisal processes. In R. Schwarzer & R. Schwarzer (Eds.), *Self-efficacy: Thought control of action.* (pp. 195–213). Washington, DC: Hemisphere Publishing.

Kline, R. B. (2011). *Principles and practice of structural equation modeling* (3rd ed.). New York: Guilford Press.

Kumar, K., & Kadhiravan, S. (2009). Stress, proactive coping and perceived self-efficacy of college students. *Journal of Psychosocial Research, 4*(2), 299–306.

Lackaye, T., Margalit, M., Ziv, O., & Ziman, T. (2006). Comparisons of self-efficacy, mood, effort, and hope between students with learning disabilities and their non-LD-matched peers. *Learning Disabilities Research & Practice, 21*(2), 111–121. doi:10.1111/j.1540-5826.2006.00211.x

Lang, F. R., Weiss, D., Gerstorf, D., & Wagner, G. G. (2013). Forecasting life satisfaction across adulthood: Benefits of seeing a dark future? *Psychology and Aging*, *28*(1), 249–261. doi:10.1037/a0030797

Law, F. M., & Guo, G. J. (2016). Correlation of hope and self-efficacy with job satisfaction, job stress, and organizational commitment for correctional officers in the Taiwan prison system. *International Journal of Offender Therapy and Comparative Criminology*, *60*(11), 1257–1277.

Levi, U., Einav, M., Ziv, O., Raskind, I., & Margalit, M. (2014). Academic expectations and actual achievements: The roles of hope and effort. *European Journal of Psychology of Education*, *29*(3), 367–386. doi:10.1007/s10212-013-0203-4

Ling, Y., Huebner, E. S., Liu, J., Liu, W.-L., Zhang, J., & Xiao, J. (2015). The origins of hope in adolescence: A test of a social–cognitive model. *Personality and Individual Differences*, *87*, 307–311. doi:10.1016/j.paid.2015.08.016

Lopes, M. P., & Cunha, M. P. e. (2008). Who is more proactive, the optimist or the pessimist? Exploring the role of hope as a moderator. *The Journal of Positive Psychology*, *3*(2), 100–109. doi:10.1080/17439760701760575

Luszczynska, A., Gutiérrez-Doña, B., & Schwarzer, R. (2005). General self-efficacy in various domains of human functioning: Evidence from five countries. *International Journal of Psychology*, *40*(2), 80–89. doi:10.1080/00207590444000041

Luszczynska, A., Scholz, U., & Schwarzer, R. (2005). The general self-efficacy scale: Multicultural validation studies. *The Journal of Psychology: Interdisciplinary and Applied*, *139*(5), 439–457. doi:10.3200/JRLP.139.5.439-457

Luthans, F., Avolio, B. J., Avey, J. B., & Norman, S. M. (2007). Positive psychological capital: Measurement and relationship with performance and satisfaction. *Personnel Psychology*, *60*(3), 541–572. doi:10.1111/j.1744-6570.2007.00083.x

Luthans, F., Avolio, B. J., Walumbwa, F. O., & Li, W. (2005). The psychological capital of Chinese workers: Exploring the relationship with performance. *Management and Organization Review*, *1*(2), 249–271. doi:10.1111/j.1740-8784.2005.00011.x

Madan, S., & Pakenham, K. (2014). The stress-buffering effects of hope on adjustment to multiple sclerosis. *International Journal of Behavioral Medicine*, *21*(6), 877–890. doi:10.1007/s12529-013-9384-0

Magaletta, P. R., & Oliver, J. M. (1999). The hope construct, will, and ways: Their relations with self-efficacy, optimism, and general well-being. *Journal of Clinical Psychology*, *55*(5), 539–551. doi:10.1002/(SICI)1097-4679(199905)55:5<539:AID-JCLP2>3.0.CO;2-G

May, E. M., Hunter, B. A., Ferrari, J., Noel, N., & Jason, L. A. (2015). Hope and abstinence self-efficacy: Positive predictors of negative affect in substance abuse recovery. *Community Mental Health Journal*, *51*(6), 695–700. doi:10.1007/s10597-015-9888-y

O'Keefe, V. M., & Wingate, L. R. (2013). The role of hope and optimism in suicide risk for American Indians/Alaska Natives. *Suicide and Life-Threatening Behavior*, *43*(6), 621–633. doi:10.1111/sltb.12044

O'Sullivan, G. (2011). The relationship between hope, stress, self-efficacy, and life satisfaction among undergraduates. *Social Indicators Research*, *101*(1), 155–172. doi:10.1007/s11205-010-9662-z

Peleg, G., Barak, O., Harel, Y., Rochberg, J., & Hoofien, D. (2009). Hope, dispositional optimism and severity of depression following traumatic brain injury. *Brain Injury*, *23*(10), 800–808. doi:10.1080/02699050903196696

Peterson, C., & Seligman, M. E. P. (2004). *Character strengths and virtues: A handbook and classification*. New York: Oxford University Press.

Peterson, S. J., Luthans, F., Avolio, B. J., Walumbwa, F. O., & Zhang, Z. (2011). Psychological capital and employee performance: A latent growth modeling approach. *Personnel Psychology*, *64*(2), 427–450. doi:10.1111/j.1744-6570.2011.01215.x

Phan, H. P. (2013). Examination of self-efficacy and hope: A developmental approach using latent growth modeling. *The Journal of Educational Research*, *106*(2), 93–104. doi:10.1080/00220671.2012.667008

Rand, K. L. (2009). Hope and optimism: Latent structures and influences on grade expectancy and academic performance. *Journal of Personality*, *77*(1), 231–260.

Rand, K. L., Martin, A. D., & Shea, A. M. (2011). Hope, but not optimism, predicts academic performance of law students beyond previous academic achievement. *Journal of Research in Personality*, *45*(6), 683–686. doi:10.1016/j.jrp.2011.08.004

Raub, S., & Liao, H. (2012). Doing the right thing without being told: Joint effects of initiative climate and general self-efficacy on employee proactive customer service performance. *Journal of Applied Psychology*, *97*(3), 651–667. doi:10.1037/a0026736

Rego, A., Sousa, F., Marques, C., & Cunha, M. P. E. (2012). Retail employees' self-efficacy and hope predicting their positive affect and creativity. *European Journal of Work and Organizational Psychology*, *21*(6), 923–945. doi:10.1080/1359432X.2011.610891

Roesch, S. C., Duangado, K. M., Vaughn, A. A., Aldridge, A. A., & Villodas, F. (2010). Dispositional hope and the propensity to cope: A daily diary assessment of minority adolescents. *Cultural Diversity and Ethnic Minority Psychology*, *16*(2), 191–198. doi:10.1037/a0016114

Rosenstreich, E., Feldman, D. B., Davidson, O. B., Maza, E., & Margalit, M. (2015). Hope, optimism and loneliness among first-year college students with learning disabilities: A brief longitudinal study. *European Journal of Special Needs Education*, *30*(3), 338–350. doi:10.1080/08856257.2015.1023001

Ryan, R. M., & Deci, E. L. (2001). On happiness and human potentials: A review of research on hedonic and eudaimonic well-being. In S. Fiske (Ed.), *Annual review of psychology* (Vol 52, pp. 141–166). Palo Alto, CA: Annual Reviews, Inc.

Scheier, M. F., & Carver, C. S. (1985). Optimism, coping, and health: Assessment and implications of generalized outcome expectancies. *Health Psychology*, *4*(3), 219–247. doi:10.1037/0278-6133.4.3.219

Scheier, M. F., Carver, C. S., & Bridges, M. W. (1994). Distinguishing optimism from neuroticism (and trait anxiety, self-mastery, and self-esteem): A reevaluation of the Life Orientation Test. *Journal of Personality and Social Psychology*, *67*(6), 1063–1078. doi:10.1037/0022-3514.67.6.1063

Scheier, M. F., Matthews, K. A., Owens, J. F., Magovern, G. J., Lefebvre, R. C., Abbott, R. A., & Carver, C. S. (1989). Dispositional optimism and recovery from coronary artery bypass surgery: The beneficial effects on physical and psychological well-being. *Journal of Personality and Social Psychology*, *57*(6), 1024–1040. doi:10.1037/0022-3514.57.6.1024

Scheier, M. F., Weintraub, J. K., & Carver, C. S. (1986). Coping with stress: Divergent strategies of optimists and pessimists.

Journal of Personality and Social Psychology, 51(6), 1257–1264. doi:10.1037/0022-3514.51.6.1257

Schwarzer, R., Boehmer, S., Luszczynska, A., Mohamed, N. E., & Knoll, N. (2005). Dispositional self-efficacy as a personal resource factor in coping after surgery. *Personality and Individual Differences, 39*(4), 807–818. doi:10.1016/j.paid.2004.12.016

Sezgin, F., & Erdogan, O. (2015). Academic optimism, hope and zest for work as predictors of teacher self-efficacy and perceived success. *Kuram ve Uygulamada Eğitim Bilimleri, 15*(1), 7–19. doi:10.12738/estp.2015.1.2338

Sherer, M., Maddux, J. E., Mercandante, B., Prentice-dunn, S., Jacobs, B., & Rogers, R. W. (1982). The Self-Efficacy Scale: Construction and validation. *Psychological Reports, 51*(2), 663–671. doi:10.2466/pr0.1982.51.2.663

Shorey, H. S., Little, T. D., Rand, K. L., Snyder, C. R., Monsson, Y., & Gallagher, M. W. (2009). *Validation of the Revised Snyder Hope Scale (HS-R2): The will, the ways, and now the goals for positive future outcomes.*

Shorey, H. S., Snyder, C. R., Yang, X., & Lewin, M. R. (2003). The role of hope as a mediator in recollected parenting, adult attachment, and mental health. *Journal of Social and Clinical Psychology, 22*(6), 685–715. doi:10.1521/jscp.22.6.685.22938

Snyder, C. R. (1994). *The psychology of hope: You can get there from here.* New York: Free Press.

Snyder, C. R. (2000). *Handbook of hope: Theory, measures, and applications.* San Diego, CA: Academic Press.

Snyder, C. R. (2002). Hope theory: Rainbows in the mind. *Psychological Inquiry, 13*(4), 249–275.

Snyder, C. R., Berg, C., Woodward, J. T., Gum, A., Rand, K. L., Wrobleski, K. K., . . . Hackman, A. (2005). Hope against the cold: Individual differences in trait hope and acute pain tolerance on the cold pressor task. *Journal of Personality, 73*(2), 287–312.

Snyder, C. R., Harris, C., Anderson, J. R., Holleran, S. A., Irving, L. M., Sigmon, S. T., . . . Harney, P. (1991). The will and the ways: Development and validation of an individual-differences measure of hope. *Journal of Personality and Social Psychology, 60*(4), 570–585.

Snyder, C. R., Shorey, H. S., Cheavens, J., Pulvers, K. M., Adams, V. H. III, & Wiklund, C. (2002). Hope and academic success in college. *Journal of Educational Psychology, 94*(4), 820–826.

Suls, J., & Fletcher, B. (1985). The relative efficacy of avoidant and nonavoidant coping strategies: A meta-analysis. *Health Psychology, 4*(3), 249–288. doi:10.1037/0278-6133.4.3.249

Tennen, H., Affleck, G., & Tennen, R. (2002). Clipped feathers: The theory and measurement of hope. *Psychological Inquiry, 13*(4), 311–317.

Thimm, J. C., Holte, A., Brennen, T., & Wang, C. E. A. (2013). Hope and expectancies for future events in depression. *Frontiers in Psychology, 4.* doi:10.3389/fpsyg.2013.00470

Tucker, R. P., Wingate, L. R., O'Keefe, V. M., Mills, A. C., Rasmussen, K., Davidson, C. L., & Grant, D. M. (2013). Rumination and suicidal ideation: The moderating roles of hope and optimism. *Personality and Individual Differences, 55*(5), 606–611. doi:10.1016/j.paid.2013.05.013

Wong, S. S., & Lim, T. (2009). Hope versus optimism in Singaporean adolescents: Contributions to depression and life satisfaction. *Personality and Individual Differences, 46*(5-6), 648–652. doi:10.1016/j.paid.2009.01.009

Wright, M. A., Wren, A. A., Somers, T. J., Goetz, M. C., Fras, A. M., Huh, B. K., . . . Keefe, F. J. (2011). Pain acceptance, hope, and optimism: Relationships to pain and adjustment in patients with chronic musculoskeletal pain. *The Journal of Pain, 12*(11), 1155–1162.

Wrobleski, K. K., & Snyder, C. R. (2005). Hopeful thinking in older adults: Back to the future. *Experimental Aging Research, 31*(2), 217–233. doi:10.1080/03610730590915452

Yang, Y.-L., Liu, L., Wang, X.-X., Wang, Y., & Wang, L. (2014). Prevalence and associated positive psychological variables of depression and anxiety among Chinese cervical cancer patients: A cross-sectional study. *PLoS One, 9*(4).

Zeidner, M., & Hammer, A. L. (1992). Coping with missile attack: Resources, strategies, and outcomes. *Journal of Personality, 60*(4), 709–746. doi:10.1111/j.1467-6494.1992.tb00271.x

Self-Determination and Hope

Michael L. Wehmeyer *and* Karrie A. Shogren

Abstract

This chapter introduces the self-determination construct and examines relationships between self-determination and hope, with an emphasis on issues pertaining to the development of self-determination. Self-determination is a construct situated in theories of human agentic behavior and autonomous motivation. People who are self-determined self-regulate action to satisfy basic psychological needs and to act as causal agents in their lives. The self-determination and hope constructs share common theoretical foundations in goal-oriented action, and understanding research in self-determination will assist in understanding pathways thinking, particularly in hope theory. The chapter ends with a summary and a list of questions for readers to consider.

Key Words: self-determination, autonomous motivation, casual agent, agentic behavior, goal-oriented action, pathways thinking

This chapter introduces the self-determination construct and examines relationships between self-determination and hope, with an emphasis on issues pertaining to the development of self-determination. *Self-determination* is a "general psychological construct within the organizing structure of theories of human agentic behavior" (Wehmeyer, Little, & Sergaent, 2009, p. 357). According to Little, Hawley, Henrich, and Marsland (2002), an agentic person is the "origin of his or her actions, has high aspirations, perseveres in the face of obstacles, sees more and varied options for action, learns from failures, and overall, [and] has a greater sense of wellbeing" (p. 390). Human agentic theories "share the meta-theoretical view that organismic aspirations drive human behaviors" (Little, Snyder, & Wehmeyer, 2006, p. 61). Organismic theories view people as active contributors to their behavior; as agents in their lives. Agentic action is self-regulated and goal directed; it is motivated by both biological and psychological needs and directed toward self-governance of behavior (Wehmeyer et al., 2009).

Origins and Uses of the Self-Determination Construct
Self-Determination in Philosophy

The origins of the self-determination construct are found in the philosophical doctrines of determinism and free will. Determinism, and specifically causal determinism, is the philosophical doctrine positing that every event is preceded by antecedent events and conditions together with the laws of nature. Free will is conceptualized as the human capacity to act (or not) as we choose or prefer, without external compulsion or restraint. This question of free will verses determinism is generally identified by philosophers to be one of the most enduring philosophical problems of all time, bound inextricably with religious theologies about the free will of man versus the control and authority (determinism) of God.

In his important work, *An Essay Concerning Human Understanding*, published in 1690, John Locke provided a synopsis of the "free will problem." Trying to illustrate the importance of connections in human thought to understanding, Locke wrote:

this proposition "men can determine themselves" is drawn in or inferred from this, "that they shall be punished in the other world." For here the mind, seeing the connexion there is between the idea of men's punishment in the other world and the idea of God punishing; between God punishing and the justice of the punishment; between justice of punishment and guilt; between guilt and a power to do otherwise; between a power to do otherwise and freedom; and between freedom and self-determination, sees the connexion between men and self-determination. (Locke, 1690)

All human ideas and knowledge, according to Locke, emerge from experience (sensation) and from reflection on that experience or sensation. Further, according to Locke, the human mind has the active power of beginning or ceasing its own operations as activated by a preference. The exercise of that power is volition or will.

With the turn of the 20th century and the emergence of psychology as a discipline distinct from philosophy, as discussed subsequently, the philosophical discussion of determinism and self-determination as it pertains to human action and behavior became overshadowed by discoveries and theories in biology, psychology, and anthropology. Nevertheless, even as the meaning or sense of the construct changed as it was used in other disciplines, it is important to remember that the construct's roots lie in the free will problem that was the basis of philosophic discussions for centuries; self-determination still refers fundamentally to and its meanings derive directly from the philosophical debates around determinism.

Self-Determination in Social Work and Social Welfare

Since the early 20th century, a guiding principle of social work has been the client right to self-determination (Biestek, & Gehrig, 1978). Owing much to the sense of the term as a national or political right, which also emerged in the early 20th century and which is discussed subsequently, the emphasis in social work on client self-determination became a principle that guided the way in which services should be provided by social workers. More than just a right of people in general, however, the use of the construct in social work embodies a respect and value for the rights of individuals to make choices and decisions and to, in essence, live autonomous lives.

Self-Determination in Politics and Governance

As noted earlier, an alternate meaning of self-determination is as a national or political construct referring to the rights of peoples to self-governance. Heater (1994) attributed much of the notoriety for self-determination and its relative importance in 20th century politics to Woodrow Wilson's "Fourteen Points" speech to a joint session of Congress on January 8, 1918, during which he outlined 14 points for a postwar settlement that would lead to world peace, six of which referred specifically to ensuring that nations who were defeated in the war would be assured the opportunity for national self-determination. Heater noted that the 20th-century preference for national self-determination emerged from twin 18th-century notions that the people, not monarchs, are sovereign and that the people are to be thought of as "the nation." Through the 19th century, the belief that people should have the right and opportunity to determine their own government spread and gained wide acceptance and by the 20th century became a principal of international justice.

Self-Determination in Psychology

The philosophical discussions of freedom versus determinism were picked up by theorists as the discipline of personality psychology emerged in the early 20th century. Andras Angyal, writing in 1951, proposed that:

> The over-all pattern of personality function can be described from two different vantage points. Viewed from one of these vantage points, the human being seems to be striving basically to assert and to expand his self-determination. He is an autonomous being, a self-governing entity that asserts itself actively instead of reacting passively like a physical body to the impacts of the surrounding world. This fundamental tendency expresses itself in a striving of the person to consolidate and increase his self-government, in other words to exercise his freedom and to organize of self. This tendency—which I have termed "the trend toward increased autonomy"— expresses itself in spontaneity, self-assertiveness, striving for freedom and for mastery. In an objective fashion this tendency can be described as follows: the human being is an autonomous unity that, acting upon the surrounding world, molds and modifies it. His life is a resultant of self-determination on the one hand and the impacts of the surrounding world, the situation, on the other. (pp. 131–132)

Angyal posed this vantage point, autonomous-determinism, with heteronomous-determinism—self-caused action versus other-caused action. Self-determination, then, as a psychological construct, refers to self- (vs. other-) caused action—to people acting volitionally, based on their own will. Volition is the capability of conscious choice, decision, and intention.

Self-Determination in Education

As the 20th century went on, the political or national sense of construct, pertaining to the "right of a peoples of a nation to self-governance," was adapted by other groups of people who were not identified as being the citizens of a country but instead were self-identified by some factor (racial identity, disability status) that, in turn, was seen to result in the loss of a corporate right to self-governance. For example, one of the days of the African American holiday Kwanzaa is Kujichagulia, a Swahili word meaning self-determination, referring to the rights of African Americans to define and speak for themselves, rather than having others do so.

In turn, this sense of the corporate or political sense of the term was used by people with disabilities to demand their corporate and individual right to control their lives. This sense of the term is captured best by Robert Williams (1989), a national leader in the disability rights effort and a man with a disability, who stated:

> But, without being afforded the right and opportunity to make choices in our lives, we will never obtain full, first class American citizenship. So we do not have to be told what self-determination means. We already know that it is just another word for freedom. We already know that self-determination is just another word for describing a life filled with rising expectations, dignity, responsibility, and opportunity. That it is just another word for having the chance to live the American Dream. (p. 16)

The disability adoption of the term embodied both the political and self-governance "rights-based" sense, as well as the psychological implications of volitional action. In time, the application of the self-determination construct within the disability context became a leading issue in the application of strengths-based approaches and positive psychological constructs to disability (Wehmeyer, 2013).

Psychological Theories of Self-Determination
Self-Determination Theory

The most visible application of the self-determination construct has been self-determination theory (SDT), a prominent approach to studying human motivation (Deci & Ryan, 1985; Deci & Ryan, 2002; Ryan & Deci, 2000). In fact, SDT is a macro-theory based on the organismic paradigm that "details the origins and outcomes of human agentic action (Adams, Little, & Ryan, 2017). Self-determination theory posits three basic psychological needs—competence, autonomy, and relatedness—that must be met to support healthy psychological development (Deci & Ryan, 2012). The *need for competence* reflects humans' desire to effectively master their environment and experience a sense of competence in it. According to SDT, humans experience satisfaction of the need for competence not necessarily as an absolute level of achievement but instead as a "phenomenological" experience in which a person experiences increasing mastery and effectance (Deci, Ryan, & Guay, 2013, p. 112). The *need for autonomy* is satisfied when people experience choice and volition in their action and perceive themselves to be the origin of their actions. Autonomous actions are those that are self-endorsed and congruent with one's values and interest (Vansteenkiste, Niemiec, & Soenens, 2010). The *need for relatedness* is associated with social belonging. Relatedness is a satisfaction derived from a sense of connectedness with others—to care and be cared for by others (Deci et al., 2013; Ryan & Deci, 2000).

According to SDT, social environment supports are critical to address these three basic psychological needs. In social environments that support the satisfaction of these needs, optimal growth and positive development are expected, whereas in social environments that thwart satisfaction of any of these fundamental these needs, greater passivity, alienation, and ill-being are expected.

Deci and Ryan (2012) incorporated these basic psychological needs into six mini-theories, each addressing different problems of motivation theory. The six mini-theories (cognitive evaluative theory, causality orientations theory, organismic integration theory, basic psychological needs theory, goal content theory, and relationships motivation theory) each explain a set of observed motivation phenomena in many domains (Adams et al., 2017).

Cognitive evaluation theory explains the types of external events that enhance or diminish intrinsic motivation, identifies autonomy supportive social contexts versus controlling social contexts, and explains the interactions of external events and social contexts and their effects on intrinsic motivation (Deci & Ryan, 2012). *Causality orientations theory* proposes three different personality orientations based on the source of initiation and regulation of behavior: autonomous, controlled, and impersonal (Deci & Ryan, 1985). The autonomous orientation is associated with orienting toward internal and external cues in a way that supports one's autonomy and the informational significance of cues. The controlled orientation is associated with perceiving internal and external cues as controlling and demanding. Finally, the impersonal orientation is associated with perceiving cues as indicators of incompetence and is linked with amotivation.

Organismic integration theory explains behavior that is externally motivated but also either controlled or autonomous (Deci & Ryan, 1985). Motivation, this theory explains, exists on a continuum and is dependent on an individual's traits and the environmental and social context. Deci and Ryan proposed five types of motivation on a continuum from extrinsic to intrinsic: external regulation, introjected regulation, identified regulation, integrated regulation, and intrinsic motivation. *Basic psychological needs theory* was formulated based on findings that environments and contexts that support psychological needs satisfaction were associated with greater feelings of well-being, psychological health, and greater positive affect in both work- and nonwork-related environments (Ryan, Bernstein, & Brown, 2010).

Goal content theory posits that extrinsic goals such as financial wealth, image, and fame are less likely to satisfy the three basic psychological needs compared to intrinsic goals such as personal growth, community and emotional closeness (Ryan, Kasser, Sheldon & Deci, 1996). Empirical evidence for goal content theory indicates that pursuing extrinsic goals leads to less well-being and poorer performance whereas pursuing intrinsic goals leads to greater well-being, presumably due to increased satisfaction of the basic psychological needs (Deci & Ryan, 2012).

Finally, Deci and Ryan (2014) articulated *relationships motivation theory* to describe the need supportive elements most likely to lead to sustained and satisfying relationships. Beyond the idea that intimacy is about warmth, involvement., and security, this theory argues that true relationship satisfaction depends on respect and caring for the *self* of the other. Relationships motivation theory helps explain variations in security of attachment as a function of autonomy support (e.g., La Guardia, Ryan, Couchman, & Deci, 2000), and why parental styles such as contingent regard hamper both motivation and emotional wellness (e.g., Roth, Assor, Niemiec, Ryan & Deci, 2009).

Self-determination theory has been applied to understanding motivation in social issues such as health behavior and maintenance, education and school adjustment, psychotherapy, and sport and physical activity (Adams et al., 2017) and provides a multidimensional view of the effects of goal purposes and contents on individuals' behavior, well-being, performance, and social engagement. Thus the foundational concept of intrinsic versus extrinsic goal engagement provides a detailed framework for understanding human agency.

Causal Agency Theory

Causal agency theory explains how people become self-determined—that is, how they define the actions and beliefs necessary to engage in self-caused, autonomous action (e.g., causal action) in response to basic psychological needs and autonomous motivation as well as contextual and environmental challenges. Within the context of causal agency theory, self-determination is defined as a

> dispositional characteristic manifested as acting as the causal agent in one's life. Self-determined people (i.e., causal agents) act in service to freely chosen goals. Self-determined actions function to enable a person to be the causal agent is his or her life. (Shogren et al., 2015, p. 258)

Within causal agency theory, self-determination is conceptualized as a *dispositional characteristic*, referring to an enduring tendency used to characterize and describe differences between people. While the assumption is that self-determined people have a tendency to act or think in a particular way, there is also a presumption of contextual variance (i.e., people behave in more or less self-determined ways as a function of the context or situation). *Causal agency*, another key term in causal agency theory, refers to the fact that it is the individual who makes or causes things to happen in his or her life. Causal agency implies that the person acts with an eye toward causing an effect to accomplish a specific end or to cause or create change. Self-determined actions enable a person to act as a causal agent.

Causal agency theory is grounded in human agentic theories, which assume that action is self-caused. Human agentic theories differentiate between self-determination as self-caused action and self-determination as controlling one's behavior. Self-determined action refers to the degree to which action is self-caused, volitional, and agentic, driven by beliefs about the relationships between actions (or means) and ends. Volitional and agentic action and action-control beliefs are central to causal agency theory and reflect the essential characteristics of self-determined action under causal agency theory.

The theory posits three essential characteristics—volitional, agentic, and action-control beliefs—that contribute to causal agency and the development of self-determination. These essential characteristics refer not to specific actions performed or the beliefs that drive action but to the function the action serves for the individual—that is, whether the action enabled the person to act as a causal agent and enhances the development of self-determination.

VOLITIONAL ACTION

Self-determined people act volitionally. Volitional action is based on conscious choices that reflect one's preferences. Conscious choices are intentionally conceived, deliberate acts that occur without direct external influence. As such, volitional actions are self-initiated and function to enable a person to act autonomously (i.e., engage in self-governed action). Volitional actions involve the initiation and activation of causal capabilities—the capacity to cause something to happen—in one's life (Shogren & Wehmeyer, in press).

AGENTIC ACTION

Agentic actions are the means by which something is done or achieved. Agentic actions are self-directed and goal focused. When acting agentically, self-determined people identify pathways that lead to a specific ends or cause or create change (which, as discussed subsequently, provides the link between self-determination and hope). The identification of pathways, or pathways thinking, is a proactive, purposive process. When acting agentically, action is self-regulated and self-directed and enables progress toward freely chosen goals. Volitional actions involve the initiation and activation of agentic capabilities—the capacity to sustain action toward a goal.

ACTION-CONTROL BELIEFS

In applying volitional and agentic actions, self-determined people develop a sense of personal empowerment. They believe they have what it takes to achieve freely chosen goals. They perceive a link between their action and the outcomes they experience; they develop adaptive action-control beliefs. To account for these beliefs and actions, causal agency theory incorporates basic tenets of action-control theory (Little et al., 2002), which posits three types of action-control beliefs: beliefs about the link between the self and the goal (control expectancy beliefs; "When I want to do ____, I can"); beliefs about the link between the self and the means for achieving the goal (capacity beliefs; "I have the capabilities to do _____"); and beliefs about the utility or usefulness of a given means for attaining a goal (causality beliefs; "I believe my effort will lead to goal achievement" vs. "I believe other factors—luck, access to teachers, or social capital—will lead to goal achievement"). As adaptive action-control beliefs emerge, people are better able to act with self-awareness and self-knowledge in a goal-directed manner.

The Development of Self-Determination

Drawing from research with SDT and causal agency theory, Wehmeyer, Shogren, Little, and Lopez (in press) proposed a model of the development of self-determination, depicted in Figure 5.1.

At the start of this system are basic psychological needs—organismic necessities for psychological growth, integrity, and wellness—for autonomy, competence, and relatedness proposed by SDT. Satisfaction of these basic needs facilitates autonomous motivation, defined as intrinsic motivation and well-internalized extrinsic motivation (Deci & Ryan, 2012, p. 88). Consistent with assumptions of organismic theories, the interplay between the context and the individual's psychological needs satisfaction is complex and reciprocal. When a motive or motives are salient, people are in a position to select goals on the basis of their expectations about the satisfaction of these motives (Deci & Ryan, 1985, p. 235). These psychological needs serve as the "energizer of behavior" (Deci & Ryan, 2012, p. 101) and initiate a *causal action sequence* that, through interaction with environmental supports and opportunities, enables the development of a "synergistic set of action-control beliefs and behaviors that provide the self-regulatory foundation that is called upon to negotiate the various tasks and challenges of the life course" (Little et al, 2002,

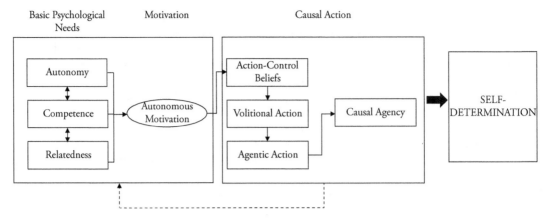

Fig. 5.1. The development of self-determination (Shogren & Wehmeyer, 2014).

p. 396). As organisms take action to meet these three basic psychological needs, this energizes the development of autonomous motivation, consisting of intrinsic motivation (doing an activity because it is enjoyable) and/or internalized extrinsic motivation (doing an activity because it leads to a valued consequence separate from the activity itself; Deci & Ryan, 2012, p. 88). The interaction between the organism's efforts to meet basic psychological needs and the resultant autonomous motivation stimulates causal action.

As discussed previously, self-determined action is self-caused action. Organisms act volitionally and self-initiate action based on conscious choices that reflect one's preferences in pursuit of goals that enhance personal well-being. The interaction between causal action and the context or environment is complex but reflects the organism's response to opportunities or threats in the environment. Opportunity refers to situations or circumstances that provoke the organism to engage in causal action to achieve a planned, desired outcome that is available because of the situation or circumstance. Opportunity implies that the situation or circumstance provides a chance for the person to create change or make something happen based on his or her individual causal capability (knowledge and abilities leading to volitional action, discussed subsequently). Opportunities can be "found" (unanticipated, happened upon through no effort of one's own) or "created" (the person acts to create a favorable circumstance).

The second challenge condition, threat, involves situations or circumstances that threaten the organism's self-determination and provokes the organism to exercise causal action to maintain a preferred outcome or to create change that is consistent with

its own values, preferences, or interests and not the values, preferences or interests of others. The interplay between autonomous motivation and these challenge conditions is, as mentioned previously, complex. In the case of created opportunities, it is the organism's autonomous motivation that directly motivates the effort to create the opportunity. In the case of found opportunities or threats, these contextual challenges emerge unsolicited by the organism, so that it is the context or the condition that triggers the autonomous motivation to take advantage of the opportunity or minimize the impact of the threat. In all cases, though, the emergence of these environmental and contextual conditions lead to the innervation of a set of *action-control beliefs* that mediate volitional and causal action.

The interaction between the organism's efforts to meet basic psychological needs and the resultant autonomous motivation and the environmental conditions of opportunity or threat stimulates causal action, beginning with "self-perceptions about the means and competencies one has to reach one's goals" (Little et al., 2002, p. 396). Action-control beliefs refer to beliefs about the link between the self and the goal (control expectancy beliefs), the links between the self and the means that are available for use to address a challenge (agency beliefs), and beliefs about which specific means are most effective for reaching one's goals (causality beliefs) (Little et al., 2002, p. 396). These beliefs interact with and mediate volitional and agentic actions (employing causal and agentic capabilities), resulting in causal agency.

These interrelated action-control beliefs contribute jointly to the initiation of volitional action but also contribute uniquely. Control expectancy beliefs are more generalized beliefs about one's ability to set and attain goals, influencing both capacity and agency beliefs as well as the initiation of volitional action. Capacity beliefs contribute more directly to the initiation of volitional action (and specific causal capabilities), while agency beliefs contribute more directly to agentic action and the agentic capabilities that energize that action.

These action-control beliefs are self-perceptions about a person's means and competencies he or she has to reach goals that are in service of meeting basic psychological needs and initiating causal action. The causal action sequence consists of volitional and agentic action, as described in causal agency theory. Volitional action is based on conscious choices that reflect one's preferences. Conscious choices are intentionally conceived, deliberate acts that occur without direct external influence. As such, volitional actions are self-initiated and function to enable a person to act autonomously (i.e., engage in self-governed action). Volitional actions involve the initiation and activation of causal capabilities—the capacity to cause something to happen—in one's life. As noted previously, agentic actions are the means by which something is done or achieved. These actions enable people to sustain action toward a goal as initiated by volitional action.

This is an iterative process. Causal action enables the individual to fulfill basic psychological needs pertaining to competence, relatedness, and autonomy, leading to autonomous motivation to address further environmental challenges, leading to repeated experiences with causal action. Repeated experiences with the causal action sequence leads to multiple experiences with causal agency and, as a result, enhanced self-determination.

Self-Determination and Hope

We consider, in this section, the relationships between hope and self-determination with a particular focus on the role of hope in causal agency theory and in the development of self-determination, as described in the previous section.

Hope and Causal Agency Theory

As articulated by Marques and Lopez (2017), as well as elsewhere through this text, hope reflects people's perceptions "regarding their capacities to: (1) clearly conceptualize goals; (2) develop the specific strategies to reach those goals (pathways thinking); and (3) initiate and sustain the motivation for using these strategies (agency thinking)." Given the previous discussion pertaining to causal agency theory, it is readily apparent that there is

considerable overlap between causal action and hope theory. Agentic action, according to causal agency theory, refers to the process of identifing pathways that lead to specific ends and engaging in self-directing and self-regulating action to navigate environmental opportunities and threats. Causal agency theory explicitly identifies the primary elements of hope theory (e.g., pathways thinking, agency thinking) in explaining both causal action and—because repeated experiences with causal action lead to perceptions of causal agency and the development of self-determination—ultimately, elements of self-determination.

It is important to differentiate from among the clearly related constructs of self-determination, hope, and such issues as goal setting and attainment. Self-determination refers, in causal agency theory, to a dispositional characteristic manifested as acting as the causal agent in one's life. People who are causal agents act in service to freely chosen goals. It is this issue of volitional action that is at the heart of self-determination, as underscored by the SDT framework emphasis on autonomous motivation. Self-determination, as a construct, emphasizes action that is autonomously motivated and volitional; goal-setting and attainment is in service to achievement of the basic psychological needs identified in SDT. Within hope theory, goal-directed action is in service to "a hierarchically organized system of beliefs regarding one's ability to successfully engage" in a goal-directed cognitive process (Marques & Lopez, 2017, p. 2713). Marques and Lopez identify four levels of abstraction in which to organize the "hierarchically organized system of beliefs": global or trait hope, domain-specific hope, goal-specific hope, and state hope. It is beyond the scope of this chapter to elaborate on these levels, but it is worth repeating that it is "[p]eoples' overall evaluation of their capacity to construct sufficient pathways and generate the agency thoughts necessary to achieve goals" (Marques & Lopez, 2017, p. 273) that constitutes hope (at a global or trait level). Thus, pathways thinking contributes to agentic action through, in essence, this organized system of beliefs regarding one's ability to successfully engage in goal-directed action, which, in turn, contributes to experience of causal action and causal agency.

Research on Hope and Self-Determination

There is only a limited research base directly examining relationships between self-determination and hope and among other, similar constructs. At the level of research on hope and basic psychological needs (autonomy, competence, relatedness) posited by SDT, Wandeler and Bundick (2011) found a positive, reciprocal longitudinal relationship between hope and satisfaction of the need for competency among over 400 young adults in work training circumstances. In essence, these researchers found that higher perceived competence predicted higher hope and higher hope predicted higher perceived competence. There were not similar relationships, however, with the other psychological needs (autonomy, relatedness). Similarly, Kenny, Walsh-Blair, Blustein, Bempachat, and Seltzer (2010) examined the contributions of work-based beliefs and autonomy supports as a predictor of adaptive achievement-related beliefs. They found that work hope, career planning, and autonomy support shared a significant amount (37%) of the variance with achievement-related beliefs and that work hope and teacher autonomy support further contributed unique variance in explaining these beliefs. In a study examining protective factors at school, Van Ryzin (2011) measured perceptions of school environments (as based on characteristics of autonomy-supportive classrooms established by SDT) and hope and found that student perceptions of the school environment predicted engagement in learning, which in turn predicted academic achievement and greater hope. Like the Wandeler and Bundick findings, hope had a reciprocal relationship with perceptions of environment.

Shogren, Lopez, Wehmeyer, Little, and Pressgrove (2006) conducted a study of the associations between hope, optimism, locus of control, self-determination, and life satisfaction in adolescents with and without cognitive disabilities. Self-determination was measured by an assessment incorporating elements of causal agency theory, so instead of measuring perceptions of psychological need, as did the previously mentioned studies, this study measured adolescent causal agency. Using structural equation modeling, Shogren et al. found that hope, optimism, locus of control, and self-determination were strongly correlated, and hope and optimism predicted life satisfaction in adolescents with and without cognitive disabilities.

Conclusion

There is much yet to be done with regard to examinations of the relationships between and unique or combined contributions of hope and self-determination. The research that does exist shows that each construct contributes uniquely to outcomes such as academic achievement or lifestyle satisfaction, but there is more research needed to parcel out those contributions. Hope and self-determination are both goal-focused constructs but examine differing aspects of goal-oriented action: self-determination focuses on understanding and explaining causal agency including volitional and agentic action; hope focuses on understanding the system of beliefs regarding one's ability to successfully engage in a goal-directed cognitive process. As described in the section on the development of self-determination, it is clear that these constructs (and their respective theoretical frameworks of hope theory and causal agency theory) work synergistically, along with motivational constructs (as elucidated by SDT) and action-control beliefs (as identified by action-control theory) to enable people to respond to threats and opportunities in their environments in ways that enable them not only to become more hopeful and self-determined but to live healthier, more satisfying, lives.

Review Questions

• What is self-determination, and how does it relate to theories of human agentic behavior?

• Self-determination theory posits three basic psychological needs. What are these, and how does the satisfaction of these needs lead to enhanced self-determination?

• The fulfillment of basic psychological needs results in autonomous motivation. What relationship exists between autonomous motivation and causal action?

• What is causal agency and how is it related to self-determination?

• Causal agency theory refers to self-determination as a dispositional characteristic. What is a dispositional characteristic, and why would self-determination be conceptualized as such?

• Self-determined action is volitional and agentic. How is this different from independent behavior or function?

• Discuss the intersection between self-determination and hope theory.

• How are hope and self-determination similar? What theoretical and practical themes do they share?

• What does the research on hope and self-determination suggest with regard to the two constructs?

• Why is it important to consider issues pertaining to self-determination in conceptualizing hope?

References

Adams, N., Little, T. D., & Ryan, R. M. (2017). Self-determination theory. In M. L. Wehmeyer, K. A. Shogren, T. D. Little, & S. J. Lopez (Eds.), *Development of self-determination across the life course* (pp. 47–67). New York: Springer.

Angyal, A. (1951). A theoretical model for personality studies. *Journal of Personality, 20*(1), 131–142. http://dx.doi.org/10.1111/j.1467-6494.1951.tb01517.x.

Biestek, F. P., & Gehrig, C. C. (1978). *Client self-determination in social work: A fifty-year history.* Chicago: Loyola University Press.

Deci, E. L., & Ryan, R. (1985). *Intrinsic motivation and self-determination in human behavior.* New York: Plenum Press. http://dx.doi.org/10.1007/978-1-4899-2271-7.

Deci, E. L., & Ryan, R. M. (2012). Motivation, personality, and development within embedded social contexts: An overview of self-determination theory. In R. M. Ryan (Ed.), *Oxford handbook of human motivation* (pp. 85–107). Oxford: Oxford University Press. http://dx.doi.org/10.1093/oxfordhb/9780195399820.013.0006

Deci, E. L., & Ryan, R. M. (2014). Autonomy and need satisfaction in close relationships: Relationships motivation theory. In N. Weinstein (Ed.), *Human motivation and interpersonal relationships: Theory, research and applications* (pp. 53–73). Dordrecht: Springer. http://dx.doi.org/10.1007/978-94-017-8542-6_3

Deci, E. L., & Ryan, R. M. (Eds.). (2002). *Handbook of self-determination research.* Rochester, NY: University of Rochester Press.

Deci, E. L., Ryan, R. M., & Guay, F. (2013). Self-determination theory and actualization of human potentials. In D. M. McInerney, H. W. Marsh, R. G. Craven, F. Guay, & D. M. McInerney (Eds.), *Theory driving research: New wave perspectives on self-processes and human development* (pp. 109–133). Charlotte, NC: Information Age Publishing.

Heater, D. (1994). *National self-determination: Woodrow Wilson and his legacy.* New York: St. Martin's Press. http://dx.doi.org/10.1007/978-1-349-23600-8

Kenny, M. E., Walsh-Blair, L. Y., Blustein, D. L., Bempechat, J., & Seltzer, J. (2010). Achievement motivation among urban adolescents: Work hope, autonomy support, and achievement-related beliefs. *Journal of Vocational Behavior, 77*(2), 205–212. http://dx.doi.org/10.1016/j.jvb.2010.02.005

La Guardia, J. G., Ryan, R. M., Couchman, C. & Deci, E. L. (2000). Within-person variations in attachment style and their relations to psychological need satisfaction. *Journal of Personality and Social Psychology, 79,* 367–384. http://dx.doi.org/10.1037/0022-3514.79.3.367

Little, T. D., Hawley, P. H., Henrich, C. C., & Marsland, K. (2002). Three views of the agentic self: A developmental synthesis. In E. L. Deci & R. M. Ryan (Eds.), *Handbook of self-determination research* (pp. 389–404). Rochester, NY: University of Rochester Press.

Little, T. D., Snyder, C. R., & Wehmeyer, M. (2006). The agentic self: On the nature and origins of personal agency across the lifespan. In D. K. Mroczek & T. D. Little (Eds.), *Handbook of personality development* (pp. 61–80). Mahwah, NJ: Lawrence Erlbaum.

Locke, J. (1690). An essay on human understanding. Retrieved from http://www.ilt.columbia.edu/projects/digitexts/locke/understanding/title.html

Marques, S.C. & Lopez, S.J. (2017). The development of hope. In M. L. Wehmeyer, K. A. Shogren, T. D. Little, & S. Lopez (Eds.), *Development of self-determination across the life course* (pp. 271–281). New York: Springer.

Roth, G., Assor, A., Niemiec, C. P., Ryan, R. M., & Deci, E. L. (2009). The emotional and academic consequences of parental conditional regard: Comparing conditional positive regard, conditional negative regard, and autonomy support as parenting practices. *Developmental Psychology, 45,* 1119–1142. http://dx.doi.org/10.1037/a0015272

Ryan, R. M., Bernstein, J. H., & Brown, K. W. (2010). Weekends, work, and well-being: Psychological need satisfactions and day of the week effects on mood, vitality, and physical symptoms. *Journal of Social and Clinical Psychology, 29,* 95–122. http://dx.doi.org/10.1521/jscp.2010.29.1.95

Ryan, R. M., & Deci, E. L. (2000). Self-determination theory and the facilitation of intrinsic motivation, social development, and well-being. *American Psychologist, 55,* 68–78. http://dx.doi.org/10.1037/0003-066X.55.1.68

Ryan, R. M., Kasser, T., Sheldon, K. M. & Deci, E. L. (1996). All goals are not created equal: An organismic perspective on the nature of goals and their regulation. In P. M. Gollwitzer, J. A. Bargh, P. M. Gollwitzer, & J. A. Bargh (Eds.), *The psychology of action* (pp. 7–26). New York: Guilford Press.

Shogren, K. A., Lopez, S. J., Wehmeyer, M. L., Little, T. D., & Pressgrove, C. L. (2006). The role of positive psychology constructs in predicting life satisfaction in adolescents with and without cognitive disabilities: An exploratory study. *Journal of Positive Psychology, 1,* 37–52. http://dx.doi.org/10.1080/17439760500373174

Shogren, K. A., & Wehmeyer, M. L. (2014). *The development of self-determination.* Lawrence, KS: Beach Center on Disability.

Shogren, K. A., & Wehmeyer, M. L. (in press). Causal agency theory. In M. L. Wehmeyer, K. A. Shogren, T. D. Little, & S. Lopez (Eds.), *Handbook on the development of self-determination.* New York: Springer.

Shogren, K. A., Wehmeyer, M. L., Palmer, S. B., Forber-Pratt, A., Little, T., & Lopez, S. (2015). Causal agency theory: Reconceptualizing a functional model of self-determination. *Education and Training in Autism and Developmental Disabilities, 50*(3), 251–263

Van Ryzin, M. J. (2011). Protective factors at school: Reciprocal effects among adolescents' perceptions of the school environment, engagement in learning, and hope. *Journal of Youth and Adolescence, 40*(12), 1568–1580. http://dx.doi.org/10.1007/s10964-011-9637-7

Vansteenkiste, M., Niemiec, C., & Soenens, B. (2010). The development of the five mini-theories of self-determination theory: An historical overview, emerging trends, and future directions. In T. Urdan & S. Karabenick (Eds.), *Advances in motivation and achievement: Vol. 16, The decade ahead* (pp. 105–165). London: Emerald Publishing.

Wandeler, C.A., & Bundick, M.J. (2011). Hope and self-determination of young adults in the workplace. *The Journal of Positive Psychology, 6*(5), 341–354. http://dx.doi.org/10.1080/17439760.2011.584547

Wehmeyer, M. L. (2013). *Handbook of positive psychology and disability*. Oxford: Oxford University Press. http://dx.doi.org/10.1093/oxfordhb/9780195398786.001.0001

Wehmeyer, M. L., Little, T., & Sergeant, J. (2009). Self-Determination. In S. Lopez & R. Snyder (Eds.), Handbook of positive psychology (2nd Ed., pp. 357–366). Oxford: Oxford University Press.

Williams, R. R. (1989). Creating a new world of opportunity: Expanding choice and self-determination in lives of Americans with severe disability by 1992 and beyond. In R. Perske (Ed.), *Proceedings from the National Conference on Self-Determination* (pp. 16–17). Minneapolis: Institute on Community Integration.

How Hope Influences Goal-Directed Behavior

Gabriele Oettingen *and* Malin Patricia Chromik

Abstract

This chapter explores how hope affects goal-directed behavior. In contrast to expectancy-based hope theories, hope is defined as positive fantasies about the future despite having low expectations of reaching the desired future. Depending on whether people indulge in these positive fantasies or mentally contrast them with the present reality, and depending on the situational contexts, such positive fantasies can serve different functions. In situations in which action alternatives are possible, positive fantasies complemented with obstacles of the present reality allow people to selectively pursue desired futures. People invest their limited resources in feasible futures. However, in situations in which action alternatives are not possible and people can neither reach their desired future nor disengage from it, indulging in positive fantasies without contrasting them with the reality can help people to endure the difficult situations. The chapter also considers affective aspects of hope and discusses directions for future research.

Key Words: hope, positive fantasies, expectations, mental contrasting, goal-directed behavior

I have positive fantasies about my parents being around for my children. I have always wanted my parents to be around when I have kids; I want them to come over for dinner, I want them to babysit and spoil my children. Most importantly, I want my children to not only know about, but to get to know my parents. I want to keep positively fantasizing about my parents being around for my children, because the reality is, I don't actually think they will be around for as long as I want them to be. ... I don't mind fantasizing about it even if it means no action will ever take place.

As this excerpt from a student's essay shows, positive fantasies may portray an idealized future and allow people to enjoy the wished for future in the present reality (Oettingen & Mayer, 2002). Importantly, positive fantasies are not constrained by the perceived likelihood that the event will actually occur (Klinger, 1990; Singer, 1966). Although the student believes that there is a low likelihood

that her future children will get to know her parents, she vividly imagines various aspects of the desired future. She does not expect the desired future to occur, but she remains hopeful and enjoys dreaming about it. We define hope as positive fantasies about the future that occur despite having low expectations of fulfilling the desired future event (Oettingen, 1997b).

This chapter investigates how hope influences goal-directed behavior. The chapter has five parts. We first provide an overview of the existing approaches in psychological research on hope and describe different expectancy-based hope theories. As our definition of hope differs from expectancy-based theories, the second section differentiates between the two forms of thinking positively about the future: beliefs about the future (expectations) versus free images about the future (fantasies). We describe hope in terms of positive fantasies and discuss its mechanisms and origins. The third section will explain fantasy realization theory, which specifies how positive fantasies can be used to ful-fill desired future events. The next section then discusses how context can affect hope. We explain under which circumstances positive future fan-tasies serve different functions and why such fan-tasies can be of particular importance for creating hope in people with pessimistic expectations about their future. The following section moves beyond cognitive hope theories related to expectancies and describes the affective aspects of hope. We end by discussing the theoretical and practical implications of the different approaches to the research on hope and suggesting a series of studies that should further elucidate the significance of hope in our everyday lives and long-term development.

Hope: Overview
Conceptualization

One of the most significant works on hope stems from the German philosopher Ernst Bloch. In *The Principle of Hope* (Bloch, 1954, 1955, 1959), he describes "[h]ow richly people have always dreamed about this, dreamed of the better life that might be possible" (Bloch, 1996, p. 3). For Bloch, hope is the proactive part of these daydreams that leads people to actively strive for a better future (Schnoor, 1988). We define hope as daydreams or positive fantasies about the future despite hav-ing low expectations of fulfilling the desired future event (Oettingen, 1997b). In contrast to Bloch, we argue that, rather than leading to an active action, hope leads people to *hang in*—to passively endure despite the fact that the perceived likelihood of the desired future is low.

In psychological research hope is primarily con-ceptualized in terms of positive expectations for the future (e.g., Erikson, 1964; Gottschalk, 1974; Snyder, 2000; Stotland, 1969). According to these expectancy-based hope theories, hope is an overall perception that goals are attainable (Snyder, Irving, & Anderson, 1991). This conceptualization leads to the question of whether hope versus expectancy-based constructs such as self-efficacy and optimism are distinct constructs (e.g., Aspinwall & Leaf, 2002; Bryant & Cvengros, 2004; Gallagher & Lopez, 2009; Magaletta & Oliver, 1999). We argue that expectations play an important role for hope, but, rather than equate hope with expectancy-based constructs, hope should emerge when people per-ceive the probability of attaining a goal as low. Before outlining our concept of hope in detail, we provide a short overview of expectancy-based hope theories.

Expectancy-Based Hope Theories
THEORIES OF HOPE

One of the earliest expectancy-based definitions of hope comes from Erikson (1964) who described hope as "the enduring belief in the attainability of fervent wishes" (p. 118). For Erikson, hope is a crucial aspect of healthy human development. Shortly thereafter, Stotland (1969) conceptualized hope as a positive expectation of achieving a goal. According to Stotland's hope theory, hope emerges when people perceive the probability of attaining a goal as greater than zero. Gottschalk (1974) also linked hope to positive expectations and defined hope as optimism about the likelihood that favor-able outcomes will occur. Taking the cognitive as well as the affective aspects of hope into account, Staats (1989) proposed that the cognitive aspect of hope is based on the interaction between expecta-tions and wishes.

Currently, the most accepted theory of hope in psychological research is Snyder's (2000) hope theory. Drawing on Stotland's (1969) ideas, Snyder argues that hope (i.e., positive expectations of achiev-ing a goal) can be classified into agency-related and pathways-related hope thoughts. According to the theory, agency-related hope thoughts refer to the individual's determination that chosen goals can be achieved, whereas pathways-related hope thoughts refer to the individual's belief that successful plans can be generated to achieve the goals. The combi-nation of agency-related and pathways-related hope thoughts leads to the perception of a relatively high likelihood that the goal can be attained (Snyder et al., 1991).

THEORIES OF HOPELESSNESS

As we turn from hope to hopelessness, the litera-ture on depression becomes relevant. In their hope-lessness theory of depression, Abramson, Metalsky, and Alloy (1989) have postulated that hopeless-ness can cause depressive symptoms. Specifically, hopelessness is seen as a proximal sufficient cause of a subtype of depression referred to as hopeless-ness depression. Hopelessness is characterized by the expectation that negative outcomes will occur and that nothing can be done to prevent or change these future outcomes. Following up on Stotland's (1969) hope theory, Beck, Weissman, Lester, and Trexler (1974) designed a hopelessness scale in a similar vein. They defined hopelessness as negative expectancies regarding oneself and the future and designed a 20-item scale to assess these negative expectancies.

The aforementioned definitions of hope and hopelessness are in line with Seligman's (1991) and Scheier and Carver's (1992) concepts of optimism as beliefs or expectations about the future that are grounded on past experience of success. Peterson and Seligman (1984) operationalized these optimistic expectations as using stable and global attributions to a greater extent for explaining positive events than for explaining negative events. Scheier and Carver (1985) measured dispositional optimism by asking people directly about their expectations regarding good outcomes in their future life. Thus it is not surprising that optimists are often associated with a hopeful view of the future (e.g., Affleck & Tennen, 1996).

In sum, in psychological research, hope is primarily operationalized in terms of positive expectations. In line with these theories, expectations are defined as judgments about the likelihood of attaining a desired future (e.g., Ajzen, 1991; Atkinson, 1957; Bandura, 1977, 1997; Bandura & Locke, 2003; Mischel, 1973; Roese & Sherman, 2007; Taylor, Kemeny, Reed, Bower, & Gruenewald, 2000). Based on past experiences, expectations specify the probability of whether an event or behavior will occur.

Our definition of hope differs from this conceptualization. We argue that hope arises when people positively fantasize about the future despite the fact that they have low expectations of fulfilling the desired future. While positive expectations and positive fantasies are both forms of positively thinking about the future, they differ in substantial aspects.

Hope as Positive Fantasies
Positive Fantasies versus Positive Expectations

On the basis of the different conceptualizations of thinking positively about the future, Oettingen and Mayer (2002) suggest that two forms of thinking about the future can be differentiated: beliefs about the future (expectations) and images about the future (fantasies). Beliefs and images were first differentiated by William James (1890): "Everyone knows the difference between imagining a thing and believing in its existence, between supposing a proposition and acquiescing in its truth" (p. 283). Accordingly, thoughts can appear in one's mind regardless of whether the person believes in its truth or not. While James was referring to beliefs and images from the past or the present, Oettingen and Mayer (2002) applied this idea to

future thought and distinguished between expectations and fantasies. As described already, expectations are beliefs in the form of judgments. These expectancy judgments refer to the likelihood that certain events or behaviors will happen in the future (Bandura, 1977; Mischel, 1973; see review by Roese & Sherman, 2007). People base their expectancy judgments on experiences in the past and thus on their performance history. Expectations can refer to (a) whether one can perform a specific behavior in its relevant context (self-efficacy expectations; Bandura, 1997); (b) whether performing a specific behavior will lead to the desired outcome (outcome expectations; Bandura, 1997); (c) whether a specific event will occur, thereby involving both self-efficacy and outcome expectations (general expectations, Heckhausen, 1991; Oettingen & Wadden, 1991); or (d) whether the future in general will be positive or negative (generalized expectations; Scheier & Carver, 1992).

Conversely, positive fantasies are positively experienced daydreams or mental images about the future that freely appear in the mind, regardless of whether people believe that they will come true (Klinger, 1990; Oettingen & Mayer, 2002; Singer, 1966). In contrast to expectations, positive fantasies are not constrained by factual information, and thus people can freely indulge in future scenarios without considering their past performance. For example, despite a low perceived probability of starting an intimate relationship with his "crushee," a student can indulge in positive fantasies about having a great relationship with that person. While expectations are measured by participants' judgments of the probability that a certain future will or will not occur, fantasies are measured with projective tests that ask participants to freely respond to a given stimuli. Oettingen and Wadden (1991), for example, measured positive fantasies by semiprojective techniques asking participants to describe their fantasies regarding a hypothetical scenario and subsequently rate these fantasies for their experienced positivity versus negativity. One of the strengths of this method is that it combines the advantages of projective tests (or operant measures; McClelland, 1980) with the advantages of questionnaires (or respondent measures; Oettingen & Mayer, 2002).

Positive Fantasies and Success

As outlined, positive expectations and positive fantasies are two different ways of positively thinking about future events, which have both been associated with hope. The question arises of whether these forms of future thought have different effects on effort and success in fulfilling the desired future. Research consistently finds that positive expectations foster effort and performance (Bandura, 1997; Heckhausen, 1991; Seligman, 1991). For example, positive expectations are associated with task persistence (Carver, Blaney, & Scheier, 1979), school achievement (Caprara et al., 2008), and successful coping (Bandura, 1986), as well as with happiness, productivity, and creativity (Taylor & Brown, 1988). Do positive fantasies have the same beneficial effects on effort and performance?

CORRELATIONAL STUDIES

Oettingen and Wadden (1991) examined the effects of positive expectations versus positive fantasies in a study with obese women who had enrolled in a weight-reduction program. At pretreatment, participants indicated how many pounds they wanted to lose in the program. To measure expectations of successfully attaining the weight goal, participants indicated how likely they thought it was that they would lose the amount of weight they specified. To measure the positivity of fantasies, the researchers asked the participants to complete four hypothetical weight- and food-related scenarios. After writing down their thoughts and images to each open-ended scenario, participants rated the positivity and negativity of their mental images. Participants with positive fantasies about successfully losing weight lost fewer pounds over the next year than participants with negative fantasies. The reverse pattern emerged regarding positive expectations: Participants with positive expectations about successfully losing weight lost more pounds than participants with negative expectations.

Other correlational studies replicated these results. Again, the more positive the participants' fantasies were, the lower was their effort and success in fulfilling the desired future events. Positive fantasies predicted, for example, less success in finding a job after graduation from college, starting a romantic relationship, achieving strong grades, and recovering after hip replacement surgery (Oettingen & Mayer, 2002). Moving from the individual and interpersonal level to the society as a whole, Sevincer, Wagner, Kalvelage, and Oettingen (2014) investigated the relationship between positive fantasies in historical documents and economic development. To test if a cultural climate of positive fantasies can predict economic downturn in a society, the researchers used computerized content analysis (Linguistic Inquiry and Word Count; Pennebaker, Chung, Ireland, Gonzales, & Booth, 2007) of newspaper reports and presidential addresses. Indeed, one study (Sevincer et al., 2014, Study 1) showed that during the financial crisis from 2007 to 2009, the more newspaper articles on the economy page of *USA Today* entailed positive thinking about the future, the lower the Dow Jones Industrial Average was in the subsequent week and after one month. Another study (Sevincer et al., 2014, Study 2) revealed that between the New Deal era and the present day, the more presidential inaugural addresses contained positive thinking about the future, the more the gross domestic product and the employment rate decreased in the subsequent presidential terms.

EXPERIMENTAL STUDIES

Experimental studies that induced positive fantasies about an idealized future (vs. questioning fantasies, negative fantasies, factual thoughts, or no thoughts) are in line with the correlational research described earlier. For example, in three studies, Kappes, Sharma, and Oettingen (2013) found that when participants were led to positively fantasize about their successful charitable giving, they were *less* willing to give time or money when helping demanded a large number of resources. Positive fantasies did not affect the likelihood of charitable giving when helping demanded a relatively small number of resources. These results suggest that positive fantasies dampen effort not only for a person's own accomplishments but also for giving to others. They also imply that positive fantasies unfold their problematic effects especially when reaching the desired future is challenging and demands many resources.

MECHANISMS

Further experimental work induced positive fantasies to investigate the underlying mechanisms that cause their effort-hampering effects. Oettingen and Mayer (2002) assumed that positively fantasizing a desired future would lead people to act as if they had already accomplished the desired future event. Ferguson and Bargh (2004) have shown that people automatically evaluate instrumental objects more positively while they pursue their goals, as compared to when they have completed their goal pursuit. Therefore, Kappes, Kappes, and Oettingen (2015) hypothesized that positive fantasies lead to less positive automatic evaluations of expressions that are related to their desired future, as they feign goal completion. Indeed, when students were induced to generate positive fantasies about the idealized experience of taking a neuroenhancing drug, their automatic evaluations of terms related to neuroenhancing drugs were less positive compared to students that were induced to generate questioning fantasies, negative fantasies, or no thoughts. The researchers concluded that one reason why positive fantasies predict low effort and success is that positive fantasies lead to mental attainment of the desired experience, leaving little motivation to invest effort in fulfilling the desired future.

A second reason for the effort-hampering effects of positive fantasies was found in a series of studies that measured participants' level of energy. Energy plays a crucial role in fulfilling desired futures (Brehm & Self, 1989; Klinger, 1975; Oettingen et al., 2009) and has a long tradition in motivation psychology. Energy or energization can be caused by engaging in actual effort, as well as by anticipating the investment of effort in upcoming challenges (Contrada, Wright, & Glass, 1984). Kappes and Oettingen (2011) hypothesized that, by leading to mental attainment, positive fantasies should obscure the need for energy. Indeed, in four studies, induced positive fantasies led to lower energization (measured by self-report and physiological measures) compared to questioning, negative, or neutral fantasies. These results suggest that positive fantasies allow people to enjoy the desired future in the present moment and thus hinder the mobilization of energy required to fulfill the desired future event.

Origins of Positive Fantasies

If positive fantasies are not based on past experience, how do they emerge? Kappes, Schwörer, and Oettingen (2012) hypothesized that aroused needs would spur fantasies that are experienced as particularly positive. Indeed, the researchers found in four studies that people with an aroused need generated more positive fantasies about future scenarios addressing the need than people without this need. For example, in one study (Kappes et al., 2012, Study 1), the researchers aroused the need for meaning in life by asking people to read an article that linked their present employment status (being unemployment or employed) to meaninglessness in life. To measure need-relevant fantasies, participants fantasized the ending to a scenario that allowed them to increase meaning in life by becoming employed or finding more meaningful work than they presently had, respectively. Thereafter, participants indicated the positivity and negativity of the thoughts and images they had generated.

Participants with an aroused need for meaning generated more positive fantasies than control participants. These results were found with physiological as well as psychological needs (need for water, for relatedness, or for power) regardless of whether the needs were manipulated or measured.

In sum, while positive expectations, as they are based on past experiences, predict high effort and successful performance, positive fantasies that are detached from past experience predict low effort and little success. If positive fantasies are detrimental for effort and performance, what can be done with these thoughts to help people find success in fulfilling the desired future outcomes? Can people effectively use their positive fantasies and dreams about the future to take action, as suggested by Bloch (1954, 1955, 1959), or do we need to give up hope for hope?

Fantasy Realization Theory

Fantasy realization theory (Oettingen, 1996, 2012) investigates the effects of fantasies on fulfilling the desired future. According to the theory, positive fantasies can lead to effective pursuit of desired futures if people mentally contrast them with the present reality. In mental contrasting (Oettingen, 2000; Oettingen, Pak, & Schnetter, 2001), people first imagine the fulfillment of a specific desired future (e.g., leading a group project at work), and thereafter they imagine the present reality that stands in the way of fulfilling the desired future (e.g., one's shyness). Imagining the desired future followed by the present reality links the future to reality, revealing that one has to act in the present reality in order to fulfill the desired future (e.g., overcoming the present shyness). As a consequence, expectations of success become activated and guide subsequent effort and performance. When expectations are high, people increase their effort to fulfill the desired future; when expectations are low they decrease their effort. Thus mental contrasting causes selective effort and performance, which helps people to invest their resources in feasible futures and prevents them from wasting their resources on unfeasible ones.

Many studies show that mental contrasting leads to expectancy-guided effort and performance. The pattern of results evinces in a wide variety of life domains, covering interpersonal, health, academic, and work contexts, with diverse populations including children, students, managers, and patients, as well as different cultures such as Germany and the United States. It is found with different indictors of wish fulfillment (e.g., cognitive, emotional, motivational, and behavioral) no matter whether these indicators were measured via self-report or observation, directly after the experiment or weeks later, whether it was in the laboratory or in the field, and whether expectations were measured or manipulated (for an overview, see Oettingen, 2012).

In sum, these experimental studies show that Bloch (1954, 1955, 1959) was right: Daydreams (i.e., positive fantasies) can be used to help people actively strive for a better future. Contrasting positive fantasies with the present reality activates expectations of success, and thus people can wisely regulate their limited resources (e.g., time, energy, effort; Brehm & Self, 1989, Wright, 1996). People who mentally contrast invest their resources only in feasible futures and refrain from spending their resources on unfeasible ones.

The Hopeful Pessimist
Hopeful in Dark Moments

In situations in which different action alternatives are possible, a selective pursuit of desired futures allows people to invest their limited resources wisely. However, there are several instances in real life where people cannot reach their desired future nor can they disengage (Oettingen, 1997b). For example, a young man who has been diagnosed with a life-threatening chronic disease should not follow his low expectations to be able to survive, because these expectations will lead him to disengage from his desired future to survive. Here, focusing solely on his positive fantasies will help him *stay in the field*. In addition to constrained situations like this, there are certain cultural or political environments that lay down boundaries for action, thereby preventing individuals from selecting and striving for their desired futures. For example, traditional societies that adhere to strictly norm-oriented rituals may convey normative commitments, which specify the direction of action without allowing the individual's input (Oettingen, 1997a). In these cultures, indulging in positive fantasies will help "to overcome the experience of normative constraint in the present by providing hope for a better future" (Oettingen, 1997a, p. 371). Thus, even in light of pessimistic expectations about the future (e.g., terminal cancer, frailty in old age, normative constraints), positive fantasies should encourage people to stay committed and patiently deal with the situation. In such constrained situations, positive fantasies should help people to endure.

Indeed, research on fantasy realization theory shows that indulging in positive fantasies without contrasting them with the present reality leads to unchanged engagement regardless of the expectations to fulfill the desired future. Figure 6.1 shows the typical pattern of expectations and goal commitment in participants induced to mentally contrast versus indulge. Participants in the mental contrasting condition showed expectancy-dependent goal commitment: When expectations were high, participants who mentally contrasted committed themselves to fulfill the desired future; when expectations were low, they refrained from doing so and thus were able to pursue alternative wishes and desired futures. Participants in the indulging condition showed expectancy-*in*dependent goal commitment: Regardless of whether expectations where high or low, their commitment remained unchanged. Specifically, when expectations were high, they committed less than mental contrasting participants; when expectations were low, they committed more than mental contrasting participants. In other words, positive fantasies in the face of low expectations led people to stay in the field; that is, they were more engaged than seemed justified on

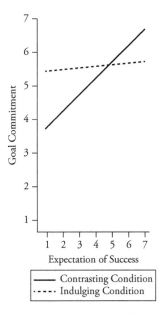

Fig. 6.1. Regression lines depict the link between expectation of success and goal commitment as a function of mental contrasting and indulging. From "Mental contrasting and goal commitment: The mediating role of energization," by G. Oettingen, D. Mayer, A. T. Sevincer, E. J. Stephens, H. Pak, & M. Hagenah (2009). *Personality and Social Psychology Bulletin, 35*, 608–622. Copyright 2009 by the Society for Personality and Social Psychology, Inc. Reprinted with permission.

the basis of their expectations. They were pessimistic and hopeful at the same time (Oettingen, 1996). While mentally contrasting the desired future with insurmountable obstacles of reality would emphasize how precarious the situation is, indulging in positive fantasies will give people the hope that one day the situation may still come to a good end. Thus hopefully indulging in their positive fantasies may help people to emotionally cope with apparently insoluble situations (Oettingen, 1997b).

Other Benefits of Positive Fantasies

As described earlier, people who positively fantasize about desired futures for which their expectations are low become hopeful pessimists. Being a hopeful pessimist is helpful in constrained situations where neither engagement nor disengagement is possible or beneficial. In such forlorn situations, positive fantasies can help people to endure despite their low expectations. In the following section, we discuss four additional circumstances in which positive fantasies can prove useful.

PATIENT WAITING

First, people frequently face situations in which they simply have to wait without any possibilities to take purposeful action. People may have to wait for a diagnosis, a court decision, or academic test results. In these constrained situations where people cannot do anything about their upcoming results, positive fantasies can help people to wait patiently. Positively fantasizing helps people to perceive the waiting period as passing by quickly and thus enables them to effectively deal with impatience (Oettingen, 1997a). However, even though positive fantasies enable people to patiently wait, research has also shown that individuals who foresaw a positive outcome while waiting for exam results experienced more unpleasant surprise when they failed and less pleasant surprise when they passed (Sweeny, Reynolds, Falkenstein, Andrews, & Dooley, 2016).

TEMPORARY RELIEF

Second, hopefully indulging in positive fantasies can provide short-term pleasure and temporary relief. For example, Salomons, Moayedi, Erpelding, and Davis (2014) found that focusing on positive thoughts helped people when they were suffering from physical pain. A brief cognitive-behavioral intervention that taught people to reappraise their negative thoughts and focus on the positivity of the situation reduced pain unpleasantness and secondary hyperalgesia, an indicator for central sensitization.

Oettingen, Mayer, and Portnow (2016) showed that positive thoughts and images not only relate to lower physical pain but also to lower psychological pain. The researchers demonstrated in four studies that the positivity of fantasies related to fewer symptoms of depression when measured concurrently. However, the positivity of fantasies related to more symptoms of depression when measured over time. A parallel pattern was found with suicide attempts. While intrapersonal positive thinking related to low suicidal ideation when participants were in the crisis (i.e., in the hours following a suicide attempt), it predicted repeat suicide attempts over the subsequent 15 months (O'Connor, Smyth, & Williams, 2015). The patterns of these studies suggest that positive fantasies are a risk factor in the long term, even though they are protective in the short term. When people are in a crisis and need immediate relief from their psychological or physical pain, positively fantasizing seems to help them deal with the painful situation.

RELAXATION AND ENJOYMENT

Third, positively fantasizing can help people to calm down and relax. Positive fantasies enable enjoyment of the wished-for future in the here and now and lead to a relaxed state. People not only subjectively feel less energized but also show a decrease in physiological energization measured by systolic blood pressure (Kappes & Oettingen, 2011). These findings imply that one could, for example, use positive fantasies to wind down and relax after a long workday. Because there is no more need to act, one can indulge to create a calm and relaxed state during recovery time.

MENTAL EXPLORATION

Fourth, positive fantasies provide the opportunity to mentally explore the various possibilities of the future. The explorative use of dreams enables people to mentally experience different future scenarios. By hopefully fantasizing what the future may look like, people can virtually experience the fulfilment of their wishes without the necessity of taking action and without being urged to make a commitment. As positive fantasies stem from need states, which signal a deprivation (Kappes et al., 2012), they serve the important function of keeping a person's unsatisfied needs in mind. People can explore what *feels* right and thereby identify what they really want and need.

In sum, positively fantasizing about the future can prove useful in a variety of different circumstances.

Importantly, positive fantasies can encourage people to not give up in situations that offer no action alternatives even when the expectations to fulfill the desired future are low. Furthermore, they can support people during waiting periods, in crisis situations in which people need immediate relief, during relaxation times, and when a person wants to discover what his or her hopes and wishes for the future actually are.

The Emotion of Hope

So far we have focused on the cognitive and behavioral aspects of hope. Research has also investigated hope as an emotion (e.g., Averill, Catlin, & Chon, 1990; McInnis & de Mello, 2005). However, there are fewer emotion-based hope theories than theories based on cognition (Snyder, Cheavens, & Michael, 2005). Furthermore, the emotion-based hope theories usually contain cognitive elements (Lopez, Snyder, & Pedrotti, 2003). One early emotion-based definition of hope originates from Mowrer (1960) who studied hope in animals using a stimulus-response paradigm. Mowrer identified four basic emotions—fear, relief, hope, and disappointment—and discussed the respective situations that evoke them. According to Mowrer, the emotion of hope is aroused by the onset of a stimulus that indicates the imminent occurrence of a pleasurable experience. To the contrary, fear is seen as the antithesis of hope and is aroused by the onset of a stimulus that indicates the imminent occurrence of a noxious experience.

Later on, Averill and colleagues (1990) proposed that hope is a cognitively orientated emotion. According to their model, the emotion of hope most likely occurs when people possess goals that are midrange in their probability of achievement, personally important, under some control, and socially as well as morally acceptable. Another emotion-based definition by MacInnis and de Mello (2005) describes hope as "a positively valenced emotion evoked in response to an uncertain but possible goal-congruent outcome" (p. 2). We agree that hope includes elements of cognition as well as emotion. On the basis of their positive fantasies, people can sustain the feeling of hope even though they rationally know from their past experience that it is unlikely that these dreams will come true. Thus, in emotion terms, hope can be described as the anticipation of being positively surprised.

In sum, emotion-based hope theories have received far less attention than cognition-based theories. Furthermore, most of the theories that are based on emotions include a cognitive aspect in their theory. Our definition of hope attempts to combine the cognitive and affective components of hope and describes the emotion of hope as the anticipation of being positively surprised.

Future Directions

As we have highlighted throughout this chapter, past research has provided a variety of definitions for the concept of hope, which have fundamentally different consequences for goal-directed behavior. Thus it is very important that future research elucidate whether hope is conceptualized as a positive expectation, a positive fantasy, a specific emotion, or in some other way. As lay theories (i.e., intuitive theories people use in their everyday life) impact people's cognitions, emotions, and behaviors (Hong, Levy, & Chiu, 2001), future research should investigate how people differ in the way they conceive hope and if these lay theories have different consequences for people's behavior. Furthermore, it would be important to explore the extent to which people from different cultures differ in their lay beliefs about hope. Averill and colleagues (1990) provided an important first step in this direction exploring how people from the United States and Korea experience and interpret hope. Distinguishing hope from wants and desires, the researchers asked students to describe something they want or desire but that they do not hope for. While students from the United States primarily described wants and desires that involved material goods, interpersonal relationships, or achievement, students from Korea primarily described hedonistic pursuits, material goods, or freedom from social and personal obligations. As reasons that distinguish wants and desires from hope, US students emphasized that they do not hope for these wants and desires because they are impossible or unrealistic. Students from Korea, on the contrary, emphasized that they do not hope for their described wants and desires because of potential disadvantages should they be realized as well as concerns about the violation of personal and/or social values.

Future studies may also elucidate what role expectations versus fantasies play when it comes to lay conceptions of hope in different cultures. Specifically, people from cultures with normative constraints may conceive hope as positive fantasies, whereas people from cultures that allow them to guide their own actions conceive hope in terms of positive expectations. Future studies may also experimentally manipulate participants' contexts (e.g., constrained: yes vs. no) and as dependent variables assess their lay beliefs about hope.

Research is also needed to further examine the affective aspects of hope. We argue that the emotion of hope is triggered by an anticipation of a positive surprise. To test this assumption, future research may analyze the facial expressions when people are asked to look hopeful. The Facial Action Coding System (Ekman, Friesen, & Hager, 2002) may be used to investigate if people indeed express the combination of surprise and happiness when they subjectively experience the emotion of hope. It would also be interesting to test whether people's facial and bodily expressions of hope change as a function of inducing various existing theoretical constructs of hope (e.g., expectancy- versus fantasy-based). Finally, future efforts might be directed at inducing hope versus fear as well as hope versus hopelessness before assessing participants' facial and bodily expressions.

In sum, it is important that future research on hope clearly identifies the specific concept of hope on which it is built. An interesting question that should be addressed in future research is how people's lay theories about hope differ and to what extent differences in these lay theories depend on people's sociocultural backgrounds. Finally, future studies should further investigate the affective aspects of hope.

Conclusion

The construct of hope plays a crucial role for people's lives. However, there are many different perspectives regarding what hope really is. The predominant perspective on hope in psychological research is an expectancy-based conceptualization that associates high hope with the perception of a high probability to fulfill the desired future.

In contrast, we have argued that rather than equate hope with expectations, hope should emerge when people uphold fantasies about the desired future despite low expectations of fulfilling their desired future. As the example at the beginning of the chapter—a student dreaming of her parents being around for her future children—showed, people positively fantasize about their future even when they rationally judge that the probabilities of the desired event coming true are low. In other words, people can be hopeful pessimists. When they do not have the possibility to take purposeful action, hopefully indulging in positive fantasies helps them to deal with the dire circumstances instead of disengaging from them. The student cannot influence whether or not her parents will be able to play with her future children, but her positive fantasies help her to cope with the prospect that they probably will not.

However, if purposeful action is possible and needed, hopefully indulging in positive fantasies will not be enough. People will not exercise more, quit smoking, get better grades, or ask their crushee out if they simply positively fantasize about these scenarios. Rather, they need to contrast these positive fantasies with the obstacles of the reality that stand in the way in order to take action and achieve the desired future.

Thus, when discussing how hope influences goal-directed behavior, it is important to consider the specific context. When people can take purposeful action to fulfill their desired future, they need to contrast their positive fantasies with the obstacles of reality in order to fully engage or disengage from it. When people can neither actively reach for their desired future nor disengage, they can overcome the painful experience by hoping for a better future.

References

Abramson, L. Y., Metalsky, G. I., & Alloy, L. B. (1989). Hopelessness depression: A theory-based subtype of depression. *Psychological Review, 96*, 358–372. doi:10.1037//0033295X.96.2.358

Affleck, G., & Tennen, H. (1996). Construing benefits from adversity: Adaptational significance and dispositional underpinnings. *Journal of Personality, 64*, 899–922. doi:10.1111/j.1467-6494.1996.tb00948.x

Ajzen, I. (1991). The theory of planned behavior. *Organizational Behavior and Human Decision Processes, 50*, 179–211. doi:10.1016/0749-5978(91)90020-T

Aspinwall, L. G., & Leaf, S. L. (2002). In search of the unique aspects of hope: Pinning our hopes on positive emotions, future-oriented thinking, hard times, and other people. *Psychological Inquiry, 13*, 276–288. doi:10.1207/S15327965PLI1304_02

Atkinson, J. W. (1957). Motivational determinants of risk-taking behavior. *Psychological Review, 64*, 359–372. doi:10.1037/h0043445

Averill, J. R., Catlin, G., & Chon, K. K. (1990). *Rules of hope.* New York, NY: Springer-Verlag.

Bandura, A. (1977). Self-efficacy: Toward a unifying theory of behavioral change. *Psychological Review, 84*, 191–215. doi:10.1037/0033-295X.84.2.191

Bandura, A. (1986). *Social foundation of thought and action.* Englewood Cliffs, NJ: Prentice Hall.

Bandura, A. (1997). *Self-efficacy: The exercise of control.* New York, NY: Freeman.

Bandura, A., & Locke, E. A. (2003). Negative self-efficacy and goal effects revisited. *Journal of Applied Psychology, 88*, 87–99. doi:10.1037/0021-9010.88.1.87

Beck, A. T., Weissman, A., Lester, D., & Trexler, L. (1974). The measurement of pessimism: The hopelessness scale. *Journal of Consulting and Clinical Psychology, 42*, 861–865.

Bloch, E. (1954). *Das Prinzip Hoffnung I* [The principle of hope I]. Frankfurt am Main, Germany: Suhrkamp.

Bloch, E. (1955). *Das Prinzip Hoffnung II* [The principle of hope II]. Frankfurt am Main, Germany: Suhrkamp.

Bloch, E. (1959). *Das Prinzip Hoffnung III* [The principle of hope III]. Frankfurt am Main, Germany: Suhrkamp.

Bloch, E. (1996). *The principle of hope: Vol. 1.* Cambridge, MA: MIT Press.

Brehm, J. W., & Self, E. A. (1989). The intensity of motivation. *Annual Review of Psychology, 40,* 109–131. doi:10.1146/annurev.ps.40.020189.000545

Bryant, F. B., & Cvengros, J. A. (2004). Distinguishing hope and optimism: Two sides of a coin, or two separate coins? *Journal of Social and Clinical Psychology, 23,* 273–302. doi:10.1521/jscp.23.2.273.31018

Caprara, G. V., Fida, R., Vecchione, M., Del Bove, G., Vecchio, G. M., Barbaranelli, C., & Bandura, A. (2008). Longitudinal analysis of the role of perceived self-efficacy for self-regulated learning in academic continuance and achievement. *Journal of Educational Psychology, 100,* 525–534. doi:10.1037/0022-0663.100.3.525

Carver, C. S., Blaney, P. H., & Scheier, M. F. (1979). Reassertion and giving up: The interactive role of self-directed attention and outcome expectancy. *Journal of Personality and Social Psychology, 37,* 1859–1870. doi:10.1037/0022-3514.37.10.1859

Contrada, R. J., Wright, R. A., & Glass, D. C. (1984). Task difficulty, type A behavior pattern, and cardiovascular response. *Psychophysiology, 21,* 638–646. doi:10.1111/j.14698986.1984.tb00250.x

Ekman, P., Friesen, W. V., & Hager, J. C. (2002). *Facial Action Coding System* [E-book]. Salt Lake City, UT: Research Nexus.

Erikson, E. H. (1964). *Insight and responsibility.* New York, NY: Norton.

Ferguson, M. J., & Bargh, J. A. (2004). Liking is for doing: The effects of goal pursuit on automatic evaluation. *Journal of Personality and Social Psychology, 87,* 557–572. doi:10.1037/0022-3514.87.5.557

Gallagher, M. W., & Lopez, S. J. (2009). Positive expectancies and mental health: Identifying the unique contributions of hope and optimism. *The Journal of Positive Psychology, 4,* 548–556. doi:10.1080/17439760903157166

Gottschalk, L. A. (1974). A hope scale applicable to verbal samples. *Archives of General Psychiatry, 30,* 779–785. doi:10.1001/archpsyc.1974.01760120041007

Heckhausen, H. (1991). *Motivation and action.* Heidelberg, Germany: Springer.

Hong, Y. Y., Levy, S. R., & Chiu, C. Y. (2001). The contribution of the lay theories approach to the study of groups. *Personality and Social Psychology Review, 5,* 98–106. doi:10.1207/S15327957PSPR0502_1

James, W. (1890). *The principles of psychology.* New York, NY: Holt.

Kappes, H. B., Kappes, A., & Oettingen, G. (2015). *When attainment is all in your head.* Unpublished manuscript, Department of Psychology, New York University, New York.

Kappes, H. B., & Oettingen, G. (2011). Positive fantasies about idealized futures sap energy. *Journal of Experimental Social Psychology, 47,* 719–729. doi:10.1016/j.jesp.2011.02.003

Kappes, H. B., Schwörer, B., & Oettingen, G. (2012). Needs instigate positive fantasies of idealized futures. *European Journal of Social Psychology, 42,* 299–307. doi:10.1002/ejsp.1854

Kappes, H. B., Sharma, E., & Oettingen, G. (2013). Positive fantasies dampen charitable giving when many resources are demanded. *Journal of Consumer Psychology, 23,* 128–135. doi:10.1016/j.jcps.2012.02.001

Klinger, E. (1975). Consequences of commitment to and disengagement from incentives. *Psychological Review, 82,* 1–25. doi:10.1037/h0076171

Klinger, E. (1990). *Daydreaming: Using waking fantasy and imagery for self-knowledge and creativity.* Los Angeles, CA: Tarcher.

Lopez, S. J., Snyder, C. R., & Pedrotti, J. T. (2003). Hope: Many definitions, many measures. In S. J. Lopez & C. R. Snyder (Eds.), *Positive psychological assessment: A handbook of models and measures* (pp. 91–107). Washington, DC: American Psychological Association.

MacInnis, D. J., & de Mello, G. E. (2005). The concept of hope and its relevance to product evaluation and choice. *Journal of Marketing, 69,* 1–14. doi:10.1509/jmkg.69.1.1.55513

Magaletta, P. R., & Oliver, J. M. (1999). The hope construct, will, and ways: Their relations with self-efficacy, optimism, and general well-being. *Journal of Clinical Psychology, 55,* 539–551. doi:10.1002/(SICI)1097-4679(199905)55:5<539:AID-JCLP2>3.0.CO;2-G

McClelland, D. C. (1980). Motive dispositions: The merits of operant and respondent measures. In L. Wheeler (Ed.), *Review of personality and social psychology* (Vol. 1, pp. 10–41). Beverly Hills, CA: SAGE.

Mischel, W. (1973). Toward a cognitive social learning reconceptualization of personality. *Psychological Review, 80,* 252–283. doi:10.1037/h0035002

Mowrer, O. H. (1960). *Learning theory and behavior.* New York, NY: Wiley.

O'Connor, R. C., Smyth, R., & Williams, J. M. G. (2015). Intrapersonal positive future thinking predicts repeat suicide attempts in hospital-treated suicide attempters. *Journal of Consulting and Clinical Psychology, 83,* 169–176. doi:10.1037/a0037846

Oettingen, G. (1996). Positive fantasy and motivation. In P. M. Gollwitzer & J. A. Bargh (Eds.), *The psychology of action: Linking cognition and motivation to behavior* (pp. 236–259). New York, NY: Guilford Press.

Oettingen, G. (1997a). Culture and future thought. *Culture & Psychology, 3,* 353–381. doi:10.1177/1354067X9733008

Oettingen, G. (1997b). *Psychologie des Zukunftsdenkens* [The psychology of thinking about the future]. Göttingen, Germany: Hogrefe.

Oettingen, G. (2000). Expectancy effects on behavior depend on self-regulatory thought. *Social Cognition, 18,* 101–129. doi:10.1521/soco.2000.18.2.101

Oettingen, G. (2012). Future thought and behaviour change. *European Review of Social Psychology, 23,* 1–63. doi:10.1080/10463283.2011.643698

Oettingen, G., & Mayer, D. (2002). The motivating function of thinking about the future: Expectations versus fantasies. *Journal of Personality and Social Psychology, 83,* 1198–1212. doi:10.1037/0022-3514.83.5.1198

Oettingen, G., Mayer, D., & Portnow, S. (2016). Pleasure now, pain later: Positive fantasies about the future predict symptoms of depression. *Psychological Science, 27,* 345–353. doi:10.1177/0956797615620783

Oettingen, G., Mayer, D., Sevincer, A. T., Stephens, E. J., Pak, H., & Hagenah, M. (2009). Mental contrasting and goal commitment: The mediating role of energization. *Personality* and Social Psychology Bulletin, 35, 608–622. doi:10.1177/0146167208330856

Oettingen, G., Pak, H., & Schnetter, K. (2001). Self- regulation of goal setting: Turning free fantasies about the future into binding goals. Journal of Personality and Social Psychology, 80, 736–753. doi:10.1037/0022-3514.80.5.736

Oettingen, G., & Wadden, T. A. (1991). Expectation, fantasy, and weight loss: Is the impact of positive thinking always positive? Cognitive Therapy and Research, 15, 167–175. doi:10.1007/BF01173206

Pennebaker, J. W., Chung, C. K., Ireland, M., Gonzales, A. L., & Booth, R. J. (2007). The development and psychometric properties of LIWC2007. Austin, TX: LIWC.net.

Peterson, C., & Seligman, M. E. P. (1984). Causal explanations as a risk factor for depression: Theory and evidence. Psychological Review, 91, 347–374. doi:10.1037/0033-295X.91.3.347

Roese, N. J., & Sherman, J. W. (2007). Expectancy. In A. W. Kruglanski & E. T. Higgins (Eds.), Social psychology: Handbook of basic principles (pp. 91–115). New York, NY: Guilford Press.

Salomons, T. V., Moayedi, M., Erpelding, N., & Davis, K. D. (2014). A brief cognitive-behavioural intervention for pain reduces secondary hyperalgesia. Pain, 155, 1446–1452. doi:10.1016/j.pain.2014.02.012

Scheier, M. F., & Carver, C. S. (1985). Optimism, coping, and health: Assessment and implications of generalized outcome expectancies. Health Psychology, 4, 219–247. doi:10.1037/0278-6133.4.3.219

Scheier, M. F., & Carver, C. S. (1992). Effects of optimism on psychological and physical well-being: Theoretical overview and empirical update. Cognitive Therapy and Research, 16, 201–228. doi:10.1007/BF01173489

Schnoor, H. (1988). Psychoanalyse der Hoffnung: Die psychische und psychosomatische Bedeutung von Hoffnung und Hoffnungslosigkeit [Psychoanalysis of hope: The psychological and psychosomatic meaning of hope and hopelessness]. Heidelberg, Germany: Asanger.

Seligman, M. E. P. (1991). Learned optimism. New York; NY: Knopf.

Sevincer, A. T., Wagner, G., Kalvelage, J., & Oettingen, G. (2014). Positive thinking about the future in newspaper reports and presidential addresses predicts economic downturn. Psychological Science, 25, 1010–1017. doi:10.1177/0956797613518350

Singer, J. L. (1966). Daydreaming. New York, NY: Random House.

Snyder, C. R. (2000). Handbook of hope: Theory, measures, and applications. San Diego, CA: Academic Press.

Snyder, C. R., Cheavens, J. S., & Michael, S. T. (2005). Hope theory: History and elaborated model. In J. A. Elliott (Ed.), Interdisciplinary perspectives on hope (pp. 101–118). Hauppauge, NY: Nova Science.

Snyder, C. R., Irving, L. M., & Anderson, J. R. (1991). Hope and health. In C. R. Snyder & D. R. Forsyth (Eds.), Handbook of social and clinical psychology: The health perspective (pp. 285–305). Elmsford, NY: Pergamon.

Staats, S. R. (1989). Hope: A comparison of two self-report measures for adults. Journal of Personality Assessment, 53, 366–375. doi:10.1207/s15327752jpa5302_13

Stotland, E. (1969). The psychology of hope. San Francisco, CA: Jossey-Bass.

Sweeny, K., Reynolds, C. A., Falkenstein, A., Andrews, S. E., & Dooley, M. D. (2016). Two definitions of waiting well. Emotion, 16, 129–143. doi:10.1037/emo0000117

Taylor, S. E., & Brown, J. D. (1988). Illusion and well-being: A social psychological perspective on mental health. Psychological Bulletin, 103, 193–210. doi:10.1037/0033-2909.103.2.193

Taylor, S. E., Kemeny, M. E., Reed, G. M., Bower, J. E., & Gruenewald, T. L. (2000). Psychological resources, positive illusions, and health. American Psychologist, 55, 99–109. doi:10.1037/0003-066X.55.1.99

Wright, R. A. (1996). Brehm's theory of motivation as a model of effort and cardiovascular response. In P. M. Gollwitzer & J. A. Bargh (Eds.), The psychology of action: Linking cognition and motivation to behavior (pp. 424–453). New York, NY: Guilford Press.

PART **II**

Measuring Hope

Hope Measurement

Sage Rose *and* Nicole Sieben

Abstract

This chapter covers the multiple measures currently used to assess hope theory. Hope, as theorized by Snyder and colleagues, was originally determined to be a global construct measuring agency and pathways toward goal attainment. Using much of the original theory, hope research has expanded, resulting in multiple measures across different applications and domains. By exploring the context specificity, these scales have been shown to consistently predict outcomes across differing domains, supporting the reliability and validity of new hope measurement. It is anticipated that with more specific hope measurement, the more accurate hope assessment and intervention can become. Concepts covered in this chapter include academic hope, math hope, writing hope, work hope, children's hope, employment hope, and state hope.

Key Words: hope, academic hope, work hope, children's hope, state hope, goals

Hope is a cognitive-motivational construct within positive psychology that affects perceptions of future success and goal-directed behavior (Snyder et al., 1991). According to Snyder (2000), hope has three major components: agency, pathways, and goals. Agency is the volitional response to goal pursuits that energizes and excites an individual. The pathways are the perceived strategies or means to achieve meaningful goals. According to Snyder et al. (1991), pathways and agency thinking are highly correlated factors, but they are factorially distinct from one another. They work together to support engagement and prevent disengagement of goal pursuit.

Unlike other cognitive-motivational constructs (e.g., self-efficacy, self-regulation, optimism), hope theory places equal emphasis on all of the goal-pursuit components (i.e., motivation, regulation, affect, and strategies; Snyder, 2002). Hope is characterized by a reciprocal relationship between efficacy expectancies (agency) and outcome expectancies (pathways). Since agency and pathways beliefs are both directed toward goals, they react reciprocally with one another during the goal journey. Hope theory incorporates a person's intention to act rather than just his or her confidence in his or her ability to act, as is the case in other self-theories like self-efficacy theory (Berg et al., 2011; Padilla-Walker et al., 2011; Snyder et al., 2002). In hope theory, the two expectancies are reciprocally present and work together for successful goal pursuit.

In past studies, hope has frequently been linked to academic achievement. Research reveals that children, adolescents, and adults with higher hope levels perform better in school and athletics and have better problem-solving skills (Chang, 1998; Snyder, 2002; Snyder et al., 2002). In a study of college students, Chang found that high-hope students had better problem-solving skills and employed less disengagement strategies during stressful academic situations than low-hope students did. Regardless of coping strategies, hope was a significant predictor of academic satisfaction as well (Chang, 1998). Additionally, a study of college student-athletes (Curry, Snyder, Cook, Ruby, & Rehm, 1997) found that hope significantly predicted student-athletes' semester grade point averages (GPAs), more so than cumulative GPA and overall self-worth did. Additional studies have supported these findings and have continued to show that hope has been related to athletic performance (Curry & Snyder, 2000), academic achievement (Gilman, Dooley, & Florell, 2006), as well as life meaning (Feldman & Snyder, 2005).

In a meta-analysis of hope studies involving academic achievement, Snyder (2002) found that higher hope levels led to better academic outcomes overall. People with higher hope levels set specific goals and have a desired pathway to achieve those goals but see other pathways as options if the desired pathway is not possible. High-hope individuals anticipate setbacks, recover from failure more easily, and set goals in many different aspects of their lives so that if one goal is obstructed, another goal can be pursued (Snyder et al., 1991). On the contrary, people with lower hope levels tend to set vague goals, have difficulty determining pathways to achieve those goals, and experience greater stress as a result of obstructed goals or failure (Snyder et al., 1991).

In order for people to have hope, they must have belief in their abilities to accomplish the set goal and positive motivation toward the attainment of the goal.

> According to hope theory, hope reflects individuals' perceptions of their capabilities to (1) clearly conceptualize goals; (2) develop the specific strategies to reach those goals (pathways thinking); and (3) initiate and sustain the motivation for using those strategies (agency thinking). (Lopez et al., 2004, p. 388)

High-hope persons tend to generate many pathways as opposed to just a few and can utilize these multiple paths when faced with challenges or obstacles. By having multiple pathways, high-hope individuals are more likely to achieve their desired goals. Goals are the anchoring system for hope (Snyder, Ilardi, Michael, & Cheavens, 2000). It is important to note that Snyder (2002) theorized hope and goal completion as reciprocal influences on one another. High-hope individuals are more likely to accomplish their goals through perceived agency and viable pathways application. In response, goal success will heighten and support these hope perceptions during the next goal pursuit. Emotions are theorized to happen as a result of hope, and experiences of blocked pathways or failed goal attempts produce negative emotions while successful goal achievement results in positive emotions (Snyder, 2002).

For those counseling low-hope individuals, it is assumed the cognitive element of hope provides guidance for goal efforts while the emotional element mobilizes goal efforts (Buechler, 1995). Because hope is such a strong indicator of goal-directed behaviors, research has shown hope to impact multiple aspects, such as lowering depression levels and increasing life satisfaction (Rustøen, Cooper, and Miaskowski, 2010), helping those with disabilities overcome obstacles (Snyder, Lehman, Kluck, & Monsson, 2006), aiding in usage of positive coping skills for those with spinal cord injuries (Smedema, Catalano, & Ebener, 2010), and increasing tolerance to pain (Snyder et al., 2005). Each of these studies suggests that high-hope individuals can achieve their goals even in the most difficult situations. Because positive hope perceptions result in many successful outcomes, there are a multitude of assessments available in the literature that attempt to capture different aspects of hope.

Within positive psychology, hope theory and measurement is not limited to the research of Snyder and colleagues. Peterson and Seligman (2004) developed the Values in Action (VIA) measurement system that classifies a person's character strengths and virtues. This 240-item classification system includes 24 strengths that are grouped under six different virtues. This instrument uses self-reported information to identify the individual's top strengths (about four to seven strengths). Using one's signature strengths in work and relationships can improve aspects of life and overall meaning in life (Seligman et al., 2005). Hope is a character strength and falls under the virtue of transcendence. It is defined as "Expecting the best in the future and working to achieve it; believing that a good future is something that can be brought about" (Park, Peterson, & Seligman, 2004, p. 606). Hope, as a character strength, is similar to optimism. It does not include the agency and pathways components that was a part of the hope theory developed by Snyder et al., (1991). In addition, the VIA items for hope do not maintain a focus on goals or goal development. This type of hope is typically used within a package of strengths (e.g., gratitude and zest) and is not used as an independent measurement to predict success or well-being. The VIA has demonstrated strong validity and reliability (Peterson & Seligman, 2004).

Adult Dispositional Hope Scale

Snyder et al., (1991) developed the Adult Dispositional Hope Scale (DHS) in order to measure hope levels in adults (ages 15 and older). The

12-item scale is psychometrically strong with high validities and reliabilities. The total scores of the various samples had Cronbach alphas that ranged from .74 to .84 and test–retest reliabilities of .80 or above (Snyder et al., 1991). These correlation coefficients reveal that the DHS has strong internal consistency reliability. In past and recent studies, when factor analyses of the DHS were conducted, the two-factor structure (i.e., pathways and agency) of the hope construct emerged (Babyak, Snyder, & Yoshinobu, 1993; Lopez et al., 2000; Sieben, 2013; Snyder et al., 1991).

The DHS has strong concurrent construct validity as it has been moderately correlated (.50 to .60) with measures of optimism, expectancy for attaining goals, the amount of expected control, and self-esteem (Lopez et al., 2000). These moderate, positive correlations reveal that hope is a separate construct from these similar theories but is significantly related to them. Additionally, the DHS has strong divergent validity because it is inversely correlated ($r = -.51$) with the Hopelessness Scale (Lopez et al., 2000).

In the DHS, there are a total of 12 items with four items measuring agency, four items measuring pathways, and the final four items serving as distracter items. Respondents record their level of agreement with each of the items ranging from 1 (*definitely false*) to 8 (*definitely true*). Sample items include "I can think of many ways to get out of a jam" and "I energetically pursue my goals" (Lopez et al., 2000). For college and non-college student samples, the average DHS score is about 48 when using the 8-point Likert scale (Lopez et al., 2000). The highest possible score on the DHS is 64 and the lowest is 8. Snyder et al. (1991) initially determined the means and standard deviations of the scale using six different samples: four samples composed of undergraduate college students and two composed of people receiving psychological treatment. Based on the validity and reliability of the DHS, the scale has been used in many studies to predict psychological components and academic achievement outcome expectancies (Lopez et al., 2000). For example, a recent study of first-year college students' self-beliefs used the DHS to measure college students' general hope levels as compared to their writing hope levels (Sieben, 2013). In this study, the calculated internal consistency reliability for the DHS was high ($\alpha = .88$) and factor analyses again revealed two distinct factors in the hope construct: agency and pathways (Sieben, 2013).

The DHS has been tested among diverse samples, and the typical finding is no significant difference between men and women, but there are mixed results regarding ethnic differences and hope. Roesch and Vaughn (2006) performed a confirmatory factor analysis for the DHS designed to examine the validity of the agency and pathways subscales within a multiethnic sample ($N = 1,031$), a considerably larger sample than most diverse samples used in the past. Their study confirmed a two-factor model that fit well across genders and ethnicities. Further, the study found the two-factor model to be a better fit than a one-factor model. Other research has shown ethnic differences across hope, hopelessness, and suicidal behavior across ethnicities. One study found that African Americans who were hopeless were much more at risk for suicide than those who just had lower hope (Hirsch, Visser, Chang, & Jeglic, 2012). The researchers suggested this might be attributed to the racially based discriminatory factors African Americans face when attempting to achieve desired goals. For Hispanics and Caucasians, hope but not hopelessness was the best predictor for depression and suicide, suggesting that hope may work similarly for these groups. Unlike the other ethnic groups, hope and hopelessness did not affect depression and suicide for Asian Americans. Culturally speaking, hope and hopelessness may work differently across ethnicities or cultures when buffering depressive symptoms and predicting suicidal behaviors.

State Hope Scale

While Snyder et al., (1991) has theorized that individuals maintain a generalized hopeful disposition, research has suggested that there is a more immediate hope as it applies to current goal-oriented thinking (Snyder et al., 1996). Dispositional hope appears to be more focused on the distal goals that remain further out on the horizon of an individual's goal pursuit, while state hope pertains to the proximal goals that one is more immediately pursuing. State hope is reliant on the dispositional hope in that the higher the level of hope a person has, the higher the range of state hope that individual will experience. Past research (Snyder et al., 1996) developed the State Hope Scale (SHS) using the DHS as a base and transformed items to reflect a more current orientation to goal pursuit. The SHS contains three agency items and three pathways items. Each item was reworked from the DHS to have a greater focus on the present. For example, an "agency item 'I energetically pursue my goals' was changed to

'At the present time, I am energetically pursuing my goals'" (Snyder et al., 1996, p. 322). To keep the participant in the present, the instructions ask respondents to consider what is going on in their lives at that moment and to estimate on a Likert scale how hopeful they are in the "here and now."

The SHS mirrored the validity and reliability of the original hope scale. The initial validation study described a factor analysis on the six-item SHS to produce a two-factor structure that accounted for 71.4% of the total variance (Snyder et al., 1996). Cronbach alphas were very high in the reliability testing of the scale, ranging from .82 to .95 with test–retest reliability hovering around .80 for a 10-week period. Based on responses of over 400 college students, strong correlations were found between the SHS and dispositional hope ($r = .78$ to.79), state self-esteem ($r = .65$ to.79), state positive affect ($r = .55$ to.65), and state negative affect ($r = -.47$ to -50), supporting the convergent and divergent validity of the scale. Further, SHS scores were positively related with the number of responses students got correct on a complex learning task measuring verbal skills ($r = .27$), supporting the predictive validity of the scale in tracking a continuous goal-related performance.

In other studies researchers find that state hope is related to performance in various conditions. Often research has examined state hope and the presence of positive or negative feedback (Peterson, Gerhardt, & Rode, 2006; Ziv, Chaim, & Itamar, 2011) and the effect of state hope on athletic performance (Curry et al., 1997). According to Ziv et al. (2011), when individuals were required to perform on a flying simulator that produced negative feedback about performance, participants who had high dispositional hope tended to also have high state hope pathways even when informed they had failed the performance. This effect was magnified when classical music was playing in the background. Participants who had low dispositional hope had lower state hope after negative feedback regardless of whether music played in the background or not. It was not clear how music interacted with state hope, but there does appear to be a connection between the state hope and their level of dispositional hope. Similarly, past research (Curry et al., 1997) found that state hope acts as a viable mediator for dispositional hope in athletic performance among athletes. When dispositional hope and state hope were included together in a regression analysis, they accounted for 56% of the total variance in predictive athletic performance for

runners. Peterson et al. (2006) confirmed that the relationship between dispositional hope and task performance is mediated by state hope. Participants were given an anagram task and assigned to a low-hope or high-hope condition in which they would receive negative or positive verbal cues. A surprising finding in their study suggested that negative verbal persuasion lowered state hope; however, positive verbal persuasion did not increase state hope scores. Regardless of task, it appears that state hope and dispositional hope interact with one another, and the amount of general hope an individual has affects the levels of state hope he or she experiences even while negotiating negative feedback.

Children's Hope Scale

Snyder et al., (1997) developed a measure of children's hope with the assumption that children would have similar hope-based perceptions in comparison to adults regarding agency, pathways, and goals. Children's hope is a cognitive set that includes the self-beliefs about movement toward goal attainment (agency) and the workable routes to make those goals happen (pathways). The belief that goals are attainable relates to perceptions of control and competence and can elicit positive emotions in the individual. The Child Hope Scale (CHS) contains six items that were developed to be developmentally appropriate for youth ages 8 to 16, but it is also valid for use with individuals up to age 19. Based on these assumptions, Snyder and colleagues did find that high-hope children experience higher levels of optimism, self-esteem, problem-solving capabilities, and academic achievement (Valle, Huebner, & Suldo, 2004).

Past research has shown the CHS to have strong reliability ranging from .72 to .86 and a test–retest relationship of .73 (Snyder et al., 1997). To support convergent validity, Snyder and colleagues found the measure to correlate with parental assessments of the child's hope ($r = .57$, $p < .01$), perceptions of self-worth ($r = .52$, $p < .01$), and depression ($r = -.48$, $p < .01$). Using factor analysis, Valle and Suldo (2004) found that a two-factor model (agency and pathways) produced a significantly better fitting model than a single-factor model when they analyzed the CHS responses of over 400 high school students. Positive correlations ($r = .53$ to .55, $p < .01$) between the CHS and life satisfaction, social support, temperament, and life events support the criterion validity of the measure (Valle & Suldo, 2004). The CHS has been translated into multiple languages that maintain similar findings with the English version of the scale. Marques, Pais-Ribeiro, and Lopez (2009) developed a Portuguese version of the CHS that produced a two-factor structure and total scores significantly correlated with satisfaction with life ($r = .63$, $p < .01$), global self-worth ($r = .60$, $p < .01$), and mental health ($r = .45$, $p < .01$).

Goal-Specific Hope Scale

In more recent research, the Goal-Specific Hope Scale (GSHS; Feldman, Rand, & Kahle-Wrobleski, 2009) was created to specifically address the goal-directed nature of hope that is not measured directly in the DHS. Though past research (Feldman & Snyder, 2002) has attempted to tap into the goal aspect of hope, empirically it has been difficult to prove that hope actually predicts success on goal-specific outcomes. Feldman et al. slightly altered items on the original SHS to produce six items that specifically focus in on three goal-directed agency statements and three goal-directed pathways statements. The measure had high reliability with alphas that ranged from .74 to .88, and the GSHS was also positively correlated with the original hope scale, supporting convergent validity. Using confirmatory factor analysis, a two-factor model (agency and pathways) was found to produce a better fitting model than a one-factor model. To determine predictive validity, 162 college students completed the measure, and results indicated that goal-directed agency but not goal-directed pathways predicted goal attainment. The researchers also found that participants adjusted their hope levels based on the level of success or failure experienced with the goals they valued, primarily within the Agency subscale. This study suggests that the GSHS might be more predictive of goal attainment than the measure of general hope, especially when examining goal-directed agency.

Domain-Specific Hope

Snyder originally theorized hope to be a general construct that covered all life domains; however, research has examined domain-specific hope and found that individuals tend to differ in hope perceptions depending on context. This encouraged the development of the Domain-Specific Hope Scale (DSHS; Sympson, 1999) and launched several studies investigating how hope may be more context-specific. The DSHS began as a 48-item scale assessing agency and pathways across life domains such as social relationships, romantic relationships, leisure, family, work, and academics. Like other published hope measures, participants were to respond in level of agreement across an 8-point Likert scale. Examining perceptions of success in context-specific ways is not new to motivational research. Self-efficacy perceptions are situation-specific and most accurate when they are task-specific as well (Pintrich & Schunk, 2002). In self-efficacy theory, the best way to predict success is through domain specificity. For example, according to Lackaye and Margalit (2006), in order to best predict academic success it is necessary to measure academic self-efficacy. Because hope and self-efficacy have been considered similar constructs (Snyder et al., 2002), it is possible that hope would be most accurately assessed when taking domain or context into account.

A few recent studies reveal the predictive nature of domain-specific hope on specific learning outcomes (Berg et al., 2011; Robinson & Rose, 2010; Sieben, 2013; Sympson, 1999). As previously stated, in domain-specific hope theory, hope functions within specific contexts, therefore necessitating measures of hope to reflect specific contexts as well (Berg et al., 2011; Robinson & Rose, 2010; Snyder et al., 1996). Some research has pulled specific areas from the DSHS and examined them as separate measures. Campbell and Kwon (2001) modified the DSHS to collapse the life domains into two measures: interpersonal hope (social, family, and romantic hope) and achievement-oriented hope (academic and work hope). They compared these DSHS subscores to dysphoria, autonomy, and interpersonal security. Results showed that dysphoria was negatively associated with interpersonal hope ($r = -.33$, $p < .01$) and achievement-oriented hope ($r = -.34$, $p < .01$). Further, interpersonal hope, autonomy, and interpersonal security were significant predictors of dysphoria, whereas achievement-oriented hope was not a significant contributor to the regression analysis. Additional research (Kwon, 2002) continued the investigation of domain-specific hope and how it related to adjustment typologies among college undergraduates. Correlations showed that domains within the DSHS matched up with adjustment types such as social relationship hope with social life adjustment ($r = .61$, $p < .01$) and academic hope with student work role adjustment ($r = .47$, $p < .01$). Correlations such as these supported the convergent validity of the specific subscales of the DSHS showing the subtle differences in hope that would not be accessible using a global measure of hope.

Math Hope Scale

Robinson and Rose (2010) took domain specificity a step further and examined academic domain-specific hope. Using the format of the Academic Hope Scale, the researchers modified the six items to go from general academic statements to statements oriented toward math achievement in math-based courses. Items like "I can think of many ways to make good grades" were altered to "I can think of many ways to make good grades in math classes" to create the Math Hope Scale (MHS). The MHS (see Appendix 7A) contained three agency items and three pathways items that measured perceptions about math success. By transforming the Academic Hope Scale to be even more academic domain-specific, it was anticipated that a better measure of hope could be obtained, especially given that many students feel stronger in certain subject areas over others. The authors make the case that more academic domain-specific hope measures are needed to assess specific areas in which students may be struggling and experiencing low hope.

To ensure that math hope was distinct from academic hope and dispositional hope, Robinson and Rose (2010) performed a principal axis factor analysis using a Promax rotation due to the theoretical overlap among the three scales. The factor solution produced a three-factor model with all three hope scales extracting out as separate factors, accounting for 62.3% of the variance. Math hope accounted for nearly 38% of the variance, academic hope accounted for 15% of the variance, and dispositional hope accounted for about 9% of the variance. Even though each scale did not factor out by agency and pathways subcomponents, there was a clear distinction between the item domains. Math, academic, and dispositional hope were separate factors but were found to be significantly correlated (correlations ranged from .35 to .44) supporting the convergent validity of the instrument. Math hope produced high internal consistency (α = .95) compared to academic hope (α = .89) and dispositional hope (α = .82).

Identifying that math hope is a separate construct from its related scales of academic hope and dispositional hope is one step in validating it as an authentic measure. Next the researchers investigated the predictive validity of the MHS. Because their validation study took place with a college-student population, Rose and Robinson (2010) examined to what extent the three scales would predict final course grade in an introductory college course, the cumulative GPA, and GPA for math courses. Regression analysis showed that academic hope outpredicted dispositional hope and math hope in predicting final course grade (β = .27, $p < .05$) and cumulative GPA (β = .43, $p < .01$); however, math hope was the best predictor of math GPA (β = .39, $p < .05$). These hope measures predicted achievement outcomes beyond self-efficacy, optimism, and mastery orientation. This study was one of the first investigations into academic domain-specific hope, and the results support the idea that the more specific the instrument is, the more sophisticated hope measurement can become.

Writing Hope Scale

Another domain-specific hope construct that has been recently validated and used in academic settings is "writing hope" (Sieben, 2013). Writing hope is a recently established, academic domain-specific, psychometrically sound construct utilized in the teaching and learning of writing to determine the will (agency) and the ways (pathways) that a person has to accomplish worthwhile writing goals (Sieben, 2013). Based on a synthesis of the literature on writing education (Beaufort, 2007; Ferrari, Bouffard, & Rainville, 1998; Gallagher, 2006; Graham & Perin, 2007; Lavelle, 2009; Saddler & Graham, 2007; Smagorinsky, 1992, 2009; Street & Stang, 2009), positive psychology (Snyder et al., 2011), and hope theory (Lopez et al., 2004; Snyder et al., 2002), Sieben (2013) has developed the new theoretical framework of writing hope as the belief that one (a) possesses the necessary cognitive skills and a motivated disposition for writing success and (b) has knowledge of multiple writing strategies to effectively pursue writing goals. Additionally, writing hope includes the self-belief that obstacles during a writing process are possible to overcome by problem-solving and applying alternative strategies when challenges are present.

In response to Robinson and Rose's (2010) assertion that more academic domain-specific hope measures are needed, an academic domain-specific hope scale was created to measure students' hope levels about writing in order to assess areas in which students may be struggling and experiencing low hope with writing. Sieben and Rose (2012) developed the Writing Hope Scale (WHS) to measure students' motivations about and pathways toward accomplishing writing goals. The scale was designed to follow the two-factor model of other previously established valid and reliable hope scales. The six-item WHS (see Appendix 7B) contains three agency items and three pathways items. The scale uses an 8-point Likert scale ranging from 1 (*definitely false*) to 8 (*definitely true*). Sample items in the WHS include "I can think of many ways to improve my writing" and "I actively pursue my writing interests in English classes and other courses." Sieben and Rose established content validity of the measure through development and refinement of the items before the instrument was given to participants.

In the initial study that established the newly created WHS as a valid and reliable measure, a principal component factor analysis with a Promax rotation of the DHS (Snyder et al., 1991) and the WHS indicated the DHS and the WHS are similar scales but distinct constructs (Sieben & Rose, 2012). This study also established writing hope as a separate, domain-specific construct as compared to general hope (Sieben & Rose, 2012). When factoring all survey items of both scales together, two distinct factors emerged: general hope and writing hope. Both of these factors accounted for 63.92% of the total variance in hope scores, with general hope accounting for 46.15% of the variance and writing hope accounting for 17.77% of the variance. A correlation of the total scores from the WHS and the DHS revealed that general hope and writing hope are significantly, directly correlated ($r = .45$, $p < .01$). This moderate, direct correlation further supports the assertion that hope and writing hope are in fact related, yet distinct constructs, thus establishing convergent validity of the writing hope measure.

In order to identify agency (will) and pathways (ways) items in the WHS, Sieben and Rose (2012) conducted another principal component factor analysis with a Promax rotation using the items from the WHS only. This factor analysis revealed the presence of two distinct factors—(a) writing hope pathways and (b) writing hope agency—which together accounted for 81.11% of the total variance in writing hope scores of college students. Writing hope pathways accounted for 72.92% of the total variance in writing hope scores, and writing hope agency accounted for 8.19% of the variance. The presence of the two factors in the WHS supports the measure's construct validity as past studies on hope measures have shown the hope construct to contain both pathways and agency components (Lopez et al., 2000; Snyder, 1996, 2002). Additionally, all items in the structure matrix of the factor analysis showed correlation coefficients

between .77 and .94, thus supporting construct validity of the WHS (Sieben & Rose, 2012). Further statistical tests showed the WHS to have strong reliability as Cronbach's alpha revealed the internal consistency reliability of the measure to be extremely high ($\alpha = .91$).

In a recent study that measured hope and writing hope levels of first-year college students alongside students' writing competency levels, writing hope was able to reliably predict writing ability in college students more so than general hope, revealing predictively validity of the WHS (Sieben, 2013). In fact, writing hope was the only significant predictor of writing ability in college students in the hierarchical multiple regression model that considered general hope, writing hope, writing self-efficacy, and writing self-regulation as predictors in the model (Sieben, 2013). Additionally, a confirmatory factor analysis of all self-belief scales used in the study also revealed writing hope to be a distinct yet related construct to general hope and writing self-efficacy, indicating the scale has strong convergent validity (Sieben, 2013). A second factor analysis of the six-item scale represented the WHS as two factors: (a) writing hope pathways and (b) writing hope agency (Sieben, 2013). In this study, the Cronbach alpha reliability coefficient was a moderately high .78.

Work Hope

Academics is only one area in which hope domain specificity has been applied. Research has also investigated what affects hope has on vocational experiences. Juntunen and Wettersten (2006) developed the Work Hope Scale, which showed strong validity in measuring the work hope individuals perceived to have based on their economic resources. The researchers designed the scale to investigate populations transitioning from welfare to work environments. They were also interested in other populations who may have difficult transitions such as those escaping interpartner violence, those experiencing mental health issues, those with low self-concept, or those lacking social support or child care. The scale consisted of 28 items scored on a Likert scale from 1 (*strongly disagree*) to 7 (*strongly agree*). The Work Hope Scale showed an acceptable factor structure that delineated participants' senses of work hope agency and work hope pathways. However, unlike the original hope scale, Juntunen and Wettersten included a third factor designed to measure work hope goals. Their analysis did not provide strong support for hope as a three-factor model. The total Work Hope Scale was correlated with similar scales like career decision-making, self-efficacy and vocational identity, supporting convergent validity and a moderate correlation with optimism, which the researchers interpreted as support for divergent validity. The internal consistency reliability for the overall scale was high ($\alpha = .90$), and subscales reflected moderate to high reliability as well, (agency = .79; pathways = .85; goals = .84).

This scale may facilitate career counselors in their work with individuals who struggle to produce and maintain realistic work goals. According to the authors, the scale allows a platform for work counselors to do much more than other scales have allowed. First, counselors can address client issues with work hope using a theoretical base, one with empirical evidence and not a reliance on anecdotes or lay interpretations. Second, the Work Hope Scale is a comprehensive assessment of work-related agency, pathways, and goals that the client may be struggling with but may not have the language to disclose. This in-depth assessment provides a deeper investigation into specific problems clients may be dealing with at work and in work transitions. Third, the Work Hope Scale can be administered to groups or individuals, and either context benefits from simple interpretation and assessment that can be applied right away. This also facilitates a directed discussion about how clients may be struggling with hope in general and how they can begin to identify hope-related strategies to improve hopeful outlooks not just for work but also in other life domains.

Employment Hope

Hong, Polanin, and Pigott (2012) developed the Employment Hope Scale (EHS) to determine the impact of psychological well-being in developing economic self-sufficiency and forward movement in the labor market. It was anticipated that the EHS would help monitor the perceptions of individual empowerment and program success during job training or assist agencies designed to support self-sufficiency (Hong et al., 2012). A total of 14 total items capture hope in the employment realm of an 11-point Likert-type scale ranging from 0 to 10. Like Snyder's hope scale, the EHS has two sub-components: (a) psychological empowerment or agency and (b) a movement process toward future goals or pathways. The scale had high internal consistency reliability ($\alpha = .94$). Through factor analysis, the EHS showed a strong two-factor structure representing the pathways and agency components, and these were shown to have strong reliability

(agency = .90, pathways = .93). The EHS was also correlated with the Trait Hope Scale ($r = .40$, $p < .01$) and the Work Hope Scale ($r = .28$, $p < .01$). Examining one's employment hope is one step toward self-sufficiency. Building beliefs of empowerment or agency about employment is a means of facilitating those who are struggling to become more competent workers that can better benefit from training, education, and job experiences.

Conclusion

Extensive research has supported the validity and reliability of hope measurement across genders, ethnicities, adults and children, and differing life domains. According to the early work of Snyder et al., (1991) hope began as a general dispositional theory, one that applied agency and pathways perceptions in a universal manner. This general approach to hope has provided strong evidence that the agency and pathways factors are stable across populations and can consistently predict outcomes related to goal achievement. With the development of the DHS (Sympson, 1999), there was a shift to applying hope in a context-specific way. Assessing hope in certain domains gained traction, and further research produced academic domain-specific hope and work hope. Robinson and Rose (2010) were able to create a math hope measure that outpredicts other hope measures in math-related outcomes; Sieben and Rose (2012) developed a writing hope measure that predicts writing ability. Within the work realm, two instruments (Juntunen & Wettersten, 2006; Hong et al., 2012) were created to expose the hope beliefs of employees and those entering the workforce. Drilling into more specific domains like these allows researchers to utilize more sophisticated measures of hope in assessing perceptions of agency and pathways. Continued exploration of the context-specificity of hope may benefit researchers in locating the main factor affecting one's hope, lending to successful interventions. Hope interventions are available in the literature; however, they have shown to be moderately effective.

Weis and Speridakos (2011) conducted a meta-analysis of studies on the effectiveness of hope interventions. Across the intervention studies they found 19 studies using the Adult Hope Scale or the Children's Hope Scale and seven studies using another hope measure to determine if hope had increased. Results showed that strategies increasing hopefulness were significant but with small effect sizes. The researchers called into question the malleability of hope. An alternative explanation is that participant hope was not being addressed at the domain-specific level and therefore was less effective. All of the studies used a global hope measure. Perhaps more subtle changes in hope could be viewed with a more specific measure. This has been effective in self-efficacy research where specificity is a part of the pre- and postassessments surrounding the intervention. Schwoerer, May, Hollensbe, and Mencl (2008) found that when individuals were trained to cope with challenging work situations, their work specific self-efficacy was significantly increased at the end of the intervention, more so than general self-efficacy.

Future Directions

• Can we better assess hope intervention success through domain-specific hope scales?

• Is domain-specific hope a better predictor of intervention success than global hope?

• Are there certain hope domains that are more responsive to interventions than others?

• Much work has been done to create more domain-specific hope; it is time to use these tools to continue the investigation on the malleability of hope?

References

Babyak, M. A., Snyder, C. R., & Yoshinobu, L. (1993). Psychometric properties of the Hope Scale: A confirmatory factor analysis. *Journal of Research in Personality, 27*, 154–169. doi:10.1006/jrpe.1993.1011.

Beaufort, A. (2007). *College writing and beyond: A new framework for university writing instruction.* Logan: Utah State University Press.

Berg, C. J., Ritschel, L. A., Swan, D. W., An, L. C., & Ahluwalia, J. S. (2011). The role of hope in engaging in healthy behaviors among college students. *American Journal of Health Behavior, 35*, 402–415. doi:10.5993/AJHB.35.4.3

Buechler, S. (1995). Hope as inspiration in psychoanalysis. *Psychoanalytic Dialogues, 5*, 63–74. doi:10.1080/10481889509539050

Campbell, D. G., & Kwon, P. (2001). Domain-specific hope and personal style: Toward an integrative understanding of dysphoria. *Journal of Social and Clinical Psychology, 20*, 498–520. doi:10.1521/jscp.20.4.498.22400

Chang, E. C. (1998). Hope, problem-solving ability, and coping in a college student population: Some implications for theory and practice. *Journal of Clinical Psychology, 54*, 953–962. doi:10.1002/(SICI)1097-4679(199811)54:73.3.CO;2-W

Curry, L. A., & Snyder, C. R. (2000). Hope takes the field: Mind matters in athletic performances. In C. R. Snyder (Ed.), *Handbook of hope: Theory, measures, and applications* (pp. 243–259). San Diego, CA: Academic Press. doi:10.1016/B978-012654050-5/50015-4

Curry, L. A., Snyder, C. R., Cook, D. L., Ruby, B. C., & Rehm, M. (1997). Role of hope in academic and sport achievement. *Journal of Personality and Social Psychology, 73*, 1257–1267. doi:10.1037/0022-3514.73.6.1257

Feldman, D. B., Rand, K. L., & Kahle-Wrobleski, K., (2009). Hope and goal attainment: Testing a basic prediction of hope theory. *Journal of Social and Clinical Psychology, 28*(4), 479–497. doi:10.1521/jscp.2009.28.4.479

Feldman, D. B., & Snyder, C. R. (2002). The State Hope Scale. In J. Maltby, C. A. Lewis, & A. Hill (Eds.), *A handbook of psychological tests.* Lampeter, UK: Edwin Mellen.

Feldman, D. B., & Snyder, C. R. (2005). Hope and the meaningful life: Theoretical and empirical associations between goal-directed thinking and life meaning. *Journal of Social and Clinical Psychology, 24*, 401–421. doi:10.1521/jscp.24.3.401.65616

Ferrari, M., Bouffard, T., & Rainville, L. (1998). What makes a good writer? Differences in good and poor writers' self-regulation of writing. *Instructional Science, 26*, 473–488. doi:10.1023/A:1003202412203

Gallagher, K. (2006). *Teaching adolescent writers.* Portland, ME: Stenhouse Publishers.

Gilman, R., Dooley, J., & Florell, D. (2006). Relative levels of hope and their relationship with academic and psychological indicators among adolescents. *Journal of Social and Clinical Psychology, 25*, 166–178. doi:10.1521/jscp.2006.25.2.166

Graham, S., & Perin, D. (2007). What we know, what we still need to know: Teaching adolescents to write. *Scientific Studies of Reading, 11*, 313–335. doi:10.1080/10888430701530664

Hirsch, J. K., Visser, P. L., Chang, E. C., & Jeglic, E. L. (2012). Race and ethnic differences in hope and hopelessness as moderators of the association between depressive symptoms and suicidal behavior. *Journal of American College Health, 60*(2), 115–125. doi:10.1080/07448481.2011.567402

Hong, P., Polanin, J. R., & Pigott, T. D. (2012). Empirical explanation of the employment hope measure using exploratory factor analysis. *Research on Social Work Practice, 22*, 322–333.

Juntunen, C. L., & Wettersten, K. B. (2006). Work hope: Development and initial validation of a measure. *Journal of Counseling Psychology, 53*, 94–106. doi:10.1037/0022-0167.53.1.94

Kwon, P. (2002). Hope, defense mechanisms, and adjustment: Implications for false hope and defensive hopelessness. *Journal of Personality, 70*, 207–230. doi:10.1111/1467-6494.05003

Lackaye, T., & Margalit, M. (2006). Comparison of achievement, effort, and self-perceptions among students with learning disabilities and their peers from different achievement groups. *Journal of Learning Disabilities, 39*, 432–446. doi:10.1177/00222194060390050501

Lavelle, E. (2009). Writing through college: Self-efficacy and instruction. In R. Beard, D. Myhill, J. Riley, & M. Nystrand (Eds.), *The SAGE handbook of writing development* (pp. 415–422). London: SAGE

Lopez, S. J., Ciarlelli, R., Coffman, L., Stone, M., & Wyatt, L. (2000). Diagnosing for strengths: On measuring hope building blocks. In C.R. Snyder (Ed.), *Handbook of hope: Theory, measures, and applications* (pp. 57–85). San Diego: Academic Press. doi:10.1016/B978-012654050-5/50006-3

Lopez, S. J., Snyder, C. R., Magyar-Moe, J. L., Edwards, L. M., Pedrotti, J. T., Janowski, K., . . . Pressgrove, C. (2004). Strategies for accentuating hope. In P. Linley & S. Joseph (Eds.), *Positive psychology in practice* (pp. 388–404). Hoboken, NJ: Wiley. doi:10.1002/9780470939338.ch24

Marques, S. C., Pais-Ribeiro, J. L., & Lopez, S. J (2009). Validation of the Portuguese version of the Children's Hope

Scale. *School Psychology International, 30*(5), 538–551. doi:10.1177/0143034309107069

Padilla-Walker, L. M., Hardy, S. A., & Christensen, K. J. (2011). Adolescent hope as a mediator between parent-child connectedness and adolescent outcomes. *Journal of Early Adolescence, 31*, 853–879. doi:10.1177/0272431610376249

Park, N., Peterson, C., & Seligman, M. E. P. (2004). Strengths of character and well-being. *Journal of Social and Clinical Psychology, 23*(5), 603–619. doi:10.1521/jscp.23.5.603.50748

Peterson, S. J., Gerhardt, M. W., & Rode, J. C. (2006). Hope, learning goals, and task performance. *Personality and Individual Differences, 40*(6), 1099–1109. doi:10.1016/j.paid.2005.11.005

Peterson, C., & Seligman, M. E. P. (2004). *Character strengths and virtues: A classification and handbook.* New York: Oxford University Press.

Pintrich, P. R., & Schunk, D. H. (2002). *Motivation in education: Theory, research, and applications* (2nd ed.). Upper Saddle River, NJ: Prentice Hall.

Robinson, C., & Rose, S. (2010). Predictive, construct, and convergent validity of general and domain-specific measures of hope for college student academic achievement. *Research in the Schools, 17*(1), 38–52.

Rustøen, T., Cooper, B. A., & Miaskowski, C. (2010). The importance of hope as a mediator of psychological distress and life satisfaction in a community sample of cancer patients. *Cancer Nursing, 33*, 258–267. doi:10.1097/NCC.0b013e3181d6fb61.

Saddler, B., & Graham, S. (2007). The relationship between writing knowledge and writing performance among more and less skilled writers. *Reading & Writing Quarterly, 23*, 231–247. doi:10.1080/10573560701277575

Seligman, M. E. P., Steen, T. A., Park, N., & Peterson, C., (2005). Positive psychology progress: Empirical validations of interventions. *American Psychologist, 60*(5), 410–421. doi:10.1037/0003-066X.60.5.410

Sieben, N. (2013). *Writing hope, self-regulation, and self-efficacy as predictors of writing ability in first-year college students.* Doctoral dissertation. Hofstra University, Hempstead, NY.

Sieben, N., & Rose, S. (2012, August). *Self-regulation, self-efficacy, and hope as predictors of writing ability.* Paper presented at the annual convention of the American Psychological Association, Orlando, FL.

Smagorinsky, P. (1992). How reading model essays affects writers. In J. W. Irwin & M. A. Doyle (Eds.), *Reading/writing connections: Learning from research* (pp. 160–176). Newark, DE: International Reading Association.

Smagorinsky, P. (2009). The architecture of textuality: A semiotic view of composing in and out of school. In R. Beard, D. Myhill, J. Riley, & M. Nystrand (Eds.), *The SAGE handbook of writing development* (pp. 363–373). London: SAGE. doi:10.4135/9780857021069.n25

Smedema, S. M., Catalano, D., & Ebener, D. J. (2010). The relationship of coping, self-worth, and subjective well-being: A structural equation model. *Rehabilitation Counseling Bulletin, 53*, 131–142. doi:10.1177/0034355209358272

Snyder, C. R. (2002). Hope theory: Rainbows in the mind. *Psychological Inquiry, 13*, 249–275. doi:10.1207/S15327965PLI1304_01

Snyder, C. R. (Ed.). (2000). *Handbook of hope: Theory, measures, and applications.* San Diego, CA: Academic Press.

Snyder, C. R., Berg, C., Woodward, J. T., Gum, A., Rand, K. L., . . . Hackman, A. (2005). Hope against the cold: Individual differences in trait hope and acute pain tolerance on the cold pressor task. *Journal of Personality, 73*, 287–312. doi:10.1111/j.1467-6494.2005.00318.x

Snyder, C. R., Harris, C., Anderson, J. R., Holleran, S. A., Irving, L. M., Sigmon, S. T., . . . Harney, P. (1991). The will and the ways: Development and validation of an individual-differences measure of hope. *Journal of Personality and Social Psychology, 60*, 570–585. doi:10.1037/0022-3514.60.4.570

Snyder, C. R., Hoza, B., Pelham, W. E., Rapoff, M., Ware, L., Danovsky, M., . . . Stahl, K. J. (1997). The development and validation of the Children's Hope Scale. *Journal of Pediatric Psychology, 22*(3), 399–421. doi:10.1093/jpepsy/22.3.399

Snyder, C. R., Ilardi, S., Michael, S. T., & Cheavens, J. (2000). Hope theory: Updating a common process for psychological change. In C. R. Snyder & R. E. Ingram (Eds.), *Handbook of psychological change: Psychotherapy processes and practices for the 21st century* (pp. 128–153). New York: Wiley.

Snyder, C. R., Lehman, K. A., Kluck, B., & Monsson, Y. (2006). Hope for rehabilitation and vice versa. *Rehabilitation Psychology, 51*, 89–112. doi:10.1037/0090-5550.51.2.89

Snyder, C. R., Lopez, S. J., & Pedrotti, J. T. (2011). *Positive psychology: The scientific and practical explorations of human strengths.* Thousand Oaks, CA: Sage.

Snyder, C. R., Shorey, H. S., Cheavens, J., Pulvers, K. M., Adams, V. H. III, & Wiklund, C. (2002). Hope and academic success in college. *Journal of Educational Psychology, 94*, 820–826. doi:10.1037//0022-0663.94.4.820

Snyder, C. R., Sympson, S. C., Ybasco, F. C., Border, T. F., Babyak, M. A., & Higgins, L. R., (1996). Development and validation of the State Hope Scale. *Journal of Personality and Social Psychology, 70*(2), 321–335. doi:10.1037/0022-3514.70.2.321

Street, C., & Stang, K. K. (2009). In what ways do teacher education courses change teacher's self-confidence as writers? *Teacher Education Quarterly, 36*(3), 75–94.

Sympson, S.C. (1999). *Validation of the Domain Specific Hope Scale: Exploring hope in life domains.* Unpublished doctoral dissertation, University of Kansas, Lawrence.

Teramoto Pedrotti, J., Edwards, L., & Lopez, S.J., (2008). Promoting hope: Suggestions for school counselors. *Professional School Counseling, 12*(2), 100–107. doi:10.5330/PSC.n.2010-12.100

Valle, M. F., Huebner, E. S., & Suldo, S. M. (2004). Further evaluation of the Children's Hope Scale. *Journal of Psychoeducational Assessment, 22*(4), 320–337. doi:10.1177/073428290402200403

Valle, M. F., & Suldo, S. M. (2004). Further evaluation of the Children's Hope Scale. *Journal of Psychoeducational Assessment, 22*, 320–337.

Weis, R., & Speridakos, E. C. (2011). A meta-analysis of hope enhancement strategies in clinical and community settings. *The Psychology of Well-Being: Theory, Research and Practice, 1*(5), 1–16. doi:10.1186/2211-1522-1-5.

Ziv, N., Chaim, A. B., & Itamar, O. (2011). The effect of positive music and dispositional hope on state hope and affect. *Psychology of Music, 39*, 3–17. doi:10.1177/0305735609351920

Appendix 7A
Math Hope Scale

Directions: Read each item carefully. Think about your classes and your coursework that have involved math and math-related skills. If you are not currently taking a math course, think back to the courses you have had in the past. Using the scale shown below, please select the number that best describes you (1 = *definitely false*, 8 = *definitely true*).

1	2	3	4	5	6	7	8
Definitely False	Mostly False	Somewhat False	Slightly False	Slightly True	Somewhat True	Mostly True	Definitely True

_____ 1. I can think of many ways to make good grades in math classes.
_____ 2. I actively pursue my school work in math.
_____ 3. There are several ways to meet the challenges of any math class.
_____ 4. I am motived to do well in math classes.
_____ 5. I can think of ways to do well in math classes that are important to me.
_____ 6. I am energized when it comes to my school work in math.

Source: Robinson and Rose (2010).

Appendix 7B
Writing Hope Scale

Directions: Please take a moment to contemplate your experiences with writing. Think about your classes and your coursework that have involved writing such as creative writing, persuasive writing, expository writing, narrative writing, poetry writing, research writing, or any other areas that contain writing. If you are not currently taking a writing course, think back to the courses you have had. Once you have this in mind, answer the following questions using the scale provided.

1	2	3	4	5	6	7	8
Definitely False	Mostly False	Somewhat False	Slightly False	Slightly True	Somewhat True	Mostly True	Definitely True

_____ 1. I can think of many ways to improve my writing.
_____ 2. I actively pursue my writing interests in English classes and other courses.
_____ 3. There are several ways to meet the challenges of any writing assignment.
_____ 4. I expect to be successful when I write.
_____ 5. I can think of ways to perform well on writing assignments that are important to me.
_____ 6. I am energized when it comes to writing.

Source: Sieben and Rose (2012).

A Cultural Context Lens of Hope

Lisa M. Edwards *and* Jessica B. McClintock

Abstract

This chapter explores hope theory, measurement (i.e., Children's Hope Scale and Adult Dispositional Hope Scale), and research with regard to diverse racial and ethnic groups. Utilizing a cultural context lens, a case study of a Latina adolescent without documentation is used to illustrate how culture influences goals, obstacles, agency, and pathways. Research about the equivalence of hope across groups, including racial and ethnic groups within the United States as well as in other countries, is reviewed. The chapter concludes with a summary of findings regarding hope measurement and hope theory as they apply to various cultural groups and suggestions for future research in the field.

Key Words: hope, goals, agency, pathways, cultural context, equivalence, Children's Hope Scale, Adult Dispositional Hope Scale

Hope is the perceived ability to produce energy and avenues around obstacles to work toward goals. As such, hope is relevant to everyone and can be utilized by all. Hope has existed across time and cultures and has been demonstrated in the individual and collective feats of all humans (Lopez et al., 2000). While hope may be a universal construct that all can access and develop, it is clear that people use and conceptualize hope in very different ways (Lopez, Snyder, & Teramoto Pedrotti, 2003). From the goals that people develop to the obstacles they face, as well as the factors they use to maintain motivation toward achieving their goals, all exist within a cultural context. Therefore, in order to best understand hope, or any human strength, it is critical to consider cultural context (Sandage, Hill, & Vang, 2003; Sue & Constantine, 2003). In this chapter we attempt to summarize the state of hope measurement and research with regard to diverse groups, utilizing a cultural context lens of hope. We describe how hope might differ across cultures from both theoretical and measurement perspectives. Specifically, we focus on racial and ethnic differences (e.g., multicultural differences) as

well as differences based on country of origin (e.g., cross-cultural differences). For the most part, we also focus on research that has been conducted with the purpose of exploring culture and hope, rather than just studies that have included small groups of participants of different demographic backgrounds. We describe findings about hope measurement and hope theory as they apply to various cultural groups and conclude with suggestions for future research in the field.

A Cultural Context Lens

Goals are the building blocks of hope theory, such that hope necessitates having the ability to develop meaningful goals and work toward them. Goals naturally vary in size, temporal frame (e.g., short-term or long-term), specificity, value, and importance (Rand & Touza, 2016). They should be aspirational and must be valued by the individual (Snyder, 2002). Given the diversity of human experience, it is not hard to imagine, then, the vast array of goals that individuals, families, and communities might develop. These goals will be influenced by any number of cultural background characteristics, including age, gender, disability status, immigration history, sexual orientation, spirituality, and many others. One person's idea of a "positive" or "appropriate" goal might be seen by someone else as inappropriate, pointless, or even harmful. As such, understanding the role of cultural context in goal development and achievement is critical.

In addition to goals, hope theory suggests that all people will encounter obstacles during their goal pursuit (Snyder, 2002). These roadblocks are inevitable and may vary in size. Part of having hope is contending with these obstacles and deciding how to continue to proceed toward goals. Similar to goals, obstacles also should be understood from a cultural context. Individuals across groups may share certain obstacles, such as lack of social support or a lack of self-confidence, yet some obstacles are unique to certain groups. Within the United States, for example, members of marginalized groups such as racial and ethnic minorities often experience systemic obstacles to goal attainment (Lopez et al., 2000). Poverty, lack of access to culturally relevant services, and racism/discrimination are all obstacles that are more commonly experienced by individuals and communities of color, which might make hope particularly relevant (Snyder, 1994). These obstacles have been shown to relate to poorer health and mental health outcomes, as well as academic attainment, financial stability, and many other outcomes (Office of the Surgeon General, 2001). Expecting that an individual's goals would be completely thwarted by these obstacles would clearly be problematic, yet not recognizing that these larger, sociopolitical obstacles exist is equally concerning. Indeed the balance between maintaining hope in spite of challenges, while also acknowledging that some obstacles are insurmountable, is a difficult one.

Finally, the cultural context of *agency* (willpower) and *pathways* (waypower) is critical to understanding hope. Hope theory defines agency as the belief that one has the motivation to reach one's goals and waypower as the belief that one knows how to reach one's goals (Snyder, Rand, & Sigmon, 2002). Without each of these, hope is not present (Edwards, Rand, Lopez, & Snyder, 2007). All individuals can utilize their strengths and supports to maintain motivation and make progress toward goals, but this will likely look different for each person. Some will utilize internal resources, while others may seek help from others in the family or community. We believe it is important to consider culturally relevant strengths, many which have only recently been investigated by the field, as potential resources for maintaining agency and pathways. In particular, we describe cultural values (e.g., familism) and ethnic identity as two strengths that can be utilized by individuals of color.

Cultural values serve as lenses for interacting with the social world and refer to the role of the family, interpersonal interactions, and gender roles, as well as religious and spiritual values (Edwards & Cardemil, 2015). Among Latinos, for example, the cultural value of *familismo* refers to strong feelings of attachment, commitment, loyalty, and obligation to family members (Arredondo & Perez, 2003; Gloria, Ruiz, & Castillo, 2004; Lugo Steidel & Contreras, 2003). Highly familistic individuals tend to conceptualize the family as a source of support that is readily available and provided when needed and may be less inclined to seek external sources of support (Campos et al., 2008). The value of family has been noted in many other cultures, particularly those that are collectivistic in nature, and as such can serve as both a motivational source (e.g., agency; "I'm going to keep working toward this goal because this is something that is important to me and my family") and a resource for support (e.g., pathways; "I'm going to talk to a family member to get advice about how to tackle this obstacle").

Another culturally related strength, ethnic identity, can be a useful agency and pathways resource for ethnically diverse individuals. Ethnic identity is a part of one's self-concept that manifests from a sense of belonging, knowledge, pride, and esteem related to membership with an ethnic group (Piña-Watson, Ojeda, Castellon, & Dornhecker, 2013; Tajfel, 1981). Rather than feeling shameful, alienated, or disconnected, individuals with ethnic identity are proud and feel a sense of affirmation toward their ethnic group. Adolescents with a strong sense of ethnic identity tend to have higher self-esteem, better coping with discrimination, higher academic achievement, and less engagement in risky behaviors, among other positive outcomes (Guilamo-Ramos, 2009; Piña-Watson et al., 2013; Roberts et al., 1999; Umaña-Taylor, Diversi, & Fine, 2002). As such, capitalizing on ethnic identity can serve as agency (e.g., "I'm not giving up because I want to be the first African American in my cohort to accomplish this") and pathways (e.g., "There are skills I have learned from my background that I can use to navigate this obstacle").

There are many other strengths that emerge from cultural traditions and practices that can serve as the pathways and agency components of hope. Pamela Hays (2008) provides a list of culturally related strengths and supports that may be relevant to individuals of diverse backgrounds, which she delineates as personal/individual, interpersonal, and environmental. Some of the individual strengths include religious faith, bilingual or multilingual skills, ethnic pride, and wisdom. Interpersonal supports may be extended families, traditional celebrations and rituals, and cultural or group-specific networks. Finally, examples of environmental conditions include cultural foods, animals, a space for prayer or meditation, and an altar to honor deceased ancestors.

A Case Example: Rocio

To illustrate a cultural context lens for hope theory, consider the case of Rocio, a Latina high school student who is undocumented. Rocio has dreams of going to college and becoming a professional in health sciences. Her goals are long term, but she continuously works toward shorter term goals in her coursework and activities. In many ways she is a typical high schooler, with a very busy schedule, good friends and family, and many dreams for the future. She has been successful in school thus far, obtaining a high grade point average (GPA) in difficult science and math classes, thereby distinguishing herself to the teachers and staff at her high school as someone with great potential for college.

Despite her hard work and success within the academic arena, however, Rocio is keenly aware of the systemic obstacles that she faces because she is undocumented. Each day she fears that her citizenship status might be revealed and that her parents may be deported. She has many unanswered questions about her future and the United States climate toward immigrants. Due to being undocumented, she is unable to obtain a driver's license or an after-school job that could be aligned with her career interests in health sciences and help her save money for college. Rocio is also aware she may not receive admission to a university because of her documentation status, and it is unclear if she will qualify for in-state tuition or scholarships.

Using a cultural context lens of hope theory, Rocio's goals and obstacles show similarities and differences to those of other adolescents her age. She is working toward getting admitted to college, which many youth do, and she is naturally faced with obstacles (e.g., time management, hard courses) to her goal attainment. Additionally, Rocio is faced with challenges not encountered by many of her peers as a result of her lack of US citizenship. These obstacles come from the sociopolitical system in which she lives, and they are unable to be directly changed by Rocio or her family.

Like many culturally diverse individuals, Rocio's agency and pathways may reflect her cultural background. When Rocio finds herself particularly overwhelmed by her financial future, she reminds herself that there are some universities and colleges where she might obtain financial aid and that she will continue to work hard in the next year and summer to save as much money as possible. With these agency thoughts, she is propelled to continue to show up on time for work each day, even though her job is not related to her future goals and to talk with her parents about the family finances. Rocio also decides to phone a financial aid counselor at a nearby college to ask basic questions about budgeting and tuition fees. Though she is not comfortable disclosing her name, she asks general questions about opportunities for aid for someone who is undocumented. Learning practical information about the finances helps her manage concerns about her goal.

At other times Rocio gets discouraged about how much work she is doing in her courses, and she must call upon her agency thoughts to keep going. Rocio reminds herself that her parents came to the United States to help ensure that she could have opportunities and that she is going to be the first to go to college in her family. She knows she wants this goal for herself and for her family, and this is her primary motivation. These agency thoughts work in conjunction with the pathways that she must identify to get around her obstacles. When Rocio is unsure of how to get everything done in her classes or does not understand a concept, she must reach out to her teachers for guidance, and she sometimes talks to her older brother. She also combats her doubts and stress by praying and marshaling her personal faith.

As can be seen by the case of Rocio, all aspects of hope exist in a cultural context. Each person faces unique obstacles, and each individual has unique cultural strengths and resources that might be used to maintain hope. It is also important to note that the added obstacles that individuals from marginalized groups face are sometimes insurmountable, even when the individual is hopeful. Assuming that any motivational or cognitive construct is enough to make any goal possible would be akin to believing that simply having hope could cure a terminal illness. That said, the significant evidence that suggests that being hopeful is important and related to well-being, health, mental health, and athletic and academic outcomes implies that being hopeful may be more useful than not in the face of personal and systemic obstacles (Lopez et al., 2000). Hope can give individuals an edge to achieving their goals, it can help them navigate obstacles better, and it may also help them modify goals when appropriate.

Hope Measurement across Cultures

If hope is relevant to all people, then it would seem as though measuring and understanding hope across cultures would be a simple task. However, as has been discussed, just because hope might be relevant to many does not mean that it means the same thing to everyone or that the measures used to assess hope in one population are valid for another population (Lopez et al., 2003).

Measurement issues across groups are important to consider for any construct before making test selection and interpretation decisions (Ægisdóttir, Gerstein, & Çinarbaş, 2008). Specifically, using measures that have been normed primarily on the mainstream population may create problems with cross-cultural equivalence. In this context, equivalence refers to the comparability of test scores across cultures (Ægisdóttir et al., 2008). Several types of equivalence have been noted in the field, including: functional, conceptual, metric, and linguistic (Ægisdóttir et al., 2008; Lonner, 1985). Functional equivalence addresses the meaning the behavior under investigation (e.g., hope) has in different cultures. Thus, if similar behaviors have different meaning across cultures, they cannot be compared. Conceptual equivalence addresses the connection in meaning ascribed to a behavior or notion. In other words, behaviors and notions may differ in meaning in various cultures. Metric equivalence refers to the psychometric properties of a scale or tool developed to measure the same concept across cultures. In other words, if the psychometric data from multiple cultural groups are identical or very close, the measure is cross-culturally equivalent. Last, linguistic equivalence addresses the phrasing of items in different language versions of an instrument, including the reading difficulty and the natural ease of the items in translated form (Ægisdóttir et al., 2008; Lonner, 1985).

In addition to equivalence issues, bias can also affect generalizability of measures or constructs across cultures. Common sources of bias are construct, method, and item bias (Ægisdóttir et al., 2008). Construct bias occurs when the construct (e.g., hope) being measured is not identical across cultures. Sources for this form of bias are when there is not a complete overlap of how the construct is described across cultural groups and when there are language differences in relation to item content between two versions of an instrument. Nonequivalence is the product of construct bias. Method bias occurs when characteristics or administration methods create differences in scores across cultural groups. Potential sources of this type of bias are differences in response styles, communication problems between researchers and participants, and variations in physical conditions during the administration of the instrument across cultures. Finally, item bias may produce a threat to cross-cultural comparison. Item bias is a form of bias related to measurement at the item level. This form of bias can result from inadequate translation or unsatisfactory item construction. In addition, item bias can occur because item content may not have the same relevance for the cultural groups being compared (Ægisdóttir et al., 2008).

Because providing support for linguistic equivalence is fundamental for translated measures for cross-cultural research, Brislin (1986) has suggested translation methods that increase linguistic equivalence. The first procedure is to translate the instrument using bilingual individuals who speak both the original and the target language. The next procedure is back translation, whereby the translated version of a measure is independently translated back to the original language by different individuals than those who developed the original translation. The two versions are compared to refine and ensure equivalence (Brislin et al., 1973). Once the translation and back translation of the instrument have occurred, various pretest measures are utilized to evaluate the equivalence of the instrument.

Providing support for equivalence is an ongoing process and one that can be complicated. Authors have proposed different terms and guidelines for various types of equivalence, and researchers have utilized different methods depending on the guidelines they are following. Hope measurement across culturally diverse groups has progressed a great deal in the last years, with some studies directly addressing issues of equivalence. In the next section, we review the most commonly used and researched hope measures—the Children's Hope Scale (CHS; Snyder et al., 1997) and the Adult Dispositional Hope Scale (Snyder et al., 1991) —and describe efforts made to provide evidence of equivalence across different racial and ethnic groups.

Hope Scales
Children's Hope Scale

The CHS (Snyder et al., 1997) is a six-item self-report measure of children's hope validated for use with children ages 7 to 17, second grade and beyond (Lopez et al., 2000). The scale is easily hand-scored in about 3 minutes. In accordance with Snyder's model of hope, three of the six items tap into agency ("I believe I'm doing fairly well"), and three are designed to assess pathways ("I have the ability to come up with many ways to solve any problems I may experience"). Participants taking the CHS are instructed to rate statements using a 6-point Likert scale ranging from 1 (*none of the time*) to 6 (*all of the time*). The agency and pathways subscale scores can range from 3 to 18, while total scores (sum of both agency and pathways scores) can range from 6 to 36.

The CHS was standardized using multiple samples of 1,115 schoolchildren in four states, some of who were diagnosed with attention deficit hyperactivity disorder or who had a history physical health issues such as arthritis, sickle cell anemia, or cancer. The norming samples were predominately European American, and, according to Snyder and colleagues (1997) only two samples had sufficient numbers of children from diverse racial/ethnic groups to conduct statistical comparisons. The first sample included 12 African American, 70 Caucasian, and 59 Hispanic children. The racial demographics of the second group included in the scale development were African American ($n = 26$), Caucasian ($n = 130$), and other ($n = 5$).

Internal consistency was demonstrated by the Cronbach alphas computed for the normative samples that ranged from .72 to .86, with a median alpha of .77 (Snyder et al., 1997). The test–retest correlations over a one-month period were found to be both positive and significant, ranging from .70 to .80 (Snyder et al., 1997). Concurrent construct validity was supported in a number of ways. For example, parents' judgments of their child's hope level was found to be correlated positively with their children's scores on the CHS. Youth's CHS scores were also found to be positively correlated with scores on various measures of children's self-perceptions and control-related attributions. Self-perceptions were assessed in the areas of scholastics, social acceptance, athletics, physical appearance, and behavioral conduct (Lopez et al., 2000; Snyder et al., 1997). Children's Hope Scale scores were negatively correlated with scores on the Children's Depression Inventory (Kovacs, 1984). The fact that higher scores on the CHS were not associated with intelligence provided evidence for discriminant validity. However, scores on the CHS were positively correlated with cumulative percentile scores on the Iowa Test of Basic Skills (Snyder et al., 1997).

Studies of Equivalence of the Childen's Hope Scale

In an early study that sought to further evaluate the psychometric properties of the CHS with an ethnically diverse (50% African American) group of high school students, Valle, Huebner, and Suldo (2004) found support for the two-factor structure of the scale. Similarly, Edwards, Ong, and Lopez (2007) assessed the psychometric properties of the CHS in a sample of 135 Mexican American adolescents and found support for the two-factor model. More recently, Shadlow, Boles, Roberts, and Winston (2015) completed a construct validation study of the CHS with a sample of 96 Native American children. Participants were administered the CHS as well as questions from a hope interview ("Tell me about your hopes" and "Is hope important to you? Why?") to ascertain how youth described hope. The results indicated a similar conceptualization and factor structure of hope for the children in this sample, thereby providing support for its equivalence.

The CHS has also been translated to Portuguese (Marques, Pais-Ribeiro, & Lopez, 2009) through the process of translation, back translation, and validation with 367 Portuguese students. The results suggest that the psychometric properties of the translated version are similar to the English version of the scale, providing support for metric and linguistic equivalence of the measure.

Adult Dispositional Hope Scale

The Adult Dispositional Hope Scale or Hope Scale (Snyder et al., 1991) is a 12-item self-report measure of hope developed for use with ages 15 and older. During administration the Hope Scale is referred to as the "Goals Scale" as way to disguise the purpose of the assessment. Participants taking the Adult Hope Scale are instructed to rate statements using a 4-point Likert scale ranging from 1 (*definitely false*) to 4 (*definitely true*). Recently an 8-point Likert scale has been used to encourage score diversity. Four items measure agency ("I've been pretty successful in life"), four measure pathways ("I think of many ways to get out of a jam"), and four items are distracters ("I feel tired most of the time"; Snyder et al., 1991).

The Hope Scale was normed on six separate samples of University of Kansas introductory psychology students and two samples (one outpatient and one inpatient) of individuals in psychological treatment. No information was given about the racial background of the norming sample, though it is assumed to be predominately Caucasian. During the process of norming the Hope Scale, Snyder et al. (1991) found that the average score for college and non-college student samples was 24 using the 4-point scale and 48 using the 8-point scale. Those seeking psychological treatment had lower hope scores; however, these treatment sample participants scored on the hopeful end of the Hope Scale (i.e., approximately a 3 on the 4-point response scale for each hope item).

Reliability coefficients were determined by assessing six samples of undergraduate college students and two samples of individuals in psychological treatment. Cronbach alphas ranged from .74 to .84, and test–retest correlations of .80 or above were found for a period of over 10 weeks (Snyder et al., 1991). Concurrent construct validity was assessed by comparing Hope Scale responses to responses on similar scales of psychological processes (Snyder et al., 1991). For example, Hope Scale scores were found to be correlated in the range of .50 to .60 with measures of optimism (Lopez et al., 2000; Scheier & Carver, 1985). Construct validity was evaluated by testing hope's application to daily life. For example, it was found that high-hope people view their goals in a more positive manner (Snyder et al., 1991). Finally, discriminant validity was supported by comparing Hope Scale scores to unrelated measures, such as the Self-Conscious Scale (Fenigstein, Scheier, & Buss, 1975), and no significant correlations were found (Lopez et al., 2000).

Studies of Equivalence of the Adult Dispositional Hope Scale

Snyder (1995) originally suggested that ethnic minority individuals, in comparison to European Americans, would have less hope due to larger obstacles and differential goal availability. Research suggests, however, that there are not strong differences in levels of hope among ethnically diverse college students (Chang & Banks, 2007; Hirsch, Visser, Chang & Jeglic, 2012). Congruent with hope theory, Chang and Banks also found that hope is significantly related to other variables (e.g., problem orientation) among Latino, African American,

and Asian American college students. Finally, in a study of 1,031 multiethnic adults, Roesch and Vaughn (2006) sought to test the factorial validity and structure of the Hope Scale and found invariance across ethnic groups as well as support for the two-factor model of hope.

The Adult Dispositional Hope Scale has been translated into several languages, including Arabic (Abdel-Khalek & Snyder, 2007), Chinese (Sun, Ng, & Wang, 2012), Dutch (Brouwer, Meijer, Weekers, & Baneke, 2008), French (Gana, Daigre, & Ledrich, 2013), Japanese (Kato & Snyder, 2005), Portuguese (Marques, Lopez, Fontaine, Coimbra, & Mitchell, 2014; Pacico, Bastianello, Zanon, & Hutz, 2013), Slovak (Halama, 1999, 2001), and Spanish (Galiana, Oliver, Sancho, & Tomás, 2015). Of the studies noted previously, several (Galiana et al., 2015; Gana et al., 2013; Marques et al., 2014; Pacico et al., 2013; Sun et al., 2012) used the process of translation and back translation as first steps toward establishing linguistic equivalence.

Support for construct equivalence (e.g., the two-factor structure of hope) was found in samples in China (Sun et al., 2012), France (Gana et al., 2013), Japan (Kato & Snyder, 2005), and Portugal (Marques et al., 2014). In contrast, studies in Brazil (Pacico et al., 2013), Spain (Galiana et al., 2015), and the Netherlands (Brouwer et al., 2008) found that hope was better conceptualized as one factor (Rand & Touza, 2016). In a study comparing Portuguese and American college students, Hutz, Midgett, Pacico, Bastianello, and Zanon (2014) found that relationships between hope and variables such as optimism, life satisfaction, and self-esteem were different, as were levels of hope.

Researchers in Taiwan (Luo, Huang, Lin, & Hwang, 2010) and Japan (Kato, 2006) have sought to expand hope theory by incorporating aspects of each respective culture (Rand & Touza, 2016). Kato's expansion of hope theory included hopeful thinking related to others, while Luo et al. found support for two constructs from Chinese culture in addition to pathways and agency: transcendental adaptation and persisting effort. Together these new constructs formed "peaceful hope," which was shown to predict lower levels of hopelessness than agency and pathways.

How Hope Operates in Diverse Cultural Groups

In addition to studies providing support for equivalence of the construct of hope and hope measurement within racial and ethnic groups both within and outside of the United States, a growing number of studies have attempted to understand hope and its relation to other constructs. Chang and Banks' (2007) study of college students suggested that while levels of hope were similar across ethnic groups and hope was associated with other positive constructs, there were variations in the predictors of agency and pathways for specific groups. For example, the strongest predictor of agency differed for Africans Americans (negative problem orientation), Asian Americans (positive affect), Latinos (rational problem-solving), and European Americans (life satisfaction).

Using a daily diary methodology, Roesch, Duangado, Vaughn, Aldridge, and Villodas (2010) investigated hope in a diverse sample of 126 low-socioeconomic status (SES), minority adolescents. The study assessed CHS hope components (i.e., agency, pathways) on the use of daily coping strategies over a five-day period. The analysis revealed that pathways thinking predicted direct problem-solving (Roesch et al., 2010) among all participants. In addition, the agency component of hope predicted greater seeking of instrumental support. While differences in hope among specific ethnic/racial groups were not explored, this study helped to provide support for the relationship between hope and related variables in a low-SES diverse sample.

Authors have investigated the role of hope, depression, and suicidal risk in ethnically diverse samples. In one study of college students, Hirsch, Visser, Chang, and Jeglic (2012) found that higher levels of hope buffered the relationship between depressive symptoms and suicidality among White and Hispanic participants but not among African American participants. Among Latino college students, Chang el al. (2013) found that hope significantly predicted hopelessness and suicide risk. Importantly, findings also revealed that a positive problem orientation uniquely predicted suicide risk, such that "doubling up" on positive future cognitions (through both hope and problem orientation) might be most useful against hopelessness and suicidal behavior.

A series of studies by Adams and colleagues (Adams, 2002; Adams & Jackson, 2000; Adams & Nelson, 2001) examined hope in African Americans of various ages. Adams and Jackson analyzed a national survey of African Americans and found a correlation between high hope and increased satisfaction. Similarly, Adams and Nelson examined life satisfaction among African American fathers and indicated that hope predicted perceptions of their ability to support their families above and beyond parental strain and self-esteem. Analogous findings were found in a study examining African American mothers (Adams et al., 2003).

A few researchers have investigated hope and its relationship to discrimination. In one study, Danoff-Burg, Prelow, and Swenson (2004) examined hope and coping with race-related stress on life satisfaction in a sample of 100 African American undergraduate college students. Results indicated that high-hope students reported more use of problem-focused and greater coping efficacy with race-related stressors than students with low hope. Of note, high-hope participants' life satisfaction was associated with fewer active coping strategies and vice versa for low-hope students. Coping and hope had no effect on life satisfaction, a finding that contrasts previous research about hope among White populations.

In a larger study of African American college students, Banks, Singleton, and Kohn-Wood (2008) similarly found that individuals with high hope reported experiencing more depressive symptoms when reporting discrimination compared to low-hope individuals. In contrast to the idea that hope may serve as a buffer to discrimination, these findings instead suggest that at high levels of discrimination hope is no longer protective because the obstacle may be too large. The authors remind us that though hope may not buffer the negative effects of discrimination for African American students, it is still a useful construct because of its relation to positive adjustment variables. Nonetheless, professionals working with African American college students should be aware of the complex relationship between these variables in order to best work with this population.

In one of the few qualitative studies of hope, McClintock (2015) utilized grounded theory methodology (Strauss & Corbin, 1990) to explore how resilient African American youth use hope in their lives. The participants included in the study met criteria for possessing a "hopeful profile," which included high hope scores (29 or above), resilience factors (presence of risk and protective factors such as low SES, family and friend support), a high GPA (3.0 or above), and teacher/counselor ratings' of positive adaptation. Seventeen adolescents (5 male, 12 female) participated in individual interviews in which they were queried about their goals as well as how they created pathways and maintained movement toward their goals when faced with obstacles.

The storyline or theory that emerged from the analysis revealed that resilient African American youth use hope to facilitate academic and long-term life goals by calling upon multiple support systems and persevering to combat obstacles such as racial discrimination and procrastination. Participants revealed that they were primarily pursuing academic goals that were influenced by family role models and aspirations for an improved quality of life. Goals were generally academic in nature possibly due to the study being conducted in the school setting. In order to accomplish their goals in the face of a variety of obstacles (e.g., racial discrimination, procrastination), participants utilized various social support systems (e.g., family, friends, teachers) and personal coping strategies (e.g., perseverance). Furthermore, participants offered ideas for other youth to reach their goals.

Future Directions

Research in the area of hope across cultures has seen a large increase recent years. From investigations about hope in specific groups to translation of hope measures that can now be used with individuals in many different countries, the field has clearly begun to attend to cultural context with this construct. As can be seen from this review, one of the most important findings from this growing body of research is that hope looks similar and can be measured in the same way in some groups but not in others. In some cases, it appears that the structure and definition of hope may differ for groups, and in other cases predictors and correlates of hope may differ. Indeed, the early cautions (e.g., Lopez et al., 2003) against assuming that hope can be used in the same way by all were wise.

While the findings about hope and hope measurement among diverse cultural groups have given us a flavor for some of the complexities of this construct, there is still much more work to be done. Generally speaking, there is still a dearth of research about individuals of color and hope as compared to European Americans (Chang & Banks, 2007) and a need for more attention to translations of the CHS. Additionally, studies are needed that describe *how* individuals utilize pathways and agency thinking toward goal pursuits (Edwards, Rand, Lopez, & Snyder, 2007). Qualitative studies are particularly useful for exploring phenomena such as these, and McClintock's (2015) project about how African Americans use hope is an example of this work. Finally, more research is needed that explores how hope might change over the life course or as diverse individuals cope with general and culture-specific obstacles. The complex processes and interactions between experiences of discrimination and poverty and the resilience exhibited by ethnic minority youth and adults, for example, provides an area ripe for investigation with longitudinal methods.

It is inspiring to see that theorists and researchers alike now commonly acknowledge the importance of context in understanding human emotions and behavior. Indeed, using a cultural context lens to consider the role of hope helps to reveal the unique aspects and functioning of this construct. Existing research with culturally diverse individuals suggests there are compelling nuances that still must be further understood, however, and it is hoped that researchers will take this charge and continue to move the field forward.

Future Directions

• In what ways does the structure and meaning of hope differ across culturally diverse groups?
• How do individuals utilize pathways and agency thinking toward goal pursuits?
• How can hope help culturally diverse individuals cope with stressors such as discrimination and poverty?

References

Abdel-Khalek, A., & Snyder, C. R. (2007). Correlates and predictors of an Arabic translation of the Snyder Hope Scale. *The Journal of Positive Psychology, 2*(4), 228–235. doi:10.1080/17439760701552337

Adams, V. III. (2002). *Changes in African mothers' hope and life satisfaction between 1980 and 1999.* Unpublished manuscript, Department of Psychology, University of Kansas, Lawrence.

Adams, V. H. III, & Jackson, J. S. (2000). The contribution of hope to the quality of life among aging African Americans: 1980–1992. *International Journal of Aging & Human Development, 50*(4), 279–295. doi:10.2190/awb4-7clu-a2ep-bqlf

Adams, V. III, & Nelson, J. (2001). Hope, happiness, and African American fathers: Changes between 1980 and 1992. *African American Research Perspectives, 7*(1), 148–156.

Adams, V. III, Rand, K. L., Kahle, K., Snyder, C., Berg, C., King, E. A., & Rodrigues-Hanley, A. (2003). African Americans' hope and coping with racism stressors. In R. Jacoby & G. Keinan (Eds.), *Between stress and hope: From a disease-centered to a health-centered perspective* (pp. 235–249). Westport, CT: Praeger.

Ægisdóttir, S., Gerstein, L. H., & Çinarbaş, D. C. (2008). Methodological issues in cross-cultural counseling research equivalence, bias, and translations. *The Counseling Psychologist, 36*(2), 188–219. doi:10.1177/0011000007305384

Arredondo, P., & Perez, P. (2003). Expanding multicultural competence through social justice leadership. *The Counseling Psychologist, 31*(3), 282–289. doi:10.1177/0011000003031003003

Banks, K. H., Singleton, J. L., & Kohn-Wood, L. P. (2008). The influence of hope on the relationship between racial discrimination and depressive symptoms. *Journal of Multicultural Counseling and Development, 36*, 231–244. doi:10.1002/j.2161-1912.2008.tb00085.x

Brislin, R. N. (1986). The wording and translation of research instruments. In W. J. Lonner & J. W. Berry (Eds.), *Field methods in cross cultural research* (pp. 159–163). Beverly Hills, CA: SAGE.

Brislin, R. W., Lonner, W. J., & Thorndike, R. M. (1973). Cross-cultural research methods. New York: Wiley.

Brouwer, D., Meijer, R. R., Weekers, A. M., & Baneke, J. J. (2008). On the dimensionality of the Dispositional Hope Scale. *Psychological Assessment, 20*(3), 310. doi:10.1037/1040-3590.20.3.310

Campos, B., Schetter, C. D., Abdou, C. M., Hobel, C. J., Glynn, L. M., & Sandman, C. A. (2008). Familialism, social support, and stress: Positive implications for pregnant Latinas. *Cultural Diversity and Ethnic Minority Psychology, 14*(2), 155–162. doi:10.1037/1099-9809.14.2.155

Chang, E. C., & Banks, K. H. (2007). The color and texture of hope: Some preliminary findings and implications for hope theory and counseling among diverse racial/ethnic groups. *Cultural Diversity and Ethnic Minority Psychology, 13*(2), 94–103. doi:10.1037/1099-9809.13.2.94

Chang, E. C., Elizabeth, A. Y., Kahle, E. R., Jeglic, E. L., & Hirsch, J. K. (2013). Is doubling up on positive future cognitions associated with lower suicidal risk in Latinos?: A look at hope and positive problem orientation. *Cognitive Therapy and Research, 37*(6), 1285–1293. doi:10.1007/s10608-013-9572-x

Danoff-Burg, S., Prelow, H. M., & Swenson, R. R. (2004). Hope and life satisfaction in Black college students coping with race-related stress. *Journal of Black Psychology, 30*(2), 208–228. doi:10.1177/0095798403260725

Edwards, L. M., & Cardemil, E. V. (2015). Clinical approaches to assessing cultural values among Latinos. In K. F. Geisinger (Ed.), *Psychological testing of Hispanics: Clinical, cultural, and intellectual issues* (2nd ed., pp. 215–236). Washington, DC: American Psychological Association. doi:10.1037/14668-012

Edwards, L. M., Ong, A.D., & Lopez, S. J. (2007).Hope measurement in Mexican American youth. *Hispanic Journal of Behavioral Sciences, 29*, 225–241. doi:10.1177/0739986307299692

Edwards, L. M., Rand, K. L., Lopez, S. J., & Snyder, C. R. (2007). Understanding hope: A review of measurement and construct validity research. In A. D. Ong & M. H. M. van Dulmen (Eds.), *Oxford handbook of methods in positive psychology* (pp. 83–95). New York: Oxford University Press.

Fenigstein, A., Scheier, M. F., & Buss, A. H. (1975). Public and private self-consciousness: Assessment and theory. *Journal of Consulting and Clinical Psychology, 43*(4), 522–527. doi:10.1037/h0076760

Galiana, L., Oliver, A., Sancho, P., & Tomás, J. M. (2015). Dimensionality and validation of the Dispositional Hope Scale in a Spanish sample. *Social Indicators Research, 120*(1), 297–308. doi:10.1007/s11205-014-0582-1

Gana, K., Daigre, S., & Ledrich, J. (2013). Psychometric properties of the French version of the Adult Dispositional Hope Scale. *Assessment, 20*(1), 114–118. doi:10.1177/1073191112468315

Gloria, A. M., Ruiz, E. L., & Castillo, E. M. (2004). Counseling and psychotherapy with Latino and Latina clients. In T. B. Smith (Ed.), *Practicing multiculturalism: Affirming diversity in counseling and psychology* (pp. 167–189). Boston: Pearson.

Guilamo-Ramos, V. (2009). Maternal influence on adolescent self-esteem, ethnic pride and intentions to engage in risk behavior in Latino youth. *Prevention Science, 10*(4), 366–375. doi:10.1007/s11121-009-0138-9

Halama, P. (1999). Snyder's Hope Scale. *Studia Psychologica, 41*(4), 329–332.

Halama, P. (2001). Slovenská verzia Snyderovej Škály Nádeje: Preklad a adaptácia. = The Slovak version of Snyder's Hope Scale: Translation and adaptation. *Československá Psychologie, 45*(2), 135–142.

Hays, Pamela A., (2008). Addressing cultural complexities in practice: Assessment, diagnosis, and therapy (2nd ed., pp. 21–39). Washington, DC: American Psychological Association. doi:10.1037/11650-000

Hirsch, J. K., Visser, P. L., Chang, E. C., & Jeglic, E. L. (2012). Race and ethnic differences in hope and hopelessness as moderators of the association between depressive symptoms and suicidal behavior. *Journal of American College Health, 60*(2), 115–125. doi:10.1080/07448481.2011.567402

Hutz, C. S., Midgett, A., Pacico, J. C., Bastianello, M. R., & Zanon, C. (2014). The relationship of hope, optimism, self-esteem, subjective well-being, and personality in Brazilians and Americans. *Psychology, 5*(6), 514–522. doi:10.4236/psych.2014.56061

Kato, T. (2006). Role of hope and coping behavior in interpersonal stress. *Japanese Journal of Health Psychology, 19*(1), 25–36.

Kato, T., & Snyder, C. R. (2005). The relationship between hope and subjective well-being: Reliability and validity of the Dispositional Hope Scale, Japanese version. *Japanese Journal of Psychology, 76*, 227–234.

Kovacs, M. (1984). The Children's Depression, Inventory (CDI). *Psychopharmacology Bulletin, 21*(4), 995–998.

Lonner, W. J. (1985). Issues in testing and assessment in cross-cultural counseling. *The Counseling Psychologist, 13*(4), 599–614. doi:10.1177/0011000085134004

Lopez, S. J., Gariglietti, K. P., McDermott, D., Sherwin, E. D., Floyd, R. K., Rand, K., Snyder, C. R. (2000). Hope for the evolution of diversity: On leveling the field of dreams. In C. R. Snyder (Ed.), *Handbook of hope: Theory, measures and applications* (pp. 223–244). San Diego, CA: Academic Press.

Lopez, S. J., Synder, C. R., & Pedrotti, J. T. (2003). Hope: Many definitions, many measures. In S. J. Lopez & C. R. Snyder (Eds.), *positive psychological assessment: A handbook of models and measures* (pp. 91–107). Washington, DC: American Psychological Association. doi:10.1037/10612-006

Luo, Y.-C., Huang, L.-L., Lin, Y.-C., & Hwang, K.-K. (2010). The duality of hope: The development and validation of a new scale. *Chinese Journal of Psychology, 52*(3), 265–285.

Marques, S. C., Lopez, S. J., Fontaine, A. M., Coimbra, S., & Mitchell, J. (2014). Validation of a Portuguese version of the Snyder Hope Scale in a sample of high school students. *Journal of Psychoeducational Assessment, 32*(8), 781–786. doi:10.1177/0734282914540865

Marques, S. C., Pais-Ribeiro, J. L., & Lopez, S. J. (2009). Validation of a Portuguese version of the Children's Hope Scale. *School Psychology International, 30*(5), 538–551. doi:10.1177/0143034309107069

McClintock, J. B. (2015). *Hope among resilient African American adolescents.* Unpublished doctoral dissertation. Marquette University, Milwaukee, WI.

Office of the Surgeon General, Center for Mental Health Services, National Institute of Mental Health. (2001). *Mental health: Culture, race, and ethnicity: A supplement to mental health: A report of the Surgeon General*. Rockville, MD: Substance Abuse and Mental Health Services Administration. Retrieved from http://www.ncbi.nlm.nih.gov/books/NBK44249/

Pacico, J. C., Bastianello, M. R., Zanon, C., & Hutz, C. S. (2013). Adaptation and validation of the Dispositional Hope Scale for adolescents. *Psicologia: Reflexão e Crítica, 26*(3), 488–492. doi:10.1590/S0102-79722013000300008

Piña-Watson, B., Ojeda, L., Castellon, N. E., & Dornhecker, M. (2013). Familismo, ethnic identity, and bicultural stress as predictors of Mexican American adolescents' positive psychological functioning. *Journal of Latina/o Psychology, 1*(4), 204–217. doi:10.1037/lat0000006

Rand, K., & Touza, K.K. (in press). Hope theory. In S. J. Lopez, L. M. Edwards, & S. Marques (Eds.), *Handbook of positive psychology* (3rd ed.). New York: Oxford University Press.

Roberts, R. E., Phinney, J. S., Masse, L. C., Chen, Y. R., Roberts, C. R., & Romero, A. (1999). The structure of ethnic identity of young adolescents from diverse ethnocultural groups. *The Journal of Early Adolescence, 19*, 301–322. doi:10.1177/0272431699019003001

Roesch, S. C., Duangado, K. M., Vaughn, A. A., Aldridge, A. A., & Villodas, F. (2010). Dispositional hope and the propensity to cope: A daily diary assessment of minority adolescents. *Cultural Diversity and Ethnic Minority Psychology, 16*(2), 191. doi:10.1037/a0016114

Roesch, S. C., & Vaughn, A. A. (2006). Evidence for the factorial validity of the Dispositional Hope Scale: Cross-ethnic and cross-gender measurement equivalence. *European Journal of Psychological Assessment, 22*(2), 78–84. doi:10.1027/1015-5759.22.2.78. doi:10.1027/1015-5759.22.2.78

Sandage, S. J., Hill, P. C., & Vang, H. C. (2003). Toward a multicultural positive psychology: Indigenous forgiveness and Hmong culture. *The Counseling Psychologist, 31*(5), 564–591. doi:10.1177/0011000003325650

Scheier, M. F., & Carver, C. S. (1985). Optimism, coping, and health: Assessment and implications of generalized outcome expectancies. *Health Psychology, 4*(3), 219–247. doi:10.1037/0278-6133.4.3.219

Shadlow, J. O., Boles, R. E., Roberts, M. C., & Winston, L. (2015). Native American children and their reports of hope: Construct validation of the Children's Hope Scale.

Journal of Child and Family Studies, 24(6), 1707–1714. doi:10.1007/s10826-014-9974-8

Snyder, C. R. (1994). *The psychology of hope: You can get there from here*. New York: Free Press.

Snyder, C. R. (2002). Hope theory: Rainbows in the mind. *Psychological Inquiry, 13*(4), 249–275. doi:10.1207/S15327965PLI1304_01

Snyder, C. R., Harris, C., Anderson, J. R., Holleran, S. A., Irving, L. M., Sigmon, S. T., . . . Harney, P. (1991). The will and the ways: Development and validation of an individual-differences measure of hope. *Journal of Personality and Social Psychology, 60*(4), 570–585. doi:10.1037/0022-3514.60.4.570

Snyder, C. R., Hoza, B., Pelham, W. E., Rapoff, M., Ware, L., Danovsky, M., . . . Stahl, K. J. (1997). The development and validation of the Children's Hope Scale. *Journal of Pediatric Psychology, 22*(3), 399–421. doi:10.1093/jpepsy/22.3.399

Snyder, C. R., Rand, K. L., & Sigmon, D. R. (2002). Hope theory: A member of the positive psychology family. In C. R. Snyder, S. J. Lopez, C. R. Snyder, & S. J. Lopez (Eds.), *Handbook of positive psychology* (pp. 257–276). New York: Oxford University Press.

Steidel, A. G. L., & Contreras, J. M. (2003). A new familism scale for use with Latino populations. *Hispanic Journal of Behavioral Sciences, 25*(3), 312–330. doi:10.1177/0739986303256912

Strauss, A. L., & Corbin, J. M. (1990). *Basics of qualitative research: Grounded theory procedures and techniques/Anselm Strauss, Juliet Corbin*. Newbury Park, CA: SAGE.

Sue, D. W., & Constantine, M. G. (2003). Optimal human functioning in people of color in the United States. *Counseling Psychology and Optimal Human Functioning, 34*, 151–169. doi:10.1177/0011000005281318

Sun, Q., Ng, K., & Wang, C. (2012). A validation study on a new Chinese version of the Dispositional Hope Scale. *Measurement & Evaluation in Counseling & Development, 45*(2), 133–148. doi:10.1177/0748175611429011

Tajfel, H. (1981). *Human groups and social categories: Studies in social psychology*. New York: Cambridge University Press.

Umaña-Taylor, A. J., Diversi, M., & Fine, M. A. (2002). Ethnic identity and self-esteem of Latino adolescents distinctions among the Latino populations. *Journal of Adolescent Research, 17*(3), 303–327. doi:10.1177/0743558402173005

Valle, M. F., Huebner, E., & Suldo, S. M. (2004). Further evaluation of the Children's Hope Scale. *Journal of Psychoeducational Assessment, 22*, 320–337. doi:10.1177/073428290402200403

Promoting Hope

The Will and the Ways in School: Hope as a Factor in Academic Success

Jennifer Teramoto Pedrotti

Abstract

The school environment is a key place in which to address development of numerous positive traits and characteristics. Hope is a one construct that addresses goal-setting and progress and is linked to many other positive behaviors and characteristics including resilience, optimism, school and athletic achievement, and well-being in general. Grounding today's children in skills and mindsets that assist them in determining how to get the things they what they want in life may help them to stay on healthy tracks academically throughout their scholastic career. Past and current research has shown that hope is easily instilled and that it can be increased through simple interventions in a variety of different populations. School personnel such as teachers, counselors, and administrators can all play a role in the development of this trait and can help to direct parents in using the hope model with children as well.

Key Words: hope, academic achievement, school, children, interventions

Children across the world spend a significant amount of their time in school classrooms. As such, the school environment becomes a key place to instill behaviors and character traits that will be useful in life both in and outside of the classroom. Investigating the potential for increasing these types of positive psychological constructs within the school environment becomes a very worthwhile area of research. Hope is a construct that has been oft studied in schools and in relation to success in life in general. The simplicity of the hope model defined by Snyder and colleagues (1991) and the evidence that shows that it is a malleable trait (Pedrotti, Edwards, & Lopez, 2008) make it a prime candidate for inclusion in multiple ways in the school environment.

Definitions

Snyder and colleagues (1991) conceptualize hope as a two-factor construct aimed at explaining goal-directed processes. In this model, the *pathways* component is described as the ability to delineate routes to find a way toward one's goals, and to find new routes around obstacles if necessary, whereas the *agency* component is the ability to sustain motivation to move along these identified routes. Snyder and colleagues are clear in the fact that both components are necessary in order for individuals to make progress toward their goals. In addition, Snyder and colleagues address the ability of a high-hope individual to move around various *obstacles* that may occur in the middle of previously identified pathways; a high-hope individual is able to create new routes when thwarted in this way. Hope has been shown to be correlated with many other positive characteristics and traits, including optimism (Feldman & Kubota, 2015), self-efficacy (Gallagher, Marques, & Lopez, 2017; Phan, 2013), life satisfaction (Chang, 1998; Choma, Busseri, & Sadava, 2014), and general positive psychological functioning (Marques, Lopez, Fontaine, Coimbra, & Mitchell, 2015; Snyder et al., 1991). In addition, it has been shown to correlate with less depression (Kwon, 2000; Mathew, Dunning, Coats, & Whelan, 2014) and better physical health (Barnett, 2014; Wrobleski & Snyder, 2005). All of these positive characteristics may assist a child or adolescent in his or her academic process.

Measuring Hope in Schools

Measures for different age groups have been created including the original Adult Hope Scale (Snyder et al., 1991), the Children's Hope Scale (Snyder et al., 1997), and the Young Children's Hope Scale (McDermott et al., 1997). Finally, Snyder, Feldman, Shorey, and Rand (2002) have shown that it is possible for individuals to have high global hope, though this does not translate to higher hope in academic domains, thus these researchers encourage measurement of hope in specific domains in addition to global hope using the Domain Specific Hope Scale (Sympson, 1999) or the Children's Domain Specific Hope Scale (Woodruff, 2003). Knowledge about ways in which hope can be measured, particularly relevant to school settings, helps to determine how hope can be increased in these environments. In addition, once levels of hope have been established for particular groups, charting can occur with regard to increases and/or decreases that happen due to particular events or circumstances or as a result of various interventions (Pedrotti et al., 2008).

Academically Relevant Correlates to Hope

It is well established that hope as a construct is consistently linked to areas of academic achievement. From the beginning of Snyder and colleagues' (1991) validation of their Adult Hope Scale, significant and positive correlations have been found between hope scores and grade point averages at many levels of schooling (e.g., Snyder et al., 2002). Many researchers have sought to elucidate the way this relationship functions and have found that hope (sometimes along with other positive characteristics such as self-efficacy) contributes significantly to the variance found in academic performance across a number of different groups (Adelabu, 2008; Phan, 2013). Many have discussed the value of hope in academic success as a form of its relationships to intentional and motivational factors (Onwuegbuzie & Snyder, 2000), as well as a future-oriented perspective (Adelabu, 2008), both of which have shown to be pathways toward academic achievement. In addition, others have discussed links between hope and effort, such that effort appears to contribute to hope development and maintenance in academic arenas (Levi, Einav, Ziv, Raskind, & Margalit, 2014). As an example, a hopeful student is able to conceive of a reasonable goal they would like to achieve (i.e., having a future-oriented time perspective) and is planful (i.e., able to intentionally use pathways) about the types of steps they take toward this particular goal, while being motivated (i.e., possessing effort or agency) to move along those pathways, has a good chance of success. This may be particularly relevant in school-related pursuits, which often have concrete steps that one might take toward the completion of a course, certificate, or degree.

It follows, then, that hope is also related to and influential in development of other positive cognitive characteristics that appear to assist in making progress academically. Self-efficacy, for example, is a common correlate found in studies investigating hope and has been shown to contribute to academic success as well. In a study investigating the pathways toward academic success, Phan (2013) showed that self-efficacy plays a significant role. In this study, the researcher looked at the dynamic interplay between the constructs of hope and self-efficacy and found, via latent growth modeling, that self-efficacy seemed to influence the development of hope in the adolescent sample. Specifically, "students who reported higher initial levels of self-efficacy beliefs for academic learning tended to show a more rapid increase in hope over time compared with students who reported lower initial levels of self-efficacy" (Phan, 2013, p. 100). Phan discusses the possibility of self-efficacy beliefs either enhancing or hindering the development of hope about future goals and states that this might be particularly relevant during adolescence. Understanding the dynamic interaction between these constructs asserts the value of each to the other and helps to clarify use relevant to academic achievement and progress.

Several researchers have developed models that include hope to better define the process that may occur in terms of the links found here. Levi and colleagues (2014) for example, used structural equation modeling to show pathways between hope, three types of self-efficacy (academic, social, and emotional), effort, expected grades, and actual grades. In this study, indirect links were found between hope and actual grades, though hope influenced expected grades very strongly ($r = .69$), which in turn were strongly and positively linked to actual grades achieved ($r = .59$). Thus much empirical data supports connections between hope and academic success in the form of grades.

Hope also has been found to be linked to various affective variables that might assist in strong academic performance or positive association with school in general. Though hope is associated with positive affect in many studies, Ciarrochi, Heaven, and Davies (2007) looked at this association in the context of academic achievement and found that hope was the strongest predictor of positive affect as well as the strongest predictor of grades (even after controlling for academic skill). As positive affect has been shown elsewhere to be linked to better coping and potentially broader thinking in general (Fredrickson, 2000), this may provide a clue to the impact of hope on academic achievement as well. Perhaps even more interesting to parents and today's teachers, hope was significantly negatively associated with sadness and hostility, both characteristics that may disrupt academic goals and success (Ciarrochi et al., 2007).

In another school context, Fite and colleagues (2014) studied the buffering effect of hope against behaviors that thwart academic achievement (e.g., delinquency, substance use, etc.) in Latino adolescents. Results showed that use of some substances (e.g., marijuana, tobacco) appeared to depend on levels of hope, with higher hope adolescents choosing to forgo these activities. In addition, hope was a moderator in the relationship between alcohol use and depressive symptoms, such that alcohol and depressive symptoms were only linked in low-hope students in this study (Fite et al., 2014). These are, again, important findings for use in other settings.

Unsurprisingly, hope is also found to be connected to career goals and efficacy in moving toward these goals. Described by Juntunen and Wettersten (2006) as *work hope*, this construct is defined as the ability to move along various pathways and with motivation toward succeeding in career arenas. In a study by Taylor et al. (2015), work-based education was found to stimulate work hope and the creation of goals regarding career and work plans. It has been posited that "work hope may have particular relevance for better understanding the vocational needs of disenfranchised populations" (Juntunen & Wettersten, 2006, p. 96), and as such more study in this area has broad benefits toward increasing understanding of the role work-based education in the development of hope.

Hope in a Multicultural Context

As is true with all psychological constructs, cultural context must be considered with regard to hope, both in terms of the equivalence across groups and utility with multiple cultural groups. Though the original validation of the Adult Hope Scale (Snyder et al., 1991) and its other versions did not include culturally diverse samples, several studies since have investigated hope in multicultural populations. Some of these findings have shown that hope might be differentially linked to a variety of other variables in different cultural groups; however, hope still has utility in different cultural populations. A few of these studies are reviewed here as they have much relevance in today's increasingly diverse school environments.

Chang and Banks (2007), in a groundbreaking study, investigated the construct of hope in adults from several different racial and ethnic groups: African American, Latino/a, Asian American, and White Americans. In this study, the authors conducted analyses to determine the best predictors of the two components of hope (pathways and agency) in these different racial and ethnic groups. Findings showed that different constructs and traits were the best predictor in the different groups. For example, with regard to agentic thinking, in the Latino sample the best predictor was rational problem-solving, though it was life satisfaction in the White American sample, negative problem-solving in the African American sample, and positive affect in the Asian American sample. Similarly, different constructs were the best predictors of pathways thinking, with positive problem orientation best predicting this for both African American and Asian American samples, life satisfaction for the Latino sample, and positive affect for the White American sample (Chang & Banks, 2007). It is important to note that hope and its overall correlations with these other variables were significant and still in the direction that one might predict, so hope still has utility in each of these populations. That said, the way in which it might be stimulated or manifested could be slightly different depending on ethnic group. These differences are important to take into account particularly when interpreting and disseminating findings.

Specific to the school setting, there may be some variables such as ethnic identity that must be considered particularly in non-White populations as being valuable to the development of hope and/or achievement. In a study by Adelabu (2008), regression analysis showed that both hope and ethnic identity account for a large amount of the variance in academic achievement of African American adolescents. Further, hope and ethnic identity were found to be significantly and positively correlated with one another (Adelabu, 2008). Of note, however, is the fact that ethnic identity was a stronger predictor of academic achievement in comparison to hope, showing the importance of attending to ethnic identity when looking at links between hope and academic achievement in diverse populations.

Other researchers have found similar results when hope has been targeted with African American children with the goal of increasing and preserving academic achievement through positive encouragement toward ethnic identity development. Ani (2013) states that clear links exist theoretically and conceptually between Mazama's (2001) descriptions of *Afrocentricity*, which describes culturally relevant ways of thinking of oneself and moving forward in the African American community, and Snyder's (1991) concept of hope. Ani conducted qualitative research with six African American children and found that a strong sense of ethnic identity appeared to generate hope for these participants, which in turn appeared to lead to higher desires and a positive feeling of a responsibility to achieve. The fact that the participants in Ani's study were from impoverished backgrounds and environments also shows that finding hope in these situations and making use of goals to move toward better circumstances is a valuable course of study with regard to similar populations.

Finally, measurement issues with regard to hope in different cultural groups must be attended to within multicultural populations. Though *linguistic* equivalence has been established in Spanish, for example, not much is known about the *construct* equivalence of hope across various cultural groups. Further investigation of the definition of hope used in different cultural groups to ascertain if there are cultural differences in definition and manifestation must be conducted. Though this type of research is beginning, there is not currently enough information to draw conclusions (Christopher & Howe, 2014). In addition, Snyder and colleagues' (1991) definition is both linear and Western focused in terms of its future-oriented nature, and this may limit its utility in some non-Western groups (Lopez, Pedrotti, & Snyder, 2015). Thus care must be taken in interpreting the results in these samples.

Enhancing and Engendering Hope

As it has been established that hope is a useful construct in the area of academic success, working to develop hope is a valued pursuit. Methods of enhancing of hope may differ depending on role in the school process, however. The next sections focus on ways to enhance and engender hope in different parts of the school environment.

School Counselors Promoting Hope

Several ideas and strategies for increasing hope in youth in both individual and groups have been presented in the literature (e.g., Pedrotti et al., 2008). Individually, school counselors may help students to develop personally relevant goals that can be pursued throughout a time frame and potentially spanning a variety of life domains. This idea of *relevance* is particularly important, and school counselors might assist students in developing lists of potential goals and then rank-ordering them in terms of personal priority (Pedrotti et al., 2008). School counselors can then work with students to move through Snyder's hope model to develop reasonable pathways, consider possible obstacles, and identify sources of agency or motivation to help them to stay on track with these valued goals. A student who has the goal of raising his math grade, for example, might list specific pathways such as obtaining a tutor, asking the teacher for help, or spending a particular amount of time on this subject per day toward his overall goal. Next the counselor might strategize with this student about how to move along these various pathways with role-play, suggestions, and dialogue. Agency would also need to be attended to here, and various sources might be identified together such as pride in self to achieve this goal, happiness of teacher or parents regarding the student's success, or remembering that this grade may help with future goals of college or work in the future. Last, obstacles would need to be identified (e.g., lack of money for a tutor, a nonhelpful teacher, etc.), and plans could be worked out to move around these obstacles should they occur. There are several ways in which this task could be described to children. One discussed by Lopez (2012) is the creation of a HopeMap, a tangible way of writing down the goal process in several stages. In this way, the goal and the steps it takes to get there are concretized in the mind of the goal pursuer.

In terms of group techniques, many different programs have been developed over the years aimed at increasing hope in youth. One of the first interventions aimed at increasing hope in children was developed by McDermott, Callahan, Gingerich, Hastins, and Gariglietti (1997) and involved eight weekly sessions in classrooms with first- through sixth-graders. The program consisted of 30-minute sessions that involved listening to stories about high-hope children, with an accompanying group discussion about hope and goal-setting. Children involved then identified goals talked about by the protagonists of the stories and investigated ways to use hope concepts in their own lives. Results of this program showed slight increases in scores on the Children's Hope Scale (Snyder et al., 1997) from

Session 1 to 8, and teacher ratings of hope supported the increases. These results laid a promising groundwork for other programs to follow.

The Making Hope Happen program (MHH; Pedrotti, Lopez, & Krieshok, 2000) is another example of this type of school-based hope intervention. The MHH involved a five-week (45-minute sessions), school-based program delivered to junior high school students as a part of a family and consumer sciences class. Each group contained 8 to 10 students and was led by two graduate students. Week 1 focused on the introduction of the concept of hope, pathways, agency, and obstacles and called for the development of individual positive and specific goals that students planned to make progress toward over the course of the five weeks. Various stories were shared with the groups to assist the identification of these concepts in actual situations. In addition, in Week 1, "hope buddies" were formed; these were pairs determined by the researchers after assessing baseline hope and consisted of a higher hope student and a lower hope student to facilitate modeling. Interestingly, very few of these partnerships reflected friendships that had existed previously; the students who scored high on hope tended to associate with one another, as did those who scored lower on hope. Implications for these types of natural relationships are important as well and should be studied further. Week 2 reintroduced the concepts via the use of new narratives and presented the acronym of G-POWER, in which each letter stood for a component in the hope process (goal, pathways, obstacles, willpower (i.e., agency), evaluate, rethink and try again; Pedrotti et al., 2000) to help students remember the main components of the process. Weeks 3 and 4 utilized different manipulatives (e.g., a hope board game and "Hope Talk" worksheets) to further help students to understand the concepts and begin to use them in their lives. The Hope Game (Pedrotti et al., 2000) required players to obtain both pathways and willpower cards to move forward along a path and reiterated the need to possess both components to make progress toward a goal. The Hope Talk worksheets asked students to rework various sentences that were not particularly hopeful ("I will never be good at writing") to still-truthful statements that included hopeful elements ("Writing is a hard subject for me, but I can get help and keep trying"). In each of the four sessions students met with their hope buddies to review progress and help each other to stay motivated. Finally, participants discussed progress made over the five weeks of the program in their last week in a hope story-sharing session. Students offered encouragement, feedback, and ideas for future steps during this celebratory session.

The Children's Hope Scale (Snyder et al., 1997) was administered to all participants prior to the first session of the MHH program and then again following the five weeks. Significant gains were shown to have occurred in overall hope, pathways, and agency over the five weeks, and increases in these scores were found to be significantly larger than those found in a control group (students taking an alternate class to the family and consumer sciences class). These gains remained sustained after a six-week follow-up assessment (Pedrotti et al., 2000), suggesting that students continued to utilize the basic ideas and tenets presented in the MHH program. This type of program was a manageable endeavor when integrated into a class period and might be something that school counselors could refine or emulate in its entirety in their school as a part of their role there. Other examples (e.g., MHH for elementary [Edwards & Lopez, 2000] and high school [Bouwkamp & Lopez, 2001]) are reviewed elsewhere (Pedrotti et al., 2008).

Teachers' Roles in Enhancing Hope

There are multiple ways that teachers can utilize hope in the classroom on a day-to-day basis. Teaching the model and encouraging use of it to tackle both small and larger goals can easily be assimilated into everyday activity in the classrooms. In addition, utilizing hope to make progress on group goals or class goals may assist in strengthening agency and pathways for future endeavors. Taking time to develop class pathways toward success and identifying sources of agency are worthwhile practices in the classroom. Using "hope talk" as described in MHH (Pedrotti et al., 2000) may be another way that teachers can bring hope into the classroom. Teachers might help their students to reframe self-talk (e.g., "I am too nervous to take a test" into "Testing is hard for me, but I can use strategies to succeed.") to potentially influence outcomes on various activities. Other authors have noted that, like emotions, hope appears to be "contagious," in the sense that a hopeful person's presence may encourage others to be more hopeful as well (Lopez, 2013). Lopez discusses modeling hope, as well as including it as a piece of instrumental or intrusive support, and cites these as ways to pass it on. Hopeful teachers are particularly situated to have this type of effect on their students and can work to increase their own hope with the goal of increasing it in their students as well.

In a study conducted with teachers of students who had been diagnosed with learning disabilities, researchers found that teachers who had the highest hope felt more confident in their abilities to work with students with learning disabilities (Levi, Einav, Raskind, Ziv, & Margalit, 2013). In this way, teachers' personal hope may not only be contagious but was linked to self-efficacy at being an effective teacher. This type of self-belief is no doubt helpful for the students of these teachers. In addition, if the teachers in this study apply the goal processes depicted in Snyder's (1991) hope theory, they may have a better ability to pass these concepts on to their students organically (Levi et al., 2013). Making sure we nurture and enhance hope in teachers as well as students might provide an exponential effect.

Last, some research explicitly shows that teacher support is linked to the development of hope. Van Ryzin (2011), in a study looking at several protective factors, found that hope was significantly correlated with student-perceived teacher support. The teacher support scale included items such as "My teachers want me to do my best in schoolwork" and "My teachers really care about me" (Van Ryzin, 2011, p. 1572). Findings in this study showed that teachers can influence development and enhancement of hope, particularly via impacts on student engagement.

Parents' Role in Hope Development

Parents may increase hope in the same ways noted earlier for teachers and/or work together with teachers to provide hopeful frameworks. Schools may be able to assist parents in creating home curriculum or tips and strategies for including hope in various ways in the home environment. A two-pronged approach (school + home) may have more impact on creating hopeful mindsets in students. Other research has shown that hope may mediate the relationship between life satisfaction in adolescents and attachment to parents (Jiang, Huebner, & Hills, 2013). As attachment to parents has been shown to assist in the development of many positive qualities in adolescents that relate to academic success and life success in general, the discussion of hope from teachers to parents has the potential to be very valuable.

Promoting Hope on the College Campus

Though much of the research on hope in school environments focuses on primary and lower secondary education, some researchers have also endeavored to create workshops or other focused interventions to promote hope in the college environment.

Davidson, Feldman, and Margalit (2012) developed an intervention for first-year college students aimed at increasing hope, among other related constructs. The workshop was designed to teach students about hope and other positive constructs with the goal of increasing these states/traits. Though there were no significant differences in grades at the time of the intervention between lower hope participants and higher hope participants, results showed that students who achieved higher levels of hope after the workshop went on to earn higher grades in the semester following the intervention; the lower hope students grades had significantly lower grades than those with high hope in this semester (Davidson et al., 2012). Feldman and Dreher (2012) found that it is possible to increase hope in college students as a result of one 90-minute session. Thus there appear to be efficient and fast ways of working to affect academic achievement via hope enhancement in a college setting.

Future Directions
Hope within a Diverse Student Body

As diversity is increasing across the United States, further investigating constructs that can be utilized with a diverse student population is critical to providing fair and inclusive opportunities in school settings. Hope has been discussed as a benefit in a number of different populations in studies that seem to suggest that hope has value for multiple types of individuals.[1]

Many have used the word "hopeless" to describe impoverished neighborhoods and disenfranchised environments when discussing the plight of low-income children and adolescents across our country. As such, use of hope to help students in these types of school settings could prove invaluable if strategies around obstacles and movement toward goals that include escape from poverty could be created. Bennett, Wood, Butterfield, Kraemer, and Goldhagen (2014) studied hope within a human capital investment framework to investigate the benefits of high hope in youth toward health. Findings showed that high hope was statistically most related to higher social capital (e.g., school, family, connectedness) and educational capital (e.g., parent education; Bennett et al., 2014). This provides implications for the benefits of developing hope via the school environment as a mode of potentially increasing benefits in other areas including physical health. Many of the circumstances that make academic success difficult that are described in impoverished neighborhoods might not able to be directly influenced by the school environment (e.g., enough food in the household, number of people living in the household, household income and purchasing capability, etc.); however, hope via social and educational capital can be affected within the school environment if care is taken by teachers and administrators to bring this topic into the curriculum and school environment at large. More research on ways to train teachers, school counselors, and administrators to accomplish this is needed.

Further, unique obstacles may exist for children and adolescents from traditionally marginalized backgrounds, and utilization of the hope model to deal with these may be particularly beneficial. Obstacles such as racism, microaggressions, heterosexism, and others must be attended to in such a way as to validate the reality of these concepts in the lives of many individuals in the United States. Some research has found that coping with obstacles such as these may lead to better overall coping strategies and resilience (Romero, Edwards, Fryberg, & Orduña, 2014). Understanding more about the ways in which the school setting can help students to develop appropriate pathways around these obstacles toward goals of academic achievement is a very valuable course of study in future hope research.

Hope has also been utilized in working with children who are atypical in terms of learning style or behavior. Some researchers are proposing that working to increase hope levels in children diagnosed with attention deficit hyperactivity disorder (ADHD) may be an effective way to assist them in developing goals. Shiri, Tenenbaum, Sapir-Budnero, and Wexler (2014) discuss the benefits that high hope could provide to these children due to the myriad obstacles that may occur for them minute to minute related to difficulty in sustaining attention, especially in the classroom. One of the main problems, Shiri and colleagues state with regard to utilizing this model, is the fact that children diagnosed with ADHD may have difficulty in "creating and holding images" that could be a major part of envisioning the goal process. As a way of working around this issue, Shiri and colleagues suggest a virtual reality program in which images are created and manifested visually for the children so that they can attend to them long enough to flesh out strong pathways and move along them. This type of innovative research has the potential to broaden the utility of hope in the classroom in ways that have previously not been attempted.

Children who have suffered trauma or other kinds of experiences that have affected them in negative ways in the past may benefit greatly from exposure to the hope model. In a program called the Hope Project, practitioners worked with refugee children from Sierra Leone, Iraq, Sudan, Pakistan, the Philippines, and China (Yohani, 2008) in a school setting. The program utilized many different modalities including art, the making of a quilt, and photography. The research conducted on this program is currently more anecdotal, but it shows the vast utility of hope in a different context. Here hope was used to help children make plans for the future and deal with obstacles including areas that reflected fear of their past experiences or even fear of daring to hope (called "the dark side of hope" by some of the participants; Yohani, 2008, p. 319). Though these children were from different contexts and countries and not in their home country when this program was implemented, the positive anecdotal feedback calls for more work in this particular area with more formal measurement. Other research has investigated the use of hope in therapy settings and other non-school environments (e.g., McCrea, 2014), but bringing this type of work into the school setting with this type of population may also be an area to explore more.

Conclusion

Nobel Peace Prize–winning author Elie Wiesel (1986) is quoted as saying "Just as despair can come to one only from other human beings, hope, too, can be given to one only by other human beings." This is a point to take to heart when working with children and adolescents in the school system. School counselors, administrators, and teachers are in prime positions to assist in the development of hope in their diverse student body—or its demise. Hope is beneficial to academic achievement both directly (as related to correlations connected with markers such as grade point averages) and in conjunction with other characteristics (e.g., self-efficacy, optimism, life satisfaction, etc.) that may aid in achievement (Snyder et al., 2002). It has been shown to be useful within many different types of populations and in different ways. More research is needed on hope within diverse populations, but here, too, preliminary study is promising. As such, helping schools to develop hopeful classrooms and campuses is a worthy pursuit.

Future Direction Questions:

• How might hope function differently in groups of children from collectivist versus individualist backgrounds?

- How can we effectively train teachers, school counselors, and administrators to utilize hope more purposefully in the curriculum to assist with equality of experience across students with different socioeconomic backgrounds?
- How can the hope model help to address institutional obstacles such as racism, microaggressions, heterosexism, and other -isms in school-aged children from underrepresented groups and help them to find pathways and motivation to move around them?
- How can more opportunities to utilize the hope model be created for children dealing with diagnoses such ADHD, to assist with potential difficulty at holding onto a goal image, as Shiri and colleagues (2014) suggest?
- How might the hope model be applied and formally measured in populations that deal with what Yohani (2008) calls "the dark side of hope" (i.e., dealing with a fear of daring to hope)?

Note

1. In thinking of diversity, a broad definition is used in this chapter including areas of race, ethnicity, socioeconomic status, disability, gender, sexual orientation, and other social identity facets (Hays, 2016).

References

Adelabu, D. H. (2008). Future time perspective, hope, and ethnic identity among African American adolescents. *Urban Education, 43*, 347–360. doi:10.1177/0042085907311806

Ani, A. (2013). In spite of racism, inequality, and school failure: Defining hope with achieving Black children. *Journal of Negro Education, 82*, 408–421. doi:10.7709/jnegroeducation.82.4.0408

Barnett, M. D. (2014). Future orientation and health among older adults: The importance of hope. *Educational Gerontology, 40*, 745–755. doi:10.1080/03601277.2014.898496

Bennett, A., Wood, D., Butterfield, R., Kraemer, D. F., & Goldhagen, J. (2014). Finding hope in hopeless environments. *International Journal of Child Health and Human Development, 7*, 313–324.

Bouwkamp, J. L., & Lopez, S. J. (2001). *Making hope happen: A program for inner-city adolescents.* Unpublished master's thesis. University of Kansas, Lawrence.

Chang, E. C. (1998). Hope, problem-solving ability, and coping in a college student population: Some implications for theory and practice. *Journal of Clinical Psychology, 54*, 953–962. doi:10.1002/(SICI)1097-4679(199811)54:7<953:AID-JCLP9>3.0.CO;2-F

Chang, E. C., & Banks, K. H. (2007). The color and texture of hope: Some preliminary findings and implications for hope theory and counseling among diverse racial/ethnic groups. *Cultural Diversity and Ethnic Minority Psychology, 13*, 94–103. doi:10.1037/1099-9809.13.2.94

Choma, B. L., Busseri, M. A., & Sadava, S. W. (2014). Deciphering subjective trajectories for life satisfaction using self-versus-normative other discrepancies, self-esteem,

and hope. *European Journal of Personality, 28*, 107–119. doi:10.1002/per.1889

Christopher, J. C., & Howe, K. L. (2014). Future directions for a more multiculturally competent (and humble) positive psychology. In J. T. Pedrotti & L. M. Edwards (Eds.), *Perspectives on the intersection of multiculturalism and positive psychology* (pp. 253–266). New York: Springer Science. doi:10.1007/978-94-017-8654-6_17

Ciarrochi, J., Heaven, P. C. L., & Davies, F. (2007). The impact of hope, self-esteem, and attributional style on adolescents' school grades and emotional well-being: A longitudinal study. *Journal of Research in Personality, 41*, 1161–1178. doi:10.1016/j.jrp.2007.02.001

Davidson, O. B., Feldman, D. B., & Margalit, M. (2012). A focused intervention for 1st-year college students: Promoting hope, sense of coherence, and self-efficacy. *The Journal of Psychology: Interdisciplinary and Applied, 146*, 333–352. doi:10.1080/00223980.2011.634862

Edwards, L. M., & Lopez, S. J. (2000). Making hope happen for kids. Unpublished protocol.

Feldman, D. B., & Dreher, D. E. (2012). Can hope be changed in 90 minutes? Testing the efficacy of a single-session goal-pursuit intervention for college students. *Journal of Happiness Studies, 13*, 745–759. doi:10.1007/s10902-011-9292-4

Feldman, D. B., & Kubota, M. (2015). Hope, self-efficacy, optimism, and academic achievement: Distinguishing constructs and levels of specificity in predicting college grade-point average. *Learning and Individual Differences, 37*, 210–216. doi:10.1016/j.lindif.2014.11.022

Fite, P. J., Gabrielli, J., Cooley, J. L., Haas, S. M., Frazer, A., Rubens, S. L., & Johnson-Motoyama, M. (2014). Hope as a moderator of the associations between common risk factors and frequency of substance use among Latino adolescents. *Journal of Psychopathology and Behavioral Assessment, 36*, 653–662. doi:10.1007/s10862-014-9426-1

Fredrickson, B. L. (2000). Cultivating positive emotions to optimize health and well-being. *Prevention & Treatment, 3*. doi:10.1037/1522-3736.3.1.31a

Gallagher, M. W., Marques, S. C., & Lopez, S. J. (2017). Hope and the academic trajectory of college students. *Journal of Happiness Studies, 18*(2), 341–352. doi:10.1007/s10902-016-9727-z

Hays, P. A. (2016). *Addressing cultural complexities in practice.* Washington, DC: American Psychological Association.

Jiang, X., Huebner, E. S., & Hills, K. J. (2013). Parent attachment and early adolescents' life satisfaction: The mediating effect of hope. *Psychology in the Schools, 50*, 340–352. doi:10.1002/pits.21680

Juntunen, C. L., & Wettersten, K. B. (2006). Work hope: Development and initial validation of a measure. *Journal of Counseling Psychology, 53*, 94–106. doi:10.1037/0022-0167.53.1.94

Kwon, P. (2000). Hope and dysphoria: The moderating role of defense mechanisms. *Journal of Personality, 68*, 199–223. doi:10.1111/1467-6494.00095

Levi, U., Einav, M., Raskind, I., Ziv, O., & Margalit, M. (2013). Helping students with LD to succeed: The role of teachers' hope, sense of coherence and specific self-efficacy. *European Journal of Special Needs Education, 28*, 427–439. doi:10.1080/08856257.2013.820457

Levi, U., Einav, M., Ziv, O., Raskind, I., & Margalit, M. (2014). Academic expectations and actual achievements: The roles of hope and effort. *European Journal* of Psychology of Education, 29, 367–386. doi:10.1007/s10212-013-0203-4

Lopez, S. J. (2012). Mapping out hope. Retrieved from http://shanelopez.com/about/hope-how-tos/

Lopez, S. J. (2013). Making hope happen: Create the future you want for yourself and others. New York: Atria.

Lopez, S. J., Pedrotti, J. T., & Snyder, C. R. (2015). Positive psychology: The scientific and practical explorations of human strengths. Thousand Oaks, CA: SAGE.

Marques, S. C., Lopez, S. J., Fontaine, A. M., Coimbra, S., & Mitchell, J. (2015). How much hope is enough? Levels of hope and students' school and psychological functioning. Psychology in the Schools, 52, 325–334. doi:10.1002/pits.21833

Mathew, J., Dunning, C., Coats, C., & Whelan, T. (2014). The influence of hope on multidimensional perfectionism and depression. Personality and Individual Differences, 70, 66–71.

Mazama, A. (2001). The Afrocentric paradigm: Contours and definitions. Journal of Black Studies, 31, 387–405. doi:10.1177/002193470103100401

McCrea, K. T. (2014). How does that itsy bitsy spider do it?: Severely traumatized children's development of resilience in psychotherapy. Journal of Infant, Child, & Adolescent Psychotherapy, 13, 89–109. doi:10.1080/15289168.2014.905319

McDermott, D., Callahan, B., Gingerich, K., Hastins, & Gariglietti, K. (August, 1997). Working together to bring hope to our children. Paper presented at the annual convention of the Kansas Counselors Association, Hutchinson, KS.

McDermott, D., Hastings, S. L., Gariglietti, K. P., & Callahan, B. (1997). The development of the Young Children's Hope Scale. Unpublished manuscript, University of Kansas, Lawrence.

Onwuegbuzie, A. J., & Snyder, C. R. (2000). Relations between hope and graduate students' coping strategies for studying and examination-taking. Psychological Reports, 86, 803–806. doi:10.2466/PR0.86.3.803-806

Pedrotti, J. T., Edwards, L. M., & Lopez, S. J. (2008). Promoting hope: Suggestions for school counselors. Professional School Counseling, 12, 100–107. doi:10.5330/PSC.n.2010-12.100

Pedrotti, J. T., Lopez, S. J., & Krieshok, T. S. (2000). Making hope happen: A program for fostering strengths in adolescents. Unpublished master's thesis. University of Kansas, Lawrence.

Phan, H. P. (2013). Examination of self-efficacy and hope: A developmental approach using latent growth modeling. The Journal of Educational Research, 106, 93–104. doi:10.1080/00220671.2012.667008

Romero, A. J., Edwards, L. M., Fryberg, S. A., & Orduña, M. (2014). Resilience to discrimination stress across ethnic identity stages of development. Journal of Applied Social Psychology, 44, 1–11. doi:10.1111/jasp.12192

Shiri, S., Tenenbaum, A., Sapir-Budnero, O., & Wexler, I. D. (2014). Elevating hope among children with attention deficit and hyperactivity disorder through virtual reality. Frontiers in Human Neuroscience, 8, 198.

Snyder, C. R., Feldman, D. B., Shorey, H. S., & Rand, K. L. (2002). Hopeful choices: A school counselor's guide to hope theory. Professional School Counseling, 5, 298–307.

Snyder, C. R., Harris, C., Anderson, J. R., Holleran, S. A., Irving, L. M., Sigmon, S. T., . . . Harney, P. (1991). The will and the ways: Development and validation of an individual-differences measure of hope. Journal of Personality and Social Psychology, 60, 570–585. doi:10.1037/0022-3514.60.4.570

Snyder, C. R., Hoza, B., Pelham, W. E., Rapoff, M., Ware, L., Danovsky, M., & Stahl, K. J. (1997). The development and validation of the Children's Hope Scale. Journal of Pediatric Psychology, 22, 399–421. doi:10.1093/jpepsy/22.3.399

Sympson, S. (1999). Validation of the domain specific hope scale: Exploring hope in life domains. Unpublished doctoral dissertation, University of Kansas, Lawrence.

Taylor, C. E., Hutchison, N. L., Ingersoll, M., Dalton, S. J., Dods, J., Godden, L., & Chin, P. (2015). At-risk youth find work hope in work-based education. Exceptionality Education International, 25, 158–174.

Van Ryzin, M. J. (2011). Protective factors at school: Reciprocal effects among adolescents' perceptions of the school environment, engagement in learning, and hope. Journal of Youth and Adolescence, 40, 1568–1580. doi:10.1007/s10964-011-9637-7

Wiesel, E. (11 December, 1986). Hope, despair, and memory. Nobel lecture. Oslo, Norway.

Woodruff, T. W. (2003). Development and validation of the children's domain-specific hope scale. Dissertation Abstracts International, 63, 4962.

Wrobleski, K., & Snyder, C. R. (2005). Hopeful thinking in older adults: Back to the future. Experimental Aging Research, 31, 217–233. doi:10.1080/03610730590915452

Yohani, S. C. (2008). Creating an ecology of hope: Arts-based interventions with refugee children. Child & Adolescent Social Work Journal, 25, 309–323. doi:10.1007/s10560-008-0129-x

Promoting Hope in Children

Susana C. Marques *and* Shane J. Lopez

Abstract

This chapter provides an overview of the literature base supporting hope theory and examines milestones in the promotion of hope. Accordingly, it describes the tenets of hope theory and development and provides a review of the hope system and the instruments that can be used with young children and adolescents. Brief illustrations on how hope can be detected are provided. Moreover, the chapter summarizes the hope research conducted over the past 25 years with children and adolescents and emphasizes how to help them capitalize on their strengths and build hope, along with its implications for use by parents and schools professionals.

Key Words: children and adolescents, hope literature, hope theory, instruments, research

The concept of hope has been important since classical times. Previous reviews (e.g., Lopez, Snyder, & Teramoto Pedrotti, 2003) located more than two dozen scholarly theories or definitions of hope (and a handful of validated measures) and discussed some of their common characteristics. Generally conceptualizations of hope emphasize a person's thoughts and feelings about the future and thoughts and feelings about personal capacity to make the future better.

Snyder and his colleagues (Snyder, 1994; Snyder et al., 1991) developed a cognitive motivational model of hope based in goal-directed thinking that has received much attention both within and outside the field of psychology (Marques, Lopez, Fontaine, Coimbra, & Mitchell, 2014). According to hope theory (Snyder et al., 1991), hope reflects individuals' perceptions regarding their capacities to (a) clearly conceptualize goals, (b) develop the specific strategies to reach those goals (pathways thinking), and (c) initiate and sustain the motivation for using those strategies (agency thinking). Goals, whether short term or long term, provide the targets of mental action sequences and vary in the degree to which they are specified, but all goals

must be of sufficient value to warrant sustained conscious thought about them (Snyder, 2002). Pathways thinking refers to a person's perceived ability to generate workable routes to desired goals (Snyder, Shorey, et al., 2002) and the production of several pathways is important when encountering impediments. Agency thinking is the motivational component in hope theory that reflects a person's cognitions about his or her ability to begin and sustain goal-directed behavior (Snyder et al., 2003), therefore it takes on special significance when people encounter challenges or obstacles (Snyder, 2002). Pathways and agency thinking are positively related, additive and reciprocal, but neither component alone defines hope, nor are they synonymous. When people have a robust level of hope they will convey messages such as "I'll find a way to get this done!"; "I can do this"; and "I am not going to be stopped." Whereas other characteristics popularized by positive psychology such as optimism (Scheier & Carver, 1985) or goal theory (Covington, 2000; Dweck, 1999), and some characteristics previously established such as self-efficacy (Bandura, 1982) and problem-solving (Heppner & Petersen, 1982), give differentially weighted emphases to the goal itself or to the future-oriented agency- or pathways-related processes, hope theory equally emphasizes all of these goal-pursuit components (Snyder, 1994).

Hope Development

In detailing the importance of hope to success in life, it is necessary to elucidate first the mechanisms through which hopeful thought develops. Snyder (1994, 2000a, 2000b) established a developmental framework for how hopeful thought takes form. One of the first goals of a newborn is to predict and control its environment, a necessary ability for survival. In fact, many developmental theorists (e.g., Berlyne, 1960; Kagan, 1972) have held that feelings of disorientation and confusion motivate individuals to improve their causal understanding. These feelings reflect unfulfilled needs in infants that are ultimately sated by the development of hopeful thought (Snyder, Feldman, Shorey, & Rand, 2002). Pathways thinking is the first component of hope to develop in children. Upon birth, infants are inundated with a bewildering sensory input, but with time each sensation is imbued with meaning and linked temporally with another sensation. These connections turn into anticipatory thoughts in the infant's mind. This anticipation is the mechanism by which children later are able to cognitively chain events together to form if-then thinking, the precursor to pathways thinking.

Agency thought also develops early in life. By the age of 12 to 21 months children establish a sense of self (Kaplan, 1978) and further evince self-awareness. This self-awareness is followed by the realization that one can act as a causal agent. This sense of self, combined with the recognition that one can initiate change in the environment, is the basis of agency thought (Snyder, 1994, 2000a, 2000b).

Hopeful thought becomes more refined as the child matures. This improvement in hopeful thinking sparks developmental gains in vocabulary, memory capacity, and abstraction, skills that, in turn, help children to use hope more productively and achieve personal goals. This maturation is parallel to school entrance, and the connection between hope and school begins to assume particular importance. Along these lines, according to hope theory (Snyder, 1994; Snyder, 2002), high-hope students demonstrate superior academic performance compared to their low-hope counterparts. Performance in school, often related to one's ability to set concrete goals and then attain the goal, necessitates using adequate pathways and agency thoughts. Research has

supported this link. Linked to the development of hope, research also demonstrates that hope is built on a foundation of contingency thinking (Snyder, 1994) and that it is socially primed (Snyder, Cheavens, & Sympson, 1997). Related to this point, Marques and colleagues (2009) identified a moderate relation between children's hope and their parents' in a sample of Portuguese students, which supports previous thinking about how caregivers foster hope development in children. Nevertheless, given the recent efforts in this area, further research is needed to investigate these process mechanisms (see Hoy, Suldo, & Mendez, 2013).

Hope System and Measurement

Hope is not only a goal-directed cognitive process. It is also a hierarchically organized system of beliefs regarding one's ability to successfully engage in such a thought process. These beliefs are organized into four specific levels of abstraction: global or trait hope, domain-specific hope, goal-specific hope, and state hope. Individuals' overall evaluation of their capacity to construct sufficient pathways and generate the agency thoughts necessary to achieve goals is known as global or trait hope (Snyder, Feldman, et al., 2002). Adult and child versions of the Hope Scale have been developed to measure such global hopes (Snyder, Hoza, et al., 1997; Snyder et al., 1991). A second, more concrete level in the system of hope-related beliefs is domain-specific. Illustratively, people who are high in global hope have the tendency to manifest high hope in most life domains. However, a gap commonly is observed in students who, although quite hopeful about life in general, display low hope in the academic domain (Snyder, Shorey, et al., 2002). To fill this need, the Domain-Specific Hope Scale (Sympson, 1999) was developed to assess adolescents' and adults' hope in six life arenas: social relationships, romantic relationships, family life, academics, work, and leisure.

A more concrete level in the hope belief hierarchy is the goal-specific level, manifested regarding a specific goal. Even when an individual's global and domain-specific hope levels are quite high, it is still possible that he or she will evidence low hope regarding a specific goal. The goal-specific level of analysis, then, may be important in understanding perceived deficits in specific goal pursuits. Additionally, Snyder et al. (1996) have developed and validated the State Hope Scale for tapping a person's hope in a specific context. Without identifying the goals, the State Hope Scale measures a person's momentary hopeful thinking, providing a snapshot of his or her current goal-directed thinking. That is to say, in contrast to the more enduring type of motivational set, the State Hope Scale is related to the ongoing events in people's lives. Both trait and state are operative and useful depending on one's focus. People probably have dispositional hope that applies across situations and times, but they also have state hope that reflects particular times and more proximal events. Theoretically, dispositional hope should relate to the intensity of state hope by setting a band or range within which state hope varies. As such, it is important to pay close attention not only to global hope but also to domain- and goal-specific hope and state hope to understand the complex web of hope-related beliefs that individuals possess (Snyder, Feldman, et al., 2002).

Hope Theory: 25 Years of Systematic Research

Research over the past 25 years has honed in on what we know about hope and also has identified some of the ways that hope makes a difference in the lives of children and youth.

Hope and Social-Emotional Development

Accumulating evidence suggests that hope is positively related with life satisfaction, perceived competence, and self-worth (Marques, Pais-Ribeiro, & Lopez, 2007) and negatively associated with symptoms of depression (Snyder, Hoza, et al., 1997) and measures of internalizing and externalizing behavior problems (e.g., Gilman, Dooley, & Florell, 2006). Indeed, researchers have reported that children very high in hope (upper 10% of the distribution) differ from students with average (middle 25%) and very low hope (bottom 10%) on self-esteem and life satisfaction, with significantly higher self-esteem and life satisfaction levels for the very high-hope group (Marques, Lopez, Fontaine, Coimbra, & Mitchell, 2015). As with self-worth, extremely high and average hope is associated with mental health benefits that are not found among adolescents reporting comparatively extremely low hope levels (Marques et al., 2015). Additional longitudinal evidence suggests that adolescents with lower levels of hope (and life satisfaction) who experienced several stressful events had a higher risk of developing low mental health five years later, while those with higher levels of hope (and life satisfaction) were not exposed to this vulnerability (Marques, 2016).

Also, lower hope predicts more depressive symptoms (Kwon, 2000), and it does so independently

of appraisals and other coping strategies (Chang & DeSimone, 2001). Results from a recent meta-analysis found that hope accounted for 23% of the strength of student assets, making its greatest contributions to self-worth, optimism, and life satisfaction (Marques, Lopez, Reichard, & Dollwet, 2016). Those with high hope typically are more optimistic, are more focused on success when pursuing goals, develop many life goals, and perceive themselves as being capable of solving problems that may arise (Snyder et al., 1991; Snyder, Hoza, et al., 1997). Likewise, higher hope is linked closely to having a greater perceived purpose in life (Feldman & Snyder, 2005).

Hope, Spirituality, and Religiosity

There remains a paucity of research on the relationships between hope and spirituality and religiosity. Preliminary findings suggest no significant differences between children's hope from families that practice and do not practice religion (Santos, 2012). Longitudinal findings with adolescents (Marques, Lopez, & Mitchell, 2013) indicated that hope is moderately correlated with spirituality but shares weak relations with religious practice (as measured by attendance at a place of worship). These associations were stable six months and one year later. Nevertheless, further research from different countries and ages is clearly needed (including different indicators of religiosity).

Hope and Physical Health

Research suggests that hope may play a significant role in health. Berg, Rapoff, Snyder, and Belmont (2007) investigated the relation between hope and adherence to a daily inhaled steroid regimen among 48 asthma patients ages 8 to 12. A multivariate model with children's hope level entered in the second step predicted adherence (and no other demographic or psychosocial variables were significant predictors of adherence). These results support hope as a significant predictor of student adherence to prescribed medication. As a possible explanation for these findings is that low-hope individuals may not believe their medication will provide a pathway to their goals of improved health, or it may be that taking the medication is difficult or uncomfortable, thus affecting their agency beliefs (Snyder, 2000a). These findings highlight the need to attend to psychosocial predictors of adherence, specifically hope, which might help practitioners target these factors in their efforts to increase adherence among pediatric asthma patients.

Similarly, research on adolescents with diabetes showed that those with higher hope were more likely to adhere to a medical regimen necessary for glycemic control (Lloyd, Cantell, Pacaud, Crawford, & Dewey, 2009). Past research (Lewis & Kliewer, 1996) on children with sickle-cell disease found that those who had the disease but maintained high hope perceptions along with active coping strategies were less likely to experience the negative effects of anxiety. Hope can provide benefits for those struggling with their health, but it can also facilitate healthy behaviors. At the college level, students with high hope were less likely to binge drink and smoke, even when controlling for demographics (Berg, Ritschel, Swan, An, & Ahluwalia, 2011). Further, these high-hope students were more likely to restrict fat in their diet, and they engaged in more frequent exercise than low-hope students.

Hope and Academic Outcomes

As early as grade school, hope is significantly related to achievement test scores (Snyder, Hoza, et al., 1997). This trend continues throughout the educational sequence. For example, higher levels of hope are related to stronger academic performance, as measured by grade point average (GPA), in elementary school (Marques, Pais-Ribeiro, & Lopez, 2011, Snyder, Hoza, et al., 1997), junior high school and high school (Ciarrochi et al., 2007; Lopez, Bouwkamp, Edwards, & Terramoto Pedrotti, 2000; Snyder et al., 1991; Worrell & Hale, 2001), and college (e.g., Buckelew, Crittendon, Butkovic, Price, & Hurst, 2008; Curry, Maniar, Sondag, & Sandstedt, 1999; Snyder et al., 1991; Snyder, Shorey, et al., 2002). Additionally, there is some evidence that high-hope students are less likely to experience anxiety or engage in self-deprecatory thinking in academic situations (Onwuegbuzie & Snyder, 2000a; Snyder, 1999). This may be due in part to the tendency for high-hope students to engage in more problem-solving and positive problem orientation than low-hope students (Chang, 1998).

Hope is not merely a proxy for intelligence and personality variables often associated with academic performance. Findings suggest that the predictive power of hope remained significant even when controlling for intelligence (e.g., Day, Hanson, Maltby, Proctor, & Wood, 2010; Snyder, Hoza, et al., 1997), prior grades (e.g., Gallagher & Lopez, 2008; Snyder et al., 1991; Snyder, Shorey, et al., 2002), self-esteem (Snyder, Shorey, et al., 2002), personality (Day et al., 2010), and college entrance examination scores (Gallagher & Lopez, 2008; Snyder,

Shorey, et al., 2002), such as high school GPA and ACT/SAT scores. Furthermore, recent research has suggested that very high hope Portuguese youths (top 10%) reported significantly higher academic achievement and school engagement (Marques et al., 2015) than youths in the average (middle 25%) and very low (bottom 10%) hope groups.

Based on the longitudinal findings (Marques, 2016), students with high levels of hope at the mean age of 12 years were at a reduced risk of developing school difficulties (i.e., low levels of school engagement) at the mean age of 17. These associations remained significant after controlling for age, gender, and preexisting difficulties on school engagement at the mean age of 12. Additionally, early adolescents with lower levels of hope who experienced several stressful events had a superior risk of developing difficulties of engagement at school during early adulthood, while those with higher levels of hope were not exposed to this vulnerability (Marques et al., 2016).

On the differential analysis between agency and pathways components of hope, although most studies are suggestive of a significant positive relation between both components of hope and academic achievement (e.g., Day et al., 2010), such findings are not fully conclusive. For example, a study with a college sample of students (Buckelew et al., 2008) reported that scores on the Agency subscale correlated positively with semester GPA (even when intelligence and anxiety were controlled) but not those on the Pathways subscale and GPA.

Hope and Athletic Achievement

Research suggest that higher hope has been positively related to superior athletic (and academic) performances among student athletes (Curry et al., 1999; Curry, Snyder, Cook, Ruby, & Rehm, 1997), even after statistically controlling for variance related to their natural athletic abilities. For example, Curry and colleagues reported that high-hope student athletes performed significantly better in their track and field events than their low-hope counterparts, with trait and state hope scale scores together accounting for 56% of the variance in subsequent track performances.

Curry and colleagues (1999) examined the efficacy of a semester-long academic class aimed to raise students' levels of hope. Results from this study revealed that students have increased confidence related to their athletic ability, academic achievement, and self-esteem after taking the "hope" class. These gains were retained for at least a year after completion of the athlete class intervention. Also, high- as compared to low-hope children were less likely to consider quitting their sports (Brown, Curry, Hagstrom, & Sandstedt, 1999).

Hope, Demographics, and Social Contexts

Preliminary research has found that hope is unrelated to the type of family structure and living situation (Santos, 2012), although it is positively correlated with parents' educational level (Marques, Pais-Ribeiro, & Lopez, 2007; Santos, 2012). Moreover, hope is significantly lower among students from families with both parents unemployed compared to students with one or none of the parents unemployed (Santos, 2012).

Cross-sectional findings suggest that hope is unrelated to gender and age in the early ages (Marques et al., 2011). However, when the results are analyzed across the lifespan (using a Portuguese large sample), hope levels are average in childhood (ages 10–13) and drop during adolescent years (ages 14–17), rise gradually throughout adulthood, from ages 18 to 29 to ages 46 to 64, and then decline in old age (Marques, 2016). Further, the differences in the hope scores of children and adults across ethnic groups have been examined, and it appears that while not statistically significant, Caucasians tend to report fewer obstacles (e.g., oppression, prejudice) in their lives than their ethnic-minority counterparts. However, minority groups have been shown to produce higher average hope scores (see McDermott et al., 1997; Munoz-Dunbar, 1993) and higher average levels of agency thinking (Chang & Banks, 2007) than Caucasians.

To date, few studies have examined the relative levels of hope among special groups, such as gifted students, students with learning disorders or physical disabilities, and groups at risk (e.g., institutionalized youth). Additional research among these populations is much needed.

Agents Who Play a Significant Role in Children's Hope

Given that hope is malleable and that the hopeless can learn to be hopeful, our children need a focused effort from people who care about them and their future. Parents are the first important agents to impact children's hope. They model hope by the way they communicate ("hopeful language" in everyday life, such as "when you finish your homework we can go out" instead of "if you can finish your homework we can go out"), set goals, view challenges, and cope with problems. In the same manner, teachers play an important role in children's perceptions about their competences to achieve goals and to cope with obstacles that can arise. For example, educators should provide help students develop the capacity to think about the future in a complex way, develop flexible thinking about how to attain future goals, and learn how to renew motivation when willpower is depleted. Additionally, being a high-hope parent and teacher facilitates children's hopeful thinking, and school psychologists are well positioned to facilitate this hope transmission. See Appendix 10A for some suggestions on how to work with teachers and parents to enhance children's hope. For more detailed information about imparting goal-setting as well as pathways and agency thinking to students, parents, and teachers see McDermott and Snyder (1999) or Snyder, Hoza, et al. (2002).

In addition to parents and teachers, there are other significant influences on children's hope, such as peer groups. It is important that parents stay in touch with these influences and be active participants in their children's interests. Hope transmission between peers' interactions should also be a focus of attention in hope development. In this regard, we suggest the inclusion of peers when adults intentionally work on children's hope.

By integrating hope into curriculum or doing separate and regular hope-enhancing group sessions, the school is an ideal place to work in groups and include peers. It is possible to find ways to infuse hopeful thinking into the subject matter that children are studying. For example, history is replete with high-hope people, and students may be oriented to explore their goals, the problems that had to be overcome, and the initiative and energy it took to achieve their objectives. In literature, teachers can benefit from personal narratives and assign short stories to illustrate the hope process. In mathematics, teachers can infuse hope and at the same time may reduce math anxiety, a problem that frequently inhibits the learning of relevant skills (Snyder, 1999). For this purpose, it is important to teach the concepts in small steps and praise the child's comprehension of each step, giving a special emphasis on their efforts in addition to their achievements. In fact, mathematics may be one of the most strategic subjects in which the steps to enhance hope described later (see "Enhancing Hope in Students" section) can produce benefits in learning and in reducing anxiety. Physical education is also a critical area because the goals and movement toward them are visually perceived.

Building on a Foundation of Hope

It is theorized that children are hopeful and that they report higher hope than most adults (Snyder, 1994). Although the school years should be among the most hopeful in students' lives, recent research with a large Portuguese sample of students suggests that hope declines from late childhood (ages 10–13) to adolescence (ages 14–17; Marques, 2016). This finding seems to imply that children and adolescents are ideal targets for hope training programs. In general, a common characteristic of these programs is the specific work into three categories—goals, pathways, and agency.

Helping Students to Set Goals

Helping students to set goals is core for any intention to foster hope. Among many adolescents, who often need encouragement to set goals in various life domains, sometimes these goals relate to interpersonal matters such as wanting to feel happier or meeting new people, whereas at other times they may involve selecting a career or deciding whether to go to college. If adolescents select several goals, calibrated to the their age and specific circumstances, they can turn to another important goal when they face a profound blockage in one.

If the school-based psychologist first gives instruments that measure values, interests, and abilities, then specific goals can be designed for each given student. Likewise, the student can be asked about recent important goals that are quite meaningful and pleasurable. These recent activities then may be used to generate an appropriate future goal. Once the student, with the help of the mental health or education professional, has produced a list of goals, that student then should rank the importance of these goals. In this process, the student learns important skills about how to prioritize goals. Some students, particularly those low in hope, do not prioritize their goals (Snyder et al., 2005); instead, they have the maladaptive practice of impulsively wanting to go after any or all goals that come to their minds.

Assuming students have been helped to establish desired goals, the next step is to teach them how to set clear markers for such goals. These markers enable the students to track progress toward the goals. A common goal is the vague "getting good grades." This and similar goals may be quite counterproductive because they are sufficiently lacking in clarity that the student cannot know when they are attained (Pennebaker, 1989). Moreover, related research shows that abstract goals actually are more difficult to reach than well-specified goals (Emmons,

1992). Thus we advocate concrete markers, such as "to study an hour each day in preparation for my next biology exam." With this latter goal, students not only can tell when they have reached it, but they also can experience a sense of success.

Another important aspect of helping students is to encourage them to establish approach goals in which they try to move toward getting something accomplished. This is in contrast to avoidance goals, in which students try to prevent something from happening (Snyder, Feldman, Taylor, Schroeder, & Adams, 2000). Avoidance goals work to maintain the status quo, but they are not very reinforcing to students. We have found that high-hope students are more likely to use approach goals in their lives, whereas low-hope students tend to use avoidance goals. Thus students should be helped to abandon avoidance goal-setting and to embrace the more productive approach goal-setting (Snyder, Hoza, et al., 2002).

High-hope people also appear to be interested in other people's goals in addition to their own. Accordingly, we see advantages in instructing students to think in terms of "we" goals and their own "me" goals (Snyder, Cheavens, et al., 1997). For example, encouraging students to help each other on difficult math problems can create a sense of shared accomplishment while deemphasizing competition. This has the benefit of helping students to get along with their peers, and it makes for easier and more fulfilling interpersonal transactions. Related research (e.g., Batson, 1991) indicates that people who help others fulfill natural human altruism needs, and they thus have the pleasure of feeling good about themselves as they think about and attend to the welfare of others (Snyder, 1994).

Helping Students to Develop Pathways Thinking

Possibly the most common strategy for enhancing pathways thinking is to help students to break down large goals into smaller subgoals. The idea of such "stepping" is to take a long-range goal and separate it into steps that are undertaken in a logical, one-at-a-time sequence. Low-hope students tend to have the greatest difficulty in formulating subgoals (Snyder, Cheavens, et al., 1997). They often hold onto counterproductive and inaccurate beliefs that goals are to be undertaken in an "all at once" manner. Likewise, low-hope students may not have been given much instruction by their caregivers, teachers, or other adult figures in the planning process more generally. Such planning can be learned, however, and with practice in "stepping" students can gain confidence in the fact that they can form subgoals to any of the major goals in their lives.

Perhaps a student's deficiency is not in stepping per se but rather involves difficulty in identifying several routes to a desired goal. Blockage to desired goals happens frequently in life and, lacking alternative pathways to those goals, a student can become very dejected and give up. This may explain, in part, the previous research findings on low-hope students' high probabilities of dropping out of school (Snyder, Shorey, et al., 2002). Thus we advocate teaching students to have several routes to their desired goals—even before they set out to reach their goals. Likewise, students need to learn that if one pathway does not work, they have other routes to try.

Additionally, it is crucial for the production of future pathways—as well as for the maintenance of agency—that students learn not to attribute a blockage to a perceived lack of talent. Instead, we believe that a more productive attribution when encountering impediments is to think of that information as identifying the path that does not work—thereby helping one to search productively for another route that might.

Helping Students to Develop Agency Thinking

Although it may seem obvious that students would select goals that are important to them, such goals actually may reflect those imposed by their peers, parents, or teachers. As such, the student does not obtain an accompanying sense of motivation in pursuing these imposed goals. Related to this point, research indicates that the pleasure in meeting externally derived goals is fleeting (Sheldon & Elliot, 1999). Furthermore, when students lack personal goals that fill their needs, their intrinsic motivations and performances are undermined (Conti, 2000). Thus goals that are built on internal, personal standards are more energizing than those based on external standards.

Helping students to set "stretch" goals also is invigorating for them. These stretch goals are based on a child or adolescent's previous performances and personally established more complex goals. Stretch goals thus can enhance intrinsic motivation and perseverance when progress is hindered.

Often individuals do not realize the impact their self-talk can have on their goal attaining abilities. Having students keep a diary of their ongoing self-talk (via a small notebook or audio tape recorder) can be helpful in determining if their internal dialogues are high (e.g., "I can . . ." and "I'll keep at it . . .") or low in agency (e.g., "I won't . . ." and "I can't . . ."). Students sometimes are amazed at how negative they are in such self-talk. Students of various ages can be cruel to each other, but they also can be extremely critical of themselves. As such, there are plenty of sources for these negative self-scripts. We would suggest that the students who have low-hope internal dialogues be taught to dispute their negative, hypercritical self-talk. Emphasize to such students how they can replace the ongoing self-criticism with more realistic, positive, and productive thoughts. This approach requires repeated practice before it begins to work, so it is important to inform students of this fact so as to lessen their needless discouragement.

Hopeful children often draw on their own memories of positive experiences to keep them buoyant during difficult times. In this way, they tell themselves their own uplifting stories, or they create their own positive personal narratives (Snyder, Hoza, et al., 2002). In contrast to high-hope children, low-hope children may not have a base of positive memories to sustain them. These children, especially when in grade school, can be helped to create their own personal narratives. Telling them stories and providing them with books that portray how other children have succeeded or overcome adversity can give low-hope children a model on which to begin building their own sense of agency. For suggested children's books, listed by specific hope-related topics (e.g., adoption, alcohol, anger, arguing, attachment, communication, confidence, crying, and death), see the appendices in *The Psychology of Hope: You Can Get There From Here* (Snyder, 1994) and *Hope for the Journey: Helping Children Through the Good Times and Bad* (Snyder, Hoza, et al., 2002).

Hope: Potential for Programs and Interventions

Although hope is somewhat stable, with moderate one-, two-, and five-year test–retest coefficients (e.g., Gallagher, Marques, & Lopez, 2016; Marques, 2016; Valle, Huebner, & Suldo, 2004), research suggests that hope in children is malleable to change through intentional efforts (e.g., Lopez et al., 2000; Marques, Lopez, & Pais-Ribeiro, 2011).

The past two decades have witnessed the development of specific strategies and programs/interventions aimed to enhance hope in children and youth. Specific strategies for eliciting hope have been extensively described in *The Psychology of Hope* (Snyder, 1994), *Hope for the Journey* (Snyder, McDermott, Cook, & Rapoff, 1997), *Making Hope Happen* (McDermott & Snyder, 1999), *The Great Big Book* of *Hope* (McDermott & Snyder, 2000) and *The Handbook of Hope* (Snyder, 2000). The use of hope enhancement strategies is advocated in children and youth from the general community but also in clinical settings. For example, Nel (2010) describes how clinicians might use narrative approaches to instill hope in clinic-referred youths. Snyder, McDermott, and colleagues (1997) describe how similar hope enhancement strategies can be used to treatment attention deficit hyperactivity disorder, major depressive disorder, and oppositional defiant disorder in children. Furthermore, Lopez and colleagues (2009) describe how these strategies might be implemented in public schools "for enhancing hope in all children" (p. 42). Hope enhancement strategies have also been suggested in related disciplines, such as counseling (Larsen & Stege, 2010), family therapy (Ripley & Worthington, 2002), health psychology (Hollis, Massey, & Jevne, 2007), and nursing (Herth, 2001; Turner & Stokes, 2006).

Several promising programs have been developed to enhance hope among children and adolescents using the theoretical model and measures of the Snyder theory of hope. Table 10.1 presents a description of these hope-based programs designed for children and/or adolescents.

One of the first interventions developed to increase hope in children involved learning about hope theory and discussing stories about high-hope children (McDermott, Callahan, Gingerich, Hastings, & Gariglietti, 1997). This program involved eight weekly sessions with first- through sixth-grade students at an ethnically diverse elementary school. During each week of this program, students spent 30 minutes discussing hope and goal-setting and hearing stories about high-hope children. Through hearing and discussing these stories each week, children had the opportunity to identify goals in the lives of protagonists as well as to apply the hope concepts to their own lives. Children's hope was assessed with the Children's Hope Scale (CHS) before and after the eight-week session, and results demonstrated modest improvement on both self-report and teacher ratings of students' hope. McDermott and colleagues concluded that an eight- week session was not sufficient time to instill high hope, but they considered their results promising (Lopez et al., 2004).

The Making Hope Happen program (MHH; Pedrotti, Lopez, & Krieshok, 2000) is another school-based intervention developed to enhance hope in students through didactic teaching and group work. Making Hope Happen was first piloted at the junior high level. The MHH program consisted of five 45-minute sessions with groups of 8 to 10 junior high students, each lead by two graduate students. After beginning with a simple explanation of the hope model developed by Snyder and colleagues (1991), the MHH program was designed to move through various exercises and interactions geared at helping students use the hope model in their own lives.

Week 1 began with an introduction of the model, using various posters and cartoons to outline the main tenets of pathways, agency, and obstacles. In addition, narratives that featured high-hope protagonists were introduced during this session to help students to identify high-hope strategies and statements. Group discussions were facilitated to outline these points for all students. At the end of this first session, students were paired into "hope buddy" partnerships to be kept throughout the five weeks. These pairs were chosen by the researchers after reviewing the students' individual hope scores, and they paired high-hope children with lower hope children so as to facilitate modeling. Finally, students were asked to devise a personal goal during this session that could be pursued throughout the five weeks of the MHH program. These goals could be small or large and did not have to be achieved by the fifth week of the program; the only restriction placed on students was that the goals had to be positive (i.e., adding something to one's life) as opposed to negative (i.e., stopping a bad behavior or habit). If students devised more negative goals (e.g., "I want to stop fighting with my brother"), group leaders helped them to rework them into more positive phrasing (e.g., "I want to get along better with my brother").

In Week 2, the points made during the first session were revisited through the use of new narratives, and the concept of "G-POWER" was introduced. Each of the letters in this word stand for a particular component of the hope model: G = goals; P = pathways; O = obstacles; W = willpower; E = evaluate your process; R = rethink and try again (Pedrotti et al., 2000). Students were trained to use this acronym to help them to remember the different steps to the hope model. Week 3 followed up on this concept and the "Hope Game" was introduced. This board game was devised to reinforce the additive properties of agency and pathways and to emphasize that both are needed to facilitate goal achievement. After each of these sessions hope buddies met and discussed progress made on goals throughout the week.

In Week 4, students were given more individual work in addition to group work, and the concept of hope talk was introduced. Students were asked to change unhopeful sentences (e.g., "I will never be

Table 10.1. Programs/Intervention Studies to Foster Hope in Children and/or Adolescents

Authors	N	Intervention/Program and Sample	Research Design	Recruitment of Participants	Manualized Intervention	Outcomes Assessed	Follow-Up
Bouwkamp & Lopez (2001)	30	Making Hope Happen program for high school students	Quasi-experimental	School	Manual/protocol for students	Hope	No follow-up
Buchanan (2007)	20	Making Hope Happen program for youths in special education	Quasi-experimental	School	Manual/protocol for students	Hope, multidimensional life satisfaction	No follow-up
Kirschman et al. (2010)	391	Hope-based summer camp for at-risk youth	Quasi-experimental	Community	No manual/protocol	Hope	4-month follow-up
Marques et al. (2011)	62	Building Hope for the Future for middle school students	Quasi-experimental	School	Manual/protocol for students, teachers and parents	Hope, global life satisfaction, self-esteem, mental health, academic achievement	18-month follow-up
McDermott et al. (1997)		Learning about hope theory and discussing stories about high-hope children	No comparison group	School	No manual/protocol	Hope	No follow-up
McNeal et al. (2006)	155	Hope-based group therapy for youth in residential treatment	Quasi-experimental	psychiatric or medical facility	No manual/protocol	Hope	No information available
Pedrotti et al. (2000)	104	Making Hope Happen program for junior high school students	Quasi-experimental	School	Manual/protocol for students	Hope	6-week follow-up
Robitschek (1996)	98	Hope enhancement program for at-risk youth	Quasi-experimental	psychiatric or medical facility	No manual/protocol	Hope	No information available
Edwards & Lopez (2000)	?	Making Hope Happen for Kids	No comparison group	School	Manual/protocol for students	Hope	1 year follow-up

good at math") into more hopeful sentences (e.g., "Math is not my best subject, but I can use these strategies to succeed"). In addition, statements from historical (e.g., Martin Luther King Jr.) and local (e.g., a college basketball coach) figures were evaluated by the students for their level of hopefulness. Finally, in this week students began to write their personal hope story, which described their chosen goal and the progress made toward it during the five weeks. Last, in Week 5, students read their completed hope stories to the group. Snacks and beverages were provided on this day to promote a celebration of the completion of progress on these goals, and students were asked to offer positive feedback and future steps to each other about their goal processes.

Prior to the beginning of the MHH program, all students were given the CHS (Snyder et al., 1997). At this time, a control group also was identified and these students were administered the measure as well. Upon completion of the program, all students were again administered the CHS; increases in hope scores were found to be significantly larger in the group of students who participated in the MHH program as compared to the control group. These results were maintained six weeks post-programming (Pedrotti et al., 2000), suggesting that students continued to utilize the tenets learned in the program.

After the MHH was established at the junior high level, expansion to the elementary school level occurred. Making Hope Happen for Kids (MHHK; Edwards & Lopez, 2000) was developed to enhance hope in fourth-grade students. This five-session program involved activities and lessons designed to help students understand hope and apply the construct to their lives. The program was conducted in several classrooms with groups of 7 to 10 students each led by two graduate student cofacilitators. The first week of MHHK involved learning about the hope model and acting out the parts of the model with laminated props (Edwards & Lopez, 2000). Students pretended to be goals, obstacles, pathways, and agency using the props (e.g., a stop sign for an obstacle, an arrow for pathways and willpower) in a brief psychodrama depicting meaningful goal pursuits. In the second week, children were introduced to a story that described a young girl navigating obstacles as she worked toward the goal of learning lines for her school play. During the third week, children played a different version of the Hope Game designed for this age group. Children worked in teams to identify obstacles, pathways, and agency thoughts to accomplish a shared goal. In the fourth week, children designed hope cartoons, emphasizing

hopeful language. Finally, during the last week of the program, children developed hope stories detailing the goals on which they had been working, and then they shared their stories with one another in a final celebration. Evaluation of the MHHK program was conducted at the end of the first and second years in two different schools. The CHS (Snyder et al., 1997) was administered before and after delivery of the intervention with all children. While the evaluation of this program did not include a control group, comparisons of means at pretest and posttest demonstrated significant gains in hope scores in the students. Thus hope was enhanced in these young children (Lopez et al., 2004).

In addition, the Making Hope Happen High School (MHH-HS) program was developed specifically for use with freshmen in an urban high school (Bouwkamp & Lopez, 2001). The MHH-HS program, which is quite similar to the original MHH program, consists of five 70-minute sessions with groups of 20-plus students, each led by two trained facilitators. As in the other versions of the program, pretest measures were completed and Week 1 programming began with an introduction of hope theory and its many applications, using various posters and stories (with adolescent high-hope protagonists) to describe how goal thinking combines with pathways and agency. The "hope camera project" also was introduced during the first week. In Weeks 2, 3, and 4, additional hope stories were used to emphasize the components of hope theory and engage participants in the daily applications of hope. Progress on the hope camera projects was discussed. Completion of personal hope stories (see the description in the junior high version of MHH) reinforced that individuals can pursue important goals without much help from others, and the team project helped to introduce hope as a social phenomenon. Week 5 took on a celebratory tone with snacks, beverages, and music. Groups shared their hope camera projects, which included collages, PowerPoint presentations, a musical number, and one video. The group ended with each participant discussing future plans using hopeful language. Upon completion of the program all students completed the posttest measures, and it was found that low-hope students had achieved significant gains in hope (Bouwkamp & Lopez, 2001).

A few years later, Marques et al. (2011) developed the first hope-based program for students with the involvement of key stakeholders. "Building Hope for the Future—A Program to Foster Strengths in School Students" was designed and developed for

Portuguese middle school students, based on the theoretical and applied work of Snyder and colleagues (Lopez et al., 2000; McDermott & Snyder, 1999; Snyder, Feldman, et al., 2002). The program included four main components: (a) developing and refining clear goals, (b) producing numerous range of pathways to attainment, (c) creating and maintaining mental for goal pursuit, and (d) reframing potential obstacles as challenges to be overcome. It was designed to (a) promote the development of a hopeful therapeutic relationship between the psychologists and the students; (b) work solution-focused, narrative and cognitive-behavioral techniques; (c) help students develop psycho-educational, skills training, and group process components; and (d) include structured activities, role-playing, and guided discussion (Lopez, Floyd, Ulven, & Snyder; 2000). The intervention was conducted in a group setting based on the theoretical assumption that hopeful thinking reflects a transactional process (Snyder et al., 1997). Sixty-two students were assigned to either an intervention or no-treatment control groups, matched on demographics and pretest measures of the outcome variables. The intervention condition was divided into small groups of 8 to 12 students who participated in five weekly sessions facilitated by two psychologists.

The first session "Learning about Hope" was devoted to the introduction of the hope theory and its relevance to the change process and positive outcomes (e.g., learn the vocabulary used in the model though acting out the hope picture). In the second session, "Structuring Hope," participants were encouraged to learn how to recognize goals, pathways, and agency components of hope and obstacles and to identify personal goals (salient and attainable) that they could work with for the next four weeks (e.g., learn to identify goals, obstacles, pathways, and agency from stories or examples). In the third session "Creating Positive and Specific Goals," students refined their personal workable goals in order to be more specific, positive, and clear; created multiple pathways; and identified agency thoughts for each goal (e.g., reorganize goal with a "goal enhancer worksheet" by making it more specific and positive). In the fourth session "Practice Makes Perfect," students identified and created an "hopeful talk"; the hope model was reinforced, and personal workable goals were reviewed and introduced in a personal hope story (e.g., follow the progress of the goals through a "Hope Buddy Journal"). In the fifth session "Review and Apply for the Future," students were encouraged to review and share personal hope stories and to plan future steps (e.g., to evaluate the process, discuss next steps with the hope buddy, and share with the whole group).

To promote goal-setting and pursuit by students in the intervention condition, their parents and teachers were also provided with intervention manuals and guided through intervention principles and procedures during a single one-hour session that occurred before the commencement of the hope training with the students. The intervention manual for parents and teachers were organized in three segments: (a) "Learning about Hope," (b) "Instilling Hope" (includes "Hope Finding" and "Hope Bonding"), and (c) "Increasing Hope" (includes "Hope Enhancing" and "Hope Reminding") (see Appendix 10B). Students completed translated and validated measures of the target constructs (hope, satisfaction with life, self-worth, and mental-health). Academic achievement was obtained from school records. Results suggested that an intervention designed to foster hope in middle schoolers can produce psychological benefits: participants of the intervention group increased hope, life satisfaction and self-worth for one year and six months after the program, in comparison to a matched group. Further, this intervention had the potential to address issues of efficacy, accessibility (students, teachers, and parents), and sustainability (low cost to deliver in a group setting and completed in five weeks).

Conclusion

In summary, the literature review on children's hope details how meaningful, measureable, and malleable via intentional change efforts this construct is. All children, irrespective of their age, gender, culture, and language, need support from parents, school, and community to build their energy and ideas for the future. This body of information is vital to everyone who has the motivation to help build children's lives on a foundation of hope.

Future Directions

• What is the utility of hope in promoting health for specific groups of children and adolescents (e.g., children living with chronic illness)?

• What is the stability of hope during childhood, adolescence, and into adulthood (i.e., across the lifespan)?

• Is there any utility in refining and using scales of "multidimensional hope" in children and adolescents?

References

Bandura, A. (1982). Self-efficacy mechanism in human agency. *American Psychologist, 37*, 122–147. doi:10.1037/0003-066X.37.2.122

Batson, C. D. (1991). *The altruism question: Toward a social-psychological answer.* Hillsdale, NJ: Lawrence Erlbaum.

Berg, C. J., Rapoff, M. A., Snyder, C. R., & Belmont, J. M. (2007). The relationship of children's hope to pediatric asthma treatment adherence. *Journal of Positive Psychology, 2*, 176–184. doi:10.1080/17439760701409629

Berg, C. J., Ritschel, L. A., Swan, D. W., An, L. C., & Ahluwalia, J. S. (2011). The role of hope in engaging in healthy behaviors among college students. *American Journal of Health Behavior, 35*, 402–415. doi:10.5993/AJHB.35.4.3

Berlyne, D. E. (1960). *Conflict arousal and curiosity.* New York: McGraw-Hill.

Bouwkamp, J., & Lopez, S. J. (2001). *Making Hope Happen: A program for inner-city adolescents.* Unpublished master's thesis, University of Kansas, Lawrence .

Brown, M., Curry, L. A., Hagstrom, H., & Sandstedt, S. (1999, August). *Female teenage athletes, sport participation, self-esteem, and hope.* Paper presented at the Association for the Advancement of Applied Sport Psychology, Banff, Alberta, Canada.

Buckelew, S. P., Crittendon, R. S., Butkovic, J.D., Price, K. B., & Hurst, M. (2008). Hope as a predictor of academic performance. *Psychological Reports, 103*, 411–414. doi:10.2466/PR0.103.6.411-414

Chang, E. C. (1998). Hope, problem-solving ability, and coping in a college student population: Some implications for theory and practice. *Journal of Clinical Psychology, 54*, 953–962. doi:10.1002/(SICI)1097-4679(199811)54:7<953:AID-JCLP9>3.0.CO;2-F.

Chang, E. C., & Banks, K. H. (2007). The color and texture of hope: Some preliminary findings and implications for hope theory and counseling among diverse racial/ethnic groups. *Cultural Diversity & Ethnic Minority Psychology, 13*, 94–103. doi:10.1037/1099-9809.13.2.94.

Chang, E. C., & DeSimone, S. L. (2001). The influence of hope on appraisals, coping, and dysphoria: A test of hope theory. *Journal of Social and Clinical Psychology, 20*, 117–129. doi:10.1521/jscp.20.2.117.22262

Ciarrochi, J., Heaven, P. C., & Davies, F. (2007). The impact of hope, self-esteem, and attributional style on adolescents' school grades and emotional well-being: A longitudinal study. *Journal of Research in Personality, 41*, 1161–1178. doi:10.1016/j.jrp.2007.02.001

Conti, R. (2000). College goals: Do self-determined and carefully considered goals predict intrinsic motivation, academic performance, and adjustment during the first semester? *Social Psychology of Education, 4*, 189–211. doi:10.1023/A:1009607907509.

Covington, M. V. (2000). Goal theory, motivation, and school achievement: An integrative review. *Annual Review of Psychology, 51*, 171–200. doi:10.1146/annurev.psych.51.1.171

Curry, L. A., Maniar, S. D., Sondag, K. A., & Sandstedt, S. (1999). *An optimal performance academic course for university students and student-athletes.* Unpublished manuscript. University of Montana, Missoula.

Curry, L. A., Snyder, C. R., Cook, D. L., Ruby, B. C., & Rehm, M. (1997). Role of hope in academic and sport achievement. *Journal of Personality and Social Psychology, 73*, 1257–1267. doi:10.1037/0022-3514.73.6.1257

Day, L., Hanson, K., Maltby, J., Proctor, C., & Wood, A. (2010). Hope uniquely predicts objective academic achievement above intelligence, personality, and previous academic achievement. *Journal of Research in Personality, 44*, 550–553. doi:10.1016/j.jrp.2010.05.009

Dweck, C. S. (1999). *Self-theories: Their role in motivation, personality, and development.* Philadelphia: Taylor & Francis.

Edwards, L. M., & Lopez, S. J. (2000). *Making Hope Happen for Kids.* Unpublished protocol.

Emmons, R. A. (1992). Abstract versus concrete goals: Personal striving level, physical illness, and psychological well-being. *Journal of Personality and Social Psychology, 62*, 292–300. doi:10.1037/0022-3514.62.2.292

Feldman, D. B., & Snyder, C. R. (2005). Hope and the meaningful life: Theoretical and empirical associations between goal-directed thinking and life meaning. *Journal of Social and Clinical Psychology, 24*, 401–421. doi:10.1521/jscp.24.3.401.65616

Gallagher, M. W., & Lopez, S. J. (2008). *Hope, self-efficacy, and academic success in college students.* Poster presented at the annual convention of the American Psychological Association. Boston.

Gallagher, M. W., Marques, S. C., & Lopez, S. J. (2016). Hope and the academic trajectory of college students. *Journal of Happiness Studies, 14*, 251–261. doi:10.1007/s10902-016-9727-z

Gilman, R., Dooley, J., & Florell, D. (2006). Relative levels of hope and their relationship with academic and psychological indicators among adolescents. *Journal of Social and Clinical Psychology, 25*, 166–178. doi:10.1521/jscp.2006.25.2.166.

Heppner, P. P., & Petersen, C. H. (1982). The development and implications of a personal problem solving inventory. *Journal of Counseling Psychology, 29*, 66–75. doi:10.1037/0022-0167.29.1.66

Herth, K. A. (2001). Development and implementation of a hope intervention program. *Oncology Nursing Forum, 28*, 1009–1017.

Hollis, V., Massey, K., & Jevne, R. (2007). An introduction to the intentional use of hope. *Journal of Allied Health, 36*, 52–56.

Hoy, B., Suldo, S., & Mendez, L. (2013). Links between parents' and children's levels of gratitude, life satisfaction, and hope. *Journal of Happiness Studies, 14*, 1343–1361. http://scholarcommons.usf.edu/etd/3157

Kagan, J. (1972). Motives and development. *Journal of Personality and Social Psychology, 22*, 51–66. doi:10.1037/h0032356.

Kaplan, L. (1978). *Oneness and separateness.* New York: Simon & Schuster.

Kwon, P. (2000). Hope and dysphoria: The moderating role of defense mechanisms. *Journal of Personality, 68*, 199–223. doi:10.1111/1467-6494.00095

Larsen D. J., & Stege, R. (2010). Hope-focused practices during early psychotherapy sessions. *Journal of Psychotherapy Integration, 20*, 293–311. doi:10.1037/a0020821

Lewis, H. A., & Kliewer, W. (1996). Hope, coping, and adjustment among children with sickle cell anemia: Tests of mediator and moderator models. *Journal of Pediatric Psychology, 21*, 25–41. doi:10.1093/jpepsy/21.1.25.

Lloyd, S. M., Cantell, M., Pacaud, D., Crawford, S., & Dewey, D. (2009). Brief report: Hope, perceived maternal empathy, medical regime adherence, and glycemic control in adolescents with type 1 diabetes. *Journal of Pediatric Psychology, 34*, 1025–1029. doi:10.1093/jpepsy/jsn141

Lopez, S. J., Bouwkamp, J., Edwards, L. M., & Teramoto Pedrotti, J. (February, 2000). *Making hope happen via brief interventions*. Paper presented at the second Positive Psychology Summit, Washington, DC.

Lopez, S. J., Snyder, C. R., Magyar-Moe, J. L., Edwards, L. M., Pedrotti, J. T., Janowski, K., et al. & Pressgrove (2004). Strategies for accentuating hope. In P. A. Linley & S. Joseph (Eds.), *Positive psychology in practice* (pp. 388–404). Hoboken, NJ: Wiley.

Lopez, S. J., Snyder, C. R., & Pedrotti, J. T. (2003) Hope: Many definitions, many measures. In S. J. Lopez & C. R. Snyder (Eds.), *Positive psychological assessment: A handbook of models and measures* (pp. 91–107). Washington, DC: American Psychological Association.

Lopez, S. J., Floyd, R. K., Ulven, J. C., & Snyder, C. R. (2000). Hope therapy: Helping clients build a house of hope. In C. R. Snyder (Ed.), *Handbook of hope* (pp. 123- 150). New York, NY: Academic Press.

Marques, S. C. (2016). Age differences and short-term stability in hope: Results from a sample aged 15 to 80. Manuscript submitted for publication.

Marques, S. C., Lopez, S. J., Fontaine, A. M., & Coimbra, S. & Mitchell, J. (2014). Validation of a Portuguese version of the Snyder Hope Scale in a sample of high school students. *Journal of Psychoeducational Assessment, 32*, 781–786. doi:10.1177/0734282914540865.

Marques, S. C., Lopez, S. J., Fontaine, A. M., Coimbra, S., & Mitchell, J. (2015). How much hope is enough? Levels of hope and students' psychological and school functioning. *Psychology in the Schools, 52*, 325–334.

Marques, S. C., Lopez, S. J., & Mitchell, J. (2013). The role of hope, spirituality and religious practice in adolescents' life satisfaction: Longitudinal findings. *Journal of Happiness Studies, 14*, 251–261.

Marques, S. C., Lopez, S. J., & Pais-Ribeiro, J. L. (2011). "Building Hope for the Future"—A program to foster strengths in middle-school students. *Journal of Happiness Studies, 12*, 139–152. doi:10.1007/s10902-009-9180-3

Marques, S. C., Lopez, S. J., Reichard, R. J., & Dollwet, M. (2016). Relation of hope to academic outcomes: A meta-analysis. *Journal of Happiness Studies, 14*, 251–261.

Marques, S. C., Pais-Ribeiro, J. L., & Lopez, S. J. (2007). Validation of a Portuguese version of the Students' Life Satisfaction Scale. *Applied Research in Quality of Life, 2*, 83–94. doi:10.1007/s11482-007-9031-5

Marques, S. C., Pais-Ribeiro, J. L., & Lopez, S. J. (2009). Validation of a Portuguese version of the Children Hope Scale. *School Psychology International, 30*, 538–551. doi:10.1177/0143034309107069

Marques, S. C., Pais-Ribeiro, J. L., & Lopez, S. J. (2011). The role of positive psychology constructs in predicting mental health and academic achievement in children and adolescents: A two-year longitudinal study. *Journal of Happiness Studies, 12*, 1049–1062. doi:10.1007/s10902-010-9244-4

McDermott, D., Callahan, B., Gingerich, K., Hastings, S., & Gariglietti, K. (1997, March). *Working together to bring hope to our children*. Paper presented at the annual convention of the Kansas Counselors Association, Hutchinson, KS.

McDermott, D., & Snyder, C. R. (1999). *Making hope happen*. Oakland, CA: New Harbinger.

McDermott, D., & Snyder, C. R. (2000). The great big book of hope: Help your children achieve their dreams. Oakland, CA: New Harbinger.

McNeal, R., Handwerk, M. L., Field, C. E., Roberts, M. C., Soper, S., Huefner, J. C., et al., (2006). Hope as an outcome variable among youths in a residential care setting. *American Journal of Orthopsychiatry, 76*, 304-311.

Munoz-Dunbar, R. (1993). *Hope: A cross-cultural assessment of American college students*. Unpublished master's thesis. University of Kansas, Lawrence.

Nel, J. (2010). Putting the lid on the divorce monster: Creating hope-filled narratives with storybook therapy. In G. W. Burns (Ed.), *Happiness, healing, enhancement: Your casebook collection for applying positive psychology in therapy* (pp. 76–87). Hoboken, NJ: Wiley.

Pedrotti, J. T., Lopez, S. J., & Krieshok, T. S. (2000). *Making Hope Happen: A program for fostering strengths in adolescents*. Unpublished master's thesis, University of Kansas, Lawrence.

Pennebaker, J. W. (1989). Stream of consciousness and stress: Levels of thinking. In J. S. Uleman & J. A. Bargh (Eds.), *Unintended thought* (pp. 327–349). New York: Guilford Press.

Onwuegbuzie, A. J., & Snyder, C. R. (2000). Relations between hope and graduate students' coping strategies for studying and examination-taking. *Psychological Reports, 86*, 803–806. doi:10.2466/PR0.86.3.803–806

Ripley, J. S., & Worthington, E. L. (2002). Hope-focused and forgiveness-based group interventions to promote marital enrichment. *Journal of Counseling and Development, 80*, 452–463. doi:10.1002/j.1556-6678.2002.tb00212.x

Santos, A. (2012). *Hope, family challenges and school context*. Unpublished master thesis. Escola Superior de Altos Estudos, Instituto Superior Miguel Torga, Portugal (in Portuguese).

Scheier, M. F., & Carver, C. S. (1985). Optimism, coping, and health: Assessment and implications of generalized outcome expectancies. *Health Psychology, 4*, 219–247. doi:10.1037/0278-6133.4.3.219

Sheldon, K. M., & Elliot, A. J. (1999). Goal striving, need satisfaction, and longitudinal well-being: The self-concordance model. *Journal of Personality and Social Psychology, 76*, 482–497. doi:10.1037/0022-3514.76.3.482

Snyder, C. R. (1994). *The psychology of hope: You can get there from here*. New York: Free Press.

Snyder, C. R. (1999). Hope, goal blocking thoughts, and test-related anxieties. *Psychological Reports, 84*, 206–208.

Snyder, C. R. (2000a). Genesis: Birth and growth of hope. In C. R. Snyder (Ed.), *Handbook of hope: Theory, measures, and applications* (pp. 25–57). San Diego, CA: Academic Press.

Snyder, C. R. (2000b). Hypothesis: There is hope. In C. R. Snyder (Ed.), *Handbook of hope: Theory, measures, and applications* (pp. 3–21). San Diego, CA: Academic Press.

Snyder, C. R. (2002). Hope theory: Rainbows in the mind. *Psychological Inquiry, 13*, 249–275. doi:10.1207/S15327965PLI1304_01

Snyder, C. R., Berg, C., Woodward, J. T., Gum, A., Rand, K. L., Wrobleski, K.K., Brown, J., & Hackman, A. (2005). Hope against the cold: Individual differences in trait hope and acute pain tolerance on the cold pressor task. *Journal of Personality, 73*(2), 287–312. doi:10.1111/j.1467-6494.2005.00318.x

Snyder, C. R., Cheavens, J., & Sympson, S. C. (1997). Hope: An individual motive for social commerce. *Group Dynamics: Theory, Research, and Practice, 1*, 107–118. doi:10.1037/1089-2699.1.2.107

Snyder, C. R., Feldman, D. B., Shorey, H. S., & Rand, K. L. (2002). Hopeful choices: A school counselor's guide to hope theory. *Professional School Counseling, 5*, 298–307.

Snyder, C. R., Feldman, D. B., Taylor, J. D., Schroeder, L. L., & Adams, V. III (2000). The roles of hopeful thinking in preventing problems and enhancing strengths. *Applied and Preventive Psychology, 15,* 262–295. doi:10.1016/S0962-1849(00)80003-7

Snyder, C. R., Harris, C., Anderson, J. R., Holleran, S. H., Irving, L. M., Sigmon, S. T., . . . Harney, P. (1991). The will and the ways: Development and validation of an individual-differences measure of hope. *Journal of Personality and Social Psychology, 60,* 570–585. doi:10.1037/0022-3514.60.4.570

Snyder, C. R., Hoza, B., Pelham, W. E., Rapoff, M., Ware, L., Danovsky, M., . . . Stahl, K. L. (1997). The development and validation of the Children's Hope Scale. *Journal of Pediatric Psychology, 22,* 399–421. doi:10.1093/jpepsy/22.3.399

Snyder, C. R., Lopez, S. J., Shorey, H. L., Rand, K. L., & Feldman, D. B. (2003). Hope theory, measurements, and applications to school psychology. *School Psychology Quarterly, 18,* 122–139. doi:10.1521/scpq.18.2.122.21854

Snyder, C. R., McDermott, D., Cook, W., & Rapoff, M. (2002). *Hope for the journey* (revised ed.). Clinton Corners, NY: Percheron Press.

Snyder, C. R., Shorey, H. S., Cheavens, J., Pulvers, K. M., Adams, V. H. III, & Wiklund, C. (2002). Hope and academic success in college. *Journal of Educational Psychology, 94,* 820–826. http://dx.doi.org/10.1037/0022-0663.94.4.820

Snyder, C. R., Sympson, S. C., Ybasco, F. C., Borders, T. F., Babyak, M. A., & Higgins, R. L. (1996). Development and validation of the State Hope Scale. *Journal of Personality and Social Psychology, 70,* 321–335. doi:10.1037/0022-3514.70.2.321

Sympson, S. (1999). *Validation of the Domain Specific Hope Scale.* Unpublished doctoral dissertation, Department of Psychology, University of Kansas, Lawrence.

Turner, D., & Stokes, L. (2006). Hope promoting strategies of registered nurses. *Journal of Advanced Nursing, 56,* 363–372. doi:10.1111/j.1365-2648.2006.04017.x

Valle, M. F., Huebner, E. S., & Suldo, S. M. (2004). Further evaluation of the Children's Hope Scale. *Journal of Psychoeducational Assessment, 22,* 320–337. doi:10.1177/073428290402200403

Worrell, F. C., & Hale, R. L. (2001). The relationship of hope in the future and perceived school climate to school completion. *School Psychology Quarterly, 16,* 307–388. doi:10.1521/scpq.16.4.370.19896

Appendix 10A
Suggestions to Work and Refine with Teachers and Parents to Enhance Children's Hope

• Let teachers and parents know that children build hope through learning to trust in the ordered predictability and consistency of interactions with them.

• Explain the importance of being firm, fair, and consistent in engendering hope among their children.

• Explain the importance of creating an atmosphere of trust, where students are responsible for their actions and supported to establish growth-inducing stretch goals.

• Emphasize that children should be praised and rewarded for both their efforts and achievements.

• Encourage teachers and parents to set goals that are concrete, understandable, and broken down into subgoals.

• Work with them to focus on long-range as opposed to short-term goals.

• Emphasize the importance of preparation and planning.

• Develop an atmosphere where students are focused on expending effort and mastering the information rather than a sole focus on obtaining good outcomes (e.g., high grades or stellar athletic records).

• Encourage an atmosphere through a give-and-take process between teachers/parents and students.

• Encourage teachers to remain engaged and invested in pursuing their own important interests and life goals outside of the classroom.

• Remind parents and teachers that being a hopeful adult has many benefits. High-hope people perform better at work, have higher well-being, and live longer.

Appendix 10B
Content of the BHF

Session 1: Learning about Hope

The primary goal of this session is to improve the students' understanding of hope theory and its relevance to the change process and to achieve positive outcomes. This session offers the participants an overview of the topic of hope, including its three components (pathways, agency, and goals). Additionally, the central role that hope plays in daily communication is addressed by learning, identifying, and practicing the vocabulary used in the model.

Session 2: Structuring Hope

A major goal of this session is students learn to recognize pathways and agency components of hope and obstacles to a goal attainment. In addition, this session aims to help students build or identify personal goals (salient and attainable) they can work with for the next four weeks. This session encompasses three important elements: the discussion of stories and goal-oriented characters, the brainstorming of goal-oriented ideas from the past life, and the identification of present goals on which they would like to work.

Session 3: Creating Positive and Specific Goals

The goals of this session are to practice the model; refine personal workable goals in order to be more specific, positive, and clear; create multiple pathways; and identify agency thoughts for each personal goal. First, the introduction of new narratives and group activities offers the participants the chance to reinforce and practice the model. This session also draws on the progress of personal goals, and collaboration can occur to adjust or modify any disparities in actions or thinking that may hinder the successful achievement of the desired goals.

Session 4: Practice Makes Perfect

The goals of this session are to judge, identify, and create a "hopeful talk"; to reinforce the hope model; and to review and introduce personal workable goals in a personal hope story. Hopefulness communication patterns, as well as hopeful communication behavior, are presented, and supervised role-plays help students better identify and understand hopefulness and hopeful voices. The progress of personal goals is continually monitored.

Session 5: Review and Apply for the Future

The primary goal of this session is to enhance exchange of personal hope stories and to plan future steps. This session proposes to the students the exchange with the group on how they implement the hope theory to their unique life experiences. The process of overachievement is emphasized as well as the next steps in the goal process.

Shared Considerations across the Five Sessions

• Each session starts with a 10-minute segment dedicated to modeling and developing enthusiasm for the program and to reinforcing ideas learned in the previous session.

• The sessions are based on the theoretical and applied work of Snyder and colleagues (e.g., Lopez et al., 2000; Snyder 1994; Snyder et al. 2002; McDermott & Snyder 1999).

• The sessions integrate solution-focused, narrative, and cognitive-behavioral techniques.

• The sessions offer psycho-educational skills training and group process components and include structured activities, role-playing, brainstorming, and guided discussion.

• The program is managed by adult attention, group cohesion, social support, the discussion of hope components, sharing thoughts and feelings with peers, and engagement in session activities.

Session with Parents and Teachers

The direct work with parents and teachers is supported by a manual designed to (a) increase parents' and teachers' awareness of the principles of hope and enhance their goal-setting behavior and (b) promote goal-setting behavior in their children/students. This manual has three sections: The first section is dedicated to "Learning about Hope" (e.g., hope concept, research on hope, how hope can be cultivated, reflection questions). The second section is on "Instilling Hope," and participants are first oriented to a "Hope Finding" (e.g., self-evaluation with the Hope Scale from Snyder et al., 1991) and next to a "Hope Bonding" (how to build hopeful relationships). The third section, "Increasing Hope," is dedicated to "Hope Enhancing" (this segment provides basic steps associated with hope enhancement) and "Hope Reminding" (this segment provides strategies and practical exercises to improve their own hope and in their children/students).

Hope Therapy

Jennifer S. Cheavens *and* Madison M. Guter

Abstract

The strong association between hope and optimal psychological functioning has been empirically demonstrated repeatedly over the past two decades. In an effort to capitalize on these associations, researchers have developed and tested hope interventions aimed to increase hopeful thinking and optimal psychological functioning. Results are promising, suggesting that hope is malleable and that hope therapy reduces symptoms of distress and increases in well-being. Further, hope has been examined as a predictor of treatment success and data suggest that those with higher hope may do better in various treatments than their low-hope counterparts and that changes in hope across the course of therapy are associated with simultaneous improvements in psychological functioning. In future research, it will be important to identify specific therapeutic interventions that predict increases in hope and to determine whether or not hopeful thought is a mechanism of change in psychotherapy interventions.

Key Words: hope therapy, hope treatment, hope intervention, psychotherapy interventions, therapeutic interventions, treatment success

As defined by Snyder, Irving, and Anderson (1991), hope is comprised of pathways, the perception that one can generate various routes that connect the present to a desired future, and agency, the perception that one can successfully use said routes to reach goals. As Snyder (2002) later elucidated, cognition and thinking are at the heart of this definition of hope with emotions and feelings playing an important secondary role. In Snyder's conceptualization, goals anchor hope in that goals are the mental endpoints of hopeful thought. In other words, we hope *for* something or some goal. Emotions are outcomes of these goal pursuits; when we are successful in our goal pursuits, we experience positive emotions, and when our goals are blocked, impeded, or unsuccessful, we experience negative emotions. Hope, as an individual difference, develops over time as we learn the links between our goals and our actions in context of goal failures and successes. In this framework, a history of goal pursuit successes leads to more well-developed goals, varied

and clear routes to those goals, and strong beliefs in one's ability to reach goals, which then eventually coalesce into a stable sense of hope. Conversely, a history of goal failures and unmet desires leads to more poorly developed goals and associated difficulties finding ways to reach those goals and maintaining the energy to engage in goal pursuits, which eventually settles into a stable sense of hopelessness. Specifically, Snyder (1994, 2002) hypothesized that we develop trait-like pathways and agency thoughts through repeated attempts at making sense of causality (i.e., this leads to that; pathways) and recognition of the self as a causal agent (i.e., "I made that happen"; agency). Over time, individuals who are able to generate workable routes to their goals and maintain the requisite motivation to use these routes have more goal successes, which are accompanied by the happiness, pride, and gratitude thought to be inherent in success. The experiences of emotion provide feedback to the individual and, over time, become entwined with dispositional hope such that goals are viewed with a sense of curiosity and interest or, alternatively, with a sense of dread and apathy.

Based on this definition, it is not surprising that hope is related to both experiences of positive emotions and successful goal completion. Hope is positively related to experiences of positive emotion and psychological health and inversely associated with experiences of negative emotion and psychopathology. For example, using a daily diary methodology, Snyder and colleagues (1996) found that over the course of 28 days, hope was positively correlated with positive emotional experiences and negatively correlated with negative emotional experiences. Similarly, hope is inversely related to markers of psychopathology, including suicide ideation (Hirsch, Visser, Chang, & Jeglic, 2012) and personality pathology profiles (Cramer & Dyrkacz, 1998) as well as symptoms of depression (Chang, 2003) and anxiety (Carretta, Ridner, & Dietrich, 2014). In terms of goal pursuits, researchers have demonstrated that dispositional hope is related to academic success (e.g., Snyder, Shorey, et al., 2002), athletic accomplishment (e.g., Curry et al., 1997), development of satisfying and sustaining social networks (e.g., Snyder, Cheavens, & Sympson, 1997), and attainment of important, self-generated goals (Feldman, Rand, & Kahle-Wrobleski, 2009).

Given these associations, treatment development and outcome researchers have sought to harness the power of hope in increasing the likelihood of successful therapy outcomes. There are several ways in which hope might be incorporated into the study of psychosocial interventions. First, it has been proposed that those with high hope might be most well-suited to benefit from nonpharmacological interventions, particularly interventions that rely on the teaching and generalization of skills such as cognitive-behavioral therapy. Second, some treatment developers have focused on designing interventions to increase hopeful thought, both as a desirable outcome in its own right as well as a mechanism through which other desired changes (e.g., less depression, more meaning in life, higher self-esteem) might be accomplished. In this class of intervention research, the hope theory framework is used to inform the treatment delivered and the outcomes of interest range from increases in hopeful thought to better psychological functioning.

Does Hope Predict Treatment Response?

One of the primary questions in treatment research is for whom will treatment be most efficacious or effective? In other words, are there certain patient characteristics that predict successful completion of and benefit from intervention in general? There is reason to believe that hope might predict response to psychosocial treatments. At higher levels of hope, people are more likely to believe that treatment will be helpful in successfully overcoming current difficulties and reaching goals (Irving et al., 2004). Thus if treatment response (i.e., becoming less depressed, less anxious, more connected to the world around them) is the goal, it is possible that higher hope individuals will begin therapy with the belief that they will be able to succeed in this goal and that this stance will help to propel their treatment successes.

Although research suggests that hope is concurrently associated with both symptoms of psychopathology and markers of well-being at baseline (see chapters in this volume) and across treatment, the evidence is mixed in terms of whether baseline levels of hope predict symptom reduction over the course of treatment. Several trials have found that baseline hope does not predict symptoms at posttreatment (e.g., Irving et al., 2004; Ritschel, Cheavens, & Nelson, 2012; Thornton et al., 2014). There are, however, two studies that contradict these null findings. First, in a study of eight weeks of group hope therapy, Cheavens et al. (2006) found that baseline hope scores predicted posttreatment symptoms of depression and anxiety (in separate models) after accounting for pretreatment symptoms scores. In this trial, the hope therapy protocol did not include any other treatment components (e.g., mindfulness, other forms of cognitive-behavioral therapy); thus it is possible that higher hope at baseline increases the likelihood of successfully mastering and using hope skills and that this advantage is specific to hope therapy. However, Gilman, Schumm, and Chard (2012) also found that pretreatment hope scores predicted symptoms at posttreatment. Gilman and colleagues examined the role of hope in the treatment of veterans with posttraumatic stress disorder (PTSD) using cognitive processing therapy (CPT; Resick, Monson, & Chard, 2008). Pretreatment levels of hope were significantly associated with midtreatment and posttreatment symptoms of PTSD and depression, including both self-reported and observer-rated reports of PTSD. Thus, even in a treatment that did not specifically target hopeful thought, baseline hope scores were associated with lower posttreatment symptoms. In sum, across all tested treatments, those with higher hope reported less severe symptoms of depression and anxiety at each assessment time point, whether that was pretreatment, during treatment, or posttreatment; the evidence regarding baseline hope levels predicting treatment outcome is more mixed, with some investigators reporting that pretreatment hope is associated with less severe posttreatment symptoms (Cheavens et al., 2006; Gilman et al., 2012) and others reporting no association (Irving et al., 2004; Ritschel et al., 2012; Thornton et al., 2014).

What Is Hope Therapy?

Interventions to increase hope are comprised of the requisite skills for both pathways and agency thinking. Specifically, hope interventions provide participants with pathways skills related to generating multiple workable routes to a goal, anticipating and planning around obstacles, and evaluating pathways in terms of likelihood of success, costs to enact, and progress over the course of the goal pursuit. Examples of pathways skill building include exercises such as goal-mapping (i.e., drawing viable pathways, as well as the anticipated roadblocks to using those pathways, likely to result in successful goal pursuit), conducting a pros and cons evaluation of the generated pathways in order to determine the most promising route to one's goal, and evaluating progress on a given pathway at various times over the course of a goal pursuit.

In terms of agency, hope interventions tend to rely on cognitive-behavioral strategies to target goal-relevant self-talk (i.e., increasing statements such as "I believe I can do this" and "I know the best way to accomplish this goal"), increasing self-care, and maintaining and/or increasing goal-relevant motivation by determining the optimal level of challenge inherent in goals. For example, a participant with an agency deficit might be able to think of several ways through which others could reach important goals but have difficulty believing that he or she can successfully navigate those same pathways or that the desired outcomes are available. In such cases, hope therapy interventions would focus on the messages we tell ourselves when in the midst of a goal pursuit. Are the internal messages energizing and motivating or depleting and discouraging? Working on noticing and changing amotivational thoughts is essential for agency interventions. Of similar importance is a focus on identifying the optimal level of challenge in terms of maintaining and increasing energy and motivation in goal pursuits. Agency is theorized to be optimized when goals, referred to as stretch or Goldilocks (i.e., they are *just* right) goals, are at the edge of an individual's ability (Cheavens & Ritschel, 2014). Goals that are too easily accomplished

diminish agency through boredom or apathy and goals that are too difficult dampen agency via lack of reinforcement and exhaustion.

Hope interventions also include skills relevant to optimal goal-setting, including defining goals in terms of subgoals with concrete endpoints, focusing on approach-oriented goals, and making public commitments to goals in order to harness the power of social networks. Participants are taught the ways in which having goals with concrete endpoints allows for acknowledgment and celebration of successes and that approach-oriented goals are associated with naturally occurring reinforcers. By setting goals that can be intrinsically reinforced, acknowledged, and celebrated with others, the positive emotions of successful goal pursuits are enhanced and future hopeful thought is likely to be strengthened through a feedback loop (Snyder, 2002).

In the context of hope theory, goals and values have been inextricably linked (e.g., Cheavens & Ritschel, 2014; Snyder, 2002). As concordance between values and goals predicts goal pursuit success (e.g., Koestner, Lekes, Powers, & Chicoine, 2002), setting and choosing optimal goals necessitates that one considers his or her values; the most fulfilling and energizing goals are thought to be those that serve one's personal values because these value-congruent goals are most likely to be associated with high levels of agency and pathways thinking. For example, someone who values material success and prestige is likely to be able to identify several paths that are most likely to lead to material reward and recognition from peers and superiors while maintaining motivation to work toward important goals even in the face of setbacks and obstacles. However, it is likely to be more difficult for this person to engage in this same level of pathways and agency generation for a goal that might serve a lesser held value.

Can Hope Be Changed?

In Snyder's conceptualization (Snyder et al., 1991; Snyder, 2002), hope is primarily considered an individual difference construct. Thus, although context-specific (Snyder et al., 1996) and domain-specific (Shorey, Roberts, & Huprich, 2012) fluctuations are expected, hope theory posits that individuals develop lasting and global hopeful thinking that remains relatively stable across time, situations, and goals (Snyder, 1994, 2002). Test–retest reliability estimates suggest that dispositional hope is indeed quite stable ($r = .80$ across 17 studies with test–retest data; Hellman, Pittman,

& Munoz, 2013). These estimates, however, tend to be generated in samples in which there is no reason to believe that participants are actively engaged in efforts to increase their levels of hope. Given the benefits associated with hope, there is an interest in determining if hope can be increased, and the associated benefits conferred, for those with low hope.

There is evidence from college-student (Feldman & Dreher, 2012), community (Cheavens et al., 2006), older adult (Klausner et al., 1998), and medically compromised (Thornton et al., 2014) samples that hope interventions do result in changes of self-reported levels of hope. In one of the first interventions based on Snyder's (1994) theory of hope, Klausner et al. randomized 13 depressed adults ages 55 years and older to either goal-focused group psychotherapy (GFGP; based on hope theory) or a reminiscence/life-review group. Each group met for a total of 11 hours (i.e., one hour per week for 11 weeks). They found that participants in the GFGP/hope group demonstrated increases in overall hope scores and agency scores from pretreatment to posttreatment. The effect size of total hope score change was quite small ($d = .08$), but the effect size associated with the increase in agency scores ($d = 1.13$) was large. The increase in hope scores for the GFGP/hope group was not significantly different than that of the participants in the reminiscence group. However, given the small sample size, it is difficult to know whether these null findings represent equivalency across the two treatments or a lack of power to detect differences.

Cheavens et al. (2006) developed and tested a comprehensive hope therapy manual that incorporated goal-setting, pathways, and agency skills. Participants from the community who responded to ads for a group to help with successful goal completion were randomized to the hope group or a wait-list control group. The hope group protocol was delivered in 16 hours (i.e., two hours per week for eight weeks). From baseline to posttreatment eight weeks later, participants in the hope group demonstrated large increases in hope ($d = 1.04$) and agency ($d = 1.20$) scores and medium increases in pathways scores ($d = .68$). Those in the hope therapy group had larger increases in total hope ($p = .07$) and agency ($p = .04$), but not pathways, compared to those participants on the waiting list. The effect size estimates for the change in agency is similar to those from the Klausner et al. (1998) intervention, although the effect size estimates for the hope total score and pathways score changes were stronger in this study than those in the Klausner et al. intervention. In

both samples, the agency changes were more robust than the pathways changes.

Lapierre, Dubé, Bouffard, and Alain (2007) compared a 12-week personal goals intervention, with components very similar to the hope therapy used in Cheavens et al. (2006), to a no-intervention control group in a Canadian sample of recent retirees who endorsed some suicidal ideation ($n = 21$). Participants in the intervention had greater increases in hope, pathways, and agency scores compared to the control group at the end of treatment. Lapierre and colleagues included a follow-up assessment six months after the end of treatment. They found that the increases in hope, pathways, and agency scores (and the relatively stronger improvements compared to the control group) were maintained six months later. This investigation makes an important contribution to the literature in two important ways. First, by focusing on a sample of older adults who endorsed suicidal ideation, the authors demonstrated that a hope intervention can be impactful even when the participants are significantly distressed. Second, by including a six-month follow-up assessment, these authors provided the first assessment of the long-term effects of a hope intervention on hopeful thinking.

The Klausner et al. (1998), Cheavens et al. (2006), and Lapierre et al. (2007) studies are all tests of a multicomponent hope intervention across many weeks (range = 8–12) with treatment-seeking participants. It is important to also know whether hope can be changed in a shorter amount of time for individuals not seeking treatment. In a sample of unselected undergraduate students, Feldman and Dreher (2012) delivered an approximately 60-minute hope intervention that focused on goal-mapping to enhance pathways thinking and visualization of goal progress to enhance agency to small groups of undergraduate students. They found that for participants in the hope condition, compared to participants in a relaxation training condition, both pathways and agency scores increased from pre- to postsession and that the increase in pathways scores was maintained one month later.

In order to examine the role of hope in treatment for medically compromised individuals, Thornton and colleagues (2014) integrated aspects of the hope therapy protocol from Cheavens et al. (2006) with mindfulness practices and a biobehavioral intervention developed by Andersen Golden-Kreutz, Emery, and Thiel (2009) and delivered this treatment to a group of women with recurrent cancer. Results indicated that hope scores increased from pretreatment to posttreatment seven months later.

However, unlike the findings from Cheavens et al., changes in hope scores in this sample were driven by a significant increase in pathways scores over the first four months and maintenance of this improvement for the remaining three months. Agency scores did not improve in this sample. The conclusion from these interventions designed to bolster hope suggests that hope can be changed and that these changes can be maintained up to six months postintervention. However, there is still much work to be done to understand the necessary conditions for hope change as well as the differential impact on agency and pathways thinking observed in some of these investigations.

In addition to treatments that directly target hope, hope may increase during the course of therapy that is not specifically designed to bolster hope due to factors common across treatments such as treatment-initiation hopefulness and belief in treatment rationale. In the context of treatment provided in a community mental health center, Irving and colleagues (2004) measured patient hope scores at multiple sessions over the course of treatment. Therapists identified with a variety of theoretical orientations (including psychodynamic, cognitive-behavioral, and family systems) and provided treatment consistent with their theoretical orientations. Irving et al. reported a linear increase in hope scores from baseline to 11 weeks into treatment, suggesting that hope increased during treatment even when this construct was not a specific target of the treatment. Similarly, Ritschel et al. (2012) assessed patients in a dialectical behavior therapy (Linehan, 1993) intensive outpatient program. They found that hope increased linearly over the course of three weeks of daily treatment, suggesting, again, that hopeful thought is a response to treatment such that more treatment is associated with more hope. Both of these investigations focused on fairly intensive interventions (at least 12 hours of therapy delivered over at least three weeks); however, Harper-Jacques and Foucault (2014) measured change in hope up to one month after a single-session problem-solving intervention delivered in a mental health walk-in clinic. These authors found that hope scores improved from pre- to postintervention and that these gains were maintained one month later. Importantly, they found moderate to large effect size increases in both pathways and agency scores. These studies, taken together, suggest that engaging in a structured activity aimed to improve mental health functioning might in and of itself be beneficial to the experience of hope. Given the host of benefits

associated with hope, it is incredibly encouraging that hope can be increased and that there are a number of avenues through which hope can be impacted. Including assessment of hope at various points in treatment trajectories across therapeutic orientations and interventions will allow future researchers to pinpoint the particular mechanisms necessary for hope change.

Can Hope Interventions Be Used to Treat Psychological Symptoms and Disorders?

Demonstrations that indicate hope can be increased are important. The results from the previous section taken as a whole suggest that hope is for the many, not just the lucky few who developed the skills of hopeful thinking in childhood. But increasing hope is not the ultimate goal for most hope interventions. In addition to increasing hope, these interventions are designed to result in optimal psychological functioning by decreasing symptoms of psychopathology and increasing markers of psychological health such as subjective well-being, meaning in life, and self-esteem. At the end of a course of hope therapy, we would anticipate that participants would be more hopeful and also happier and more meaningfully engaged, confident, and socially connected as well as less depressed and anxious.

The data to date are extremely encouraging; hope interventions result in improved psychological functioning from pre to postintervention and tend to result in larger improvements than wait-list and active control conditions. For people who present with symptoms of psychopathology, the most important outcome is likely a reduction in symptoms. Hope therapy is associated with a reduction of symptoms of both depression (Cheavens et al., 2006; Heiy & Cheavens, 2015; Klausner et al., 1998) and anxiety (Cheavens et al., 2006; Thornton et al., 2014). Additionally, hope therapy is associated with increases in markers of well-being (Cheavens et al., 2006; Thornton et al., 2014).

Depression

In terms of depression, hope therapy, compared to control conditions, results in reductions of observer-rated (Klausner et al., 1998) and self-reported (Cheavens et al., 2006; Heiy & Cheavens, 2015) symptoms of depression. In the Klausner et al. study, depressed older adults who participated in the hope group intervention demonstrated significant reductions in both observer-rated ($d = 2.5$) and self-reported ($d = .91$) symptoms of depression from baseline to posttreatment. Importantly, participants in the hope group intervention had significantly greater reductions in observer-rated depression than participants in the reminiscence therapy group. In fact, the participants in the hope group, on average, had postsession depression ratings in the remitted range. There were no between-group differences in self-reported symptoms of depression, as both groups reported reductions.

In the Klausner et al. (1998) trial, participants were only randomized to hope therapy or reminiscence therapy if they met criteria for major depressive disorder at the initiation of the study and maintained at least residual symptoms of depression after 10 weeks of treatment with psychopharmacology or psychotherapy. The sample in the Cheavens et al. (2006) test of hope therapy was unselected; however, over half of the sample met diagnostic criteria for current mood or anxiety disorders. In this trial (Cheavens et al., 2006), participants in the hope group intervention reported significant reductions in symptoms of depression from pretreatment to posttreatment ($d = .7$), and this reduction tended to be larger than the reduction in depressive symptoms for those in the wait-list control group ($p = .07$, two-tailed). Symptoms of depression for participants in the hope group intervention (and the wait-list control group) remained in a clinically significant range at posttreatment, suggesting that in order for hope therapy to be a viable stand-alone treatment for depression, the protocol or delivery dose would need to be modified in future tests.

Recently, Heiy and Cheavens (2015) developed a very brief (i.e., approximately 20 minutes) hope intervention to be delivered for patients who screened high in depressive symptoms during their primary care appointments. The primary outcome variable of this trial was seeking treatment from a mental health professional in the weeks following the hope therapy intervention; however, change in depressive symptoms was included as a secondary outcome. In this design, the hope intervention, which included delineating valued goals for treatment of depression and generating pathways for those goals while developing and encouraging related agency thoughts, was compared to psychoeducational and treatment referral control groups. When reassessed about 10 weeks later, participants in the hope therapy intervention were approximately three times more likely to have attempted to initiate treatment than participants in the other two groups. Additionally, participants in the hope intervention group reported significantly lower symptoms of depression than participants in the other

two groups. The reduction in self-reported symptoms of depression was approximately twice as large for those in the hope group than participants in the other two groups (see also Heiy, 2014).

To test the impact of a hope intervention on symptoms of depression following an acute stressor, in this case a natural disaster, Retnowati, Ramadiyanti, Suciati, Sokang, and Viola (2015) adapted the Cheavens et al. (2006) protocol to be delivered in four two-hour sessions. Following a series of volcanic eruptions and associated flooding in Indonesia, Retnowati and colleagues delivered the hope intervention to participants in one of the impacted villages and compared the outcomes of these individuals to those in another similarly impacted village. The authors found a significant time by group interaction, suggesting that the change in self-reported depression scores was greater for those in the hope group intervention compared to the no-treatment control group.

Taken together, these findings suggest that participation in hope therapy tends to result in less depression over time (see Thornton et al., 2014, however, for contradictory findings) and that these reductions tend to be greater for those in hope therapy than for those waiting for treatment or those participating in other interventions (e.g., reminiscence/life review therapy, psychoeducation). Hope therapy has never been proposed to be, or tested as, a first-line, stand-alone treatment for depression. Thus the results from these trials are most accurately interpreted as support for the use of hope therapy to reduce depressive symptoms in conjunction with other forms of treatment for depression (i.e., Heiy & Cheavens, 2015; Klausner et al., 1998) or as an intervention to decrease distress and symptoms of depression in samples of participants not diagnosed with depression (i.e., Cheavens et al., 2006; Retnowati et al., 2015).

Anxiety

Although there are fewer reports about the effects of hope therapy on levels of anxiety compared to those of depression, there is evidence that hope therapy reduces symptoms of anxiety for both community (Cheavens et al., 2006) and medically compromised (Thornton et al., 2014) samples. To date, there have not been any trials of hope therapy specifically targeting anxiety disorders, but symptoms of anxiety disorders have been assessed in two trials. First, Cheavens et al. found that symptoms of anxiety were significantly reduced over the course of hope group therapy ($d = .8$) and that the participants in the hope group had significantly greater decreases in anxiety symptoms than those in the wait-list condition ($p = .003$). Similarly, Thornton et al. reported that self-reported anxiety symptoms decreased from pre-hope treatment to post-hope treatment ($d = .6$) in a group of women with recurrent cancer diagnoses. Thornton et al. did not find reductions in symptoms of depression over time in this sample, and it is possible that symptoms of anxiety are particularly important in the context of recurrent cancer (Meyer & Mark, 1995). Hope therapy might be an especially promising intervention for symptoms of anxiety as setting approach goals, planning ways to reach one's goals, and maintaining an energetic stance toward those goals might disrupt the worry thoughts often associated with anxiety disorders.

Well-Being

One of the primary aims of positive psychology interventions, including hope therapy, is to increase well-being and move toward optimal psychological functioning, in addition to decreasing distress and psychopathology. To that end, it is important to include measures of well-being and optimal functioning as well as symptom measures in hope therapy trials. For example, Cheavens et al. (2006) found significant increases in self-reported measures of meaning in life ($d = .5$) and self-esteem ($d = .5$) in addition to reductions in symptoms of depression and anxiety; the hope group participants had significantly greater increases in both self-esteem ($p = .02$) and meaning in life ($p = .02$) compared to participants in the wait-list condition. It is possible that hope therapy, which focuses on goal pursuits, leads to better self-esteem by providing more opportunities for goal successes and that meaning in life is impacted by focusing on goals that are consistent with one's personal values. This trial did not include multiple assessments of outcome variables, and, as such, it is impossible to determine whether reductions in symptoms preceded increases in well-being markers or the converse or if these two classes of outcomes changed concurrently. However, it is clear that, over the course of eight weeks of hope therapy, mental health indicators increased and mental illness indicators decreased, suggesting that hope therapy is a promising optimal functioning intervention.

Are Changes in Hope Associated with Changes in Symptoms?

Although none of the hope therapy studies reviewed here included tests of hope as a mechanism of change for pretreatment to posttreatment psychological functioning, several provide evidence of concurrent changes in hope and psychological functioning outcomes. For example, Cheavens et al. (2006) found that change in hope scores was significantly associated with posttreatment symptoms of depression and anxiety (in separate models) after accounting for both pretreatment symptom and hope scores. Greater pretreatment to posttreatment hope change scores were associated with lower levels of residualized symptoms of both depression and anxiety at posttreatment. Similarly, in a trial of intensive outpatient dialectical behavior therapy, Ritschel et al. (2012) found that larger increases in hope from pretreatment to posttreatment were associated with lower reports of posttreatment symptoms of depression and anxiety, after accounting for initial symptom severity levels.

Gilman et al. (2012) included assessments of hope and symptom measures at multiple time points across the course of CPT for PTSD in a sample of veterans. This design allows for tests of temporal sequencing of change and provides some information regarding whether changes in hope and symptoms are concurrent or if change in one of these constructs precedes change in the other. In this sample, pretreatment hope predicted posttreatment clinician-rated PTSD severity, but pretreatment clinician-rated PTSD severity did not predict posttreatment hope. Similarly, midtreatment hope scores predicted posttreatment self-reported PTSD and depression severity, but the converse (midtreatment self-reported PTSD and depression severity predicting posttreatment hope scores) was not significant. This contribution to the hope literature is extremely important because it tests the role of hope as a non-targeted mechanism of change with a sample of individuals with diagnosed disorders. In other words, although CPT is not designed to target hope specifically in the treatment of PTSD, changes in hope did occur over the course of treatment and these changes predicted reductions in symptom severity. Changes in symptom severity did not predict changes in hope, suggesting that the relation between hope and symptom severity in the context of treatment is not bidirectional or solely concurrent.

The Next Steps in Hope Therapy Research
Hope Therapy for What/Whom?

The investigations of hope therapy to date have been conducted with a wide array of presenting problems, including samples of unselected adults with significant symptoms of depression and anxiety (Cheavens et al., 2006), depressed older adults (Klausner et al., 1998), primary care patients with high symptoms of depression (Heiy & Cheavens, 2015), women with recurrent cancer (Thornton et al., 2014), and survivors of natural disasters (Retnowati et al., 2015). In all of these trials, changes in symptoms of depression were assessed, and in about half of these trials, changes in anxiety symptoms and hope scores were also assessed. Although the diversity of these samples speaks to the potential generalizability of hope therapy, it makes it difficult to draw conclusions regarding for whom or under what circumstances hope therapy might be most efficacious. Additionally, it is too early to determine whether the promising findings replicate because the samples, methodology, and measurement practices are so distinct that any fluctuations in results can be attributed to patient characteristics, protocol differences, or design differences. The literature to date suggests that hopeful thought and symptoms of depression are promising targets of hope therapy. Additionally, the effect sizes for symptoms of anxiety suggest that the effects of hope therapy on anxiety may be as strong as or stronger than the effects of hope therapy on depression. Further, there are a number of targets that would theoretically respond to a hope intervention (e.g., pain management, interpersonal relationships, suicide ideation) that have not been tested. As proposed by Cheavens et al. (2006), it may be that hope therapy is most useful as a first-line treatment for those who are dissatisfied, distressed, or are otherwise experiencing problems in living as opposed to those who meet criteria for mental health disorders. In future research on hope therapy, it is important to determine the most promising and important targets of treatment.

Distinguishing Hope Therapy from Other Cognitive Behavioral Interventions

The potential role of hope in cognitive-behavioral treatments has been explicated numerous times (Snyder et al., 2000; Snyder, Michael, & Cheavens, 1999). Based on the work of Frank and Frank (1991), Snyder and colleagues (1999) have argued that early in treatment hope may serve as a common factors variable that allows individuals to be energized and motivated by the promise of help and the rationale offered by treatment providers across various treatment disciplines and modalities. In this way, hope would explain early treatment gains that might precede skill acquisition. Cognitive-behavioral treatments may be specifically well suited to capitalize on the hope framework. Cognitive-behavioral interventions tend to be goal focused and rely on teaching and generalizing skills. Targeting individual goals and working to problem-solve discrepancies between goals and current functioning is likely to result in an increase in pathways thinking or make use of existing strengths in pathways thinking. Similarly, the work done to reduce negative thoughts and social isolation are likely to increase agency or the impact of existing agentic thought (Snyder et al., 2000). In the development of their protocol, Cheavens et al. (2006) noted that hope therapy utilizes many strategies common in cognitive-behavioral interventions, including positive self-talk interventions, tracking of behavioral progress, and homework. In moving forward with this research agenda, it will be important to distinguish hope therapy from other forms of cognitive-behavioral therapies. For example, there needs to be some consensus on the prescribed and proscribed components of hope therapy. Additionally, including both hope therapy and other active treatments in intervention studies will allow for examination of treatment processes and outcomes that are shared and unique.

Hope as a Mechanism of Change

The implicit theory in hope interventions is that directly targeting and increasing hope will result in goal-setting, pathways, and agency skills that can be used to tackle myriad stressors across life domains. Theoretically, these skills would lead to more successful goal pursuits, which in turn would lead to more experiences of positive emotions and fewer experiences of negative emotions. In other words, increased hope would be the mechanism through which decreases in psychological distress, increases in subjective well-being, increases in goal successes, and other favorable outcomes would occur. However, to date, there are no investigations of hope therapy that allow for a test of this chain of events. To be confident that hope is a mechanism of change in treatment, we need more designs that demonstrate that changes in hope precede changes in goal pursuit behavior, which in turn precede changes in psychological and performance outcomes. Only through investigations of this nature can we pinpoint the role of hope in the change process.

Conclusion

At higher levels of hope, people tend to be happier, more productive, and more socially connected and have fewer signs of psychopathology. One of the open questions in hope theory has always been whether hope can be increased such that more people can share in these desirable outcomes or if the benefits of hope are limited to the lucky few. Several psychotherapy outcome studies now suggest that hope is responsive to intervention and can be increased in a number of treatment modalities. Additionally, hope therapy has been used to successfully reduce symptoms of depression and anxiety and increase meaning in life and self-esteem. Importantly, changes in hope are associated with changes in symptoms of depression and anxiety disorders as well as indices of well-being. Although there is still work to be done in order to understand the mechanisms of change and the necessary components of treatment, hope therapy delivers on the promise that hope and the associated benefits are for the many.

Future Directions

• For whom are hope interventions likely to be most effective? Are there particular psychological difficulties that are most likely to respond to hope interventions?

• What are the prescriptive and proscriptive components of hope therapy? How should hope interventions be distinguished from other cognitive-behavioral or positive psychology interventions?

• Do changes in goal-setting and goal-pursuit skills precede changes in hopeful thought? Do changes in goal outcomes precede or follow changes in hopeful thought?

• Is change in hope a replicable mechanism of change in symptoms of psychopathology in non-hope interventions?

• What is the most appropriate "dose" of hope interventions for lasting changes?

References

Andersen, B. L., Golden-Kreutz, D. M., Emery, C. F., & Thiel, D. L. (2009). Biobehavioral intervention for cancer stress: Conceptualization, components, and intervention strategies. *Cognitive and Behavioral Practice, 16*, 253–265. doi:10.1016/j.cbpra.2008.11.002

Carretta, C. M., Ridner, S. H., & Dietrich, M. S. (2014). Hope, hopelessness, and anxiety: A pilot instrument comparison study. *Archives of Psychiatric Nursing, 28*, 230–234. doi:10.1016/j.apnu.2014.05.005

Chang, E. C. (2003). A critical appraisal and extension of hope theory in middle-aged men and women: Is it important to distinguish agency and pathways components? *Journal of Social and Clinical Psychology, 22*, 121–143.

Cheavens, J. S., Feldman, D. B., Gum, A. Michael, S. T., & Snyder, C. R. (2006). Hope therapy in a community

sample: A pilot investigation. *Social Indicators Research, 77*, 61–78. doi:10.1007/s11205-005-5553-0

Cheavens, J. S., & Ritschel, L. A. (2014). Hope theory. In M. M. Tugade, M. N. Shiota, & L. D. Kirby (Eds.), *Handbook of positive emotions* (pp. 396–410). New York: Guilford Press.

Cramer, K. M., & Dyrkacz, L. (1998). Differential prediction of maladjustment scores with the Snyder Hope subscales. *Psychological Reports, 83*, 1035–1041. doi:10.2466/PR0.83.7.1035-1041

Curry, L. A., Snyder, C. R., Cook, D. L., Ruby, B. C., & Rehm, M. (1997). Role of hope in academic and sport achievement. *Journal of Personality and Social Psychology, 73*, 1257–1267. doi:10.1037/0022-3514.73.6.1257

Feldman, D. B., & Dreher, D. E. (2012). Can hope be changed in 90 minutes? Testing the efficacy of a single-session goal-pursuit intervention for college students. *Journal of Happiness Studies, 13*, 745–759. doi:10.1007/s10902-011-9292-4

Feldman, D. B., Rand, K. L., & Kahle-Wrobleski, K. (2009). Hope and goal attainment: Testing a basic prediction of hope theory. *Journal of Social and Clinical Psychology, 28*, 479–497. doi:10.1521/jscp.2009.28.4.479

Frank, J. D., & Frank, J. B. (1991). *Persuasion and healing* (3rd ed.). Baltimore: Johns Hopkins University Press.

Gilman, R., Schumm, J. A., & Chard, K. M. (2012). Hope as a change mechanism in the treatment of posttraumatic stress disorder. *Psychological Trauma: Theory, Research, Practice, and Policy, 4*, 270–277. doi:10.1037/a0024252

Harper-Jacques, S., & Foucault, D. (2014). Walk-in single-session therapy: Client satisfaction and clinical outcomes. *Journal of Systemic Therapies, 33*, 29–49. doi:10.1521/jsyt.2014.33.3.29

Heiy, J. E. (2014). *A brief intervention on treatment-seeking: Barriers to mental health treatment.* Doctoral dissertation. Retrieved from Proquest (3672311).

Heiy, J. E., & Cheavens, J. S. (2015). *A brief intervention in primary care: Increasing treatment-seeking and reducing symptoms of depression. Unpublished manuscript.* Department of Psychology, Ohio State University, Columbus.

Hellman, C. M., Pittman, M. K., & Munoz, R. T. (2013). The first twenty years of the will and the ways: An examination of score reliability distribution on Snyder's Dispositional Hope Scale. *Journal of Happiness Studies, 14*, 723–729. doi:10.1007/s10902-012-9351-5

Hirsch, J. K., Visser, P. L., Chang, E. C., & Jeglic, E. L. (2012). Race and ethnic differences in hope and hopelessness as moderators of the association between depressive symptoms and suicidal behavior. *Journal of American College Health, 60*, 115–125. doi:10.1080/07448481.2011.567402

Irving, L. M., Snyder, C. R., Cheavens, J., Gravel, L., Hanke, J., Hilberg, P., & Nelson, N. (2004). The relationships between hope and outcomes at the pretreatment, beginning, and later phases of psychotherapy. *Journal of Psychotherapy Integration, 14*, 419–443. doi:10.1037/1053-0479.14.4.419

Klausner, E. J., Clarkin, J. F., Spielman, L., Pupo, C., Abrams, R., & Alexopoulos, G. S. (1998). Late-life depression and functional disability: The role of goal-focused group psychotherapy. *International Journal of Geriatric Psychiatry, 13*, 707–716. doi:10.1002/(SICI)1099-1166(1998100)13:10<707:AID-GPS856>3.0.CO;2-Q

Koestner, R., Lekes, N., Powers, T., & Chicoine, E. (2002). Attaining personal goals: Self-concordance plus implementation intentions equals success. *Journal of Personality and Social Psychology, 83*, 231–244. doi:10.1037/0022-3514.83.1.231

Lapierre, S., Dubé, Bouffard, L., & Alain, M. (2007). Addressing suicidal ideations through the realization of meaningful personal goals. *Crisis, 28,* 16–25. doi:10.1027/0227-5910.28.1.16

Linehan, M. M. (1993*). Cognitive-behavioral treatment of border-line personality disorder.* New York: Guilford Press.

Meyer, T. J., & Mark, M. M. (1995). Effects of psychosocial interventions with adult cancer patients: A meta-analysis of randomized experiments. *Health Psychology, 14,* 101–108. doi:10.1037/0278-6133.14.2.101

Resick, P. A., Monson, C. M., & Chard, K. M. (2008). *Cognitive processing therapy: Veteran/military manual.* Cincinnati, OH: Veterans Administration.

Retnowati, S. Ramadiyanti, D. W., Suciati, A. A., Sokang, Y. A., & Viola, H. (2015). Hope intervention against depression in the survivors of cold lava flood from Merapi Mount. *Procedia: Social and Behavioral Sciences, 165,* 170–178. doi:10.1016/j.sbspro.2014.12.619

Ritschel, L. A., Cheavens, J. S., & Nelson, J. (2012). Dialectical behavior therapy in an intensive outpatient program with a mixed-diagnostic sample. *Journal of Clinical Psychology, 68,* 221–235. doi:10.1002/jclp.20863

Shorey, H. S., Roberts, C. R. D., & Huprich, S. K. (2012). The roles of domain specific hope and depressive personality in predicting depressive symptoms. *Personality and Mental Health, 6,* 255–265. doi:10.1002/pmh.1189

Snyder, C. R. (1994). *The psychology of hope.* New York: Free Press.

Snyder, C. R. (2002). Hope theory: Rainbows in the mind. *Psychological Inquiry, 13,* 249–275.

Snyder, C. R., Cheavens, J., & Sympson, S. C. (1997). Hope: An individual motive for social commerce. *Group Dynamics: Theory, Research, and Practice, 1,* 107–118. doi:10.1037/1089-2699.1.2.107

Snyder, C. R., Harris, C., Anderson, J. R., Holleran, S. A., Irving, L. M., Sigmon, S. T., . . . Harney, P. (1991). The will and the ways: Development and validation of an individual-differences measure of hope. *Journal of Personality and Social Psychology, 60,* 570–585. doi:10.1037/0022-3514.60.4.570

Snyder, C. R., Ilardi, S. S., Cheavens, J., Michael, S. T., Yamhure, L., & Sympson, S. (2000). The role of hope in cognitive-behavior therapies. *Cognitive Therapy and Research, 24,* 747–762. doi:10.1023/A:1005547730153

Snyder, C. R., Michael, S. T., & Cheavens, J. (1999). Hope as a psychotherapeutic foundation of common factors, placebos, and expectancies. In M. A, Huble, B. L. Duncan, & S. D. Miller (Eds.), *The heart and soul of change: What works in therapy* (pp. 179–200). Washington, DC: American Psychological Association. doi:10.1037/11132-005

Snyder, C. R., Shorey, H. S., Cheavens, J., Pulvers, K. M., Adams, V. H., & Wiklund, C. (2002). Hope and academic success in college. *Journal of Educational Psychology, 94,* 820–826. doi:10.1037/0022-0663.94.4.820

Snyder, C. R., Sympson, S. C., Ybasco, F. C., Borders, T. F., Babyak, M. A., & Higgins, R. L. (1996). Development and validation of the State Hope Scale. *Journal of Personality and Social Psychology, 70,* 321–335. doi:10.1037/0022-3514.70.2.321

Thornton, L. M., Cheavens, J. S., Heitzmann, C. A., Dorfman, C. S., Wu, S. M., & Andersen, B. L. (2014). Test of mindfulness and hope components in a psychological intervention for women with cancer recurrence. *Journal of Consulting and Clinical Psychology, 82,* 1087–1100. doi:10.1037/a0036959

Promoting Hope in Older Adults

Amber M. Gum

Abstract

As evidenced by 15 years of research, hopeful older adults reject negative stereotypes of aging; envision themselves as aging successfully; plan for later life; cope with stressors; apply wisdom; and perceive good physical, mental, and social well-being. Hopeful older adults even live longer than less hopeful older adults. Preliminary research indicates that older adults participating in individual- and small-group interventions can learn and apply strategies to improve hope, goal pursuits, and distress. The larger social and physical environments create barriers to pursuing goals in later life, including ageism and physical barriers. Thus broader social and environmental interventions may provide additional pathways to foster older adults' hope and goal pursuits, as well as to help younger generations develop more positive views of aging and prepare for successful aging.

Key Words: hope, older adults, goals, ageism, aging

Most, if not all, of us hope to live a long life in which we attain most of our chosen goals, culminating in final goals for a peaceful dying process and a legacy that contributes to loved ones and others after we die. While each of us has unique goals, as we age, we usually attempt to maintain or improve functioning in important life areas, such as health, relationships, and spirituality. In addition, we may pursue new goals as circumstances change over time, such as helping to raise grandchildren, traveling, or learning new skills after retirement. Certain life events are more common for older adults that make it more difficult to pursue goals, such as poor health, death of a life partner, or financial difficulties following retirement or health problems. At the same time, older adults may have more resources, such as time, finances, knowledge, and skills, to pursue new opportunities and goals.

Hopeful older adults pursue meaningful, feasible goals with tenacious agency and resourceful pathways, maximizing new opportunities, adjusting to losses, and resisting ageism. We can likely promote hope for older adults in a variety of ways that span

individual to global strategies. Taking on the goal of promoting hope for older adults on a global scale may sound unrealistic, but it benefits us all. We live on a planet that, as of 2017, has more older adults than children—an unprecedented demographic shift that we observe across almost all societies (World Health Organization, 2011).

The Nature of Hope for Older Adults

The (first and) last handbook chapter about hope in older adults was published in 2000 (Cheavens & Gum, 2000). It contained a citation for one published empirical study of hopeful thinking that used the Hope Scale with older adults. In contrast, this chapter contains citations for 13 different empirical studies involving older participants (not including secondary publications from the same data sets). These publications describe new cross-sectional, longitudinal, and intervention studies conducted in several different countries, including Canada, Germany, Greece, Israel, and the United States.

This research indicates that, overall, hope remains stable over time, has comparable associations with other positive attributes as earlier in life, and improves in response to individual or small-group interventions. Being able to turn one's attention from thwarted goals and invest in other meaningful goals may be particularly relevant for older adults. Nonetheless, it is clear that the basic processes of hope, pathways, and agency operate across ages.

Hope tends to be stable within older adults across time, moderately correlated ($r = .44$) over six years for older adults in Germany who participated in a large population-based, longitudinal study of aging ($N = 1,286$; Wurm, Tesch-Römer, & Tomasik, 2007). As with younger age groups, pathways and agency are correlated ($r = .57$) for older adults. Compared to lower hope older adults, those with higher hope perceive that they used more pathways in the past, have a greater chance of reaching an important future goal, and are further along toward reaching that goal (Wrobleski & Snyder, 2005). Given their use of more pathways, Wrobleski and Snyder speculated, "our results raise the intriguing speculation that hope in older age may be as much about looking back as it is about looking forward" (p. 230).

It is unclear whether average level of hope changes with age. Quite a bit of gerontological theory and research focus on the challenges of aging (i.e., goal blockages), which might lead to a hypothesis that hope declines with age. In the population-based German sample, within one wave of data, hope was slightly negative correlated with age ($r = -.14$; Wiest, Schüz, & Wurm, 2013). Another study found slightly lower total hope scores for middle-age compared to younger age groups, but the sample size within age groups was fairly small (sample sizes were 16–56 within age groups; total $N = 215$), the older adults had similar hope scores as younger groups, and the means were not very different (23 for middle-age versus 25–26 for younger age groups; Bailey & Snyder, 2007). At this time, it seems that, if hope declines with age at all, the magnitude of decline is very small, with significant differences across people.

Instead of having lower hope overall, many older adults choose to focus their efforts on select goals and disengage from other goals. The dominant theories of lifespan development identify goals as "cornerstones of developmental regulation" (Haase, Heckhausen, & Wrosch, 2013, p. 965). Using structural equation modeling from two data sets of adults across ages (including older adults), Haase and colleagues integrated 11 concepts across three leading developmental theories into three goal-related processes: goal engagement, goal disengagement, and metaregulation. Across our lives, we identify discrepancies between our existing state and desired states (i.e., a goal), and then we pursue some goals (goal engagement) while relinquishing others (goal disengagement). At a higher level (metaregulation), we choose which goals to pursue and let go, manage multiple goals, and ensure we have goals across multiple domains. In both data sets analyzed by Haase and colleagues, greater metaregulation predicted more goal engagement as well as more disengagement, both of which also predicted better well-being. Compared to younger age groups, older adults appear to use more of all three processes, pursuing goals, disengaging from goals, and managing multiple goal pursuits. And goal disengagement may be particularly important in later life, as it predicted a greater sense of purpose in life only for older adults (Haase et al., 2013). Thus many older adults actively think about, select, and pursue goals, and they also stop pursuing other goals, which is adaptive in certain situations.

One might assume that older adults disengage from more goals than younger adults due to confronting more goal blockages, but there could be other, more positive reasons too. For example, older adults may learn that some goals that occupy many younger people are not satisfying in the long term (e.g., material possessions, popularity) or that it is more rewarding and productive to live a simpler life in which they focus on fewer goals. It is important to remember that older age comes with challenges but also a wealth of experience in pursuing goals and many other strengths. Later adulthood also can come with unique opportunities, such as having more discretionary time after retirement and child-rearing.

Attributes of Hopeful Older Adults

Hopeful older adults are more likely to perceive better physical well-being, mental well-being, and attitudinal and coping resources compared to less hopeful older adults. They even live longer, perhaps due to health behaviors. It is impossible to determine causality and interrelationships of these associations, which in reality probably influence each other in myriad, cyclical ways.

Physical Well-Being

Higher hope is associated with better perceived physical health and functioning, according to studies of community-dwelling older adults in the United States (Barnett, 2014; Wrobleski & Snyder,

2005) and the epidemiological study of German older adults (Steverink, Westerhof, Bode, & Dittmann-Kohli, 2001; Wurm et al., 2007). Hope may not be strongly related to more objective indicators of physical health, such as number of physical conditions or symptoms (Wrobleski & Snyder, 2005; Wurm et al., 2007). In the German sample ($N = 1,286$), hope did not independently predict number of physical illnesses six years later, although high hope at both time points was correlated with fewer perceived physical losses concurrently and across time points (Wurm et al., 2007).

Physical limitations may have multifaceted relationships with hope and functioning, as suggested by a cross-sectional study of survivors three months following stroke in the United States (Gum, Snyder, & Duncan, 2006). Stroke survivors reported better participation in meaningful activities if they had high hope and fewer activity limitations in physical functioning, memory, and communication. On the other hand, if they had more severe activity limitations and high hope, they reported less participation than lower hope participants. It may be that high-hope stroke survivors maximize preserved abilities to participate in meaningful activities, whereas those with severe activity limitations may focus on restoring those abilities, foregoing participation goals (Gum et al., 2006).

High-hope older adults may live longer than lower hope elders, as suggested by the eight-year follow-up of the German longitudinal study (Wiest et al., 2013). In this study, high hope predicted lower mortality eight years later (hazard ratio = .80) after controlling for life satisfaction, which did not predict mortality. The statistical relationship between hope and mortality disappeared after controlling for smoking and functional health, although it interacted with life satisfaction in the final model. Thus, in the final model, participants were more likely to die within eight years if they smoked, had poorer functional health, and had low hope *and* low life satisfaction. Perhaps high-hope older adults engage in more healthy behaviors and fewer unhealthy behaviors like smoking. In support of this hypothesis, a study of younger Americans found that hope predicted health behaviors (salt/fat intake, exercise) one month later for participants who were knowledgeable about the health behavior or thought it was important (Feldman & Dreher, 2012). Also, low life satisfaction might not contribute to mortality in the presence of high hope, in which case someone might be able to change dissatisfying aspects of his or her life (Wiest et al., 2013).

In summary, high-hope older adults perceive good physical health and functioning. They may be able to maximize their physical abilities to participate in meaningful activities, although they may become single-mindedly focused on overcoming more severe physical limitations. They live longer than lower hope older adults, which may be because they take better care of themselves through various health behaviors and also because of having better mental well-being and coping.

Mental Well-Being

Compared to older adults with less hope, hopeful older adults experience better mental well-being, including lower depressive symptoms (Cheavens, Cukrowicz, Hansen, & Mitchell, 2016; Gum et al., 2006), less suicidal ideation (Cheavens et al., 2016), lower negative affect, greater positive affect, better life satisfaction (Steverink et al., 2001), and greater overall mental well-being (Barnett, 2014). These studies span diverse samples, including the German population-based study (Steverink et al., 2001), general community sample (Barnett, 2014), primary care (Cheavens et al., 2016), and stroke survivors (Gum et al., 2006) in the United States.

Hope may benefit mood in spite of physical challenges. For example, in the study of stroke survivors, hope predicted lower depressive symptoms after controlling for physical and other activity limitations (Gum et al., 2006). For older American primary care patients high in hope, their functional limitations were less strongly associated with depressive symptoms than for lower hope patients (Hirsch, Sirois, & Lyness, 2011).

It is likely that hope and mental well-being influence each other in dynamic ways. While the previously cited research examined hope as a predictor of well-being, other research suggests that affect predicts hope (Moraitou & Efklides, 2013). Specifically, using structural equation modeling with a sample of 446 community-dwelling Greek adults ranging in age from 20 to 80, positive affect predicted pathways, and positive and negative affect each predicted agency. Here, the feedback loops of pathways and agency to positive and negative affect were not significant, suggesting affect contributed more strongly to hope than vice versa. Thus older adults experiencing positive affect appear better able to identify pathways to goals and agency to pursue those goals, whereas negative affect may sap agency to pursue goals.

Thus hopeful older adults experience better mental well-being and moods than lower-hope older adults. Hope may buffer against negative moods, and moods likely impact pathways and agency as well. There are probably many mechanisms linking hope and mental well-being, including attitudes and coping resources.

Attitudes and Coping Resources

Hope in older adults is linked to several adaptive attitudes and coping resources. Hopeful older adults respond well to stress and have more wisdom, better attitudes about aging, and better social functioning than less hopeful older adults. First, it appears that high-hope older adults are particularly good at responding to stressful events. Ong and Edwards, and Bergeman (2006) conducted a daily study with 27 older Americans for 45 days. At baseline, participants completed the trait Hope Scale and other measures; then, every day for 45 days, they completed the state Hope Scale and measures of daily stressful events and negative affect. Those with high trait hope reported fewer daily stressors and higher daily hope. Across all participants, on days when hope was high, stressors that occurred those days were less strongly associated with negative affect, compared to days of lower hope. Also, for those with higher trait hope, on days they experienced more stressors, the stressors were less associated with negative affect the next day, suggesting their negative affect did not fluctuate much in response to stressors. On the other hand, lower hope participants had more negative affect the day after a stressor than on lower stress days, suggesting more fluctuations in negative affect following stressors.

Taken together, the findings by Ong and colleagues (2006) suggest that hope may help older adults to experience (or at least perceive) fewer stressors and to respond to those stressors with less distress. These findings are highly consistent with general principles of hope theory. Hopeful people are able to work toward and achieve goals while working around obstacles; this goal progress and success could prevent many stressors, such as financial planning that prevents future financial problems. Moreover, hopeful people perceive that they can "find many ways to get out of a jam," as asked by the Hope Scale (Snyder et al., 1991), so they probably respond to a stressor calmly and begin to think of goals and pathways to address it, with sufficient agency to implement the pathways.

Related to coping response, hopeful older adults are wiser than less hopeful elders. Based on the study with Greek adults (Moraitou & Efklides,

2012, 2013), across adulthood, hope is associated with wisdom, which could contribute to more adaptive coping and goal pursuits. Moraitou and Efklides conceptualized wisdom according to three components, including practical wisdom (i.e., using knowledge and experience to manage life dilemmas), dialectical thinking (i.e., perceiving multiple perspectives), and awareness of life uncertainty. In structural equation modeling, they found that agency predicted greater practical wisdom (not vice versa), and pathways predicted greater dialectical thinking (not vice versa). They suggested that agency was an "energizer" for wise thinking (Moraitou & Efklides, 2013, p. 211) and that being able to identify multiple strategies to achieve goals contributed to an ability to see future situations, goals, and problems from multiple perspectives. The older participants were not necessarily wiser than younger participants, but the combination of age and education predicted greater wisdom, especially practical wisdom (Moraitou & Efklides, 2012). The authors suggested that education might help older (more experienced) adults use their experience analytically to solve new problems and goals. This finding is interesting given hope's strong associations with educational attainment (Snyder et al., 2002), which could lead to greater wisdom in adulthood.

Older adults hold various attitudes about growing old, which likely affect their hope and goal pursuits. Overall it appears that hopeful older adults hold more positive views about aging. In the study of German older adults, hopeful participants were more likely than lower hope participants to perceive that they continued to grow as they aged; in regression analyses predicting continued growth, hope was the strongest predictor ($\beta = .46$), more so than age itself ($\beta = -.27$; Steverink et al., 2001). Perceived growth in turn predicted better life satisfaction. This relationship may be reciprocal, as perceived continued growth at baseline was correlated with hope six years later (Wurm et al., 2007). Similarly, in the Greek sample, agency predicted older adults' sense of general adaptation to aging and self control, and pathways predicted several aging attitudes, including overall perceived health, general adaptation, self control, and generativity (Moraitou, Kolovou, Papasozomenou, & Paschoula, 2006). These findings are important given that middle-aged and older adults who hold negative views of aging experience worse health, which appears to be partially mediated by lower physical activity (Beyer, Wolff, Warner, Schüz, & Wurm, 2015). Perhaps hope protects older adults from these negative attitudes and ageism from society, so they can continue to be physically active and pursue meaningful goals.

Hope also likely relates to social functioning in older adults, which is important given the strong associations of loneliness to late-life depression and suicide risk (Barg et al., 2006). In the large German study of older adults, hopeful older adults perceived less social loss (Steverink et al., 2001). In a sample of American older primary care patients, hopeful patients reported that they felt less like a burden to others and had a better sense of belongingness; these factors predicted suicidal ideation (although hope did not independently predict suicidal ideation; Cheavens et al., 2016). In a population-based study of older Israelis, those who had experienced more other-oriented adversity (i.e., adversities that had occurred to other people) were more hopeful than those with fewer other-oriented adversities (Keinan, Shrira, & Shmotkin, 2012). The authors suggested that these adverse events might have activated the individual's desire and commitment to help. These studies suggest multiple relationships among hope and social functioning. Hope may help older adults develop and maintain social relationships, and even to help others who are in distress. Moreover, other people can help older adults be hopeful, such as by encouraging, showing positive affect and regard, and helping identify or implement pathways.

As a whole, the research that has been conducted with older adults across several countries indicates that hopeful older adults have a variety of other strengths, including perceived physical health and functioning, positive moods, coping with stress, wisdom, positive attitudes about growing older, and social relationships. Consequently, we might wonder, can we enhance hope for older adults, and if so, how do they benefit?

Promoting Hope for Older Adults

The existing interventions to promote hopeful thinking and goal pursuits are individual or small-group behavioral interventions. These interventions likely benefit older adults, as they do earlier in life. Building on individual- and small-group interventions, can we think bigger yet? Could larger scale social interventions curb ageism and promote positive views of aging, hope, and goal pursuits? Could some kinds of built and natural environments facilitate older adults' goal pursuits as well?

Individual and Small-Group Interventions

Individual and small-group interventions have been tested mostly with younger ages, although a small amount of research indicates they are valuable with older adults as well. As reviewed in this handbook (see chapter 11), hope is relevant to adult psychotherapy. Across different types of psychotherapy, patients who begin therapy with higher hope experience greater reduction in depressive symptoms than those who begin therapy with less hope. Moreover, behavioral interventions that specifically target hope and goals benefit participants—participants improve in hope, depressive symptoms, and anxiety symptoms. In hope interventions, the clinician helps participants learn how to identify important life goals, how to set goals that are likely to be achieved, how to foster agency, how to generate multiple pathways, and how to deal with obstacles. Based on at least one study, a hope intervention can help participants actually make more progress toward goals (Feldman & Dreher, 2012). Recent meta-analyses have demonstrated small benefits of positive psychology interventions, including hope and goal-pursuit interventions (Bolier et al., 2013). In a meta-analysis focused on hope interventions, many of which used the Hope Scale as an outcome, hope interventions improved hopefulness and life satisfaction but not distress (Weis & Speridakos, 2011). These meta-analyses are helpful in terms of providing detailed reviews of hope and other positive psychology interventions, but there was striking heterogeneity across studies, and many studies did not select distressed individuals. Thus the conclusions from the meta-analytic statistics should be interpreted cautiously.

Intervention Research with Older Adults

Only one hope intervention has been tested with an exclusively older adult sample, a small pilot randomized controlled trial conducted in the late 1990s in the United States (Klausner et al., 1998). The sample included 13 older adults with major depression, 10 of whom had been treated previously with antidepressant medication without benefit. Klausner and colleagues developed their intervention specifically based on Snyder's hope theory, teaching participants strategies to pursue goals and enhance their agency and pathways. The findings were promising although tentative given the small sample size. Hope improved significantly for the hope group (pretreatment $M = 22.8$, posttreatment $M = 31.7$) but not the reminiscence group (pretreatment $M = 20.5$, posttreatment $M = 27.5$). The hope group improved more on depressive symptoms and hopelessness, but the difference in change scores for the Hope Scale was not significant (Klausner et al.,

1998; Klausner, Snyder, & Cheavens, 2000). These results are particularly encouraging given that this sample could be considered difficult to treat, given they had major depression and had already been taking antidepressant medication without experiencing improvement.

Similarly, a hope intervention can benefit middle-aged adults as they transition into retirement (Dubé, Lapierre, Bouffard, & Alain, 2007). The authors used a quasi-experimental design in which early retirees in Canada were recruited into a goals intervention or a study of adaptation to retirement (i.e., no-treatment control group). The control group had higher hope at baseline (as measured by the Hope Scale), and the treatment group improved to a comparable level at follow-up. The treatment group also improved more for distress, and results suggested that improvements in hope mediated improvements in outcomes, including distress and adjustment to retirement. The intervention also was beneficial for a subset of the participants who had suicidal ideation at baseline (Lapierre, Dubé, Bouffard, & Alain, 2007). Retirement is a critical time for older adults, when a major life goal is ending (one's career); a hope intervention can help such individuals put that goal in context and begin to pursue goals for a new phase of life.

Problem-solving therapy is distinct from hope interventions but has some similarities and is considered an evidence-based intervention for depressed older adults (Wyman, Gum, & Areán, 2011). In problem-solving therapy, the interventionist teaches a patient a specific, step-by-step process to solve problems. After defining the problem in detail, the second step is to identify a very specific goal that addresses the problem, and the remaining steps involve strategies to achieve that goal (brainstorm solutions, evaluate pros and cons of solutions, select one or more solutions, develop a specific action plan for the chosen solution, implement, and evaluate the outcome). The main difference seems to be that hope interventions begin by focusing on desired states (i.e., goals) instead of problems. Also, problem-solving therapy does not include a higher order consideration of one's life meaning and goals, as through the concept of metaregulation (Haase et al., 2013). Nonetheless, the research on problem-solving therapy provides additional empirical support for the general hypothesis that an intervention that teaches strategies to systematically pursue goals benefits older adults.

It is possible that hope may improve through behavioral activation, which is another evidence-based intervention (Dimidjian, Barrera, Martell, Munoz, & Lewinsohn, 2011) that improves depressive symptoms for older adults (Moss, Scogin, Di Napoli, & Presnell, 2012; Yon & Scogin, 2009). In behavioral activation, an interventionist helps a patient to identify and engage in behaviors expected to bring about a sense of enjoyment or accomplishment, in an attempt to increase rewarding experiences. Given that positive affect may bolster hope and negative affect may drain hope, it is possible that directly increasing rewarding experiences could indirectly improve hope.

When Hope Gets in the Way

A question that may arise when applying a hope or goal-focused intervention with older adults is whether a thwarted goal should be considered lost (i.e., impossible, should be given up) or blocked (i.e., still may be possible if an effective pathway is found). Hope theorists have contemplated the issue of false hope (Snyder & Rand, 2003). Almost all research has found positive associations between hope and other positive attributes, although it seems possible that hope could be harmful in particular instances. For example, high-hope stroke survivors who were more severely limited in mobility, memory, or communication were less likely to participate in meaningful activities compared to those with fewer limitations. Imagine a high-hope survivor with severe mobility limitations who is bound and determined to walk and refuses a wheelchair, thereby limiting participation (Gum et al., 2006).

To address this kind of scenario, it may be beneficial to discuss the patient's goals: What does it mean for you to walk? What does it mean for you to not walk? What other goals does walking help you achieve? What other goals would be blocked by not walking? What does it mean to use a wheelchair? What other goals would using a wheelchair serve? What other goals would be blocked by using a wheelchair? Do you have to choose only one? Is it possible to pursue both? Oftentimes, a patient insists upon a goal because it is very important and serves as a pathway to higher order, meaningful goals. In this hypothetical scenario, walking helps us get to places we want to go, it is beneficial exercise to promote health, it is enjoyable in its own right, and, perhaps more importantly, it is a symbol of independence for many people. By identifying these higher order goals, a patient may come to see walking as one of several pathways and be more willing to pursue other pathways to achieve the same goals. This patient might also even come to see using a wheelchair as a pathway to doing more and being independent. Discussing concerns about a goal also can help patients to reframe the goal or change pathways. This patient might be concerned that using a wheelchair means becoming weak from the lack of movement and giving up on walking forever. It can be very powerful to remind a patient that he or she need not choose only one goal. A provider could help the patient to realize he or she could pursue both goals and could identify strategies to make sure that using the wheelchair helps to achieve meaningful higher order goals (e.g., participating in social activities) while still working on walking (e.g., physical therapy, deciding when it is best to use the wheelchair versus trying to walk).

Thus, in at least some cases, it may not matter whether an older adult views a goal as lost or blocked, even in seemingly dire circumstances like terminal illness (Gum & Snyder, 2002). An important key seems to be to have a variety of goals, some of which are likely to be achieved and that are meaningful and fulfilling. Thus a hope interventionist could help an older person explore meaningful goals across multiple life domains and strategies to pursue more than one goal at a time. A values assessment could be useful in this regard, such as the values assessment in behavioral activation treatment for depression (Lejuez, Hopko, Acierno, Daughters, & Pagoto, 2011). This could assist with the process of metaregulation (Haase et al., 2013), helping an older adult consider his or her purpose, values, and meaning, and thereby identify multiple meaningful goals across different life domains. This process also is consistent with general research across the lifespan on goal pursuits (MacLeod, 2013), which indicates that goals benefit well-being when we select and pursue goals that are intrinsically meaningful, across multiple life domains (i.e., "don't put all your eggs in one basket") and not overly dependent on other goals or outcomes (i.e., avoid thinking "I'll only be happy when . . .").

Maximizing Older Adults' Strengths

Later adulthood not only brings blocked or lost goals but it also brings strengths. Older adults often accumulate experience, education, social networks, financial resources, and other resources that may facilitate hope. A strengths-based approach begins with a general therapeutic stance that each older person has strengths, the power to learn and change, and the ability to grow even from negative experiences (Chapin, Nelson-Becker, Macmillan, & Sellon, 2015). The older person makes decisions and sets goals for him- or herself, guided by an interventionist. The interventionist may assist by identifying strengths in the community and helping the older person access those resources. As one example, Chapin and colleagues developed a strengths assessment for use with older adults, in which the older adult identifies "what do I have going for me?" (current status), "what do I want?" (goals), and "what have I used in the past?" (resources; Chapin et al., 2015). They pilot-tested the strengths assessment and a strengths-based intervention with low-income, depressed older adults, finding that it reduced depressive symptoms and improved health-related quality of life. The strengths intervention involved an older adult volunteer who helped each participant to set and pursue personal goals (e.g., attend granddaughter's wedding in six months). The program was supervised by a social worker, who may implement additional strategies to access community resources for participants (Chapin et al., 2013). The authors observed that participants seemed to become more engaged and motivated to participate when they realized the interventionist would help them focus on their strengths and goals that were important to them (Chapin et al., 2015). Although the authors did not conceptualize their intervention using hope theory, this observation suggests that a strengths-based, client-centered approach enhances agency to set and pursue goals. Focusing on strengths also may lead to positive affect and identifying effective pathways to achieve personally relevant goals.

Older adults do not always see these strengths themselves. I often point out to older patients that, in order to have survived to old age, they have clearly solved many problems and achieved many goals over their lifetime. No one has disagreed yet. In one memorable conversation with a terminally ill woman many years ago, she recounted having raised her children alone after being widowed at a young age, sometimes working multiple jobs. She stated that she was very proud of her children and that they had all turned out well and were raising their own children well. She then asked me about my education. At the time, I had recently finished my doctoral training and had little career experience and no parenting experience. I felt very inexperienced compared to her lifetime of accomplishments, and yet when I responded that I had recently finished my doctoral training, she said, "I never accomplished much," proceeding to explain that she had not obtained an advanced education. Surprised, I replied by saying how awed I was that, in spite of losing her husband, she had accomplished much more important goals than an education by working hard and raising children well, who were in turn raising the next generation. She said she had never thought of it that way. She died within a few days with her children present. I have no idea whether my comment benefitted her, but it made an impact on me. As Wrobleski and Snyder (2005) suggested, part of our therapeutic work with older adults may be this process of helping them to look back on their lives, recognizing their accomplished goals and making sense of goals not pursued or achieved. Reflecting on goals achieved, previous pathways, strengths, and other resources the older person possesses may invigorate new agency and pathways for future goals as well.

To summarize, research is beginning to accumulate that attests to the value of hope interventions for individuals and small groups of older adults. A hope intervention may help older adults facing major transitions in life goals (e.g., retirement) or depression or other goal blockages. In working with some older adults, it may be therapeutic to grieve lost goals, and to identify new goals to pursue, even while still pursuing uncertain goals. Older adults also are likely to benefit from interventionists who are hopeful themselves—who assume older people have strengths and capability to identify and pursue meaningful goals.

The Social Environment

Turning to broader pathways of change, could we improve the social environment to help older adults feel more hopeful and achieve more goals? Could we foster more hopeful expectations that later life can be a time to pursue meaningful goals, using public health campaigns, social media, or community interventions? No research has been done regarding promoting hope through the social environment, nor on how harmful aspects of the social environment, like ageism, affect hope in older adults.

Ageism is alive and well in many societies across the world. It is very common for all ages to hold negative views of older adults as ill, cognitively impaired, unattractive, and incompetent, although warm (which induces pity). Even young children and older adults themselves hold such attitudes (North & Fiske, 2012). Ageism harms older adults' behavior. For example, priming older adults to think about negative age stereotypes impairs their performance, causing them to remember less and move more slowly (Meisner, 2012). Rates of elder

abuse, abandonment, and suicide are on the rise, particularly in countries with the highest proportions of older adults (North & Fiske, 2015). Ageism is present in many domains of society, including healthcare, the workforce, nursing homes, and the media. We do not know the causes of ageism, but it likely includes psychological factors (e.g., mortality threat) and social factors, such as competition for resources across generations and modernization (e.g., published knowledge, industrialized labor) that renders older adults' knowledge and skills irrelevant (North & Fiske, 2012, 2015). Although collectivist cultures explicitly value caring for elders, a meta-analysis suggests that collectivist cultural attitudes may be associated with worse ageism than individualistic attitudes, which may promote tolerance and respect for the individual (North & Fiske, 2015).

One piece of good news is that older adults are less affected by negative stereotypes if they do not believe them—if they resist ageist attitudes and hold positive views of their own aging (North & Fiske, 2012). People who hold a more positive view of their possible self as an older person actually prepare more for their own aging (Kornadt, Voss, & Rothermund, 2015). Studies confirm that having more positive self-views of one's aging predict several adaptive behaviors, such as physical activity, health behaviors, financial planning, coping strategies, and engaging in meaningful daily activities (Kornadt et al., 2015).

As discussed previously, positive attitudes about aging are associated with higher hope in older adults (Moraitou et al., 2006; Steverink et al., 2001; Wurm et al., 2007). Future self-views reflect individuals' goals for themselves as older adults, as they consider possible selves they desire to attain and other possibilities they desire to avoid. "Future self-views are highly relevant for personal goal setting and engagement in goal-related behaviors, as well as for developmental regulation across the life span" (Kornadt et al., 2015, p. 2). From the lens of hope theory, if a high-hope person identifies desired and undesired self-views, this person will develop specific goals and identify pathways and agency to pursue those goals, thereby preparing for a better aging process.

So, if ageism promotes negative self-views and worse performance and if some older adults (who are more hopeful) reject ageist self-views and indeed prepare and have a better later adulthood—how could we intervene on a large scale to promote more positive self-views of later life? Does hope serve as a buffer against ageism, helping individuals see later life as continued growth and success in pursuing goals? Could different generations join together on common goals, rather than view older adults as taking resources from younger generations (and thereby threatening the goals of younger generations)?

These questions suggest at least two broad social goals: promoting positive self-views (and goals) for growing old and promoting common goals to which multiple generations can contribute. Various social institutions could become involved in these goals. As even children hold ageist views, educational institutions are one promising venue, as are healthcare, workplaces, and the general media and entertainment industry. Promoting images of hopeful older adults who have achieved meaningful goals could help to promote positive self-views of aging. Hope theory suggests, however, that it will be important to communicate that the goals these older adults have achieved are within reach for others too and to communicate pathways that are likely to foster success. There are numerous possibilities for organizations that could work on social marketing and public education campaigns of this nature, such as public health organizations and aging service and advocacy organizations. These organizations range from local public health, aging service, and community organizations, all the way to national (e.g., U.S. Administration on Aging, National Council on Aging) and international (e.g., World Health Organization's Ageing and Life Course Programme, http://www.who.int/ageing/en/). An international European effort is bringing together researchers from 30 countries to study and combat ageism (www.notoageism.com). Taking a different approach to promoting positive self-views, in a recent experiment, an intervention in which older adults (age M = 81) were subliminally presented with age-positive words (e.g., "spry") resulted in improvements in age stereotypes (about older adults in general), self-views, and physical functioning eight weeks later (Levy, Pilver, Chung, & Slade, 2014). Surprisingly, the implicit intervention was more effective than an explicit intervention, where participants were asked to write a brief essay about an older adult aging well. This type of intervention is very intriguing; perhaps it could be disseminated more broadly pending additional research. At the very least, this study suggests that how images and language are portrayed will have important effects on whether large-scale social interventions can positively affect attitudes and hope for aging.

Regarding joining together on common goals across generations, when older adults are seen as altruistic and concerned about younger generations, this enhances others' perceptions of their trustworthiness and may enhance cooperation across generations (North & Fiske, 2012). It is also helpful in this regard to recognize the strengths and resources older adults have to offer in addressing many social goals for older and younger generations. As such, it behooves aging advocacy organizations to study and report on the contributions of older adults (e.g., volunteerism, economic impact) and to frame advocacy efforts for older adults within a broader goal of contributing to the well-being of all ages. It may even be valuable for aging advocacy organizations to develop volunteer initiatives to benefit other age groups and to join together with organizations that advocate for other age groups to jointly address issues that affect all ages, such as health and financial policies, and planning for urban and other physical environments.

Physical Environment

How can we enhance our built physical environment to foster older adults' hope and successful goal pursuit? How can we maximize older adults' access to natural physical landscapes to do so? No research has examined hope in relation to interventions on the physical environment, but it seems logical that certain physical structures and environments would be conducive to inspiring and supporting goals, agency, and pathways. Community leaders are making some communities more walkable, wheelchair accessible, and healthier in other ways, such as by adding sidewalks, bicycle lanes, public transportation, grocery stores and produce markets, green spaces, and spaces for social events. Housing planners are building communities that blend different kinds of households (e.g., apartments and single-family homes nearby) and have communal spaces that foster social interactions. The World Health Organization is one of many organizations working to make communities more aging-friendly, to foster older adults' activity level and interactions with other generations, as described in a report with checklists for aging-friendly cities (World Health Organization, 2007). Many studies demonstrate that characteristics of the built environment are associated with physical activity, although very little intervention research has been done to determine what kinds of changes actually cause improvements in physical activity and other outcomes (Ferdinand, Sen, Rahurkar, Engler, & Menachemi, 2012). It seems plausible that improving the built environment could potentially improve older adults' abilities to pursue multiple goals and pathways, including mobility, transportation, social interactions, physical health, spiritual involvement, and community and volunteer work. The World Health Organization's report included feedback directly from older adults in several different countries, and older adults' input was used to create the checklists for aging-friendly cities. This report demonstrates the importance of involving older adults in such planning efforts. It might be helpful to talk to them about their meaningful life goals and how the physical environment gets in the way and could be improved to help them pursue goals. Perhaps physical modifications can help older adults be more hopeful as they experience fewer barriers and a greater number of pathways to pursue their personal goals. Moreover, if physical structures could foster more positive social interactions across generations, this could have positive effects on ageism and younger adults' views of aging.

In sum, there is still a great deal to learn about specific pathways to improve hope for older adults, although the initial intervention research is promising. Hope interventions and other goal-focused interventions like problem-solving therapy do appear to benefit older adults with depressed mood. When using hope-guided intervention strategies with older adults, it may be helpful to attend to metaregulation processes (Haase et al., 2013), assessing and discussing values and higher order goals and ensuring goals are distributed across at least a few life domains. Older adults possess many strengths, and assessing and utilizing these strengths as sources of agency and pathways may be especially important for older adults, who receive many ageist messages that deflate hope. It remains to be seen whether we can scale up hope through social and physical environment interventions to tackle ageism and help all ages perceive greater hope and abilities to pursue goals in their later years.

Summary

An image of the hopeful older person is emerging, thanks to new research conducted over the past 15 years. The hopeful older adult has probably been hopeful for much of his or her life, feeling capable of applying pathways and agency to pursue goals. The hopeful older adult has rejected negative stereotypes of aging and has instead envisioned an old age in which he or she continues to grow and pursue goals. As such, the hopeful older adult has prepared and planned for later life, which in turn reduces problems and stressors and helps him or her to achieve more goals, thereby maintaining physical, mental, and social well-being. When problems or stressors arise, as they inevitably do, the hopeful older person weathers the storm, feeling less distressed and able to wisely see different perspectives and apply personal knowledge to address problems. The hopeful older adult even lives longer than less hopeful older adults.

Even though hope is generally stable into later adulthood, preliminary research suggests that we can increase hope and reduce distress or depression for those less hopeful older adults. By participating in individual or small-group hope interventions, less hopeful older adults can learn new strategies to set meaningful goals, identify pathways to pursue goals and work around obstacles, and muster agency to implement pathways. Older adults possess many strengths and resources, which an interventionist can assess and maximize. While keeping a hopeful, strengths-focused outlook regarding aging is crucial for older adults and the providers who serve them, certain goal blockages do admittedly become more common later in life, such as health problems, loss of loved ones, and loss of vocation. To address these blockages, it may be especially important in later life to apply metaregulation skills, contemplating higher order values and goals, ensuring feasible goals cross multiple life domains, and carefully selecting goals with which to engage and disengage.

There are many unanswered questions about hope in later life, including how it is affected by experiences in earlier life, the conditions that foster hope in later life, and the benefits of hope in later life. Several excellent large-scale, multinational epidemiological studies are being conducted in later life, such as the U.S. Health and Retirement Survey and the Survey of Health, Ageing, and Retirement in Europe (SHARE; which includes 20 European countries plus Israel). It would be highly informative for epidemiological studies to assess hope and/or other goal pursuit processes, as well as ageism and aging attitudes, as the SHARE Israel and the large Germany study have done, for example (Keinan et al., 2012; Steverink et al., 2001; Wiest et al., 2013; Wurm et al., 2007). Likewise, it will be valuable to assess hope, goals, and aging attitudes in younger age groups to learn how these factors predict goal pursuits, goal achievements, and well-being later in life. It is likely that a common factor among older adults considered to be successfully aging is that they have pursued and achieved meaningful life goals. In addition to large-scale epidemiological research, fine-grained daily research such as the 45-day study by Ong and colleagues (2006) would provide rich information about the many cyclical ways hope interacts with stressors, goal pursuits, achievements, other strengths, and well-being in real time.

To conduct this research, theories of goal pursuits and achievements would be advanced by integrating hope theory with theories commonly applied in gerontology related to developmental regulation (Haase et al., 2013), wisdom (Moraitou & Efklides, 2013), and aging attitudes and ageism (Kornadt et al., 2015; North & Fiske, 2012). Hope theory provides a valuable framework for goals people select and how they apply pathways and agency to pursue those goals. Other developmental theories enrich this framework by focusing on higher order processes of how people select goals, accommodate for challenges, and disengage from certain goals. By integrating these theories, researchers could learn about work that has been done over the past few decades across these fields, develop novel ideas about pursuing goals in later life, and inform intervention research.

We know little regarding specific pathways to intervene and promote hope for older adults. Larger scale research is needed to evaluate a basic hope intervention with older adults, to determine which strategies are most effective, which older adults it can work for, and what outcomes improve. Can a hope intervention help depressed or even suicidal, hopeless elders? Can it be helpful at particular life transitions when goals are changing or new challenges arise? Can we enhance hope even more for older adults who are not in distress and have average hope? Could high-hope older adults serve as peer counselors to help promote hope in others?

Thinking on a community or societal scale, how could we use hope theory to guide larger scale social interventions to reconceptualize later life as a time of continued growth and goal pursuit, negating the effects of rampant ageism? How can we design built environments to minimize barriers for older adults, facilitate their pursuit of meaningful life goals, and help older adults model successful aging to younger generations? Research and development regarding social and built environments would benefit from input directly by older people, to learn more about their higher order goals and how aspects of the environment hinder and facilitate those goals. There are numerous aging and public health organizations that could be effective in bringing various stakeholders (e.g., older adults, researchers from multiple disciplines, planners, community leaders) together to design, implement, and evaluate broad-scale social campaigns and environmental modifications to create hopeful, successfully aging societies. Although not informed by hope theory, the World Health Organization is leading the way in global initiatives to create a more aging-friendly planet, which will benefit all of us. The wide range of these research questions indicates that hope research related to older adults is still in its infancy. Questions span naturalistic research to intervention research at individual, social environment, and physical environment levels.

Conclusion

In an ideal world, we will be most likely to promote hope in older adults by starting early—by promoting hope in children and by promoting positive views of aging in children. While we work toward these lofty goals, we can also continue to promote hope in adults and older adults, as interventions even late in life can improve hope. There are many challenges, including widespread ageism and competition for resources, but they are not insurmountable. The many older adults who are hopeful in spite of these challenges are a testament to the power of hope across the ages, and they inspire the agency and pathways to forge ahead.

Future Directions

• What factors contribute to high hope in later life? What are the benefits of high hope in later life?

• Can behavioral interventions be used to help less hopeful, distressed older adults to feel more hopeful and achieve more goals? If so, what kinds of intervention strategies are most effective and for whom?

• Could social institutions (such as schools, workplaces, religious organizations, health and social service organizations, social media, popular media) promote hope, positive views about later life, and goal pursuits of older adults? If so, how?

• Likewise, could the physical environment (such as housing, transportation, public spaces, parks) promote hope, physical views about later life, and goal pursuits of older adults? If so, how?

References

Bailey, T. C., & Snyder, C. R. (2007). Satisfaction with life and hope: A look at age and marital status. *The Psychological Record, 57*(2), 233–240.

Barg, F. K., Huss-Ashmore, R., Wittink, M. N., Murray, G. F., Bogner, H. R., & Gallo, J. J. (2006). A mixed-methods approach to understanding loneliness and depression in older adults. *Journals of Gerontology: Series B: Psychological Sciences and Social Sciences, 61B*(6), S329–S339.

Barnett, M. D. (2014). Future orientation and health among older adults: The importance of hope. *Educational Gerontology, 40*(10), 745–755. doi:10.1080/03601277.2014.898496

Beyer, A.-K., Wolff, J. K., Warner, L. M., Schüz, B., & Wurm, S. (2015). The role of physical activity in the relationship between self-perceptions of ageing and self-rated health in older adults. *Psychology & Health, 30*(6), 671–685. doi:10.1080/08870446.2015.1014370

Bolier, L., Haverman, M., Westerhof, G. J., Riper, H., Smit, F., & Bohlmeijer, E. (2013). Positive psychology interventions: A meta-analysis of randomized controlled studies. *BMC Public Health, 13*, 119. doi:10.1186/1471-2458-13-119

Chapin, R. K., Nelson-Becker, H., Macmillan, K., & Sellon, A. (2015). Strengths-based and solution-focused practice with older adults: New applications. In D. Kaplan & B. Berkman (Eds.), *The Oxford handbook of social work in health and aging* (pp. 63–71). New York: Oxford University Press.

Chapin, R. K., Sergeant, J. F., Landry, S., Leedahl, S. N., Rachlin, R., Koenig, T., & Graham, A. (2013). Reclaiming joy: Pilot evaluation of a mental health peer support program for older adults who receive Medicaid. *The Gerontologist, 53*(2), 345–352. doi:10.1093/geront/gns120

Cheavens, J. S., Cukrowicz, K. C., Hansen, R., & Mitchell, S. M. (2016). Incorporating resilience factors into the interpersonal theory of suicide: The role of hope and self-forgiveness in an older adult sample. *Journal of Clinical Psychology, 72*(1), 58–69. doi:10.1002/jclp.22230

Cheavens, J. S., & Gum, A. (2000). Gray power: Hope for the ages. In C. R. Snyder (Ed.), *Handbook of hope: Theory, measures, and applications* (pp. 201–222). New York: Academic Press.

Dimidjian, S., Barrera, M., Jr., Martell, C., Munoz, R. F., & Lewinsohn, P. M. (2011). The origins and current status of behavioral activation treatments for depression. *Annual Review of Clinical Psychology, 7*, 1–38. doi:10.1146/annurev-clinpsy-032210-104535 21275642

Dubé, M., Lapierre, S., Bouffard, L., & Alain, M. (2007). Impact of a personal goals management program on the subjective well-being of young retirees. *Revue européenne de psychologie appliquée, 57*, 183–192. doi:10.1016/j.erap.2005.04.004

Feldman, D. B., & Dreher, D. E. (2012). Can hope be changed in 90 minutes? Testing the efficacy of a single-session goal-pursuit intervention for college students. *Journal of Happiness Studies, 13*(4), 745–759. doi:10.1007/s10902-011-9292-4

Ferdinand, A. O., Sen, B., Rahurkar, S., Engler, S., & Menachemi, N. (2012). The relationship between built environments and physical activity: A systematic review. *American Journal of Public Health, 102*(10), e7–e13. doi:10.2105/ajph.2012.300740

Gum, A. M., & Snyder, C. R. (2002). Coping with terminal illness: The role of hopeful thinking. *Journal of Palliative Medicine, 5*(6), 883–894. doi:10.1089/10966210260499078

Gum, A. M., Snyder, C., & Duncan, P. W. (2006). Hopeful thinking, participation, and depressive symptoms three months after stroke. *Psychology & Health, 21*(3), 319–334.

Haase, C. M., Heckhausen, J., & Wrosch, C. (2013). Developmental regulation across the life span: Toward a new synthesis. *Developmental Psychology, 49*(5), 964–972. doi:10.1037/a0029231, 10.1037/a0029231.supp

Hirsch, J. K., Sirois, F. M., & Lyness, J. M. (2011). Functional impairment and depressive symptoms in older adults: Mitigating effects of hope. *British Journal*

of Health Psychology, 16(4), 744–760. doi:10.1111/j.2044-8287.2010.02012.x

Keinan, G., Shrira, A., & Shmotkin, D. (2012). The association between cumulative adversity and mental health: Considering dose and primary focus of adversity. *Quality of Life Research: An International Journal of Quality of Life Aspects of Treatment, Care & Rehabilitation, 21*(7), 1149–1158. doi:10.1007/s11136-011-0035-0

Klausner, E. J., Clarkin, J. F., Spielman, L., Pupo, C., Abrams, R., & Alexopoulos, G. S. (1998). Late-life depression and functional disability: The role of goal-focused group psychotherapy. *International Journal of Geriatric Psychiatry, 13*(10), 707–716.

Klausner, E. J., Snyder, C. R., & Cheavens, J. (2000). A hope-based group treatment for depressed older adult outpatients. In G. M. Williamson, D. R. Shaffer, P. A. Parmelee, G. M. Williamson, D. R. Shaffer, & P. A. Parmelee (Eds.), *Physical illness and depression in older adults: A handbook of theory, research, and practice.* (pp. 295–310). Dordrecht: Kluwer Academic.

Kornadt, A. E., Voss, P., & Rothermund, K. (2015). Hope for the best, prepare for the worst? Future self-views and preparation for age-related changes. *Psychology and Aging, 30*(4), 967–976. doi:10.1037/pag0000048,10.1037/pag0000048.supp

Lapierre, S., Dubé, M., Bouffard, L., & Alain, M. (2007). Addressing suicidal ideations through the realization of meaningful personal goals. *Crisis: The Journal of Crisis Intervention and Suicide Prevention, 28*(1), 16–25. doi:10.1027/0227-5910.28.1.16

Lejuez, C. W., Hopko, D. R., Acierno, R., Daughters, S. B., & Pagoto, S. L. (2011). Ten year revision of the brief behavioral activation treatment for depression: Revised treatment manual. *Behavior Modification, 35*(2), 111–161. doi:10.1177/0145445510390929 21324944

Levy, B. R., Pilver, C., Chung, P. H., & Slade, M. D. (2014). Subliminal strengthening: Improving older individuals' physical function over time with an implicit-age-stereotype intervention. *Psychological Science, 25*(12), 2127–2135. doi:10.1177/0956797614551970

MacLeod, A. (2013). Goals and plans: Their relationship to well-being. In A. Efklides & D. Moraitou (Eds.), *A positive psychology perspective on quality of life* (pp. 33–50). Dordrecht: Springer.

Meisner, B. A. (2012). A meta-analysis of positive and negative age stereotype priming effects on behavior among older adults. *The Journals of Gerontology: Series B: Psychological Sciences and Social Sciences, 67B*(1), 13–17. doi:10.1093/geronb/gbr062

Moraitou, D., & Efklides, A. (2012). The Wise Thinking and Acting Questionnaire: The cognitive facet of wisdom and its relation with memory, affect, and hope. *Journal of Happiness Studies, 13*(5), 849–873. doi:10.1007/s10902-011-9295-1

Moraitou, D., & Efklides, A. (2013). Wise thinking, hopeful thinking, and positive aging: Reciprocal relations of wisdom, hope, memory, and affect in young, middle-aged, and older adults. In A. Efklides, D. Moraitou, A. Efklides, & D. Moraitou (Eds.), *A positive psychology perspective on quality of life* (Vol. 51, pp. 189–218). New York: Springer Science + Business Media.

Moraitou, D., Kolovou, C., Papasozomenou, C., & Paschoula, C. (2006). Hope and adaptation to old age: Their relationship with individual-demographic factors. *Social Indicators Research, 76*(1), 71–93. doi:10.1007/s11205-005-4857-4

Moss, K., Scogin, F., Di Napoli, E., & Presnell, A. (2012). A self-help behavioral activation treatment for geriatric depressive symptoms. *Aging & Mental Health, 16*(5), 625–635. doi:10.1080/13607863.2011.651435 22304676

North, M. S., & Fiske, S. T. (2012). An inconvenienced youth? Ageism and its potential intergenerational roots. *Psychological Bulletin, 138*(5), 982–997. doi:10.1037/a0027843

North, M. S., & Fiske, S. T. (2015). Modern attitudes toward older adults in the aging world: A cross-cultural meta-analysis. *Psychological Bulletin, 141*(5), 993–1021. doi:10.1037/a0039469

Ong, A. D., Edwards, L. M., & Bergeman, C. S. (2006). Hope as a source of resilience in later adulthood. *Personality and Individual Differences, 41*(7), 1263–1273. doi:10.1016/j.paid.2006.03.028

Snyder, C. R., Harris, C., Anderson, J. R., Holleran, S. A., Irving, L. M., Sigmon, S. T., . . . Harney, P. (1991). The will and the ways: Development and validation of an individual-differences measure of hope. *Journal of Personality and Social Psychology, 60*(4), 570–585.

Snyder, C. R., & Rand, K. L. (2003). The case against false hope. *American Psychologist, 58*, 820–822.

Snyder, C. R., Shorey, H. S., Cheavens, J., Pulvers, K. M., Adams, V. H. III, & Wiklund, C. (2002). Hope and academic success in college. *Journal of Educational Psychology, 94*(4), 820–826. doi:10.1037/0022-0663.94.4.820

Steverink, N., Westerhof, G. J., Bode, C., & Dittmann-Kohli, F. (2001). The personal experience of aging, individual resources, and subjective well-being. *The Journals of Gerontology: Series B: Psychological Sciences and Social Sciences, 56B*(6), P364–P373. doi:10.1093/geronb/56.6.P364

Weis, R., & Speridakos, E. C. (2011). A meta-analysis of hope enhancement strategies in clinical and community settings. *Psychology of Well-Being, 1*, 5.

Wiest, M., Schüz, B., & Wurm, S. (2013). Life satisfaction and feeling in control: Indicators of successful aging predict mortality in old age. *Journal of Health Psychology, 18*(9), 1199–1208. doi:10.1177/1359105312459099

World Health Organization. (2007). *Global age-friendly cities: A guide.* Geneva: Author.

World Health Organization. (2011). *Global health and aging.* Geneva: Author.

Wrobleski, K. K., & Snyder, C. R. (2005). Hopeful thinking in older adults: Back to the future. *Experimental Aging Research, 31*(2), 217–233. doi:10.1080/03610730590915452

Wurm, S., Tesch-Römer, C., & Tomasik, M. J. (2007). Longitudinal finding aging-related cognitions, control beliefs, and health in later life. *The Journals of Gerontology: Series B: Psychological Sciences and Social Sciences, 62B*(3), P156–P164. doi:10.1093/geronb/62.3.P156

Wyman, M. F., Gum, A., & Areán, P. A. (2011). Psychotherapy with older adults. In G. M. M. E. Agronin (Ed.), *Geriatric psychiatry: Evaluation and management* (pp. 179–202). Baltimore, MD: Lippincott, Williams & Wilkins.

Yon, A., & Scogin, F. (2009). Behavioral activation as a treatment for geriatric depression. *Clinical Gerontologist: The Journal of Aging and Mental Health, 32*(1), 91–103. doi:10.1080/07317110802478016

PART IV

Hope and
Physical Health

Hope and Physical Health

Heather N. Rasmussen, Kristin Koetting O'Byrne, Marcy Vandament, *and* Brian P. Cole

Abstract

This chapter introduces the research on hope and physical health. The various conceptualizations and measures of hope in the medical literature are addressed, although the research covered focuses on Snyder's hope theory. The research on hope and health behaviors is presented, followed by a critical discussion of research on hope and specific areas of health outcomes, including pain, cancer, spinal cord injury, rehabilitation/injury, and chronic illness. Some of the mechanisms through which hope influences health are discussed, and the concepts of related health behaviors and health outcomes are explored. These health effects include coping and buffering against stress and depression. This chapter concludes with questions for future research.

Key Words: hope, physical health, coping, health behaviors, health outcomes, hope theory

In this chapter, we review the major findings on physical health and hope. This is an extensive topic, and we do not purport to have fully surveyed all of the relevant research on hope and physical health. Rather, we focus on specific areas of health, such as pain, or populations (e.g., patients with cancer, individuals with spinal cord injury [SCI]) in which most research has been conducted.

We begin the chapter by reviewing some of the conceptualizations of hope and commonly used measures of hope within the health psychology and health outcomes literature. Other chapters in this volume provide a deeper explanation of these constructs, but we also briefly discuss them to provide a context for the physical health literature. Then we discuss the differences between the constructs of hope and hopelessness. Next, there is a brief discussion of hope and health behaviors, including preventive behaviors. The bulk of the chapter is focused on reviewing the literature on hope and physical health and is organized by health topics that have been addressed in the hope literature. We should note that we limited the scope of our review to focus on hope as conceptualized by Snyder and colleagues

(1991) and to those studies in which the researchers measured hope using scales (e.g., the Hope Scale; Snyder et al., 1991) based on hope theory proposed by Snyder and colleagues (1991, 1994).

Conceptualizations and Measures of Hope in Physical Health

The idea that hope is related to physical health has existed throughout history, from the writings of Aristotle and within the Judeo-Christian tradition. Scholars in the last century, such as Erikson (1950) and Frank (1968), also discussed the importance of hope for those who were dealing with illness or their mortality. The systematic study of hope, though, began with Stotland (1969). Stotland conducted a comprehensive review of the literature and developed a theory of hope. Stotland operationalized hope as an expectation of goal attainment, along with the importance of the goal to the individual. From this conceptualization, other researchers used Stotland's model to develop instruments to measure hope. Instruments based upon Stotland's conceptualization include the Hope Index (1989) and the Multidimensional Hope Scale (1994).

Researchers in the late 1970s and early 1980s further explored the dimensions of hope, expanding Stotland's (1969) narrow definition of hope to include interpersonal elements and a future-oriented sense of hope. The Stoner Hope Scale (Stoner, 1982) and the Miller Hope Scale (Miller & Powers, 1988) were developed to measure the multiple dimensions of hope. Research presented in this chapter is based on hope theory (Snyder et al., 1991) and related measures. It is worth noting that researchers investigating hope and physical health often use conceptualizations and measures of hope that are remarkably different than Snyder's (1991) theory and measures. In addition, the theoretical basis for these other measures is not always clear. For example, Notwotny (1989) developed a scale for use with cancer patients, although it focuses on future expectations, it does not address goals. The previously mentioned Miller Hope Scale (Miller & Powers, 1988) was developed to measure the multiple dimensions related to hope, including (a) satisfaction with self, others, and life; (b) avoidance of hope threats; and (c) anticipation of a future. Scholars, such as Herth (1992), argued that other instruments contained too many items to be clinically useful and lacked study in populations of seriously ill and elderly persons. Subsequently, the Herth Hope Index (HHI) was developed for nurses as a screening measure for clinical populations to measure three dimensions of hope, including (a) temporality and future, (b) positive readiness and expectancy, and (c) interconnectedness. The HHI has been widely used to assess hope in acute and chronic illnesses. According to Herth (1990), hope is "an inner power that facilitates the transcendence of the present situation and movement toward new awareness and enrichment of being" (p. 1256). Other scales such as the Integrative Hope Scale have been used with medical populations but measure different dimensions such as (a) trust and confidence, (b) positive future orientation, (c) social relations and personal value, and (d) lack of perspective (Schrank et al., 2011).

The most widely studied and cited theory of hope in the psychological literature was developed by Snyder and colleagues (1991, 1994). They noted that human actions are goal-directed and humans work to attain their goals, even if they are uncertain as to whether they will reach the desired goal. To attain their goals, people (a) must have the perception that they can achieve their goals and (b) must be able to generate multiple, workable routes to their goals. They purported that the cognitions related to

pursuing goals cause emotions. Positive emotions are a result of successful goal pursuit, whereas negative emotions can flow from unsuccessful goal pursuits (Snyder, Rand, & Sigmon, 2002). They developed a measure of hope called the Hope Scale (also known as the Goals Scale, and trait, state, and child versions exist; Snyder et al., 1991; Snyder et al., 1996; Snyder, Hoza, et al., 1997). Measurements based on hope theory consist of agency (i.e., perceived capacity to reach desired goals) and pathways (i.e., generating workable routes to desired goals) factors, along with an overarching total hope factor. In our review of the hope and physical health literature, we focus on the research findings of this hope scale (and related versions) and physical health.

Hopelessness

A discussion on hope would be incomplete without mention of hopelessness. One of the most widely noted conceptualizations of hopelessness was developed by Beck, Weissman, Lester, and Trexler (1974). They theorized that hopelessness consists of negative expectancies about oneself and future outcomes. This model and accompanying measure, the Beck Hopelessness Scale (Beck, Steer, Kovacs, & Garrison, 1985), was developed from a medical model with an emphasis on the deficits of the person. The Hopelessness Scale also emphasizes the emotional state of the respondent. Hopelessness has been linked to physical health outcomes including suicide (Hirsch et al., 2012), cancer, myocardial infarction, and mortality (Everson et al., 1996). Although hopelessness is a risk factor for physical health problems, the focus of this chapter is on hope, the positive psychological strength, studies using Snyder's theory of hope, and how hope (even low hope) is related to physical health.

The Utility of Snyder's Hope Scales in Illness/Injury

Although hopelessness is a risk factor for morbidity and mortality, hope can be a protective factor and an asset to health. Indeed, researchers have determined that hope is relevant in health challenges such as pain tolerance (Snyder et al., 2005), cancer (Stanton et al., 2002), as well as major life changes/injuries like SCI (Smedema et al., 2014), visual impairment (Jackson et al., 1998) traumatic injuries (Creamer et al., 2009), and chronic illness (Hirsch & Sirois, 2016). In addition, Snyder's Hope Scales are appropriate tools to measure hope in illness/injury-stricken populations. For example, Smedema et al. (2013) recently studied 242 individuals with spinal cord injuries and found that the Trait Hope Scale (THS) is a reliable tool with this population. In addition, the two-factor structure of the THS holds in this population. Among 1,025 individuals with traumatic injuries (due to transportation accidents, work injuries, falls, violent assaults, etc.), Snyder's Dispositional Hope Scale had similar psychometric properties, including the two-factor structure, as when administered to noninjured or nontraumatized populations (Creamer et al., 2009). The two-factor structure also held when the THS was administered orally to visually impaired older veterans (Jackson et al., 1998).

Hope and Health Behaviors

Individuals with high hope are likely to take action in the present to ensure a healthy future. They are able to generate many paths to reaching a goal and reroute when faced with obstacles. They are also able to sustain motivation and discipline and harness resources to persevere despite obstacles in reaching their goals. Using weight loss as an example, individuals with high hope would theoretically be able to generate different paths to weight loss and have the agency, including motivation, and discipline, engaging social support, to reach those goals. Indeed, researchers have found that hope is related to behaviors relevant to primary prevention, which involves actions or thoughts intended to reduce or eliminate future health problems (Kaplan, 2000). For example, high hope is linked to being a nonsmoker (Berg et al., 2011; Berg, Schauer, Rodgers, & Naurula, 2012), fruit and vegetable consumption (Nollen et al., 2008), and engaging in behavioral strategies for diet (e.g., self-monitoring, planning, preparation/buying food, portion control, social interactions, limiting fat intake; Berg et al., 2011; Nothwehr et al, 2013). Hope is also related to behaviors related to physical activity (self-monitoring physical activity, social interactions for physical activity, and number of days of physical activity; Berg et al., 2011; Nothwehr et al., 2013). Not surprisingly, individuals with low hope are significantly more likely to binge-drink (Berg et al., 2011). Feldman and Sills (2013) found that although hope alone did not predict behavior change, the interaction of hope with knowledge and/or perceived importance of a behavior did. In addition, the results varied by ethnicity. For example, among Latinos, the interaction of hope and perceived importance of dietary change predicted reduced salt/fat intake and the interaction of hope and the perceived importance of exercise change

predicted increased exercise. However, among Asian Americans, the combination of hope and knowledge predicted reduced salt/fat intake, physician visits, and cardiovascular disease information-seeking. Although hope predicts engaging in behavioral strategies, it also has important relationships with other factors (e.g., perceived importance) that may influence behavior.

Hope and Specific Health Outcomes

Hope is relevant in its promotion of engaging in healthy behaviors to prevent disease and disability, but it is also important in coping or adjusting to illness once it occurs, adhering to medical or rehabilitative regimens, enhancing quality of life, and coping with stress. Most of the literature on health outcomes focuses on the impact of hope on mental health outcomes such as depression or life satisfaction in specific populations (e.g., cancer patients) struck with physical illness (e.g., cancer) or physical injury (e.g., SCI). There are some studies that include research on hope and physical health outcomes, some of which are subjective (e.g., physical quality of life, perceived pain, fatigue functional ability) and some objective outcomes (e.g., the relationship between hope and hemoglobin, or hope and functional ability). The next part of the chapter reviews some of these findings in major areas in which the hope and physical health connection has been examined, including pain, cancer, SCI, rehabilitation and injury, and chronic illness.

Pain

Pain has many dimensions and can impact many aspects of a person's life such as mood and overall functioning. Pain is difficult to manage, in part due to the many areas of one's functioning that are impacted but also because it can last for varying time periods. In some cases, pain can last for only seconds or, in its disordered form (chronic pain), can last months or even years. Mental health and health professionals have attempted to understand the best methods for treating pain sufferers through research on hope.

Hope has been studied in various medical conditions and has been found to be associated with positive coping with illness. Hope is also related to an individual's overall ability to adjust to physical health changes (Kwon, 2002). Several studies have examined the role of hope in relationship to pain. Findings regarding individuals who are high in hope have greatly informed research on hope and physical pain. The idea behind this research is that high hope is related to an individual's ability to ignore pain and to focus on his or her individual goals (Snyder et al., 2005).

In a two-part study, Snyder et al. (2005) examined the relationship between pain onset, pain tolerance, and hope. In the first part of the study individuals with low and high hope, as measured by the THS, participated in a cold pressor task (CPT). Results from this study indicate that individuals with high hope were able to keep their hands in the water longer than those with low hope. Based on these results, it would appear that individuals high in hope have a higher pain tolerance.

In the second part of the study, researchers sought to further understand if positive individual differences and pathology made a difference in an individual's response to pain (Snyder et al., 2005). The researchers measured hope, as well as other positive individual differences, and depression. Due to previous findings regarding the potential confounding role of hand size, researchers also measured participant's hands prior to the start of the study to determine if size of hand made a difference in pain onset or tolerance.

The results from the second part of the study indicated that hope remained a significant predictor of pain onset and tolerance (Snyder et al., 2005). Individuals who had higher hope were able to keep their hand in the water longer than those with low hope. Regarding area of hand, the size (i.e. length, width, and distance) was significantly related to pain tolerance. Other positive traits and pathology were not significantly related to pain onset or pain tolerance. Overall, the findings from both parts of the study demonstrate a relationship between pain onset/tolerance and hope.

Hope also appears to play a key role in a person's response to pain. Therefore, it is important to consider factors that may contribute to someone having low or high hope. One factor that can be a negative contributor to hope and pain tolerance is "pain catastrophizing." Chronic pain sufferers are often found to have a pain-catastrophizing response to pain symptoms, which is an exaggerated and negative response toward actual or anticipated pain. Pain catastrophizing often results in individuals feeling hopeless about their symptoms and functioning and increases their focus on pain (Sullivan, Bishop, & Pivik, 1995).

Hood et al. (2012) found that hope and pain catastrophizing were correlated. Individuals low in hope or optimism had more frequent reports of pain and higher pain catastrophizing. The results

also demonstrated that rumination, magnification, and helplessness mediate the relationship between hope, optimism, and pain report. These findings indicate that hope and other positive traits are associated with lower pain catastrophizing. Researchers postulate that the ability to find alternate routes to reach their goals is one possible reason individuals higher in hope report lower pain reports and catastrophizing. Thus pain symptoms may be perceived as less debilitating to these individuals.

Understanding the effects of hope on pain is important and can further our understanding of how to treat individuals with a chronic pain disorder. Berg, Snyder, and Hamilton (2008) developed a brief hope-based intervention to examine its impact on pain tolerance and perception of pain. Participants were chosen for the study based having a THS–Revised score below the median. Participants were randomly assigned to a treatment or control group. All participants completed measures of mood, self-presentation, and pain catastrophizing.

After completion of the measures, participants in the intervention group received the hope-based intervention, while participants in the control group received an alternative manipulation. The hope-based intervention lasted approximately 15 minutes. During the intervention, participants were exposed to a guided imagery about a goal they wanted to achieve, dialogue about the goal and motivations surrounding it, strategies for reaching the goal, and a worksheet where they were asked to recall a positive experience with goal-setting and the self-talk and strategies utilized to accomplish the goal. All participants were asked to complete the THS after the manipulation or intervention. Finally, the participants completed the CPT and self-reported the onset of pain.

Researchers found that females who received the intervention had increased hope and there was an increase in pain tolerance for all of the participants. Regardless of condition, men had an increase of hope after the intervention. Overall, men tolerated the CPT longer than women. Participants who received the intervention were able to tolerate the CPT longer than participants in the control group. While these findings were not statistically significant, they demonstrate how hope can be an important component to the pain treatment process.

It is essential to further understand how hope-based interventions can help chronic pain sufferers increase mood and functionality. Howell, Jacobson, and Larsen (2015) developed a study involving individuals from a community-based mental health agency in a chronic pain group. Due to the dearth of literature in the area of interventions, the researchers elected to conduct a pilot study in addition to the main study. The studies were identical in nature including a weekly two-hour hope-orientated intervention in a group setting. Additionally, the participants received a pre- and postintervention assessment that included the State Hope Scale (SHS) and measures of acceptance of chronic pain and pain catastrophizing.

In the pilot study researchers found that after the intervention participants had significant changes in the pain experience (Howell et al., 2015). During the posttest assessment, participants were found to have higher well-being and pain acceptance than during the pretest assessment. The findings in the main study were almost identical to that of the pilot study. Individuals had higher hope, better well-being, and lower pain catastrophizing in the posttest. Additionally, across both the pilot and main study SHS scores and change in hope predicted an increase in overall well-being. However, one difference in the main study was that there was no difference in pain acceptance between pre- and posttest.

One of the most notable findings from the Howell et al. (2015) study was the increase in well-being for participants after receiving the hope intervention. This demonstrates that even when a psychological intervention is brief, clients can still experience a significant improvement in overall well-being. It is important to note that the intervention in this study was more perspective focused than goal or pathway focused. The findings regarding increases in scores on the SHS indicate that hope can be increased over time and is not static.

Overall, the study of hope and hope-based interventions appear to provide a valuable contribution to chronic pain treatment. Designing interventions that are consistent with hope theory can have a significant impact on pain management. Interventions that focus on goals, problem-solving strategies, and increasing the self-efficacy of the individuals could drastically change the way the individual perceives their chronic pain disorder.

Cancer

Early research on relations between hope and cancer utilized analogue designs that explored hypothetical coping responses among individuals without cancer. Irving and colleagues (1998) found that women with high levels of hope reported more knowledge about cancer and increased self-reports of engagement in positive coping behaviors in

hypothetical phases of cancer including prevention, detection, course, and impact. In the past 20 years, a number of studies have picked up where this study left off by examining the relationship between hope and cancer among children and adults with a variety of cancer diagnoses.

Examinations of hope among individuals diagnosed with cancer mirror analogue findings that hope is predictive of coping with cancer. For example, Ho and colleagues (2010) found that high hope was associated with increased resilience following genetic testing for colorectal cancer. Relatedly, levels of hope appear to be predictive of coping behaviors related to the diagnosis and treatment of cancer. Stanton and colleagues (2000) conducted a longitudinal study to explore women's adjustment to breast cancer. In this sample, women reporting high levels of hope were more likely to engage in emotionally expressive coping, have positive perceptions of their physical health, and report high levels of positive emotions three months posttreatment than women that were low in hope. Moreover, hope predicted engagement in emotionally expressive coping, reported lower levels of psychological distress, and fewer medical appointments for cancer-related morbidities but only for women who were high in hope. This interaction of hope and coping strategies was also found to be predictive of lower levels of distress, increased positive functioning, and lower fear of recurrence (Stanton, Danoff-Burg, & Huggins, 2002). Furthermore, the interaction of hope and coping accounted for as much as 36% of variance in outcomes among women with breast cancer at one-year follow-up (Stanton et al., 2002). Stanton and colleagues hypothesized that whereas women with high hope had positive outcome expectancies and engagement in more active coping behaviors, women with low hope engaged in reappraisal that is more akin to wishing (i.e., lacking agency, pathways thinking, and goal directedness) and increased avoidant coping behaviors. These findings were mirrored within a sample of religious women with breast cancer, such that hope mediated the relationship between religiosity and coping behaviors. Women who were high in hope reported coping consistent with a "fighting spirit," whereas women that were low in hope were more likely to report negative adjustment including hopelessness, helplessness, fatalistic acceptance, and anxious preoccupation with their diagnosis (Hasson-Ohayon, Braun, Galinsky, & Baider, 2009).

It is hypothesized that when high-hope individuals are diagnosed with cancer, they are better prepared to reprioritize their life goals, generate new pathways to reach their goals, and maintain the agency to utilize pathways to their goals (Ho, Ho, Bonanno, Chu, & Chan, 2010). Thus it should come as no surprise that high hope is associated with numerous positive outcomes among individuals with cancer. For example, hope agency thinking was positively associated with happiness and positive affect and negatively associated with depression and negative outcomes among a sample of long-term prostate cancer survivors (Blank & Bellizzi, 2006). Jafari and colleagues (2010) found that hope accounted for 7% of the variance in life satisfaction among a sample of men and women seeking cancer treatment. Moreover, hope was positively correlated with levels of spiritual, religious, and existential well-being among these patients (Jafari et al., 2010). Similar findings have emerged among childhood cancer survivors, with hope correlated to lower levels of depression, anxiety, and negative cancer-related rumination (Yuen, Ho, & Chan, 2014). Furthermore, children with low hope were more susceptible to effects of anxiety as the result of negative rumination than those with moderate and high levels of hope (Yuen et al., 2014).

Finally, it appears that hope is predictive of the occurrence of posttraumatic growth among cancer survivors (Ho, Rajandram, et al., 2010; Yuen et al., 2014). Posttraumatic growth is positive psychological change that occurs as a result of navigating traumatic life events. Posttraumatic growth occurs as the result of processing adversity, reframing negative life events as challenges to be overcome, and benefit finding. As a result of this process, individuals who are high in posttraumatic growth often experience decreased negative emotionality and reactivity as well as faster recovery in response to future stressful events (Tedeschi & Calhoun, 2004; for a systematic review of the literature on posttraumatic growth and life threatening physical illness, see Hefferon, Grealy, & Mutrie, 2009.). When experiencing traumatic life events such as cancer, hope accounts for approximately 16% of the variance in the occurrence of posttraumatic growth. Examination of pathways thinking, agency thinking, and optimism revealed that pathways thinking is significantly associated with the occurrence of posttraumatic growth following treatment for oral cavity cancer (Ho et al., 2010). Similarly, high hope was predictive of the experience of posttraumatic growth among childhood cancer survivors. Thus hope may be an important mechanism for facilitation of posttraumatic growth and the resilience needed to successfully cope with future stressful events such as cancer relapse or recurrence.

Spinal Cord Injury

Sustaining a SCI can be a life-changing and traumatic event. Individuals often experience depression, anxiety, and suicidal thoughts at the onset of SCI. However, hope is still relevant and may be a key to better psychosocial outcomes in the aftermath of SCI. Smeda et al. (2013) found that individuals with SCI were somewhat hopeful about their lives and, although life satisfaction was lower than average for participants in this study, it was significantly correlated with both pathways thinking and agency thinking. The relationship between life satisfaction and hope in individuals with SCI is supported by other studies (Kortte et al., 2010; Smedema et al., 2010; Smedema et al. 2014). The relationship between hope and life satisfaction has been investigated in prospective studies with individuals with SCI. Kortte et al. found that, along with positive affect, hope predicted life satisfaction during initial rehabilitation. Three months postdischarge from an acute rehabilitation unit, not only did hope (along with positive affect) predict greater life satisfaction, but it also accounted for a significant amount of variance above and beyond barriers to life satisfaction such as depression, negative affect, and avoidant coping.

Other studies on hope in individuals with SCI focus on different outcomes such as depression and psychosocial impairment. For example, Elliott et al. (1991) found that among individuals with traumatically acquired SCI, high levels of hope predicted lower levels of depression and psychosocial impairment. Similarly, pathways was a significant predictor of psychosocial impairment, but agency was not. High hope was also related to quality of life (Kortte et al., 2010), core self-evaluations, level of community participation (Smedma et al., 2014), and more. Low hope was related to negative coping measures such as perceived stress, dysfunctional attitudes about disease, and catastrophizing about pain (Smedema et al., 2010).

Researchers have some insight as to how hope impacts positive outcomes in individuals with SCI. Hope has also been linked with positive individual factors such as core self-evaluations, self-esteem, and disability acceptance (Smedema et al., 2010) which may influence outcomes directly and indirectly via the use of healthier coping strategies. Indeed, Kennedy et al. (2009) found that hope predicts which coping strategy individuals with SCI use. Although the bulk of the literature focuses on Lazarus and Folkman's (1988) perspective that appraisals predict what coping strategies people use, Kennedy et al. (2009) found that hope was a better predictor of coping strategies than appraisals and that high hope was related to use of adaptive coping styles (e.g., fighting spirit) and low hope was related to use of maladaptive coping. Hope agency was a significant predictor of acceptance of injury, and overall hope was related to threat appraisal as SCI individuals with lower levels of hope appraised their injury as more threatening. This is important as hope may be more powerful than appraisal, and there is a strong relationship between hope and coping.

Injury and Rehabilitation

Hope has been investigated with individuals with injuries and undergoing rehabilitation. Visually impaired individuals were given a modified verbal administration of the THS and gave answers verbally (Jackson et al., 1998). Among these 63 adults (average age 63.3), higher hope was associated with higher levels of self-reported ability and with healthier, proactive, sociable coping styles. Individuals lower on hope reported using more avoidant or inhibited coping styles. Trait hope scores, as well as agency and pathways individually, were significantly correlated with perceived functional ability and psychosocial adjustment. Lower hope was also related to depressive symptoms and using symptoms for secondary gain. These results suggest that higher hope scores are associated with less distress and fewer physical symptoms, more positive coping, and fewer adverse reactions to stress. Some of the methodological weaknesses of Jackson et al.'s (1998) study included that it was a cross-sectional design and they used self-report measures of functional ability. However, Kortte et al.'s (2012) study used a longitudinal design and clinician ratings of outcomes in their study of 174 adults who were participating in in-patient rehabilitation for various reasons, including spinal cord dysfunction, stroke, amputation, or orthopedic surgery recovery. They found that hope at baseline was a significant predictor of functional skill level, as rated by a clinician, three months postdischarge. Baseline hope also predicted three-month postdischarge outcomes in terms of functional role participation overall as well as specific indicators such as social integration and occupational engagement. It should be noted that positive affect was not a significant predictor of these longitudinal outcomes.

More recently, Lu and Hsu (2013) found that trait hope (and both pathways and agency individually) and social support predicted rehabilitation beliefs, coping, appraisal of severity of injury, and subjective well-being among Taiwanese collegiate athletes. However, only hope agency predicted compliance with regimens. There was an interaction between hope and social support and the relationship with subjective well-being. For injured athletes with low pathways scores, more perceived social support was associated with greater subjective well-being. However, in those with high pathways scores, social support had only a small association with subjective well-being.

In other studies of hope and rehabilitation, findings are not as conclusive. For example, in a study of older adults receiving hip or knee replacement surgery, Hartley et al. (2008) found that although higher hope was predictive of lower depression presurgery, it was not predictive of postsurgery depression or functional ability. Although hope, but not self-efficacy, was a significant contributor to predicting lower depression presurgery; self-efficacy, but not hope, was a significant predictor of postsurgery depression. In addition, hope was not a predictor of presurgery pain or change in pain from presurgery to postsurgery.

Chronic Illness

The goal for chronic illness is not necessarily rehabilitation or cure, but goals can shift to having better quality of life, adjusting to illness, and coping with illness and illness-related stress. When goals shift appropriately, hope can have a major impact on psychological and physical outcomes. Hope was a predictor of quality of life in individuals with postpolio syndrome, although compared to healthy matched controls, individuals with postpolio syndrome had lower quality of life (Szramka-Pawlak et al., 2014). Similarly, Madan and Pakenham (2014) found that hope was related to adjustment in individuals with multiple sclerosis (MS). Although there was a direct relationship between agency and adjustment to MS, pathways had a stress buffering impact on adjustment to MS by moderating the relationship between stress and adjustment. Hope also buffered the relationship between stress and fatigue in individuals with inflammatory chronic illnesses, including fibromyalgia, arthritis, and inflammatory bowel disease (Hirsch & Sirois, 2016). In this same study, across all samples of individuals with inflammatory chronic illness, both state and trait hope were associated with less pain, perceived stress, and fatigue. Additional analysis revealed that perceived stress was positively associated with pain and fatigue and that perceived stress explained—in part—the association between hope and fatigue; those with higher levels of hope report less stress and, in turn, less fatigue.

However, among individuals with end-stage renal failure who would eventually need dialysis, Billington et al. (2008) found hope did not play as important a role with regard to physical symptoms and physical quality of life, which were more determined by factors such as satisfaction with physical support and number of comorbid illnesses, respectively. However, hope was a significant predictor of anxiety, depression, effects and symptoms of kidney disease, and mental health quality of life.

It may be as diseases become more severe, physical outcomes are determined by other factors, such as more by support for practical disease management. This would support Vieth et al.'s (1997) findings among individuals with diabetes. They found hope was not predictive of disease status in measures of psychosocial functioning or objective physical measures like hemoglobin.

Too Much Hope May Not Always Be Beneficial to Health

Although much of this chapter presents positive or inconclusive findings, it is important to address the research indicating situations in which having high hope may be harmful. Hope is theorized to be a protective factor in mental and physical health, not a risk factor. However, Jackson and colleagues (2003) found individuals with higher levels of hope were significantly less likely to enter a substance abuse treatment programs when needed, while individuals with lower levels of hope were more likely to enter substance abuse programs. It may be that because individuals with high hope are able to generate multiple pathways to reach a goal, they may be too self-reliant. It is also possible that entering substance abuse treatment is an option they would choose when all of their other pathways have been exhausted. Or perhaps they feel they can handle the issue themselves or that it will resolve. It is also possible that (at least in part because of their high hope), they may not be willing to admit that their problem warrants professional help.

However, more strikingly paradoxical results come from a study by Riolli and Savicki (2012). In their study of physical and psychological outcomes of firefighters in various stress conditions, they investigated two groups of firefighters in the same geographic region. One group of firefighters participated in the search and rescue operations in the aftermath of the World Trade Center on 9/11; the other group stayed home during the search and rescue operations but continued their regular emergency-related work. The former group was the traumatic stress group and the latter group was the nontraumatic stress or control group. For the individuals in the nontraumatic stress group, as expected, psychological symptoms decreased as hope increased. However, the researchers found paradoxical results in the individuals in the traumatic stress group. As both hope agency and hope pathways increased, so did both their psychological symptoms and physical symptoms. In the traumatic stress group, higher hope was significantly related to worse outcomes.

Individuals with high hope, who know they can cope and have abilities to manage stress, may experience stressors that are insurmountable. It is possible that having higher hope can make them more vulnerable to adverse outcomes because they have such a strong reliance on their intrapersonal resources like hope, and when it does not work, they fare worse than individuals having low hope, who do not rely on those resources. Certain environmental conditions or situations may block hope from being effective, and for individuals with high hope, this may be more adverse.

Conclusion

Hope plays an important role in physical health. Individuals with high hope are more likely to engage in healthy behaviors and less likely to engage in health risk behaviors. In investigations of individuals with a disease or disability, the majority of the research focuses on the relationship between hope and psychological constructs, such as life satisfaction, depression, coping, stress, and so on in these medically afflicted populations. However, there are some studies that link hope directly to physical health outcomes, such as pain, functional ability, and fatigue. It is not clear exactly how hope works in these contexts. In some cases it buffers against stress and depression; in others, it facilitates religiosity and coping. Hope may also facilitate positive emotions and the mobilization of social support, which in turn influences health. There is still much that is unknown in terms of how hope influences physical health. Although there are some studies with paradoxical results, overall hope appears to generally be beneficial to physical health. More research in the area needs to be conducted to further tease out the mechanisms by which hope influences physical health.

Future Directions

• Are there specific physiological mechanisms through which hope impacts health?

• Which is a better predictor of adherence, coping, or outcomes—total hope, agency, or pathways?

• What is the overall population relationship between hope and physical health outcomes?

• Is Snyder's theory of hope more strongly related to health than other theories or measures?

• What is the mechanism behind the relationship between hope and social support?

• Is hope more strongly related to subjective or objective outcomes of physical health?

Acknowledgments

This chapter is dedicated to the memory of Dr. Shane J. Lopez. He was our mentor and friend . . . and we miss him very much. We are creating ripples in your honor, Shane.

References

Beck, A. T., Steer, R. A., Kovacs, M., & Garrison, B. (1985). Hopelessness and eventual suicide: A 10-year prospective study of patients hospitalized with suicidal ideation. *American Journal of Psychiatry, 142*, 559–563.

Beck, A. T., Weissman, A., Lester, D., & Trexler, L. (1974). The measurement of pessimism: The hopelessness scale. *Journal of Clinical and Consulting Psychology, 42*, 861–865.

Berg, C. J., Ritschel, L. A., Swan, D. W., An, L. C., & Ahluwalia, J. S. (2011). The role of hope in engaging in healthy behaviors among college students. *American Journal of Health Behavior, 35*(4), 402–415.

Berg, C. J., Schauer, G. L., Rodgers, K., Naurula, S. K. (2012). College student smokers: Former versus current and non-smokers. *American Journal of Preventive Medicine, 43*(5 Suppl. 3), S229–S236.

Berg, C. J., Snyder, C. R., & Hamilton, N. (2008). The effectiveness of a hope intervention in coping with cold pressor pain. *Journal of Health Psychology, 13*(6), 804–809. doi:10.1177/1359105308093864

Billington, E., Simpson, J., Unwin, J. Bray, D. & Giles, D. (2008). Does hope predict adjustment to end-stage renal failure and consequent dialysis? *British Journal of Health Psychology, 13*, 683–699.

Blank, T. O. & Bellizzi, K. M. (2006). After prostate cancer: Predictors of well-being among long-term prostate cancer survivors. *Cancer, 106*, 2128–2135. doi:10.1002/cncr.21865

Creamer, M., O'Donnell, M. L., Carboon, I., Lewis, V., Densley, K., McFarlane, A., … & Bryant, R. A. (2009). Evaluation of the Dispositional Hope Scale in injury survivors. *Journal of Research in Personality, 43*(4), 613–617.

Elliott, T. R., Witty, T. E., Herrick, S., & Hoffman, J. T. (1991). Negotiating reality after physical loss: Hope, depression, and disability. *Journal of Personality and Social Psychology, 61*(4), 608–613.

Erikson, E. (1950). *Childhood and society.* New York: Norton.

Everson, S. A., Goldberg, D. E., Kaplan, G. A., Cohen, R. D., Pukkala, E., Tuomilehto, J., Salonen, J. T. (1996). Hopelessness and risk of mortality and incidence of myocardial infarction and cancer *Psychosomatic Medicine, 58*, 113–121.

Feldman, D. B., & Sills, J. R. (2013). Hope and cardiovascular health-promoting behavior: Education alone is not enough. *Psychology & Health, 28*(7), 727–745. doi:10.1080/08870446.2012.754025

Frank, J. (1968). The role of hope in psychotherapy. *International Journal of Psychiatry, 5*, 383–395.

Hartley, S. M, Vance, D. E., Elliott, T. R., Cuckler, J. M., & Berry, J. W. (2008). Hope, self-efficacy, and functional recovery after knee and hip replacement surgery. *Rehabilitation Psychology, 53*(4), 521–529.

Hasson-Ohayon, I., Braun, M., Galinsky, D., & Baider, L. (2009). Religiosity and hope: A path for women coping with a diagnosis of breast cancer. *Psychosomatics, 50*, 525–533. doi:10.1176/appi.psy.50.5.525

Hefferon, K., Grealy, M., & Mutrie, N. (2009) Post-traumatic growth and life threatening physical illness: A systematic review of the qualitative literature. *British Journal of Health Psychology, 14*, 343–378. doi:10.1348/135910708X332936

Herth, K. (1990). Fostering hope in terminally ill people. *Journal of Advanced Nursing, 15*(11), 1250–1259.

Herth, K. (1992). Abbreviated instrument to measure hope: Development and psychometric evaluation. *Journal of Advanced Nursing, 17*, 1251–1259.

Hirsch, J. K., & Sirois, F. M. (2016). Hope and fatigue in chronic illness: The role of perceived stress. *Journal of Health Psychology, 21*(4), 451–456.

Hirsch, J. K., Visser, P. L., Chang, E. C., & Jeglic, E. L. (2012). Race and ethnic differences in hope and hopelessness as moderators of the association between depressive symptoms and suicidal behavior. *Journal of American College Health, 60*(2), 115–125.

Ho, S., Ho, J., Bonanno, G., Chu, A., & Chan, E. (2010). Hopefulness predicts resilience after hereditary colorectal cancer genetic testing: A prospective outcome trajectories study. *BMC Cancer, 10*, 279–288. doi:10.1186/1471-2407-10-279

Ho, S., Rajandram, R. K., Chan, N., Samman, N., McGrath, C., & Zwahlen, R. A. (2010). The roles of hope and optimism on posttraumatic growth in oral cavity cancer patients. *Oral Oncology, 47*, 121–124. doi:10.1016/j.oraloncology.2010.11.015

Hood, A., Pulvers, K., Carrillo, J., Merchant, G., & Thomas, M. D. (2012). Positive traits linked to less pain through lower pain catastrophizing. *Personality and Individual Differences, 52*, 401–405. doi:10.1016/j.paid.2011.10.040

Howell, A. J., Jacobson, R. M., & Larsen, D. J. (2015). Enhanced psychological health among chronic pain clients engaged in hope-focused group counseling. *The Counseling Psychologist, 43*(4), 586–613. doi:10.1177/0011000014551421

Irving, L. M., Snyder, C. R., & Crowson, J. J. Jr. (1998). Hope and coping with cancer by college women. *Journal of Personality, 66*, 195–214.

Jackson, R., Wernicke, R., & Haaga, D. A. F. (2003). Hope as a predictor of entering substance abuse treatment. *Addictive Behaviors 28*, 13–28.

Jackson, W. T., Taylor, R. E., Palmatier, A. D., Elliott, T. R., & Elliott, J. L. (1998). Negotiating the reality of visual impairment: Hope, coping, and functional ability. *Journal of Clinical Psychology in Medical Settings, 5*(2), 173–185. doi:10.1023/A:1026259115029

Jafari, E., Najafi, M., Sohrabi, F., Reza Dehshiri, G., Soleymani, E., & Heshmati, R. (2010). Life satisfaction, spirituality well-being and hope in cancer patients. *Procedia Social and Behavioral Sciences, 5*, 1362–1366. doi:10.1016/j.sbspro.2010.07.288

Kaplan, R. M. (2000). Two pathways to prevention. *American Psychologist, 55*(4), 382.

Kennedy, P., Evans, M., & Sandhu, N. (2009). Psychological adjustment to spinal cord injury: The contribution of coping, hope and cognitive appraisals. *Psychology, Health & Medicine, 14*(1), 17–33.

Kortte, K., Gilbert, M., Gorman, P., & Wegener, S. (2010). Positive psychological variables in the prediction of life satisfaction after spinal cord injury. *Rehabilitation Psychology, 55*, 40–47.

Kortte, K. B., Stevenson, J. E., Hosey, M. M., Castillo, R. & Wegener, S. T. (2012). Hope predicts positive functional role outcomes in acute rehabilitation populations. *Rehabilitation Psychology, 57*(3), 248–255.

Kwon, P. (2002). Hope, defense mechanisms, and adjustment: Implications for false hope and defensive hope. *Journal of Personality, 70*(2), 207–231. doi:10.1111/1467-6494.05003

Lu, F. J. H., & Hsu, Y. (2013). Injured athletes' rehabilitation beliefs and subjective well-being: The contribution of hope and social support. *Journal of Athletic Training, 48*(1), 92–98. doi:10.4085/1062-6050-48.1.03

Madan, S., & Pakenham, K. I. (2014). The stress-buffering effects of hope on adjustment to multiple sclerosis. *International Journal of Behavioral Medicine, 21*, 877–890. doi:10.1007/s12529-013-9384-0

Miller, J., & Powers, M. (1988). Development of an instrument to measure hope. *Nursing Research, 37*, 6–10.

Nollen, N., Befort, C., Pulvers, K., James, A.S., Kaur, H., Mayo, M.S., . . . Ahluwalia, J. S. (2008). Demographic and psychosocial factors associated with increased fruit and vegetable consumption among smokers in public housing enrolled in a randomized trial. *Health Psychology, 27*(3 Suppl.), S252–S259.

Nothwehr, F., Clark, D. O., & Perkins, A. (2013). Hope and the use of behavioral strategies related to diet and physical activity. *Journal of Human Nutrition and Dietetics, 26*(Suppl. 1), 159–163. http://doi.org/10.1111/jhn.12057

Nowotny, M. L. (1989). Assessment of hope in patients with cancer: Development of an instrument. *Oncology Nursing Forum, 16*(1), 57–61.

Riolli, L., & Savicki, V. (2012). Firefighters' psychological and physical outcomes after exposure to traumatic stress: The moderating roles of hope and personality. *Traumatology, 18*(3), 7–15.

Schrank, B., Woppman, A., Sibitz, I., & Lauber, C. (2011). Development and validation of an integrative scale to assess hope. *Health Expectations, 14*(4), 417–428.

Smedema, S. M., Chan, J. Y., & Phillips, B. N. (2014). Core self-evaluations and Snyder's hope theory in persons with spinal cord injuries. *Rehabilitation Psychology, 59*(4), 399–406.

Smedema, S. M., Pfaller, J., Moser, E., Tu, W., & Chang, G. (2013). Measurement structure of the trait hope scale in persons with spinal cord injury: A confirmatory factor analysis. *Rehabilitation, Research, Policy and Education, 27*(3), 206–212.

Snyder, C. R., Berg, C., Woodward, J. T., Gum, A., Rand, K. L., Wrobleski, K. K., . . . Hackman, A. (2005). Hope against the cold: Individual differences in trait hope and acute pain tolerance on the cold pressor task. *Journal of Personality, 73*(2), 287–312. doi:10.1111/j.1467-6494.2005.00318.x

Snyder, C. R., Harris, C., Anderson, J. R., Holleran, S. A., Irving, L. M., Sigmon, S. T., . . . Harney, P. (1991). The will and the ways: Development and validation of an individual differences measure of hope. *Journal of Personality and Social Psychology, 60*, 570–585.

Snyder, C. R., Hoza, B., Pelham, W. E., Rapoff, M., Ware, L., Danovsky, M., . . . Stahl, K. J. (1997). The development and validation of the Children's Hope Scale. *Journal of Pediatric Psychology, 22*, 399–421.

Snyder, C. R., Irving, L. M., & Anderson, J. R. (1991). Hope and health: Measuring the will and the ways. In C. R. Snyder & D. R. Forsyth (Eds.), *Handbook of social and clinical psychology: The health perspective* (pp. 285–305). Elmsford, NY: Pergamon.

Snyder, C. R., Rand, K. L., & Sigmon, D. R. (2002). Hope theory. In C. R. Snyder & S. J. Lopez (Eds.), *Handbook of positive psychology* (pp. 257–276). New York: Oxford University Press.

Snyder, C. R., Sympson, S. C., Ybasco, F. C., Borders, T. F., Babyak, M. A., & Higgins, R. L. (1996). Development and validation of the State Hope Scale. *Journal of Personality and Social Psychology, 70*, 321–335.

Stanton, A. L., Danoff-burg, S., & Huggins, M. E. (2002). The first year after breast cancer diagnosis: hope and coping strategies as predictors of adjustment. *Psycho-Oncology, 11*(2), 93–102.

Stoner, M. H. (1982). Hope and cancer patients. *Dissertation Abstracts International, 43*, 1983B–2592B.

Stotland, E. (1969). *The psychology of hope.* San Francisco, CA: Jossey-Bass.

Sullivan, M. J. L., Bishop, S. R., & Pivik, J. (1995). The pain catastrophizing scale: Development and validation. *Psychological Assessment, 7*(4), 524–532. doi:10.1037/1040-3590.7.4.524

Szramka-Pawlak, B., Hornowska, E., Walkowiak, H., & Żaba, R. (2014). Hope as a psychological factor affecting quality of life in patients with psoriasis. *Applied Research in Quality of Life, 9*, 273–283.

Tedeschi, R. G., & Calhoun, L. G. (2004). Posttraumatic growth: Conceptual foundations and empirical evidence. *Psychological Inquiry, 1*, 1–18.

Vieth, A. Z., Hagglund, K. J., Clay, D.L., Frank, R. G., Thayer, J. F., Johnson, J. C., & Goldstein, D. E. (1997). The contribution of hope and affectivity to diabetes-related disability: An exploratory study. *Journal of Clinical Psychology in Medical Settings, 4*(1), 65–77.

Yuen, A. N., Ho, S. M., & Chan, C. K. (2014). The mediating roles of cancer?related rumination in the relationship between dispositional hope and psychological outcomes among childhood cancer survivors. *Psycho-Oncology, 23*(4), 412–419.

Hope and Children's Health

Michael Rapoff *and* Ron Freche

Abstract

Childhood is a critical time to develop hopeful thinking that can help children cope with challenges in general and those related to maintaining or improving their health. The purpose of this chapter is to (a) define hope as it applies to children and the growth of hope across developmental stages; (b) describe the way family members, teachers, and other significant adults can foster hope in children; (c) review studies on the relationship between hope and pediatric health and illness, including studies on health promotion, adherence to chronic pediatric diseases, and coping with a chronic pediatric disease; and (d) share knowledge related to patients with chronic pediatric diseases and how they maintain hope given the additional challenges they face in their lives.

Key Words: hope, children, health, adherence, coping, pediatric disease

We often say, "children are not little adults." Childhood is a critical time for developing lifelong knowledge and skills, including hopeful thinking. At each stage of development, children are learning pathways to their goals and are being motivated to pursue their goals. Critical to that process is the support of significant adults in the lives of children, including parents, caregivers, grandparents, uncles, aunts, and teachers. Negotiating relationships with siblings and peers is also critical in learning to pursue one's goals in a social context, without impinging on the goals of others.

In this chapter, we have four main objectives. The first is to define hope in children and discuss the growth of hope at different stages of development. The second is to describe how family members, teachers, and other caregivers can foster hope in children. The third is to review studies on the relationship between hope and pediatric health and illness, including studies on health promotion and management, adherence to medical regimens for chronic pediatric diseases, and coping with a chronic pediatric disease. Our final objective is to provide details on what we learned from our

patients about how to foster hope in children with chronic pediatric illnesses.

Hope in Children and Developmental Stages

Hope has been defined as our perceived capability to devise routes to desired goals (pathways thinking) and the motivation to use those routes (agency thinking). What is different about hope in children is that they are developing from infancy through adolescence the capacity to formulate goals and pathways to reach their goals, and they are motivated to achieve their goals through the much-needed assistance of parents, teachers, siblings, and other significant people in their lives.

Infants and Toddlers (0–2 Years)

In infancy, raw sensory input (visual, auditory, tactile, gustatory, and olfactory) in a normally developing child begins to be stored, organized, and comprehended. For example, an infant learns to perceive particular facial features as not just any face but the face that is his or her mom. Infants also begin to understand cause and effect. They learn to coordinate their movements and that their movements create effects, like grabbing a toy and placing it in their mouth. Although we cannot know what babies are thinking, we can surmise that until they develop language to articulate their goals they do not have the internal language to formulate goals. However, they do engage in what appears to be goal-directed activity, when for example they swipe at a mobile again and again to see an object move or make a noise.

They learn to form simple goals, particularly when they move into toddlerhood and use language and gestures to obtain objects and generally influence those around them. They also learn the give and take in their play activities. These are all ways of developing pathways to their goals (even if they are not formally articulated). The agency aspect of hope is developing during this period as children learn that they are the agents of their actions, illustrated by the often-heard phrase from toddlers, "I can do it."

Preschoolers (3–6 Years)

The language repertoire of preschoolers virtually explodes during this period. In their groundbreaking direct observational study of language development in American children from lower to higher socioeconomic (SES) families, Hart and Risley (1995) recorded in one month an average of over 600 vocabulary words uttered by children from middle/lower SES strata to over 1,000 words by children from higher SES strata. All the components of hopeful thinking, including goal-setting and agency and pathway thinking, are possible because of language. Language is critical in communicating with others and generating internal dialogues, which increasingly guide the actions of young children. Preschoolers are also beginning to understand perspective-taking. They begin to empathize with others and understand that the pursuit of one's goals occurs in a social context where others want to pursue their goals. They learn to select goals that do not threaten their peers or caregivers.

Middle Years (7–12 Years)

Children learn to read for pleasure and for obtaining useful information during these years. They benefit from reading stories about real people or imaginary characters that have encountered obstacles to reaching their goals and have stayed the course and found ways to overcome obstacles to their goals. These stories model hopeful thinking for children who are very impressionable at this stage

of development. The memory capacity of children increases from the preschool to middle years. Just as a higher capacity of memory helps computer process more efficiently, the same happens for children who can store and process information more efficiently. This helps them in choosing goals and engaging in agency and pathway thinking. Children during this stage also develop strong friendships. They learn to share goals with their friends and support each other in pursuing their own individual goals. Social support is an important way to motivate children and support them in their pursuit of their goals.

Adolescents (13–18 Years)

During this stage of development, teenagers are solidifying their views of themselves and what they what to accomplish as they move into adulthood. They are seeking autonomy, and they are dealing with their own sexuality. They are formulating their own personal beliefs (often quite congruent with their parents), and they have developed their preferences for leisure activities. At this point in their development, teenagers have had many experiences of pursing goals, encountering obstacles, and finding ways to reach their goals or modify their goals to achieve success. In spite of the cultural stereotype that adolescence is the period of "storm and stress," teenagers do want to communicate and seek advice and support from significant adults in their lives, such as parents and teachers.

Fostering Hope in Children

Although other individuals such as teachers, peers, and community members have important effects on young people, parents have the closest connection and thus the greatest impact on their children. Hope begets hope. If parents want their children to be hopeful thinkers, they must provide hope-inducing models for their children. Parents can tell their children stories about how they encountered obstacles to reaching their goals and how they overcame these obstacles by figuring out different pathways to reach their goals and having positive self-talk about their ability to pursue their goals.

Parents can also help their children construct individualized stories about a developmental issue a child is facing or a particular problem he or she is dealing with like fear of the dark. Dr. Bill Cook has recommended the use of therapeutic stories to help children manage emotional and behavioral problems (Cook, Taylor, & Silverman, 2004; Painter, Cook, & Silverman, 1999). The basic steps for developing a story as outlined by Dr. Cook are as follows:

1. Introduce the main character(s). At this step the main character has a name similar to the child and the same central characteristics like gender, hair and eye color, size, and age. This way the child can readily identify with the main character.

2. Tell about the problem. The child in the story has a problem or goal and has encountered obstacles to solving the problem or meeting a goal (just like the one the target child is experiencing).

3. Have the character talk to a wise person. This could be a wise man or wise grandmother who lives in a magic tree house. This person is not only wise but very empathic.

4. Have the character try out a new approach. The child in the story explores strategies suggested by the wise person for solving the problem or reaching a goal.

5. Summarize the lesson. After the story ends, the child has an opportunity to ask questions, make comments, or give alternative suggestions. The child then tries out the strategies in real-life situations with parents and teachers, referring back to the story and what the character learned from the wise person.

Parents and teachers can construct these hope-inducing stories and motivate children to meet their goals and find pathways to meet their goals.

As can be seen in Box 14.1, there are ways that significant adults in children's' lives can help them set achievable goals, such as matching their goals with their talents. They can also enhance children's willpower thinking (i.e., agency thinking), for example, by praising them when they show determination to meet their goals (see Box 14.2). Significant adults can also enhance children's waypower thinking (i.e., pathways thinking), for example, by building their skill bases in scholastics, athletics, and social matters (see Box 14.3).

Studies on Hope and Health and Coping with Chronic Pediatric Diseases

Although Snyder's hope theory has been used in research with adults with chronic illnesses and the parents of chronically ill children and adolescents, there has been surprisingly little work done investigating hope and health or chronic illness with children and adolescents. The available research with children has examined the relationships between hope and subjective well-being and life adjustment during treatment and social and familial support

> **Box 14.1.** Tips for Helping Children Set Achievable Goals
>
> • Help your babies to identify and name desired objects in their environment.
> • Teach your children to use words to specify precisely what they want.
> • Listen carefully to your children so you can know what they really want.
> • Make sure your children consider a few attractive goals before settling on one.
> • Instruct your children in making stretch goals that build on previous performances.
> • Help your children to match their goals with their talents.
> • Show interest and ask about your children's goals.
> • If your children have conflicting goals, show how this can be a problem and help them select one goal.
> • Remind your children to set goals they want, rather than seeking things others want.
> • Whenever possible, let your children make the decision about their goals.
> • Praise your children when they make goals for themselves.
>
> Reprinted in part with permission from "A Goals Checklist," pages 171–172 in *The Psychology of Hope*, by C. R. Snyder, PhD (New York: Free Press, 1994).

and hope as predictors of adherence to medical regimens. Often, these studies prove useful in suggesting ways hope can be facilitated to improve the health and psychosocial functioning of healthy and chronically ill young people.

Hope and Adjustment to Chronic Illness or Injury

In one of the earliest studies to consider the effect of hope on children's adjustment to a disease, Lewis and Kliewer (1996) examined the relationships between hope, coping strategies, and adjustment among a group of children with sickle-cell disease. The researchers found that children with higher hope experienced less anxiety about their disease. Additionally, those children who were high in hope and able to engage in more active coping strategies (e.g., distraction, seeking social support) reported less anxiety than other children who were also high in hope but were only able to engage in more avoidant coping strategies. Research with

Box 14.2. Tips for Helping Children Enhance Willpower Thinking

• Take every opportunity make your children realize that they were the ones who made something happen.
• Praise your children whenever they show determination to get what they want (assuming it is a goal condoned in the family).
• Teach your children to have positive mental tapes playing in their heads about how they can do things.
• Help your children accentuate their strengths and minimize their weaknesses.
• Emphasize the roadblocks area a normal part of life and are to be anticipated.
• Tell your children about roadblocks you encountered in your childhood and how you coped successfully and unsuccessfully with them.
• Suggest that barriers should be viewed as challenges rather than preludes to failure.
• Coach your children to recall how they have overcome previous barriers when they encounter new roadblocks.
• Help your children to laugh at themselves and their predicaments.
• Teach your children to be patient and to wait when they are not getting what they want.
• Encourage your children to enjoy the process of getting to their goals, rather than concentrating only on the outcome.
• Point out that being mentally drained sometimes is normal and that we need to recharge when we feel this way.
• Allow your children to take time-outs from their goal pursuits.
• Make sure your children are exercising and getting enough rest.

Reprinted in part with permission from "A Willpower Checklist," pages 189–190 in *The Psychology of Hope,* by C. R. Snyder, PhD (New York: Free Press, 1994).

Box 14.3. Tips for Helping Children Enhance Waypower Thinking

• With infants, constantly show them how causality works (i.e., this leads to that).
• Supply objects (e.g., drums, pull-toys, building blocks) that, when used, show your youngsters how they are causing something to happen.
• Teach toddlers why things happen and have them talk about such linkages.
• Listen to your children's explanations or stories about why something happened.
• Whenever possible, build your children's skill bases in scholastics, athletics, and social matters.
• Instruct your children to have mental scripts about the chain of activities that occur in certain situations.
• Use children's stories, nursery rhymes, and songs to teach your children to anticipate how words go together in a sequence.
• Help your children break a long pathway leading to a goal into smaller, doable steps.
• Teach your children that it is helpful to think about failures as being due to the use of an ineffective strategy rather than their lack of talent.
• Talk with your children about their plans for reaching their goals.

Reprinted in part with permission from "A Waypower Checklist," page 204 in *The Psychology of Hope,* by C. R. Snyder, PhD (New York: Free Press, 1994).

burn survivors and matched controls by Barnum, Snyder, Rapoff, Mani, and Thompson (1998) expands on these findings between hope and coping. Despite few differences between the groups, when examining predictors of adjustment (e.g., social support, family environment, burn characteristics, demographics, and hope), the authors found that adolescents who reported higher levels of hope engaged in less externalizing behavior problems and

experienced better self-worth. The authors suggest that high-hope thinking may facilitate more effective functioning in the face of challenges both during recovery from burns and with obstacles in life in general. In turn, adolescents may feel more adept in their activation and use of adaptive, problem-solving coping behaviors.

Another study provides useful insight into how time may also affect the experience of hope in young people living with cancer (McKnight-Hexdall & Huebner, 2008). Researchers found that, for children with cancer, hope bears the strongest relationship with subjective well-being. They also found that as the number of months since diagnosis increased, levels of hope in the children also increased while life satisfaction and positive affect remained stable. The authors posit that cancer (and perhaps any other chronic or life-threatening illness) is more disruptive at diagnosis to hope than it is to life satisfaction or positive affect. Children and adolescents dealing with cancer might regard the diagnosis as disrupting important aspects of life, their goals, and their dreams. The authors proposed that as pediatric patients move through the treatment process, they and their family members engage with the community of other patients and receive social support from other children who are coping with the same illness. In turn, they are exposed to others who have survived cancer, and they learn that they too can survive. As a result, they experience an increase in hope. Additionally, when dealing with chronic disease, family functioning plays an important role in the utility of social support during the experience of hope.

Among a sample of children living with juvenile rheumatoid arthritis (JRA), Connelly (2005) found that when parents reported dissatisfaction with family functioning, children reported lower levels of hope. Connelly suggested that nurses can assess levels of hope in children with JRA and help facilitate higher hope by helping children set goals and generate strategies for meeting their goals.

Hope and Adherence to Medical Treatments

Lloyd, Cantell, Pacaud, Crawford, and Dewey (2009) found that among adolescents with type 1 diabetes, hope was a significant mediator of the relationships between perceptions of maternal empathy and medication adherence and glycemic control. Adolescents who reported higher levels of maternal empathy were more likely to report higher levels of adherence if they also reported higher levels of hope. This mediational relationship also was supported for glycemic control. A second study with a sample of Brazilian adolescents with type 1 diabetes found that youth experiencing higher levels of hope had lower HbA1c levels (better disease control) and lower rates of depressive symptomology (Santos et al., 2015).

Researchers have also studied the relationships between hope, depression, and medication adherence among a sample of children and adolescents who were organ donor recipients (Maikrantz, Steele, Dreyer, Stratman, & Bovaird, 2007). They found that those patients who experienced higher levels of hope while being less sure about the efficacy of their treatments had higher rates of adherence than those patients who were lower in hope but more secure about the efficacy of their treatments. While hope and uncertainty were associated with depressive symptoms and anxiety, hope and adherence to treatment were fully mediated by depressive symptoms. Those patients who were high in hope but low in uncertainty about the efficacy of their treatment were only more likely to adhere to the treatment regimen when they were not experiencing symptoms of depression.

Additionally, children's adherence to an asthma treatment regimen was also predicted by higher levels of hope (Berg, Rapoff, Snyder, & Belmont, 2007). Researchers measured adherence to a daily inhaled steroid regimen by electronically monitoring the patients' use of a metered-dose inhaler over a 14-day period. While no demographic or psychosocial variables predicted adherence, hope was a significant and positive predictor of adherence to the treatment regimen.

Together these studies suggest that developing interventions to increase hope (e.g., helping children set goals, build motivation, and develop strategies for meeting goals) might be beneficial in improving adherence. Also, interventions that tackle cognitive distortions about treatment efficacy via restructuring of goals and outcome expectancies might effectively combat depressive symptomology while also increasing protective factors, such as hope.

Interventions Targeting Hope to Improve Health

There have been very few intervention studies that involve increasing hope or using hope to facilitate better health outcomes among children and adolescents. One study with a sample of obese children found intervention participants were able to decrease waist circumference and cholesterol levels via use of pathway-related hope thinking (Beale, 2014). The authors theorized that pathway-related hopeful thinking works to facilitate goal attainment and positive health outcomes by increasing self-efficacy and problem-solving coping. Additionally, studies that take students out of the "sick role" and place them in new environments (such as summer camps for the chronically ill) are able to facilitate developing a sense of mastery and self-esteem from participating in the activities of summer camp. Research has proposed that these activities and increases in efficacy and ability work to facilitate increases in youths' sense of hope (Warady, Carr, Hellerstein, & Alon, 1992). Another study looked at the experience of 102 youth with various chronic illnesses who attended a summer camp and found that increases in pathway hope subscale scores drove increases in total hope scores from pre- to post-camp, suggesting that youth developed effective problem-solving strategies to meet their goals through the camp experiences. Interestingly, agency post-camp subscale scores significantly predicted post-camp health-related quality of life scores, while the pathway scores did not (Woods, Mayes, Bartley, Fedele, & Ryan, 2013).

Finally, one intervention focused on increasing hope to facilitate changes in physical activity as part of a weight management program (Van Allen & Steele, 2012). Researchers found that increases in hope were associated with changes in physical activity, regardless of gender, ethnicity, or socioeconomic status.

Working to increase self-efficacy, motivation, and persistence via goal-setting behavior may be particularly useful for children and adolescents who are living with chronic illnesses (e.g., cystic fibrosis, asthma) that require detailed and time-consuming medical treatments that can become burdensome and difficult to manage. For instance, interventions designed to increase hope might result in increased setting of specific goals (i.e., "I need to find a good time to do my airway clearance techniques"), more effective problem-solving (i.e., picking a time in the day to perform airway clearance techniques that does not commonly involve interruptions), and more persistence and adaptive adjustments when a strategy does not work (i.e., changing the time for airway clearance when the first choice is frequently interrupted).

Fostering Hope in Children with Chronic Pediatric Illnesses

The first author has had over 37 years of experience doing research with and providing clinical services for children and adolescents with chronic pediatric illnesses, including asthma, cystic fibrosis, juvenile idiopathic arthritis, and migraine headaches. Beyond the usual developmental tasks, children with chronic health problems have to face other physical, social, and emotional challenges, like pain, fatigue, limitations in daily activities, and changes in their appearance. They also have to follow complicated regimens involving medications, special exercises, and restrictive diets. One would think that with all these challenges, these children with be low on hope. But the research and our experience does not bear this out.

We have observed and interviewed many young people with chronic diseases and their families who have successfully coped with a child's illness. These children and families have clear goals, including the usual ones that are critical to daily life, plus goals specific to managing a chronic illness and containing its negative effects. These children and their families can generate multiple pathways to reach their goals. This is particularly critical to hopeful thinking as chronic diseases present many obstacles. The children and their families also have the mental energy, commitment, and determination to overcome obstacles and meet their goals. Our lives are enriched by the stories of hope that emanate from the experiences of chronically ill children and their families. So how do they maintain hope under challenging life circumstances?

Acceptance: Getting Past "Why Me?"

When the first author's son was diagnosed with asthma at age nine, he had moderately severe symptoms. Like many children with asthma, he had to cope with intermittent and sometime unpredictable asthma attacks that have been described as trying to breathe with an elephant sitting on one's chest. He was an active and athletic boy who was frustrated at times that his asthma interfered with his active life. Soon after being diagnosed he asked, "Why did this happened to me?" The only answer we could give him is that we do not know why certain children develop asthma and others do not. But in one sense this question was really rhetorical and was really a question about fairness. The "why me?" question is a way of expressing this unfairness of having to cope with a chronic health condition.

Children with chronic diseases successfully confront this issue of "why me" in several ways. First, they express their negative feelings such as fear, sadness, and anger about having to deal with their condition. Second, they are helped by their parents, teacher, and healthcare providers to understand that their illness is not a punishment for wrongdoing. Third, they come to accept the illness and treatment regimen as part of their lives and overcome obstacles in pursuit of their goals.

The world-class Olympic track star Jackie Joyner-Kersee has been an excellent role model for how people with asthma cope with their disease. Diagnosed with asthma as a teenager, Joyner-Kersee was reluctant to accept her illness and was not consistent in following her treatment program. Her wake-up call came one day when she was rushed to the emergency room after a serious asthma attack. After this life-threatening experience, she focused on controlling her asthma instead of letting if control her. As she said, "Asthma is part of who I am. If I want to continue to be great on the athletic field, I have to discipline myself to do things needed to win.

Taking my medication every day is just one of them" (Joyner-Kersee, 1996). She discovered that acceptance leads to better control of her illness. Hopeful children and families accept the realities of living with a chronic disease. They do not deny the negatives, but they do not dwell on them either. They focus their energies on meeting the challenges of managing a chronic disease and finding ways to overcome these challenges to meet their goals.

Adherence to Medical Regimens

A major challenge for children with chronic disease is following medical treatment programs that are often complex (e.g., involving medications, exercises, self-injections, or special diets), are not always immediately effective in relieving symptoms, and sometimes produce negative side-effects. It is not surprising that about 50% of children with a chronic disease have problems consistently following their medical regimens (Rapoff, 2010). Children and families with high hope are better able to follow their treatment regimens for several reasons. First, as active partners in their treatment, children can help set treatment goals in collaboration with their doctor, nurse, or therapist. This gives them a clear focus and energizes their efforts to improve and maintain their health. Second, parents and healthcare providers can provide guidance and positive reinforcement, which helps to further energize children in pursuit of health-enhancing goals. Finally, parents and health care providers can help children generate multiple pathways to reach their treatment goals, particularly when they encounter barriers. There are effective adherence-enhancing treatment programs that teach children how to overcome barriers to following their medical regimens. The more recent trend is to take effective face-to-face interventions and convert them to "e-health" platforms, such as web-based and phone application programs that can be more widely disseminated (Rapoff, 2013).

The Role of Humor

Dr. Rick Snyder had a saying: "If you don't laugh at yourself, you've missed the biggest joke of all." The health-promoting properties of humor have long been recognized (Cousins, 1979; Lefcourt & Davidson-Katz, 1991; Moody, 1978). Children with chronic illnesses who maintain a sense of humor find it enhances their willpower to continue to cope with the demands of their illness and its

effects. The first author had a patient with cystic fibrosis who had a well-developed sense of humor. She was the first patient to think up a way to make others laugh by filling an IV bag with water and goldfish and pretending that it was attached to her by an intravenous needle. This was quite a shock for residents and staff when they first encountered this setup. Like many young people with cystic fibrosis, she also had clubbed digits, where the tips of the fingers and thumbs become swollen and bulbous in appearance because of inadequate oxygen profusion. Most people did not notice these "fat" fingertips unless she painted her fingernails. On one occasion as a teenager, she did just that and went to school. Another child noticed one of her fingers and asked if she had slammed it in the car door. Seeing the humor in this, she replied, "If that's true, I would have to be awfully clumsy, because I would have had to smash all of them in the door." She could laugh at herself and the absurdity of the situation. Humor helps children with chronic illness maintain their energy for pursuing their goals.

Focusing on "Can Do's" Rather Than "Can't Do's"

All of us have strengths and weaknesses in coping with life challenges. It is not different for children with chronic health conditions. An important way to help children who are chronically ill is to help them focus on what they can do rather than what they cannot do.

By focusing on what they can do, children with chronic illnesses can remain flexible in pursuing their goals. They can shift to alternate activities that are within their capabilities and learn to excel in these new areas. A patient of the first author who had severe arthritis played on her basketball team but had to quit because of physical limitations caused by joint damage and inflammation. She was very angry and frustrated the she could no longer play with her team. She thought of several alternative pathways, including quitting (which she did not want to do), playing with her limitations and pain (which would have been very difficult), or being the manager of the team. She chose to be the manager, which allowed her to enjoy being part of the team and contributing to their efforts. Another young man with bone cancer was told he could no longer play football, which was very frustrating to him. Instead of moping and being angry, he chose to pick up a new sport, golf, which he could play and at which he could excel. This is hope in action, as young people with physical challenges remain energized and find new goals and pathways to their goals.

Getting by With a Little Help from Family, Friends, and Others

Like all children and, maybe to a greater extent, children with chronic illness need the support of significant people in their lives. They have to cope with the usual developmental challenges plus challenges their illnesses present to them. They need social support more than youngsters without these illness challenges.

In the social support literature, it is emphasized that what is being measured is "perceived support" because the person's perception of the amount and type of support being provided is most important. There is also thought to be at least four different types of support, each with different functions (Wills & Shinar, 2000):

1. Emotional support (affirming a person's worth and self-esteem, providing encouragement).

2. Instrumental support (practical support like providing tangible support, resources, and behavioral assistance).

3. Companionship support (inviting the person into a social group, socializing with the person).

4. Validation (giving valuable feedback and providing social comparisons for the person to validate their behaviors and feelings).

Different people in the person's social network may provide different types of support. For example peers may provide more emotional support, while parents might provide more instrumental support, such as behavioral assistance with managing medical regimens (La Greca et al., 1995).

Support, however, is not always perceived as positive. There is a concept in the literature titled "miscarried helping" whereby caregivers believe they are supporting their youngsters with a chronic condition but their efforts are not helpful and cause poorer family functioning, which contributes to poor management of the child's chronic condition (Fales, Essner, Harris, & Palermo, 2014; Harris et al., 2008).

PARENTS

Parents of children with chronic disease also have to meet the usual needs of their children plus the additional challenges related to their children's disease, such as following complicated medical regimens on a daily basis. They are asked to take time for doctor's appointments and to see their children go through complicated and sometimes painful medical treatments. They have to be advocates for their children and provide emotional as well as concrete assistance, such as encouraging their children to manage their illness and medical treatments. Parents also have to be supportive of each other as having a child with a chronic disease can create conflicts and challenges to their relationship. Having a child with a serious illness can make or break marriages. Those couples who "make it" seem to be able to share their feelings, comfort each other, maintain open communication, balance responsibilities, and find time for each other. They energize each other and help each other discover ways to cope with adversity. In short, they have high levels of hope.

SIBLINGS

Having siblings brings to children the reality that they are not the center of the universe. They have to make room for other person(s) in their lives. Siblings can be a source of both care and conflict for children with chronic illnesses. Their brothers or sisters provide companionship by playing games, drawing, talking, and just hanging out with them, particularly when they are in the hospital or have to stay indoors. Such sibling support helps children with chronic illness to generate alternative pathways to social and recreational goals. Siblings also assist children with their medical treatments and encourage them to take their medicine, follow their diets, or do special exercises. To a lesser degree, siblings of children with chronic disease can resent the extra attention given to their brother or sister from parents and relatives. These resentful feelings can be mixed with guilt as siblings realize that their sibling cannot help that he or she has a chronic illness. Overall, most siblings provide companionship and direct assistance to their chronically ill brother or sister.

GRANDPARENTS

Grandparents provide needed support to children with chronic illnesses and their families. Fortunately, healthcare providers recognize this and allow grandparents unlimited visitation in the hospital, as well as involving them more directly (with parental permission) in discussions about children's illness and treatments. Grandparents provide affection and companionship and relate hopeful stories to their grandchildren. Because grandparents often deal with the physical challenges caused by illness and aging, they can give living testimonials about overcoming obstacles and living productive lives.

FRIENDS

As the saying goes, a friend is someone who knows you and still likes you. Friends are an important source of companionship and intimacy for children. This is critical for children with chronic illnesses because their illness can interfere with opportunities to develop and maintain friendships. One of the most important things friends can do is treat chronically ill children "normally." They do not care if their ill friend has lost his or her hair to chemotherapy or has a hard time keeping up physically. Because children with chronic disease often try to "protect" the feelings of their parents and other relatives, friends are sometimes the only people to whom they confide their frustrations and fears. Thus friends can be hope-givers too. They help children with chronic illnesses remain energized and generate alternative pathways to their social goals. Peers can be particularly supportive of their chronically ill friend following their treatment regimen. For children with diabetes, they can encourage them to follow their diet and eat the same foods required of their friend and remind them to test their blood glucose levels (Bearman & La Greca, 2002).

TEACHERS

With advances in treatments for once-fatal diseases, more children recover from serious illnesses or are able to live with them. School is an important part of children's intellectual and social life and teachers play a major role in nurturing hope. Many medical treatment teams now include teachers who help chronically ill children keep up with their schoolwork and provide valuable emotional support while they are in the hospital. Also, after a child is diagnosed with a chronic illness, these teachers often will visit the children's classrooms to discuss the child's medical condition and encourage classroom teachers and students to treat them normally.

The classroom teachers of children with chronic illnesses also provide valuable support. They often arrange for their classes to send personal notes, pictures, and get-well cards to children when they are in the hospital. These messages communicate that their teachers and classmates have not forgotten them, still care for them, and will welcome them back when they return to school. Teachers also share narratives that promote a positive and more balanced view of chronic illness: namely, that someone may have a serious illness or physical limitations but that does not mean he or she is a different person than before or that he or she is to be pitied.

HEALTHCARE PROVIDERS

Children with chronic disease have frequent contact with the medical system, including doctors, nurses, and therapists. These healthcare providers provide education and support and are important sources of support. For example, nurses have been at the forefront of efforts to assess and reduce children's pain from illness and medical procedures. They were the first professionals to challenge the long-standing belief that children, especially neonates, experienced pain to a lesser degree than adults and, therefore, did not need as much pain relief. Fortunately this situation has changed, and nurses have continued to be leaders in efforts to control children's pain. Such efforts are vital because unrelieved pain often leads to feelings of hopelessness and depression and can retard the restorative powers of the immune system. Nurses and other healthcare providers not only help relieve pain but encourage children to follow their medical treatments, and they provide emotional support during hospital stays. Pediatric psychologists are also frequently part of the medical team, particularly at university medical centers and children's hospitals. They offer inpatient consultations and outpatient therapy for chronically ill children and their families. Thus healthcare providers are significant givers of hope to children with chronic diseases.

Conclusion

As we have tried to show, the nutrients for developing hope in children must be delivered from infancy and throughout development. There are many ways that important adults in the lives of children can help them learn to set achievable goals and develop agency and pathway thinking. We have also reviewed the empirical literature on how hope can positively impact coping and adjustment and adherence to medical regimens and promote health in children with or without chronic disease. Finally, we concluded based on clinical experience how our patients with chronic health problems have taught us how they maintain hope, sometime under great adversity. Our desire is that parents, teachers, therapists, extended family members, siblings, and healthcare providers do their part in fostering the health of children by helping them engage in hopeful thinking.

Acknowledgments

This chapter is dedicated to the memory of Dr. Rick Snyder who lived and breathed hope during his too-short stay with us. We remember him with great affection and appreciation for his mentorship and friendship. Parts of this chapter were adapted from *Hope for the Journey: Helping Children through Good Times and Bad*, by R. Snyder, D. McDermott, W. Cook, and M. Rapoff (Boulder, CO: Westview Press, 1997). Box 14.1, Box 14.2, and Box 14.3 were adapted with permission from checklists published in *The Psychology of Hope*, by Rick Snyder (New York: Free Press, 1994), pages 176–177, 189–190, and 204–205, respectively.

References

Barnum, D. D., Snyder, C. R., Rapoff, M. A., Mani, M. M., & Thompson, R. (1998). Hope and social support in the psychological adjustment of children who have survived burn injuries and their matched controls. *Children's Health Care, 27*(1), 15–30.

Beale, B. D. (2014). *The role of hope and resilience in pediatric obesity intervention outcomes.* Unpublished doctoral dissertation. Wright State University, Washington, DC.

Bearman, K. J., & La Greca, A. M. (2002). Assessing friend support of adolescents diabetes care: The Diabetes Social Support Questionnaire–Friends version. *Journal of Pediatric Psychology, 27,* 417–428.

Berg, C. J., Rapoff, M. A., Snyder, C. R., & Belmont, J. M. (2007). The relationship of children's hope to pediatric asthma treatment adherence. *Journal of Positive Psychology, 2,* 176–184. doi:10.1080/17439760701409629

Connelly, T. W. (2005). Family functioning and hope in children with juvenile rheumatoid arthritis. *The American Journal of Maternal/Child Nursing, 30*(4), 245–250. doi:10.1097/00005721-200507000-00008

Cousins, N. (1979). *Anatomy of an illness as perceived by the patient.* New York: Norton.

Cook, W.J., Taylor, L.A. & Silverman, P. (2004). The application of therapeutic storytelling techniques with preadolescent children: A clinical description with illustrative case study. *Cognitive and Behavioral Practice, 11* (*12*), 243-248.

Fales, J. L., Essner, B. S., Harris, M. A., & Palermo, T. M. (2014). When helping hurts: Miscarried helping in families of youth with chronic pain. *Journal of Pediatric Psychology, 39,* 427–437.

Harris, M. A. Antal, H., Oelbaum, R., Buckloch, L. M., White, N. H., & Wysocki, T. (2008). Good intentions gone awry: Assessing parental "miscarried helping" in diabetes. *Families, Systems, & Health, 26,* 393–403.

Hart, B., & Risley, T. R. (1995). *Meaningful differences in the everyday experience of young American children.* Baltimore: Paul H. Brookes.

Joyner-Kersee, J. (1996). Jackie Joyner-Kersee world record holder with a winning asthma strategy. *Air Currents, 3,* p. 8.

La Greca, A. M., Auslander, W. F., Greco, P., Spetter, D., Fisher, E. B., & Santiago, J. V. (1995). I get by with a little help from my family and friends: Adolescents' support for diabetes care. *Journal of Pediatric Psychology, 20,* 449–476.

Lefcourt, H. M., & Davidson-Katz, K. (1991). The role of humor and the self. In C.R. Snyder & D. R. Forsyth (Eds.), *Handbook of social and clinical psychology: The health perspective* (pp. 41–56). New York: Pergamon.

Lewis, H., & Kliewer, W. (1996). Hope, coping, psychological, and physical adjustment among children with sickle cell disease: Tests of mediator and moderator models. *Journal of Pediatric Psychology, 21,* 23–41.

Lloyd, S. M., Cantell, M., Pacaud, D., Crawford, S., & Dewey, D. (2009). Brief report: Hope, perceived maternal empathy, medical regimen adherence, and glycemic control in adolescents with type 1 diabetes. *Journal of Pediatric Psychology, 34*(9), 1025–1029. doi:10.1093/jpepsy/jsn141

Maikrantz, J. M., Steele, R. G., Dreyer, M. L., Stratman, A. C., & Bovaird, J. A. (2007). The relationship of hope and illness-related uncertainty to emotional adjustment and adherence among pediatric renal and liver transplant recipients. *Journal of Pediatric Psychology, 32*(5), 571–581. doi:10.1093/jpepsy/jsl046

McKnight-Hexdall, C., & Huebner, E. S. (2008). Subjective well-being in pediatric oncology patients. *Applied Research in Quality of Life, 2,* 189–208. doi:10.1007/s11482-008-9037-7

Moody, R. A. (1978). *Laugh after laugh: The healing power of humor.* Jacksonville, FL.: Headwaters Press.

Painter, L.T., Cook, W.J., & Silverman, P.S. (1999). The effects of therapeutic storytelling and behavioral parent training on noncompliant behavior in young boys. *Child & Family Behavior Therapy, 21*(2), 47-66.

Rapoff, M. A. (2010). *Adherence to pediatric medical regimens* (2nd ed.) New York: Springer.

Rapoff, M. A. (2013). E-health interventions in pediatrics. *Clinical Practice in Pediatric Psychology, 1,* 309–313.

Santos, F. R. M., Sigulem, D., Areco, K. C. N., Gabbay, M. A. L., Dib, S. A., & Bernardo, V. (2015). Hope matters to the glycemic control of adolescents and young adults with type 1 diabetes. *Journal of Health Psychology, 20*(5) 681–689. doi:10.1177/1359105315573429

Warady, B. A., Carr, B., Hellerstein, S., & Alon, U. (1992). Residential summer camp for children with end-stage renal disease. *Child Nephrology and Urology, 12*(4), 212–215.

Wills, T. A., & Shinar, O. (2000). Measuring perceived and received social support. In S. Cohen., L. G. Underwood., & B. H. Gottlieb (Eds.), *Social support measurement and intervention: A guide for health and social scientists* (pp. 86–135). Oxford: Oxford University Press.

Woods, K., Mayes, S., Bartley, E., Fedele, D., & Ryan, J. (2013). An evaluation of psychosocial outcomes for children and adolescents attending a summer camp for youth with chronic illness. *Children's Health Care, 42*(1), 85–98. doi:10.1080/02739615.2013.753822

Van Allen, J., & Steele, R.G. (2012). Associations between change in hope and change in physical activity in a pediatric weight management program. *Children's Health Care, 41*(4), 344–359. doi:10.1080/02739615.2012.721724

Hope and Athletic Performance

Henrik Gustafsson, Leslie Podlog, *and* Paul Davis

Abstract

A substantial body of empirical work has demonstrated links between hope and positive psychosocial functioning within the general field of psychology. Surprisingly little attention has been paid to the importance of hope within the athletic domain. The minimal research that does exist suggests that hope is associated with enhanced athlete well-being and performance. The reasons for such associations, however, remain uncertain. Potential mechanisms underlining the hope–performance relationship may include more efficacious goal-setting practices, increased effort, diminished anxiety, and enhanced pain tolerance. Further research is needed to elucidate potential mediators of the hope–performance relationship, the antecedents of hope, the implications of hope for individual and team performance, and the value of hope interventions in augmenting athlete well-being, coping, and athletic performance.

Key Words: hope interventions, goal-setting, athletes, hope–performance relationship, team performance, athlete well-being

"An athlete cannot run with money in his pockets. He must run with hope in his heart and dreams in his head."

—*Emil Zatopek*

The only individual to be Olympic champion at the 5,000m, 10,000m, and marathon distances at the same Olympics, Emil Zapotek, suggests hope is essential in achieving high-level athletic attainment. Indeed, many athletes acknowledge hope serves an important motivational function enabling them to persist through the myriad of challenges they face in training and competition. Recognizing the potentially pivotal role of hope in sport performance, sport psychology researchers over the past decade have turned their attention to the role of hope in enhancing sport performance, promoting athlete well-being, and diminishing deleterious states such as burnout. This chapter addresses the central role of hope in sport across four sections. First, we summarize research on hope in the sport domain. Second, given the relative dearth of empirical research, we highlight the relevance of hope theory constructs for sport performance with a specific focus on its implications for injury rehabilitation, career transitions, and performance slumps. Third, interventions and therapies designed to foster dispositional and state hope are described. Finally, we offer suggestions for further inquiry.

In advance of synthesizing the research on hope and sport performance, we provide a brief description of hope constructs. As highlighted in previous chapters, hope theorists initially described hope as a positive expectation of goal attainment (Melges & Bowlby, 1969; Stotland, 1969); Lazarus (2000) later suggested that fear or anxiety may be an inherent aspect of hope, proposing the core relational theme as "fearing the worst but yearning for better, and believing improvement is possible" (p. 234). In contrast, Snyder and colleagues (1991) make no mention of fear in their definition, suggesting that "hope is a positive motivational state based on an interactively derived sense of successful agency thinking (goal-directed energy) and goal pathways (i.e., planning to meet goals)" (p. 287). Pathway thinking relates to one's perceived capacity to create feasible ways or routes to achieve desired goals. Agency thinking is the motivational aspect of hope and corresponds to an individual's perceived power or ability to initiate and continue using routes to goal attainment. Thus, in the definition of hope proposed by Snyder and colleagues, the two goal-pursuit components, namely agency and pathway thinking, are considered equally important. According to Curry and Snyder (2000), hope represents a metaconstruct insofar as pathway and agency thinking are considered reciprocal and mutually reinforcing elements related to athletic achievement.

A vital tenet of hope theory is that high-hope individuals are imbued with feelings of agency, perceptions of self-efficacy (i.e., "I can do this"), and anticipation about the prospects of developing personal capacities (Snyder, 2002; Snyder et al., 1991). High-hope individuals are also able to envision alternative routes in the face of goal blockage, develop multiple strategies for overcoming obstacles, and display high levels of dedication and energy in pursuing desirable goals (Rodriguez-Hanley & Snyder, 2000; Snyder, Rand, King, Feldman, & Woodward, 2002). Conversely, low-hope individuals feel diminished agency and have difficulty imagining viable or alternative routes to their goals. As a consequence, such individuals typically apply less energy and drive in pursuit of their goals (Snyder et al., 1991).

Researchers have also characterized hope both as a dispositional tendency and a state-like characteristic. Perceptions about pathways and agency thoughts are suggested to be iterative as individuals pursue goals, with each reinforcing one another in the case of successful goal pursuit (Snyder, Rand, et al., 2002). Consequently, pathways and agency thoughts change with perceived success, resulting in hope as an ongoing and fluctuating state. Such state hope, however, is thought to be influenced by a dispositional tendency to conceive viable pathways and agency across situations (Snyder et al., 1991; Snyder et al., 2002).

Hope and Sport Research

Although hope research within sport is still in its infancy, a substantial body of research exists on the constituent elements of hope, namely goal pathways and agency-related constructs. For instance, literature reviews summarizing the abundant research on goal setting (Kyllo & Landers, 1995) and concepts similar to agency such as self-efficacy (Moritz, Feltz,

Fahrbach, & Mack, 2000) and achievement goals (Lochbaum & Gottardy, 2015) are available. For the purposes of this chapter, we delimit our discussion to investigations focusing explicitly on hope. The relatively limited research that has been conducted has focused on three issues: the role of hope in enhancing sport performance, the promotion of athlete well-being. and diminishing deleterious states, namely burnout.

Hope and Sport Performance

The relationship between hope and sport performance has been examined in four studies (Curry, Snyder, Cook, Ruby, & Rehm, 1997; Gould, Dieffenbach, & Moffett, 2002; Woodman et al., 2009). In a longitudinal study of nine cross-country runners, Curry et al. found that both dispositional and state hope significantly predicted performance (56%) but that other psychological measures such as self-esteem, self-confidence, and mood did not. Furthermore, in a second study by Curry and colleagues involving 106 female track-and-field National Collegiate Athletic Association Division I runners, high-hope runners achieved a significantly higher national qualifying mark than low-hope athletes, and hope predicted performance even when controlling for athletic ability as well as positive and negative performance-related affect. Echoing these findings, Gould et al. found that high levels of dispositional hope characterized the 10 Olympic champions participating in their mixed-method study (a mean score of 55.9 [standard deviation (SD) = 3.48] with a range of 51 to 61). Athletes exhibited extremely high agency (a mean score of 29.1 [SD = 2.13] with a range of 24 to 31) and pathway subscale scores (a mean score 26.8 [SD = 2.35] with a range of 23 to 31 scores). Gould et al. suggested that hope is an especially interesting construct to explore because sport psychology goal-setting research has typically focused on specific goal characteristics. As indicated previously, however, the hope model provides a meta- or holistic system for analyzing goal-setting with both dispositional and state components, the specific goals one sets, potential pathways for goal attainment, and motivational strategies for dealing with obstacles that block goal achievement (Snyder, 2002).

In an experimental study investigating the implications of state hope on cognitive performance, Woodman et al. (2009) examined the influence of hope and anger on athletes' reaction times. Imagery scripts were used to manipulate the emotional states of 18 semiprofessional British male soccer players prior to them completing a task that assessed their soccer-related reaction times. Hope was found to yield significantly faster reaction times than in an emotion-neutral condition, and performance in the anger and emotion-neutral conditions did not significantly differ. Further, hope was found to increase athletes' self-reports of perceived mental effort invested in concentrating on the task. Anger was similarly associated with a significant increase in mental effort; however it did not manifest in improved performance. One potential explanation for this finding may relate to Lazarus's (2000) proposed core relational theme of hope (i.e., yearning for better) being directed to the execution of the task; conversely, anger's core relational theme and associated action tendency (e.g., lashing out) may not have aligned with the task demands requiring fine motor control.

Extending these findings, data from the authors' unpublished work suggests that hope may also be positively associated with increased training hours and that international caliber athletes may have higher hope than their national, regional, or local counterparts. Correlation analysis indicated that hope was positively associated with increased training hours ($r = .32$, $p < .01$). Furthermore, linear regression analysis revealed that trait hope accounted for 10% variability (adjusted $r^2 = .10$, $p < .0001$) in the number of training hours per week. One-way analysis of variance also revealed a statistically significant difference in hope scores for the four competitive levels [$F(3, 290) = 3$, $p = .02$]. International caliber athletes had significantly higher hope (mean = 6.46, $SD = .86$) than their national (mean = 5.77, $SD = .99$), regional (mean = 5.45, $SD = 1.32$), or local (mean = 5.7, $SD = .92$) counterparts. These preliminary data support previous theorizing suggesting that the means by which hope may enhance performance is through its impact on factors such as effort or drive in pursuit of one's goals. That hope was positively associated with increased training time suggests that high-hope athletes' may be more inclined to put in time, energy, and effort toward their goals because they believe that doing so will result in goal attainment. Although, it is acknowledged that further research is needed to corroborate this finding. Collectively, results from studies on hope and sport performance demonstrate that high-hope individuals have enhanced performance in comparison to low-hope individuals. Tentative findings also indicate that hope may be beneficial in the promotion of training, a key ingredient in successful athletic performance (Hodges & Starkes, 1996).

Hope and Athlete Well-Being

Not only has hope been shown to enhance performance, but it has demonstrated efficacy in promoting athlete well-being (Gustafsson, Skoog, Podlog, Lundqvist, & Wagnsson, 2013; Lu & Hsu, 2013). Using a sample of 224 injured Taiwanese collegiate student-athletes, Lu and Hsu found that pathway ($r = .34$) and agency ($r = .29$) thinking were positively associated with positive affect. The researchers also found interaction effects between hope pathways and social support, such that for participants with low-hope pathways, the perception of more social support was associated with higher levels of subjective well-being. Conversely, social support only had a relatively low association with subjective well-being in participants with high-hope pathways. The latter finding suggests that social support may be of lesser importance in promoting athlete well-being among individuals high in dispositional hope. Such a contention requires further empirical scrutiny.

The positive association between hope and positive affect was also found in a second investigation with 238 competitive Swedish soccer players (Gustafsson et al., 2013). Using the Positive and Negative Affect Schedule (Watson, Clark, & Tellegen, 1988) and Perceived Stress Scale (Cohen, Karmarck, & Mermelstein, 1983) to assess athlete well-being, Gustfasson and colleagues found a negative association between dispositional hope and negative affect ($r = -.22^{**}$, $p < .01$) and a positive correlation between dispositional hope and positive affect ($r = .35^{**}$ $p < .01$). The same pattern was found when the two components of hope (pathways and agency) were studied separately. Pathway thinking was negatively associated with negative affect and stress, while a moderately positive association was found between pathways and positive affect. Agency thinking was also negatively related to stress and negative affect and positively related to positive affect. Thus the more hopeful athletes were, the less they perceived their life situations as stressful, the fewer negative emotions they reported, and the more likely they were to report positive affect.

Hope and Sport Burnout

Adding to the aforementioned research, recent work has focused on the relationship between hope and negative performance states, namely athlete burnout. In two investigations, Gustafsson and colleagues (2010; see also Gustafsson, Hassmén, & Podlog, 2013) examined relationships among hope and burnout in samples of competitive youth athletes. Consistent with hope theory contentions, it was predicted that low-hope individuals would be susceptible to burnout because they are prone to experience goal blockage, frustration, and negative affect, all of which would likely increase the risk of burnout (Rodriguez-Hanley & Snyder, 2000). In the 2010 investigation, Gustafsson et al. examined the relationship between state hope and athlete burnout among 178 competitive athletes (63 females and 115 males) ages 15 to 20 years. Hope was significantly and negatively correlated with all three burnout subscales: emotional/physical exhaustion, a reduced sense of accomplishment, and sport devaluation. Moreover, results of a multivariate analysis of variance showed that low-hope athletes scored significantly higher than medium- and high-hope athletes on all three burnout dimensions. Finally, results revealed that agency thinking was a significant negative predictor of all burnout dimensions.

In the previously mentioned investigation, Gustafsson and colleagues (2013) examined the relationship between trait hope and burnout in elite junior soccer players and whether stress and positive and negative affect mediated this relationship. Participants were 238 Swedish soccer players (166 males, 71 females; one did not indicate gender) ages 15 to 19 years who completed questionnaires measuring trait hope, perceived stress, positive and negative affect, and athlete burnout (i.e., emotional/physical exhaustion, a reduced sense of accomplishment, and sport devaluation). Bivariate correlations were consistent with hope theory contentions indicating significant negative relationships between hope and all three burnout dimensions. The relationship between hope and emotional/physical exhaustion was fully mediated by stress and positive affect. For sport devaluation and a reduced sense of accomplishment, stress and positive affect partially mediated the relationship with hope. In contrast, negative affect did not mediate the relationship between hope and any of the burnout dimensions. Together findings from these studies suggest that frustration over unmet goals and a perceived lack of agency, a characteristic of low-hope athletes, might pose a risk factor in athlete burnout, whereas being able to maintain hope appears to be associated with health and well-being. Findings also suggest that high-hope athletes may experience less stress and therefore less burnout. In short, promoting hope may be beneficial in reducing the likelihood of this detrimental syndrome.

Relevance of Hope Theory for Sport

A burgeoning corpus of research suggests that hope may be relevant for athlete performance and well-being. As research on hope in sport is still relatively new, it seems instructive to highlight the potential relevance of hope theory constructs in relation to three prominent areas of sport psychology research: injury rehabilitation, career transitions, and performance slumps.

Hope and Injury Rehabilitation

Athletes spend countless hours training in an effort to master their craft, to perfect their physical and mental skills, and to perform at the highest level in critical moments. Perhaps no other event threatens athletic performance and well-being more so than injury. Injury disrupts athletes' sense of self, creates uncertainties about the potential for future athletic attainment, and forces competitors to question their athletic capabilities and skills (Podlog, Heil, & Schulte, 2014). In short, injury represents an existential threat to athletic performance and athlete well-being. Based on hope theory research it seems reasonable to suggest that fostering hope could be advantageous in optimizing injury rehabilitation processes (Snyder, Lehman, Kluck, & Monsson, 2006), specifically by helping athletes set appropriate goals, increasing their pathway thinking, and instilling greater agency. Despite its apparent relevance to injured athletes, empirical examination of hope in a sport rehabilitation setting has been limited (Lu & Hsu, 2013; Smith & Sparkes, 2005). Smith and Sparkes examined expressions of hope and the meaning it had in the lives of 14 former male rugby union players suffering spinal cord injury. The researchers also sought to examine how different kinds of hope were framed by three narrative types—the restitution narrative, the quest narrative, and the chaos narrative—common in Western cultures. Eleven men described a sense of concrete hope in which medical and technological advances would enable them to return to their former capabilities. Such concrete hope was grounded in a restitution narrative that followed a similar storyline, namely, "Yesterday I was able-bodied, today I'm disabled, but tomorrow I'll be able-bodied again" (p. 1096). Those subscribing to the restitution narrative typically clung to the hope that a medical cure would return them to their former physical selves and in the process alleviate the profound dissatisfactions associated with their current limitations.

A second form of hope, transcendent hope, was focused not so much on achieving a fixed or specific outcome but instead embraced a quest narrative characterized by a receptivity to "uncertainty and finitude" and the celebration of "surprise, play, novelty, mystery and openness to change" (Smith & Sparkes, 2005, p. 1099). The two men espousing transcendent hope, suggested that they became a "different," "better," or "more well-rounded" person following their spinal cord injury. Their hope was not grounded in aspirations of finding a cure and becoming abled bodied again but in enjoying the mysteries and uncertainties of what the future held and in proactively shaping their own future and sense of self. As one participant commented:

> Being able to change and develop personally has
> been made possible by other disabled people,
> and nondisabled people who have taught me that
> breaking my neck isn't necessarily the end. The social
> position on disability I've heard about. It's society
> that mainly disables people, has helped me make
> some sense of disability and how to live. Certainly,
> I think the advice offered to me since becoming
> disabled has helped me resist the tragic role given
> to disabled people and the expectation that we all
> want to walk again which, for me, just isn't the case
> now. In fact, not hoping for a cure doesn't tie me
> down to one way of seeing things. As I've come to
> learn, I certainly don't think for some people it's very
> healthy to live your life solely with the hope that a
> cure will arrive. I mean, what happens if it doesn't?
> The media, and a lot of disabled people don't think
> about that. They aren't cautious or critical about it,
> when in fact a cure is probably a long way off. For
> myself, I couldn't develop knowing the hope for a
> cure was hanging over me day after day (p.1101).

Finally, one individual described an absence of hope, relaying stories of how he had descended into a life of despair, one without meaning or purpose. The following sentiment highlights a chaos narrative, which according to Frank (1995), suggests that life is never going to get better:

> I don't. I'm no one. [7 s silence] I have no future,
> no. Then, I won't walk again. It's just, just. You have
> an accident in life. I don't know, but, but it's, it's, a
> jumble. I've been given a chance of life, but it's not
> a life, not living. It's, then, then, see, the accident
> happened and I can't do anything now. That's the way
> it is. What can I do? My life, it's, it's, not here. It's over.
> I have nothing left to live. I have no hope of a life.
> I have nothing. There is no hope for me. (p. 1101)

As previously described, Lu and Hsu (2013) also examined the relevance of hope among injured athletes. They found that trait hope had

positive implications for injured athletes' well-being. Findings also revealed that both agency and pathway thinking were positively linked with athletes' rehabilitation beliefs. In particular, pathway and agency thinking were positively associated with greater perceptions of treatment efficacy, self-efficacy, and rehabilitation value. Put differently, athletes who believed there was a path toward achieving their rehabilitation goals and felt they had the personal abilities to achieve such goals were more likely to believe in the effectiveness of their treatment, had greater confidence in achieving rehabilitation goals, and saw the benefit of engaging in a rehabilitation regimen. Not surprisingly, these individuals also self-reported greater adherence to the rehabilitation protocol. Given the acknowledged importance of rehabilitation beliefs (Bone & Fry, 2006) and adherence (Granquist, Podlog, Engel, & Newland, 2014) to overall rehabilitation success, the finding that hope was related to these crucial rehabilitation elements is of clear importance. As difficulties with rehabilitation adherence have been recognized previously (Brewer, 1998), results suggest that hope may be essential in facilitating injured athlete compliance with rehabilitation programs. The goal pathway component of hope may be crucial for envisaging a route to future goal attainment (Snyder, Lehman, Kluck, & Monsson, 2006). Athletes have reported a lack of clarity, uncertainty, and direction regarding the path toward full recovery, particularly in the case of chronic injuries where the diagnosis and length of injury recovery may be uncertain (Podlog & Eklund, 2006). Articulating a clear route toward a return to full competitive activity may, when feasible, be particularly relevant for chronically injured athletes. Certainly, there is support for the benefits of goal-setting and the value of functional progressions within sport injury settings (Kenow & Podlog, 2015).

The agency component of hope may also be useful in fostering perceptions of ability to assert influence over the course of recovery and to focus on factors under one's control (Snyder et al., 2006). Injured athletes have reported feeling ill-equipped to handle rehabilitation demands, including (but not limited to) pain management, completing challenging rehabilitation exercises, maintaining fitness and skill execution, complying with rehabilitation/activity restrictions, and managing negative moods and frustrations (Podlog, 2015). It may be that athletes with a tendency to perceive greater agency in dealing with challenging rehabilitation circumstances or asserting control over injury-related uncertainties have greater rehabilitation adherence and more positive return-to-sport outcomes (e.g., less reinjury anxiety, enhanced performance, greater mental toughness). Research regarding the role of agency thinking—both state and trait—in surmounting the aforementioned rehabilitation demands and uncertainties seems prudent. Furthermore, given the motivational signature of agency thinking, the construct would appear relevant among athletes struggling with the motivational challenges associated with rehabilitation. Taking into account the tedious, repetitive nature of many rehabilitation programs, sport physiotherapists have acknowledged the importance of enhancing athlete motivation for the recovery process, particularly in instances with extended rehabilitation periods (Granquist et al., 2014). Testing the relevance of agency thinking in overcoming motivational decrements during the rehabilitation period seems worthwhile and of practical value.

Hope and Career Transitions

A second research area in which hope theory concepts may be pertinent is for athletes' career transitions—both within and out of sport. Hope may be essential for athletes making upward, downward, or lateral transitions within the sport system. For the athlete attempting an upward transition, the ability to conceive a path (pathway thinking) from current proficiency levels to a higher skill level may be a critical determinant of successful upward transition. Moreover, a requisite level of motivation or will (agency thinking) may be needed to achieve the higher level. With regard to motivation and upward sport transitions, Pummell, Harwood, and Lavallee (2008) found that motivation for the transition was a critical component of British adolescent equestrian riders' ability to transition from a club to a regional level. In particular, motivation-related behaviors for the transition including a high work ethic, maximizing opportunities for selection, and "aiming for the transition" (p. 434), as well as intrinsic motivation (love of the sport, love of the horse, voluntary sacrifices for the sport) were essential elements of the ability to make an effective upward transition. These findings are consistent with hope theory contentions in which high-hope individuals develop multiple strategies for successful goal attainment and display high levels of dedication and energy in pursuing desirable goals (Rodriguez-Hanley & Snyder, 2000; Snyder, Rand, et al., 2002).

Just as hope may be critical for those attempting upward sport transitions, it may also be of value for

those transitioning from higher to lower levels of competition. For example, the Major League baseball player who is sent to the Minor Leagues may require agency and conceivable pathways if he is to successfully return to previous performance levels. Similarly, the professional athlete making a horizontal transition from one team to the next may be sustained by the hope that she can remain a pivotal player within the structure or system of her new team. Such hope may increase the likelihood of an effective transition to the new team. The previous contentions require further scrutiny.

Perceptions of hope may also be pivotal in facilitating adjustment out of sport, particularly in the case of nonnormative or unpredictable transitions (Stambulova, Alfermann, Statler, & Coté 2009). Examples of nonnormative transitions include deselection from a team, injury, the loss of a personal coach, or unexpected success. Such transitions can be harder to cope with given their unexpected nature and the fact that the athlete has little control or autonomy over the situation (see Smith & McManus [2008] for a review). In the case of nonnormative transitions, the transition out of sport may be characterized by a reduction in the gradualness of the adaptation process, the non-accomplishment of sports-related goals, and a lack of preparation for a new life direction (McManus & Smith, 2008). Premature retirement from sport may therefore be associated with psychosocial difficulties such as a lack of positive identity and self-respect, feelings of anger, anxiety and depression, and substance abuse (Lavallee & Robinson, 2007; Warriner & Lavallee, 2008). Hope theory tenets may provide the means through which intervention efforts can be initiated. For example, helping retiring athletes articulate a clear career path as well as intermediate goals may be important from an intervention standpoint. Furthermore, athletes who are given opportunities to develop agency through various means such as career education programs, life development initiatives (Lavallee, 2005), or assistance with retirement decision-making processes (Park, Lavallee, & Tod, 2013), may experience greater feelings of personal control, a key factor influencing an individual's ability to cope with transition (Schlossberg, Waters, & Goodman, 1995). Finally, the value of hope-based interventions in mitigating negative emotions—particularly among those facing unexpected sport termination—is evident. The efficacy of hope-based interventions in facilitating smooth career transitions requires further examination.

Hope and Performance Slumps

A third topic of research in which hope theory tenets may be particularly germane is in the area of performance slumps. Taylor (1988) suggests that a slump is characterized by "an unexplained decline in performance from a previously determined baseline level of a particular athlete that extends longer than would be expected from normal cyclic variations in performance in a given sport" (p. 40). Given the unexplained nature of the performance decrement, the duration of the performance drop, and uncertainties regarding if or when performance may return to (or exceed) baseline levels, it would be easy to imagine how an athlete might lose hope during a slump. Decreases in state hope could conceivably have detrimental consequences for athletes' effort levels, concentration, self-efficacy, and subsequent performance. Empirical examination of this sequel seems valuable for those interested in better understanding cyclic variations in performance.

Interestingly, in developing a "slump-busting" program for reducing slumps, Taylor (1988) suggested the importance of goal-setting. Following identification of the physical, technical, technological, and psychological causes of a slump, Taylor highlighted the importance of identifying goals that address the causes and that alleviate the slump. In particular, he underscored the importance of a long-term "return-to-form" goal (p. 45) as well as intermediate and short-term daily goals. The value of a goal-setting plan is consistent with hope theory tenets highlighting the need for clear goal pathways—both short and long term—in attaining relevant outcomes (McDermott & Snyder, 2000). The importance of a goal-setting plan in overcoming a slump also highlights the essential nature of pathway thinking in counteracting slumps. Furthermore, it may be the case that high-hope athletes are less likely to get into slumps in the first place. That is, trait pathway and agency thinking may serve as protective factors in preventing slumps. The athlete who sees clear goal pathways and believes in his or her capacities to assert influence over performance outcomes may be more likely to maintain effort, dedication, and self-efficacy in pursuit of goals than his or her low-hope counterpart. Such effort, dedication, and efficacy may in turn help to prevent performance slumps. In summary, decreases in hope may not only account for drops in performance but may provide the key to enhancing performance in periods of poorer execution. In addition, trait hope may help mitigate the initial occurrence of slumps. Certainly, further work examining the relevance of hope constructs in relation to performance slumps would be valuable.

Interventions and Therapies for Promoting Hope

Despite the recognized benefits of hope for athletic performance (Curry et al., 1997; Gould et al., 2002; Woodman et al., 2009) and athlete well-being (Gustafsson et al., 2013; Snyder et al., 1996), few sport researchers have examined the efficacy of hope interventions. In one exception, Curry and Maniar (2003) developed an academic course with a multimodal approach including both psychological skills training as well as life skills education with student athletes (see Curry & Maniar [2004] for a detailed description of the program). Using a 15-week program, they found significant improvements in trait hope, self-esteem, and sport confidence in comparison with a control group (who did not receive any intervention). Furthermore, their coaches rated the course-taking students higher in leadership, playing with confidence, peaking under pressure, coping with adversity, and achievement to date. Similarly, Rolo and Gould (2007) investigated the effectiveness of a six-week hope-enhancing intervention among student-athletes. They found that the collegiate athletes' state hope increased in comparison with a control group (students who did not receive any intervention). No differences emerged, however, between experimental and control groups in terms of dispositional hope, academic and athletic domain hope, or perceptions of athletic and academic performance. These studies provide preliminary evidence of the potential value of hope-enhancing interventions. Importantly, although both studies used control groups, and controls did not receive any treatment in either investigation, thus raising the possibility that the observed effects might be due to the Hawthorne effect (attention given to participants from the researchers; McCarney, et al., 2007). Further studies should therefore employ the use of attention-control groups. In addition, research investigating objective measures of performance or behavior change would be beneficial.

Directions for Future Hope Research

As highlighted, initial research in the sport domain indicates positive relationships between hope and performance (Curry et al., 1997). There is, however, a need to further support these findings. Research demonstrating the value of hope in increasing academic (e.g., Snyder, Lopez, Shorey, Rand, & Feldman, 2003) and job performance (Adams et al., 2002; Peterson & Byron, 2008) give support for the role of hope in performance. Possible explanations as to why high-hope individuals may perform better than their low-hope counterparts include (but are not limited to) enhanced problem-solving skills (Chang, 1998), greater agency thoughts as reflected in their positive self-talk (Snyder, LaPointe, Crowson, & Early, 1998), and lower anxiety and stress in test situations (Onwuegbuzie, 1998; Onwuegbuzie & Snyder, 2000). Of relevance to sport scholars is research showing that high-hope individuals appear better able to handle pain (in a cold pressure task) than low-hope individuals (Snyder et al., 2005)—a capability that would certainly seem beneficial for athletes where the ability to handle fatigue and exhaustion (e.g., long-distance running) are paramount to successful athletic performance. Such relationships should be tested in sport to increase understanding of how athletes may benefit from hopeful thinking in cultivating their athletic development and performance.

Research examining individuals' ability to regulate emotions has significantly increased over the past decades (Gross, 2014); in particular emotion regulation has been identified as being central to goal achievement, performance outcomes, well-being, and harmonious relationships in sport (Davis & Davis, 2016; Jones, 2003; Moore & Gardner, 2011; Tamminen & Crocker, 2013; Wagstaff, 2014; Woodcock, Cumming, Duda, & Sharp, 2012). Core features of emotion regulation relate to the activation of a goal to modify the emotion-generative process, the trajectory of the emotion, and the potential outcomes of the emotion (Gross, 2014; Gross, Sheppes, & Urry, 2011). To date, limited research has examined the regulation of the specific emotion of hope. However, opposing emotions such as anxiety and anger have been the focus of emotion-regulation research in sport (Hill & Davis, 2014; Tamminen & Crocker, 2013) with the predominant aim of diminishing their occurrence, intensity, and duration. A number of emotion-regulation strategies have been forwarded for use in sport; by extension, these strategies may be used to regulate hope. For example, implementation intentions or "if-then" plans have been shown to be an effective self-regulation technique in sport (Achtziger, Gollwitzer, & Sheeran 2008) and been proposed for use to minimize the effects of athletes' and coaches' anxiety (Davis & Davis, 2016). The framework of the if-then plan appears to align with Lazarus's (2000) relational theme for hope (fearing the worst yet believing improvement is possible). Researchers may investigate the potential efficacy of implementation plans directed toward increasing hope. Further, if coaches and athletes effectively apply implementation intentions, the potential negative (and positive) effects of emotion contagion within a team can be minimized (or enhanced; e.g., Totterdell, 2000).

The concepts of emotion contagion and interpersonal emotion regulation have been identified within team sports (Friesen et al., 2013; Totterdell, 2000); however, neither the contagion of hope nor collective levels of hope on a team level have been explored. Collective efficacy has been linked with empathy and the consideration of situational factors that can impact team members' emotions (Shearer, Holmes, & Mellalieu, 2009). A potentially fruitful line of research may be to explore the role of hope within collective efficacy. Further, examining the role of the coach in promoting hope within a team may elucidate the influence of related mechanisms that underpin collective efficacy (e.g., interpersonal emotion regulation; Davis & Davis, 2016).

The determinants of hope in athletes are of great interest, and the social context in which they train and compete is therefore important to investigate. The role of coaches, parents, and peers are important contributors in these processes. Using research from achievement goal theory (cf. Roberts, Treasure, & Conroy, 2007) and role of the motivational climate could be an interesting venue for future research. The motivational climate can be described as the specific situational and contextual circumstances in which the athlete performs their sport (cf. Ames, 1992). Research indicates that the individual's subjective perception of the motivational climate can affect the psychological and behavioral responses in athletes (for a review, see Harwood, Keegan, Smith, & Raine, 2015). Thus studying how athletes perceive their motivational climate and how this is related to hope could be valued in future research.

Conclusion

Although research on hope within the broad field of psychology has showed the benefits of being hopeful, it appears that empirical examination of hope has been somewhat neglected in the sport context. The minimal research that does exist suggests that hope is associated with enhanced athlete well-being and performance. The reasons under-lining the benefits of hope, however, need further exploration. Potential mechanisms accounting for the hope–performance relationship may include more efficacious goal-setting practices, increased effort, diminished anxiety, and enhanced pain tol-erance. Further research is needed to elucidate potential mediators of the hope--performance rela-tionship; the antecedents of hope; the implications of hope for individual and team performance; and finally, the value of hope interventions in aug-menting athlete well-being, coping, and athletic performance.

Future Directions

• What are the potential mechanisms in the hope–performance relationship? Do hopeful athletes employ more efficient goal-setting strategies than less hopeful athletes? Is it that hopeful athletes have lower levels of performance anxiety? Do hopeful athletes simply train more than their low-hope counterparts?

• Is hope always adaptive in sport? Are there circumstances in which hope might lead to negative sport outcomes (e.g., persisting beyond reasonable limits)?

• Can hope interventions with injured athletes lead to greater adherence to rehabilitation programs and increased well-being?

• How is hope influenced by significant others in the sport environment? Do coach-, peer-, and parent-induced motivational climates impact upon hope in athletes?

• Is hope related to collective efficacy? Can a coach promote athletes' hope and collective team hope? Can emotionally intense relationships be improved by hope interventions?

References

Achtziger, A., Gollwitzer, P., & Sheeran, P. (2008). Implementation intentions and shielding goal striving from unwanted thoughts and feelings. *Personality and Social Psychology Bulletin, 34*, 381–393. doi:10.1177/0146167207311201

Ames, C. (1992). Classrooms: goals, structures, and student motivation. *Journal of Educational Psychology, 84*, 261–271.

Bone, J. B., & Fry, M. D. (2006). The influence of injured athletes' perceptions of social support from ATC's on their beliefs about rehabilitation. *Journal of Sport Rehabilitation, 15*, 156–167.

Brewer, B. W. (1998) Adherence to sport injury rehabilitation programs. *Journal of Applied Sport Psychology, 10*, 70–82. doi:10.1080/10413209808406378

Chang, E. C. (1998). Hope, problem-solving ability, and cop-ing in a college student population: Some implications for theory and practice. *Journal of Clinical Psychology, 54*, 953–962. doi:10.1002/(SICI)1097-4679(199811)

Cohen, S., Kamarck, T., & Mermelstein, R. (1983). A global measure of stress. *Journal of Health and Social Behavior, 24*, 385–396. doi:10.2307/2136404

Curry, L., & Maniar, S. (2003). Academic course combining psychological skills training and life skills education for uni-versity students and student-athletes. *Journal of Applied Sport Psychology, 15*(3), 270–277. doi:10.1080/10413200305384

Curry, L. A., & Maniar, S. D. (2004). Academic course for enhancing student-athlete performance in sport. *Sport Psychologist, 18*(3), 297–316.

Curry, L. A., & Snyder, C. R. (2000). Hope takes the field: Mind matters in athletic performance. In C. R. Snyder (Ed.), *Handbook of hope: Theory, measures and applications* (pp. 243–259). San Diego, CA: Academic Press.

Curry, L. A., Snyder, C. R., Cook, D. L., Ruby, B. C., & Rehm, M. (1997). Role of hope in academic and sport achievement. *Journal of Personality and Social Psychology, 73*(6), 1257. doi:10.1037/0022-3514.73.6.1257

Davis, P. A., & Davis, L. (2016). Emotions and emotion reg-ulation in coaching. In P. A. Davis (Ed.), *The psychology of effective coaching and management. (pp. 285–306)* New York: Nova Science.

Friesen, A. P., Lane, A. M., Devonport, T. J., Sellars, C. N., Stanley, D. N., & Beedie, C. J. (2013). Emotion in sport: Considering interpersonal regulation strategies. *International Review of Sport and Exercise Psychology, 6*(1), 139–154. doi:10.1080/1750984X.2012.742921

Gould, D., Dieffenbach, K., & Moffett, A. (2002). Psychological characteristics and their development in Olympic champi-ons. *Journal of Applied Sport Psychology, 14*(3), 172–204. doi:10.1080/10413200290103482

Granquist, M. D., Podlog, L., Engel, J. R., & Newland, A. (2014). Certified athletic trainers' perspectives on rehabili-tation adherence within collegiate athletic training settings. *Journal of Sport Rehabilitation, 23*, 123–133. doi:10.1123/JSR.2013-0009

Gross, J. J. (2014). Emotion regulation: Conceptual and empir-ical foundations. In J. J. Gross (Ed.), *Handbook of emotion regulation* (2nd ed., pp. 3–22). New York: Guilford Press.

Gross, J. J., Sheppes, G., & Urry, H. L. (2011). Emotion gen-eration and emotion regulation: A distinction we should make (carefully). *Cognition and Emotion, 25*, 765–781. doi:10.1080/02699931.2011.555753

Gustafsson, H., Hassmén, P., & Podlog, L. (2010). Exploring the relationship between hope and burnout in competitive sport. *Journal of Sports Sciences, 28*(14), 1495–1504. doi:10.1080/02640414.2010.521943

Gustafsson, H., Skoog, T., Podlog, L., Lundqvist, C., & Wagnsson, S. (2013). Hope and athlete burnout: Stress and affect as mediators. *Psychology of Sport and Exercise, 14*(5), 640–649. doi:10.1016/j.psychsport.2013.03.008

Harwood, C. G., Keegan, R. J., Smith, J. M., & Raine, A. S. (2015). A systematic review of the intrapersonal correlates of motivational climate perceptions in sport and physical activ-ity. *Psychology of Sport and Exercise, 18*, 9–25.

Hill, A., & Davis, P. A. (2014). Perfectionism and emotion regulation in coaches: A test of the 2 × 2 model of disposi-tional perfectionism. *Motivation and Emotion, 38*, 715–726. doi:10.1007/s11031-014-9404-7

Hodges, N. J., & Starkes, J. L. (1996). Wrestling with the nature expertise: A sport specific test of Ericsson, Krampe and Tesch-Römer's (1993) theory of "deliberate practice." *International Journal of Sport Psychology, 27*(4), 400–424.

Jones, M. V. (2003). Controlling emotions in sport. *The Sport Psychologist, 17,* 471–486.

Kenow, L., & Podlog, L. (2015). Psychosocial aspects of return-to-participation. In M. D. Granquist, J. Hamson-Utley, L. Kenow, & J. Stiller-Ostrowski (Eds.), *Psychosocial strategies for athletic trainers: An applied and integrated approach.* (pp. 269–296). Philadelphia, PA: F. A. Davis.

Kyllo, L. B., & Landers, D. M. (1995). Goal setting in sport and exercise: A research synthesis to resolve the controversy. *Journal of Sport & Exercise Psychology, 17,* 117–137.

Lavallee, D. (2005). The effect of a life development intervention on sports career transition adjustment. *The Sport Psychologist, 19,* 193–202.

Lavallee, D., & Robinson, H. (2007). In pursuit of an identity: A qualitative exploration of retirement from women's artistic gymnastics. *Psychology of Sport and Exercise, 8,* 119–141.

Lazarus, R. S. (2000). How emotions influence performance in competitive sports. *The Sport Psychologist, 14,* 229–252.

Lochbaum, M., & Gottardy, J. (2015). A meta-analytic review of the approach-avoidance achievement goals and performance relationships in the sport psychology literature. *Journal of Sport and Health Science, 4,* 164–173. doi:10.1016/j.jshs.2013.12.004

Lu, F. J., & Hsu, Y. (2013). Injured athletes' rehabilitation beliefs and subjective well-being: the contribution of hope and social support. *Journal of athletic training, 48*(1), 92–98.

McCarney, R., Warner, J., Iliffe, S., Van Haselen, R., Griffin, M., & Fisher, P. (2007). The Hawthorne effect: A randomised, controlled trial. *BMC Medical Research Methodology, 7*(1), 30. doi:10.1186/1471-2288-7-30

McDermot, D., & Snyder, C. R. (2000). *The great big book of hope: Help your children achieve their dreams.* Oakland, CA: New Harbinger.

Melges, F. T., & Bowlby, J. (1969). Types of hopelessness in psychopathological process. *Archives of General Psychiatry, 20,* 690–699.

Moore, Z. E., & Gardner, L. F. (2011). Understanding models of performance enhancement from the perspective of emotion regulation. *Athletic Insight: The Online Journal of Sport Psychology, 13*(3). Retrieved from http://www.athleticinsight.com/Vol13Iss3/Feature.htm

Moritz, S. E., Feltz, D. L., Fahrbach, K. R., & Mack, D. E. (2000). The relation of self-efficacy measures to sport performance: A meta-analytic review. *Research Quarterly for Exercise and Sport, 71*(3), 280–294. doi:10.1080/02701367.2000.10608908

Onwuegbuzie, A. J. (1998). Role of hope in predicting anxiety about statistics. *Psychological Reports, 82,* 1315–1320.

Onwuegbuzie, A. J., & Snyder, C. R. (2000). Relations between hope and graduate students' studying and test-taking strategies. *Psychological Reports, 86,* 803–806.

Park, S., Lavallee, D., & Tod, D. (2013). Athletes' career transition out of sport: A systematic review. *International Review of Sport and Exercise Psychology, 6*(1), 22–53.

Peterson, S. J., & Byron, K. (2008). Exploring the role of hope in job performance: Results from four studies. *Journal of Organizational Behavior, 29*(6), 785–803.

Podlog, L. (2015). Sport injury in sport psychology. In S. Schinke, K., McGannon, & B. Smith (Eds.), *The Routledge international handbook of sport psychology* (pp. 167–175). New York: Routledge.

Podlog, L., Heil, J., & Schulte, S. (2014). Psychosocial factors in sports injury rehabilitation and return to play. *Physical Medicine and Rehabilitation Clinics of North America, 25,* 915–930. doi:10.1016/j.pmr.2014.06.011

Pummell, B., Harwood, C., & Lavallee, D. (2008). Jumping to the next level: A qualitative examination of within-career transition in adolescent event riders. *Psychology of Sport & Exercise, 9,* 427–447. doi:10.1016/j.psychsport.2007.07.004

Roberts, G. C., Treasure, D. C., & Conroy, D. E. (2007).Understanding the dynamics of motivation in sport and physical activity: An achievement goal interpretation. In G. Tenenbaum & R. C. Eklund (Eds.), *Handbook of sport psychology* (3rd ed., pp. 3–30). Hoboken, NJ: Wiley.

Rodriguez-Hanley, A., & Snyder, C. R. (2000). The demise of hope: On losing positive thinking. In C. R. Snyder (Ed.), *Handbook of hope: Theory, measures and applications* (pp. 39–54). San Diego, CA: Academic Press.

Rolo, C., & Gould, D. (2007). An intervention for fostering hope, athletic and academic performance in university student-athletes. *International Coaching Psychology Review, 2*(1), 44–61.

Schlossberg, N., Waters, E. B., & Goodman, J. (1995). *Counseling adults in transition: Linking practice with theory.* New York: Springer.

Smith, J. L., & McManus, A. (2008). A review on transitional implications for retiring elite athletes: What happens when the spotlight dims. *The Open Sports Sciences Journal, 1,* 45–49.

Smith, B., & Sparkes, A. C. (2005). Men, sport, spinal cord injury, and narratives of hope. *Social Science & Medicine, 61*(5), 1095–1105. doi:10.1016/j.socscimed.2005.01.011

Snyder, C. R. (2002). Hope theory: Rainbows in the mind. *Psychological Inquiry, 13*(4), 249–275. doi:10.1207/S15327965PLI1304_01

Snyder, C. R., Berg, C., Woodward, J. T., Gum, A., Rand, K. L., Wrobleski, K. K., . . . Hackman, A. (2005). Hope against the cold: Individual differences in trait hope and acute pain tolerance on the cold pressor task. *Journal of Personality, 73*(2), 287–312. doi:10.1111/j.1467-6494.2005.00318.x

Snyder, C. R., Harris, C., Anderson, J. R., Holleran, S. A., Irving, L. M., Sigmon, S. T., . . . Harney, P. (1991). The will and the ways: Development and validation of an individual-differences measure of hope. *Journal of Personality and Social Psychology, 60*(4), 570–585. doi:10.1037/0022-3514.60.4.570

Snyder, C. R., LaPointe, A. B., Crowson, J. J. Jr., & Early, S. (1998). Preferences of high- and low hope people for self-referential input. *Cognition & Emotion, 12,* 807–823. doi:10.1080/026999398379448

Snyder, C. R., Rand, K. L., King, E. A., Feldman, D. B., & Woodward, J. T. (2002). "False" hope. *Journal of Clinical Psychology, 58*(9), 1003–1022. doi:10.1002/jclp.10096

Snyder, C. R., Shorey, H. S., Cheavens, J., Pulvers, K. M., Adams, V. H. III, & Wiklund, C. (2002). Hope and academic success in college. *Journal of Educational Psychology, 94*(4), 820–826. doi:10.1037/0022-0663.94.4.820

Snyder, C. R., Sympson, S. C., Ybasco, F. C., Borders, T. F., Babyak, M. A., & Higgins, R. L. (1996). Development and validation of the State Hope Scale. *Journal of Personality and Social Psychology, 70*(2), 321–335. doi:10.1037/0022-3514.70.2.321

Stambulova, N., Alfermann, D., Statler, T., & Côté, J. E. A. N. (2009). ISSP position stand: Career development and transitions of athletes. *International Journal of Sport and Exercise Psychology, 7*(4), 395–412.

Stotland, E. (1969). *The psychology of hope.* San Francisco, CA: Jossey-Bass.

SungHee, P., Lavallee, D., & Tod, D. (2013). A conceptual model of the athlete retirement decision-making process. *International Journal of Sport Psychology, 44*(5), 409–428.

Shearer, D. A., Holmes, P., & Mellalieu, S. D. (2009). Collective efficacy in sport: The future from a social neuroscience perspective. *International Review of Sport and Exercise Psychology, 2*(1), 38–53. doi:10.1080/17509840802695816

Tamminen, K. A., & Crocker, P. R. (2013). "I control my own emotions for the sake of the team": Emotional self-regulation and interpersonal emotion regulation among female high-performance curlers. *Psychology of Sport and Exercise, 14*(5), 737–747. doi:10.1016/j.psychsport.2013.05.002

Taylor, J. (1988). Slumpbusting: A systematic analysis of slumps in sports. *The Sport Psychologist, 2*(1), 39–48.

Totterdell, P. (2000). Catching moods and hitting runs: Mood linkage and subjective performance in professional sport teams. *Journal of Applied Psychology, 85*(6), 848–859. doi:10.1037//0021-9010.85.6.848

Wagstaff, C. (2014). Emotion regulation and sport performance. *Journal of Sport & Exercise Psychology, 36*(4), 401–412. doi:10.1123/jsep.2013-0257

Warriner, K., & Lavallee, D. (2008). The retirement experience of elite female gymnasts: Self identity and the physical self. Journal of Applied Sport Psychology, 20, 301–317.

Watson, D., Clark, L. A., & Tellegen, A. (1988). Development and validation of brief measures of positive and negative affect: The PANAS scales. *Journal of Personality and Social Psychology, 54*(6), 1063–1070. doi:10.1037/0022-3514.54.6.1063

Woodcock, C., Cumming, J., Duda, J. L., & Sharp, L (2012). Working within an individual zone of optimal functioning (IZOF) framework: Consultant practice and athlete reflections on refining emotion regulation skills. *Psychology of Sport and Exercise, 13*, 291–302. doi:10.1016/j.psychsport.2011.11.011

Woodman, T., Davis, P. A., Hardy, L., Callow, N., Glasscock, I., & Yuill-Proctor, J. (2009). Emotions and sport performance: An exploration of happiness, hope, and anger. *Journal of Sport & Exercise Psychology, 31*(2), 169–188.

Hope in the Midst of Terminal Illness

Douglas L. Hill *and* Chris Feudnter

Abstract

Although palliative and hospice care services are increasingly available, many adults and children still die without this kind of support or receive it only in the last few days of life, as many patients, family members, and clinicians equate the initiation of these services with loss of hope. This chapter presents a model of how hopeful patterns of thinking and a balance of positive and negative affect may facilitate a regoaling process in which individuals transition from cure-seeking goals to other personally meaningful goals that are attainable at the end of life or while living with a serious chronic illness. Understanding different forms of hopeful thinking, goals, and self-concepts among dying patients and their families can help clinicians provide support through this difficult experience and achieve better quality of life and symptom management for patients and better quality of life and long-term adjustment for family members.

Key Words: hope, hopeful thinking, regoaling, chronic illness, end of life, palliative care, hospice care, quality of life, self-concept, affect

Patients with a serious illness face many difficult challenges and often experience pain, discomfort, fear, and sadness. Some patients reach a point where the chances of a full recovery are unlikely, no effective treatments remain, and they must manage a chronic life-threating illness indefinitely or accept that they are likely to die in the near future. Many of these patients would benefit from a transition from aggressive cure-seeking care to palliative or hospice care that focuses on managing symptoms and maintaining quality of life. Unfortunately, even as palliative and hospice care options become more available (National Hospice and Palliative Care Organization [NHPCO], 2014), many patients continue to undergo aggressive, cure-seeking treatments at the end of life that increase the patient's suffering with very little chance of benefit (Earle et al., 2008). One reason many patients, family members, and clinicians fail to consider initiating palliative or hospice care is that they equate these forms of end-of-life care with the loss of hope.

In this chapter we argue that patients, family members, and clinicians can benefit from a clearer recognition that hopeful thinking does not always mean—exclusively—hoping for a cure. We suggest that initiating palliative or hospice care is a specific form of regoaling and that facilitating a transition from one set of highly valued, personally meaningful goals to another set of goals that are attainable at the end of life will be beneficial for many patients and their family members. At the same time, we recognize that initiating palliative or hospice care earlier will not be the right choice for everyone. The purpose of the approaches described in this chapter are not to encourage practicioners to pressure or persuade patients and family members to make a specific decision but rather to ensure they are able to understand and consider alternatives to the default approach of cure-seeking care.

We use the terms "family members" or "loved ones" broadly to refer to spouses, siblings, parents, friends, and anyone else who is close to the patient and provides support. We use the term "parents" to refer to an adult who is the primary caretaker who is responsible for healthcare decisions for a child or a patient with intellectual disability including biological parents, grandparents, stepparents, adoptive parents, foster parents, guardians, or another family member or adult who takes care of the patient. We use the term "clinicians" to refer to any healthcare professional who provides care for the patient including physicians, physician's assistants, nurse practitioners, nurses, psychologists, social workers, and therapists.

Our chapter starts by first setting the stage regarding palliative and hospice care options for adults and children then expands our notions of hope, hopes, and hopeful patterns of thinking in the context of serious illness. We then introduce the concept of regoaling, outline various barriers to regoaling, and finish the chapter by proposing how we can support the regoaling process amidst serious illness and thereby work with the full capacity of hopeful patterns of thinking.

Palliative and Hospice Care

Palliative care, pediatric palliative care, and hospice programs have increased dramatically in the past 20 years (Institute of Medicine, 2015; NHPCO, 2014). Palliative care is patient- and family-centered care that optimizes quality of life by anticipating, preventing, and treating suffering and addressing physical, intellectual, emotional, social, and spiritual needs of patients and families throughout the course of an illness (Friebert & Williams, 2015). Palliative care services are usually coordinated by an interdisciplinary team that collaborates and communicates about care needs with patients, families, and nonpalliative health care providers (NHPCO, 2014). Although palliative care focuses on maintaining quality of life and dignity of patients rather than trying to cure the underlying condition, palliative care can occur concurrently with or independently of cure-seeking or life-prolonging care. While some palliative care patients are near death, many live for years with chronic diseases that are incurable. Palliative care usually occurs in hospital settings but can take place in the home as well (Jones, 2011).

Pediatric palliative care supports children with chronic, complex, or life-threatening conditions and also supports caregivers and families, including bereavement support (Friebert & Williams, 2015). Pediatric palliative care provides care for patients (and their families) ranging from prenatal to young adult, and in some cases care continues after patients reach 21 years of age (Feudtner et al., 2013). These providers recognize that pediatric patients have different trajectories of illness than adult patients and may require different pain and symptom management interventions (Friebert & Williams, 2015). Prognosis is often difficult to predict for pediatric patients, and many patients receive palliative care for years as they cope with an incurable, life-shortening illness. In addition, some patients may be hospitalized and dependent on mechanical ventilation for extended periods (Feudtner et al., 2002). Improvements in prenatal care, surgical techniques, and care for children with complex chronic conditions have reduced the number of children who die quickly of many serious conditions but have increased the number of children who would benefit from pediatric palliative care (Feudtner et al., 2001).

Hospice care can be considered a subcategory of palliative care for patients with a life-limiting or terminal illness who are expected to die in the near future and have discontinued all cure-seeking treatment (Friebert & Williams, 2015). Hospice provides quality, compassionate, expert medical care, pain management, and emotional and spiritual support tailored to the patients and loved ones needs and wishes (NHPCO, 2014). Hospice is more likely to take place in the patient's home but can also take place in freestanding hospice centers, hospitals, nursing homes, and other long-term care facilities. Pediatric hospice programs are still rare, and the majority of hospice programs do not have formal pediatric programs (Friebert & Williams, 2015).

Benefits of Palliative and Hospice Care

Research has found that patients receiving palliative care experience higher quality of life, receive higher quality information, have better communication with clinicians, are more likely to have access to home care, receive more emotional and spiritual support, experience greater well-being and dignity, receive better care at the time of death, and experience a lower symptom burden (Casarett et al., 2008; Gomes, Calanzani, Curiale, McCrone, & Higginson, 2013; Rabow et al., 2013; Temel et al., 2010). Patients who receive home-based palliative care may experience fewer symptoms and be more likely to fulfill their desire of dying at home instead of in a hospital without increasing burden on caregivers (Gomes, et al., 2013). One study found that earlier initiation of palliative care was associated with lower reports of stress and depression among caregivers (Dionne-Odom et al., 2015). Personal accounts describe how choosing palliative care over painful, debilitating treatments can allow patients to enjoy months or years of remaining life (Berman, 2015).

Pediatric palliative care is associated with higher reported quality of life for the child and the family (Gans et al., 2012). Medical providers report that pediatric hospice programs focused on end-of-life care provide benefits beyond those of pediatric palliative care services that do not include referral to hospice, including reducing the need for hospitalization and allowing patients to die at home (Dickens, 2010).

Hospice patients with terminal illness report higher levels of satisfaction than similar patients receiving standard care (Kane, Klein, Bernstein, Rothenberg, & Wales, 1985). Family members report that hospice improves care for patients with dementia (Teno et al., 2011). Family members of nursing home residents were more satisfied with the quality of care after hospice was initiated (Baer & Hanson, 2000), and family members report higher satisfaction with home hospice care compared to care provided in hospitals and nursing homes and by home health agencies (Teno et al., 2004).

One study found that the significant others of patients receiving hospice care report lower anxiety and greater satisfaction with involvement in care (Kane, et al., 1985). Other studies have found that hospice services and being prepared for the death of the patient is associated with lower rates of psychological disorders among bereaved caregivers (Bradley et al., 2004).

Problems with End-of-Life Care

Unfortunately, many patients at the end of life do not receive they care they would prefer and may have unmet needs for pain management, dyspnea, anxiety, depression, and spirituality (Teno, Freedman, & Kasper, 2015; US Department of Health and Human Services, 2008). Patients often die in hospitals after undergoing many aggressive procedures that may increase their suffering including chemotherapy, feeding tubes, mechanical ventilation, and cardiopulmonary resuscitation. Some studies have shown that aggressive treatment for adults at the end of life has increased over time and may represent poor quality care including overuse of chemotherapy very near death; misuse of treatments resulting in high rates of emergency room visits, hospitalization, or intensive care unit stays for terminal patients; and lack of or late referral to

hospice (Earle et al., 2008). Aggressive care at the end of life is associated with lower quality of life for patients (Temel, et al., 2010; Wright et al., 2008), and adults who know they are dying often do not want to receive aggressive care (Weeks et al., 1998).

Teenagers and children with terminal conditions may be more likely than adults to receive aggressive care at the end of life, and many pediatric patients experience substantial suffering in their final weeks of life when efforts to manage their symptoms fail (Mack et al., 2015; Wolfe, Grier, et al., 2000). Some parents report regretting choosing to continue cancer-directed therapy for a child with incurable cancer if they felt the child suffered as a result of the therapy (Mack, Joffe, et al., 2008). Most children die in hospitals in spite of parent and child preferences that the child be at home (Jones, 2011; Knapp, Shenkman, Marcu, Madden, & Terza, 2009). In some cases, clinicians report experiencing moral distress when they are asked to provide aggressive care that they feel is increasing the suffering of a seriously ill child (Klein, 2009).

Parents of seriously ill children and caretakers of ill adults report lower quality of life (Hodges, Humphris, & Macfarlane, 2005; Palos et al., 2011). Research studies have found that high levels of stress over time can have negative effects on physical and mental health for caretakers of sick adults (Rohleder, Marin, Ma, & Miller, 2009; Vitaliano, Zhang, & Scanlan, 2003) and for parents of medically fragile children (Kuster & Badr, 2006; Rosenberg et al., 2014). Caregivers are at greater risk for negative health outcomes such as hypertension and hyperlipidemia, cardiovascular disorders, diabetes, and infectious diseases (Gouin, Hantsoo, & Kiecolt-Glaser, 2008; Vitaliano et al., 2003). The death of a loved one also has long-term negative psychological and physical health consequences for caregivers (Stroebe, Schut, & Stroebe, 2007). Parents who experience the death of a child (an extremely stressful life event) appear to show higher rates of early mortality compared to nonbereaved parents (Li, Precht, Mortensen, & Olsen, 2003).

Based on this evidence, the Institute of Medicine and the Department of Health and Human Services have emphasized the importance of discussing end-of-life care preferences with patients and caregivers, providing high-quality palliative and hospice care to children and adults at the end of life, and supporting family members throughout this process (Institute of Medicine, 2015; US Department of Health and Human Services, 2008). Unfortunately, many patients, family members, and clinicians are reluctant to discuss palliative or hospice care because they worry about losing one of their most important resources in their fight against serious illness: hope.

Hope, Hopes, and Hopeful Thinking in Serious Illness

Many health researchers recognize hope as being particularly important for patients coping with serious illness as well as caregivers and parents of children with chronic illness (Dufault & Martocchio, 1985; Horton & Wallander, 2001). Patients and caregivers report that hope is vital for helping them get through these difficult experiences (Herth, 1989; Reder & Serwint, 2009), and healthcare providers report that part of their job is to help patients and families maintain hope (Herth, 2000; Hinds, 1988). Some researchers describe hope as a buffer for stress and as a prerequisite to effective coping that may predict better psychosocial outcomes while recovering from a serious illness (Herth, 1989).

Researchers have argued that family members and caretakers can play an important role both in maintaining or reinforcing the hope of the patient, as well as maintaining their own hope (Duggleby et al., 2010; Miller, 1991). Another study found that hope predicted higher quality of life for both stroke survivors and their caregivers (Bluvol & Ford-Gilboe, 2004). Levels of caregiver and patient hope are important determinants of the level of burden experienced by caregivers (Utne, Miaskowski, Paul, & Rustoen, 2013). Parents of seriously ill children report that hope is an important part of coping with their child's illness (Carroll, Mollen, Aldridge, Hexem, & Feudtner, 2012; Reder & Serwint, 2009). In a study of both parental and provider hope during a high-risk pregnancy (Roscigno et al., 2012), researchers identified that parents used hope as an emotional motivator, providing "energy to cope with recommended treatments" (p. 1236).

Fundamental Error of Hope at the End of Life

Family members of critically ill patients report experiencing a tension between wanting accurate prognostic information and not wanting to lose hope (Schenker et al., 2013). Clinicians often worry that unrealistic hopes or expectations for a miracle cure might be dangerous for patients, especially if unrealistic hope sets them up for future disappointment (Reder & Serwint, 2009; Tomko, 1985). Hope can be conceptualized in multiple ways including an expectancy that a specific outcome

is possible (Gottschalk, 1974) and the opposite of feeling powerless over one's life, environment, or health (Miller, 1992) or in broader sense that positive outcomes are possible in life and that life overall has meaning (Dufault & Martocchio, 1985).

Concerns about losing hope or false hope in the context of terminal illness are based in a fundamental error of equating all hopeful thinking with one desired outcome: achieving a cure for serious illness. We argue that, in the context of end-of-life care, hopeful thinking must be seen as an engagement toward a set of goals, not just one current goal or target. Indeed, we suggest that hope can be compared to water: that is, able to be solid (particular *hopes* linked to a particular outcome), liquid (*hopeful patterns of thinking* that flow and change in response to the situation), or gaseous (*hope,* a general optimistic feeling that things will work out; Feudtner, 2014). This broader conceptualization of hopeful thinking can be a powerful force in changing one's perspective on one's goals at the end of life. A cure is clearly the most desirable outcome for a serious illness, but this solid or specific hope is not the only thing that patients and families can hope for. If patients and families can engage in hopeful patterns of thinking (a more flexible, liquid mindset), they may be able to find new targets and goals to hope for that are appropriate in their difficult situation (Gum & Snyder, 2002).

Our conceptualization of hopeful thinking in the face of terminal illness is based on C. R. Snyder's popular theory and measure of hopeful thinking that focuses on goals (Snyder et al., 1991). In Snyder's theory, hope is a set of goal-directed cognitive processes that influence and are influenced by emotion. The theory has two major parts: "agency" is an individual's sense of being generally successful in meeting goals and "pathways" is an individual's sense of being able to generate successful plans to achieve those goals (Snyder, 2000; Snyder et al., 1991). People with patterns of hopeful thinking show high levels of both agency and pathways, tend to generate more goals overall, are better at working to achieve their goals, are more likely to think of new ways of achieving a blocked goal, and are more likely to substitute another goal for a blocked goal (Snyder et al., 1991; Snyder et al., 1996). High-hope individuals experience less negative and more positive emotion when they are unable to achieve a goal. In contrast, low-hope individuals are more likely to experience negative emotions after a setback, are more likely to give up, and are less able to set new goals. Snyder and others have shown that his measure of hope captures something separate from optimism and self-efficacy (Gallagher & Lopez, 2009; Snyder et al., 1991). Studies have supported Synder's hope theory by finding that high-hope individuals have better psychosocial outcomes after burn injuries (Barnum, Snyder, Rapoff, Mani, & Thompson, 1998), report higher levels of well-being after the death of a loved one (Michael & Snyder, 2005), experience better adjustment after spinal cord injuries (Elliott, Witty, Herrick, & Hoffman, 1991), and are less likely to experience distress when taking care of children with chronic health conditions (Horton & Wallander, 2001).

Developing new hopes at the end of life involves moving beyond the death that the patient and family fear and thinking about what they can still desire and move toward. Under these circumstances, hope changes but does not disappear (Feudtner, 2009). The focus may change from the long term to simply "being" in the present (Herth, 1993). In this perspective, hopeful thinking is more important than ever at the end of life. One study of caregivers of terminally ill patients found that caregivers reported a variety of strategies to maintain hope and that the physical and emotional comfort of the patient was key to maintaining hope among caregivers (Herth, 1993).

Research studies have shown that patients and their caregivers are often able to find other ways to be hopeful even after accepting that death is inevitable including hoping for effective pain management, maintaining dignity, improving relationships with others, finding spiritual meaning, achieving inner peace, or making one last trip to the beach (Clayton, Butow, Arnold, & Tattersall, 2005; Reder & Serwint, 2009). Some dying patients refer to hopes of leaving a legacy and maintaining or deepening their relationships with family and other loved ones (Eliott & Olver, 2009). Some patients and families focus on achieving a "good death" including pain and symptom management, clear decision-making, preparation for death, completion, contributing to others, and affirmation of the whole person (Steinhauser et al., 2000). Critical care nurses report ways to provide a good death include facilitating dying with dignity, managing discomfort, knowing and following patients' wishes for end-of-life care, and promoting earlier cessation of treatment or not initiating aggressive treatment at all (Beckstrand, Callister, & Kirchhoff, 2006). Research has shown that some individuals are able to face death with peaceful acceptance (Mack, Nilsson, et al., 2008; Ray et al., 2006).

Many authors have argued that hope can be a resource for parents of children and adolescents with potentially incurable cancer (Kylma & Juvakka, 2007). Some bereaved parents report finding hope and comfort in the idea that their child's life touched others and was meaningful. Families make a particular effort to keep the memory of the child alive by participating in ritual, creating and treasuring keepsakes, and helping the child be known by others (Davies, 2004; Klass, 1993). Some parents start nonprofits in memory of their children. Learning about these kinds of meaningful activities may give parents of dying children concrete goals to hope for and work toward.

Patients and families may also be able to maintain both realistic and unrealistic hopes at the same time. Parents of dying children report continuing to hope for a miraculous recovery while being quite aware of the severity of the child's illness and making practical preparations for the undesired outcome and preparing for loss (De Graves & Aranda, 2008; Mack et al., 2007). Patients may talk about activities they would like to do in the future such as enjoying a Christmas dinner with their family while later in the same conversation acknowledging they will probably die in the near future (Clayton, et al., 2005; Eliott & Olver, 2009). Some researchers draw a distinction between expectancies as outcomes that an individual thinks are likely to happen versus hopes as ideal outcomes that people may maintain even if they recognize that the ideal outcome is unlikely to happen (Leung, Silvius, Pimlott, Dalziel, & Drummond, 2009).

Hopeful Thinking and Regoaling in Terminal Illness

Some patients and caregivers are able to maintain hope and meaningful goals after initiating palliative or hospice care, but others focus on aggressive cure-seeking treatments until the patient's death. What helps patients and families make this transition from highly valued cure-seeking goals to initiating palliative or hospice care? We have previously suggested, in the context of pediatric palliative care, that parents sometimes go through a difficult regoaling process in which they disengage from one highly valued goal (e.g., help my child get better) and generate and reengage in new goals (e.g., keep my child comfortable; Hill et al., 2014). We suggest that some amount of negative emotion such as sadness plays a critical role in disengaging from highly valued goals and reprioritizing other goals (Wrosch & Miller, 2009). Negative mood can trigger a deliberative mindset in which a person switches from working toward a goal to reevaluating whether the goal is realistically attainable (Brandstätter & Schüler, 2013). In contrast, hopeful thinking and positive mood may help individuals reengage in new meaningful goals (Figure 16.1). Some level of positive affect and hopeful thinking may help patients and family members manage the negative affect associated with giving up on a valued goal and help them start to think about new goals.

A key assumption of our model is that both negative and positive affect are necessary for regoaling. Individuals who experience only negative affect are more likely to be overwhelmed with despair and relinquish their initial cure-seeking goals without generating any new goals. Individuals who experience only positive affect are unlikely to give up on their initial goals or consider new goals (hence the negative dashed line between positive affect and critiquing initial goals in Figure 16.1). Individuals who experience a mix of positive and negative affect and who are able to engage in hopeful thinking will be more likely to disengage from initial cure-seeking goals (or at least reduce the amount of effort invested in them) and reengage in new goals that are meaningful and consistent with initiating palliative

or hospice care. Studies have found that, even in extreme situations, caregivers experience both positive and negative affect (Feudtner et al., 2010; Moskowitz, Shmueli-Blumberg, Acree, & Folkman, 2012). In addition to feelings of sadness and distress about their child's condition, parents of seriously ill children report being overwhelmed with feelings of love for their child and of gratitude for the support they have received. Patients with terminal illness report making the most of good days when they feel well and incorporating the things they enjoy into their life (Clayton et al., 2005).

Parents of seriously ill children do seem to change their hopes over time depending on the child's prognosis. One study found that parents of children with difficult-to-treat cancer changed their hopes over time depending on changes in the child's health (Granek et al., 2013). Parents of children who were doing better than expected shifted to more future-oriented hopes over time, whereas parents of children who were not doing well focused on more immediate hopes such as hoping their child would not suffer or experience complications. In our research with parents of children receiving palliative care, we have found that as the child's perceived health status worsened, parents with higher

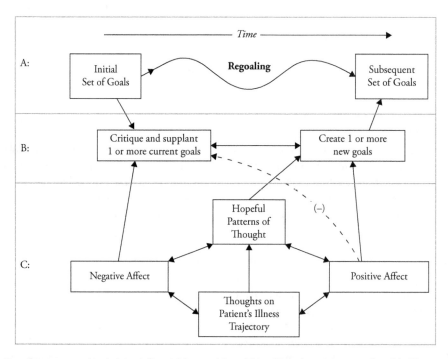

Fig. 16.1. Regoaling process and underlying influential factors. Adapted from "Regoaling: A conceptual model of how parents of children with serious illness change medical care goals," by D. L. Hill, V. Miller, J. K. Walter, K. W. Walter, W. E. Morrison, D. A. Munson, T. I. Kang, P. S. Hinds & C. Feudtner (2014). *BMC Palliative Care, 13,* 5. Copyright 2014 by authors. Adapted with permission.

levels of hope (compared to parents with lower levels of hope) were more likely to decide to limit interventions, such as by having a do-not-attempt-resuscitation order (Feudtner et al., 2010).

Barriers to Regoaling and Initiating Palliative and Hospice Care

We argue that patients, family members, and clinicians often start off working toward a set of appropriate cure-seeking goals and that initially the goal of finding a cure and getting better overrides all other goals. As the patient's health declines, the cure-seeking goals become less realistic, but for a variety of reasons everyone involved may fail to consider initiating palliative or hospice care. Next we discuss potential barriers to the transition from cure-seeking goals to initiating palliative or hospice care.

FAILURES IN COMMUNICATION AND UNDERSTANDING

Some patients and family members may never even realize that their initial cure-seeking goals need to be reevaluated. Many studies and anecdotal reports show that communication between clinicians and dying patients and their families is often poor and patients and family members may not be aware that the patient is dying (Hancock, . . . Hagerty, 2007). Talking about the possibility of death is uncomfortable and upsetting, and sometimes patients, family members, and clinicians avoid the topic or refer to it only in vague euphemistic terms (Anselm et al., 2005; Durall, Zurakowski, & Wolfe, 2012; Hancock, . . . Tattersall, 2007). Unfortunately, this means that patients and family members sometimes do not realize that their cure-seeking goals are no longer realistic and need to be reevaluated until the patient is actively dying or dead. In some cases, clinicians think they have clearly communicated this information, when in fact the patient and family are still confused about what is happening. In some cases, patients do not seem to know that they have a terminal illness or do not realize that they are receiving palliative care (Greer et al., 2014). Some bereaved parents report never discussing end-of-life treatment with clinicians or regretting cancer treatments their child received at the end of life (Hechler et al., 2008), while others report wishing that clinicians had better prepared them for the possibility of their child's death (Midson & Carter, 2010). In some cases, physicians may be aware that a child is dying months before the parents understand that the child will not recover (Wolfe, Klar, et al., 2000).

INABILITY TO DISENGAGE FROM VALUED GOAL

Patients and families may understand how poor the prognosis is but find the possibility of death so upsetting that they are simply unable to let go of their original cure-seeking goals. Models of goal regulation suggest that if individuals feel they are making adequate progress toward their goals, they experience positive affect. If they feel they are not making progress, they are more likely to experience negative affect. This negative affect serves as a cue that the goal may need to be reevaluated. Initially, the individual will work harder to achieve the goal and try alternate strategies (Carver & Scheier, 1998). If additional effort is unsuccessful, individuals may fall into despair.

Some studies have found that the ability to disengage from goals that are no longer realistic and reengage in new goals is associated with better psychological and physical health outcomes (Wrosch, Amir, & Miller, 2011; Wrosch, Miller, Scheier, & de Pontet, 2007). In these studies, the goals that individuals disengage from are highly valued (e.g., academic majors or career aspirations). These participants are usually giving up on one valued goal to work toward a goal of equal or higher value. Other studies have looked at how goals change over the lifespan. As people get older, they often have to give up on some goals that are no longer realistic. They realize their chances of being a professional athlete or an astronaut are unlikely, and they may have to give up on their initial college major, their dream career, or an unrequited love. As they get older, they may have to accept that they are unlikely to get married or have children if they have not already done so, and other goals may become increasingly unlikely with age (Schulz & Heckhausen, 1996).

Disengaging from dreams of a successful career or having a family is difficult and upsetting. Dying patients and their family members face a much more difficult crisis, a literal existential crisis in which they must confront the fact that they (or the loved one) may no longer be alive in the future. In this case, it can be much more difficult to find acceptable alternative goals to work toward because staying alive (or helping your loved one stay alive) is generally the highest level goal. Patients with terminal illness and their family members may get stuck in a cycle of recognizing they are not getting any closer to a cure, feeling overwhelmed by despair, and then redoubling their efforts to find some way to beat the illness. These individuals may focus all of their attention on cure-seeking treatments, no matter how unlikely a cure may be, because thinking about the alternative is too overwhelming. Patients and family members often report a period of despair when they come to understand that achieving a cure is no longer likely. Some deal with this despair by simply rejecting what the doctors have said, deciding they will be the one case in 100 that survives, or focusing all efforts on miracle cures.

NEGATIVE BELIEFS ABOUT PALLIATIVE AND HOSPICE CARE

Patients and family members may understand and accept how poor the prognosis is but maintain their cure-seeking goal because they (and possibly their clinicians) hold negative beliefs about palliative and hospice care, making it an unacceptable option. For example, they may believe that once palliative or hospice care is initiated, the patient will die faster. Doctors may worry that discontinuing cure-seeking treatments and using stronger opioid pain medicines will shorten the patient's life (Connor, Pyenson, Fitch, Spence, & Iwasaki, 2007). This expectation often appears to be confirmed when patients die soon after starting hospice care. Researchers note this is actually an illusory correlation in cases where healthcare providers and patients wait to initiate this kind of care until the patient is very close to death (Good, Cavenagh, & Ravenscroft, 2004; Irwin, Greer, Khatib, Temel, & Pirl, 2013).

In fact, studies have found that patients who receive palliative care often show no significant difference in survival time compared to patients receiving cure-seeking care (Irwin et al., 2013), and, in some cases, especially among patients with metastatic non-small-cell lung cancer, patients who receive palliative care may show a longer median survival rate in spite of receiving less aggressive cure-seeking treatments (Bakitas et al., 2015; Murakami et al., 2015; Palos et al., 2011; Temel et al., 2010). Similar results have been reported for hospice patients with one study finding the Medicare patients who chose hospice had longer mean and median survival time across all diseases (Pyenson, Connor, Fitch, & Kinzbrunner, 2004) and another study finding hospice patients with many conditions such as lung cancer, congestive heart failure, pancreatic cancer, and colon cancer appear to live significantly or marginally longer than nonhospice patients, with no differences in survival for other conditions such as breast and prostate cancer (Connor et al., 2007; Saito et al., 2011). Other research has shown that the stronger opioids used to manage symptoms in palliative and hospice care

are not associated with shorter survival (Good, Ravenscroft, & Cavenagh, 2005).

If patients, family members, and clinicians know that choosing to initiate palliative or hospice care does not necessarily mean a shorter life expectancy (and in some cases may even lead to a longer life expectancy), they may be more likely to choose to initiate palliative and hospice care.

LACK OF MEANINGFUL ALTERNATIVE GOALS

Even if patients and families do not have negative beliefs about palliative and hospice care, they may not have positive beliefs about them. Individuals are generally happier and healthier if they are working toward meaningful goals. Individuals without clear self-relevant goals may experience low self-esteem and depression. Goals can be further divided into approach and avoidance goals (e.g., working toward a positive outcome versus trying to avoid a negative outcome; Elliot & Church, 1997; Elliot & Thrash, 2002). Individuals who focus primarily on avoidance goals (e.g., avoiding failure) or toward goals set by others (e.g., trying to make others happy) may have higher levels of anxiety and depression. Individuals who focus on self-directed approach goals tend to have higher levels of well-being and psychological health and are more flexible when facing a challenge, while those who focus primarily on other-directed avoidance goals tend to have lower levels of psychological well-being and be more rigid when facing a crisis (Brandstätter & Schüler, 2013; Ryan & Deci, 2000).

Terminal illness poses a unique challenge because it eliminates most of the familiar highly valued approach goals concerning the long-term future. Many patients and family members see themselves stuck between an unattainable goal that they are working toward (curing the disease) and some unacceptable outcomes they are working to avoid (death, suffering, loss of dignity). Even if patients and family members see palliative care as a way to reduce suffering, they may still see this as something negative they are avoiding and prefer to focus on working toward a positive goal of a cure, even if they know this goal is unlikely.

Patients and family members may be more receptive to palliative and hospice care if they are able to focus on something positive that they are doing, since family members may experience distress if they feel like they are doing nothing and just watching as their loved one is dying. In some cases, parents who have always had clear preferences for a do not resuscitate order for their child call 911 as the child is dying because they cannot bear to do nothing as the child is dying. Reframing the situation from "doing nothing" to "holding and comforting your child to the end" may help them alleviate this distressing situation.

VIOLATION OF SELF-CONCEPT AND WORLDVIEW

Goals are often closely tied to self-concepts and one's worldview, both of which are radically challenged when facing one's own death or the death of a loved one. Individuals work harder toward goals that affirm positive, highly valued aspects of their self-concept and deliberately avoid actions that will damage their self-concept (both in their own perception and in the perception of others). Many individuals have visions of a positive possible future self that they strive toward and a negative possible future self that they wish to avoid (Markus & Nurius, 1986). Falling short of these self-concepts can result in anxiety and depression (Higgins, 1987). These self-concepts are often based in culture (Markus & Kitayama, 2003) and involve personal narratives, the story the person tells about his or her own life (McLean, Pasupathi, & Pals, 2007).

Disengaging from these high-level, self-relevant goals and personal narratives is particularly difficult because it requires changing basic beliefs about the self and how the world works, including beliefs such as "the world is a just place," "doctors can cure people when they are sick," "children don't suffer and die," or "parents who love their children can protect them and save them from anything" (Janoff-Bulman, 1992). Many studies have shown that people who face a crisis such as losing a loved one may either fall into despair or experience a form of posttraumatic growth where they emerge with a changed self-concept (Davis & Nolen-Hoeksema, 2001; Tedeschi & Calhoun, 2004).

Parents of children with serious illness report that acting as a "good parent" is very important to them (Hinds et al., 2009; October, Fisher, Feudtner, & Hinds, 2014). Being a good parent includes values such as advocating for the child, making informed medical decisions, and making sure the child feels loved (Feudtner et al., 2015). Some parents may reject the idea of palliative care because their idea of a "good parent" is someone who never gives up on his or her child. Some parents see part of their responsibility as staying positive or being a "bearer of hope" even when the situation seems negative, which can put them in conflict with clinicians who try to get them to adopt more realistic goals (Reder & Serwint, 2009). In some cases, parents and other

family members of patients may be able to reevaluate some of these core values and place a greater value on keeping the patient comfortable and making sure the patient feels loved and supported. These family members may be able focus on a new positive self-concept, as the loving and supportive family member who does everything possible to keep the patient comfortable and make the final days meaningful.

CONCERN ABOUT BEING PERCEIVED NEGATIVELY BY OTHERS

Initiating palliative or hospice care may (accurately or not) be perceived as letting down others. Patients sometimes report that if they stop fighting for a cure, they will feel as if they are letting down all of the family members, friends, and healthcare providers who have supported them through their ordeal. They may also worry about upsetting their loved ones by raising the possibility that they are probably going to die even if they continue cure-seeking treatment. Family members may also worry that bringing up the possibility of death will undermine the patient's hope and suggest that they see patient as a burden.

Regoaling in the Context of Health Threats

To summarize, patients and families will be more likely to successfully transition from cure-seeking goals to palliative goals if (a) they clearly understand the situation and their options, (b) they are not overwhelmed by sadness or despair (or have time to recover from an initial period of despair), (c) they do not equate palliative and hospice care with shortening survival time, (d) they can identify meaningful goals to work toward at the end of life other than cure-seeking ones, (e) they can integrate these goals into positive aspects of their self-concept, and (f) they are not worried that others will see considering or initiating palliative or hospice care as a betrayal.

Some researchers have suggested models for how health goals can change over time that may be relevant to initiating palliative care and hospice. Leung et al. (2009) suggest that individuals can maintain separate hopes and expectancies (e.g., might hope for a miracle cure but not really expect it to happen) and regularly reevaluate their health goals depending upon available information. Researchers in the field of lifespan and geriatrics have proposed a lines of defense model that suggests that individuals adjust their goals over time as they experience declining physical health, abilities, and independence (Heckhausen, Wrosch, & Schulz, 2013). These individuals start with an initial set of goals appropriate for being healthy and disease free, and over time they retreat from goals that are no longer realistic (walking unaided) and adopt new goals and strategies that are more realistic for a person with a subclinical disease, chronic disease, or terminal illness. For example, over time a person might go from taking walking for granted, to walking using a walker, to getting around using a wheelchair, to maintaining some quality of life while bedbound. In some cases, individuals are able to regain lost ground (e.g., learn to walk again after rehab). This model includes the final stages of terminal illness in which the individual focuses on minimizing psychological and physical suffering while promoting existential acceptance (e.g., focusing on family relationships and leaving a legacy). We suggest that individuals who are able to maintain patterns of hopeful thinking and a balance of positive and negative affect will be more likely to be able to reevaluate their goals and adjust their lines of defense when necessary.

Supporting Hopeful Thinking and Regoaling

Clinicians can use several strategies for helping patients and families cope with this stressful situation and potentially engage in regoaling. First, once clinicians know that the patient will probably not fully recover, they must give clear and accurate information about the patient's prognosis, make sure that that the patient and family understand the information (ideally by having them state their understanding in their own words), and be ready to repeat the information multiple times as needed. Clinicians should be explicit about the limitations of medical care and which treatments are no longer likely to be beneficial for the patient (Clark & Dudzinski, 2011). Clinicians should give the patient and family time to understand and accept the news while acknowledging and supporting their emotional reactions ("I can see how hard this is"). Clinicians should also be honest if the patient's prognosis is uncertain and not get stuck in an endless cycle of additional tests waiting for a clear answer that may never emerge (Smith, White, & Arnold, 2013). Ideally clinicians will discuss end-of-life care preferences with the family and address common fears and misconceptions about palliative care and hospice before a health crisis places the patient and family under time pressure to make a difficult decision. Palliative care and hospice can be framed positively as something that is offered to patients to keep them comfortable rather than as the absence of care (Fadul et al., 2009).

Clinicians can try to create small positive experience by praising patients and their family members and recognizing how much they are doing ("I can see how much you and your wife care about each other"; Back, Arnold, Baile, Edwards, & Tulsky, 2010). Clinicians can then explore the breadth of hopes that patients and families hold and gently guide them toward new goals (Feudtner, 2007, 2009). When the patient and family seem ready, providers can carefully prompt them to think about new hopes and goals by asking what they are hoping for given the current situation. Some patients and families may immediately identify other goals, such as going home, reducing the number of painful interventions, having a family reunion, having an early birthday party, or taking one last trip together. Others may need time to think of new goals. Providers may be able to provide suggestions ("What some loving families have done in this situation is . . .") or co-create goals ("If that doesn't work out, then what would you hope for?"). Once patients and families start to talk about additional hopes or goals, providers can focus on the most realistic possibilities and offer suggestions of how those goals can be achieved. They can help the patients and families achieve hopeful thinking by supporting both pathways ("Here are ways you can achieve this goal, and here is how we can help") and agency ("I know this is hard, but you will be able to do this").

If patients or families seem to be stuck and unable to decide whether to initiate palliative care, it may help to ask them to think about their goals in terms of four different questions: (a) What are the potential benefits of continuing cure-seeking treatment? (b) What are the potential harms of continuing cure-seeking treatment? (c) What are the benefits of initiating palliative care? (d) What are the potential harms of initiating palliative care? Discussing these questions may help patients and family members express their hopes and fears more clearly and may allow the clinician to address concerns that are based on inaccurate beliefs.

Pediatric palliative care providers can help parents identify what it means to them personally to be a good parent to their child in this difficult situation and how they can meet their good parent goals as the child gets closer to death (Hinds et al., 2009; October et al., 2014). Adult palliative care providers may be able to help other family members explore ways they can show their love for the patient (e.g., be a good spouse, sibling, or son/daughter).

Clinicians often must find a balance between being honest with patients and their families about the seriousness of the situation while not necessarily directly challenging unrealistic hopes. In some cases patients and family members may simply need time to adjust to the upsetting new reality. In other cases, unrealistic hopes may serve as a pleasant daydream or coping strategy that helps them feel a little better for a brief period even if they know the daydream is unlikely to happen in real life.

If possible, clinicians must also give patients and families time to accept this upsetting situation and to generate new meaningful goals. Some patients may already be familiar with palliative and hospice care and not need much time to change their worldview and goals. Others are forced to question their most basic beliefs and rebuild their worldview and their place in the world from scratch. Patients and family members may become angry if they feel that clinicians are aggressively pushing them to give up too quickly. At the other end, clinicians should recognize that patients and family members do sometimes go through radical changes in goals. A parent who initially vehemently rejects palliative care for her child may gradually become more receptive as she sees that the medical staff are not just trying to get rid of her child.

Patients and family members may also seem to go back and forth in their decision for reasons that are not immediately clear to clinicians. In one case, a pediatric intensive care team was caught off guard when the mother of a baby who was close to death suddenly seemed to change her mind and wanted to "do everything" (Lee & Dupree, 2008). After further discussion, it became clear that the mother did not want to be by herself when her baby died and just wanted enough time for the grandmother arrive at the bedside.

Clinicians may also be able to incorporate elements of interventions to increase hope and improve quality of life among seriously ill patients and caregivers including group sessions, videos, journaling, creating a hope collection, writing letters, making a joy collage, making lists of supportive individuals, identifying values and beliefs that are important and strength giving, and identifying small joys worthy of celebration (Duggleby et al., 2013; Herth, 2001; Rustoen, Cooper, & Miaskowski, 2011). Finally, clinicians can recognize that even if attempts at cure-seeking treatment have stopped, they can still help the family by being present and supportive rather than handing them off to palliative care and disappearing.

The goal of end-of-life care discussions should not be to persuade the patient and family to choose palliative care or hospice. The goal should be to make sure patients and families fully understand the situation and what palliative care or hospice can offer and are able to clearly articulate what they are hoping for. Palliative care may not be the right choice for all patients. Some patients may have serious medical conditions that are incurable but stable and still allow for a good quality of life. Some parents are frustrated and offended when medical staff raise the issue of whether a child's code status should be changed to do not resuscitate when the child has what the parents believe to be a good quality of life and is not suffering (Pearson, 2015). In other cases patients may understand their situation and the low likelihood of benefit from aggressive treatment but still strongly prefer to "fight until the end" (Harrington & Smith, 2008). Some patients and family members may reject palliative care and hospice for religious reasons or beliefs that doctors should do everything possible to keep patients alive (Pew Research Center, 2013).

Conclusion

Palliative and hospice care services have increased dramatically in the past 20 years, but many patients still die without this kind of support. Understanding different forms of hopeful thinking, goals, and self-concepts among dying patients and their families can help clinicians support them through this difficult experience and achieve better quality of life and symptom management for patients, a slightly longer life for some patients, and better quality of life and long-term adjustment for family members.

Future Directions

• What interventions help patients with serious illness build or maintain patterns of hopeful thinking to generate new goals that are personally meaningful and attainable? How should these interventions be delivered, by whom, and when in the course of the illness? What would be the impact of such interventions on the experience of being seriously ill and on patient-valued outcomes regarding quality of life and the nature of how dying is managed and death occurs?

• What interventions can similarly help family members and friends of patients with serious illness to also work with patterns of hopeful thinking to generate or accept new goals of care as being best for the seriously ill patient? What would be the long-term physical and mental health benefits for families members of early initiation of this hope and regoaling work?

• What interventions can augment or support clinicians' own personal processes of hopeful thinking and regoaling when caring for patients with serious illness and their families? Would such interventions lower the chances that clinicians experience burnout or heighten their satisfaction of caring for seriously ill patients? Would they also heighten the satisfaction of seriously ill patients and family members?

• What interventions can help interdisciplinary teams of clinicians recognize when patterns of hopeful thinking and regoaling need to be mindfully brought into the care of the seriously ill patient and when hospice and palliative care are appropriate options and communicate about these options effectively with other team members, patients, and family members? Would these team-based interventions also prevent clinician burnout and heighten satisfaction on several fronts?

References

Anselm, A. H., Palda, V., Guest, C. B., McLean, R. F., Vachon, M. L. S., Kelner, M., & Lam-McCulloch, J. (2005). Barriers to communication regarding end-of-life care: Perspectives of care providers. *Journal of Critical Care, 20*(3), 214–223. doi:http://dx.doi.org/10.1016/j.jcrc.2005.05.012

Back, A. L., Arnold, R. M., Baile, W. F., Edwards, K. A., & Tulsky, J. A. (2010). The art of medicine: When praise is worth considering in a difficult conversation. *The Lancet, 376*(9744), 866–867. doi:http://dx.doi.org/10.1016/S0140-6736(10)61401-8

Baer, W. M., & Hanson, L. C. (2000). Families' perception of the added value of hospice in the nursing home. *Journal of the American Geriatrics Society, 48*(8), 879–882.

Bakitas, M. A., Tosteson, T. D., Li, Z., Lyons, K. D., Hull, J. G., Dionne-Odom, J. N., . . . Ahles, T. A. (2015). Early versus delayed initiation of concurrent palliative oncology care: Patient outcomes in the ENABLE III randomized controlled trial. *Journal of Clinical Oncology 33*(13), 1438–1445. doi:10.1200/jco.2014.58.6362

Barnum, D. D., Snyder, C. R., Rapoff, M. A., Mani, M. M., & Thompson, R. (1998). Hope and social support in the psychological adjustment of children who have survived burn injuries and their matched controls. *Children's Health Care, 27*(1), 15–30. doi:10.1207/s15326888chc2701_2

Beckstrand, R. L., Callister, L. C., & Kirchhoff, K. T. (2006). Providing a "good death": Critical care nurses' suggestions for improving end-of-life care. *American Journal of Critical Care, 15*(1), 38–45.

Berman, A. (2015, September 28). A nurse with fatal breast cancer says end-of-life discussion saved her life. *The Washington Post.* Retrieved from https://http://www.washingtonpost.com/national/health-science/a-nurse-with-fatal-breast-cancer-says-end-of-life-discussions-have-saved-her/2015/09/28/1470b674-5ca8-11e5-b38e-06883aacba64_story.html

Bluvol, A., & Ford-Gilboe, M. (2004). Hope, health work and quality of life in families of stroke survivors. *Journal of Advanced Nursing, 48*(4), 322–332. doi:10.1111/j.1365-2648.2004.03004.x

Bradley, E. H., Prigerson, H., Carlson, M. D., Cherlin, E., Johnson-Hurzeler, R., & Kasl, S. V. (2004). Depression among surviving caregivers: Does length of hospice enrollment matter? *American Journal of Psychiatry, 161*(12), 2257–2262.

Brandstätter, V., & Schüler, J. (2013). Action crisis and cost-benefit thinking: A cognitive analysis of a goal-disengagement phase. *Journal of Experimental Social Psychology, 49*(3), 543–553.

Carroll, K. W., Mollen, C. J., Aldridge, S., Hexem, K. R., & Feudtner, C. (2012). Influences on decision making identified by parents of children receiving pediatric palliative care. *AJOB Primary Research, 3*(1), 1–7.

Carver, C. S., & Scheier, M. F. (1998). *On the self-regulation of behavior.* New York: Cambridge University Press.

Casarett, D., Pickard, A., Bailey, F. A., Ritchie, C., Furman, C., Rosenfeld, K., . . . Shea, J. A. (2008). Do palliative consultations improve patient outcomes? *Journal of the American Geriatrics Society, 56*(4), 593–599.

Clark, J. D., & Dudzinski, D. M. (2011). The false dichotomy: Do "everything" or give up. *The American Journal of Bioethics, 11*(11), 26–27.

Clayton, J. M., Butow, P. N., Arnold, R. M., & Tattersall, M. H. (2005). Fostering coping and nurturing hope when discussing the future with terminally ill cancer patients and their caregivers. *Cancer, 103*(9), 1965–1975. doi:10.1002/cncr.21011

Connor, S. R., Pyenson, B., Fitch, K., Spence, C., & Iwasaki, K. (2007). Comparing hospice and nonhospice patient survival among patients who die within a three-year window. *Journal of Pain and Symptom Management, 33*(3), 238–246. doi:10.1016/j.jpainsymman.2006.10.010

Davies, R. (2004). New understandings of parental grief: Literature review. [Review]. *Journal of Advanced Nursing, 46*(5), 506–513. doi:10.1111/j.1365-2648.2004.03024.x

Davis, C. G., & Nolen-Hoeksema, S. (2001). Loss and meaning: How do people make sense of loss? *American Behavioral Scientist, 44*(5), 726–741. doi:http://dx.doi.org/10.1177/00027640121956467

De Graves, S., & Aranda, S. (2008). Living with hope and fear—the uncertainty of childhood cancer after relapse. *Cancer Nursing, 31*(4), 292–301. doi:10.1097/01.NCC.0000305745.41582.73

Dickens, D. S. (2010). Comparing pediatric deaths with and without hospice support. *Pediatric Blood & Cancer, 54*(5), 746–750.

Dionne-Odom, J. N., Azuero, A., Lyons, K. D., Hull, J. G., Tosteson, T., Li, Z., . . . Akyar, I. (2015). Benefits of early versus delayed palliative care to informal family caregivers of patients with advanced cancer: Outcomes from the ENABLE III randomized controlled trial. *Journal of Clinical Oncology, 33*(13), 1446–1452.

Dufault, K., & Martocchio, B. C. (1985). Symposium on compassionate care and the dying experience. Hope: Its spheres and dimensions. *The Nursing Clinics of North America, 20*(2), 379–391.

Duggleby, W., Holtslander, L., Kylma, J., Duncan, V., Hammond, C., & Williams, A. (2010). Metasynthesis of the hope experience of family caregivers of persons with chronic illness. *Qualitative Health Research, 30*(2), 148–158.

Duggleby, W., Williams, A., Holstlander, L., Cooper, D., Ghosh, S., Hallstrom, L. K., . . . Hampton, M. (2013). Evaluation of the living with hope program for rural women caregivers of persons with advanced cancer. *BMC Palliative Care, 12*(1), 36. doi:10.1186/1472-684X-12-36

Durall, A., Zurakowski, D., & Wolfe, J. (2012). Barriers to conducting advance care discussions for children with life-threatening conditions. *Pediatrics, 129*(4), e975–e982. doi:10.1542/peds.2011-2695

Earle, C. C., Landrum, M. B., Souza, J. M., Neville, B. A., Weeks, J. C., & Ayanian, J. Z. (2008). Aggressiveness of cancer care near the end of life: Is it a quality-of-care issue? *Journal of Clinical Oncology, 26*(23), 3860–3866.

Elliot, A. J., & Church, M. A. (1997). A hierarchical model of approach and avoidance achievement motivation. *Journal of Personality and Social Psychology, 72*(1), 218–232. doi:http://dx.doi.org/10.1037/0022-3514.72.1.218

Elliot, A. J., & Thrash, T. M. (2002). Approach-avoidance motivation in personality: Approach and avoidance temperaments and goals. *Journal of Personality and Social Psychology, 82*(5), 804–818. doi:http://dx.doi.org/10.1037/0022-3514.82.5.804

Elliott, T. R., Witty, T. E., Herrick, S. M., & Hoffman, J. T. (1991). Negotiating reality after physical loss: Hope, depression, and disability. *Journal of Personality and Social Psychology, 61*(4), 608–613. doi:10.1037/0033-2909.103.2.193

Eliott, J. A., & Olver, I. N. (2009). Hope, life, and death: A qualitative analysis of dying cancer patients' talk about hope. *Death Studies, 33*(7), 609–638. doi:10.1080/07481180903011982

Fadul, N., Elsayem, A., Palmer, J. L., Del Fabbro, E., Swint, K., Li, Z., . . . Bruera, E. (2009). Supportive versus palliative care: What's in a name? *Cancer, 115*(9), 2013–2021.

Feudtner, C. (2007). Collaborative communication in pediatric palliative care: A foundation for problem-solving and decision-making. *Pediatric Clinics of North America, 54*(5), 583–607. doi:10.1016/j.pcl.2007.07.008

Feudtner, C. (2009). The breadth of hopes. *The New England Journal of Medicine, 361*(24), 2306–2307. doi:10.1056/NEJMp0906516

Feudtner, C. (2014). Hope is like water. *Perspectives in Biology and Medicine, 57*(4), 555–557.

Feudtner, C., Carroll, K. W., Hexem, K. R., Silberman, J., Kang, T. I., & Kazak, A. E. (2010). Parental hopeful patterns of thinking, emotions, and pediatric palliative care decision making: A prospective cohort study. *Archives of Pediatrics & Adolescent Medicine, 164*(9), 831–839. doi:10.1001/archpediatrics.2010.146

Feudtner, C., Christakis, D. A., Zimmerman, F. J., Muldoon, J. H., Neff, J. M., & Koepsell, T. D. (2002). Characteristics of deaths occurring in children's hospitals: Implications for supportive care services. *Pediatrics, 109*(5), 887–893.

Feudtner, C., Friebert, S., Jewell, J., Carter, B., Hood, M., Imaizumi, S., & Komatz, K. (2013). Pediatric palliative care and hospice care commitments, guidelines, and recommendations. *Pediatrics, 132*(5), 966–972.

Feudtner, C., Hays, R. M., Haynes, G., Geyer, J. R., Neff, J. M., & Koepsell, T. D. (2001). Deaths attributed to pediatric complex chronic conditions: National trends and implications for supportive care services. *Pediatrics, 107*(6), E99.

Feudtner, C., Walter, J. K., Faerber, J. A., Hill, D. L., Carroll, K. W., Mollen, C. J., . . . Hinds, P. S. (2015). Good-parent

beliefs of parents of seriously ill children. [Research Support, NIH, Extramural]. *JAMA Pediatrics, 169*(1), 39–47. doi:10.1001/jamapediatrics.2014.2341

Friebert, S. E., & Williams, C. (2015). *NHPCO facts and figures: Pediatric palliative and hospice care in America.* Alexandria, VA: National Hospice and Palliative Care Organization.

Gallagher, M. W., & Lopez, S. J. (2009). Positive expectancies and mental health: Identifying the unique contributions of hope and optimism. *The Journal of Positive Psychology, 4*(6), 548–556. doi:http://dx.doi.org/10.1080/17439760903157166

Gans, D., Kominski, G. F., Roby, D. H., Diamant, A. L., Chen, X., Lin, W., & Hohe, N. (2012). *Better outcomes, lower costs: Palliative care program reduces stress, costs of care for children with life-threatening conditions.* Los Angeles, CA : UCLA Center for Health Policy Research.

Gomes, B., Calanzani, N., Curiale, V., McCrone, P., & Higginson, I. J. (2013). Effectiveness and cost-effectiveness of home palliative care services for adults with advanced illness and their caregivers. *Cochrane Database of Systematic Reviews, 6*, CD007760. doi:10.1002/14651858.CD007760.pub2

Good, P. D., Cavenagh, J., & Ravenscroft, P. J. (2004). Survival after enrollment in an Australian palliative care program. *Journal of Pain and Symptom Management, 27*(4), 310–315. doi:10.1016/j.jpainsymman.2003.12.011

Good, P. D., Ravenscroft, P. J., & Cavenagh, J. (2005). Effects of opioids and sedatives on survival in an Australian inpatient palliative care population. *Internal Medicine Journal, 35*(9), 512–517. doi:10.1111/j.1445-5994.2005.00888.x

Gottschalk, L. A. (1974). A hope scale applicable to verbal samples. *Archives of General Psychiatry, 30*(6), 779–785. doi:http://dx.doi.org/10.1001/archpsyc.1974.01760120041007

Gouin, J. P., Hantsoo, L., & Kiecolt-Glaser, J. K. (2008). Immune dysregulation and chronic stress among older adults: A review. *Neuroimmunomodulation, 15*(4–6), 251–259. doi:10.1159/000156468

Granek, L., Barrera, M., Shaheed, J., Nicholas, D., Beaune, L., D'Agostino, N., . . . Antle, B. (2013). Trajectory of parental hope when a child has difficult-to-treat cancer: A prospective qualitative study. *Psycho-Oncology, 22*(11), 2436–2444. doi:10.1002/pon.3305

Greer, J. A., Pirl, W. F., Jackson, V. A., Muzikansky, A., Lennes, I. T., Gallagher, E. R., . . . Temel, J. S. (2014). Perceptions of health status and survival in patients with metastatic lung cancer. *Journal of Pain and Symptom Management, 48*(4), 548–557. doi:10.1016/j.jpainsymman.2013.10.016

Gum, A., & Snyder, C. (2002). Coping with terminal illness: The role of hopeful thinking. *Journal of Palliative Medicine, 5*(6), 883–894.

Hancock, K., Clayton, J. M., Parker, S. M., Walder, S., Butow, P. N., Carrick, S., . . . Hagerty, R. (2007). Discrepant perceptions about end-of-life communication: A systematic review. *Journal of Pain and Symptom Management, 34*(2), 190–200.

Hancock, K., Clayton, J. M., Parker, S. M., Walder, S., Butow, P. N., Carrick, S., . . . Tattersall, M. H. (2007). Truth-telling in discussing prognosis in advanced life-limiting illnesses: A systematic review. *Palliative Medicine, 21*(6), 507–517.

Harrington, S. E., & Smith, T. J. (2008). The role of chemotherapy at the end of life: "When is enough, enough?" *JAMA, 299*(22), 2667–2678.

Hechler, T., Blankenburg, M., Friedrichsdorf, S. J., Garske, D., Hubner, B., Menke, A., . . . Zernikow, B. (2008). Parents' perspective on symptoms, quality of life, characteristics of death and end-of-life decisions for children dying from cancer. *Klinische Padiatrie, 220*(3), 166–174. doi:10.1055/s-2008-1065347

Heckhausen, J., Wrosch, C., & Schulz, R. (2013). A lines-of-defense model for managing health threats: A review. *Gerontology, 59*(5), 438–447.

Herth, K. (1989). The relationship between level of hope and level of coping response and other variables in patients with cancer. *Oncology Nursing Forum, 16*(1), 67–72.

Herth, K. (1993). Hope in the family caregiver of terminally ill people. *Journal of Advanced Nursing, 18*, 538–548.

Herth, K. (2000). Enhancing hope in people with a first recurrence of cancer. *Journal of Advanced Nursing, 32*(6), 1431–1441.

Herth, K. (2001). Development and implementation of a hope intervention program. *Oncology Nursing Forum, 28*(6), 1009–1017.

Higgins, E. T. (1987). Self-discrepancy: A theory relating self and affect. *Psychological Review, 94*(3), 319–340. doi:http://dx.doi.org/10.1037/0033-295X.94.3.319

Hill, D. L., Miller, V., Walter, J. K., Carroll, K. W., Morrison, W. E., Munson, D. A., . . . Feudtner, C. (2014). Regoaling: A conceptual model of how parents of children with serious illness change medical care goals. *BMC Palliative Care, 13*(1), 9. doi:10.1186/1472-684X-13-9

Hinds, P. S. (1988). The relationship of nurses' caring behaviors with hopefulness and health care outcomes in adolescents. *Archives of Psychiatric Nursing, 2*(1), 21–29.

Hinds, P. S., Oakes, L. L., Hicks, J., Powell, B., Srivastava, D. K., Spunt, S. L., . . . Furman, W. L. (2009). "Trying to be a good parent" as defined by interviews with parents who made phase 1, terminal care, and resuscitation decisions for their children. *Journal of Clinical Oncology, 27*(35), 5979–5985. doi:10.1200/JCO.2008.20.0204

Hodges, L., Humphris, G., & Macfarlane, G. (2005). A meta-analytic investigation of the relationship between the psychological distress of cancer patients and their carers. *Social Science & Medicine, 60*(1), 1–12.

Horton, T. V., & Wallander, J. L. (2001). Hope and social support as resilience factors against psychological distress of mothers who care for children with chronic physical conditions. *Rehabilitation Psychology, 46*(4), 382–399. doi:10.1037/0090-5550.46.4.382

Institute of Medicine. (2015). *Dying in america: Improving quality and honoring individual preferences near the end of life.* Washington, DC: National Academies Press.

Irwin, K. E., Greer, J. A., Khatib, J., Temel, J. S., & Pirl, W. F. (2013). Early palliative care and metastatic non-small cell lung cancer: Potential mechanisms of prolonged survival. *Chronic Respiratory Disease, 10*(1), 35–47. doi:10.1177/1479972312471549

Janoff-Bulman, R. (1992). *Shattered assumptions: Towards a new psychology of trauma.* New York: Free Press.

Jones, B. W. (2011). The need for increased access to pediatric hospice and palliative care. *Dimensions of Critical Care Nursing, 30*(5), 231–235.

Kane, R. L., Klein, S. J., Bernstein, L., Rothenberg, R., & Wales, J. (1985). Hospice role in alleviating the emotional stress of terminal patients and their families. *Medical Care, 23*(3), 189–197.

Klass, D. (1993). Solace and immortality: Bereaved parents' continuing bond with their children. *Death Studies, 17*(4), 343–368. doi:http://dx.doi.org/10.1080/07481189308252630

Klein, S. M. (2009). Moral distress in pediatric palliative care: A case study. *Journal of Pain and Symptom Management, 38*(1), 157–160.

Knapp, C. A., Shenkman, E. A., Marcu, M. I., Madden, V. L., & Terza, J. V. (2009). Pediatric palliative care: Describing hospice users and identifying factors that affect hospice expenditures. *Journal of Palliative Medicine, 12*(3), 223–229.

Kuster, P. A., & Badr, L. K. (2006). Mental health of mothers caring for ventilator-assisted children at home. *Issues in Mental Health Nursing, 27*(8), 817–835.

Kylma, J., & Juvakka, T. (2007). Hope in parents of adolescents with cancer—Factors endangering and engendering parental hope. *European Journal of Oncology Nursing, 11*(3), 262–271. doi:10.1016/j.ejon.2006.06.007

Lee, K. J., & Dupree, C. Y. (2008). Staff experiences with end-of-life care in the pediatric intensive care unit. *Journal of Palliative Medicine, 11*(7), 986–990.

Leung, K. K., Silvius, J. L., Pimlott, N., Dalziel, W., & Drummond, N. (2009). Why health expectations and hopes are different: The development of a conceptual model. *Health Expectations, 12*(4), 347–360.

Li, J., Precht, D. H., Mortensen, P. B., & Olsen, J. R. (2003). Mortality in parents after death of a child in Denmark: A nationwide follow-up study. *The Lancet, 361*(9355), 363–367.

Mack, J. W., Chen, L. H., Cannavale, K., Sattayapiwat, O., Cooper, R. M., & Chao, C. T. (2015). End-of-life care intensity among adolescent and young adult patients with cancer in Kaiser Permanente Southern California. *JAMA Oncology, 1*(5), 592–600. doi:10.1001/jamaoncol.2015.1953

Mack, J. W., Joffe, S., Hilden, J. M., Watterson, J., Moore, C., Weeks, J. C., & Wolfe, J. (2008). Parents' views of cancer-directed therapy for children with no realistic chance for cure. *Journal of Clinical Oncology, 26*(29), 4759–4764. doi:JCO.2007.15.6059

Mack, J. W., Nilsson, M., Balboni, T., Friedlander, R. J., Block, S. D., Trice, E., & Prigerson, H. G. (2008). Peace, equanimity, and acceptance in the cancer experience (PEACE). *Cancer, 112*(11), 2509–2517.

Mack, J. W., Wolfe, J., Cook, E. F., Grier, H. E., Cleary, P. D., & Weeks, J. C. (2007). Hope and prognostic disclosure. *Journal of Clinical Oncology, 25*(35), 5636–5642. doi:10.1200/JCO.2007.12.6110

Markus, H., & Kitayama, S. (2003). Culture, self, and the reality of the social. *Psychological Inquiry, 14*(3–4), 277–283.

Markus, H., & Nurius, P. (1986). Possible selves. *American Psychologist, 41*(9), 954.

McLean, K. C., Pasupathi, M., & Pals, J. L. (2007). Selves creating stories creating selves: A process model of self-development. *Personality and Social Psychology Review, 11*(3), 262–278.

Michael, S. T., & Snyder, C. R. (2005). Getting unstuck: The roles of hope, finding meaning, and rumination in the adjustment to bereavement among college students. *Death Studies, 29*(5), 435–458. doi:10.1080/07481180590932544

Midson, R., & Carter, B. (2010). Addressing end of life care issues in a tertiary treatment centre: Lessons learned from surveying parents' experiences. *Journal of Child Health Care, 14*(1), 52–66. doi:10.1177/1367493509347060

Miller, J. F. (1991). Developing and maintaining hope in families of the critically ill. *AACN Clinical Issues in Critical Care Nursing, 2*(2), 307–315.

Miller, J. F. (1992). *Coping with chronic illness: Overcoming powerlessness* (2nd ed.). Philadelphia: F. A. Davis.

Moskowitz, J. T., Shmueli-Blumberg, D., Acree, M., & Folkman, S. (2012). Positive affect in the midst of distress: Implications for role functioning. *Journal of Community & Applied Social Psychology, 22*(6), 502–518.

Murakami, N., Tanabe, K., Morita, T., Kadoya, S., Shimada, M., Ishiguro, K., . . . Kashii, T. (2015). Going back to home to die: Does it make a difference to patient survival? *BMC Palliative Care, 14*, 7. doi:10.1186/s12904-015-0003-5

National Hospice and Palliative Care Organization. (2014). NHPCO facts and figures: Hospice care in America. Alexandria, VA: Author.

October, T. W., Fisher, K. R., Feudtner, C., & Hinds, P. S. (2014). The parent perspective: "Being a good parent" when making critical decisions in the PICU. *Pediatric Critical Care Medicine, 15*(4), 291–298. doi:10.1097/PCC.0000000000000076

Palos, G. R., Mendoza, T. R., Liao, K.-P., Anderson, K. O., Garcia-Gonzalez, A., Hahn, K., . . . Lynch, G. R. (2011). Caregiver symptom burden: The risk of caring for an underserved patient with advanced cancer. *Cancer, 117*(5), 1070–1079.

Pearson, A. (2015). Never say never about our child. *BMJ, 350*, h1246.

Pew Research Center. (2013). Views on end-of-life medical treatments. Washington, DC: Author.

Pyenson, B., Connor, S., Fitch, K., & Kinzbrunner, B. (2004). Medicare cost in matched hospice and non-hospice cohorts. *Journal of Pain and Symptom Management, 28*(3), 200–210. doi:10.1016/j.jpainsymman.2004.05.003

Rabow, M., Kvale, E., Barbour, L., Cassel, J. B., Cohen, S., Jackson, V., . . . Stevens, D. (2013). Moving upstream: A review of the evidence of the impact of outpatient palliative care. *Journal of Palliative Medicine, 16*(12), 1540–1549.

Ray, A., Block, S. D., Friedlander, R. J., Zhang, B., Maciejewski, P. K., & Prigerson, H. G. (2006). Peaceful awareness in patients with advanced cancer. *Journal of Palliative Medicine, 9*(6), 1359–1368.

Reder, E. A., & Serwint, J. R. (2009). Until the last breath: Exploring the concept of hope for parents and health care professionals during a child's serious illness. *Archives Pediatrics & Adolescent Medicine, 163*(7), 653–657. doi:10.1001/archpediatrics.2009.87

Rohleder, N., Marin, T. J., Ma, R., & Miller, G. E. (2009). Biologic cost of caring for a cancer patient: Dysregulation of pro-and anti-inflammatory signaling pathways. *Journal of Clinical Oncology, 27*(18), 2909–2915.

Roscigno, C. I., Savage, T. A., Kavanaugh, K., Moro, T. T., Kilpatrick, S. J., Strassner, H. T., . . . Kimura, R. E. (2012). Divergent views of hope influencing communications between parents and hospital providers. *Qualitative Health Research, 22*(9), 1232–1246. doi:10.1177/1049732312449210

Rosenberg, A. R., Wolfe, J., Bradford, M. C., Shaffer, M. L., Yi-Frazier, J. P., Curtis, J. R., . . . Baker, K. S. (2014). Resilience and psychosocial outcomes in parents of children with cancer. *Pediatric Blood & Cancer, 61*(3), 552–557.

Rustoen, T., Cooper, B. A., & Miaskowski, C. (2011). A longitudinal study of the effects of a hope intervention on levels of hope and psychological distress in a community-based sample of oncology patients. *European Journal of Oncology Nursing, 15*(4), 351–357. doi:10.1016/j.ejon.2010.09.001

Ryan, R. M., & Deci, E. L. (2000). Self-determination theory and the facilitation of intrinsic motivation, social development, and well-being. *American Psychologist, 55*(1), 68–78.

Saito, A. M., Landrum, M. B., Neville, B. A., Ayanian, J. Z., Weeks, J. C., & Earle, C. C. (2011). Hospice care and survival among elderly patients with lung cancer. *Journal of Palliative Medicine, 14*(8), 929–939.

Schenker, Y., White, D. B., Crowley-Matoka, M., Dohan, D., Tiver, G. A., & Arnold, R. M. (2013). "It hurts to know . . . and it helps": Exploring how surrogates in the ICU cope with prognostic information. *Journal of Palliative Medicine, 16*(3), 243–249.

Schulz, R., & Heckhausen, J. (1996). A life span model of successful aging. *American Psychologist, 51*(7), 702.

Smith, A. K., White, D. B., & Arnold, R. M. (2013). Uncertainty: The other side of prognosis. *The New England Journal of Medicine, 368*(26), 2448–2450.

Snyder, C. R. (Ed.). (2000). *Handbook of hope: Theory, measures, and applications.* San Diego, CA: Academic Press.

Snyder, C. R., Harris, C., Anderson, J. R., Holleran, S. A., Irving, L. M., Sigmon, S. T., . . . Harney, P. (1991). The will and the ways: Development and validation of an individual-differences measure of hope. *Journal of Personality and Social Psychology, 60*(4), 570–585.

Snyder, C. R., Sympson, S. C., Ybasco, F. C., Borders, T. F., Babyak, M. A., & Higgins, R. L. (1996). Development and validation of the State Hope Scale. *Journal of Personality and Social Psychology, 70*(2), 321–335.

Steinhauser, K. E., Clipp, E. C., McNeilly, M., Christakis, N. A., McIntyre, L. M., & Tulsky, J. A. (2000). In search of a good death: Observations of patients, families, and providers. *Annals of Internal Medicine, 132*(10), 825–832.

Stroebe, M., Schut, H., & Stroebe, W. (2007). Health outcomes of bereavement. *The Lancet, 370*(9603), 1960–1973.

Tedeschi, R. G., & Calhoun, L. G. (2004). Target article: Posttraumatic growth: Conceptual foundations and empirical evidence. *Psychological Inquiry, 15*(1), 1–18. doi:http://dx.doi.org/10.1207/s15327965pli1501_01

Temel, J. S., Greer, J. A., Muzikansky, A., Gallagher, E. R., Admane, S., Jackson, V. A., . . . Lynch, T. J. (2010). Early palliative care for patients with metastatic non-small-cell lung cancer. *The New England Journal of Medicine, 363*(8), 733–742. doi:10.1056/NEJMoa1000678

Teno, J. M., Clarridge, B. R., Casey, V., Welch, L. C., Wetle, T., Shield, R., & Mor, V. (2004). Family perspectives on end-of-life care at the last place of care. *JAMA, 291*(1), 88–93.

Teno, J. M., Freedman, V. A., & Kasper, J. D. (2015). Is care for the dying improving in the United States? *Journal of Palliative Medicine, 18*(8), 662–666.

Teno, J. M., Gozalo, P. L., Lee, I. C., Kuo, S., Spence, C., Connor, S. R., & Casarett, D. J. (2011). Does hospice improve quality of care for persons dying from dementia? *Journal of the American Geriatrics Society, 59*(8), 1531–1536.

Tomko, B. (1985). The burden of hope. *Hospice Journal, 1*(3), 91–97. doi:http://dx.doi.org/10.1300/J011v01n03_06

US Department of Health and Human Services. (2008). *Advance directives and advance care planning: Report to Congress.* Washington, DC: Author.

Utne, I., Miaskowski, C., Paul, S. M., & Rustoen, T. (2013). Association between hope and burden reported by family caregivers of patients with advanced cancer. *Supportive Care in Cancer, 21*(9), 2527–2535. doi:10.1007/s00520-013-1824-5

Vitaliano, P. P., Zhang, J., & Scanlan, J. M. (2003). Is caregiving hazardous to one's physical health? A meta-analysis. *Psychological Bulletin, 129*(6), 946–972.

Weeks, J. C., Cook, E. F., O'Day, S. J., Peterson, L. M., Wenger, N., Reding, D., . . . Connors, A. F. Jr. (1998). Relationship between cancer patients' predictions of prognosis and their treatment preferences. *JAMA, 279*(21), 1709–1714.

Wolfe, J., Grier, H. E., Klar, N., Levin, S. B., Ellenbogen, J. M., Salem-Schatz, S., . . . Weeks, J. C. (2000). Symptoms and suffering at the end of life in children with cancer. *The New England Journal of Medicine, 342*(5), 326–333. doi:10.1056/NEJM200002033420506

Wolfe, J., Klar, N., Grier, H. E., Duncan, J., Salem-Schatz, S., Emanuel, E. J., & Weeks, J. C. (2000). Understanding of prognosis among parents of children who died of cancer: Impact on treatment goals and integration of palliative care. *JAMA, 284*(19), 2469–2475. doi:joc00623

Wright, A. A., Zhang, B., Ray, A., Mack, J. W., Trice, E., Balboni, T., . . . Maciejewski, P. K. (2008). Associations between end-of-life discussions, patient mental health, medical care near death, and caregiver bereavement adjustment. *JAMA, 300*(14), 1665–1673.

Wrosch, C., Amir, E., & Miller, G. E. (2011). Goal adjustment capacities, coping, and subjective well-being: The sample case of caregiving for a family member with mental illness. *Journal of Personality and Social Psychology, 100*(5), 934–946. doi:10.1037/a0022873

Wrosch, C., & Miller, G. E. (2009). Depressive symptoms can be useful: Self-regulatory and emotional benefits of dysphoric mood in adolescence. *Journal of Personality and Social Psychology, 96*(6), 1181–1190. doi:10.1037/a0015172

Wrosch, C., Miller, G. E., Scheier, M. F., & de Pontet, S. B. (2007). Giving up on unattainable goals: Benefits for health? *Personality and Social Psychology Bulletin, 33*(2), 251–265. doi:10.1037/0003-066x.54.3.165

PART V

Hope and Mental Health

Hope and Depression

Lorie A. Ritschel *and* Christopher S. Sheppard

Abstract

This chapter examines the relationship between hopeful thinking and major depressive disorder. Hope is a positive psychology construct that comprises goals, agency thinking, and pathways thinking and has been associated with psychological and physical well-being and psychosocial outcomes. Depression is inversely correlated with hope and is characterized by a host of symptoms and psychological correlates, including feelings of sadness, negative self-talk, amotivation, and difficulties in problem-solving and concentrating. This chapter explores the empirical evidence regarding the relationship between hope and depression, including the relationship between the subcomponents of hope (i.e., pathways and agency thinking) and the biological (e.g., neural reward systems) and cognitive (e.g., executive functioning) correlates of depression. In addition, the evidence for hope as a viable route for remediating depressive symptoms is reviewed, and future directions are proposed.

Key Words: hope, depression, goals, pathways thinking, agency thinking, positive psychology

Major depressive disorder (MDD) is a highly prevalent mental disorder and a serious public health problem that is strongly correlated with substantial psychosocial impairment. Prevalence data show that approximately 18.8 million adults in the United States (i.e., 9.5% of the entire adult population) suffer from depression in a given year (Beck & Alford, 2009). Globally, the World Health Organization estimates that 350 million people are affected by depression, and depression is now the leading cause of disability worldwide (World Health Organization, 2015). A substantial number of depressed individuals do not receive treatment; current estimates suggest that between a third and half of depressed individuals in developed nations are untreated, and upwards of 76% of depressed individuals in less developed countries receive treatment (Lépine & Briley, 2011).

Depression is characterized by negative mood (e.g., sadness), anhedonia, negative self-concept, self-punitive wishes, feelings of guilt or worthlessness, hopelessness, changes in sleep or eating patterns, and changes in activity level (Beck & Alford, 2009). In addition, depression is a major risk factor for both attempted and completed suicide (Qin & Nordentoft, 2005). Depression is associated with a host of impairments in learning, memory, and cognition; for example, individuals with MDD tend to show generally negative biases in their thinking style (Alloy & Abramson, 1999; Alloy et al., 1999, 2000, 2006; Blackburn, Jones, & Lewin, 1986), greater deficits in learning and episodic memory (McDermott & Ebmeier, 2009), greater negative bias in memory (Joormann, Teachman, & Gotlib, 2009; Williams et al., 2007), a greater tendency toward a ruminative thinking style (Nolen-Hoeksema & Morrow, 1991; Thomsen, 2006), and greater difficulty shifting their attention between tasks (Murphy et al., 1999). Together, these symptoms are relevant to the relationship between hope and depression, which we explore in this chapter.

A number of theories have been proposed to characterize the experience of depression (for a review, see Ritschel, Gillespie, Arnarson, & Craighead, 2013), most of which can be categorized as behavioral, cognitive, or biological. In general, these theories have not only articulated a hypothesis about the etiology of depression but also have formulated the bases for developing targeted treatments for depression. For example, behavioral theorists propose that depression results from the cycle created from an insufficient reinforcement system and increasing levels of behavioral withdrawal. By extension, behavioral therapies target avoidant behaviors and are designed to help depressed individuals more readily come into contact with environmental rewards. Similarly, biological theorists propose that depression results from deficiencies or alterations in functioning of various aspects of the central nervous system (e.g., the serotinergic system), and biological interventions for depression are designed to remediate these deficiencies.

For the purposes of the present discussion, cognitive conceptualizations of depression are most relevant, as hope is generally thought of as a cognitive construct (but see Cheavens & Ritschel [2014] for a discussion of whether hope is better characterized as a cognition or an emotion). Broadly speaking, cognitive theorists propose that distorted cognitions (e.g., "I'll never pass this test"; "She's canceling dinner plans because she doesn't like me") and unhealthy schemas or basic beliefs about the self (e.g., "I'm unloveable"; "I'm powerless") are the cornerstone of the depressive experience (Beck, Rush, Shaw, & Emery, 1979). By extension, cognitive therapy was designed to help patients identify and modify these distorted thoughts and beliefs about themselves as the primary route to improving depression (Beck, 1995). Several cognitive constructs are relevant to the relationship between depression and hope. In the next section, we explore the links between helplessness, hopelessness, and depression, as these constructs set the stage for a framework for thinking about the relationship between specific aspects of depression and how they relate to hope theory.

The Helplessness and Hopelessness Theories of Depression

As a robust literature has shown, depression is intricately related to the constructs of helplessness and hopelessness. In the 1970s, Seligman (1975) proposed the *learned helplessness theory of depression* (see also Peterson & Seligman, 1993), in which they hypothesized that individuals become depressed because they see their personal situations as futile and they see themselves as incapable of bringing about desired change. Seligman proposed that individuals who are prone to depression are those whose attributional styles (i.e., the way a person explains a situation to him- or herself) are global, stable, and internal; that is, depressed people tend to view themselves negatively across situations (global), believe that their situation and inability to overcome situations will not change (stable), and believe that they are the cause of their aversive situation (internal). Numerous studies support this theory across a range of populations. In a meta-analysis of 104 studies involving nearly 15,000 adult participants, Sweeney, Anderson, and Bailey (1986) found that this attributional style was reliably and significantly linked to depression. The same results have been found in youth samples; Gladstone and Kaslow (1995) conducted a meta-analysis of 28 studies involving 7,500 children and adolescents and found a significant relationship between depression and internal, stable, and global attributions about negative outcomes.

In the 1980s, Abramson and colleagues (1989) reformulated the learned helplessness theory of depression and renamed it the *hopelessness theory of depression*. According to this theory, individuals with a negative cognitive style are more vulnerable to the development of depressive symptoms when faced with negative life events. More specifically, hopelessness depression is a subtype of depression wherein hopelessness is "an expectation that highly desired outcomes will not occur or that highly aversive outcomes will occur coupled with an expectation that no response in one's repertoire will change the likelihood of occurrence" (Abramson et al., 1989, p. 359). Abramson and colleagues proposed that hopelessness is a proximal and sufficient cause (rather than a symptom) of depression. In addition, they placed a greater emphasis on the importance of the outcome to the individual (i.e., negative outcomes in events that are not important to the individual are not likely to lead to depression) and to the inferences people draw about the causes and consequences of negative events. A number of studies have provided support for the hopelessness theory of depression in both adult and youth samples (see Hankin, Abramson, & Siler, 2001; Liu & Alloy, 2010).

Although these theories have their differences, they share several key elements that are relevant to the relationship between hope and depression. First, the empirical data borne out of studies of helplessness and hopelessness support the notion that depression is associated with negative outcomes of life events, particularly when the outcome is important to the person. Second, merely the perception or expectation of a negative outcome is sufficient for a negative mood induction. In other words, the way a person talks to him- or herself about real or imagined outcomes is critical—perhaps even more so than the actual situations or outcomes themselves. Third, depressed people have a difficult time generating ways to change the negative outcome that they wish to avoid, instead perceiving that the outcome is a foregone conclusion. As we discuss in the next section, each of these three elements map directly onto the hope construct.

Hope Theory

Hope theory is a cognitive construct comprising three distinct yet interrelated components: goals, pathways thinking, and agency thinking (see Geraghty, Wood, & Hyland [2010] for an analysis of the distinction between the components of hope). According to Snyder's model (Snyder et al., 1991), goals are the mental end points of all purpose-driven behavior. Goals may be approach- or avoidance-oriented; that is, one can have a goal to move toward a particular outcome that is not currently in place (e.g., a promotion at work), or one can have a goal to move away from an aversive outcome or status (e.g., to quit smoking). Goals can differ in their degree of difficulty, ranging from the easily attainable (e.g., going outside once a day) to the nigh impossible (e.g., winning an Olympic medal). Six distinct goal domains have been articulated: social relationships (e.g., friendships), romantic relationships, family life, academics, work, and leisure activities. In comparison to low hopers, high hopers tend to have a greater number of goals across a number of these domains, set approach rather than avoidance goals, and set goals that are just slightly out of reach, rather than being too easy or completely unattainable (Averill, Catlin, & Chon, 1990; Snyder et al., 1991).

Pathways thinking is the ability to develop routes or strategies to achieve goals. Although only one pathway is technically required for goal attainment, people often encounter obstacles as they pursue their goals and must generate a new pathway. As a first step in this process, people must first accurately perceive that they have encountered a goal blockage. Next, they must be able to correctly evaluate whether a new route is needed; if so, they must be able to generate a new route, disengage from the previous route, and continue their goal pursuit. Early studies of hope theory demonstrated that high hopers tend to be able to generate multiple routes to getting what they want. In addition, they tend to be better than low hopers at mobilizing a secondary route if the primary route is blocked (Irving, Snyder, & Crowson, 1998; Snyder et al., 1991).

Agency thinking comprises the motivational aspect of the hope construct; it is the self-talk that individuals engage in as they work toward their goals. Agency thinking, which overlaps with Bandura's (1982) concept of self-efficacy, reflects a person's belief about his or her ability to be successful and to reach goals. Higher hope individuals tend to engage in positive, self-referential agency thinking (e.g., "I can do it") and to be able to remain positive in their self-talk when they encounter a goal blockage (Irving et al., 1998). Moreover, they gravitate to positive statements and examples of self-talk more generally. In a series of studies conducted by Snyder, LaPointe, Crowson, and Early (1998), participants were given the choice of listening to prerecorded messages that were either positively or negatively valenced in general (Study 1) or that contained messages of successful versus unsuccessful goal pursuit (Study 2). As compared to low hopers, high hopers preferred the audiotapes containing positive and successful messages.

Hope can be conceptualized as both a state and a trait variable. Snyder (2002) posited that people's goal-related learning history is particularly relevant to their trait hope and approach to goal pursuits; that is, a person with a history of successful goal pursuits is more likely to have higher dispositional hope, generally positive affect, and an approach to goals that is marked by curiosity, openness, and enthusiasm. Conversely, a person with a history of unsuccessful goal pursuits is more likely to have lower levels of dispositional hope, poorer affect, and an approach to goals that is marked by doubtfulness, disinterest, or hopelessness. At a trait level, individuals who are considered "high hopers" are those who set numerous goals across multiple life domains and who demonstrate high levels of both agency and pathways thinking. Trait level hope is associated with general life satisfaction and overall well-being. By comparison, state hope describes positive affect as it occurs in a more concentrated time span; however, Mascaro and Rosen (2005) found that state hope and meaning in life (i.e., a trait variable) were positively correlated as well.

A robust literature has demonstrated that hope and emotion are closely related (for a review, see Cheavens & Ritschel, 2014). Three points bear mentioning for the current discussion. First, goal attainment is associated with increases in positive affect, whereas goal blockage or failure is associated with increases in negative affect (Jones, Papadakis, Orr, & Strauman, 2013). In fact, Snyder and colleagues (1991) proposed that merely the *perception* of goal stagnation or failure is sufficient to prompt negative affect. Moreover, higher hope has been shown to relate not only to better short-term positive affect (i.e., a state variable) but also to better subjective and psychological well-being more generally (i.e., a trait variable). That is, over the long term, repeated goal successes or failures appear to be related to more consistent positive or negative moods, respectively. Second, hope appears to be a protective factor in the face of life stressors (e.g., environmental or health-related stressors). For example, in a sample of survivors of Hurricane Katrina, higher hope was protective against post-traumatic stress disorder, and hope moderated the relationship between avoidant coping and psychological distress (Glass, Flory, Hankin, Kloos, & Turecki, 2009). Third, hope has been shown to be inversely correlated with a number of measures of psychopathology (Snyder et al., 1991), including major depression.

Depressive Symptomatology: Relevance to Hope Theory

Depression is characterized by a host of symptoms and psychological correlates, including pervasive feelings of sadness, anergia, negative self-talk, amotivation, and difficulties in problem-solving and concentrating. Conceptually, all nine of the *Diagnostic and Statistical Manual of Mental Disorders* (fifth edition; American Psychiatric Association, 2013) criteria for MDD can be conceptualized through the lens of hope theory (see Cheavens, 2000; Snyder, 1994). In fact, the depression literature shows that many individuals can point to some sort of triggering event (real or perceived) that preceded the onset of their depression. Viewed through the lens of hope theory, these triggering events can be conceptualized as goal blockages. For example, losing an important relationship is a common trigger for depression. Such a loss could be considered a blockage for a person who has a goal of having a happy, successful marriage. Alternatively, being passed over for a promotion at work could be considered a blockage for a person who has a goal of climbing the corporate ladder. In theory, the blockage of a particularly important goal or numerous blockages that occur across a range of goals could produce more pervasive feelings of sadness,

worthlessness, or even suicidality. Because the three components of hopeful thinking are interrelated (Snyder et al., 1996), the emotion that results from a goal blockage is likely to impact a person's agency and pathways thinking negatively as well. As feelings of sadness become more pervasive in the context of major depression, people generally experience reductions in their motivation and energy to pursue goals. Both of these symptoms are theoretically linked to agency thinking. Specifically, when individuals are depressed and lose interest in activities they typically enjoy, or when they experience reductions in the psychological or physical energy needed to sustain movement toward goals, it makes sense that their motivation to engage in goal pursuit decreases accordingly.

The research literature on depression and its behavioral and biological correlates supports the theoretical relationship between the components of hopeful thinking and depressive symptomatology. With regard to the relationship between goal pursuit and emotion, numerous studies have shown that depression is associated with a disruption of reward systems in the brain (Forbes, 2009; Naranjo, Tremblay, & Busto, 2001; Russo & Nestler, 2013). Studies using functional magnetic resonance imaging have found an association between depression and hypoactivation of the promotion system, which results in reduced enjoyment in trying to complete approach goals and a reduction in reward sensitivity even when goals are achieved (Klenk, Strauman, & Higgins, 2011).

With regard to agency thinking, reductions in interest (i.e., anhedonia), energy, and motivation are cardinal symptoms of major depression, and plentiful evidence has demonstrated that depression is associated with these symptoms (Watson, Clark, & Carey, 1988; Clark & Watson, 1991). In comparison to their nondepressed peers, depressed individuals show evidence of reductions on measures of the behavioral activation system, which is an approach-based positive reinforcement system; conversely, depressed individuals show increases in measures of the behavioral inhibition system, which is associated with avoidance behaviors and threat sensitivity (Kasch, Rottenberg, Arnow, & Gotlib, 2002; Pinto-Meza et al., 2006; Vergara & Roberts, 2011). Depressed individuals also have strong tendencies to engage in negative self-talk (Blackburn, Jones, & Lewin, 1986; Olinger, Kuiper, & Shaw, 1987; Weissman & Beck, 1978); in fact, cognitive behavioral therapy (CBT), which is the most well-studied treatment for major depression, is based on the premise that changing this negative self-talk is effective in treating depression (Beck, Rush, Shaw, & Emery, 1979).

Depression is also characterized by numerous cognitive deficits, including impaired executive functioning and slower processing speed (Snyder, 2013). These symptoms can be theoretically linked to pathways thinking, which requires an individual to follow a stepwise plan to achieve a goal. Executive functioning is defined as "higher-level cognitive processes, which control and regulate lower-level processes (e.g., perception, motor responses) to effortfully guide behavior towards a goal, especially in non-routine situations" (Snyder, 2013, p. 81). In a recent meta-analysis, Snyder reported that patients with major depression show significant impairments across a range of neuropsychological tests of executive functioning and that these results hold even after controlling for the processing speed deficits that also are a hallmark of depression. Of particular relevance to the current discussion, results showed that depressed patients have greater difficulties than healthy controls with shifting (i.e., the ability to flexibly move back and forth between tasks), inhibition (i.e., the ability to override an immediate response, which is critical to one's ability to think before acting), updating (i.e., the ongoing monitoring, adding, and subtracting of items in one's working memory), and planning (which includes the ability to formulate goals, identify a sequence of steps for goal achievement, and monitor progress toward goals). Clearly, deficits in these skill domains are related to pathways thinking and one's ability to devise alternate routes in the face of goal blockage.

Empirical Studies of the Relationship Between Hope and Depression

Numerous studies have demonstrated an inverse relationship between hope and depression (for a review, see Alacron, Bowling, & Khazon, 2013). To date, this relationship has been examined in college students (e.g., Chang & DeSimone, 2001; Feldman & Snyder, 2005; Geiger & Kwon, 2010; Mathew, Dunning, Coats, & Whelan, 2014), individuals who have suffered a traumatic injury (Elliot, Witty, Herick, & Hoffman, 1991; Peleg, Barak, Harel, Rochberg, & Hoofien, 2009; Strom & Kosciulek, 2007), individuals with chronic illness (Lynch, Kroenck, & Denney, 2001), middle school students (Ashby, Dickson, Gnilka, & Noble, 2011), parents of children with intellectual disabilities and chronic illnesses (Lloyd & Hastings, 2009; Venning, Eliott, Whitford, & Honnor, 2007), spouses of individuals

with obsessive-compulsive disorder (Geffken et al., 2003), and general community samples (Chang, Yu, & Hirsch, 2013).

Research to date indicates that the strength of the relationship between hope and depression varies as a function of both time and symptom intensity. Thimm and colleagues (2013) found that currently depressed individuals have lower levels of hope than both previously depressed individuals whose symptoms are in remission and individuals who have never experienced depression. Furthermore, previously depressed individuals in remission had lower levels of hope than never depressed individuals. In a multiwave longitudinal study conducted with college students, Arnau and colleagues (2007) found that higher levels of hope (and, specifically, the agency component of hope) predicted lower depression scores at one-month follow-up. In addition, they found that depression was unrelated to later levels of hope, suggesting that hope may be a trait variable that is unaffected by the occurrence of major depressive episodes. Given that this study was conducted with a sample of college students (rather than a sample of clinically depressed individuals), further research on this question is needed.

Some studies have found important distinctions between depressed and nondepressed individuals regarding goal pursuit. Dickson, Moberly, and Kinderman (2011) compared depressed individuals to a sample of people who had never experienced depression and found that depressed individuals generate just as many goals as their peers but tend to be more pessimistic about the possibility that they will achieve their goals. In addition, the depressed group felt that they had significantly less control over the outcome of their goal pursuit compared to controls. Depressed individuals also tend to create less specific goals and generate less specific reasons for why a goal was or was not accomplished (Dickson & Moberly, 2013), and they report lower intrinsic motivation for approach goals (Winch, Moberly, & Dickson, 2015). Depressed individuals also are more likely than nondepressed individuals to seek out situations and pursue goals that will lead to increased experiences of sadness (Millgram, Joormann, Huppert, & Tamir, 2015). Finally, conflicting evidence has emerged on the topic of whether the number and type of goals set is impacted by depression; some studies have found that depressed individuals do not differ from nondepressed individuals in terms of the number of approach and avoidance goals they set (Dickson & Moberly, 2013; Dickson, Moberly, & Kinderman,

2011); however, other studies have found that depressed individuals generate more avoidance goals than nondepressed individuals (Vergara & Roberts, 2011). Given the correlation between low hope and depression, it should be noted that these findings are counterintuitive vis à vis early studies by Snyder and colleagues (1991), in which they reported that low hopers generate fewer goals than high hopers (note, however, that the low hopers in those studies did not meet full criteria for major depression).

Several studies have examined hope as a moderator or mediator between risk factors for or correlates of depression and depressive symptomology. For example, Hirsch, Sirois, and Lyness (2011) found that hope moderates the relationship between functional impairment (i.e., difficulty performing daily activities due to physical illness) and depression in older adults, even after controlling for illness burden and cognitive status. In another study, Hirsch, Visser, Chang, and Jeglic (2012) found that hope moderates the relationship between depression and suicidal ideation in Caucasian and Latino college students; results showed that hope did not moderate this relationship in African American students.

A robust literature has demonstrated that both rumination and perfectionism are significant risk factors for depression, both in terms of depression severity (Donaldson & Lam, 2004) and likelihood of relapse or recurrence (Michalak, Hölz, & Teismann, 2011). Rumination is the tendency to think perseveratively about one's problems or symptoms in a passive way that does not involve active problem-solving and is a well-known risk factor for the development, maintenance, and recurrence of major depression (for a review, see Nolen-Hoeksema, Wisco, & Lyubomirsky, 2008). Rumination is tightly related to other depressive constructs, such as negative cognitive style, neuroticism, pessimism, perfectionism, and hopelessness, although studies have shown that rumination is an independent construct that is strongly correlated with depression even after controlling for all of these variables. The tendency to ruminate has been shown to exacerbate depressed mood and is predictive of elevated levels of depressive symptoms (Just & Alloy, 1997; Morrow & Nolen-Hoeksema, 1990; Papageorgiou & Wells, 2003).

Recent studies have shown that hope moderates the relationship between rumination and depression. In a sample of college students, Geiger and Kwon (2010) found that individuals with high hope experienced lower levels of depression in the presence of high rumination compared to individuals with low hope. Hope was not found to impact the relationship between rumination and depression at low levels of rumination. Building on these findings, Tucker and colleagues (2013) found that both hope and optimism moderate the relationship between rumination and suicidal ideation, even after controlling for depressive symptomology. In a sample of Chinese college students, Sun and colleagues (2014) found that rumination was not a significant factor in depressive severity for students in the high-hope group; conversely, students in the low-hope group with high levels of rumination endorsed more significant levels of depression. In fact, Sun and colleagues propose that rumination may differ fundamentally in high-hope individuals than in low-hope individuals in that high hopers may be able to leverage perseverative thought to mobilize their own problem-solving abilities.

Perfectionism is another construct that is strongly related to major depression. Trait perfectionism creates a greater vulnerability for depression and can worsen symptoms of depression (Enns & Cox, 1999; Hewitt & Flett, 1990; Hewitt, Flett, & Ediger, 1996). Studies examining the impact of hope on the relationship between perfectionism and depression found that high levels of maladaptive perfectionism increase depression except in the presence of high levels of hope in both middle school students (Ashby et al., 2011) and college students (Mathew et al., 2014). More specifically, Mathew and colleagues found that while agency and pathways thinking both mediated the relationship between perfectionism and depression, pathways thinking had a larger impact on maladaptive perfectionism and depression and agency thinking had a larger impact on adaptive perfectionism and depression.

Hope also has been studied as a protective factor against the emergence of depression in the wake of negative or stressful life events (see Cheavens & Ritschel, 2014). Studies have found that high hope reduces levels of depression when experiencing mild or moderate life events (e.g., failing an exam, time-limited illness) or serious life events (e.g., severe physical disabilities, traumatic brain injury) in both college students and general adult populations (Elliot et al., 1991; Peleg et al., 2009; Visser, Loess, Jeglic, & Hirsch, 2013). More specifically, hope has been shown to serve a protective effect against depressive symptoms for individuals who have suffered a stroke (Gum et al., 2006), been diagnosed with end-stage renal failure (Billington, Simpson, Unwin, Bray, & Giles, 2008), experienced low to moderate levels of peer victimization (Cooley &

Ritschel, 2012), and recently given birth (Thio & Elliott, 2005). Two particularly interesting findings have emerged from this research. First, high levels of pathways thinking after a physically-disabling event is correlated with lower levels of depression independent of time, whereas high levels of agency thinking as a protective factor diminishes as more time passes after the life event (Elliot et al., 1991). That is, positive self-talk as it relates to goal attainment appears to be less effective for the prevention of depression following serious physical injury than is the ability to derive multiple routes to goal attainment. Second, compared to high levels of optimism, high hope is a greater predictor of lower levels of depression following serious physical disability (Chang et al., 2013; Peleg et al., 2009).

Hope-Based Interventions

Several hope-based interventions have been developed, and results have demonstrated that hopeful thinking can be taught (Berg, Snyder, & Hamilton, 2008; Cheavens, Feldman, Gum, Michael, & Snyder, 2006; Curry, Maniar, Sondag, & Sandstedt, 1999; Klausner et al., 1998; Rolo & Gould, 2007). Improvements in hope have been shown to be associated with improvements on a range of different outcomes, including life satisfaction, academic achievement, and self-worth (Davidson, Feldman, & Margalit, 2012; Marques, Lopez, & Pais-Ribeiro, 2011). The majority of these interventions were designed to improve hopeful thought in individuals without identified psychopathology (e.g., athletes, students). To our knowledge, only two studies have investigated changes in depression following a hope-based intervention. Klausner and colleagues examined a hope-building intervention conducted in group format with older adults with major depression. Patients were randomized to either the hope group or a reminiscence group and were treated for 11 weeks. Results showed that patients in the hope group demonstrated significant increases in overall hope scores and had significant reductions in depression, hopelessness, anxiety, and disability over the course of treatment.

In a second study, Cheavens and colleagues (2006) investigated the effects of a hope-building intervention that was delivered over eight weeks in a group setting to individuals without psychopathology. The intervention was not designed to target depression; however, over half of the sample (n = 32 treatment completers) met criteria for a psychiatric diagnosis, with depression and anxiety scores in the clinically significant range on relevant measures.

Participants were randomized to either the hope group or a wait-list control. Compared to the control condition, results showed that participants in the hope group had greater reductions in anxiety and increases in self-esteem, meaning in life, and agency thinking. In addition, results showed trends toward significant increases in overall hope scores and decreases in depressive symptoms (p = .07). These findings are noteworthy given that the original intent of the study was to evaluate whether hopeful thinking could be taught in the absence of psychopathology and thus did not include any materials specific to depression or anxiety; the results suggest that hope-based interventions that directly target depression may be even more effective in ameliorating depressive symptoms.

A confluence of factors would suggest that a hope-based intervention developed explicitly for the treatment of depression makes sound theoretical sense. First, as we have reviewed in this chapter, the hope literature shows that hope and depression are inversely correlated, that hopeful thinking can be taught, and that improvements in hope appear to be related to reductions in depressive symptoms. Second, a type of treatment for depression called problem-solving therapy (PST; Nezu, Nezu, & Perri, 1989) has been shown to be effective in the treatment of depression (Bell & D'Zurilla, 2009). The underlying principles of PST map onto the tenets of pathways thinking: the focus of the treatment is on helping patients develop more adaptive problem-solving skills as well as more adaptive attitudes toward problem-solving. Third, CBT (Beck, Rush, Shaw, & Emery, 1979) is perhaps the most well-known and well-studied treatment for depression. The underlying principles of CBT map onto the tenets of agency thinking: CBT focuses on helping patients identify distorted cognitions and learn to talk to themselves in healthier, more effective ways. Thus, empirically supported treatments exist that focus on helping patients develop routes to solving their problems as well as more effective ways to talk to themselves. The benefit of developing a novel treatment is that a hope-based intervention would (a) tie together the principles of both PST and CBT, (b) include an explicit focus on goals and goal development across a variety of life domains, (c) help patients develop future-oriented goals and thinking skills, and (d) focus on building strengths rather than focusing more exclusively on a patient's weaknesses or deficits, as is typically the case in treatments for psychological disorders (see Seligman, 2002).

Conclusion

An ample literature shows that depression is strongly related to each of the three components of hopeful thinking. Difficulties with goal-setting and attainment have been shown to precede the onset of major depression, and negative emotions also have been shown to follow goal blockage; thus, goals and emotions are cyclically linked and appear to have reciprocal influences on one another. In addition, depressed individuals have difficulty generating routes to goals, rerouting in the face of goal blockage, and talking to themselves in ways that promote positive movement toward goals. By extension, hope theory offers a lens through which to view the onset and maintenance of depression. Recent studies suggest that hope theory may offer a novel route for the treatment of depressive symptoms. The hope construct as a treatment strategy theoretically fuses existing empirically supported treatments for depression into a cogent package that could help compensate for deficits in executive functioning and enable depressed individuals to re-engage with pleasant activities and pursue their goals in a value-consistent way. Individuals suffering from major depression would very likely benefit from help in setting a more diverse set of goals across a range of life domains, improving their ability to generate multiple viable pathways to goal attainment, and improving their self-talk as it specifically occurs in the context of goal pursuit and goal blockage. A focus on hopeful thought as an intervention strategy would serve a dual benefit: ameliorating the symptoms of depression (i.e., decreasing sadness) as well as bolstering well-being and meaning in life (i.e., improving happiness).

Future Directions

• Can a hope-based intervention that directly targets depressive symptoms be developed and tested with a clinical population? Does such an intervention remediate depressive symptoms?

• What is the impact of a hope-based intervention on preventing relapse in major depression? Does hope confer a protective advantage?

• What is the long-term relationship between hope and depression? Do additional depressive episodes erode hope over time?

• Does hope moderate the relationship between clinically significant depression and known cognitive correlates of depression, such as executive functioning?

• In trials of existing treatments for depression (e.g., CBT, antidepressant medication), does baseline hope predict outcomes in depressed individuals? That is, are higher hope individuals more likely to be classified as treatment responders?

References

Abramson, L. Y., Metalsky, G. I., & Alloy, L. B. (1989). Hopelessness depression: A theory-based subtype of depression. *Psychological Review, 96*(2), 358–372. doi:10.1037/0033-295X.96.2.358

Alacron, G. M., Bowling, N. A., & Khazon, S. (2013). Great expectations: A meta-analytic examination of optimism and hope. *Personality and Individual Differences, 54*(7), 821–827. doi:10.1016/j.paid.2012.12.004

Alloy, L. B., & Abramson, L. Y. (1999). The Temple–Wisconsin Cognitive Vulnerability to Depression Project: Conceptual background, design, and methods. *Journal of Cognitive Psychotherapy, 13*(3), 227–262. Retrieved from http://www.springerpub.com/journal-of-cognitive-psychotherapy.html

Alloy, L. B., Abramson, L. Y., Hogan, M. E., Whitehouse, W. G., Rose, D. T., Robinson, M. S., . . . Lapkin, J. B. (2000). The Temple–Wisconsin Cognitive Vulnerability to Depression Project: Lifetime history of Axis I psychopathology in individuals at high and low cognitive risk for depression. *Journal of Abnormal Psychology, 109*(3), 403–418. doi:10.1037/0021-843X.109.3.403

Alloy, L. B., Abramson, L. Y., Whitehouse, W. G., Hogan, M. E., Panzarella, C., & Rose, D. T. (2006). Prospective incidence of first onsets and recurrences of depression in individuals at high and low cognitive risk for depression. *Journal of Abnormal Psychology, 115*(1), 145–156. doi:10.1037/0021-843X.115.1.145

Alloy, L. B., Abramson, L. Y., Whitehouse, W. G., Hogan, M. E., Tashman, N. A., Steinberg, D. L., . . . Donovan, P. (1999). Depressogenic cognitive styles: Predictive validity, information processing and personality characteristics, and developmental origins. *Behaviour Research and Therapy, 37*(6), 503–531. doi:10.1016/S0005-7967(98)00157-0

American Psychiatric Association. (2013). *Diagnostic and statistical manual of mental disorders* (5th ed.). Washington, DC: Author.

Arnau, R. C., Rosen, D. H., Finch, J. F., Rhudy, J. L., & Fortunato, V. J. (2007). Longitudinal effects of hope on depression and anxiety: A latent variable analysis. *Journal of Personality, 75*(1), 43–64. doi:10.1111/j.1467-6494.2006.00432.x

Ashby, J. S., Dickson, W. L., Gnilka, P. B., & Noble, C. L. (2011). Hope as a mediator and moderator of multidimensional perfectionism and depression in middle school students. *Journal of Counseling and Development, 89*, 131–139. doi:10.1002/j.1556-6678.2011.tb00070.x

Averill, J. R., Catlin, G., & Chon, K. K. (1990). *Rules of hope: Recent research in psychology*. New York: Springer-Verlag.

Bandura, A. (1982). Self-efficacy mechanism in human agency. *American Psychologist, 37*(2), 122–147. doi:10.1037/0003-066X.37.2.122

Beck, J. S. (1995). *Cognitive therapy: Basics and beyond.* New York: Guilford Press.

Beck, A. T., & Alford, B. A. (2009). *Depression: Causes and treatment* (2nd ed.). Philadelphia: University of Pennsylvania Press.

Beck, A. T., Rush, A. J., Shaw, B. F., & Emery, G. (1979). *Cognitive therapy of depression*. New York: Guilford Press.

Bell, A. C., & D'Zurilla, T. J. (2009). Problem-solving therapy for depression: A meta-analysis. *Clinical Psychology Review*, *29*(4), 348–353. doi:10.1016/j.cpr.2009.02.003

Berg, C. J., Snyder, C. R., & Hamilton, N. (2008). The effectiveness of a hope intervention in coping with cold pressor pain. *Journal of Health Psychology*, *13*, 804–809. doi:10.1177/1359105308093864

Billington, E., Simpson, J., Unwin, J., Bray, D., & Giles, D. (2008). Does hope predict adjustment to end-stage renal failure and consequent dialysis? *British Journal of Health Psychology*, *13*, 683–699. doi:10.1348/135910707X248959

Blackburn, I. M., Jones, S., & Lewin, R. J. P. (1986). Cognitive style in depression. *British Journal of Clinical Psychology*, *25*(4), 241–251. doi:10.1111/j.2044-8260.1986.tb00704.x

Chang, E. C. (2003). A critical appraisal and extension of hope theory in middle-aged men and women: Is it important to distinguish agency and pathway components? *Journal of Social and Clinical Psychology*, *22*(2), 121–143. doi:10.1521/jscp.22.2.121.22876

Chang, E. C., & DeSimone, S. L. (2001). The influence of hope on appraisals, coping, and dysphoria: A test of hope theory. *Journal of Social and Clinical Psychology*, *20*(2), 117–129. doi:10.1521/jscp.20.2.117.22262

Chang, E. C., Yu, E. A., & Hirsch, J. K. (2013). On the confluence of optimism and hope on depressive symptoms in primary care patients: Does doubling up on *bonum futurun* proffer any added benefits? *Journal of Positive Psychology*, *8*(5), 404–411. doi:10.1080/17439760.2013.818163

Cheavens, J. (2000). Hope theory: Updating a common process for psychological change. In C. R. Snyder, S. Ilardi, & S. T. Michael (Eds.), *Handbook of psychological change: Psychotherapy process & practices for the 21st century* (pp. 128–150). Hoboken, NJ: Wiley.

Cheavens, J. S., Feldman, D. B., Gum, A., Michael, S. T., & Snyder, C. R. (2006). Hope therapy in a community sample: A pilot investigation. *Social Indicators Research*, *77*(1), 61–78. doi:10.1007/s11205-005-5553-0

Cheavens, J. S., & Ritschel, L. A. (2014). Hope theory. In M. Tugade, M. Shiota, & L. Kirby (Eds.), *Handbook of positive emotions* (pp. 396–410). New York: Guilford Press.

Clark, L. A., & Watson, D. (1991). Tripartite model of anxiety and depression: Psychometric evidence and taxonomic implications. *Journal of Abnormal Psychology*, *100*(3), 316–336. doi:10.1037/0021-843X.100.3.316

Cooley, J. L., & Ritschel, L. A. (August, 2012). *Hope as a protective factor against the effects of peer victimization*. Poster presented at the 2012 annual meeting of the American Psychological Association Convention, Orlando, FL.

Curry, L. A., Maniar, S. D., Sondag, K. A., & Sandstedt, S. (1999). *An optimal performance academic course for university students and student-athletes*. Unpublished manuscript, University of Montana, Missoula.

Davidson, O. B., Feldman, D. B., & Margalit, M. (2012). A focused intervention for 1st-year college students: Promoting hope, sense of coherence, and self-efficacy. *The Journal of Psychology: Interdisciplinary and Applied*, *146*(3), 333–352. doi:10.1080/00223980.2011.634862

Dickson, J. M., & Moberly, N. J. (2013). Reduced specificity of personal goals and explanation for goal attainment in major depression. *PLoS One*, *8*(5):e64512. doi:10.1371/journal.pone.0064512

Dickson, J. M., Moberly, N. J., & Kinderman, P. (2011). Depressed people are not less motivated by personal goals but are more pessimistic about attaining them. *Journal of Abnormal Psychology*, *120*(4), 975–980. doi:10.1037/a0023665

Donaldson, C., & Lam, D. (2004). Rumination, mood and social problem-solving in major depression. *Psychological Medicine*, *34*(7), 1309–1318. doi:10.1017/S0033291704001904

Elliot, T. R., Witty, T. E., Herrick, S., & Hoffman, J. T. (1991). Negotiating reality after physical loss: Hope, depression, and disability. *Journal of Personality and Social Psychology*, *61*(4), 608–613. doi:10.1037/0022-3514.61.4.608

Enns, M. W., & Cox, B. J. (1999). Perfectionism and depression symptom severity in major depressive disorder. *Behavior Research and Therapy*, *37*(8), 783–794. doi:10.1016/S0005-7967(98)00188-0.

Feldman, D. B., & Snyder, C. R. (2005). Hope and the meaningful life: Theoretical and empirical associations between goal-directed thinking and life meaning. *Journal of Social and Clinical Psychology*, *24*, 401–421. doi:10.1521/jscp.24.3.401.65616

Forbes, E. E. (2009). Where's the fun in that? Broadening the focus on reward function in depression. *Biological Psychiatry*, *66*(3), 199–200. doi:10.1016/j.biopsych.2009.05.001

Geffken, G. R., Storch, E. A., Duke, D. C., Monaco, L., Lewin, A. B., & Goodman, W. K. (2003). Hope and coping in family members of patients with obsessive-compulsive disorder. *Anxiety Disorders*, *20*(5), 614–629. doi:10.1016/j.janxdis.2005.07.001

Geiger, K. A., & Kwon, P. (2010). Rumination and depressive symptoms: Evidence for the moderating role of hope. *Personality and Individual Differences*, *49*(5), 391–395. doi:10.1016/j.paid.2010.04.004

Geraghty, A. W. A., Wood, A. M., & Hyland, M. E. (2010). Dissociating the facets of hope: Agency and pathways predict dropout from unguided self-help therapy in opposite directions. *Journal of Research in Personality*, *44*(1), 155–158. doi:10.1016/j.jrp.2009

Gladstone, T. R., & Kaslow, N. J. (1995). Depression and attributions in children and adolescents: A meta-analytic review. *Journal of Abnormal Child Psychology*, *23*(5), 597–606. doi:10.1007/BF01447664

Glass, K., Flory, K., Hankin, B. L., Kloos, B., & Turecki, G. (2009). Are coping strategies, social support, and hope associated with psychological distress among Hurricane Katrina survivors? *Journal of Social and Clinical Psychology*, *28*(6), 779–795. doi:10.1521/jscp.2009.28.6.779

Gum, A., Snyder, C. R., & Duncan, P. W. (2006). Hopeful thinking, participation, and depressive symptoms three months after stroke. *Psychology & Health*, *21*, 319–334. doi:10.1080/14768320500422907

Hankin, B. L., Abramson, L. Y., & Siler, M. (2001). A prospective test of the hopelessness theory of depression in adolescence. *Cognitive Therapy and Research*, *25*(5), 607–632. doi:10.1023/A:1005561616506

Hewitt, P., L., & Flett, G. L. (1990). Perfectionism and depression: A multidimensional analysis. *Journal of Social Behavior and Personality*, *5*(5), 423–438. Retrieved from https://www.sbp-journal.com/index.php/sbp

Hewitt, P. L., Flett, G. L., & Ediger, E. (1996). Perfectionism and depression: Longitudinal assessment of specific vulnerability hypothesis. *Journal of Abnormal Psychology*, *105*(2), 276–280. doi:10.1037/0021-843X.105.2.276

Hirsch, J. K., Sirois, F. M., & Lyness, J. M. (2011). Functional impairment and depressive symptoms in older adults: Mitigating effects of hope. *British Journal of Health Psychology*, *16*(4), 744–760. doi:10.1111/j.2044-8287.2010.02012.x

Hirsch, J. K., Visser, P. L., Chang, E. C., & Jeglic, E. L. (2012). Race and ethnic differences in hope and hopelessness as moderators of the association between depressive symptoms and suicidal behavior. *Journal of American College Health*, *60*(2), 115–125. doi:10.1080/07448481.2011.567402

Irving, L. M., Snyder, C. R., & Crowson, J. J. Jr. (1998). Hope and coping with cancer by college women. *Journal of Personality*, *66*(2), 195–214. doi:10.1111/1467-6494.00009

Joormann, J., Teachman, B. A., & Gotlib, I. H. (2009). Sadder and less accurate? False memory for negative material in depression. *Journal of Abnormal Psychology*, *118*(2), 412–417. doi:10.1037/a0015621

Just, N., & Alloy, L. B. (1997). The response styles theory of depression: Test and extension of the theory. *Journal of Abnormal Psychology*, *106*(2), 221–229. doi:10.1037/0021-843X.106.2.221

Jones, N. P., Papadakis, A. A., Orr, C. A., & Strauman, T. J. (2013). Cognitive processes in response to goal failure: A study of ruminative thought and its affective consequences. *Journal of Social and Clinical Psychology*, *32*(5), 482–503. doi:10.1521/jscp.2013.32.5.482

Kasch, K. L., Rottenberg, J., Arnow, B. A., & Gotlib, I. H. (2002). Behavioral activation and inhibition systems and the severity and course of depression. *Journal of Abnormal Psychology*, *111*(4), 589–597. doi:10.1037/0021-843X.111.4.589

Klausner, E. J., Clarkin, J. F., Spielman, L., Pupo, C., Abrams, R., & Alexopoulos, G. S. (1998). Late-life depression and functional disability: The role of goal-focused group psychotherapy. *International Journal of Geriatric Psychiatry*, *13*(10), 707–716. doi:10.1002/(SICI)1099-1166(1998100)13:10<707:AID-GPS856>3.0.CO;2-Q

Klenk, M. M., Strauman, T. J., & Higgins, E. T. (2011). Regulatory focus and anxiety: A self-regulatory model of GAD-depression comorbidity. *Personality and Individual Differences*, *50*(7), 935–943. doi:10.1016/j.paid.2010.12.003

Lépine, J. P., & Briley, M. (2011). The increasing burden of depression. *Neuropsychiatric Disease and Treatment*, *7*, 3–7. doi:10.2147/NDT.S19617

Liu, R. T., & Alloy, L. B. (2010). Stress generation in depression: A systematic review of the empirical literature and recommendations for future study. *Clinical Psychology Review*, *30*(5), 582–593. doi:10.1016/j.cpr.2010.04.010

Lloyd, T. J., & Hastings, R. (2009). Hope as a psychological resilience factor in mothers and fathers of children with intellectual disabilities. *Journal of Intellectual Disability Research*, *53*(12), 957–968. doi:10.1111/j.1365-2788.2009.01206.x

Lynch, S. G., Kroenck, D. C., & Denney, D. R. (2001). The relationship between disability and depression in multiple sclerosis: The role of uncertainty, coping, and hope. *Multiple Sclerosis*, *7*(6), 411–416. doi:10.1177/135245850100700611

Marques, S. C., Lopez, S. J., & Pais-Ribeiro, J. L. (2011). "Building Hope for the Future": A program to foster strengths in middle-school students. *Journal of Happiness Studies*, *12*(1), 139–152. doi:10.1007/s10902-009-9180-3

Mascaro, N., & Rosen, D. H. (2005). Existential meaning's role in the enhancement of hope and prevention of depressive symptoms. *Journal of Personality*, *73*(4), 985–1014. doi:10.1111/j.1467-6494.2005.00336.x

Mathew, J., Dunning, C., Coats, C., & Whelan, T. (2014). The mediating influence of hope on multidimensional perfectionism and depression. *Personality and Individual Differences*, *70*, 66–71. doi:10.1016/j.paid.2014.06.008

McDermott, L. M., & Ebmeier, K. P. (2009). A meta-analysis of depression severity and cognitive function. *Journal of Affective Disorders*, *119*, 1–8. doi:10.1016/j.jad.2009.04.022

Michalak, J., Hölz, A., & Teismann, T. (2011). Rumination as a predictor of relapse in mindfulness-based cognitive therapy for depression. *Psychology and Psychotherapy: Theory, Research and Practice*, *84*(2), 230–236. doi:10.1348/147608310X520166

Millgram, Y., Joormann, J., Huppert, J. D., & Tamir, M. (2015). Sad as a matter of choice? Emotion-regulation goals in depression. *Psychological Science*, *26*(8), 1216–1228. doi:10.1177/0956797615583295

Morrow, J., & Nolen-Hoeksema, S. (1990). Effects of response to depression on the remediation of depressive affect. *Journal of Personality and Social Psychology*, *58*(3), 519–527. doi:10.1037/0022-3514.58.3.519

Murphy, F. C., Sahakian, B. J., Rubinsztein, J. S., Michael, A., Rogers, R. D., Robbins, T. W., & Paykel, E. S. (1999). Emotional bias and inhibitory control processes in mania and depression. *Psychological Medicine*, *29*(6), 1307–1321. doi:10.1017/S003329179001233

Naranjo, C. A., Tremblay, L. K., & Busto, U. E. (2001). The role of the brain reward system in depression. *Progress in Neuro-Psychopharmacology and Biological Psychiatry*, *25*(4), 781–823. doi:10.1016/S0278-5846(01)00156-7

Nezu, A. M., Nezu, C. M., & Perri, M. G. (1989). *Problem-solving therapy for depression: Theory, research, and clinical guidelines.* Oxford: Wiley.

Nolen-Hoeksema, S., & Morrow, J. (1991). A prospective study of depression and posttraumatic stress symptoms after a natural disaster: The 1989 Loma Prieta earthquake. *Journal of Personality and Social Psychology*, *61*(1), 115–121. doi:10.1037/0022-3514.61.1.115

Nolen-Hoeksema, S., Wisco, B. E., & Lyubomirsky, S. (2008). Rethinking rumination. *Perspectives on Psychological Science*, *3*(5), 400–424. doi:10.1111/j.1745-6924.2008.00088.x

Olinger, L. J., Kuiper, N. A., & Shaw, B. F. (1987). Dysfunctional attitudes and stressful life events: An interactive model of depression. *Cognitive Therapy and Research*, *11*(1), 25–40. doi:10.1007/BF01183130

Papageorgiou, C., & Wells, A. (2003). An empirical test of a clinical metacognitive model of rumination and depression. *Cognitive Therapy and Research*, *27*(3), 261–273. doi:10.1023/A:1023962332399

Peleg, G., Barak, O., Harel, Y., Rochberg, J., & Hoofien, D. (2009). Hope, dispositional optimism and severity of depression following traumatic brain injury. *Brain Injury*, *23*(10), 800–808. doi:10.1080/02699050903196696

Peterson, M. C., & Seligman, M. E. P. (1993). *Learned helplessness: A theory for the age of personal control.* New York: Oxford University Press.

Pinto-Meza, A., Caseras, X., Soler, J., Puigdemont, D., Perez, V., & Torrubia, R. (2006). Behavioral inhibition and behavioral activation systems in current and recovered depression participants. *Personality and Individual Differences*, *40*(2), 215–226. doi:10.1016/j.paid.2005.06.021

Qin, P., & Nordentoft, M. (2005). Suicide risk in relation to psychiatric hospitalization: Evidence based on longitudinal registers. *Archives of General Psychiatry*, *62*(4), 427–432. doi:10.1001/archpsyc.62.4.427

Ritschel, L. A., Gillespie, C. F., Arnarson, E., & Craighead, W. E. (2013). Major depressive disorder. In W. E. Craighead, D. J. Miklowitz, & L. W. Craighead (Eds.), *Psychopathology: History, theory, and diagnosis for clinicians* (2nd ed., pp. 285–333). New York: Wiley.

Rolo, C., & Gould, D. (2007). An intervention for fostering hope, athletic, and academic performance in university student-athletes. *International Coaching Psychology Review*, *2*, 44–61. Retrieved from http://www.bps.org.uk/publications/member-network-publications/member-publications/international-coaching-psychology-review

Russo, S. J., & Nestler, E. J. (2013). The brain reward circuitry in mood disorders. *Nature Reviews Neuroscience*, *14*(9), 609–625. doi:10.1038/nrn3381

Seligman, M. E. P. (1975). *Helplessness: On depression, development, and death*. (Series of Books in Psychology). San Francisco: Freeman.

Seligman, M. E. P. (2002). Positive psychology, positive prevention, and positive therapy. In C. R. Snyder and S. J. Lopez (Eds.), *Handbook of positive psychology* (pp. 3–12). New York: Oxford University Press.

Snyder, C. R. (1994). *The psychology of hope: You can get there from here*. New York: Free Press.

Snyder, C. R. (2002). Hope theory: Rainbows in the mind. *Psychological Inquiry*, *13*, 249–275. doi:10.1207/S15327965PLI1304_01

Snyder, H. R. (2013). Major depressive disorder is associated with broad impairments on neuropsychological measures of executive function: A meta-analysis and review. *Psychological Bulletin*, *139*(1), 81–132. doi:10.1037/a0028727

Snyder, C. R., Harris, C., Anderson, J. R., Holleran, S. A., Irving, L. M., Sigmon, S. T., . . . Harney, P. (1991). The will and the ways: Development and validation of an individual-differences measure of hope. *Journal of Personality and Social Psychology*, *60*(4), 570–585. doi:10.1037/0022-3514.60.4.570

Snyder, C. R., LaPointe, A. B., Crowson, J. J., & Early, S. (1998). Preferences of high- and low-hope people for self-referential input. *Cognition and Emotion*, *12*(6), 807–823. doi:10.1080/026999398379448

Snyder, C. R., Sympson, S. C., Ybasco, F. C., Borders, T. F., Babyak, M. A., & Higgins, R. L. (1996). Development and validation of the State Hope Scale. *Journal of Personality and Social Psychology*, *70*(2), 321. doi:10.1037/0022-3514.70.2.321

Strom, T. Q., & Kosciulek, J. (2007). Stress, appraisal and coping following mild traumatic brain injury. *Brain Injury*, *21*(11), 1137–1145. doi:10.1080/02699050701687334

Sun, H., Tan, Q., Fan, G., & Tsui, Q. (2014). Different effects of rumination on depression: Key role of hope. *International Journal of Mental Health Systems*, *8*(1), 83–87. doi:10.1186/1752-4458-8-53

Sweeney, P. D., Anderson, K., & Bailey, S. (1986). Attributional style in depression: A meta-analytic review. *Journal of Personality and Social Psychology*, *50*(5), 974–991. doi:10.1037/0022-3514.50.5.974

Thimm, J. C., Holte, A., Brennen, T., & Wang, C. E. A. (2013). Hope and expectancies for future events in depression. *Frontiers in Psychology*, *4*, 1–6. doi:10.3389/fpsyg.2013.00470

Thio, I. M., & Elliott, T. R. (2005). Hope, social support, and postpartum depression: Disentangling the mediating effects of negative affectivity. *Journal of Clinical Psychology in Medical Settings*, *12*(4), 293–299. doi:10.1007/s10880-005-7814-0

Thomsen, D. K. (2006). The association between rumination and negative affect: A review. *Cognition and Emotion*, *20*(8), 1216–1235. doi:10.1080/02699930500473533

Tucker, R. P., Wingate, L. R., O'Keefe, V. M., Mills, A. C., Rasmussen, K., Davidson, C. L., & Grant, D. M. (2013). Rumination and suicidal ideation: The moderating roles of hope and optimism. *Personality and Individual Differences*, *55*(5), 606–611. doi:10.1016/j.paid.2013.05.013

Venning, A. J., Eliott, J. Whitford, H., Honnor, J. (2007). The impact of a child's chronic illness on hopeful thinking in children and parents. *Journal of Social and Clinical Psychology*, *26*(6), 708–727. doi:10.1521/jscp.2007.26.6.708

Vergara, C., & Roberts, J. E. (2011). Motivation and goal orientation in vulnerability to depression. *Cognition and Emotion*, *25*(7), 1281–1290. doi:10.1080/02699931.2010.542743

Visser, P. L., Loess, P., Jeglic, E. L., & Hirsch, J. K. (2013). Hope as a moderator of negative life events and depressive symptoms in a diverse sample. *Stress and Health*, *29*(1), 82–88. doi:10.1002/smi.2433

Watson, D., Clark, L. A., & Carey, G. (1988). Positive and negative affectivity and their relation to anxiety and depressive disorders. *Journal of Abnormal Psychology*, *97*(3), 346–353. doi:10.1037/0021-843X.97.3.346

Weissman, A. N., & Beck, A. T. (1978). *Development and validation of the Dysfunctional Attitude Scale: A preliminary investigation*. Paper presented at the annual meeting of the Association for the Advancement of Behavior Therapy, Chicago.

Williams. J. M. G., Barnhofer, T., Crane, C., Hermans, D., Raes, F., Watkins, E., & Dalgleish, T. (2007). Autobiographical memory specificity and emotional disorder. *Psychological Bulletin*, *133*(1), 122–148. doi:10.1037/0033-2909.133.1.122

Winch, A., Moberly, N. J., & Dickson, J. M. (2015). Unique associations between anxiety, depression, and motives for approach and avoidance goal pursuit. *Cognition and Emotion*, *29*(7), 1295–1305. doi:10.1080/02699931.2014.976544

World Health Organization. (2015). Depression Fact Sheet N°369. Retrieved from http://www.who.int/mediacentre/factsheets/fs369/en/

Hope and Anxiety

Randolph C. Arnau

Abstract

This chapter compares and contrasts two current theories of hope, as operationalized by the Snyder Hope Scale and the Herth Hope Scale. The primary focus is on theoretical and empirical relationships between hope and anxiety. The differences between panic-related and anxious apprehension (general anxiety) as per Barlow's model are described, and it is argued that hope has stronger theoretical links to general anxiety than to panic-related anxiety. Specifically, linkages between the goal pursuit feedback loops described by hope theory and Barlow's anxious apprehension model are highlighted, illustrating how hope may be negatively related to anxious apprehension and how anxious apprehension may interfere with hope during pursuit of a goal. The current empirical literature relating hope to anxiety is critically reviewed, and suggestions for future research are discussed.

Key Words: Snyder Hope Scale, Herth Hope Scale, hope theory, anxiety, anxious apprehension

Hope is a motivational and cognitive construct. At the most basic level, hope provides motivation for action and involves cognitions related to the possibility of goal attainment. Early work on hope (e.g., Frankl, 1963, Menninger, 1959) conceptualized hope to be essentially be a positive expectation future goal attainment, or as Stotland (1969) put it, "an expectation greater than zero of achieving a goal" (p. 2). More recently, it has become clear that hope is a multidimensional construct and is more than just an expectation of achieving a goal. Hope theory, as described by C. R. Snyder, builds upon and extends that of Stotland. Starting with the assumption that the core of hope involves having goals with some minimal level of importance to the individual as well as some positive expectation of attainment of such goals, Snyder and colleagues (Snyder et al, 1991; Snyder, 1994), expanded on this idea to include two cognitive sets comprising hope: agency and pathways. Agency, which is sometimes referred to as "willpower," is a cognitive set consisting of having important goals and believing that one is able to initiate and sustain action toward

attainment of those goals. Pathways, which is sometimes referred to as "waypower," refers to an individual's perceived ability to find one or more effects ways to reach their goals, and beliefs that they have to ability to formulate alternative plans when coming up against obstacles. Snyder (1994) emphasized that these interrelated dimensions of hope commonly co-occur but that this is not always the case and that both agency and pathways thinking are necessary for the operation of hope. In other words, if one has strong agency thoughts about wanting to achieve goals and having the ability to take action but does not have positive thoughts about one's ability to find routes to the goal, one is not likely to take any action toward goal achievement. On the other hand, one might believe they have routes to a goal but not have motivation to initiate action (i.e., low agency), and thus no action is taken. The Snyder Hope Scale (SHS; Snyder et al., 1991) was developed to operationalize this construct at a trait or dispositional level, and the State Hope Scale (Snyder et al., 1996) was developed to measure the construct at a state level.

Although Snyder's hope theory is the most commonly used conceptualization of hope in the clinical and personality literature, other theories have been put forth. A complete review of all such theories is beyond the scope of this chapter and is available elsewhere (see Farran, Herth, & Popovich, 1995). I describe one that I believe is particularly useful and that also bears some similarities to, and distinct differences from, Snyder's theory. Based upon a qualitative study of the concept of hope by Dufault and Martocchio (1985), Kaye Herth developed a multidimensional measure of hope (Herth, 1991), initially designed to tap into three dimensions: cognitive-temporal, affective-behavioral, and affiliative-contextual. As has been noted previously (see Arnau, Martinez, Nino de Guzman, Herth, & Konishi, 2010), the first two dimensions bear resemblance to the agency and pathways thinking components from Snyder's hope theory. The cognitive-temporal dimension refers to "the perception that the desired outcome is realistically probable" (Farran et al., 1995, p. 62), which bears some resemblance to Snyder's model in that there is the expectation greater than zero of goal attainment, and it implies that there is a desired goal in mind. The affective-behavioral dimension contains elements of behaviors being initiated toward goal attainment, as well as an affective judgment of the adequacy of such behaviors. More specifically, it taps into "a feeling of confidence with the initiation of plans" for goal attainment (Farran et al., p. 62). As such, this dimension also bears resemblance to Snyder's model, as this dimensions seems to resemble a combination of agency thinking and pathways thinking. The third dimension, affiliative-contextual, is where Herth's model more clearly diverges from Snyder's model. This dimension has been referred to as a "recognition of interdependence and interconnectedness between self and others and between self and spirit" (Farran et al., p. 62), and essentially reflects a perception of social and spiritual support.

The Herth Hope Scale (HHS; Herth, 1991) was developed as a self-report measure to capture those three dimensions of hope. An initial factor analysis found evidence for three factors largely corresponding to the three dimensions described previously but were given the labels temporality and future, positive readiness and expectancy, and interconnectedness (Herth, 1991). More recently, Arnau (2002; see also Arnau & Rosen, 2005) found a somewhat different structure of responses to the HHS. Using both exploratory and confirmatory methods, both a three-factor and a four-factor model garnered relatively equal support. In the three-factor model, the factors were labeled optimism/support, agency, and hopelessness. The optimism and support factor was composed of items reflecting a general sense of optimism as well as a perception of spiritual and social support. The agency factor was labeled as such given the strong correspondence of items loading on this factor with Snyder's concept of agency (i.e., most items were related in some way to having important goals and an initiation of action and planning for goal attainment). The four-factor solution was essentially the same but with social support splitting off into its own factor. The four-factor solution was replicated in an independent sample of Peruvian college students (Arnau et al, 2010). The HHS (Herth, 1991), along with a short form, the Herth Hope Index (HHI; Herth, 1992) have primarily been used for research in the nursing literature but have been used in some studies appearing in the psychological literature (e.g., Arnau, 2002; Arnau & Rosen, 2005; Arnau, Rosen, & Green, 2006; Arnau et al., 2010; Cassaretto & Martínez, 2009), some of which are reviewed here, when relevant to the topic of hope and anxiety.

In response to Herth's model, Snyder (2000) notes that his model "emphasizes thinking in contrast to other emotion-based models" (p. 13). Snyder further explains that this is an important distinction within hope theory and that "emotions are a by-product of goal-directed thought," rather than a component of hope itself (p. 13). Although I agree with the importance of this distinction, I would not characterize Herth's model as emotion-based. Although the model does capture an emotional component, it captures thinking components as well. While it does make sense, as Snyder emphasizes, to delineate the positive emotions resulting from goal attainment (the primary emotion likely being joy), this does not preclude an emotional component to related to the experience of hope that is distinguishable from such emotions resulting from goal attainment—if not a separable "hopeful" emotion then at least some positive emotions that occur simultaneously with the hopeful, goal-oriented thinking. Thus there remains the possibility that an emotional component could be an important dimension in the definition of the hope construct. Of course, whether such a dimension adds to the predictive utility of the measurement is an empirical question.

Distinguishing Types of Anxiety: Theoretical Framework in Relation to Hope

When thinking about the theoretical and empirical links between hope and anxiety, it would be more useful to use more specific terms other than just "anxiety." Although anxiety is often measured as a broad construct, there are also a number of more narrow-bandwidth and specific constructs of anxiety, such as generalized anxiety, panic-related anxiety, and phobic anxiety. It may be the case that hope relates to anxiety in general and relates equally to the more specific types of anxiety. However, based on hope theory and what we know about these specific types of anxiety, we may expect hope to be more strongly related to certain types of anxiety over others. If such is the case, then studies measuring anxiety at a broad level (such as is the case with the State-Trait Anxiety Inventory) may reveal effects that are attenuated relative to what we might find if we used measures of more specific types of anxiety.

The most important delineation for hope theory may be the distinction between generalized anxiety and panic-related anxiety. Sometimes these two constructs are distinguished as fear versus anxiety. One major way these constructs differ is the temporal focus of the emotions. Fear (or panic-related anxiety) can be described as a present-oriented emotion, whereas anxiety (or generalized anxiety or anxious apprehension) is a future-oriented emotion (Barlow, 2000; Nolen-Hoeksema, 2007). When one perceives a threat in the environment, fear is elicited via the sympathetic nervous system, and the fight-or-flight response is activated. Characterizing the emotion as present-oriented comes from the fact that cognitions are focused on the present. When experiencing fear, thoughts are focused on ways of escape or defending oneself, not on what one might do Friday night or cook for dinner. The physiology of the fight-or-flight response, which physically prepares one's body for the physical demands of fighting for one's life, and the corresponding narrowing of one's attention on the threat and survival are such that focus on any other goal or task becomes impossible. Of course, this system is quite adaptive when in the presence of real danger but is quite maladaptive when it is triggered in the absence of real danger, what Barlow (2000) refers to as a "false alarm" and what we would generally label as a panic attack. Generalized anxiety, on the other hand, is a future-oriented emotion, in that cognitions are focused on the future or, more specifically, possible future misfortunes. To better reflect to future-oriented focus

of the emotion, Barlow (2000) suggests that a better term would be "anxious apprehension." As opposed to the fight-or flight response, which is focused on dealing with an imminent threat to life, anxious apprehension is an emotion where "one is ready or prepared to attempt to cope with upcoming negative events" (Barlow, 2000, p. 1249).

Barlow (2000) also describes a process model of anxious apprehension, which, in part, theorizes the causal impacts of the emotion on attentional focus, behavioral performance, and subsequent attempts to cope with the possibility of a future negative event. It is here that hope theory appears to have the most direct theoretical links with anxiety. Thus this model is described in some detail, and then the connections with hope theory are highlighted. Barlow proposes a process of anxious apprehension that is triggered by cues indicating a potentially negative event combined with a "perceived inability to predict, control, or obtain desired results or outcomes" (p. 1249). This activates a physiological response in order to prepare to deal with the event, and attention shifts to self-evaluative cognitions in which "one's (inadequate) capabilities to deal with the threat is prominent" (Barlow, 2000, p. 1250). In Barlow's model, this then triggers a feedback loop where the shift in attention to helplessness and inadequacy further increases arousal, induces hypervigilance, and activates cognitive biases related to the threat, which in turn further impairs performance. If the anxiety becomes too uncomfortable, efforts to cope shift from active, problem-focused behaviors to either avoidance behaviors or ruminative worrying. Thus worrying is a primary component of chronic or intense generalized anxiety (anxious apprehension), and thoughts are preoccupied not so much with the present but with possible bad things that may occur in the future.

When we consider emotional and cognitive processes in conjunction with active goal pursuit within Snyder's hope theory, there are distinct parallels with and links to Barlow's (2000) model of anxious apprehension. First, of course, when considering anxiety in relation to goal pursuit, it makes the most sense to consider pursuit of a goal that is of high importance to an individual (which is necessary for hope to be activated and/or even relevant). Further, anxiety would be most relevant when there is the perception (real or imagined) that such goal pursuit may fail. Thus hope theory would seem to be most relevant to anxious apprehension when such anxiety is in regard to either the potential for failure or actual failure in attainment of an important goal.

Put another way, although Barlow's model describes a general process of anxious apprehension, it should apply equally well to the more specific context of anxious apprehension in relation to goal pursuit. In this context, the "future threat or negative event" that is anticipated (as in Barlow's model of anxious apprehension) would be failure in pursuit of a very important goal. Within this context, Barlow's (2000) characterization of anxiety as "a state of helplessness, because of a perceived inability to predict, control, or obtain desired results" (p. 1249) appears to be practically the opposite of hope, and thus it is reasonable to hypothesize that anxiety would impair or even completely block hopeful thinking when in the pursuit of an important goal.

Hope Theory: Goal Pursuit Feedback Loops

Next, consider the sequential forward and feedback loops relating the value of goals, agency and pathways thinking, and goal attainment, as described by Snyder et al. (2000). For our purposes, I skip the learning history and pre-event components of the model and focus on the event sequence (see Snyder et al., 2000, p. 750). When considering hope regarding a goal with some minimal level of outcome value to be considered worth pursuing, agency thoughts (e.g., "I have the will and the energy to do it") and pathways thoughts ("I have a plan and have workable routes to accomplish it") work together both additively and iteratively to motivate action toward goal attainment. They work additively in that both add "fuel" to the motivational "fire" but also iteratively, in that increases in one can naturally lead to increases the other. Two of the feedback loops that come into play result from the outcome of goal-driven behavior (i.e., either goal attainment or nonattainment). The end result then drives cognitive feedback loops to both pathways and agency thoughts, such that if the goal is attained, there is an increase in agency and pathways thoughts, and if the goal-seeking fails, there is a decrease in such thoughts. In other words, chronic, repeated achievement of goals leads to higher levels of hope over time, given that pathways and agency thinking is strengthened with each accomplishment. Although not explicitly described by Snyder, I think it important to note here that "goal attainment/nonattainment" in the model can also represent attainment of smaller subgoals or objectives along the way to a larger goal. In other words, actions toward a goal, motivated in part by hope, may be repeatedly reinforced by accomplishment of a number of subgoals required to achieve the overall goal, with repeated feedback functioning to

maintain or increase agency and pathways thoughts along the way. This could even occur in the absence of specifically delineated subgoals and could include any externally perceived signal indicating at least some *movement* toward the goal, just as any perception of blockage of goal attainment can increase anxious apprehension. This would seem consistent with findings from the positive psychology literature indicating that positive emotions result not only from goal achievement but also in response to the perception that progress is being made toward a goal. Thus, just as Barlow (2000) described anxiety as a "unique and coherent cognitive-affective structure within our defensive motivational system" (p. 1249), likewise it makes sense to think of hope as a unique and coherent cognitive-affective structure within our approach motivational system. Being less hopeful during goal pursuit likely increases the chances of perception of a possible negative outcome (impending failure), thus increasing anxious apprehension and impeding adaptive focus on the goal. Low hope, in and of itself, may serve to cue such failure signals. Thus this provides a theoretical link between hope and anxious apprehension.

As noted earlier, fear (or panic-related anxiety) is a present-oriented mood state. The focus of cognitions is on the here and now, and not just that, but the potentially life threatening here and now. Hope is not likely to be theorized as having an effect on this particular type of anxiety or to even be activated in the alarm cognitions associated with this emotion. Of course, hope can be activated in the here and now (i.e., state hope), but even state hope would be theorized to be activated in the presence of goal pursuit, focused on the here and now action (or inaction) toward goal attainment, not environmental threats. Also, fear is adaptive if there is a real threat (such as coming across a bear in the woods) but maladaptive if the panic response is being triggered by non-life-threatening stimuli, such as is the case with the "false alarms" associated with panic disorder, that are often brought about by a classical conditioning that occurs during a panic attack brought about by high stress. The vulnerability to be high strung and experience a panic response under stress tends to run in families (Barlow, 2000; Nolen-Hoeksema, 2007), and the classical conditioning that occurs during such an extreme emotional response would not be thought to be affected by high trait or state hope or lack thereof. Thus it would be reasonable to hypothesize that hope is less strongly related to panic-related anxiety than to anxious apprehension or generalized anxiety.

Empirical Studies of Hope and Anxiety

A number of empirical studies have provided consistent evidence for higher levels of hope being associated with lower levels of anxiety, where anxiety has been measured most often at the more general level, without differentiation of different types or components of anxiety. A study of a French version of the SHS indicated that hope was negatively correlated with negative affectivity and anxiety (Gana, Daigre, & Ledrich, 2013; see also Abdel-Khalek & Snyder, 2007, for similar findings with an Arabic version of the SHS), although the effects were smaller than might be expected ($r = -.23$ and $-.25$, respectively). In this particular study, anxiety was operationalized by scores on the Anxiety subscale of the Hospital Anxiety and Depression Scale (Zigmond & Snaith, 1983). The subscale is only comprised of seven items and achieved an internal consistency of .75 in the study, which is reasonable but also attenuates the maximum possible observed effect. A more important question is how anxiety is operationalized by this scale. Inspection of items from this measure indicates that the scale contains a mix of different types and dimensions of anxiety, including anxious apprehension ("worried thoughts"), stress and physiological arousal ("tense and wound up"), as well as cognitive symptoms of panic-related anxiety ("sudden feelings of panic"). Thus if hope does relate differentially to different types and/or dimensions of anxiety, then one would expect an attenuated effect when measured at the more general level, such as is the case with this study.

Hope has also been investigated in relation to the clinical scales from the Minnesota Multiphasic Personality Inventory (MMPI). Hope was significantly negatively correlated with most of the MMPI clinical scales, indicating that hope is inversely related to a variety of psychological distress and maladjustment symptoms. In regards to anxiety, the two most relevant correlations were with the MMPI scales Hypochondriasis ($r = -.30$) and Psychasthenia ($r = -.52$; Irving et al., 1990, as cited in Snyder et al., 1991). Psychasthenia is the best index of anxiety from the clinical scales of the MMPI, although it should be noted that, as is the case with most of the MMPI clinical scales, this scale is quite multidimensional in content. It does contain much anxiety-related content (such as feeling anxious, tense, worried, and fearful) but is saturated by other content as well, such as feeling sad, unhappy, and self-critical, and is best thought of as a scale reflecting "psychological turmoil and discomfort" (Graham, 2006, p. 80). Hypochondriasis

certainly is not a measure of anxiety per se, but the scale does contain some elements of anxiety, albeit specific to anxiety about health and illness. In addition, the scale taps into concerns about physical functioning and poor health, but also people scoring high on this scale tend to be cynical and pessimistic (Graham, 2006). Thus a significant but relatively smaller correlation of hope with this scale compared to Psychasthenia would be expected.

Also suggesting an inverse relation between hope and anxiety was a study by Anderson (1988, as cited in Snyder et al., 1991) where the incremental validity of hope in the prediction of mental health symptoms was evaluated. Specifically, hope scores were used to predict scores on a mental health symptom checklist and were found to still predict unique variance after controlling for several other relevant variables, including life stressors, locus of control, and even optimism. The dependent variable was not anxiety per se, but the checklist did include a number of anxiety-related symptoms, such as general anxiety, phobic anxiety, and paranoid ideation.

Holleran and Snyder (1990; as cited in Snyder et al., 1991) evaluated the correlation of hope with anxiety in a sample of introductory psychology students. They found that the SHS correlated with scores from the Taylor Manifest Anxiety Scale ($r = -.47$) and the Trait scale of the State Trait Anxiety Inventory (STAI; $r = -.58$). Feldman & Snyder (2005), also using the trait form of the STAI, found that hope predicted unique variance in anxiety, even when controlling for measures of life meaning. So again, hope correlated with anxiety as hypothesized and to a noteworthy degree. Nevertheless, it still would be useful to know if specific types of anxiety are driving this correlation or whether the relation is ubiquitous to anxiety in general. The Trait scale of the STAI, while reasonable as a rough indicator of anxiety, is far from ideal as a measure of anxiety. Although it does contain items that are distinctly about anxiety, such as "nervous and restless" and "worry too much," many of the items are only tangentially related to anxiety and are possibly better characterized as other constructs. For example, items such as "satisfied with myself" and "happy" are better described as subjective well-being, and items such as "I feel inadequate" and "feel like a failure" seem to be more like depression or self-esteem items than anxiety. As such, this scale probably taps into neuroticism more so than anxiety per se, so it is hard to draw firm conclusions from this study regarding the correlation of hope with anxiety. One might guess that the Taylor Manifest Anxiety Scale, based upon the name of the instrument, is a much more specific measure of anxiety, but again inspection of the items from this scale is important for interpreting the results of this study. The scale taps several components of anxiety. There are items covering physiological arousal, with content such as sweating, pounding heart, and blushing. There are also items related to the affective and cognitive components of anxiety (e.g., worrying, anxiety, feeling nervous), as well as physical aspects of stress (e.g., headaches, gastrointestinal upset, tiring easily). However, there is also content related to interpersonal sensitivity and self-consciousness (e.g., fear of blushing, easily embarrassed, self-conscious). In addition, there are items related to low self-confidence and low self-esteem. Thus, as is the case with the STAI, this measure definitely taps into anxiety but certainly is not specific to that particular negative emotion.

Looking at hope as a state, as opposed to a trait, the State Hope Scale, in which respondents rate the items in regard to how they feel right at the moment, has been found to be negatively correlated with state negative affect ($r = -.47$ and $-.50$ at days 1 and 29 of the study, respectively; Snyder et al., 1996). These larger effects are expected given that both hope and affect were measured at the state level as opposed to the trait level. It is notable that the correlations were practically the same within the same subjects almost a month apart, providing evidence of the stability of the effect. Of course, these findings, although suggestive of a relationship between hope and anxiety, are not definitive, given that a number of negative emotions comprise negative affect.

One limitation of all of studies reviewed so far is that they all use cross-sectional designs, and so no conclusions can be drawn about causality. Although it would be reasonable to theorize that the causality goes in both directions, longitudinal studies would still be useful to help tease apart such reciprocal effects. One study addressed this question using a longitudinal design. Arnau, Rosen, Finch, Rhudy, and Fortunato (2007) used a latent variable modeling approach to test the longitudinal effects of hope on anxiety in college students. Hope and anxiety were measured at three time points (beginning, middle, and end of the semester) with a one-month lag between assessments. Another particularly interesting aspect of this study was that latent agency and pathways factors were included independently in the model, as opposed to modeling a single latent hope factor. As such, the unique of effects of agency and pathways could be evaluated for a more fine-grained test of Snyder's hope theory. Structural

equation modeling was used to test a cross-lagged panel analysis, with agency, pathways, and anxiety all reciprocally effecting each other over time. The results indicated that agency, but not pathways, made a unique and statistically significant prediction of decreased anxiety one month later. This effect was found for both the time 1–time 2 relationship and the time 2–time 3 relationship. Although the effect was small, as Arnau et al. noted, the effect is noteworthy, given that the variance in anxiety being predicted was variance remaining after controlling for levels of anxiety at the previous time points. The lack of a statistically significant effect of pathways on anxiety seems counter to hope theory, which clearly says agency and pathways thinking are both required for the positive effects of hope. However, there are a couple of reasons why this may have occurred. First, as Arnau et al. indicated, it could have been that pathways was predicting the same variance in anxiety as was predicted by agency, which statistically leads to one path parameter significant and the other nonsignificant (see Courville & Thompson, 2001). But still, if both are required, it would have been expected that both would make unique contributions to the prediction of anxiety. On the other hand, this study was not evaluating hope in relation to specific efforts toward a goal or whether or not a goal was achieved, and perhaps it is only in relation to goal behavior that both agency and pathways are required, whereas perhaps dispositional agency by itself is all that is needed to reduce an anxious mood. Finally, one other possibility, which was not tested in this study, is that agency and pathways *interact* in predicting outcomes such as anxiety. Given that interaction effects are statistically independent of main effects, the lack of a main effect for pathways would not preclude the possibility of an interaction between agency and pathways. All of these possibilities would be fruitful areas to explore further in future studies.

There is a limitation of the Arnau et al. (2007) study that is the same as many other studies critiqued here, and that is the lack of measurement of a *specific* types of anxiety. Arnau et al. used scores from two subscales of the Depression Anxiety Stress Scales (DASS; Lovibond & Lovibond, 1995) as indicators of the latent anxiety variable. These scales from the DASS are more specific measures of anxiety compared to the measures of anxiety used in the studies reviewed here, given that scores are yielded for two separate anxiety subscales: Anxiety and Stress. The Stress scale taps more into anxious apprehension and physical symptoms of stress, whereas the Anxiety scale measures cognitive symptoms of panic and extreme physiological arousal. However, Arnau et al. used the scores from these two subscales as two indicators of the latent anxiety variable in the structural model. Thus, although the measure used did tease apart these two primary types of anxiety symptoms, the latent anxiety variable in the study represented variance common to both and thus still tapped a very general construct of anxiety. It would be interesting to repeat this study with separate models for panic and anxious apprehension.

A couple of studies have compared Herth's (1991) model to Snyder's model in the relation of hope and anxiety (Arnau, 2002; Carretta, Ridner, & Dietrich, 2014). Carretta et al. evaluated correlations of hope with anxiety using SHS, the HHI, and the Miller Hope Scale, which is theoretically similar to the HHS. Anxiety was measured at both the state and trait level (using the STAI). They reported the following correlations trait anxiety with hope: SHS ($r = -.51$), HHI ($r = -.65$), and Miller Hope Scale ($r = -.67$). Correlations with state anxiety were someone smaller (ranging from $r = -.26$ for the SHS to $r = -.56$ for the HHI). Somewhat smaller correlations would be expected correlating a trait or disposition with a state. The authors also found a large correlation between hopelessness and trait anxiety ($r = .86$), but whether hopelessness is simply the low end of the single dimension of hope or a construct distinguishable from hope is open to debate and beyond the scope of this chapter. Although it appears that the HHI correlated somewhat more strongly with anxiety, especially state anxiety, the researchers did not test the statistical significance of the differences. In addition, as Carretta et al noted, the instruction set of the HHI and the Miller Hope Scale indicate that respondents should rate how they feel "right now" and thus are better characterized as measures of state hope, rather than trait hope. The small sample size ($N = 23$) is a major limitation of this study, but the results generally are consistent with the larger body of evidence reviewed here.

Arnau (2002) evaluated the correlation of the HHS and SHS with the Anxiety and Stress subscales of the DASS using a sample of over 500 college students. Zero-order correlations with panic-related anxiety (DASS Anxiety scale) were comparable to those with anxious apprehension (DASS Stress scale), but there were differences between the SHS (r from $-.24$ to $-.25$) and the HHS (r from $-.45$

to $-.41$). Interestingly, the larger correlation for the HHS seems to be driven by the HHS hopelessness factor (r from .48 to .51) relative to the HHS optimism/support (r from $-.34$ to $-.37$) and HHS agency (r from $-.18$ to $-.27$) factors (see Arnau, 2002, p. 62). As mentioned previously, it is still an open question whether hopelessness is best considered as a separate construct or as the extreme lower end of the continuum of hope. However, the finding of the HHS hopelessness factor correlating notably more strongly with DASS Anxiety and Stress scales compared to the other hope factors, as opposed to demonstrating correlations of comparable magnitude (albeit in the opposite direction), might suggest hopelessness as a construct distinct form hope. On the other hand, the HHS hopelessness factor has been found to load on a higher order factor of hope in both exploratory and confirmatory factor analyses of the HHS (see Arnau, 2002; Arnau et al., 2010), which suggests that the factor is a component of the broader hope construct.

Hierarchical regression analyses were also conducted to evaluate the predictive value of both the HHS and SHS together, as well as the incremental validity of the HHS and the SHS over each other, in predicting a number of outcome variables. In regard to panic-related anxiety as the outcome variable, the SHS and HHS together predicted about 28% of the variance in DASS Anxiety scores. Although structure coefficients indicated that all SHS and HHS subscales were significantly correlated with predicted Anxiety scores, the HHS scales yielded incremental predictive validity over the SHS scales but not vice versa (Arnau, 2002; Arnau & Rosen, 2005). The same pattern of results was found when predicting anxious apprehension, using the DASS Stress scale as the dependent variable. For both of these analyses, as was the case with the zero-order correlations, the HHS Hopelessness is clearly driving the results for the HHS providing incremental validity over the SHS, evidenced by the large standardized beta for Hopelessness compared to the other subscales. As a whole, the extant literature provides strong evidence of a negative relationship between hope and anxiety, but an important next step for future studies is to better determine to what degree hope relates to specific types and dimensions of anxiety. One specific type of anxiety for which studies of hope exist is that of test anxiety.

Hope and Test Anxiety

A couple of studies have evaluated the effects of hope on test-related anxiety. Onwuegbuzie (1998), found that hope was negatively correlated with anxiety about statistics in a sample of students taking a statistics course. Given this finding, Snyder (1999) posed the question of why lower hope may be related to greater anxiety about taking tests, proposing potential mechanisms for this effect from the perspective of hope theory. First, Snyder emphasized that one must appreciate the high importance of test performance that is placed on school-aged children. Thus this makes hope directly relevant to a test-taking situation, to the extent that there is a desired goal with a reasonably high level of importance. Snyder goes on to suggest that "repeated and intrusive thoughts about how one is blocked in academic performance are posited to be associated with elevated test-related anxieties" (p. 207). This also makes sense in light of Barlow's model of anxious apprehension because, more generally speaking, if one has thoughts that block one's performance in the pursuit of an important goal, this is a signal of an impending future negative event, which should lead to anxiety. Then, as Snyder notes, these intrusive thoughts lead to impairment in performance, further increasing anxiety. On the other hand, if students have high hope regarding test performance, theoretically they should have fewer intrusive thoughts about failure, because they are confident in their ability to sustain action toward and find routes to achieve their goal. Of course, this is also important for long-term cultivation of hope and experiences of success, given that failure can have a negative impact on hope for future goal pursuits, via the feedback loops discussed earlier.

Alexander and Onwuegbuzie (2007) evaluated the relation between hope and two factors of procrastination (fear of failure and task aversiveness) in a sample of graduate students taking an research methods course. Although they did not explicitly evaluate anxiety in this study, procrastination can be seen potentially as an outcome of anxious apprehension in regard to an important goal pursuit, especially when considering the fear of failure factor. When thinking about procrastination in relation to anxious apprehension, procrastination can be conceptualized as a product of anxious apprehension to the extent that it is used as an avoidant coping strategy to deal with the anxiety. Indeed, as Alexander and Onwuegbuzie point out, previous researchers have found that procrastination is related to avoidance coping (Flett, Blankstein, & Martin, 1995, as cited in Alexander & Onwuegbuzie, 2007) and it can be seen as a reaction to anxiety (Ferrari, Johnson, & Mcown, 1995, as cited in Alexander

& Onwuegbuzie, 2007). Once a person begins to engage in procrastination, it is also reasonable to see how it could further contribute to anxiety, given that the behavior is impeding progress toward the goal, making the possibility of a negative outcome greater and greater. In this study, the researchers used canonical correlation analysis to evaluate the multivariate relationship of agency and pathways with the two factors of procrastination. They found one canonical function to be noteworthy and statistically significant, with a combination of both agency and pathways predicting lower procrastination scores but with only the Fear of Failure subscale making a notable contribution to the procrastination side of the function. Thus a combination of both strong agency and pathways thinking predicts less procrastination but only procrastination driven by anxiety. Procrastination due to aversiveness of the task is unrelated to hope. This finding makes sense considering the expected negative relationship between hope and anxiety related to a goal pursuit, as well as seeing procrastination driven by a fear of failure as either a component of or a reaction to anxious apprehension about the potential negative outcome of a goal pursuit.

Conclusion

It is clear that higher hope is related to lower anxiety and that levels of hope can even predict future decreases in anxiety. However, there is much still to be learned about this relationship as well as potential mechanisms by which this effect manifests. As mentioned previously, one important focus for future research should be measurement of specific types and/or dimensions of anxiety, rather than measurement as a single-broadband construct. Specifically delineating the relationship of hope with panic-related anxiety, anxious apprehension, and physiological hyperarousal will not only expand the nomological network of the hope construct but will better inform future interventions for anxiety that incorporate hope theory. In addition, anxiety does not frequently occur in isolation but rather often co-occurs with depression. It would be useful if future studies of hope related to mood variables to assess all specific components of comprehensive models of mood, such as the tripartite model (Clark & Watson, 1991). As Clark and Watson demonstrated (see also Watson et al., 1995), there are components of mood shared by anxiety and depression (i.e., negative affect) as well as components that are unique to each (i.e., lack of positive affect for depression, physiological hyperarousal for anxiety), and they developed the Mood and Anxiety Symptom Questionnaire (Watson & Clark, 1991) to hierarchically measure each of those factors. More recently, the model has been expanded to include the multiple factors of anxiety disorder symptoms into what has been called the hierarchical model (Mineka, Watson, & Clark, 1998) in order to better account for the heterogeneity of anxiety symptoms and the differential relationships of anxiety disorders to each other and to depression (Prenoveau et al., 2010). Thus it would be beneficial for future studies of hope, mood, and psychopathology to utilize measures that yield multidimensional, hierarchical scores, such as the battery of measures used by Prenoveau et al. (2010) to cover all domains of the hierarchical model, or the MMPI-2-Restructured Form (Ben-Porath & Tellegen, 2011).

Another fruitful area of future research would be mediational studies testing for possible mechanisms of the effect that hope has on anxiety. For example, appraisals and coping styles have been found to be mediators of the relationship between hope and dysphoria (Chang & DeSimone, 2001). Given the theoretical links between hope, anxious appraisal, and cognitions associated with goal pursuit, it is reasonable to hypothesize that an effect of hope on cognitive appraisals during pursuit of important goals would partially mediate the effect of hope on anxiety.

Some other areas of future research, although not directly focused on the link between hope and anxiety, are important. As mentioned previously, there still is not a definitive answer to the question of whether hopelessness is a best conceptualized as the extreme low end of a bipolar hope continuum or a separate but related construct. It may be that a hopelessness dimension better predicts negative outcomes and maladjustment (such as anxiety and depress), whereas hope better predicts positive outcomes, such as flourishing, life satisfaction, and mental health. One can be relatively happy and satisfied with life and still struggle with symptoms such as anxiety and depression, as these are not completely orthogonal constructs. If such is the case, then it may be important to more explicitly capture hopelessness, either via a separate measure (if it is a separable construct) or via more explicit hopelessness items in the measurement of hope (as is the case for the HHS). Within measurement theory, such items would likely be more difficult items, tapping into a lower level of the construct than what is captured by denial of items worded in the positive direction. Such items may be necessary for prediction of more maladaptive outcomes, such as psychopathology.

On the other hand, if hopelessness is actually a separate but related construct, then statistically it will be important to remove such items from measures of hope and include a measurement of hopelessness by itself for use in predictive models.

Another area worthy of study is evaluating Herth's conceptualization of hope as compared to Snyder's model. So far, the research empirically comparing the two is minimal, but, as described earlier in this chapter, the existing research does suggest the possibility that the Herth model may better predict some outcomes and the Snyder model may better predict others. Perhaps more importantly, from a measurement perspective, it will be important to design research to test whether the additional components included in the broader construct of hope of the Herth model are best conceptualized as components of hope or as associated constructs that interact with and modify or enhance the effects of hope. I believe it is clear that the additional components captured by the Herth model are indeed important psychological constructs, but more specific measurement and structural models could tease apart more definitively the question of whether they are best measured as components of hope or as independent constructs. Longitudinal studies with competing structural models are needed to more specifically address this question, where all of the theoretical components of hope (from both the Herth and Snyder measures) are modeled as predictors of important outcomes such as different types of anxiety, depression maladjustment, happiness, and flourishing. Within such models, the question of the additive and/or interactive effects of agency and pathways thinking can be addressed. Although agency and pathways are theorized to both be necessary for hope to be operative in terms of a motivation to behavioral action toward goals, there may be some outcomes better predicted by one versus the other. Even more interesting would be the question of whether agency and pathways interact in the prediction of some outcomes such as anxiety and depression. It is important to note that if there is an interaction effect, it is statistically independent of main effects, and it is possible to have an strong interaction effect in the absence of any main effects (Thompson, 1994). Thus, given that most studies have not modeled an agency by pathways interaction, the predictive validity of hope may in fact be underestimated. Future studies using hope as a predictor should test for such interactions to address this question.

Finally, another area of future study is to evaluate hope as a moderator variable. Specifically, we should test whether hope serves as a buffer for stress or, in other words, moderates the relationship between stressful life events and adaptive and maladaptive outcomes. Much of the work on hope and anxiety (and maladjustment in general) has focused on the main effects of hope predicting anxiety and depression. However, it might be that case that hope is an even stronger predictor of such outcomes for people with many recent stressful life events, compared to those with low levels of stress. In addition, hope may also interact with certain genetic vulnerabilities to psychopathology. For example, hope has been found to buffer the effects of life stressors on depressive symptoms in medical students with genotypic vulnerability to depression related to the serotonin transporter gene (Rosen et al., 2010). Thus future studies of genetic vulnerability to stress-related psychopathology could include a measure of hope to investigate this possibility.

Future Directions

• Does hope buffer the relationship between stressful life events and maladjustment?
• Does the four-factor model of the HHS yield incremental validity above the two-factor agency and pathways model of the SHS in predicting relevant outcomes?
• How does hope relate to more specific measures of anxiety, such as panic-related anxiety, generalized anxiety, and physiological hyperarousal?
• What are the longitudinal, reciprocal effects of state hope and anxious arousal on each other during the pursuit of a specific goal?

References

Abdel-Khalek, A., & Snyder, C. R. (2007). Correlates and predictors of an Arabic translation of the Snyder Hope Scale. *The Journal of Positive Psychology, 2*, 228–235. doi:10.1080/17439760701552337

Alexander, E. S., & Onwuegbuzie, A. J. (2007). Academic procrastination and the role of hope as a coping strategy. *Personality and Individual Differences, 42*(7), 1301–1310. doi:10.1037/t09250-000

Anderson, J. R. (1988). *The role of hope in appraisal, goal-setting, expectancy, and coping.* Unpublished doctoral dissertation, University of Kansas, Lawrence.

Arnau, R. C. (2002). Hope: Its measurement and relationships with personality and mental health. *Dissertation Abstracts International, 63*(7B), 3463.

Arnau, R. C., Martinez, P., Nino de Guzman, I., Herth, K., & Konishi, C. Y. (2010). A Spanish-language version of the Herth Hope Scale: Development and psychometric evaluation in a Peruvian sample. *Educational and Psychological Measurement, 70*, 808–824. doi:10.1177/0013164409355701

Arnau, R. C., & Rosen, D. H. (2005, August). *Psychometric evaluation of the Herth Hope Scale.* Poster presented at the 2005 convention of the American Psychological Association, Washington, DC.

Arnau, R. C., Rosen, D. H., Finch, J. F., Rhudy, J. L, & Fortunato, J. V. (2007). Longitudinal effects of hope on depression and anxiety: A latent variable analysis. *Journal of Personality, 75*, 43–63. doi:10.1111/j.1467-6494.2006.00432.x

Arnau, R. C., Rosen, D. H., & Green, B. A. (2006, January). *Predicting coping styles from the Snyder Hope Scale and Herth Hope Scale: A comparative validity study.* Poster presented at the annual convention of the Society for Personality and Social Psychology, Palm Springs, CA.

Barlow, D. H. (2000). Unraveling the mysteries of anxiety and its disorders from the perspective of emotion theory. *American Psychologist, 55*(11), 1247–1263. doi:10.1037/0003-066X.55.11.1247

Ben-Porath, Y. S., & Tellegen, A. (2011). *Minnesota Multiphasic Personality Inventory—2 Restructured Form: Manual for administration, scoring, and interpretation.* Minneapolis: University of Minnesota Press. (Original work published 2008)

Carretta, C. M., Ridner, S. H., & Dietrich, M. S. (2014). Hope, hopelessness, and anxiety: A pilot instrument comparison study. *Archives of Psychiatric Nursing, 28*, 230–234. doi:10.1037/t21563-000

Cassaretto, M., & Martínez, P. (2009). Validación de la Escala del Sentido del Humor en estudiantes universitarios. *Revista de Psicología, 27*(2), 287–309.

Chang, E. C., & DeSimone, S. L. (2001). The influence of hope on appraisals, coping, and dysphoria: A test of hope theory. *Journal of Social and Clinical Psychology, 20*, 117–129. doi:10.1521/jscp.20.2.117.22262

Clark, L. A., & Watson, D. (1991). Tripartite model of anxiety and depression: Psychometric evidence and taxonomic implications. *Journal of Abnormal Psychology, 100*, 316–336. doi:10.1037/0021-843X.100.3.316

Courville, T., & Thompson, B. (2001). Use of structure coefficients in published multiple regression articles: β is not enough. *Educational and Psychological Measurement, 61*, 229–248. doi:10.1177/00131640121971211

Dufault, K., & Martocchio, B. (1985). Hope: Its spheres and dimensions. *Nursing Clinics of North America, 20*, 379–391.

Farran, C. J., Herth, KI. A., & Popovich, J. M. (1995). *Hope and hopelessness: Critical clinical constructs.* Thousand Oaks, CA: SAGE.

Feldman, D. B., & Snyder, C. R. (2005). Hope and the meaningful life: Theoretical and empirical associations between goal-directed thinking and life meaning. *Journal of Social and Clinical Psychology, 24*, 401–421. doi:10.1521/jscp.24.3.401.65616

Ferrari, J. R., Johnson, J. L., & McCown, W. G. (1995). *Procrastination and task avoidance: Theory, research, and treatment.* New York: Plenum Press.

Flett, G. L., Blankstein, K. R., & Martin, T. R. (1995). Procrastination, negative self-evaluation, and stress in depression and anxiety: A review and preliminary model. In J.R. Ferrari, J. L. Johnson, W. G. McCown (Eds.), *Procrastination and task avoidance: Theory, research, and treatment.* New York: Plenum Press, pp. 137-167.

Frankl, V. E. (1963). *Man's search for meaning.* New York: Washington Square Press.

Gana, K., Daigre, S., & Ledrich, J. L. (2013). Psychometric properties of the French version of the Adult Dispositional Hope Scale. *Assessment, 20,* 114–118. doi:10.1177/1073191112468315

Graham, J. R. (2006). *MMPI-2: Assessing personality and psychopathology* (4th ed.). New York: Oxford University Press.

Herth, K. (1991). Development and refinement of an instrument to measure hope. *Scholarly Inquiry for Nursing Practice: An International Journal, 5,* 39–51.

Herth, K. (1992). An abbreviated instrument to measure hope: Development and psychometric evaluation. *Journal of Advanced Nursing, 17,* 1251–1259. doi:10.1111/j.1365-2648.1992.tb01843.x

Holleran, S., & Snyder, C. R. (1990). *Discriminant and convergent validation of the Hope Scale.* Unpublished manuscript, University of Kansas, Lawrence.

Irving, L. M. Crenshaw, W., Snyder, C. R., Francis, P., & Gentry, G. (1990, May). *Hope and its correlates in a psychiatric inpatient setting.* Paper presented at the 62nd annual meeting of the Midwestern Psychological Association, Chicago.

Lovibond, S. H., & Lovibond, P. F. (1995). *Manual for the Depression Anxiety Stress Scales* (2nd ed.). Sydney: Psychology Foundation.

Menninger, K. (1959). The academic lecture on hope. *The American Journal of Psychiatry, 116,* 481–491.

Mineka, S., Watson, D., & Clark, L. A. (1998). Comorbidity of anxiety and unipolar mood disorders. *Annual Review of Psychology, 49,* 377–412. doi:10.1146/annurev.psych.49.1.377

Nolen-Hoeksema, S. (2007). *Abnormal psychology* (4th ed.). New York: McGraw-Hill.

Onwuegbuzie, A. J. (1998). Role of hope in predicting anxiety about statistics. *Psychological Reports, 82,* 1315–1320. doi:10.2466/PR0.82.3.1315-1320

Prenoveau, J. M., Zinbarg, R. E., Craske, M. G., Mineka, S., Griffith, J. W., Epstein, A. M. (2010). Testing a hierarchical model of anxiety and depression in adolescents: A trilevel model. *Journal of Anxiety Disorders, 24,* 334–344. doi:10.1016/j.janxdis.2010.01.006

Rosen, D., Mascaro, N., Arnau, R., Escamilla, M., Tai-Seale, M., Ficht, A., . . . Stephenson, K. (2010). Depression in medical students: Gene-environment interactions. *Annals of Behavioral Science and Medical Education, 16*(2), 8–14. doi:10.1007/BF03355125

Snyder, C. R. (1994). *The psychology of hope.* New York: The Free Press.

Snyder, C. R. (1999). Hope, goal-blocking thoughts, and test-related anxieties. *Psychological Reports, 84,* 206–208. doi:10.2466/pr0.1999.84.1.206

Snyder, C. R. (2000). The past and possible futures of hope. *Journal of Social and Clinical Psychology, 19,* 11–28. doi:10.1521/jscp.2000.19.1.11

Snyder, C. R., Harris, C., Anderson, J. R., Holleran, S. A., Irving, L. M., Signmon, S. T., . . . Harney, P. (1991). The will and the ways: Development and validation of an individual-differences measure of hope. *Journal of Personality and Social Psychology, 60,* 570–585. doi:10.1037/0022-3514.60.4.570

Snyder, C. R., Ilardi, S. S., Cheavens, J., Michael, S. T., Yamhure, L., & Sympson, S. (2000). The role of hope in cognitive-behavioral therapies. *Cognitive Therapy and Research, 24*(6), 747–762. doi:10.1023%2FA%3A1005547730153

Snyder, C. R., Sympson, S. C., Ybasco, F. C., Borders, T. F., Babyak, M. A., & Higgins, R. L. (1996). Development and validation of the State Hope Scale. *Journal of Personality and Social Psychology, 70*(2), 321–335. doi:10.1037/0022-3514.70.2.321

Stotland, E. (1969). *The psychology of hope.* San Francisco, CA: Jossey-Bass.

Thompson, B. (1994, February). *Why multivariate methods are usually vital in research: Some basic concepts.* Paper presented at the biennial meeting of the Southwestern Society for Research in Human Development, Austin, TX. Eric Document Reproduction Service (ED 367 687).

Watson, D., & Clark, L. A. (1991). *The Mood and Anxiety Symptom Questionnaire.* Unpublished manuscript, University of Iowa, Department of Psychology, Iowa City.

Watson, D., Weber, K., Assenheimer, J. S., Clark, L. A., Strauss, M. E., & McCormick, R. A. (1995). Testing a tripartite model: I. Evaluating the convergent and discriminant validity of anxiety and depression symptom scales. *Journal of Abnormal Psychology, 104,* 3–14. doi:10.1037/0021-843X.104.1.3

Zigmond, A. S., & Snaith, R. P. (1983). The Hospital Anxiety and Depression Scale. *Acta Psychiatrica Scandinavica, 67,* 361–370. doi:10.1111/j.1600-0447.1983.tb09716.x

Hope and Posttraumatic Stress Disorder

Laura J. Long *and* Matthew W. Gallagher

Abstract

Traumatic events can have a debilitating effect on mental health, and may lead to the development of posttraumatic stress disorder (PTSD). However, most people can adjust after adversity, and some even experience posttraumatic growth (PTG). Hope theory suggests that hope provides a psychological resource that can help individuals to respond to trauma with resilience. This chapter explores the role of hope as a protective factor preventing the development of PTSD, the relationship between hope and coping in the context of PTSD, and how hope may facilitate PTG. It also discusses how hope may act as a common factor across psychotherapies for the treatment of PTSD. Future research directions include investigating hope as a mechanism of change in psychotherapy for PTSD and the degree to which hope can incrementally predict PTSD and PTG beyond related types of positive thinking.

Key Words: hope, posttraumatic stress disorder, PTSD, trauma, posttraumatic growth, resilience

Hope plays an important role in promoting mental health. Hopeful thinking is linked to high levels of adjustment, positive affect, life satisfaction, purpose in life, well-being, quality of life, and social support (Ciarrochi, Parker, Kashdan, Heaven, & Barkus, 2015; Gallagher & Lopez 2009; Germann et al., 2015; Khodarahimi, 2013; Stoyles, Chadwick, & Caputi, 2015). Low levels of hope are associated with mental health problems including anxiety, depression, and posttraumatic stress disorder (Ai, Tice, Peterson, & Huang, 2005; Gerard & Booth, 2015; Kortte et al., 2010; Madan & Pakenham, 2015; Snyder et al, 1991; Weinberg, Besser, Zeigler-Hill, & Neria, 2016). Though a traumatic event may temporarily dampen hopeful thinking, hope may also act as a protective factor against the development of posttraumatic stress disorder. Fortunately, interventions targeting hope are available, and treatments for posttraumatic stress disorder appear to improve hopeful thinking. Even in the presence of distress, a traumatic event presents the potential for personal growth, which appears to be facilitated by hope. In this chapter, we further explore these ideas in a discussion of the relationship between hope and trauma, hope's role as a protective factor against the development of posttraumatic stress disorder, the relationship between hope and posttraumatic growth, and hope in the context of therapy for posttraumatic stress disorder.

Hope and Trauma

The majority of Americans will experience or have experienced a traumatic event at some point in their lives, with lifetime prevalence estimates as high as 89.7% (Kilpatrick et al., 2013). However, the national lifetime prevalence of posttraumatic stress disorder is between 6% and 8% (Kessler, 1995; Kilpatrick et al., 2013). Thus most survivors of trauma respond with resilience, and comparatively few individuals go on to develop posttraumatic stress disorder. Some may even experience significant personal growth in the aftermath of a traumatic experience (Tedeschi & Calhoun, 2004). In the face of challenging circumstances, hope is thought to be an important source of resilience. Snyder's (2002) model of hope is cognitively based and comprised of the subcomponents pathways and agency, which have an iterative relationship. Pathways thinking involves the ability to identify the necessary routes to reach goals, including generating alternate routes around obstacles. Agency thinking involves the perceived ability to use these pathways to reach goals and serves to generate motivational energy. Together, pathways and agency thinking allow us to actively pursue these goals and response adeptly to a challenge.

One way hope may be beneficial to trauma survivors is by promoting positive coping. Hope has been associated with more adaptive forms of coping (Affleck & Tennen, 1996; Snyder et al., 1991), and thus may facilitate more adaptive responses to traumatic events, which are particularly stressful and demanding. In the context of stress and coping theory (Lazarus & Folkman, 1984), stress is contingent on the appraisal that the demands of a situation outweigh one's ability to cope. Hope also involves self-appraisals that should influence stress appraisals. The enhanced sense of agency found in those high in hope, as well as their confidence in their ability to find alternate pathways to their goals, should cause them to perceive their circumstances as less stressful (Snyder, 2002). Stress should decrease with more goal-directed thoughts and accompanying actions over time, reflecting the process of coping. Folkman (2010) also suggests that hope and coping are intimately linked and appear to have a bidirectional relationship. When coping with stressors, hope has been associated with benefit finding and problem-focused coping, as well as more productive emotional approach-oriented coping (Affleck & Tennen, 1996; Snyder et al., 1991). Those low in hope are more likely to engage in avoidance/disengaged coping (Chang, 1998; Snyder, 1999). Avoidance is a proposed maintenance factor as well as a symptom of posttraumatic stress disorder (Foa, Steketee, & Rothbaum, 1989), and avoidant coping is associated with posttraumatic stress disorder symptoms (Finklestein, Laufer, & Solomon, 2012; Jacobsen et al., 2002; Tiet et al., 2006) as well as other forms of psychopathology including anxiety disorders (Hughes, Budd, & Greenaway, 1999; Kaplan et al., 2012) and depression (Dunkley et al., 2016; Rodríguez-Naranjo & Caño, 2016).

Unfortunately, the experience of a life-changing trauma may temporarily impact levels of hope. Traumatic experiences can be disorienting, disrupting people's understanding of the world around them (Janoff-Bulman, 1992). They may involve personal loss, whether of possessions in the case

of a natural disaster, or of a loved one. Traumatic events can also obstruct our basic desires for safety and well-being. For some, the event may represent a significant obstacle. In the context of hope theory (Snyder, 1996, 2000, 2002), problems, obstacles, and loss are conceptualized as goal blockages, which can drain a person's sense of agency and motivation. Over time we develop familiar routines through which we interact with long-standing goals. Once these goals are gone or obstructed, the associated habitual pathways-related thoughts that remain serve as reminders of this fact and trigger thoughts of lost agency. Such circumstances may result in dysphoria, anger, and frustration. Snyder also argues that unsuccessful goal pursuits are catalogued in our memories by the emotions they elicited and are therefore primed by negative emotions. Due to the gravity of a traumatic event, negative emotions prompt trauma-associated thoughts and memories that can be overwhelming. Thus traumatic events may temporarily halt goal-directed thinking, which is replaced by the intrusive thinking and re-experiencing of the trauma in response to negative emotions.

Research and theory surrounding the construct of hopelessness also supports a link between hope and posttraumatic stress disorder. Hopelessness theory evolved from Beck's helplessness research and led to the development of the hopelessness theory of depression (Abramson, Metalsky, & Alloy, 1989). This theory states that hopelessness in the face of negative life events is sufficient for causing the subtype of hopelessness depression. According to Abramson et al., hopelessness is comprised of a negative outcome expectancy, which involves negative expectations about whether a desired outcome will occur, as well as a helplessness expectancy, involving expectations that one is helpless to change the likelihood of the negative outcome occurring. Hopelessness is thought to result from stable and global attributions about why an important negative event occurred, inferences about negative consequences of the event, and resulting negative inferences about the self (particularly those that are unlikely to change) and that affect one's ability to attain highly desired positive outcomes in many spheres of life. These cognitions are more likely to occur if an individual has a tendency toward a negative attributional style.

Though hopelessness implies a lack of hope in name, hope and hopelessness are not diametric opposites on the same continuum. Hopelessness involves negative thoughts regarding the future, whereas low hope involves a lack of positive thoughts regarding the future (Grewal & Porter, 2007; MacLeod, Rose, & Williams, 1993). In addition, hopelessness theory evokes the concept of agency but does not evoke the concept of pathways, which is of equal importance in hope theory (Grewal & Porter, 2007; Snyder, 2000). Hope and hopelessness therefore appear to be best conceptualized as related but distinct and opposing constructs (Huen, Ip, Ho, & Yip, 2015; Snyder et al., 1991).

Depression and posttraumatic stress disorder share overlapping symptoms, and evidence suggests that hopelessness is predictive of both disorders (Joseph, 1999; Pérez et al., 2014; Scher & Resick, 2005). Hopelessness has also been related to negative outcomes, such as suicide after termination of therapy (Dahlsgaard, Beck, & Brown, 1998), self-injury (Fox et al., 2015), social anxiety and depression (Hamilton et al., 2013), and suicidal behavior in survivors of trauma both with and without posttraumatic stress disorder (Panagioti, Gooding, & Tarrier, 2012; Spokas, Wenzel, Stirman, Brown, & Beck, 2009).

Hope as a Protective Factor

Hope helps people persevere in the face of challenging circumstances, from minor daily hassles to life-altering traumatic events. Hope theory (Snyder, 2002) suggests that those high in hope should be quicker to regain their sense of agency and motivation after encountering obstacles. They are able to create alternate routes or switch their focus to related goals, whereas for people low in hope, goal pursuit can become derailed by apprehension and rumination (Snyder, 1999). Preliminary evidence suggests that hope acts as a protective factor against developing posttraumatic stress disorder in response to trauma. In a study of survivors of Hurricane Katrine, Glass, Flory, Hankin, Kloos, and Turecki (2009) found that hope was a robust predictor of posttraumatic stress disorder symptoms such that individuals higher in hope reported fewer symptoms. In a study examining children from schools in an Israeli city affected by rocket attacks, higher levels of hope were also associated with fewer symptoms of posttraumatic stress disorder (Kasler, Dahan, & Elias, 2008). Higher dispositional hope has been associated with less posttraumatic stress disorder symptoms as well as less burnout symptoms in medical professionals (Ho & Lo, 2011). A study by Ai et al. (2011) suggests that the relationship between hope and symptoms of posttraumatic stress disorder

may vary across different ethnic groups. Hope was associated with significantly lower posttraumatic stress disorder symptoms for African American student volunteers for Hurricane Katrina and Rita but not in European American responders, and neither optimism nor positive emotions were predictive of symptomology. More research will be needed to identify demographic and cultural variables that may influence the relationship between hope and posttraumatic stress disorder.

Hope may work in concert with other positive constructs to buffer against the development of posttraumatic stress disorder. For example, optimism and self-esteem, which are consistently associated with hope, were found to predict acute anxiety symptoms including posttraumatic stress disorder symptoms and dissociative experiences in female Israeli civilians who had been exposed to war (Besser, Weinberg, Zeigler-Hill, & Neria, 2014). Hope has also been conceptualized as a subcomponent of the psychological capital construct, along with optimism, efficacy, and resiliency (Laschinger & Nosko, 2015; Luthans & Avolio, 2014). In a study by Laschinger and Nosko, psychological capital was predictive of lower levels of posttraumatic stress disorder in nurses, as were each of its subcomponents individually. Multiple modes of positive thinking and expectations of positive outcomes following trauma may serve as sources of resilience in the face of harrowing events, preventing the development of posttraumatic stress disorder. Additional research will be required to better understand the unique contributions of different modes of positive thinking as protective factors against the development of posttraumatic stress disorder.

While extensive research has established a positive association between hope and coping (Chang, 1998; Chang & DeSimone, 2001; Roesch et al., 2010; Snyder et al, 1991, 2000), very few studies have concurrently investigated the relationships among hope, coping styles, and posttraumatic stress disorder in trauma-exposed populations. Hassija, Luterek, Naragon-Gainey, Moore, and Simpson (2012) found a relationship between hope, coping, and depression, though not posttraumatic stress symptoms, among trauma-exposed veterans. For individuals high in hope, emotional avoidance did not influence depression symptoms. However, emotional avoidance predicted greater symptoms of depression for those low in hope. These results suggest that hope may act as a buffer against the negative influence of emotional avoidance coping on depression symptoms.

Glass and colleagues (2009) found that, among Hurricane Katrina survivors, greater hope and social support were both associated with fewer posttraumatic stress disorder symptoms, while avoidant coping was associated with greater posttraumatic stress disorder symptoms. Hope moderated the relationship between avoidant coping and distress, such that avoidant coping was associated with greater distress for those with low hope compared to those with high hope. Thus preliminary evidence suggests that hope and coping interact to reduce negative outcomes for those who have experienced trauma; however, more research will be needed to address the relationship between hope, coping, and posttraumatic stress disorder.

Hope may be more strongly associated with positive coping for those suffering from posttraumatic stress disorder once they have received treatment. Irving et al. (1997) studied the relationship between hope and positive coping in veterans receiving inpatient treatment for posttraumatic stress disorder. At intake, higher levels of hope were associated with greater social support and a more active, adaptive form of avoidance coping called seeking alternative rewards, which involves pursing alternate goals in the face of stressors (Holahan, Moos, & Schaefer, 1996), but hope was not associated with approach coping methods. At termination, hope was robustly related to additional approach-oriented coping strategies such as problem-solving, logical analysis, and seeking guidance. Results also indicated that agency was more consistently associated with these coping styles than pathways. It appears that those with higher hope may be better able to engage in adaptive coping strategies once they have learned these skills in therapy. In addition, agency may be particularly important for those experiencing symptoms of posttraumatic stress disorder by bolstering the motivation to engage in approach-oriented coping strategies.

Hope and Posttraumatic Growth

A traumatic event also presents the opportunity for resilience and personal growth in the face of adversity (Tedeschi & Calhoun, 1996, 2004). Though posttraumatic stress and posttraumatic growth may appear to be opposing outcomes at first glance, evidence suggests that they are separate constructs that may even occur simultaneously (Kaye-Tzadok & Davidson-Arad, 2016; Shand, Cowlishaw, Brooker, Burney, & Ricciardelli, 2015; Stermac, Cabral, Clarke, & Toner, 2014). Posttraumatic growth involves perceived changes in the self, relationships with others, and philosophy of life (Tedeschi & Calhoun, 1996). Because traumatic events represent significant stressful experiences that challenge personal beliefs and assumptions about the world, the resulting struggle, coping, and cognitive rebuilding can lead to perceived positive changes (Tedeschi & Calhoun, 2004). Hope may help focus attention on problem-solving and adapting to new circumstances in lieu of fixating on a traumatic experience (Ai et al., 2011; Kaye-Tzadok & Davidson-Arad, 2016). The belief that one has the ability to achieve a positive resolution after a traumatic experience may also provide the motivation to grow from trauma, not just recover (Ai, Tice, Whitsett, Ishisaka, & Chim, 2007).

Hope may also contribute to posttraumatic growth by promoting meaning-focused coping, which involves revision of one's goals, reordering priorities, and focusing on strengths (Folkman, 2010). Meaning-focused coping has been associated with posttraumatic growth (Ciarrochi et al., 2015). Such coping may prevent distress levels from becoming so high as to preclude cognitive processing in response to the trauma and posttraumatic growth. In addition, those high in hope are more likely to engage in benefit-finding when coping (Affleck & Tennen, 1996), which is conceptually similar to posttraumatic growth (Tedeschi & Calhoun, 1996).

Recent research has focused on establishing the factors that are associated with posttraumatic growth and determining which are most influential in this process. There is some evidence that hope is associated with posttraumatic growth across various types of trauma, though findings are not completely uniform. Hope has been associated with posttraumatic growth for survivors of childhood sexual abuse (Gall, 2006). Similarly, a study of survivors of childhood sexual abuse by Kaye-Tzadok and Davidson-Arad (2016) found that both hope and resilience independently predicted posttraumatic growth. Among traumatized Somali refugees in Hungary, Kroo and Nagy (2011) found that hope, and not optimism, was associated with posttraumatic growth. Among interpersonal violence survivors, hope in combination with depression and symptom severity was found to predict posttraumatic growth (Cabral, 2010). In a sample of Chinese people living with chronic skin disease, hope, as well as optimism, resilience, and self-efficacy, were positively related to posttraumatic growth, including its subcomponents of self-growth and new possibilities, yet only hope and resilience significantly predicted posttraumatic growth (Zhai, Huang, Gao, Jiang, & Xu, 2014). Other cognitive strategies of self-forgiveness, realistic control, and unrealistic control were not significant predictors in this study. Among Kosovar war refugees, hope as well as cognitive coping predicted posttraumatic growth, however (Ai et al., 2007).

In certain cases, hope may influence posttraumatic growth indirectly by promoting positive coping strategies. Among cancer survivors, Baník and Gajdošová, (2014) found that pathways thinking was associated with posttraumatic growth and benefit-finding. Hope was not predictive of posttraumatic growth in patients undergoing of cardiac surgery (Ai, Hall, Pargament, & Tice, 2013), survivors of a volcanic eruption in Indonesia (Subandi, Achmad, Kurniati, & Febri, 2014), or a sample of cancer survivors (Bellizzi & Blank, 2006). As a whole, preliminary evidence suggests a relationship between hope and posttraumatic growth, but more research will be needed to determine the unique influence of hope that allows us to predict posttraumatic growth above and beyond other modes of positive thinking such as optimism and self-efficacy.

Though there is evidence to support a relationship between hope and posttraumatic growth, very few studies have investigated the mechanisms by which hope may influence this construct. A study by Yuen, Ho, and Chan (2014) suggests that one way hope may influence posttraumatic growth is through reducing negative rumination. In a sample of childhood cancer survivors, hope significantly predicted posttraumatic growth, and the relationship was partially mediated by cancer rumination. The results indicated that higher hope was related to less cancer-related rumination, which in turn allowed for the development of posttraumatic growth. Rumination mediated the relationship between hope and both anxiety and depression as well. These results are in line with other evidence that hope buffers the influence of rumination on mental health outcomes, such as depression (Geiger & Kwon, 2010).

The relationship between hope, trauma, and positive outcomes may also depend on the type and amount of adversity encountered. A recent study found that lower levels of posttraumatic stress disorder symptoms were associated with greater posttraumatic growth in survivors of sexual assault, and this relationship was mediated by hope or, more specifically, agency thinking (Stermac et al., 2014). These results suggest that survivors with lower levels of distress were able to achieve more posttraumatic growth because they have a greater sense of agency,

or motivation to achieve their goals. However, other evidence suggests that high levels of hope and well-being can accompany greater amounts of adversity. A study by Keinan, Shrira, and Shmotkin (2012) examined the dose–response model of cumulative adversity in aging Israelis who had personally experienced trauma or had a traumatic experience in relation to others (e.g. witnessing or hearing about the traumatic experience of a loved one). The results showed that those who experienced a higher number of other-oriented traumatic events (increasing up to four) showed more depression symptoms but higher quality of life and greater combined hope/optimism than those who experienced comparatively fewer (or none) of these types of events. This relationship between other-oriented adversity, hope, and well-being in the face of depression symptoms may have implications for the potential for greater posttraumatic growth following a greater amount of traumatic experiences. In addition, the experience of certain types of trauma, such as other-oriented trauma, may have less of an impact on levels of hope.

Hope in the Context of Psychotherapy

Given the proposed contribution of hopelessness to the development of posttraumatic stress disorder and the role of hope as a protective factor, it follows that hope would play a role in psychotherapy for this disorder as well. As early as 1961, Frank argued that hope acts a "common factor" promoting change across psychotherapies. Snyder (2000) also proposed that hope is a common factor, or common mechanism of change across psychotherapies, which may universally teach patients to develop greater agency and pathways. Extensive research has established cognitive-behavioral therapy (CBT) as one of the most efficacious treatment modalities across psychopathologies including posttraumatic stress disorder (e.g., Hofmann, Asnaani, Vonk, Sawyer, & Fang, 2012). Cognitive processing therapy and prolonged exposure are the two most empirically supported forms of CBT for posttraumatic stress disorder and have been designated as empirically supported by the Society of Clinical Psychology as well as many other organizations.

Evidence suggests that CBT for posttraumatic stress disorder leads to increases in hope, as reflected by findings of increased levels in hope for patients who had received cognitive-processing therapy (Gilman, Schumm, & Chard, 2012), and reductions in hopelessness in veterans resulting from both cognitive-processing therapy and prolonged exposure (Gallagher & Resick, 2012). Hope also appears to increase as a result of other therapies for various trauma types, including supportive group therapy and trauma affect regulation for incarcerated women (Ford, Chang, Levine, & Zhang, 2013), relational supportive therapy for delinquent girls (Ford, Steinberg, Hawke, Levine, & Zhang, 2012), and nature adventure rehabilitation for veterans (Gelkopf, Hasson-Ohayon, Bikman, & Kravetz, 2013).

Research examining how changes in both hope and hopelessness influence change in symptoms of posttraumatic stress disorder provide preliminary evidence that hope may act as a mechanism of change in cognitive-processing therapy as well. A study by Gilman et al. (2012) found that cognitive-processing therapy resulted in robust changes in hope and symptoms of posttraumatic stress disorder. Higher levels of hope midtreatment were associated with decreases in symptoms of posttraumatic stress disorder, pointing toward a role of hope as a mechanism of change. Similarly, Gallagher and Resick (2012) investigated the potential role of hopelessness as a mechanism of change in both cognitive-processing therapy and prolonged exposure. They theorized that cognitive-processing therapy may have a greater effect on decreasing hopelessness because the treatment places a greater emphasis on the identification and modification of maladaptive cognitions than prolonged exposure, which focuses more on exposure exercises as a means of promoting recovery. Modifying cognitions such as appraisals about one's ability to control outcomes of trauma may in turn lead to an increase in hopeful cognitions. Large reductions in hopelessness were observed in both treatments, but, as expected, greater reductions in hopelessness were observed in cognitive-processing therapy versus prolonged exposure. In addition, a statistically significant indirect effect was found such that intraindividual changes in hopelessness mediated the effect of cognitive-processing therapy on intraindividual changes in posttraumatic stress disorder. The effect size for the impact of treatment on intraindividual changes in hopelessness was large, providing strong support that decreases in hopelessness, which may also reflect an increase in hope, influence reductions in symptoms of posttraumatic stress disorder. As a whole, preliminary evidence for the role of hope as a mechanism of change in CBT for posttraumatic stress disorder is promising. Additional studies across more treatment modalities will be needed to assess the degree to which hope acts as a common mechanism of change across psychotherapies for

posttraumatic stress disorder. In addition, because hope and hopelessness are separate but related constructs, both should be examined in relation to therapeutic change.

While hope may act as a mechanism of change within CBT for posttraumatic stress disorder, the primary emphasis of this therapy is not on hope. Cheavens, Feldman, Gum, Michael, and Snyder (2006) developed hope therapy to teach patients how to set goals, develop the pathways to achieve them, identify sources of motivation, monitor their progress, and modify their goals and pathways when needed. This therapy led to improvements in agency, meaning in life, self-esteem, and symptoms of anxiety and depression in a community sample. Similarly, Feldman and Deher (2012) created a 90-minute intervention to increase hope, which was associated with increases in hope, life purpose, and vocational calling among college students. Since higher levels of hope pretherapy is associated with better therapeutic outcomes, such a therapy could also be used in conjunction with or incorporated within CBT or other therapies for posttraumatic stress disorder (Irving et al., 2004).

Conclusion

Snyder's hope theory proposes that hopeful thinking provides the will and the ways to reach one's goals, as well as the ability to navigate around obstacles. Thus hopeful thinking should facilitate adjustment in response to trauma by reducing stress and promoting more adaptive responses to challenging circumstances, including more productive forms of coping. Preliminary evidence suggests that hope predicts symptoms of posttraumatic stress disorder in those who have experienced trauma. However, hope is closely related to other forms of positive thinking that promote resiliency, and future research should attempt to determine the degree to which hope uniquely predicts posttraumatic stress disorder above and beyond these factors. In addition, few studies have investigated the relationship between hope and coping in the aftermath of various types of traumatic experiences. More research is needed to determine how hope influences coping strategies in the aftermath of trauma and how the impact of hope on adaptive coping may in turn prevent the development of posttraumatic stress disorder. Hope also appears to facilitate personal growth in response to trauma, promoting functioning beyond simply enduring the challenges that arise in its wake. Hope is predictive of posttraumatic growth, though the degree to which hope facilitates growth may depend on the amount of distress experienced in response to the trauma and the type of trauma that occurred. Preliminary research also supports the idea that hope acts as a common factor across psychotherapies, and future studies should explore its promising role as mechanism of change. In light of this evidence, it will be important to investigate ways in which hope may be increased in the context of psychotherapy to optimize therapeutic outcomes. Overall, current findings provide promising evidence that hope plays an important role in both the prevention and the treatment of posttraumatic stress disorder and the promotion of positive outcomes in the aftermath of traumatic experiences.

Future Directions

• To what degree is hope a protective factor against posttraumatic stress and a conduit of posttraumatic growth compared to other types of positive thinking (e.g. optimism, self-efficacy), and how might different forms of positive thinking interact?

• Do certain demographic factors or cultural differences moderate the relationship between hope and the development of both posttraumatic stress and posttraumatic growth?

• What are the differential contributions of pathways and agency to resiliency and growth?

• Do pathways and agency thinking show different relationships with other resiliency factors related to hope, such as coping strategies?

• Is hope a mechanism of change within all empirically supported treatments for posttraumatic stress disorder, and, if so, which treatment components are responsible for producing therapeutic gains in hope?

References

Abramson, L. Y., Metalsky, G. I., & Alloy, L. B. (1989). Hopelessness depression: A theory-based subtype of depression. *Psychological Review*, *96*(2), 358–372. https://doi.org/10.1037/0033-295X.96.2.358

Affleck, G., & Tennen, H. (1996). Construing benefits from adversity: Adaptotional significance and dispositional underpinnings. *Journal of Personality*, *64*(4), 899–922. https://doi.org/10.1111/j.1467-6494.1996.tb00948.x

Ai, A. L., Hall, D., Pargament, K., & Tice, T. N. (2013). Posttraumatic growth in patients who survived cardiac surgery: The predictive and mediating roles of faith-based factors. *Journal of Behavioral Medicine*, *36*(2), 186–198. https://doi.org/10.1007/s10865-012-9412-6

Ai, A. L., Plummer, C., Kanno, H., Heo, G., Appel, H. B., Simon, C. E., & Spigner, C. (2011). Positive traits versus previous trauma: Racially different correlates with PTSD

symptoms among Hurricane Katrina-Rita volunteers. *Journal of Community Psychology*, *39*(4), 402–420. https://doi.org/10.1002/jcop.20442

Ai, A. L., Tice, T. N., Peterson, C., & Huang, B. (2005). Prayers, spiritual support, and positive attitudes in coping with the September 11 national crisis. *Journal of Personality*, *73*(3), 763–792. https://doi.org/10.1111/j.1467-6494.2005.00328.x

Ai, A. L., Tice, T. N., Whitsett, D. D., Ishisaka, T., & Chim, M. (2007). Posttraumatic symptoms and growth of Kosovar war refugees: The influence of hope and cognitive coping. *The Journal of Positive Psychology*, *2*(1), 55–65. https://doi.org/10.1080/17439760601069341

Baník, G., & Gajdošová, B. (2014). Positive changes following cancer: Posttraumatic growth in the context of other factors in patients with cancer. *Supportive Care in Cancer*, *22*(8), 2023–2029. https://doi.org/10.1007/s00520-014-2217-0

Bellizzi, K. M., & Blank, T. O. (2006). Predicting posttraumatic growth in breast cancer survivors. *Health Psychology*, *25*(1), 47–56. https://doi.org/10.1037/0278-6133.25.1.47

Besser, A., Weinberg, M., Zeigler-Hill, V., & Neria, Y. (2014). Acute symptoms of posttraumatic stress and dissociative experiences among female Israeli civilians exposed to war: The roles of intrapersonal and interpersonal sources of resilience: Resilience and exposure to trauma. *Journal of Clinical Psychology*, *70*(12), 1227–1239. https://doi.org/10.1002/jclp.22083

Cabral, C. M. (2010). *Psychological functioning following violence: An examination of posttraumatic growth, distress, and hope among interpersonal violence survivors*. Master's thesis. University of Toronto.

Chang, E. C. (1998). Hope, problem-solving ability, and coping in a college student population: Some implications for theory and practice. *Journal of Clinical Psychology*, *54*(7), 953–962. https://doi.org/10.1002/(SICI)1097-4679(199811)54:7<953:AID-JCLP9>3.0.CO;2-F

Chang, E. C., & Desimone, S. L. (2001). The influence of hope on appraisals, coping, and dysphoria: A test of hope theory. *Journal of Social and Clinical Psychology 20*(2), 117–129. http://doi.org/10.1521/jscp.20.2.117.22262

Ciarrochi, J., Parker, P., Kashdan, T. B., Heaven, P. C. L., & Barkus, E. (2015). Hope and emotional well-being: A six-year study to distinguish antecedents, correlates, and consequences. *The Journal of Positive Psychology*, *10*(6), 520–532. https://doi.org/10.1080/17439760.2015.1015154

Dahlsgaard, K. K., Beck, A. T., & Brown, G. K. (1998). Inadequate response to therapy as a predictor of suicide. *Suicide & Life-Threatening Behavior*, *28*(2), 197–204.

Dunkley, D. M., Lewkowski, M., Lee, I. A., Preacher, K. J., Zuroff, D. C., Berg, J.-L., . . . Westreich, R. (2016). Daily stress, coping, and negative and positive affect in depression: Complex trigger and maintenance patterns. *Behavior Therapy*, *48*(3), 349–365. https://doi.org/10.1016/j.beth.2016.06.001

Finklestein, M., Laufer, A., & Solomon, Z. (2012). Coping strategies of Ethiopian immigrants in Israel: Association with PTSD and dissociation. *Scandinavian Journal of Psychology*, *53*(6), 490–498. https://doi.org/10.1111/j.1467-9450.2012.00972.x

Foa, E. B., Steketee, G., & Rothbaum, B. O. (1989). Behavioral/cognitive conceptualizations of post-traumatic stress disorder. *Behavior Therapy*, *20*(2), 155–176. https://doi.org/10.1016/S0005-7894(89)80067-X

Folkman, S. (2010). Stress, coping, and hope. *Psycho-Oncology*, *19*(9), 901–908. https://doi.org/10.1002/pon.1836

Ford, J. D., Chang, R., Levine, J., & Zhang, W. (2013). Randomized clinical trial comparing affect regulation and supportive group therapies for victimization-related PTSD with incarcerated women. *Behavior Therapy*, *44*(2), 262–276. https://doi.org/10.1016/j.beth.2012.10.003

Ford, J. D., Steinberg, K. L., Hawke, J., Levine, J., & Zhang, W. (2012). Randomized trial comparison of emotion regulation and relational psychotherapies for PTSD with girls involved in delinquency. *Journal of Clinical Child and Adolescent Psychology*, *41*(1), 27–37. https://doi.org/10.1080/15374416.2012.632343

Fox, K. R., Franklin, J. C., Ribeiro, J. D., Kleiman, E. M., Bentley, K. H., & Nock, M. K. (2015). Meta-analysis of risk factors for nonsuicidal self-injury. *Clinical Psychology Review*, *42*, 156–167. https://doi.org/10.1016/j.cpr.2015.09.002

Frank, J. D. (1961). *Persuasion and healing: A comparative study of psychotherapy*. Oxford: Johns Hopkins University Press. Retrieved from http://ezproxy.lib.uh.edu/login?url=http://search.ebscohost.com/login.aspx?direct=true&db=psyh&AN=1962-03184-000&site=ehost-live

Gall, T. L. (2006). Spirituality and coping with life stress among adult survivors of childhood sexual abuse. *Child Abuse & Neglect*, *30*(7), 829–844. https://doi.org/10.1016/j.chiabu.2006.01.003

Gallagher, M. W., & Lopez, S. J. (2009). Positive expectancies and mental health: Identifying the unique contributions of hope and optimism. *The Journal Of Positive Psychology*, *4*(6), 548–556. doi:10.1080/17439760903157166

Gallagher, M. W., & Resick, P. A. (2012). Mechanisms of change in cognitive processing therapy and prolonged exposure therapy for PTSD: Preliminary evidence for the differential effects of hopelessness and habituation. *Cognitive Therapy and Research*, *36*(6), 750–755. https://doi.org/10.1007/s10608-011-9423-6

Geiger, K. A., & Kwon, P. (2010). Rumination and depressive symptoms: Evidence for the moderating role of hope. *Personality and Individual Differences*, *49*(5), 391–395. https://doi.org/10.1016/j.paid.2010.04.004

Gelkopf, M., Hasson-Ohayon, I., Bikman, M., & Kravetz, S. (2013). Nature adventure rehabilitation for combat-related posttraumatic chronic stress disorder: A randomized control trial. *Psychiatry Research*, *209*(3), 485–493. https://doi.org/10.1016/j.psychres.2013.01.026

Gerard, J. M., & Booth, M. Z. (2015). Family and school influences on adolescents' adjustment: The moderating role of youth hopefulness and aspirations for the future. *Journal of Adolescence*, *44*, 1–16. https://doi.org/10.1016/j.adolescence.2015.06.003

Germann, J. N., Leonard, D., Stuenzi, T. J., Pop, R. B., Stewart, S. M., & Leavey, P. J. (2015). Hoping is coping: A guiding theoretical framework for promoting coping and adjustment following pediatric cancer diagnosis. *Journal of Pediatric Psychology*, *40*(9), 846–855. https://doi.org/10.1093/jpepsy/jsv027

Gilman, R., Schumm, J. A., & Chard, K. M. (2012). Hope as a change mechanism in the treatment of posttraumatic stress disorder. *Psychological Trauma: Theory, Research, Practice, and Policy*, *4*(3), 270–277. https://doi.org/10.1037/a0024252

Glass, K., Flory, K., Hankin, B. L., Kloos, B., & Turecki, G. (2009). Are coping strategies, social support, and hope associated with psychological distress among Hurricane Katrina survivors? *Journal of Social and Clinical Psychology*, *28*(6), 779–795. https://doi.org/10.1521/jscp.2009.28.6.779

Grewal, P. K., & Porter, J. E. (2007). Hope theory: A framework for understanding suicidal action. *Death Studies*, *31*(2), 131–154. https://doi.org/10.1080/07481180601100491

Hamilton, J. L., Shapero, B. G., Stange, J. P., Hamlat, E. J., Abramson, L. Y., & Alloy, L. B. (2013). Emotional maltreatment, peer victimization, and depressive versus anxiety symptoms during adolescence: Hopelessness as a mediator. *Journal of Clinical Child & Adolescent Psychology*, *42*(3), 332–347. https://doi.org/10.1080/15374416.2013.777916

Hassija, C. M., Luterek, J. A., Naragon-Gainey, K., Moore, S. A., & Simpson, T. (2012). Impact of emotional approach coping and hope on PTSD and depression symptoms in a trauma exposed sample of veterans receiving outpatient VA mental health care services. *Anxiety, Stress & Coping*, *25*(5), 559–573. https://doi.org/10.1080/10615806.2011.621948

Ho, S. M. Y., & Lo, R. S. Y. (2011). Dispositional hope as a protective factor among medical emergency professionals: A preliminary investigation. *Traumatology*, *17*(4), 3–9. https://doi.org/10.1177/1534765611426786

Hofmann, S. G., Asnaani, A., Vonk, I. J. J., Sawyer, A. T., & Fang, A. (2012). The efficacy of cognitive behavioral therapy: A review of meta-analyses. *Cognitive Therapy and Research*, *36*(5), 427–440. https://doi.org/10.1007/s10608-012-9476-1

Holahan, C. J., Moos, R. H., & Schaefer, J. A. (1996). Coping, stress resistance, and growth: Conceptualizing adaptive functioning. In M. Zeidner, N. S. Endler, & M. Zeidner (Eds.), *Handbook of coping: Theory, research, applications* (pp. 24–43). Oxford: Wiley. Retrieved from http://ezproxy.lib.uh.edu/login?url=http://search.ebscohost.com/login.aspx?direct=true&db=psyh&AN=1996-97004-002&site=ehost-live

Huen, J. M. Y., Ip, B. Y. T., Ho, S. M. Y., & Yip, P. S. F. (2015). Hope and hopelessness: The role of hope in buffering the impact of hopelessness on suicidal ideation. *PLoS One*, *10*(6), e0130073. https://doi.org/10.1371/journal.pone.0130073

Hughes, I., Budd, R., & Greenaway, S. (1999). Coping with anxiety and panic: A factor analytic study. *British Journal of Clinical Psychology*, *38*(3), 295–304. https://doi.org/10.1348/014466599162872

Irving, L. M., Snyder, C. R., Cheavens, J., Gravel, L., Hanke, J., Hilberg, P., & Nelson, N. (2004). The relationships between hope and outcomes at the pretreatment, beginning, and later phases of psychotherapy. *Journal of Psychotherapy Integration*, *14*(4), 419–443. https://doi.org/10.1037/1053-0479.14.4.419

Irving, L. M., Telfer, L., & Blake, D. D. (1997). Hope, coping, and social support in combat-related posttraumatic stress disorder. *Journal of Traumatic Stress*, *10*(3), 465–479. https://doi.org/10.1023/A:1024897406135

Jacobsen, P. B., Sadler, I. J., Booth-Jones, M., Soety, E., Weitzner, M. A., & Fields, K. K. (2002). Predictors of posttraumatic stress disorder symptomatology following bone marrow transplantation for cancer. *Journal of Consulting and Clinical Psychology*, *70*(1), 235–240. https://doi.org/10.1037/0022-006X.70.1.235

Janoff-Bulman, R. (1992). *Shattered assumptions*. New York: Free Press.

Joseph, S. (1999). Attributional processes, coping and post-traumatic stress disorders. In W. Yule (Ed.), *Post-traumatic stress disorders: Concepts and therapy* (pp. 51–70). New York: Wiley. Retrieved from http://ezproxy.lib.uh.edu/

login?url=http://search.ebscohost.com/login.aspx?direct=tru
e&db=psyh&AN=1999-02527-003&site=ehost-live

Kaplan, J. S., Arnkoff, D. B., Glass, C. R., Tinsley, R., Geraci, M., Hernandez, E., . . . Carlson, P. J. (2012). Avoidant coping in panic disorder: a yohimbine biological challenge study. *Anxiety, Stress & Coping, 25*(4), 425–442. https://doi.org/10.1080/10615806.2011.609587

Kasler, J., Dahan, J., & Elias, M. J. (2008). The relationship between sense of hope, family support and post-traumatic stress disorder among children: The case of young victims of rocket attacks in Israel. *Vulnerable Children And Youth Studies, 3*(3), 182-191. http://doi:10.1080/17450120802282876

Kaye-Tzadok, A., & Davidson-Arad, B. (2016). Posttraumatic growth among women survivors of childhood sexual abuse: Its relation to cognitive strategies, posttraumatic symptoms, and resilience. *Psychological Trauma: Theory, Research, Practice, and Policy, 8*(5), 550–558. https://doi.org/10.1037/tra0000103

Keinan, G., Shrira, A., & Shmotkin, D. (2012). The association between cumulative adversity and mental health: Considering dose and primary focus of adversity. *Quality of Life Research, 21*(7), 1149–1158. https://doi.org/10.1007/s11136-011-0035-0

Kessler, R. C. (1995). Posttraumatic stress disorder in the National Comorbidity Survey. *Archives of General Psychiatry, 52*(12), 1048. https://doi.org/10.1001/archpsyc.1995.03950240066012

Khodarahimi, S. (2013). Hope and flourishing in an Iranian adults sample: Their contributions to the positive and negative emotions. *Applied Research in Quality of Life, 8*(3), 361–372. https://doi.org/10.1007/s11482-012-9192-8

Kilpatrick, D. G., Resnick, H. S., Milanak, M. E., Miller, M. W., Keyes, K. M., & Friedman, M. J. (2013). National estimates of exposure to traumatic events and PTSD prevalence using *DSM-IV* and *DSM-5* criteria: *DSM-5* PTSD prevalence. *Journal of Traumatic Stress, 26*(5), 537–547. https://doi.org/10.1002/jts.21848

Kortte, K. B., Gilbert, M., Gorman, P., & Wegener, S. T. (2010). Positive psychological variables in the prediction of life satisfaction after spinal cord injury. *Rehabilitation Psychology, 55*(1), 40–47. https://doi.org/10.1037/a0018624

Kroo, A., & Nagy, H. (2011). Posttraumatic growth among traumatized Somali refugees in Hungary. *Journal of Loss and Trauma, 16*(5), 440–458. https://doi.org/10.1080/15325024.2011.575705

Laschinger, H. K. S., & Nosko, A. (2015). Exposure to workplace bullying and post-traumatic stress disorder symptomology: The role of protective psychological resources. *Journal of Nursing Management, 23*(2), 252–262. https://doi.org/10.1111/jonm.12122

Lazarus, R. S., & Folkman, S. (1984). *Stress, appraisal, and coping.* New York: Springer.

Luthans, F., & Avolio, B. J. (2014). Brief summary of psychological capital and introduction to the special issue. *Journal of Leadership & Organizational Studies, 21*(2), 125–129. https://doi.org/10.1177/1548051813518073

MacLeod, A. K., Rose, G. S., & Williams, J. M. G. (1993). Components of hopelessness about the future in parasuicide. *Cognitive Therapy and Research, 17*(5), 441–455. https://doi.org/10.1007/BF01173056

Madan, S., & Pakenham, K. I. (2015). The stress-buffering effects of hope on changes in adjustment to caregiving in multiple sclerosis. *Journal of Health Psychology, 20*(9), 1207–1221. https://doi.org/10.1177/1359105313509868

Panagioti, M., Gooding, P. A., & Tarrier, N. (2012). Hopelessness, defeat, and entrapment in posttraumatic stress disorder: Their association with suicidal behavior and severity of depression. *The Journal of Nervous and Mental Disease, 200*(8), 676–683. https://doi.org/10.1097/NMD.0b013e3182613f91

Pérez, S., Galdón, M. J., Andreu, Y., Ibáñez, E., Durá, E., Conchado, A., & Cardeña, E. (2014). Posttraumatic stress symptoms in breast cancer patients: Temporal evolution, predictors, and mediation. *Journal of Traumatic Stress, 27*(2), 224–231. https://doi.org/10.1002/jts.21901

Rodríguez-Naranjo, C., & Caño, A. (2016). Daily stress and coping styles in adolescent hopelessness depression: Moderating effects of gender. *Personality and Individual Differences, 97*, 109–114. https://doi.org/10.1016/j.paid.2016.03.027

Roesch, S. C., Duangado, K. M., Vaughn, A. A., Aldridge, A. A., & Villodas, F. (2010). Dispositional hope and the propensity to cope: A daily diary assessment of minority adolescents. *Cultural Diversity And Ethnic Minority Psychology, 16*(2), 191-198. https://doi:10.1037/a0016114

Scher, C. D., & Resick, P. A. (2005). Hopelessness as a risk factor for post-traumatic stress disorder symptoms among interpersonal violence survivors. *Cognitive Behaviour Therapy, 34*(2), 99–107. https://doi.org/10.1080/16506070510008434

Shand, L. K., Cowlishaw, S., Brooker, J. E., Burney, S., & Ricciardelli, L. A. (2015). Correlates of post-traumatic stress symptoms and growth in cancer patients: A systematic review and meta-analysis. *Psycho-Oncology, 24*(6), 624–634. https://doi.org/10.1002/pon.3719

Snyder, C. R. (1996). To hope, to lose, and to hope again. *Journal of Personal and Interpersonal Loss, 1*(1), 1–16. https://doi.org/10.1080/15325029608415455

Snyder, C. R. (1999). Hope, goal-blocking thoughts, and test-related anxieties. *Psychological Reports, 84*(1), 206. https://doi.org/10.2466/PR0.84.1.206-208

Snyder, C. R. (2000). The past and possible futures of hope. *Journal of Social and Clinical Psychology, 19*(1), 11–28. https://doi.org/10.1521/jscp.2000.19.1.11

Snyder, C. R. (2002). Hope theory: Rainbows in the mind. *Psychological Inquiry, 13*(4), 249–275. https://doi.org/10.1207/S15327965PLI1304_01

Snyder, C. R., Harris, C., Anderson, J. R., Holleran, S. A., Irving, L. M., . . . Harney, P. (1991). The will and the ways: Development and validation of an individual-differences measure of hope. *Journal of Personality and Social Psychology, 60*(4), 570–585. https://doi.org/10.1037/0022-3514.60.4.570

Snyder, C. R., Illardi, S., Michael, S. T., & Cheavens, J. (2000). Hope theory: Updating a common proves for psychological Change. In C. R. Snyder & R. E. Ingram (Eds.), *Handbook of psychological change: Psychotherapy processes & practices for the 21st Century* (pp. 128–153). Hoboken, NJ, US: John Wiley & Sons Inc. Retrieved from http://ezproxy.lib.uh.edu/login?url=http://search.ebscohost.com/login.aspx?direct=tru e&db=psyh&AN=2001-00353-007&site=ehost-live

Spokas, M., Wenzel, A., Stirman, S. W., Brown, G. K., & Beck, A. T. (2009). Suicide risk factors and mediators between childhood sexual abuse and suicide ideation among male and female suicide attempters. *Journal of Traumatic Stress, 22*(5), 467–470. https://doi.org/10.1002/jts.20438

Stermac, L., Cabral, C. M., Clarke, A. K., & Toner, B. (2014). Mediators of posttraumatic mental health in sexual assault survivors. *Journal of Aggression, Maltreatment*

& *Trauma, 23*(3), 301–317. https://doi.org/10.1080/10926771.2014.881948

Stoyles, G., Chadwick, A., & Caputi, P. (2015). Purpose in life and well-being: The relationship between purpose in life, hope, coping, and inward sensitivity among first-year university students. *Journal of Spirituality in Mental Health, 17*(2), 119–134. https://doi.org/10.1080/19349637.2015.985558

Subandi, M. A., Achmad, T., Kurniati, H., & Febri, R. (2014). Spirituality, gratitude, hope and post-traumatic growth among the survivors of the 2010 eruption of Mount Merapi in Java, Indonesia. *Australasian Journal of Disaster and Trauma Studies, 18*(1), 19–26.

Tedeschi, R. G., & Calhoun, L. G. (1996). The Posttraumatic Growth Inventory: Measuring the positive legacy of trauma. *Journal of Traumatic Stress, 9*(3), 455–471. https://doi.org/10.1002/jts.2490090305

Tedeschi, R. G., & Calhoun, L. G. (2004). Target article: Posttraumatic growth: Conceptual foundations and empirical evidence. *Psychological Inquiry, 15*(1), 1–18. https://doi.org/10.1207/s15327965pli1501_01

Tiet, Q. Q., Rosen, C., Cavella, S., Moos, R. H., Finney, J. W., & Yesavage, J. (2006). Coping, symptoms, and functioning outcomes of patients with posttraumatic stress disorder. *Journal of Traumatic Stress, 19*(6), 799–811. https://doi.org/10.1002/jts.20185

Weinberg, M., Besser, A., Zeigler-Hill, V., & Neria, Y. (2016). Bidirectional associations between hope, optimism and social support, and trauma-related symptoms among survivors of terrorism and their spouses. *Journal of Research in Personality, 62*, 29–38. https://doi.org/10.1016/j.jrp.2016.03.002

Yuen, A. N. Y., Ho, S. M. Y., & Chan, C. K. Y. (2014). The mediating roles of cancer-related rumination in the relationship between dispositional hope and psychological outcomes among childhood cancer survivors: Dispositional hope, rumination and cancer adjustment. *Psycho-Oncology, 23*(4), 412–419. https://doi.org/10.1002/pon.3433

Zhai, J., Huang, Y., Gao, X., Jiang, H., & Xu, J. (2014). Posttrauma growth in a mainland Chinese population with chronic skin disease. *International Journal of Dermatology, 53*(4), 450–457. https://doi.org/10.1111/j.1365-4632.2012.05734.x

Hope and Coping in Individuals with Specific Learning Disorder

Michal Al-Yagon *and* Malka Margalit

Abstract

This chapter reviews and integrates empirical findings regarding hope as a major personal resource among individuals with specific learning disorder (SLD). First, it describes the *Diagnostic and Statistical Manual of Mental Disorders* (fifth edition; DSM-5) diagnostic criteria for SLD and briefly illustrates the major difficulties that individuals with SLD may experience in the academic, social, emotional, and behavioral domains. Next, it presents an overview of the empirical literature regarding hope as reported by children and adolescents with SLD in different age groups and its relations with additional personal resources such as the sense of coherence and coping with age-appropriate academic and social challenges. Possible factors that may contribute to the lower resources found in SLD and their implications are explored, as well as future research directions and interventional implications.

Key Words: specific learning disorder, SLD, hope, personal resources, sense of coherence, coping, DSM-5

This chapter reviews and integrates the research findings regarding manifestations of hope as a major personal resource among children and youth with specific learning disorder (SLD). Hope is defined as "the perceived capability to derive pathways to desired goals, and motivate oneself via agency thinking to use those pathways" (Snyder, 2002, p. 249). This is a cognitive-motivational construct that reflects individuals' psychological strength and personal resources (e.g., Margalit, 2014; Snyder, 2000). Of particular importance, whereas most studies on individuals with SLD focus on their past experiences and current struggles with academic demands and social adjustment, the hope construct enables investigation of awareness about the future, thus complementing the time perspective paradigm. Time perspective describes one's subjective orientation toward the importance of the present, past, and future in one's life (King & Gaerlan, 2015), which may be a significant factor in shaping current behavior (Guthrie, Butler, Lessl, Ochi, & Ward, 2014). A present- or past-oriented perspective of time focuses one's thoughts and fears on

recent, immediate, or past experiences. A future-oriented perspective of time favors future considerations and motivation to invest today toward the prospect of fulfilling future goals (Zimbardo & Boyd, 1999). Thus research has reported that those adolescents who are oriented toward the future tend to academically outperform their peers (Adelabu, 2008). Our goal is to present research on the future orientation reflected by hope, as reported by individuals with SLD who may be at risk for maladjustment.

In this chapter, we first describe the SLD diagnostic criteria from the *Diagnostic and Statistical Manual of Mental Disorders* (fifth edition [DSM-5]; American Psychiatric Association, 2013) and briefly illustrate the major difficulties that youth with SLD may experience in the academic, social, emotional, and behavioral domains. Next, we present an overview of the empirical literature regarding hope among children and adolescents with SLD. Possible explanations for the lower personal resources found in the SLD population compared to their typically developing peers are proposed. We end with discussions of future research directions and implications for intervention.

Individuals with SLD: Prevalence, Diagnostic Criteria, and General Features

SLD is one of the most common disorders in school-age children, with 5% to 15% prevalence rates across different languages and cultures (DSM-5, American Psychiatric Association, 2013). Four major criteria for SLD are presented in the DSM-5:

1. Difficulties in learning and using academic skills, including word reading, reading comprehension, spelling, written expression, and various mathematic aspects.

2. The affected academic skills are substantially and quantifiably below those expected for the individual's chronological age, and they cause significant interference with academic or occupational performance or with activities of daily living.

3. The learning difficulties began during the school years but may not have become fully manifested until the demands for those affected academic skills have exceeded the individual's limited capacities.

4. The learning difficulties are not better accounted for by the existence of alternative disabilities.

Moreover, as suggested by the DSM-5, SLD commonly co-occurs with other neurodevelopmental disorders such as attention deficit hyperactivity disorder (ADHD) or developmental coordination disorder, or it may co-occur with other mental disorders such as anxiety or depressive disorders. For example, as reported by prior studies, the comorbidity of SLD and ADHD is relatively high, with an estimated 31% to 45% of youngsters with ADHD also exhibiting SLD and vice versa (DuPaul, Gormley, & Laracy, 2013; Sexton, Gelhorn, Bell, & Classi, 2012). Individuals with SLD are also noted for their difficulties in executive functions (Horowitz-Kraus, 2014) and emotion regulation (Bauminger & Kimhi-Kind, 2008). "Executive functioning" is an umbrella term describing distinct cognitive processes carried out by the prefrontal cortex, including planning, working memory, attention, inhibition, self-monitoring, self-regulation, and initiation (Goldstein, Naglieri, Princiotta, & Otero, 2014). Barkley (2011) has defined executive functions as "a self-directed set of actions intended to alter a delayed outcome" (p. 11), and, as such, he has linked executive functioning to goal pursuit, which involves self-regulation, including management of emotions, problem-solving, and analysis, as well as the development of behavioral strategies.

Along with documenting the effects of SLD difficulties on academic and cognitive functioning (Kudo, Lussier, & Swanson, 2015), studies have also highlighted diverse difficulties in the social, emotional, and behavioral domains experienced by individuals with SLD (e.g., Al-Yagon & Margalit, 2013; Cook, Li, & Heinrich, 2015; Estell et al., 2008; Nelson & Harwood, 2011; Swanson, Harris, & Graham, 2013). Data from these studies pinpointed various intrapersonal and interpersonal difficulties.

For example, within the intrapersonal domain, research reported that youngsters with SLD experienced higher levels of depression, anxiety, loneliness, and withdrawal compared to their non-SLD peers (e.g., Nelson & Harwood, 2011; Wiener & Schneider, 2002). Children and adolescents with SLD also more frequently manifested lower levels of various self-concept measures and higher levels of stress compared to their non-SLD peers (Capozzi et al., 2008; Feurer & Andrews, 2009).

In the interpersonal realm, studies evidenced these youngsters' poorer social skills, higher peer rejection, and lower peer acceptance compared to their non-SLD counterparts (Estell et al., 2008). Likewise, compared to their non-SLD peers, children and adolescents with SLD were less likely to report secure attachment with mothers and fathers (Al-Yagon, 2011; Murray & Greenberg, 2001) or to appraise teachers as a secure base (Al-Yagon & Mikulincer, 2004b; Murray & Greenberg, 2006). Findings on adolescents with SLD also underscore their greater vulnerability to developing externalizing behaviors like aggression and antisocial conduct than typically developing adolescents (e.g., Al-Yagon, 2015; Capozzi et al., 2008; McNamara, Vervaeke, & Willoughby, 2008).

In line with the resilience construct, which explores individuals' strengths in addition to their difficulties (e.g., Luthar & Cicchetti, 2000; Masten, 2014, 2015), studies have also examined successful youngsters with SLD (Margalit, 2004, 2006). For example, in exploring elementary-school children with and without SLD, Al-Yagon and Mikulincer (2004a) identified a substantial subgroup of children with SLD (13%) who revealed a high level of socioemotional adjustment. This subgroup of children with SLD demonstrated difficulties that remained isolated to the academic domain, and they reported low levels of loneliness and high coping resources.

Furthermore, studies have also investigated the possible role of diverse protective factors that may contribute to well-adjusted functioning in youngsters with SLD (e.g., Margalit & Idan, 2004). These studies focused attention on the role of protective variables at different levels such as the individual, family, and community levels (e.g., Al-Yagon, 2016; Murray & Greenberg, 2001), and hope may be considered such a protective factor.

Hope and Individuals with SLD

Considering the ongoing difficulties experienced by children and adolescents with SLD, it is not surprising that they often report lower appraisals of hope compared to their non-SLD peers in various age groups, such as 8- to 11-year-olds in a study of 205 mother–child dyads (e.g., Al-Yagon, 2010), 9- to 12-year-olds in a large sample ($n = 1,024$) from 28 elementary schools (Sharabi & Margalit, 2014), and 15- to 18-year-old adolescents ($n = 856$; Idan & Margalit, 2014). At the same time, in every sample of children and adolescents with SLD, a unique resilient subgroup could be identified who reported high levels of hope (Margalit, 2012).

As a cognitive-motivational construct reflecting psychological strength (e.g., Gallagher & Lopez, 2009), hope involves two major components (Snyder, 2002): *pathway thinking* and *agency thinking*. *Pathway thinking* concerns one's perceived capacity to generate the workable routes necessary for attaining future goals, whereas *agency thinking* is the motivational component that ensures that a person will be able to initiate and sustain the effort necessary to follow movement along his or her chosen pathways to achieve desired goals. *Goals* provide the targets of mental action sequences; they can be short or long term and may vary significantly with respect to their importance and probability of attainment (Snyder, 2000).

As advocated by Valle, Huebner, and Suldo (2006), three major findings support the claim that the cognitive-motivational construct of hope may be considered a psychological strength. First, hope scores were found to predict adolescent adjustment measures. Second, hope scores showed moderate test–retest reliability over a one-year period, therefore demonstrating some trait-like properties. Third, hope levels were found to function as a moderator of the relationship between stressful or negative life events and mental health outcomes.

Studies over recent decades have underscored the importance of hope among typically developing children, adolescents, and adults. Previous studies indicated that feelings of hope were associated with a variety of adjustment measures, including the ability to cope with stressful situations (e.g., Parveen & James, 2007; Snyder, 2002). Higher hope scores in children and adolescents with typical development were linked with higher rates of positive social interactions, self-esteem, optimism, global life satisfaction, and academic achievement and with lower rates of internalizing and externalizing behavior difficulties (e.g., Levi, Einav, Ziv, Raskind, & Margalit, 2013; Marques, Lopez, Fontaine, Coimbra, & Mitchell, 2015). Similarly, higher hope scores in adults with typical development yielded associations with increased self-esteem and well-being and decreased levels of depression and externalizing behavior (see Snyder [2002] for a review).

In exploring individuals with SLD, Al-Yagon (2007) reported that, as a group, children ages 8 to 12 years with SLD revealed lower perceptions of hope than their typically developing peers. These significant differences emerged in both subscales of the Children's Hope Scale (Snyder et al., 1997): the Agency subscale (goal-directed energy), and the Pathways subscale (planning to meet goals). Significantly lower hope scores also emerged among additional studies of elementary school–age children with SLD who were compared to their non-SLD peers (Al-Yagon, 2010).

These studies on elementary-school ages with SLD showed significant associations between hope and a variety of adjustment measures such as social distress in terms of loneliness and self-confidence in terms of sense of coherence (SOC; see later elaboration of this personal resource). Thus results indicated that school-age children with highly hopeful thinking, as manifested by high agency thinking (e.g., "I meet the goals that I set for myself") and high pathway thinking (e.g., "I can think of many ways to get the things in life that are important to me"), reported lower feelings of loneliness and higher SOC levels than children who manifested less hopeful thinking.

Likewise, significant group differences also emerged in a sample of elementary school–age children with comorbid SLD and ADHD, as compared to their typically developing peers (Al-Yagon, 2009). Results indicated that school-age children diagnosed with SLD as well as ADHD reported lower feelings of hope and lower levels of academic effort compared to their typically developing counterparts. "Effort" referred to youngsters' level of investment, intensity, and persistence in academic task accomplishment (Meltzer et al., 2004).

The study of adolescents with SLD has also emphasized the important role of hopeful thinking in explaining a variety of adjustment measures such as academic achievements and effort engagement (Lackaye & Margalit, 2006). Teachers and parents often attribute students' success and failure to effort investment. For example, in Lackaye and Margalit's study of 571 seventh-graders with and without SLD, students with SLD reported lower levels of hope and less effort investment than typical students who succeeded in their studies. The examination of the relations between hope and effort revealed that hope predicted academic engagement for adolescents with SLD as well as for their peers.

Differences on hope also emerged in a sample of 856 adolescents with and without SLD ages 16 to 18 years, attending Grades 10 to 12 in seven high schools (Idan & Margalit, 2014). Results of this study indicated that adolescents with SLD reported lower hope than their peers without SLD. The significance of these results was further emphasized by the finding that hope played a mediating role between risk and protective factors and academic self-efficacy. Thus adolescents seemed to need hopeful thoughts to positively reinforce their goal-pursuit process and to increase their levels of self-efficacy for attaining desired goals. These outcomes also underlined the significance of hope in promoting students' motivation, general academic self-efficacy, as well as subject-specific self-efficacy, effort, and learning achievements.

Furthermore, these findings showed that adolescent girls in the SLD group reported the highest levels of hope, compared to the other girls and boys from both groups. These results may confirm prior findings (Crosnoe, Riegle-Crumb, & Muller, 2007) arguing that girls diagnosed with SLD tend to attribute their poor academic performance to external explanations rather than to their own internal aptitudes, which may protect their academic self-competence from the negative evaluations of others, possibly leading to higher scores.

A recent study on college students emphasized the important role of hope as a mediator for young adults with SLD (Feldman, Davidson, Ben-Naim, Maza, & Margalit, 2016). In this study, hope levels mediated the relations between SLD and adjustment to academic demands. Interestingly, when these students first entered college, the SLD directly predicted their levels of academic self-efficacy, loneliness, and hope. However, after a month of academic studies, the students' levels of hope were found to mediate the contribution of SLD to their academic

self-efficacy and loneliness, thereby demonstrating that those students with SLD who reported higher levels of hope experienced reduced levels of loneliness and enhanced academic self-efficacy.

In summary, this review demonstrated that, as a group, children and adolescents with SLD tend to manifest lower levels of hopeful thinking than their non-SLD peers. The roots of these differences can be attributed to various sources: personal, reflecting the unique characteristic of the disorder; familial, revealing the impact of the SLD on families; social, suggesting the role of social rejection and alienation; and educational, indicating the outcomes of academic frustrations.

Factors Related to Lower Hope in SLD

Overall, there is a paucity of research empirically examining possible antecedents or predictors of hopefulness, despite the individual differences found in hope levels. Some researchers have discussed possible variables related to such individual differences in typical development (e.g., Bernardo, 2010; Du, Bernardo, & Yeung, 2015). For example, Bernardo recently suggested extending hope theory by adding the locus-of-hope dimension, referring to whether the components of trait hope involve internal or external agents and internally or externally generated pathways. "Internal locus of trait hope" refers to the individual as the resource and the agent of goal-attainment cognitions, whereas "external locus of trait hope" refers to significant others and external forces as the resources and agents of goal-attainment cognitions.

These internal and external factors can be considered primary and secondary factors that may propose explanations for the lower levels of hope found among individuals with SLD. Although the differentiation between primary factors and secondary factors should be treated with caution in line with dynamic transactional developmental models (Sameroff & Mackenzie, 2003) that emphasize the importance of the dynamic ongoing interactions among developmental processes, we propose these distinctions here for conceptual purposes.

Primary (Internal) Factors
NEUROLOGICAL FACTORS AND ONGOING DIFFICULTIES

SLD is defined by individuals' difficulties in the complex set of executive functions associated with the metacognitive capacities that allow one to perceive stimuli in one's environment, respond adaptively, flexibly change direction, anticipate future goals, consider consequences, and respond in an integrated way (Horowitz-Kraus, 2014; Moura, Simões, & Pereira, 2015). Although children and adults with SLD and ADHD have heterogeneous behavioral and neuropsychological profiles, they are noted for their longer processing speed and lower abilities in inhibiting, controlling, shifting, and dynamically regulating their cognitive processing and behavior, compared to typically developing peers. Indeed, when individuals forecast and plan the future, they are mindful of their past. They rely on prior experiences to make the future planning and decisions (Morewedge, Gilbert, & Wilson, 2005). Hence, it is not surprising that such individuals—whose diagnosed disorder is defined by significant problems in cognitive functioning such as attention, memory, planning, or impulsiveness—may also disclose lower abilities in anticipating goals as well as in planning pathways and shifting to alternative pathways in order to reach goals (Roberts, Martel, & Nigg, 2013). Variables such as information-processing disorders and performance deficits, which affect individuals academic and social skills (see Al-Yagon & Margalit [2013] for a review), may in turn impair the development of their hopeful thinking.

COPING RESOURCES: SENSE OF COHERENCE

In addition, several studies have focused attention on the lower internal personal resources revealed among individuals with SLD and ADHD in terms of their SOC, which has been shown to predict hope levels in several studies (Margalit, 2012). The term SOC was coined by Antonovsky (1979, 1987) and comprises the core variable within his health promotion model, which he termed salutogenesis in contrast to pathogenesis. Overall, the salutogenic model suggests a complementary approach to the pathological model of human functioning and investigates individuals' strategies and coping resources in dealing with stressors (Antonovsky & Sagy, 1986). The salutogenic construct presents a dynamic model arguing that individuals are constantly moving along a continuum characterized by the endpoints of health ease and health dis-ease (Antonovsky, 1987). Antonovsky defined the SOC as a global orientation that expresses the extent to which one has a pervasive, enduring, though dynamic feeling of confidence that (a) the stimuli deriving from one's internal and external environments are structured, predictable, and explicable; (b) resources are available to meet the demands posed by these stimuli; and (c) these demands are challenges worthy of investment and engagement.

The SOC develops gradually through the interactions between children and their environments, and it becomes a stable trait in young adulthood, which can be significantly altered only by traumatic life exposure (Antonovsky, 1987). There is wide agreement that SOC can be regarded as a personal strength that holds implications for perception of and coping with various types of stressful situations (e.g., Hart, Wilson, & Hittner, 2006; Marsh, Clinkinbeard, Thomas, & Evans, 2007). For instance, research reported that individuals with high levels of SOC are less likely to perceive stressful situations as threatening and anxiety provoking and often appraise such situations as manageable challenges. It is not surprising that youngsters with SLD revealed lower SOC levels compared to their non-SLD peers (Al-Yagon & Mikulincer, 2004b). For example, in samples of children with SLD versus their typically developing peers attending the same public elementary schools, Al-Yagon (2007, 2014) consistently reported significant group differences in SOC levels. These studies demonstrated that, from the beginning of their school years, children with SLD as a group reported lower SOC than their peers with typical development. Similar findings emerged for children with comorbid SLD and ADHD (Al-Yagon, 2009) as well as for early adolescents with SLD in Grade 7 of junior high school (Lackaye & Margalit, 2006) and in later adolescence among high school students with SLD in Grades 10 to 12 (Idan & Margalit, 2014). Of particular importance, several of these studies also highlighted the role of SOC in understanding differences in these at-risk youngsters' socioemotional and behavioral functioning. For instance, Al-Yagon (2011) identified the cumulative vulnerability/protection models of individual-level factors and family-level factors as explaining differences in socioemotional and behavioral adjustment among children with SLD or typical development, ages 8 to 12. Structural equation modeling analysis revealed the significant contribution of children's SOC in explaining their levels of hope and loneliness. Thus children with higher SOC expressed higher levels of hope as well as decreased loneliness compared to children with lower SOC. Furthermore, in exploring adolescents in high school ($n = 327$ with SLD, $n = 529$ with typical development), Idan and Margalit reported a significant contribution of adolescents' SOC levels in predicting their levels of hopeful thinking.

INTERNAL WORKING MODELS OF ATTACHMENT

Research on SLD has suggested the possible importance of youngsters' patterns of attachment to significant others in explaining levels of hope (e.g., Al-Yagon, 2014). Over the past few decades, researchers have considered Bowlby's (1973, 1969/1982) attachment theory as a highly relevant framework for investigating developmental outcomes and differences in adjustment across the lifespan (Cassidy & Shaver, 2008; Mikulincer & Shaver, 2007). Researchers have argued that individuals' stable internal working models of attachment representations (i.e., secure, avoidant, or anxious) lead to interpretive filters that guide their beliefs and expectations about the social world, including peers and teachers. Prior studies had indicated that, compared to their non-SLD peers, children and adolescents with SLD were less likely to experience secure attachment with significant others (Al-Yagon, 2012; Al-Yagon & Mikulincer, 2004a, 2004b; Murray & Greenberg, 2006).

Specifically, research demonstrated that higher secure-attachment scores with mothers (Al-Yagon, 2007) or with fathers (Al-Yagon, 2014) were associated with the children's higher levels of hopeful thinking. For example, in the case of attachment to fathers, those children with SLD who viewed themselves as more securely attached to the father reported a higher level of hope, which refers to higher pathway thinking (i.e., the perceived capacity to generate strategies for attaining goals) and higher agency thinking (i.e., perceptions involving one's capacity to initiate and sustain movement along the chosen pathways), compared to those children with SLD who viewed themselves as less securely attached to the father.

In addition, outcomes from Al-Yagon's (2007) study showed that the group of children with SLD seemed more vulnerable to the mother's level of avoidant attachment style than the non-SLD group. Only in the group of children with SLD did a high maternal score on attachment avoidance—indicating that the mother frequently distrusted her relationship partner's goodwill or maintained emotional distance from significant others—seem to place her child with SLD at risk for experiencing lower feelings of hope.

Together, these results on attachment expand Snyder's (2002) argument regarding the association between children's attachment relations and hope. According to Snyder, attachment to the caregiver is crucial for learning goal-directed thinking. Moreover, he argued that goal-directed hopeful actions emerge in the context of other people. However, beyond the association found between these two variables, these studies also suggest the contribution of the mother's own attachment relations to her child's feelings of hope.

Secondary (External) Factors
PARENTS' EMOTIONAL AND COPING RESOURCES

Outcomes of prior studies suggested the possible role of parents' emotional and coping resources as possible external factors in explaining their children's hopeful thinking. In general, having a child with SLD has a pronounced impact on the parents, especially on their quality of life (Ginieri-Coccossis et al., 2013). Of particular importance, several previous studies confirmed that lower emotional and coping resources were found among parents of children with SLD than among parents of children with typical development (e.g., see Al-Yagon & Margalit [2012] for a review). Specifically, research pinpointed higher levels of fathers and mothers' stress, more conflicts regarding parenting styles, difficulties in interacting with the school, and mixed effects on siblings (e.g., Antshel & Joseph, 2006; Dyson, 2003, 2010). Parents must develop meaningful solutions to meet their children's increased needs for academic help and support, and many fathers and mothers experience frustrations, fatigue, anxiety, anger, and loneliness (Margalit, Raskind, Higgins, & Russo-Netzer, 2010). These difficulties are exacerbated by conflicts with schools and by parents' frequent beliefs that teachers do not understand their child with SLD and do not provide the requested remedial programs. Unsurprisingly, the outcomes of these stressors and beliefs are manifested in parental resources measures, which are a predictor of children's hope levels.

With regard to parents' emotion resource, Al-Yagon (2010) reported that mothers' negative affect explained individual differences in children's level of hope among 8- to 11-year-olds with SLD. These results resemble prior research on children with typical development, which previously underscored the impact of mothers' anxious or depressed mood on children's adjustment, even in the absence of serious maternal psychopathology (Campbell, 2003). The greater number of significant connections (direct paths) found in Al-Yagon's study between maternal affect and children's adjustment (including hope) among the SLD group versus the non-SLD group suggests that the children with SLD may be more vulnerable to subtleties in maternal emotional expression than their typical counterparts, as found elsewhere for sensitivity to differences in parental style (e.g., Belsky & Barends, 2002; Greenberg, Speltz, DeKlyen, & Jones, 2001).

Another suggested secondary factor associated with lower hope among high-risk populations is the supportive role of family and peer resources such as higher levels of perceived social support and family cohesion (e.g., Bernardo, 2010; Parker et al., 2015). As proposed by these studies, when high-hope individuals encounter stressors, they tend to rely on their family and friends for help and support (Merkas & Brajsa-Zganec, 2011). Indeed, all mothers need support and help with childrearing, but mothers of children with SLD may have more extensive needs for support due to their day-by-day struggles to meet the challenging needs of their child with SLD without neglecting the other family members and while trying to maintain resilience in the face of the higher drain on their own emotional and coping resources. Thus the important question that Luthar and Ciciolla (2015) asked about mothers of typically developing children— "Who mothers mommy?" (p. 1812)—may hold special relevance for mothers of children with SLD. In their study, Idan and Margalit (2014) specified the positive contribution of stronger family cohesion and the negative contribution of adolescents' higher loneliness as predicting adolescents' with SLD higher hope.

An additional contributing factor to the lower hope levels in individuals with SLD may be attributed to their prolonged academic struggles and sometimes disharmonious relations with teachers. Individuals with SLD are defined by their ongoing difficulties in reading, writing, and mathematics. They often experience frustrations and disappointments at school and among friends. They may feel different and alienated from typical children who perform well academically. Sometimes their teachers feel unprepared to meet their pronounced learning difficulties. In line with hope theory, teachers often report lower levels of hope, reduced self-efficacy, and less competence in providing these students with meaningful assistance (Levi et al., 2013). The continuous academic struggles of individuals with SLD to meet age-appropriate demands, throughout various developmental stages, may result in emotional scars and contribute to a reduced ability to develop sufficient pathway thinking (i.e., strategies for attaining goals) and agency thinking (i.e., capacity to initiate and sustain movement along the chosen pathways).

In conclusion, primary and secondary factors can be identified that may potentially explain the lower hope levels found among many children and adolescents with SLD. Yet it should be accentuated that many individuals with SLD reveal hope levels that do not significantly differ from those of their typically developing peers.

Conclusion

This chapter has presented research findings regarding hope as a major personal resource (Snyder, 2000) among youngsters with SLD. Data collected from empirical studies pinpointed several major findings and raised some important questions for future research. First, the current review indicated that, by and large, youngsters with SLD often manifest lower levels of hope than their non-SLD peers. Indeed, our review showed growing recent awareness about (a) the importance of hope in explaining individuals' adjustment measures, (b) this construct's role as a mediator of the relationship between stressors and mental health outcomes, and (c) the vulnerability of individuals with SLD to developing low levels of hope. Nonetheless, despite these recent research trends, surprisingly few studies to date have investigated the possible risk and protective factors that may contribute to the hopeful thinking and coping resources of children and adolescents with SLD. More studies are needed to deepen understanding of the dynamic interactional impacts of these factors. Research is also vital to help design effective psychoeducational interventions targeting individual variation in such dynamic interactions within subgroups of SLD and of comorbid SLD and ADHD.

Remarkably few studies have documented sex differences in individuals' sense of hope, and these have focused on adolescents and young adults. For example, Idan and Margalit (2014) reported that girls with SLD in high school demonstrated higher levels of hope compared to boys with SLD, to girls without SLD, and to boys without SLD. In addition, Feldman et al. (2016) showed the direct contribution of sex to college students' levels of hope. Future researchers may wish to examine females versus males with and without SLD in different age groups and may do well to include interviews and observations to further clarify the distinctions of hope characteristics between the sexes.

Another avenue needing further research is related to the developmental aspects of hope among individuals with SLD. According to Snyder's (2002) theory, hope is conceptualized as relatively enduring, cross-situational, subjective appraisals of goal-related capabilities. Yet research on young adults and adults with SLD or with comorbid SLD and

ADHD is rare, calling for future studies to explore the longevity of the differences found between SLD and non-SLD groups while tracing developmental trajectories. Specifically, the possible contribution of these young adults' hope resources may elucidate academic struggles during secondary education and in the transition to college. Furthermore, longitudinal follow-up studies on the impact of SLD as related to hopeful thinking should focus on different developmental stages in young adulthood and adulthood, extending to domains such as career plans and occupational performance as well as examining how the SLD is expressed in marital satisfaction, parenting styles, and family adjustment. Such extensions of hope research may provide much-needed understanding concerning the dynamic impact of hope within different roles, ages, and life contexts.

The critical role played by families and schools in nurturing hope for individuals with SLD was reflected in studies that examined attachment relations with a parent or a teacher in these systems (Al-Yagon, 2016). Future studies may use the hope construct to guide policymaking in formulating responsive familial and educational systems that will enhance and support the development of hopeful thinking in this population. Future programs should aspire to extend educators' and parents' abilities to identify the strengths of individuals with SLD without ignoring their difficulties and to support their hopeful thinking by providing meaningful assistance. In line with Shade's (2006) recommendation, the development of a community of hope and the adoption of the hope pedagogy in schools will provide children with appropriate resources to actively respond to circumstances and challenges such as SLD that impede effective educational processes. Such hopeful communities may foster the development of habitually hopeful thinking, which may help children, adolescents, and young adults with SLD to identify meaningful goals, plan pathways, and invest effort within supportive, hopeful systems.

With regard to hope-promoting interventions, the value of hope theory has been further demonstrated in designing effective intervention plans for different groups. Snyder (2002) argued that changes in levels of hope can occur over time through sustained interventions, such as counseling and educational processes. Although hope-promoting interventions with non-SLD groups have been widely explored (e.g., Bartholomew, Scheel, & Cole, 2015; Cheavens, Feldman, Gum, Michael, &

Snyder, 2006; Feldman & Dreher, 2012), only few studies have reported on such interventions among children and adolescents with SLD. For example, Kopelman-Rubin et al.'s (2013) manual-based "I Can Succeed" psychological intervention was administered to adolescents (ages 11–15 years) in an outpatient child and adolescent psychiatric department for adolescents with SLD. This intervention consists of short-term and follow-up phases over 18 months, focusing on skills and hopeful thinking that may strengthen resilience in three major areas: intrapersonal skills, interpersonal skills, and school/community skills. Pre–post comparisons showed significant decreases in adolescents' psychopathology and significant improvements in hope and effort levels.

In another intervention on young adults, Rosenstreich, Feldman, Davidson, Maza, and Margalit (2015) followed up on first-year undergraduate college students with SLD ($n = 85$) and without SLD ($n = 250$) after they received s hope-focused workshop. In the workshop, students (a) received a short introduction about hope theory and chose a goal they would like to accomplish during the next six months; (b) were guided through a goal-mapping exercise, where they wrote down the various steps they planned to take along a possible pathway to achieve this goal (identifying barriers for each step that could hamper achievement and identifying a way to circumnavigate that barrier); and (c) underwent a mental rehearsal exercise, where they were verbally guided to vividly imagine taking each step toward their goal, encountering barriers, and motivating themselves to overcome or to bypass each obstacle and celebrate sucess. Results indicated that both groups (with and without SLD) reported higher levels of hope immediately following their participation in the workshop. However, follow-up after one month revealed that the students with SLD returned to their original levels of hope, whereas the students without SLD did not. These results suggest that a hope-focused empowerment experience is not enough for students who struggle daily with their SLD. However, these interventions programs may need extended and consistent support to sustain their positive outcomes.

Finally, both in future research and intervention, it is especially important to focus on those resilient individuals with SLD who already manifest high levels of hope. According to Snyder's (2002) theory, hope is conceptualized as a variable that differs among individuals. Therefore, identifying hope among a subgroup of resilient individuals with SLD or comorbid SLD-ADHD may facilitate identification of the critical personal resources and ecological conditions that foster successful functioning and adjustment. It is also important to examine hope profiles within different subgroups with SLD, including males and females at different developmental stages and with/without comorbid ADHD, in order to support more effective, customized intervention planning that will nurture hopeful thinking to enhance resilient functioning among subgroups of youngsters and adults with SLD.

Future Directions

• What are the possible risk factors that may contribute to the low levels of hopeful thinking and coping resources found among children and adolescents with SLD or with comorbid SLD and ADHD? What are the possible protective factors?

• What factors may similarly/differently contribute to the hopeful thinking and coping resources of young adults and adults with SLD or comorbid SLD-ADHD in and higher education systems?

• What psychoeducational intervention procedures may enhance hope levels among individuals with SLD during different age stages?

• How do the hope levels of young adults with SLD or comorbid SLD-ADHD relate to their occupational satisfaction, quality of romantic partnerships, parenting style, and dimensions of family climate?

• What may differentiate individuals with SLD or comorbid SLD-ADHD who are resilient versus those who are more vulnerable to low levels of hope and coping resources?

• What are the similar and unique developmental aspects of hope manifestations among individuals with SLD or comorbid SLD-ADHD through four different stages of the lifecycle: childhood, adolescence, young adulthood, and adulthood?

References

Adelabu, D. H. (2008). Future time perspective, hope, and ethnic identity, among African American adolescents. *Urban Education, 43*, 347–360. doi:10.1177/0042085907311806

Al-Yagon, M. (2007). Socioemotional and behavioral adjustment among school-age children with learning disabilities: The moderating role of maternal personal resources. *Journal of Special Education, 40*, 205–217. doi:10.1177/00224669070400040201

Al-Yagon, M. (2009). Comorbid LD and ADHD in childhood: Socioemotional and behavioral adjustment and parents' positive and negative affect. *European Journal of Special Needs Education, 24*, 371–391. doi:10.1080/08856250903223054

Al-Yagon, M. (2010). Maternal emotional resources and socioemotional well-being of children with and without learning disabilities. *Family Relations, 59*, 152–169. doi:10.1111/j.1741-3729.2010.00592.x

Al-Yagon, M. (2011). Fathers' emotional resources and children's socioemotional and behavioral adjustment among children with learning disabilities. *Journal of Child and Family Studies, 20*, 569–584. doi:10.1007/s10826-010-9429-9

Al-Yagon, M. (2012). Adolescents with learning disabilities: Socioemotional and behavioral functioning and attachment relationships with fathers, mothers, and teachers. *Journal of Youth and Adolescence, 41*, 1294–1311. doi:10.1007/s10964-012-9767-6

Al-Yagon, M. (2014). Child-mother and child-father attachment security: Links to internalizing adjustment among children with learning disabilities. *Child Psychiatry and Human Development, 45*(1), 119–131. doi:10.1007/s10578-013-0383-9

Al-Yagon, M. (2015). Externalizing and internalizing behaviors among adolescents with learning disabilities: Contribution of adolescents' attachment to mother and negative affect. *Journal of Child and Family Studies, 24*, 1343–1357. doi:10.1007/s10826-014-9942-3

Al-Yagon, M. (2016). Perceived close relationships with parents, teachers, and peers: Predictors of social, emotional, and behavioral functioning in adolescents with LD or comorbid LD and ADHD. *Journal of Learning Disabilities, 49*(6), 597–615. doi:10.1177/0022219415620569

Al-Yagon, M., & Margalit, M. (2012). Parental coping, emotional resources, and children's adjustment: Theory, empirical evidence, and interventional implications. In B. Molinelli, & V. Grimaldo (Eds.), *Handbook of the psychology of coping: New research* (pp. 59-84). New York: Nova.

Al-Yagon, M., & Margalit, M. (2013). Social cognition of children and adolescents with LD: Intrapersonal and interpersonal perspectives. In H. L. Swanson, K. Harris, & S. Graham (Eds.), *Handbook of learning disabilities* (2nd ed., pp. 278–292). New York: Guilford Press.

Al-Yagon, M., & Mikulincer, M. (2004a). Patterns of close relationships and socioemotional and academic adjustment among school-age children with learning disabilities. *Learning Disabilities Research and Practice, 19*(1), 12–19. doi:10.1111/j.1540-5826.2004.00085.x

Al-Yagon, M., & Mikulincer, M. (2004b). Socioemotional and academic adjustment among children with learning disorders: The mediational role of attachment-based factors. *Journal of Special Education, 38*, 111–123. doi:10.1177/00224669040380020501

American Psychiatric Association. (2013). *Diagnostic and statistical manual of mental disorders* (5th ed.). Arlington, VA: American Psychiatric Publishing.

Antonovsky, A. (1979). *Health, stress and coping.* San Francisco, CA: Jossey-Bass.

Antonovsky, A. (1987). *Unraveling the mystery of health.* San Francisco, CA: Jossey-Bass.

Antonovsky, H., & Sagy, S. (1986). The development of a sense of coherence and its impact on responses to stress situations. *Journal of Social Psychology, 126*, 213–225. Retrieved from http://web.a.ebscohost.com/ehost/pdfviewer/pdfviewer?vid=4&sid=f30eb840-

1834-4f39-bba5-3692064aa64d%40sessionmgr4004& hid=4214

Antshel, K. M., & Joseph, G. R. (2006). Maternal stress in nonverbal learning disorder: A comparison with reading disorder. *Journal of Learning Disabilities, 39*, 194–295. doi:10.1007/978-1-4614-8106-5_7

Barkley, R. A. (2011). *Executive functioning and self-regulation: Integration, extended phenotype, and clinical implications.* New York: Guilford Press.

Bartholomew, T. T., Scheel, M. J., & Cole, B. P. (2015). Development and validation of the Hope for Change through Counseling Scale. *Counseling Psychologist, 43*, 671–702. doi:10.1177/0011000015589190

Bauminger, N., & Kimhi-Kind, I. (2008). Social information processing, security of attachment, and emotion regulation in children with learning disabilities. *Journal of Learning Disabilities, 41*, 315–332. doi:10.1177/0022219408316095

Belsky, J., & Barends, N. (2002). Personality and parenting. In M. H. Bornstein (Ed.), *Handbook of parenting* (2nd ed., Vol. 3, pp. 415–438). Mahwah, NJ: Lawrence Erlbaum.

Bernardo, A. B. I. (2010). Extending hope theory: Internal and external locus of trait hope. *Personality and Individual Differences, 49*, 944–949. doi:10.1016/j.paid.2010.07.036

Bowlby, J. (1982). *Attachment and loss: Attachment.* New York: Basic Books. (Original work published 1969)

Bowlby, J. (1973). *Attachment and loss: Anxiety, anger, and separation.* New York: Basic Books.

Campbell, S. B. (2003). *Behavior problems in preschool children: Clinical and developmental issues.* New York: Guilford Press.

Capozzi, F., Casini, M. P., Romani, M., De Gennaro, L., Nicolais, G., & Solano, L. (2008). Psychiatric comorbidity in learning disorder: Analysis of family variables. *Child Psychiatry and Human Development, 39*, 101–110. doi:10.1007/s10578-007-0074-5

Cassidy, J., & Shaver, P. R. (2008). *Handbook of attachment: Theory, research, and clinical applications* (2nd ed.). New York: Guilford Press.

Cheavens, J. S., Feldman, D. B., Gum, A., Michael, S. T., & Snyder, C. R. (2006). Hope therapy in a community sample: A pilot investigation. *Social Indicators Research, 77*, 61–78. doi:10.1007/s11205-005-5553-0

Cook, B. G., Li, D., & Heinrich, K. M. (2015). Obesity, physical activity, and sedentary behavior of youth with learning disabilities and ADHD. *Journal of Learning Disabilities, 48*, 563–576. doi:10.1177/0022219413518582

Crosnoe, R., Riegle-Crumb, C., & Muller, C. (2007). Gender, self-perception, and academic problems in high school. *Social Problems, 54*, 118–138. doi:10.1525/sp.2007.54.1.118.

Du, H., Bernardo, A. B. I., & Yeung, S. S. (2015). Locus-of-hope and life satisfaction: The mediating roles of personal self-esteem and relational self-esteem. *Personality and Individual Differences, 83*, 228–233. doi:10.1016/j.paid.2015.04.026

DuPaul, G. J., Gormley, M. J., & Laracy, S. D. (2013). Comorbidity of LD and ADHD: Implications of *DSM-5* for assessment and treatment. *Journal of Learning Disabilities, 46*, 43–51. doi:10.1177/0022219412464351

Dyson, L. L. (2003). Children with learning disabilities within the family context: A comparison with siblings in global self-concept, academic self-perception, and social competence. *Learning Disabilities Research & Practice, 18*, 1–9. doi:10.1111/1540-5826.00053

Dyson, L. (2010). Unanticipated effects of children with learning disabilities on their families. *Learning Disability Quarterly, 33*, 43–55. doi:10.1177/073194871003300104

Estell, D. B., Jones, M. H., Pearl, R, Van Acker, R., Farmer, T. W., & Rodkin, P. C. (2008). Peer group, popularity, and social preference trajectories of social functioning among students with and without learning disabilities. *Journal of Learning Disabilities, 41*, 5–14. doi:10.1177/0022219407310993

Feldman, D. B., Davidson, O. B., Ben-Naim, S., Maza, E., & Margalit, M. (2016). Hope as a mediator of loneliness and academic self-efficacy among students with and without learning disabilities during the transition to college. *Learning Disabilities Research & Practice, 31*(2), 63–74.

Feldman, D. B., & Dreher, D. E. (2012). Can hope be changed in 90 minutes? Testing the efficacy of a single-session goal-pursuit intervention for college students. *Journal of Happiness Studies, 13*, 745–759. doi:10.1007/s10902-011-9292-4

Feurer, D. P., & Andrews, J. J. W. (2009). School-related stress and depression on adolescents with and without learning disabilities: An exploratory study. *Alberta Journal of Educational Research, 55*, 92–108. Retrieved from http://search.proquest.com/docview/228596485?accountid=14765

Gallagher, M. W., & Lopez, S. J. (2009). Positive expectancies and mental health: Identifying the unique contributions of hope and optimism. *Journal of Positive Psychology, 4*, 548–556. doi:10.1080/17439760903157166

Ginieri-Coccossis, M., Rotsika, V., Skevington, S., Papaevangelou, S., Malliori, M., Tomaras, V., & Kokkevi, A. (2013). Quality of life in newly diagnosed children with specific learning disabilities (SpLD) and differences from typically developing children: A study of child and parent reports. *Child: Care, Health and Development, 39*, 581–591. doi:10.1111/j.1365-2214.2012.01369.x

Goldstein, S., Naglieri, J. A., Princiotta, D. & Otero, T. M. (2014). Introduction: A history of executive functioning as a theoretical and clinical construct. In S. Goldstein & J. A. Naglieri (Eds.), *Handbook of executive functioning* (pp. 3–12). New York: Springer. doi:10.1007/978-1-4614-8106-5_1

Greenberg, M. T., Speltz, L., DeKlyen, M., & Jones, K. (2001). Correlates of clinical referral for early conduct problems: Variable and person-oriented approach. *Development and Psychopathology, 13*, 255–276. Retrieved from http://journals.cambridge.org/action/displayAbstract?fromPage=online&aid=73991&fileId=S0954579401002048

Guthrie, L. C., Butler, S. C., Lessl, K., Ochi, O., & Ward, M. M. (2014). Time perspective and exercise, obesity, and smoking: Moderation of associations by age. *American Journal of Health Promotion, 29*, 9–16. doi:10.4278/ajhp.130122-QUAN-39

Hart, K. E., Wilson, T. L., & Hittner, J. B. (2006). A psychosocial resilience model to account for medical well-being in relation to sense of coherence. *Journal of Health Psychology, 11*, 857–862. doi:10.1177/1359105306069082

Horowitz-Kraus, T. (2014). Pinpointing the deficit in executive functions in adolescents with dyslexia performing the Wisconsin Card Sorting Test: An ERP study. *Journal of Learning Disabilities, 47*, 208–223. doi:10.1177/0022219412453084

Idan, O., & Margalit, M. (2014). Socioemotional self-perceptions, family climate, and hopeful thinking among students with learning disabilities and typically achieving students from the same classes. *Journal of Learning Disabilities, 47*, 136–152. doi:10.1177/0022219412439608

King, R., & Gaerlan, M. (2015). The role of time perspectives in the use of volitional strategies. *Psychological Studies, 60*, 1–6. doi:10.1007/s12646-014-0278-2

Kopelman-Rubin, D., Brunstein Klomek, A., Al-Yagon, M., Mufson, L., Apter, A., & Mikulincer, M. (2013). Psychological intervention for adolescents diagnosed with learning disorders: I Can Succeed (ICS) treatment model, feasibility and acceptability. *International Journal for Research in Learning Disabilities*, 1(1), 37–54. Retrieved from http://www.iarld.com/wp-content/uploads/2011/08/IJRLD-Vol1-no1-Dec2012-07-26-13.pdf

Kudo, M. F., Lussier, C. M., & Swanson, H. L. (2015). Reading disabilities in children: A selective meta-analysis of the cognitive literature. *Research in Developmental Disabilities*, 40, 51–62. doi:10.1016/j.ridd.2015.01.002

Lackaye, T., & Margalit, M. (2006). Comparisons of achievement, effort and self-perceptions among students with learning disabilities and their peers from different achievement groups. *Journal of Learning Disabilities*, 39, 432–446. doi:10.1177/00222194060390050501

Levi, U., Einav, M., Ziv, O., Raskind, I., & Margalit, M. (2013). Helping students with LD to succeed: The role of teachers' hope, sense of coherence and specific self-efficacy. *European Journal of Special Needs Education*, 28, 427–439. doi:10.1080/08856257.2013.820457

Luthar, S. S., & Cicchetti, D. (2000). The construct of resilience: Implications for interventions and social policies. *Development and Psychopathology*, 12, 857–885. Retrieved from http://www.ncbi.nlm.nih.gov/pmc/articles/PMC1903337/pdf/nihms21560.pdf

Luthar, S. S., & Ciciolla, L. (2015). Who mothers mommy? Factors that contribute to mothers' well-being. *Developmental Psychology*, 51, 1812–1823. doi:http://dx.doi.org/10.1037/dev0000051

Margalit, M. (2004). Second-generation research on resilience: Social-emotional aspects of children with learning disabilities. *Learning Disabilities Research & Practice*, 19, 45–48. doi:10.1111/j.1540-5826.2004.00088.x

Margalit, M. (2006). Loneliness, the salutogenic paradigm and learning disabilities: Current research, future directions, and interventional implications. *Thalamus*, 24, 38-48.

Margalit, M. (2012). *Lonely children and adolescents: Self perceptions, social exclusion and hope.* New York: Springer.

Margalit, M. (2014). Hope theory: Conceptualization, research, prevention and intervention. In R. Boles & A. Raviv (Eds.), *Educational counseling today* (pp. 295–319). Tel Aviv: Sifriat Hapoalim.

Margalit, M., & Idan, O. (2004). Resilience and hope theory: An expanded paradigm for learning disabilities research. *Thalamus*, 22, 58–64.

Margalit, M., Raskind, M., Higgins, E. L., & Russo-Netzer, P. (2010). Mothers' voices on the Internet: Stress, support and perceptions of mothers of children with LD and ADHD. *Learning Disabilities: A Multidisciplinary Journal*, 16(1), 3–14. Retrieved from http://eric.ed.gov/?id=EJ874466

Marques, S. C., Lopez, S. J., Fontaine, A. M., Coimbra, S., & Mitchell, J. (2015). How much hope is enough? Levels of hope and students' psychological and school functioning. *Psychology in the Schools*, 52, 325–334. doi:10.1002/pits.21833

Marsh, S. C., Clinkinbeard, S. S., Thomas, R. M., & Evans, W. P. (2007). Risk and protective factors predictive of sense of coherence during adolescence. *Journal of Health Psychology*, 12, 281–284. doi:10.1177/1359105307074258

Masten, A. S. (2014). Global perspectives on resilience in children and youth. *Child Development*, 85(1), 6–20. doi:10.1111/cdev.12205

Masten, A. S. (2015). Pathways to integrated resilience science. *Psychological Inquiry*, 26, 187–196. doi:10.1080/1047840X.2015.1012041

McNamara, J., Vervaeke, S., & Willoughby, T. (2008). Learning disabilities and risk-taking behavior in adolescents: A comparison of those with and without comorbid attention-deficit/hyperactivity disorder. *Journal of Learning Disabilities*, 41, 561–574. doi:10.1177/0022219408326096

Meltzer, L. J., Reddy, R., Pollica, L. S., Roditi, B., Sayer, J., & Theokas, C. (2004). Positive and negative self perceptions. *Learning Disabilities Research & Practice*, 19, 33–44. doi:10.1111/j.1540-5826.2004.00087.x

Merkas, M., & Brajsa-Zganec, A. (2011). Children with different levels of hope: Are there differences in their self-esteem, life satisfaction, social support, and family cohesion? *Child Indicators Research*, 4, 499–514. doi:10.1007/s12187-011-9105-7

Mikulincer, M., & Shaver, P. R. (2007). *Attachment in adulthood: Structure, dynamics, and change.* New York: Guilford Press.

Morewedge, C. K., Gilbert, D. T., & Wilson, T. D. (2005). The least likely of times: How remembering the past biases forecasts of the future. *Psychological Science*, 16, 626–630. doi:10.1111/j.1467-9280.2005.01585.x

Moura, O., Simões, M. R., & Pereira, M. (2015). Executive functioning in children with developmental dyslexia. *The Clinical Neuropsychologist*, 28(Suppl. 1), 20–41. doi:10.1080/13854046.2014.964326

Murray, C., & Greenberg, M. T. (2001). Relationships with teachers and bonds with school: Social emotional adjustment correlates for children with and without disabilities. *Psychology in the Schools*, 38, 25–41. doi:10.1002/1520-6807(200101)38:1<25::AID-PITS4>3.0.CO;2-C

Murray, C., & Greenberg, M. T. (2006). Examining the importance of social relationships and social contexts in the lives of children with high incidence disabilities. *Journal of Special Education*, 39, 220–233. doi:10.1177/00224669060390040301

Nelson, J. M., & Harwood, H. (2011). Learning disabilities and anxiety: A meta-analysis. *Journal of Learning Disabilities*, 44, 3–17. doi:10.1177/0022219409359939

Parker, P. D., Ciarrochi, J., Heaven, P., Marshall, S., Sahdra, B., & Kiuru, N. (2015). Hope, friends, and subjective well-being: A social network approach to peer group contextual effects. *Child Development*, 86, 642–650. doi:10.1111/cdev.12308

Parveen, K.G., & James, E. P. (2007). Hope theory: A framework for understanding suicidal action. *Death Studies*, 31, 131–154. doi:10.1080/07481180601100491

Roberts, B. A., Martel, M. M., & Nigg, J. T. (2013). Are there executive dysfunction subtypes within ADHD? *Journal of Attention Disorders*. doi:10.1177/1087054713510349

Rosenstreich, E., Feldman, D. B., Davidson, O. B., Maza, E., & Margalit, M. (2015). Hope, optimism and loneliness among first-year college students with learning disabilities: A brief longitudinal study. *European Journal of Special Needs Education*, 30, 338–350. doi:10.1080/08856257.2015.1023001

Sameroff, A. J., & Mackenzie, M. J. (2003). Research strategies for capturing transactional models of development: the limits of the possible. *Development and Psychopathology*, 15, 613–640. doi:10.1017.S0954579403000312

Sexton, C. C., Gelhorn, H., Bell, J., & Classi, P. (2012). The co-occurrence of reading disorder and ADHD: Epidemiology, treatment, psychosocial impact, and economic burden. *Journal of Learning Disabilities*, 45, 538–564. doi:10.1177/0022219411407772

Shade, P. (2006). Educating hopes. *Studies in Philosophy and Education, 25,* 191–225. doi:10.1007/s11217-005-1251-2

Sharabi, A., & Margalit, M. (2014). Predictors of positive mood and negative mood among children with learning disabilities (LD) and their peers. *International Journal for Research in Learning Disabilities, 2,* 18–41. Retrieved from http://www.iarld.com/wp-content/uploads/2015/10/IJRLD-vol-2_no-1-for-website.pdf

Snyder, C. R. (2000). The past and possible future of hope. *Journal of Social and Clinical Psychology, 19,* 11–28. doi:10.1521/jscp.2000.19.1.11

Snyder, C. R. (2002). Hope theory: Rainbows in the mind. *Psychological Inquiry, 13,* 249–275. doi:10.1207/S15327965PLI1304_01

Snyder, C. R., Hoza, B., Pelham, W. E., Rapoff, M., Ware, L., Danovsky, M., . . . Stahl, K. J. (1997). The development and validation of the children's hope scale. *Journal of Pediatric Psychology, 22,* 399–421. doi:10.1093/jpepsy/22.3.399

Swanson, H. L, Harris, K., & Graham, S. (Eds.). (2013). *Handbook of learning disabilities* (2nd ed.). New York: Guilford Press.

Valle, M. F., Huebner, E. S., & Suldo, S. M. (2006). An analysis of hope as a psychological strength. *Journal of School Psychology, 44,* 393–406. doi:10.1016/j.jsp.2006.03.005

Wiener, J., & Schneider, B. (2002). A multisource exploration of the friendship patterns of children with and without learning disabilities. *Journal of Abnormal Child Psychology, 3,* 127–141. doi:10.1023/A:1014701215315

Zimbardo, P. G., & Boyd, J. N. (1999). Putting time in perspective: A valid, reliable individual-differences metric. *Journal of Personality and Social Psychology, 77,* 1271–1288. doi:10.1037/0022-3514.77.6.1271

Hope and Stress Resilience

Anthony D. Ong, Taylor Standiford, *and* Saarang Deshpande

Abstract

A sizeable literature has implicated hopelessness in the phenomenological experience of various mood disorders, vulnerability to psychopathology, and overall poor psychological functioning. By contrast, how hope contributes to resilience and well-being has been understudied. This systematic review integrates findings from cross-sectional, longitudinal, ambulatory, and experimental studies that investigate the impact of hope and well-being outcomes in both healthy and clinical populations. Although the literature is not without theoretical gaps and methodological inconsistencies, the pattern of findings suggests that aggregate or trait measures of hope provide the most consistent evidence of a direct association between hope and well-being in healthy and clinical populations. More limited empirical data exists on the protective effects of hope. The chapter concludes that more rigorous and theoretically informed research is needed before firm conclusions can be drawn about the possible beneficial impact of hope on well-being.

Key Words: hope, health, resilience, well-being, protective effects, trait measures

Few things more poignantly reveal our remarkable capacity for resilience as our ability to sustain hope in the face of vulnerability, pain, and loss. As defined by Snyder, Irving, and Anderson (1991), "Hope is a positive motivational state that is based on an interactively derived sense of successful *agency* (goal-directed energy) and *pathways* (planning to meet goals)" (p. 287). Considerable empirical research suggests that hope is directly related to adjustment and well-being (Alarcon, Bowling, & Khazon, 2013; Gallagher & Lopez, 2009; Snyder, 2002). Robust associations between hope and measures of psychological health have been documented across a wide variety of contexts, both in within-person (Snyder et al., 1996) and between-person analyses (Snyder, Harris et al., 1991). Moreover, the robustness of these associations has been demonstrated in both clinical and nonclinical samples of children and adolescents, as well as adults (for a review, see Edwards, Rand, Lopez, & Snyder, 2006).

Based on Snyder's (1994) hope theory, hope is comprised of two relatively distinct ways of appraising or thinking about goals. *Pathways* thinking relates to the perceived ability to generate routes toward desired goals and is necessary to attain goals and navigate around obstacles. *Agency*, or willpower, is considered the mental determination and energy necessary to begin and sustain movement toward goals. Pathways and agency are positively related but describe distinct aspects, each of which is not sufficient to define hope (Chang & DeSimone, 2001; Snyder, 2002). Additionally, hope has been theoretically distinguished from constructs such as optimism (Scheier & Carver, 1985) and self-efficacy (Bandura, 1982). Unlike optimism, which focuses on the agency-like, generalized expectancies that one will experience good outcomes in the future, hope theory gives equal emphasis to pathways as well (Snyder, 2000). Similarly, self-efficacy theory primarily reflects an individual's perceived capacity to engage in actions that will provide movement toward specific goals (similar to agency thoughts) but focuses less on pathways thinking. Research by Magaletta and Oliver (1999) has demonstrated that hope produces unique variance independent of optimism and self-efficacy in the prediction of well-being.

Theoretical Perspectives on Resilience

Resilience has numerous meanings in prior research but generally refers to a pattern of functioning indicative of *positive adaptation* in the context of significant *risk* or adversity. Underlying this notion are two fundamental conditions: (a) exposure to significant risks and (b) evidence of positive adaptation despite serious threats to development. In early investigations of childhood resilience (e.g., Garmezy, Masten, & Tellegen, 1984; Rutter, 1987; Werner & Smith, 1982), risk factors were defined as discrete experiences (e.g., parental psychopathology, community violence) that carried high odds for maladjustment. In subsequent work (e.g., Luthar, 1999; Luthar & Cushing, 1999; Masten & O'Connor, 1989; Masten & Wright, 1998; Sameroff, Gutman, & Peck, 2003), the concept of risk was broadened to include cumulative risk indices (e.g., tallies of adverse life events over time), acute trauma and chronic life difficulties (e.g., sexual abuse, neighborhood disorganization), and factors that statistically predicted later maladjustment in the general population (e.g., low birth weight).

Positive adaptation, the second core component of resilience, represents adaptation that is substantially better than would be expected given exposure to significant risk. Although indicators of positive adaptation have varied across contexts, populations, and risk factors under study (for a review, see Luthar, 2006), extant conceptualizations have, in general, included three kinds of phenomena: good developmental outcomes despite high risk, sustained competence under stress, and recovery from trauma (Masten, Best, & Garmezy, 1990). Under each of these conditions, researchers have focused their attention on identifying *protective factors* that served to modify the adverse effects of risks in a positive direction. On the basis of early reviews of the childhood and adolescence literature, Garmezy (1985) described three major categories of protective factors: *individual attributes* (e.g., an engaging "easy" temperament and good self-regulation skills), *relationships* (e.g., parental qualities with high trust, warmth, cohesion, and close relationships with competent adults), and *external support systems* (e.g., quality neighborhoods and schools and connections to prosocial organizations). These set of protective factors have been remarkably reliable in predicting positive psychological functioning following adversity (Garmezy, 1987; Masten & Coatsworth, 1998; Rutter, 1987; Werner & Smith, 1992). The consistent support for these assets and resources led Masten (2001) to conclude that resilience emerges not from rare or extraordinary qualities and circumstances but from "the everyday magic of ordinary, normative human resources in the minds, brains, and bodies of children, in their families and relationships, and in their communities" (p. 201).

At the other end of the life course is the growing literature on *optimal aging* (Baltes & Baltes, 1990; Rowe & Kahn, 1987; Schulz & Heckhausen, 1996) that has delineated distinct patterns of developmental plasticity (i.e., changes in adaptive capacity) across multiple life domains. This work underscores distinctions between resilience as *recovery* from the negative consequences of adversity and resilience as *maintenance* of development in the face of cumulative risks (for a review, see Staudinger, Marsiske, & Baltes, 1995). Other research has conceptualized resilience as distinct from the process of recovery (Bonanno, 2004). This perspective derives from studies demonstrating that resilience and recovery are distinct outcome trajectories that are empirically separable following highly aversive events such as interpersonal loss (e.g., Bonanno et al., 2002) and psychological trauma (e.g., Bonanno, Galea, Bucciarelli, & Vlahov, 2006). Finally, several lines of adulthood research emphasize the need to assess positive outcomes (e.g., psychological well-being, developmental growth) in response to challenge (Ryff & Singer, 2003; Ryff, Singer, Love, & Essex, 1998; Staudinger, Marsiske, & Baltes, 1993; Staudinger et al., 1995). Studies within this tradition have elaborated how age-graded influences (e.g., Baltes, 1987; Ryff & Heidrich, 1997), normative transitions (e.g., Smider, Essex, & Ryff, 1996), nonnormative events (e.g., Baltes, Reese, & Lipsitt, 1980; Tweed & Ryff, 1991), and chronic life difficulties (e.g., Baltes & Baltes, 1990; Singer & Ryff, 1999) are linked to various aspects of adult mental and physical health.

Recent reviews of the burgeoning research on child and adulthood resilience (Bonanno, 2005; Luthar & Brown, 2007; Ryff & Singer, 2003) reveal notable parallels as well as salient differences. Although an exhaustive review of the major differences and similarities across these two literatures is beyond the scope of this chapter, we briefly highlight convergent themes and guiding principles that shore up idiosyncratic viewpoints and approaches evident in prior work. From the perspective of risk avoidance, it is noteworthy that extant studies of resilience have given limited empirical attention to the exact nature of the stressors and challenges confronting resilient children and adults. As Ryff and colleagues (1998) note, in many instances, risk factors are inferred from aversive or otherwise unfavorable contexts (e.g., poverty, parental psychopathology, widowhood) rather than empirically assessed. Within the developmental and adult literatures, most researchers additionally agree that it is important to consider adaptive functioning more broadly beyond just the avoidance of psychopathology or negative developmental outcomes (Masten et al., 1990; Ryff & Singer, 2003). Luthar and colleagues (Luthar, Cicchetti, & Becker, 2000; Luthar & Zelazo, 2003), for example, underscore the importance of considering the role of biological factors in resilience.

Both child and adult literatures (Bonanno, 2004; Luthar & Brown, 2007; Masten, 2001; Ryff & Singer, 2000) emphasize the need to assess the relative contribution of personality assets (e.g., ego resilience, positive self-concepts, hardiness) and environmental resources (e.g., access to supportive relationships, close and nurturing family bonds, quality relationships within the community) in response to challenge. Finally, understanding of specific mechanisms that underlie resilience is a central interest in both child and adulthood literatures (Luthar et al., 2000; Rutter, 2000; Ryff & Singer, 2003; Ryff et al., 1998). That is, rather than simply studying which individual assets and social resources are associated with positive adaptation, there is growing awareness of the need to consider *how* such factors contribute to resilience in the face of challenge.

Hope as a Source of Resilience

Although considerable research has documented the effects of hope on well-being, no systematic review has yet investigated the role of hope as a promotive factor, increasing the likelihood of adaptive well-being and health, or as a protective factor, decreasing vulnerability in the face of risk. Thus the aim of this chapter is to review systematically the literature on hope as a source of stress resilience for mental and physical health. We use systematic methods and standardized procedures (Moher, Liberati, Tetzlaff, & Altman, 2009; Project EPHP, 2009) for locating and evaluating the relevance and quality of cross-sectional, longitudinal, ambulatory, and experimental studies. It is a comprehensive review that includes investigations of hope and stress that may impact on health and well-being outcomes that lie on a continuum ranging from restorative to deteriorative processes. In addition to considering the direct contribution of hope to multiple well-being outcomes, including mental health, behavioral indicators, interpersonal functioning, and physical health, we review evidence regarding potential stress-buffering or protective effects of hope. We also discuss the role of underlying pathways in the association between hope and well-being. Last, we highlight important methodological limitations of extant studies and suggest directions for future research.

Methodological Approach
Database Sources and Study Screening

The review was conducted using guidelines from PRISMA (Preferred Reporting Items for Systematic Reviews and Meta-Analyses; Moher et al., 2009). A comprehensive search for all available research on the topic was performed in three electronic bibliographic databases (MEDLINE in PubMed, PsycINFO, CINAHL). Additional studies were identified through cited reference searching of included articles and known reviews. Study screening was carried out by two independent reviewers. Discrepancies were resolved by consensus. In a first step, screening was carried out to exclude articles that did not meet inclusion criteria based on the title and abstract. Full-text screening was performed on potentially relevant studies that were identified to meet inclusion criteria. To be included, a study had to (a) be a published empirical study (rather a meta-analysis or theoretical review); (b) involve human subjects; (c) include, as an independent variable, a measure of hope or a hope manipulation or intervention; and (d) include, as a dependent variable, a subjective or objective measure of mental or physical health. Studies were excluded if they (a) used a single-case research design (e.g., clinical case study), (b) assessed only the contemporaneous correlation between hope or well-being, (c) examined only the effect of well-being on hope (rather than the effect of hope on well-being), or (d) used a reversed indicator of hopelessness as a measure of hope (e.g., pessimism, depression, negative affect, hostility).

Data Extraction and Quality Assessment

In this review, we assessed the methodological quality of reported research using the Effective Public Health Practice Project (EPHPP) tool

(Project EPHP, 2009). The EPHPP is a tool for assessing quality and susceptibility to bias in observational studies and a variety of intervention-based study designs such as randomized controlled trials, pre–post, and case-control studies. The tool assesses six domains: (a) selection bias, (b) study design, (c) confounders, (d) blinding, (e) data collection, and (f) withdrawals/dropouts. The EPHPP assessment tool has been judged suitable for systematic reviews (Deeks et al., 2003) and has been reported to have content and construct validity (Jackson & Waters, 2005; Thomas, Ciliska, Dobbins, & Micucci, 2004). In this review, we developed a standardized data extraction protocol (available upon request) that included information about the publication, study design, participants, measures, and outcomes. We used an adapted form that excluded questions related to withdrawal/dropouts for the assessment of cross-sectional studies. Each domain was rated as strong, moderate, or weak, and domain scores were averaged to provide a global rating for each study.

Characteristics of Included Studies

Ninety-nine articles fulfilled the inclusion criteria and were included for review. The 99 studies recruited a total of 19,390 respondents. The average age of participants in each study ranged from 20 to 51 years old. The majority of included studies were cross-sectional (70.7%), followed by longitudinal studies (22.2%). In addition, we retrieved five ambulatory studies and two experimental studies. Two-thirds of the studies used US samples (66.7%), with the majority of the remainder coming from Canada, Israel, the United Kingdom, and Hong Kong. Table 21.1 summarizes the general characteristics of included studies. Cross-sectional studies examine the extent to which hope is associated with health and well-being outcomes. Longitudinal studies explore whether previous levels of hope predict subsequent levels of well-being across more extended periods of time. Ambulatory studies, in comparison, use intensive repeated measures methodology (e.g., experience sampling) across several days or weeks to examine how within-person variation in hope relates to well-being. Finally, experimental studies determine the effects of induced transient hope on concurrent well-being outcomes.

Quality Assessment and Strength of Evidence

The assessment of the quality of the study methodology for the five domains (selection bias, study design, confounders, blinding, and data collection)

is shown in Figure 21.1. Following the EPHPP tool, we categorized the majority of included studies (51.5%) as "weak," 34 studies (34.3%) as "moderate," and 14 studies (14.1%) as "strong." Weakness ratings were derived from the inadequate control of confounders and insufficient information regarding study design, as well as blinding. Among the 61 studies measuring mental health outcomes (e.g., life satisfaction, negative/positive affect, depression/anxiety, posttraumatic stress disorder [PTSD]), 25 were categorized as moderate quality, 27 showed weak quality, and 9 were rated as strong. For studies assessing behavior indicators (e.g., externalizing behaviors, academic achievement, suicide), 15 studies (65.2%) were rated as weak, 4 studies (17.4%) were categorized as moderate, and 4 studies (17.4%) were rated as strong. Among nine studies measuring interpersonal functioning (e.g., perceived social support, family processes, marital satisfaction) four studies (44.4%) were rated as weak, four studies (44.4%) were categorized as moderate, and one study (11.1%) was rated as strong. Finally, among the remaining nine studies that assessed physical health (e.g., illness symptoms, pain tolerance), six studies (66.7%) were rated as weak and three studies (33.3%) were rated as moderate.

Mental Health and Other Measures of Well-Being

Table 21.2 presents studies that address the potential impact of hope on multiple aspects of mental health and well-being, including life satisfaction, affective states, anxiety and depression symptoms, and PTSD and growth. Outcomes related to mental health were nearly all self-report. The majority of studies conceptualized hope as a trait (i.e., stable, enduring disposition). Most of the studies assessed trait hope using single-administration, paper-and-pencil questionnaires; however, two studies (Ong, Edwards, & Bergeman, 2006; Steffen & Smith, 2013) assessed trait hope using ecological momentary assessment approaches (measured by aggregating momentary assessment ratings over the day). The majority of mental health studies were cross-sectional (72.6%), followed by longitudinal (24.2%) and ambulatory (3.2%). Among the studies reviewed, 59 were consistent with theoretical predictions, and 2 reported null findings (i.e., Dew-Reeves, Athay, & Kelley, 2012; Wright et al., 2011). Among studies measuring both depression and anxiety, 9 were consistent with theoretical predictions for both outcome measures, 16 found hope as a predictor of reduced depression only, 1 found hope as a predictor

Table 21.1. Characteristics of Included Studies

First Author	Year	Region	Sample Size	Age Range (years)	Study Design
Ai	2007	USA	309	33–89	Longitudinal
Ai	2005	USA	457	M = 29.06	Cross-sectional
Arnau	2007	USA	522	M = 18.7	Longitudinal
Banks	2008	USA	318	M = 20	Cross-sectional
Barnum	1998	USA	15 survivors, 14 control	13–19	Cross-sectional
Berendes	2010	USA	51	M = 65	Cross-sectional
Berg	2008	USA	172	M = 19.17	Experimental
Berg	2007	USA	48	M = 9.4	Ambulatory
Besser	2014	Israel	140	M = 25.21	Cross-sectional
Besser	2012	Isreal	217	20–30	Longitudinal
Billington	2008	UK	103	28–83	Cross-sectional
Bluvol	2004	Canada	47 (families)	46–48 (survivor)	Cross-sectional
Cedeno	2010	USA	132	M = 10.20	Cross-sectional
Chang	2015	USA	325	17–58	Cross-sectional
Chang	2013	USA	160	18–46	Cross-sectional
Davidson	2013	USA	62	18–69	Cross-sectional
Davidson	2010	USA	115	18–31	Cross-sectional
Dew-Reeves	2012	USA	117	11–18	Longitudinal
Elliott	1991	USA	57	18–83	Cross-sectional
Evangelista	2003	USA	50	18–78	Cross-sectional
Farone	2007	USA	109	M = 74.87	Cross-sectional
Feldman	2013	USA	391	M = 41.51 for Asians, 51.91 for Latinos	Longitudinal
Fite	2014	USA	141	14–20	Cross-sectional
Geffken	2006	USA	67	28–78	Cross-sectional
Gilman	2006	USA	341	M = 14.58	Cross-sectional
Glass	2009	USA	228	18–79	Cross-sectional
Gustafsson	2013	Sweden	238	15–19	Cross-sectional
Gustafsson	2010	Sweden	178	15–20	Cross-sectional
Hackbarth	2012	USA	452	20–80	Cross-sectional
Hagen	2005	USA	65	6–12	Cross-sectional

(*continued*)

Table 21.1. Continued

First Author	Year	Region	Sample Size	Age Range (years)	Study Design
Hartley	2008	USA	62	35–84	Longitudinal
Hassija	2012	USA	209	M = 52.4	Cross-sectional
Hasson-Ohayon	2009	Isreal	60	M = 42.57	Cross-sectional
Hayashino	2012	Japan	836	28–81	Cross-sectional
Hernandez	2013	USA	54 families	M = 35 for patients, 54 for family members	Cross-sectional
Hirsch	2011	USA	105	M = 74.24	Cross-sectional
Ho	2011	Hong Kong	50	M = 60	Cross-sectional
Ho	2010	China	76	21–66	Longitudinal
Horton	2001	USA	111	M = 36	Cross-sectional
Howell	2015	Canada	24	20–70	Longitudinal
Irving	1998	USA	115	Intro psych students	Cross-sectional
Irving	1997	USA	72	M = 43.9	Ambulatory
Jackson	1998	USA	63	31–82	Cross-sectional
Jiang	2013	USA	565	6th–8th grade	Cross-sectional
Kashdan	2002	USA	252	M = 35.6	Cross sectional
Kasler	2008	Israel	311	9–11	Cross-sectional
Kennedy	2009	UK	54	16–83	Cross-sectional
Kortte	2012	USA	174	M = 57.58	Longitudinal
Kortte	2010	USA	87	18–85	Longitudinal
Krause	2014	USA	208	M = 36 at onset	Cross-sectional
Kwon	2010	USA	65	19–62	Longitudinal
Landeen	2000	Canada	100	19–47	Cross-sectional
Lee	2001	South Korea	122	27–63	Cross-sectional
Lloyd	2009	Canada	50	13–17	Cross-sectional
Lloyd	2009	UK	196	23–57 for mothers, 23–54 for fathers	Cross-sectional
Lu	2013	Taiwan	224	M = 20.02	Cross-sectional
Martin	2010	Canada	100	M = 33.3	Cross-sectional
Mathew	2014	Australia	171	18–54	Cross-sectional
Mednick	2007	USA	75	M = 35.3	Cross-sectional
Michael	2005	USA	158	18–37	Cross-sectional
Ng	2014	Hong Kong	150	7–12	Cross-sectional

Table 21.1. Continued

First Author	Year	Region	Sample Size	Age Range (years)	Study Design
O'Keefe	2013	USA	168	18–62	Cross-sectional
Ong	2006	USA	226	62–80	Ambulatory
Padilla-Walker	2011	USA	489	9–14	Cross-sectional
Parenteau	2006	USA	22	M = 37.41	Longitudinal
Rajandram	2011	Hong Kong	50	M = 60	Cross-sectional
Rawdin	2013	USA	78	M = 57.6	Cross-sectional
Reff	2005	USA	396	17–46	Longitudinal
Richman	2005	USA	1041	55–70	Longitudinal
Rock	2014	USA	56	M = 52.16 for patients, 52.74 for spouses	Cross-sectional
Roesch	2010	USA	126	14–18	Ambulatory
Rustoen	2010	USA	194	25–80	Longitudinal
Santos	2015	Brazil	113	11–23	Cross-sectional
Savahl	2013	South Africa	566	14–17	Cross-sectional
Schwartz	2007	Israel	82	38–81	Cross-sectional
Scioli	2012	USA	16	35–61	Longitudinal
Shiri	2012	Israel	101	M = 55.1	Cross-sectional
Shorey	2003	USA	197	18–30	Cross-sectional
Sjoquist	2013	Australia/Canada	126	30–89	Longitudinal
Smedema	2014	USA	187	20–71	Cross-sectional
Snyder	2005	USA	701	M = 29	Experimental
Snyder	2002	USA	213	18–21	Longitudinal
Steffen	2013	USA	84	M = 39.42	Ambulatory
Stoddard	2011	USA	164	M = 12	Cross-sectional
Strom	2007	USA	94	18–74	Cross-sectional
Sun	2014	China	517	19–23	Cross-sectional
Thio	2005	New Zealand	98	17–43	Cross-sectional
Truitt	2012	USA	546	21–84	Cross-sectional
Unwin	2009	UK	99	19–91	Longitudinal
Valle	2006	USA	860	10–18	Longitudinal
Van Allen	2012	USA	67	M = 11.74	Longitudinal

(continued)

Table 21.1. Continued

First Author	Year	Region	Sample Size	Age Range (years)	Study Design
Visser	2013	USA	386	18–46	Cross-sectional
Wheeler	2008	USA	101	20–49	Cross-sectional
Woods	2013	USA	102	8–19	Longitudinal
Wright	2011	USA	89	M = 53.62	Cross-sectional
Wrobleski	2005	USA	100	M = 75.9	Cross-sectional
Wu	2011	Taiwan	175	18–85	Cross-sectional
Yuen	2014	Hong Kong	89	17.2–31.3	Cross-sectional
Zhang	2014	China	138	M = 13.5	Cross-sectional

of reduced anxiety only (i.e., Mednick et al., 2007), and 2 reported null findings on anxiety (i.e., Lloyd & Hastings, 2009; Rajandram et al., 2011). Overall, findings suggest that higher levels of trait and state hope are uniquely promotive of better well-being in both healthy and patient populations. Moreover, 18 studies found evidence that hope is protective against a range of stressors, including anxiety, depression, PTSD, negative affect, and physical illness.

Behavioral Outcomes

Evidence linking hope to behavioral outcomes has been reported in 23 studies. Among the studies reviewed, six studies (26.1%) focused on internalizing/externalizing behaviors; four studies (17.4%) focused on suicide; six studies (26.1%) investigated coping strategies; three studies (13.0%) examined academic achievement and athletic achievement, and four studies (17.4%) focused on health behaviors (see Table 21.3). Like studies examining the mental health correlates of hope, the behavioral studies reviewed were largely cross-sectional (65.2%) and assessed hope and behavioral outcomes via self-report, which may inflate the strength of the association by shared methods. Among the studies considering an association between hope and behavioral processes, 22 were consistent with theoretical predictions, and 1

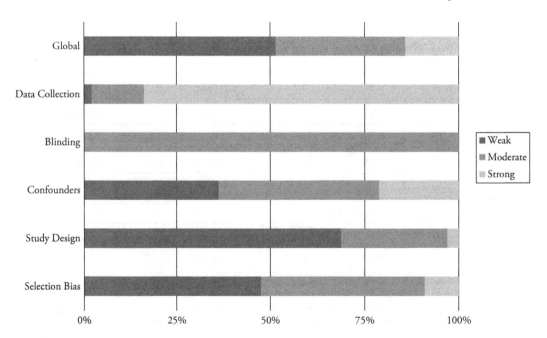

Fig. 21.1. Summary of quality assessment results from the Effective Public Health Practice Project (EPHPP) tool.

Table 21.2. Summary of Hope and Mental Health Findings in Healthy and Clinical Populations

Study	Hope Measure	Outcome Measure	Stress Measure	Comparison Group	Findings
Life satisfaction					
Smedema et al. (2014)	HS (8-item)	SWLS (5-item)	CSE (12-item)	None	Core self-evaluations had a positive relationship with life satisfaction. Agency and pathways thinking both mediate the relationship between CSE and life satisfaction.
Krause and Edles (2014)	Hope for Recovery (2-item)	SWLS (5-item)	None	None	Hope for recovery predicted higher life satisfaction.
Ng et al. (2014)	CHS (6-item)	SLSS (7-item)	None	None	Hopeful thinking was associated with increased life satisfaction.
Valle et al. (2006)	CHS (6-item)	LSIA (20-item)	LEC (46-item)	None	Stressful life events had a negative relationship with life satisfaction. The interaction between initial hope and stressful life events at T1 was predictive of higher life satisfaction scores at T2. Hopeful thinking buffered against the adverse effects of stressful life events. Hope at T1 and T2 positively predicts life satisfaction at T2.
Wrobleski and Snyder (2005)	HS (12-item)	SLSS (7-item)	None	None	Higher hope scores were associated with greater life satisfaction.
Gilman & Dooley (2006)	CHS (6-item)	SWLS (5-item)	None	None	High hope scores were associated with higher global life satisfaction.
Zhang et al. (2014)	CHS (4-item)	BMSLSS (6-item)	Perceived group based discrimination	None	Discrimination negatively predicted life satisfaction. Hope positively predicted life satisfaction. Hopeful thinking did not protect against participants' life satisfaction from the negative impact of discrimination, but it mediated the negative effect of discrimination on life satisfaction.
Jiang et al. (2013)	CHS (6-item)	SWLS (5-item)	IPPA (75-item)	None	Both parent attachment as well as hope were positively predictive of life satisfaction. Hope partially mediated the relationship between parent attachment and life satisfaction.
Strom and Kosciulek (2007)	HS (12-item)	SWLS (5-item)	PSS (10-item)	None	Perceived stress positively predicted self-reported depression. Dispositional hope was predictive of increased life satisfaction.

(continued)

Table 21.2. Continued

Study	Hope Measure	Outcome Measure	Stress Measure	Comparison Group	Findings
Kwon and Hugelshofer (2010)	ATHS (8-item)	SWLS (5-item) and PANAS (8-item; Chinese)	LGBTCI (20-item)	None	Hope was positively predictive of T2 life satisfaction. LGBTCI was not predictive of life satisfaction. Agency but not pathways served as a buffer against low workplace support climates in predicting life satisfaction.
Subjective Well-Being					
Lu and Hsu (2013)	HS (12-item)	SWLS (5-item) and PANAS (8-item; Chinese)	Injury Severity (1-item)	None	Higher hope was predictive of greater subjective well-being. Injury severity and social support were not predictive of subjective well-being. The interaction of pathways and social support was predictive of subjective well-being. Hope buffers against low social support in predicting subjective well-being.
Michael and Snyder (2005)	HS (12-item)	CES-D, (20-item), STAI (20-item), PANAS (20-item)	None	None	Hope negatively predicted depression, state anxiety, and negative affect (from PANAS) and positively predicted positive affect (from PANAS).
Savahl et al. (2013)	CHS (6-items)	KIDSCREEN-52 (52-item)	REVS (26-item)	None	Hope was a positive predictor of child well-being. Exposure to community violence was a negative predictor. Hope emerged as a stronger predictor of child well-being than exposure to community violence. No moderation was calculated.
Farone et al. (2007)	HS (12-item)	CES-D (20-item)	None	None	Higher hope was associated with more favorable outcomes of health and well-being. The association was less strong with respect to protection against somatic symptoms.
Kortte et al. (2010)	ATHS (12-item)	PANAS (20-item), SWLS (5-item), BSI (53-item)	None	None	Hope positively predicted baseline life satisfaction. Initial hope was not predictive of life satisfaction at 3-month follow up.
Quality of Life					
Billington et al. (2008)	HS (12-item)	KDQOL (36-item)	None	None	High trait hope positively predicted mental health quality of life.

Table 21.2. Continued

Study	Hope Measure	Outcome Measure	Stress Measure	Comparison Group	Findings
Evangelista et al. (2003)	HHI (12-item)	SF-12 (12-item)	None	None	Hope was a positive predictor of quality of life.
Shiri et al. (2012)	HS (12-item)	SF-36 (36-item)	Employment status in PPS and control	Age-matched subjects	Hope positively predicted total quality of life and mental health quality of life. Employment positively predicted total quality of life and physical health quality of life. The interaction of hope and employment status positively predicted both types of quality of life.
Woods et al. (2013)	CHS (6-item)	PedsQL (23-item)	None	None	Post-camp levels of agency-related hope were positively associated with post-camp health-related quality of life.
Bluvol & Ford-Gilboe (2004)	HHI (12-item)	RNLI (11-item)	None	None	Hope positively predicts quality of life.
Wheeler et al. (2008)	SHS (6-item), ATHS (12-item)	QOLI (32-item)	Parental Stress Index (36-item)	None	Trait hope positively and parenting stress negatively predicted quality of life.
Hasson-Ohayon et al. (2009)	HS (12 item)	W-QLI (58-item)	SAI-E (11-item; Hebrew)	None	Hope mediated the relationship between insight into illness and quality of life. Hope positively predicted occupational activities, physical health, social relations, daily living activities, and psychiatric symptoms. The awareness dimension of insight into mental illness negatively predicted the same categories. Hope mediated the effect of awareness on physical health, social relations, and activity of daily living.

Negative/Positive Affect

Study	Hope Measure	Outcome Measure	Stress Measure	Comparison Group	Findings
Ong et al. (2006)	SHS (6-item), ATHS (8-item)	PANAS (negative; 10-item)	Daily Stress	None	Higher daily hope was associated with lower negative affect. Additionally, daily hope served to moderate stress reactivity and mediate stress recovery.
Unwin et al. (2009)	HS (12-item)	PANAS (20-item) TAPES (15-item)	TAPES (5-item)	None	Hope at the beginning of rehabilitation positively predicted positive mood. Phantom intensity (TAPES) did not predict positive mood.

(*continued*)

Table 21.2. Continued

Study	Hope Measure	Outcome Measure	Stress Measure	Comparison Group	Findings
Steffen & Smith (2013)	SHS (6-item)	PANAS-X (60-item)	Daily Stress (1-item)	None	Within-person stress negatively predicted positive affect. Between-person hope positively predicted daily positive affect. The interaction of within-person hope and stress did not predict positive affect. When under high stress, more problem-focused coping predicted higher positive affect if the participant was high in hope.
Perceived Stress/ General Distress Horton & Wallander (2001)	HS (12-item)	BSI (53-item)	Parents of Children With Disability Inventory (40-item)	None	Higher hope was predictive of decreased maternal distress. Hope moderated the effect of disability-related stress on distress.
Glass et al. (2009)	SHS (6-item)	BSI (53-item)	IES-R (22-item)	None	Hope negatively predicted PTSD symptoms and general psychological distress. Avoidant coping positively predicted PTSD symptoms and general psychological distress. Hope moderated the relation between avoidant coping and general psychological distress.
Wright et al. (2011)	ADHS (12 item)	BSI-18 (18-item)	PDI (7-item)	None	Hope was not found to be a significant independent predictor of psychological distress.
Rustoen et al. (2011)	HHI (12-item)	IES (15-item)	None	None	Levels of hope increased and levels of psychological distress decreased immediately following hope-based intervention.
Besser and Zeigler-Hill (2014)	HS (12-item)	PSS (14-item)	SDS (3-item)	None	Hope at T1 was negatively associated with perceived stress and T2 and T3, but hope had a stronger effect on perceived stress at T2. Hope had protective effects on psychological distress, functional impairment, and self-esteem for participants.
Depression/Anxiety					
Ho et al. (2010)	HS (12-item)	HADS (14-item)	None	None	Hope negatively predicted trajectory for depression and anxiety. Hope was a positive, independent predictor of resilience against depression and anxiety.

Table 21.2. Continued

Study	Hope Measure	Outcome Measure	Stress Measure	Comparison Group	Findings
Lloyd and Hastings (2009)	HS (12-item)	HADS (14-item)	TRS (60-item)	None	Hope agency and pathways both negatively predicted depression in mothers. Hope agency negatively predicted depression and anxiety. Hope did not significantly predicted anxiety.
Arnau et al. (2007)	SHS (12-item)	BDI-II (21-item) CES-D (20-item) DASS (42-item)	Initial BDI-II (21-item) CES-D (20-item) DASS (42-item)	None	Hope agency was negatively associated with later depression and anxiety.
Billington et al. (2008)	HS (12-item)	HADS (14-item)	None	None	Hope was negatively predictive of anxiety and depression symptoms.
Mednick et al. (2007)	HS (8-item)	STAI (40-item)	None	None	Hope negatively predicted trait anxiety.
Parenteau et al. (2006)	SHS (6-item)	STAI (20-item) BDI-II (21-item)	SF-36 (36-item)	None	Hope was negatively associated with depressive symptoms and anxiety at baseline at 3- and 6-month follow-up post-surgery.
Santos et al. (2015)	HHI (12-item)	HADS (14-item)	None	None	Hope negatively predicted HbA1c (indicating better glycemic control) and depression.
Visser et al. (2013)	HS (12-item)	BDI-II (21-item) LES (43-item)	LES (43-item)	None	Hope was negatively associated with depressive symptoms. Negative life events were positively associated with depressive symptoms. Higher hope moderated the relationship between negative life events and depressive symptoms.
Sun et al. (2014)	HS (12-item)	SDS (20-item)	RRS (22-item)	None	Hope positively and rumination negatively predicted depression. Hope significantly moderated the effects of rumination on depression.
Thio and Elliott (2005)	SHS (6-item)	EPDS (10-item)	None	None	Hope negatively predicted depression. Higher levels of hope was uniquely associated with lower postpartum depression.
Hayashino et al. (2012)	HHI (12-item; Japanese)	WHO-5 (5-item)	Self-Perceived Medical Errors	None	Higher hope was negatively associated with physicians' distress. Hope worked as an effect modifier of the known associations between physicians' distress and self-perceived medical errors.

(*continued*)

Table 21.2. Continued

Study	Hope Measure	Outcome Measure	Stress Measure	Comparison Group	Findings
Ai et al. (2007)	HS (12-item)	CES-D (20-item), STAI (20-item)	CES-D (20-item)	None	Both agency and pathways were negatively associated with both preoperative and postoperative depression and anxiety. Hope mediated the favorable roles of positive religious coping style, which contributed to lower psychological distress.
Hartley et al. (2008)	HS (12-item)	CES-D (20-item)	None	None	High hope negatively predicted presurgery depression but not depression or functional ability after surgery.
Elliott et al. (1991)	HS (12-item)	IDD (22-item)	Time since injury	None	Pathways was negatively associated with depression. Agency moderated the effect of time since injury on mean impairment score in the early months and gradually faded. Pathways moderated the effect of time since injury onset on mean impairment score.
Fite et al. (2014)	CHS (6-items)	Affective Symptoms DSM-Oriented Scale (11-item)	Perceived Behavioral Norms Questionnaire (6-item), Engagement in Delinquency (14-item), Substance Use (3-item)	None	Higher depressive symptoms and peer substance abuse were correlated with tobacco, alcohol, and marijuana use frequency. Higher hope was correlated with lower tobacco, alcohol, and marijuana use frequency. Delinquency was only positively associated with frequency of tobacco and marijuana use when levels of hope were low (hope as a moderator).
Hassija et al. (2012)	HS (12-item)	PHQ-9 (9-item) TLEQ (23-item)	Brief Cope (28-item)	None	Hope was negatively associated with depression. Emotionally avoidant coping was positively associated with depression. Hope moderated the relationship between emotionally avoidant coping and depression.
Hirsch et al. (2011)	HS (12-item)	HRSD (24-item)	KPSS (%)	None	Total hope and agency were both negatively associated with depressive symptoms. Functional impairment was positively associated with depressive symptoms. Hope agency and pathways both moderated the relationship between functional impairment and depressive symptoms.

Table 21.2. Continued

Study	Hope Measure	Outcome Measure	Stress Measure	Comparison Group	Findings
Shorey et al. (2003)	HS (12-item)	MHI (38-item)	ASQ (40-item)	None	Hope partially mediated the relationship between attachment and mental health, with higher hope agency and hope pathways associated with greater positive affect, less depression, less anxiety and less perceived loss of behavioral/emotional control.
Banks et al. (2008)	HS (12-item)	CES-D (20-item)	Daily Life Experiences	None	Hope agency and pathways both negatively predicted depressive symptoms while racial discrimination positively predicted them. The interaction of hope pathways and racial discrimination positively predicted depressive symptoms. High hope buffered the effects of racial discrimination on depressive symptoms.
Geffken et al. (2006)	HOPES (20-item)	BDI (21-item)	None	None	Hope was negatively associated with depressive symptoms, symptom severity, and denial disengagement coping strategies, and positively associated with active reframing and social support coping strategies. Hope negatively predicted depression.
Sjoquist et al. (2013)	HHI (12-item)	HADS (14-item)	None	None	Trait hope was negatively correlated with anxiety and depression
Rajandram et al. (2011)	ADHS (12-item)	HADS (14-item)	None	None	Hope was negatively correlated with patient's' level of anxiety and depression. Total hope and agency were significant negative predictors of depression (pathways was not). Hope alone was not a significant predictor of anxiety, but hope and optimism together were.
Mathew et al. (2014)	HS (12-item)	CES-D (20-item)	None	None	Agency and pathways were both significantly negatively correlated with depression. Hope mediated the relationship between perfectionism and depression.
Ai et al. (2005)	ATHS (8-item)	CES-D (20-item)	None	None	Hope was negatively correlated with depression and anxiety. Hope was a negative predictor for both depression and anxiety.

Table 21.2. Continued

Study	Hope Measure	Outcome Measure	Stress Measure	Comparison Group	Findings
Reff et al. (2005)	HS (12-item)	BDI (21-item)	Exam Outcome	None	Hope was negatively associated with depression. Stress was positively associated with depression. At both low and high stress, high hope protected against increased depression for both low and high levels of defensive maturity.
Yuen et al. (2014)	HS (12-item)	PTGI (21-item)	CCRRS (12-item)	None	Dispositional hope was negatively associated with depression and anxiety.

PTSD

Kasler et al. (2008)	CHS (6-items)	The PTSD Reaction Index (20-items)	None	None	Sense of hope was negatively associated with PTSD symptoms. Hope was a significant negative predictor of PTSD and positive predictor of social support, which was also negatively correlated with PTSD.
Glass et al. (2009)	SHS (6-item)	IES-R (22-item) BSI (53-item)	Coping after Hurricane Katrina using briefCOPE (28-item)	None	High hope was negatively associated with PTSD symptoms, general psychological distress, and avoidant coping. Avoidant coping was a positive predictor for PTSD symptoms and psychological distress. Hope was a negative predictor for PTSD symptoms and psychological distress. Hope moderated the relation between avoidant coping and psychological distress.
Besser et al. (2014)	HS (12-item)	PCL-C (17-item)	None	None	Hope was negatively associated with acute PTSD and dissociative symptoms. Intrapersonal sources of resilience (hope is part of it) was a negative predictor of acute anxiety.
Wu (2011)	SHS (6-item)	C-DTS (17-item) BDI (21-item)	None	None	Hope state was one variable to mediated the effects of PTSD and depression. Hope was a positive predictor of quality of life.

Growth

Ho et al. (2011)	HS (12-item)	PTGI (21-item)	None	None	High pathways component of hope significantly predicts high PTG in patients with OC cancer. More advanced stages of cancer lead to lower PTG. No interaction term with hope and different cancer stages.

Table 21.2. Continued

Study	Hope Measure	Outcome Measure	Stress Measure	Comparison Group	Findings
Yuen et al. (2014)	HS (12-item)	PTGI (21-item)	CCRRS (12-item)	None	Dispositional hope was positively associated with PTG.
Dew-Reeves et al. (2012)	CHS-PTPB (4-item)	SFSS (26-item)	Baseline SFSS (26-item)	None	Higher levels of hope were associated with lower levels of symptom severity at baseline; however, initial level of hope was not significantly related to symptom improvement over time as reported by the youth and caregiver. Higher level of initial hope predicted slower treatment progress as recorded by the clinicians.

Note: TI = time 1; T2 = time 2; T3 = time 3; PTSD = posttraumatic stress disorder; PTG = posttraumatic growth; OC = oral cavity.

reported null findings (i.e., Davidson & Wingate, 2013). Moreover, longitudinal studies hint that hope may have long-term implications for healthy behaviors, but additional research directly assessing the effect of hope on behavioral health is needed to determine whether hope-based interventions can alter behavioral outcomes. Specifically, only two studies found hope to be a moderator (i.e., Cedeno, Elias, Kelly, & Chu, 2010; Fite et al., 2014) while the remaining studies did not directly test for moderating effects.

Interpersonal Functioning

Among the studies considering an association between hope and interpersonal functioning, eight were cross-sectional (88.8%) and one was ambulatory (11.1%). From the nine studies reviewed, all reported main effects consistent with theoretical predictions (see Table 21.4). Specifically, one study found hope to be a moderator (i.e., Elliott, Witty, Herrick, & Hoffman, 1991), one reported no moderation (i.e., Truitt, Biesecker, Capone, Bailey, & Erby, 2012), and the remaining did not conceptualize hope as a moderator. Overall, cross-sectional studies provide mixed evidence regarding potential stress-buffering or protective effects of hope. For example, hope was found to moderate the effect of time since injury on psychosocial impairment for patients who had traumatically acquired physical disabilities (Elliott et al., 1991) but not the relationship between perceived uncertainty of illness and adaptation for caregivers of children with Down syndrome (Truitt et al., 2012).

Physical Health

Minimal data are available on the effect of hope on physical health (e.g., illness symptoms and pain tolerance). Table 21.5 summarizes the identified nine studies. Despite a limited set of studies, longitudinal evidence suggests an association between hope and improved physical health in the overall population. The two longitudinal studies reviewed both provide provisional support for the link between hope and physical health found in cross-sectional work, demonstrating that this association holds even when the two variables are measured many months (ranging from 8 to 48 months) apart (i.e., Richman et al., 2005; Scioli, MacNeil, Partridge, Tinker, & Hawkins, 2012). Among the studies considering a direct association between hope and physical health, eight were consistent with theoretical predictions and one reported null findings (i.e., Rawdin, Evans, & Rabow, 2013).

Summary

This is the first systematic review to focus on the direct and moderating effects of hope on well-being. Although findings from the studies reviewed support a link in both healthy and clinical populations, the presence of basic methodological limitations among studies was frequent (according to the EPHPP criterion). Of primary concern is the limited number of longitudinal and experimental studies. Indeed, studies to date have largely been cross-sectional, making it difficult to infer the causal significance of associations. Overall, perhaps one of the most striking findings is just how few studies have addressed issues related to causality and the

Table 21.3. Summary of Hope and Behavior Findings in Healthy and Clinical Populations

Study	Hope Measure	Outcome Measure	Stress Measure	Comparison Group	Findings
Externalizing Behaviors					
Barnum et al. (1998)	THS (8-item)	CBCL (118-item)	None	Same gender friends	Burn victims had no difference from control for affective, self-esteem, or school performance variable but scored somewhat lower on internalizing and externalizing behavior. Higher hope predicted less externalizing behavior.
Fite et al. (2014)	CHS (6-item)	CSAP Student Survey (3-item)	Depressive symptoms and peer substance abuse	None	Higher depressive symptoms and peer substance abuse were correlated with tobacco, alcohol, and marijuana use frequency. Higher hope was correlated with lower tobacco, alcohol, and marijuana use frequency. Delinquency was only positively associated with frequency of tobacco and marijuana use when levels of hope were low (hope as a moderator).
Hagen et al. (2005)	CHS (12-item)	YSR (112-item)	Number of Life Stressors	None	High hope was associated with less internalizing and externalizing problems. Stress predicted internalizing behaviors and hope predicts both internalizing and externalizing behaviors. Stress and hope operated independently.
Cedeno et al. (2010)	CHS (6-item)	SSRS-T	None	None	Hope was inversely related to externalizing behaviors and positively related to self-concept. Hope moderated the effects of both direct and indirect victimization on self-concept in girls.
Martin & Stermac (2010)	HS (12-item)	LSI-OR (54-item)	None	None	Higher levels of agency, not pathways, were associated with lower estimated risk of recidivism.
Stoddard et al. (2011)	EQ-I:YV (4-item)	Add Health Student Survey (4-item)	Parent-Family Connectedness (7-item), School Connectedness (10-item)	None	Lower parent-family connectedness predicted violence involvement. Lower school connectedness marginally predicted violence involvement. Hopefulness was related to lower levels of violence even after controlling for demographic variables. The relationship between school connectedness and violence was mediated by hopefulness.
Suicide					
Chang et al. (2015)	HS (12-item)	SBQ-R (4-item)	None	No past sexual assault	Sexual assault predicted greater suicidal risk. Higher hope predicted lower suicidal risk. High hope students reported the highest levels of reasons for living independent of their experience of sexual assault. High hope students reported the lowest suicide risk independent of their experience of sexual assault.

Table 21.3. Continued

Study	Hope Measure	Outcome Measure	Stress Measure	Comparison Group	Findings
Chang et al. (2013)	HS (12-item)	SBQ-R (4-item) and BHS (20-item)	None	None	Higher hope predicted lower suicidal risk. The interaction of hope and positive problem orientation was significant in experiencing less suicide behavior.
Davidson et al. (2010)	HS-R2 (18-item)	ACSS (20-item) and HDSQ-SS (4-item)	ACSS (20-item)	None	Hope was associated with lower levels of burdensomeness but was not a significant predictor of suicidal ideation. Only optimism remained significant after hope and optimism were entered into a hierarchical regression.
O'Keefe & Wingate (2013)	THS (8-item)	ACSS (20-item) and HDSQ-SS (4-item)	None	None	American Indian ethnicity was not a significant predictor for any outcome variables. Hope, agency, and pathways all predicted thwarted belongingness negatively, perceived burdensomeness negatively, suicidal ideation negatively, and acquired capability positively.
Coping Strategies					
Roesch et al. (2010)	CHS (6-items)	CCSC HICUPS	Perceived stressful events	None	Perceived stress was positively correlated with direct problem-solving, planning, and religious coping. Hope-pathways was uniquely and positively related to direct problem-solving, planning, positive thinking, religious coping, distracting action, and overall coping. Perceived stress was not correlated with pathways or agency.
Hackbarth et al. (2012)	SHS (6-item)	F-COPES (30-item) and	None	None	State hope positively predicted family coping.
Howell et al. (2015)	SHS (6-item) CSHS (20-item)	PAQ-R (20-item)	None	None	Pretreatment hope and change in hope were predictive of improved well-being and lower pain catastrophizing in a hope-focused counseling intervention.
Jackson et al. (1998)	HS (12-item)	MBHI (150-item)	None	None	Higher hope was associated with more sociable, proactive coping styles. Hope mediated the relation of coping to functional ability. The relation of hope to functional ability was not moderated by levels of inhibited/avoidant coping style.
Irving et al. (1998)	HS (12-item)	Agentic and pathways hopeful thoughts regarding cancer risk, detection, course, and impact questionnaire.	None	None	Higher hope women had more hopeful coping responses in imagined phases of cancer.

(continued)

Table 21.3. Continued

Study	Hope Measure	Outcome Measure	Stress Measure	Comparison Group	Findings
Kashdan et al. (2002)	HS (12-item)	COPES (60-item) and HDL (33-item)	LES (67-item) ISLE (61-item)	None	Hope was positively associated with parental and familial-functioning indices and negatively associated with stress measures. Hope positively predicted psychological functioning.

Academic/Athletic Achievement

Study	Hope Measure	Outcome Measure	Stress Measure	Comparison Group	Findings
Snyder et al. (2002)	HS (8-item)	GPA, Graduation Status	None	None	Hope positively predicted GPA and likelihood of graduating from college.
Gustafsson et al. (2010)	SHS (6-item)	ABQ (15-item)	None	None	State agency and pathways both negatively correlated with all burnout dimensions. Athletes low in hope experienced greater burnout than medium-hope and high-hope counterparts.
Gustafsson et al. (2013)	THS (12-item)	ABQ (15-item)	PSS (10-item)	None	Agency and pathways were negatively correlated with all burnout dimensions and stress. Stress fully mediated the relationship between hope and burnout.

Health Behaviors

Study	Hope Measure	Outcome Measure	Stress Measure	Comparison Group	Findings
Kortte et al. (2012)	HS (12-item)	FIM (13-item) and CHART (19-item)	None	None	Hope positively predicted functional role participation.
Feldman and Sills (2013)	HS (12-item)	Health Promoting Behaviors (4-item)	None	None	In Asians, the hope and knowledge interaction term positively predicted reduced salt/fat intake and visiting doctors. In Latinos, the hope and diet change importance term predicted reduced salt/fat intake and the hope and exercise change importance term predicted increased exercise.
Van Allen and Steele (2012)	CHS (6-item)	PAQ-C (9-item) or PAQ-A (8-item)	None	None	Change in hope positively predicted physical activity at time 2.
Berg et al. (2011)	CHS (6-item)	MDIC (14-day)	FEV1	None	Hope was a significant predictor of adherence to metered-dose inhalers beyond FEV1 levels.

direction of association between hope and well-being. In addition to providing a more rigorous assessment of mechanistic pathways, prospective, multiwave, longitudinal studies are critically important in advancing the science of hope and well-being because they (a) allow for tests of theoretical models that assume stability of relations over time; () help address questions regarding duration of hope and whether sustained hope over time is associated with health outcomes above and beyond a single report; and (c) provide evidence against reverse-causality arguments, which posit that individuals who are ill may also report less hope. Similarly, as noted earlier, controlled experimental studies investigating

Table 21.4. Summary of Hope and Interpersonal Functioning Findings in Healthy and Clinical Populations

Study	Hope Measure	Outcome Measure	Stress Measure	Comparison Group	Findings
Interpersonal Functioning					
Elliott et al. (1991)	HS (12-item)	SIP (136-item)	TSI	None	Hope-pathway predicted psychosocial impairment and depression. Time since injury was not predictive of depression or impairment. Sense of agency moderated impairment in early months following injury and this relationship faded. Pathways moderated degrees of psychosocial impairment as time passed.
Kashdan et al. (2002)	HS (12-item)	SAS-SR (54-item) DAS (33-item) FES (90-item) P-CRQ (19-item)	LES (67-item), ISLE (61-item)	None	High hope was associated with cohesion, intellectual orientation, active-recreational orientation, and positive parenting factor and significantly predicted greater adaptive individual and familial functioning.
Truitt et al. (2012)	HS (12-item)	Adaptation Scale (20-items)	PPUS (31-item)	None	Uncertainty (negative) and hope (positive) independently predicted caregiver adaptation (includes social integration). Hope did not moderate the relationship between uncertainty and adaptation.
Hernandez et al. (2013)	Hope for Patient's Future Scale (20-items)	FBIS (20-item)	PANSS (30-item), Duration of illness	None	Longer duration of illness was correlated with lower family burden. High hope predicted lower family burden (fewer problems affecting routine activities, family interaction, and effect of mental health on others).
Padilla-Walker et al. (2011)	CHS (6-items)	SCS (9-item)	SCS (9-item)	None	Child-report family connectedness was positively associated with prosocial behavior and negatively with internalizing. Hope positively predicted prosocial behavior and negatively predicted internalizing. Hope mediated the relation between child-reported family connectedness and adolescents' prosocial behavior, school engagement, and internalizing behavior.

(continued)

Table 21.4. Continued

Study	Hope Measure	Outcome Measure	Stress Measure	Comparison Group	Findings
Irving et al. (1997)	HS (8-item)	PSS (40-item) CRI (58-item)	None	None	Higher hope was associated with greater perceived social support from family and friends and the use of adaptive coping strategies.
Lee (2001)	HHI (12-item)	Psychosocial Adjustment to Breast Cancer Factor	PFS-R (22-item)	None	Hope significantly explained 7% of the variance in psychosocial adjustment after controlling for fatigue. Fatigue explained 38% after controlling for hope. There was no significant interaction between fatigue and hope in accounting for psychosocial adjustment variance.
Rock et al. (2014)	AHS (12-item)	POMS (65-item)	None	None	Higher patient hope predicted greater patient marital satisfaction. The interaction of patient optimism and partner hope significantly predicted patient marital satisfaction.
Schwartz and Hadar (2007)	HS (12-item)	Caregiving Benefit Questionnaire (14-item)	Subjective and Objective Burden (29-item)	None	Higher hope was predictive of increased caregiving benefits.

the effect of hope on health outcomes are especially scarce. Thus prospective and experimental studies addressing the causal relationship between hope and well-being are urgently needed.

Other methodological challenges concern the measurement of hope, stress, and well-being, as well as adequate assessment of potential confounders. The vast majority of included studies relied upon self-report measures of hope, with very few studies examining the effects of manipulated hope on health and well-being outcomes. Moreover, so few investigations of hope and health have been conducted using objective health assessment tools (e.g., changes in respiration, skin conductance, brain activity) that conclusions must be made cautiously. Considering the significant heterogeneity across studies in measures of hope and stress, measurement error remains an issue that may contribute to biases associated with effect estimation (Hutcheon, Chiolero, & Hanley, 2010). Likewise, the inclusion of confounding variables, such as optimism and personality constructs (Bryant & Cvengros, 2004; Gallagher & Lopez, 2009), varied widely among

studies. Finally, considering the relative paucity of studies assessing positive outcomes (e.g., psychological well-being, developmental growth) in response to challenge, attention to how hope enhances restorative processes as well as protects from deteriorative ones is critical and presents an important avenue for future research.

Importantly, very limited work has been done to evaluate the potential moderating or protective effects of hope. Only a minority of studies (19.1%) demonstrated a moderating or stress-buffering effect of hope on health and well-being. Indeed, in many cases, risk factors or stressors were inferred from aversive or otherwise unfavorable contexts (e.g., poverty, parental psychopathology) rather than empirically assessed. Thus there is a critical need for additional studies examining the protective effects of hope on well-being in both healthy and clinical populations.

Limitations

The present review has some limitations that deserve attention. First, it is a narrative review and

Table 21.5. Summary of Hope and Physical Health Findings in Healthy and Clinical Populations

Study	Hope Measure	Outcome Measure	Stress Measure	Comparison Group	Findings
Illness Symptoms					
Berendes et al. (2010)	ATHS (8-item)	BFI (9-item) and QLQ-LC13	None	None	Hope was inversely associated with major symptoms of cancer (pain, fatigue, and cough) and lower depression.
Rawdin et al. (2013)	HHI (12-item)	BPI (9-item)	None	None	Hope scores were negatively correlated with average pain intensity. However, after controlling for covariates, the relationship between pain intensity and hope was no longer significant.
Santos et al. (2015)	HHI (12-item)	HbA1c levels	None	None	High levels of the construct hope were positively associated with improved glycemic control for patients with type 1 diabetes. Hope negatively predicted depression.
Billington et al. (2008)	HS (12-item)	KDQOL (36-item)	None	None	Hope had a significant inverse relationship with the effects and symptoms of kidney disease. Hope negatively predicted anxiety, depression, and effects and symptoms of kidney disease and positively predicted mental health quality of life.
Lloyd et al. (2009)	CHS (6-item)	HbA1c levels	None	None	Higher levels of hope were correlated with better glycemic control. Hope was positively correlated with perceived maternal empathy. Hope significantly predicted glycemic control.
Richman et al. (2005)	Ellsworth and Smith Emotion Scale	Health outcomes (HT, RTIs, DM)	None	None	Across three disease outcomes, higher levels of hope were associated with a decreased likelihood of having or developing a disease.
Scioli et al. (2012)	Comprehensive Trait Hope Scales (56-item)	SF-36, CD4 values	None	None	Greater total hope was associated with higher self-reported physical functioning as well as greater immunological status.
Pain Tolerance					
Berg et al. (2008)	HSR (18-item), Hope interventions	CPT, PCS	None	No Hope Intervention	Receiving the hope intervention resulted in a greater increase in hope, increased pain tolerance, and a marginally significant increase in pain severity.
Snyder et al. (2005)	THS (8-item)	CPT	None	None	Hope was positively correlated with length of time keeping their hands in water.

consequently does not provide a quantitative summary of data across studies. A meta-analysis was not feasible because we considered diverse measures of hope and stress in various forms (e.g., continuous vs. categorical), as well as a diverse set of outcomes. Thus, due to the wide variety of methods and study deigns used to investigate the associations between hope, stress, and well-being, we did not believe a meta-analysis would have been an appropriate tool to communicate the goals of this review. Although a number of qualitative and quantitative reviews of the link between hope and well-being have been conducted (Alarcon et al., 2013; Snyder, 2002), our goal in this chapter was to comprehensively review previous work to assess the state of the current research on hope and stress resilience and discuss methodological challenges and directions for future research. Additionally, we note that the risk of publication bias is inherent in any systematic review of empirical evidence. Positive publication bias can cause studies that report null or inconclusive associations between hope, stress, and well-being to remain unpublished. Such a bias may also result in a failure to publish disconfirming evidence (Stern & Simes, 1997).

Conclusion

In this chapter, we focus on what is currently known regarding hope a source of stress resilience for mental and physical health, giving emphasis to theoretical predictions, underlying mechanisms, and methodological gaps that currently exist in the literature. Although there is growing support for an association between hope and well-being in healthy and clinical populations, full understanding of the phenomenon is far from complete. The main issues limiting the validity and generalizability of the results include inadequate control of confounders, insufficient information regarding study design, small heterogeneous samples, and a paucity of longitudinal and experimental studies. Thus more carefully conducted and theoretically informed research is needed before one can have confidence that hope affects well-being in a favorable way. Overall, the pattern of findings suggests that aggregate or trait-like measures provide the most consistent evidence of a direct association between hope and well-being. At present, less evidence exists for protective effects of hope. A critical direction for future research is to elucidate the mechanisms by which hope contributes to adaptive health outcomes in the face of adversity.

To the extent that progress can be made on these issues, efforts to combat hopelessness may play an important role in improving well-being, minimizing chronic illness, and prolonging life.

Future Directions

- What are the causal pathways linking hope and physical health?
- What are the limiting conditions by which hope influences health and well-being in both healthy and patient populations?
- What is the contribution of age and disease severity to the relationship between hope and health?
- What is the role of variability and level of hope in conferring vulnerability to poor health?
- To what extent does sustained hope over time show stronger associations with health and well-being than a single hope assessment?

Glossary of Terms

ABQ	Athlete Burnout Questionnaire
ACSS	Acquired Capability for Suicide Scale
ADHS	Adult Dispositional Hope Scale
AOAQ	Adaptation to Old Age Questionnaire
ASE	academic self-efficacy
ASQ	Attachment Style Questionnaire
ATHS	Adult Trait Hope Scale
BDII	Beck Depression Inventory
BFI	Brief Fatigue Inventory
BHI	Basic Hope Inventory
BHS	Beck Hopelessness Scale
BMSLSS	Brief Multidimensional Student's Life Satisfaction Scale
BPI	Brief Pain Inventory
BSI	Brief Symptom Inventory
CBCL	Child Behavior Checklist
CCRRS	Chinese Cancer-Related Rumination Scale
CCSC	Children's Coping Strategies Checklist
CES-D	Center for Epidemiological Studies Depression Scale
CHART	Craig Handicap Assessment and Reporting Technique
CHS	Children's Hope Scale
CPT	cold pressure task
CSAP	Center for Substance Abuse Prevention
CSE	core self-evaluations
CSHS	Comprehensive State Hope Scale

DAS	Dyadic Adjustment Scale	PCL-C	PTSD Checklist—Civilian Version
DASS	Depression Anxiety Stress Scale	PCS	Pain Catastrophizing Scale
DLQI	Dermatology Life Quality Index	PDI	Pain Disability Index
EPDS	Edinburgh Post-Natal Depression Scale	PedsQL	Pediatric Quality of Life Inventory
		PFS-R	Piper Fatigue Scale—Revised
EPDS	Edinburgh Post-Natal Depression Scale	PHQ	Patient Health Questionnaire
EQ-:YV	Emotional Quotient Inventory	POMS	Profile of Mood States—Standard Form
F-COPES	Family Crisis Oriented Personal Evaluation Scale	PPUS	Parental Perceived Uncertainty Scale
FBIS	Family Burden Interview Scale	PSS	Perceived Stress Scale
FES	Family Environment Scale	PTGI	Posttraumatic Growth Inventory
FEV1	forced expiratory volume in 1 second	QLQ-LC13	European Organization for Research and Treatment of Cancer Quality of Life Questionnaire—Lung Cancer Module
FIM	functional independence measure		
GPA	grade point average		
HADS	Hospital Anxiety and Depression Scale	QOLI	Quality of Life Inventory
HDL	Health and Daily Living Form	REVS	Recent Exposure to Violence Scale
HDSQ-SS	Hopelessness Depressive Symptom Questionnaire–Suicidality Subscale	RNLI	Reintegration to Normal Living Index
HHI	Herth Hope Index	RRS	Rumination Responses Scale
HHS	Herth Hope Scale	SAI-E	Schedule for Assessment of Insight—Expanded
HICUPS	How I Coped Under Pressure Scale		
HOPES	Hunter Opinions and Personal Expectations Scale	SAS-SR	Social Adjustment Scale—Self Report
HRSD	Hamilton Rating Scale for Depression	SBQ-R	Suicidal Behaviors Questionnaire—Revised
HS	Trait Hope Scale		
HSR	The Trait Hope Scale—Revised	SCS	Social Connectedness Scale
IDD	Inventory to Diagnose Depression	SDS	Self-Rating Depression Scale
IES	Impact of Event Scale	SF	Short Form Health Survey
IES-R	Impact of Event Scale—Revised	SHS	State Hope Scale
IPPA	Inventory of Parent and Peer Attachment	SIP	Sick Impact Profile
		SFSS	Symptoms and Functioning Severity Scale
ISLE	Inventory of Small Life Events		
KDQOL	Kidney Disease Quality of Life	SLSS	Student Life Satisfaction Scale
KPSS	Karnofsky Performance Status Scale	SSRS-T	Social Skills Rating System Survey
LEC	Life Events Checklist	STAI	Speilberger State Anxiety Scale
LES	Life Event Scale	SWLS	Satisfaction with Life Scale
LGBTCI	Lesbian, Gay, Bisexual, Transgendered Climate Inventory	TAPES	Trinity Amputation and Prosthetic Experiences Scale
LSI-OR	Level of Service Inventory–Ontario Revised	TRS	The Reiss Scales
		TSHS	The State Hope Scale
LSIA	Life Satisfaction Index—Form A	TSI	time since injury
M-Cope	Multidimensional Coping Scale	W-QLI	Wisconsin Client Quality of Life Questionnaire—Mental Health
MBHI	Millon Behavioral Health Inventory		
MBI	Maslach Burnout Inventory	WAYS	The Ways of Coping Scale
MDIC	metered-dose inhaler chronology	WCQ	Ways of Coping Questionnaire
MHI	Mental Health Inventory	WHO-5	World Health Organization—Five Well Being Index
P-CRQ	Parent-Child Relationship Questionnaire		
		WHOQOL-BREF	World Health Organization Quality of Life
PANAS	Positive and Negative Affect Scale		
PAQ	Physical Activity Questionnaire		
PAQ-R	Pain Acceptance Questionnaire —Revised	YSR	Youth Self-Report

References

Ai, A. L., Cascio, T., Santangelo, L. K., & Evans-Campbell, T. (2005). Hope, meaning, and growth following the September 11, 2001, terrorist attacks. *Journal of Interpersonal Violence, 20,* 523–548. doi:10.1177/0886260504272896

Ai, A. L., Park, C. L., Huang, B., Rodgers, W., & Tice, T. N. (2007). Psychosocial mediation of religious coping styles: A study of short-term psychological distress following cardiac surgery. *Personality and Social Psychology Bulletin, 33,* 867–882. doi:10.1177/0146167207301008

Alarcon, G. M., Bowling, A., & Khazon, S. (2013). Great expectations: A meta-analytic examination of optimism and hope. *Personality and Individual Differences, 54,* 821–827.

Arnau, R. C., Rosen, D. H., Finch, J. F., Rhudy, J. L., & Fortunato, V. J. (2007). Longitudinal effects of hope on depression and anxiety: A latent variable analysis. *Journal of Personality, 75,* 43–64. doi:10.1111/j.1467-6494.2006.00432.x

Baltes, P. B. (1987). Theoretical propositions of life-span developmental psychology: On the dynamics between growth and decline. *Developmental Psychology, 23,* 611–626. doi:10.1037/0012-1649.23.5.611

Baltes, P. B., & Baltes, M. M. (Eds.). (1990). *Successful aging: Perspectives from the behavioral sciences.* New York: Cambridge University Press.

Baltes, P. B., Reese, H. W., & Lipsitt, L. P. (1980). Life-span developmental psychology. *Annual Review of Psychology, 31,* 65–110.

Bandura, A. (1982). Self-efficacy mechanism in human agency. *American Psychologist, 37,* 122–147.

Banks, K. H., Singleton, J. L., & Kohn-Wood, L. P. (2008). The influence of hope on the relationship between racial discrimination and depressive symptoms. *Journal of Multicultural Counseling and Development, 36,* 231–244.

Barnum, D. D., Snyder, C. R., Rapoff, M. A., Mani, M. M., & Thompson, R. (1998). Hope and social support in the psychological adjustment of children who have survived burn injuries and their matched controls. *Children's Health Care, 27,* 15–30. doi:10.1207/s15326888chc2701_2

Berendes, D., Keefe, F. J., Somers, T. J., Kothadia, S. M., Porter, L. S., & Cheavens, J. S. (2010). Hope in the context of lung cancer: Relationships of hope to symptoms and psychological distress. *Journal of Pain and Symptom Management, 40,* 174–182. doi:10.1016/j.jpainsymman.2010.01.014

Berg, C. J., Ritschel, L. A., Swan, D. W., An, L. C., & Ahluwalia, J. S. (2011). The role of hope in engaging in healthy behaviors among college students. *American Journal of Health Behavior, 35,* 402–415.

Berg, C. J., Snyder, C. R., & Hamilton, N. (2008). The effectiveness of a hope intervention in coping with cold pressor pain. *Journal of Health Psychology, 13,* 804–809. doi:10.1177/1359105308093864

Besser, A., Weinberg, M., Zeigler-Hill, V., & Neria, Y. (2014). Acute symptoms of posttraumatic stress and dissociative experiences among female Israeli civilians exposed to war: The roles of intrapersonal and interpersonal sources of resilience. *Journal of Clinical Psychology, 70,* 1227–1239. doi:10.1002/jclp.22083

Besser, A., & Zeigler-Hill, V. (2014). Positive personality features and stress among first-year university students: Implications for psychological distress, functional impairment, and self-esteem. *Self and Identity, 13,* 24–44. doi:10.1080/15298868.2012.736690

Billington, E., Simpson, J., Unwin, J., Bray, D., & Giles, D. (2008). Does hope predict adjustment to end-stage renal failure and consequent dialysis? *British Journal of Health Psychology, 13,* 683–699. doi:10.1348/135910707x248959

Bluvol, A., & Ford-Gilboe, M. (2004). Hope, health work and quality of life in families of stroke survivors. *Journal of Advanced Nursing, 48,* 322–332. doi:10.1111/j.1365-2648.2004.03004.x

Bonanno, G. A. (2004). Loss, trauma, and human resilience: Have we underestimated the human capacity to thrive after extremely aversive events? *American Psychologist, 59,* 20–28.

Bonanno, G. A. (2005). Resilience in the face of potential trauma. *Current Directions in Psychological Science, 14,* 135–138.

Bonanno, G. A., Galea, S., Bucciarelli, A., & Vlahov, D. (2006). Psychological resilience after disaster: New York City in the aftermath of the September 11th terrorist attack. *Psychological Science, 17,* 181–186.

Bonanno, G. A., Wortman, C. B., Lehman, D. R., Tweed, R. G., Haring, M., Sonnega, J., . . . Nesse, R. M. (2002). Resilience to loss and chronic grief: A prospective study from preloss to 18-months postloss. *Journal of Personality and Social Psychology, 83,* 1150–1164.

Bryant, F. B., & Cvengros, J. A. (2004). Distinguishing hope and optimism: Two sides of a coin, or two separate coins? *Journal of Social and Clinical Psychology, 23,* 273–302.

Cedeno, L. A., Elias, M. J., Kelly, S., & Chu, B. C. (2010). School violence, adjustment, and the influence of hope on low-income, African American youth. *American Journal of Orthopsychiatry, 80,* 213–226. doi:10.1111/j.1939-0025.2010.01025.x

Chang, E. C., & DeSimone, S. L. (2001). The influence of hope on appraisals, coping, and dysphoria: A test of hope theory. *Journal of Social and Clinical Psychology, 20,* 117–129.

Chang, E. C., Yu, E. A., Kahle, E. R., Jeglic, E. L., & Hirsch, J. K. (2013). Is doubling up on positive future cognitions associated with lower suicidal risk in Latinos? A look at hope and positive problem orientation. *Cognitive Therapy and Research, 37,* 1285–1293. doi:10.1007/s10608-013-9572-x

Chang, E. C., Yu, T., Jilani, Z., Fowler, E. E., Yu, E. A., Lin, J., & Hirsch, J. K. (2015). Hope under assault: Understanding the impact of sexual assault on the relation between hope and suicidal risk in college students. *Journal of Social and Clinical Psychology, 34,* 221–238.

Davidson, C. L., & Wingate, L. R. (2013). The glass half-full or a hopeful outlook: Which explains more variance in interpersonal suicide risk in a psychotherapy clinic sample? *Journal of Positive Psychology, 8,* 263–272. doi:10.1080/17439760.2013.787446

Davidson, C. L., Wingate, L. R., Slish, M. L., & Rasmussen, K. A. (2010). The great Black hope: Hope and its relation to suicide risk among African Americans. *Suicide and Life-Threatening Behavior, 40,* 170–180.

Deeks, J. J., Dinnes, J., D'Amico, R., Sowden, A. J., Sakarovitch, C., Song, F., . . . Altman, D. G. (2003). Evaluating nonrandomised intervention studies. *Health Technology Assessment, 7,* 3–173.

Dew-Reeves, S. E., Athay, M. M., & Kelley, S. D. (2012). Validation and use of the Children's Hope Scale–Revised PTPB Edition (CHS-PTPB): High initial youth hope and elevated baseline symptomatology predict poor treatment outcomes. *Administration and Policy in Mental Health and Mental Health Services Research, 39,* 60–70. doi:10.1007/s10488-012-0411-2

Edwards, L. M., Rand, K. L., Lopez, S. J., & Snyder, C. R. (2006). Understanding hope: A review of measurement and construct validity research. In A. D. Ong & M. van Dulmen (Eds.), *Handbook of methods in positive psychology* (pp. 83–95). New York: Oxford University Press.

Elliott, T. R., Witty, T. E., Herrick, S., & Hoffman, J. T. (1991). negotiating reality after physical loss—Hope, depression, and disability. *Journal of Personality and Social Psychology, 61,* 608–613. doi:10.1037//0022-3514.61.4.608

Evangelista, L. S., Doering, L. V., Dracup, K., Vassilakis, M. E., & Kobashigawa, J. (2003). Hope, mood states and quality of life in female heart transplant recipients. *Journal of Heart and Lung Transplantation, 22,* 681–686. doi:10.1016/s1053-2498(02)00652-6

Farone, D. W., Fitzpatrick, T. R., & Bushfield, S. Y. (2007). Hope, locus of control, and quality of health among elder Latina cancer survivors. *Social Work in Health Care, 46,* 51–70.

Feldman, D. B., & Sills, J. R. (2013). Hope and cardiovascular health-promoting behaviour: Education alone is not enough. *Psychology & Health, 28,* 727–745. doi:10.1080/08870446.2012.754025

Fite, P. J., Gabrielli, J., Cooley, J. L., Haas, S. M., Frazer, A., Rubens, S. L., & Johnson-Motoyama, M. (2014). Hope as a moderator of the associations between common risk factors and frequency of substance use among Latino adolescents. *Journal of Psychopathology and Behavioral Assessment, 36,* 653–662. doi:10.1007/s10862-014-9426-1

Gallagher, M. W., & Lopez, S. J. (2009). Positive expectancies and mental health: Identifying the unique contributions of hope and optimism. *Journal of Positive Psychology, 4,* 548–556.

Garmezy, N. (1985). Stress-resistant children: The search for protective factors. In J. E. Stevenson (Ed.), *Recent research in developmental psychopathology: Journal of Child Psychology and Psychiatry Book Supplement* (pp. 213–233). Oxford: Pergamon Press.

Garmezy, N. (1987). Stress, competence, and development: Continuities in the study of schizophrenic adults, children vulnerable to psychopathology, and the search for stress-resistant children. *American Journal of Orthopsychiatry, 57,* 159–174.

Garmezy, N., Masten, A. S., & Tellegen, A. (1984). The study of stress and competence in children: A building block for developmental psychopathology. *Child Development, 55,* 97–111.

Geffken, G. R., Storch, E. A., Duke, D. C., Monaco, L., Lewin, A. B., & Goodman, W. K. (2006). Hope and coping in family members of patients with obsessive-compulsive disorder. *Journal of Anxiety Disorders, 20,* 614–629. doi:10.1016/j.janxdis.2005.07.001

Gilman, R., & Dooley, J. (2006). Relative levels of hope and their relationship with academic and psychological indicators among adolescents. *Journal of Social and Clinical Psychology, 25,* 166–178. doi:10.1521/jscp.2006.25.2.166

Glass, K., Flory, K., Hankin, B. L., Kloos, B., & Turecki, G. (2009). Are coping strategies, social support, and hope associated with psychological distress among Hurricane Katrina survivors? *Journal of Social and Clinical Psychology, 28,* 779–795.

Gustafsson, H., Hassmen, P., & Podlog, L. (2010). Exploring the relationship between hope and burnout in competitive sport. *Journal of Sports Sciences, 28,* 1495–1504. doi:10.1080/02640414.2010.521943

Gustafsson, H., Skoog, T., Podlog, L., Lundqvist, C., & Wagnsson, S. (2013). Hope and athlete burnout: Stress and affect as mediators. *Psychology of Sport and Exercise, 14,* 640–649. doi:10.1016/j.psychsport.2013.03.008

Hackbarth, M., Pavkov, T., Wetchler, J., & Flannery, M. (2012). Natural disasters: An assessment of family resiliency following Hurricane Katrina. *Journal of Marital and Family Therapy, 38,* 340–351. doi:10.1111/j.1752-0606.2011.00227.x

Hagen, K. A., Myers, B. J., & Mackintosh, V. H. (2005). Hope, social support, and behavioral problems in at-risk children. *American Journal of Orthopsychiatry, 75,* 211–219. doi:10.1037/0002-9432.75.2.211

Hartley, S. M., Vance, D. E., Elliott, T. R., Cuckler, J. M., & Berry, J. W. (2008). Hope, self-efficacy, and functional recovery after knee and hip replacement surgery. *Rehabilitation Psychology, 53,* 521–529. doi:10.1037/a0013121

Hassija, C. M., Luterek, J. A., Naragon-Gainey, K., Moore, S. A., & Simpson, T. (2012). Impact of emotional approach coping and hope on PTSD and depression symptoms in a trauma exposed sample of veterans receiving outpatient VA mental health care services. *Anxiety Stress and Coping, 25,* 559–573. doi:10.1080/10615806.2011.621948

Hasson-Ohayon, I., Kravetz, S., Meir, T., & Rozencwaig, S. (2009). Insight into severe mental illness, hope, and quality of life of persons with schizophrenia and schizoaffective disorders. *Psychiatry Research, 167,* 231–238.

Hayashino, Y., Utsugi-Ozaki, M., Feldman, M. D., & Fukuhara, S. (2012). Hope modified the association between distress and incidence of self-perceived medical errors among practicing physicians: Prospective cohort study. *PLoS One, 7.* doi:10.1371/journal.pone.0035585

Hernandez, M., Barrio, C., & Yamada, A. M. (2013). Hope and burden among Latino families of adults with schizophrenia. *Family Process, 52,* 697–708. doi:10.1111/famp.12042

Hirsch, J. K., Sirois, F. M., & Lyness, J. M. (2011). Functional impairment and depressive symptoms in older adults: Mitigating effects of hope. *British Journal of Health Psychology, 16,* 744–760.

Ho, S., Rajandram, R. K., Chan, N., Samman, N., McGrath, C., & Zwahlen, R. A. (2011). The roles of hope and optimism on posttraumatic growth in oral cavity cancer patients. *Oral Oncology, 47,* 121–124. doi:10.1016/j.oraloncology.2010.11.015

Ho, S. M., Ho, J. W., Bonanno, G. A., Chu, A. T., & Chan, E. M. (2010). Hopefulness predicts resilience after hereditary colorectal cancer genetic testing: A prospective outcome trajectories study. *BMC Cancer, 10,* 279.

Horton, T. V., & Wallander, J. L. (2001). Hope and social support as resilience factors against psychological distress of mothers who care for children with chronic physical conditions. *Rehabilitation Psychology, 46,* 382–399. doi:10.1037/0090-5550.46.4.382

Howell, A. J., Jacobson, R. M., & Larsen, D. J. (2015). Enhanced psychological health among chronic pain clients engaged in hope-focused group counseling. *Counseling Psychologist, 43,* 586–613. doi:10.1177/0011000014551421

Hutcheon, J. A., Chiolero, A., & Hanley, J. A. (2010). Random measurement error and regression dilution bias. *BMJ, 340,* c2289.

Irving, L. M., Snyder, C. R., & Crowson, J. J. (1998). Hope and coping with cancer by college women. *Journal of Personality, 66,* 195–214. doi:10.1111/1467-6494.00009

Irving, L. M., Telfer, L., & Blake, D. D. (1997). Hope, coping, and social support in combat-related posttraumatic stress disorder. *Journal of Traumatic Stress, 10,* 465–479. doi:10.1002/jts.2490100311

Jackson, N., & Waters, E. (2005). Criteria for the systematic review of health promotion and public health interventions. *Health Promotion International, 20,* 367–374.

Jackson, W. T., Taylor, R. E., Palmatier, A. D., Elliott, T. R., & Elliott, J. L. (1998). Negotiating the reality of visual impairment: Hope, coping, and functional ability. *Journal of Clinical Psychology in Medical Settings, 5,* 173–185.

Jiang, X., Huebner, E. S., & Hills, K. J. (2013). Parent attachment and early adolescents' life ssatisfaction: The mediating effect of hope. *Psychology in the Schools, 50,* 340–352. doi:10.1002/pits.21680

Kashdan, T. B., Pelham, W. E., Lang, A. R., Hoza, B., Jacob, R. G., Jennings, J. R., . . . Gnagy, E. M. (2002). Hope and optimism as human strengths in parents of children with externalizing disorders: Stress is in the eye of the beholder. *Journal of Social and Clinical Psychology, 21,* 441–468. doi:10.1521/jscp.21.4.441.22597

Kasler, J., Dahan, J., & Elias, M. J. (2008). The relationship between sense of hope, family support and post-traumatic stress disorder among children: The case of young victims of rocket attacks in Israel. *Vulnerable Children and Youth Studies, 3,* 182–191.

Kortte, K. B., Gilbert, M., Gorman, P., & Wegener, S. T. (2010). Positive psychological variables in the prediction of life satisfaction after spinal cord injury. *Rehabilitation Psychology, 55,* 40–47.

Kortte, K. B., Stevenson, J. E., Hosey, M. M., Castillo, R., & Wegener, S. T. (2012). Hope predicts positive functional role outcomes in acute rehabilitation populations. *Rehabilitation Psychology, 57,* 248–255. doi:10.1037/a0029004

Krause, J. S., & Edles, P. A. (2014). Injury perceptions, hope for recovery, and psychological status after spinal cord injury. *Rehabilitation Psychology, 59,* 176–182. doi:10.1037/a0035778

Kwon, P., & Hugelshofer, D. (2010). The protective role of hope for lesbian, gay, and bisexual individuals facing a hostile workplace climate. *Journal of Gay & Lesbian Mental Health, 14*(1), 3–18.

Lee, E.-H. (2001). Fatigue and hope: Relationships to psychosocial adjustment in Korean women with breast cancer. *Applied Nursing Research, 14,* 87–93.

Lloyd, S. M., Cantell, M., Pacaud, D., Crawford, S., & Dewey, D. (2009). Brief report: Hope, perceived maternal empathy, medical regimen adherence, and glycemic control in adolescents with type 1 diabetes. *Journal of Pediatric Psychology, 34,* 1025–1029. doi:10.1093/jpepsy/jsn141

Lloyd, T. J., & Hastings, R. (2009). Hope as a psychological resilience factor in mothers and fathers of children with intellectual disabilities. *Journal of Intellectual Disability Research, 53,* 957–968. doi:10.1111/j.1365-2788.2009.01206.x

Lu, F. J. H., & Hsu, Y. W. (2013). Injured athletes' rehabilitation beliefs and subjective well-being: The contribution of hope and social support. *Journal of Athletic Training, 48,* 92–98. doi:10.4085/1062-6050-48.1.03

Luthar, S. S. (1999). *Poverty and children's adjustment.* Thousand Oaks, CA: SAGE.

Luthar, S. S. (2006). Resilience in development: A synthesis of research across five decades. In D. J. Cohen & D. Cicchetti (Eds.), *Developmental psychopathology: Risk, disorder, and adaptation* (pp. 739–795). Hoboken, NJ: Wiley.

Luthar, S. S., & Brown, P. J. (2007). Maximizing resilience through diverse levels of inquiry: Prevailing paradigms, possibilities, and priorities for the future. *Development and Psychopathology, 19,* 931–955.

Luthar, S. S., Cicchetti, D., & Becker, B. (2000). The construct of resilience: A critical evaluation and guidelines for future work. *Child Development, 71,* 543–562.

Luthar, S. S., & Cushing, G. (1999). Neighborhood influences and child development: A prospective study of substance abusers' offspring. *Development and Psychopathology, 11,* 763–784.

Luthar, S. S., & Zelazo, L. B. (2003). Research on resilience: An integrative review. In S. S. Luthar (Ed.), *Resilience and vulnerability: Adaptation in the context of childhood adversities* (pp. 510–549). New York: Cambridge University Press.

Magaletta, P. R., & Oliver, J. M. (1999). The hope construct, will, and ways: Their relations with self-efficacy, optimism, and general well-being. *Journal of Clinical Psychology, 55,* 539–551.

Martin, K., & Stermac, L. (2010). Measuring hope: Is hope related to criminal behaviour in offenders? *International Journal of Offender Therapy and Comparative Criminology, 54,* 693–705. doi:10.1177/0306624x09336131

Masten, A. S. (2001). Ordinary magic: Resilience processes in development. *American Psychologist, 56,* 227–238.

Masten, A. S., Best, K. M., & Garmezy, N. (1990). Resilience and development: Contributions from the study of children who overcome adversity. *Development and Psychopathology, 2,* 425–444.

Masten, A. S., & Coatsworth, J. (1998). The development of competence in favorable and unfavorable environments: Lessons from research on successful children. *American Psychologist, 53,* 205–220.

Masten, A. S., & O'Connor, M. J. (1989). Vulnerability, stress, and resilience in the early development of a high risk child. *Journal of the American Academy of Child and Adolescent Psychiatry, 28,* 274–278.

Masten, A. S., & Wright, M. O. D. (1998). Cumulative risk and protection models of child maltreatment. *Journal of Aggression, Maltreatment and Trauma, 2,* 7–30.

Mathew, J., Dunning, C., Coats, C., & Whelan, T. (2014). The mediating influence of hope on multidimensional perfectionism and depression. *Personality and Individual Differences, 70,* 66–71. doi:10.1016/j.paid.2014.06.008

Mednick, L., Cogen, F., Henderson, C., Rohrbeck, C. A., Kitessa, D., & Streisand, R. (2007). Hope more, worry less: Hope as a potential resilience factor in mothers of very young children with type 1 diabetes. *Children's Health Care, 36,* 385–396.

Michael, S. T., & Snyder, C. R. (2005). Getting unstuck: The roles of hope, finding meaning, and rumination in the adjustment to bereavement among college students. *Death Studies, 29,* 435–458. doi:10.1080/07481180590932544

Moher, D., Liberati, A., Tetzlaff, J., & Altman, D. G. (2009). Preferred reporting items for systematic reviews and meta-analyses: The PRISMA statement. *Annals of Internal Medicine, 151,* 264–269.

Ng, E. C. W., Chan, C. C., & Lai, M. K. (2014). Hope and life satisfaction among underprivileged children in Hong Kong: The mediating role of perceived community support. *Journal of Community Psychology, 42,* 352–364. doi:10.1002/jcop.21614

O'Keefe, V. M., & Wingate, L. R. (2013). The role of hope and optimism in suicide risk for American Indians/Alaska Natives. *Suicide and Life-Threatening Behavior, 43,* 621–633. doi:10.1111/sltb.12044

Ong, A. D., Edwards, L. M., & Bergeman, C. (2006). Hope as a source of resilience in later adulthood. *Personality and Individual Differences*, *41*, 1263–1273. doi:10.1016/j.paid.2006.03.028

Padilla-Walker, L. M., Hardy, S. A., & Christensen, K. J. (2011). Adolescent hope as a mediator between parent-child connectedness and adolescent outcomes. *Journal of Early Adolescence*, *31*, 853–879. doi:10.1177/0272431610376249

Parenteau, S. C., Gallant, S., Sarosiek, I., & McCallum, R. W. (2006). The role of hope in the psychological adjustment of gastropareutic patients receiving the gastric pacemaker: A longitudinal study. *Journal of Clinical Psychology in Medical Settings*, *13*, 49–56. doi:10.1007/s10880-005-9005-4

Project EPHP. (2009). Quality assessment tool for quantitative studies. Retrieved from http://www.ephpp.ca/tools.html

Rajandram, R. K., Ho, S. M., Samman, N., Chan, N., McGrath, C., & Zwahlen, R. A. (2011). Interaction of hope and optimism with anxiety and depression in a specific group of cancer survivors: a preliminary study. *BMC Research Notes*, *4*, 519. doi:10.1186/1756-0500-4-519

Rawdin, B., Evans, C., & Rabow, M. W. (2013). The relationships among hope, pain, psychological distress, and spiritual well-being in oncology outpatients. *Journal of Palliative Medicine*, *16*, 167–172. doi:10.1089/jpm.2012.0223

Reff, R. C., Kwon, P., & Campbell, D. G. (2005). Dysphoric responses to a naturalistic stressor: Interactive effects of hope and defense style. *Journal of Social and Clinical Psychology*, *24*, 638–648. doi:10.1521/jscp.2005.24.5.638

Richman, L. S., Kubzansky, L., Maselko, J., Kawachi, I., Choo, P., & Bauer, M. (2005). Positive emotion and health: Going beyond the negative. *Health Psychology*, *24*, 422–429. doi:10.1037/0278-6133.24.4.422

Rock, E. E., Steiner, J. L., Rand, K. L., & Bigatti, S. M. (2014). Dyadic influence of hope and optimism on patient marital satisfaction among couples with advanced breast cancer. *Supportive Care in Cancer*, *22*, 2351–2359. doi:10.1007/s00520-014-2209-0

Roesch, S. C., Duangado, K. M., Vaughn, A. A., Aldridge, A. A., & Villodas, F. (2010). Dispositional hope and the propensity to cope: A daily diary assessment of minority adolescents. *Cultural Diversity & Ethnic Minority Psychology*, *16*, 191–198. doi:10.1037/a0016114

Rowe, J. W., & Kahn, R. L. (1987). Human aging: Usual and successful. *Science*, *237*, 143–149.

Rustoen, T., Cooper, B. A., & Miaskowski, C. (2011). A longitudinal study of the effects of a hope intervention on levels of hope and psychological distress in a community-based sample of oncology patients. *European Journal of Oncology Nursing*, *15*, 351–357. doi:10.1016/j.ejon.2010.09.001

Rutter, M. (1987). Psychosocial resilience and protective mechanisms. *American Journal of Orthopsychiatry*, *57*, 316–331.

Rutter, M. (2000). Resilience reconsidered: Conceptual considerations, empirical findings, and policy implications. In S. J. Meisels & J. P. Shonkoff (Eds.), *Handbook of early childhood intervention* (2nd ed., pp. 651–682). New York: Cambridge University Press.

Ryff, C. D., & Heidrich, S. M. (1997). Experience and well-being: Explorations on domains of life and how they matter. *International Journal of Behavioral Development*, *20*, 193–206.

Ryff, C. D., & Singer, B. (2000). Interpersonal flourishing: A positive health agenda for the new millennium. *Personality and Social Psychology Review*, *4*, 30–44.

Ryff, C. D., & Singer, B. (2003). Flourishing under fire: Resilience as a prototype of challenged thriving. In J. Haidt & C. L. M. Keyes (Eds.), *Flourishing: Positive psychology and the life well lived* (pp. 15–36). Washington, DC: American Psychological Association.

Ryff, C. D., Singer, B., Love, G. D., & Essex, M. J. (1998). Resilience in adulthood and later life: Defining features and dynamic processes. In J. Lomranz (Ed.), *Handbook of aging and mental health: An integrative approach* (pp. 69–96). New York: Plenum Press.

Sameroff, A., Gutman, L. M., & Peck, S. C. (2003). Adaptation among youth facing multiple risks: Prospective research findings. In S. S. Luthar (Ed.), *Resilience and vulnerability: Adaptation in the context of childhood adversities* (pp. 364–391). New York: Cambridge University Press.

Santos, F. R. M., Sigulem, D., Areco, K. C. N., Gabbay, M. A. L., Dib, S. A., & Bernardo, V. (2015). Hope matters to the glycemic control of adolescents and young adults with type 1 diabetes. *Journal of Health Psychology*, *20*, 681–689. doi:10.1177/1359105315573429

Savahl, S., Isaacs, S., Adams, S., Carels, C. Z., & September, R. (2013). An exploration into the impact of exposure to community violence and hope on children's perceptions of well-being: A South African perspective. *Child Indicators Research*, *6*, 579–592. doi:10.1007/s12187-013-9183-9

Scheier, M. F., & Carver, C. S. (1985). Optimism, coping, and health: Assessment and implications of generalized outcome expectancies. *Health Psychology*, *4*, 219–247.

Schulz, R., & Heckhausen, J. (1996). A life span model of successful aging. *American Psychologist*, *51*, 702–714.

Schwartz, C., & Hadar, L. (2007). Parents caring for adult children with physical disabilities: The impact of hope and closeness on caregiving benefits. *Families in Society: The Journal of Contemporary Social Services*, *88*, 273–281. doi:10.1606/1044-3894.3625

Scioli, A., MacNeil, S., Partridge, V., Tinker, E., & Hawkins, E. (2012). Hope, HIV and health: A prospective study. *Aids Care*, *24*, 149–156. doi:10.1080/09540121.2011.597943

Shiri, S., Wexler, I. D., Feintuch, U., Meiner, Z., & Schwartz, I. (2012). Post-polio syndrome: Impact of hope on quality of life. *Disability and Rehabilitation*, *34*, 824–830. doi:10.3109/09638288.2011.623755

Shorey, H. S., Snyder, C. R., Yang, X. D., & Lewin, M. R. (2003). The role of hope as a mediator in recollected parenting, adult attachment, and mental health. *Journal of Social and Clinical Psychology*, *22*, 685–715. doi:10.1521/jscp.22.6.685.22938

Singer, B., & Ryff, C. D. (1999). Hierarchies of life histories and associated health risks. In M. Marmot & N. E. Adler (Eds.), *Socioeconomic status and health in industrial nations: Social, psychological, and biological pathways* (pp. 96–115). New York: New York Academy of Sciences.

Sjoquist, K. M., Friedlander, M. L., O'Connell, R. L., Voysey, M., King, M. T., Stockler, M. R., . . . Butow, P. N. (2013). Hope, quality of life, and benefit from treatment in women having chemotherapy for platinum-resistant/refractory recurrent ovarian cancer: The Gynecologic Cancer Intergroup Symptom Benefit Study. *Oncologist*, *18*, 1221–1228. doi:10.1634/theoncologist.2013-0175

Smedema, S. M., Chan, J. Y., & Phillips, B. N. (2014). Core self-evaluations and snyder's hope theory in persons with spinal cord injuries. *Rehabilitation Psychology*, *59*, 399–406. doi:10.1037/rep0000015

Smider, N. A., Essex, M. J., & Ryff, C. D. (1996). Adaptation of community relocation: The interactive influence of psychological resources and contextual factors. *Psychology and Aging, 11*, 362–372.

Snyder, C. R. (1994). *The psychology of hope: You can get there from here*: New York: Free Press.

Snyder, C. R. (2000). The past and possible futures of hope. *Journal of Social and Clinical Psychology, 19*, 11–28. doi:10.1521/jscp.2000.19.1.11

Snyder, C. R. (2002). Hope theory: Rainbows in the mind. *Psychological Inquiry, 13*, 249–275. doi:10.1207/s15327965pli1304_01

Snyder, C. R., Berg, C., Woodward, J. T., Gum, A., Rand, K. L., Wrobleski, K. K., . . . Hackman, A. (2005). Hope against the cold: Individual differences in trait hope and acute pain tolerance on the cold pressor task. *Journal of Personality, 73*, 287–312. doi:10.1111/j.1467-6494.2005.00318.x

Snyder, C. R., Harris, C., Anderson, J. R., Holleran, S. A., Irving, L. M., Sigmon, S. T., . . . Harney, P. (1991). The will and the ways: Development and validation of an individual-differences measure of hope. *Journal of Personality and Social Psychology, 60*, 570–585.

Snyder, C. R., Irving, L., & Anderson, J. R. (1991). Hope and health: Measuring the will and the ways. In C. R. Snyder & D. R. Forsyth (Eds.), *Handbook of social and clinical psychology: The health perspective* (pp. 285–305). Elmsford, NY: Pergamon.

Snyder, C. R., Shorey, H. S., Cheavens, J., Pulvers, K. M., Adams, V. H., & Wiklund, C. (2002). Hope and academic success in college. *Journal of Educational Psychology, 94*, 820–826. doi:10.1037//0022-0663.94.4.820

Snyder, C. R., Sympson, S. C., Ybasco, F. C., Borders, T. F., Babyak, M. A., & Higgins, R. L. (1996). Development and validation of the State Hope Scale. *Journal of Personality and Social Psychology, 70*, 321–335.

Staudinger, U. M., Marsiske, M., & Baltes, P. B. (1993). Resilience and levels of reserve capacity in later adulthood: Perspectives from life-span theory. *Development and Psychopathology, 5*, 541–566. doi:10.1017/S0954579400006155

Staudinger, U. M., Marsiske, M., & Baltes, P. B. (1995). Resilience and reserve capacity in later adulthood: Potentials and limits of development across the life span. In D. J. Cohen & D. Cicchetti (Eds.), *Developmental psychopathology: Risk, disorder, and adaptation* (Vol. 2, pp. 801–847). Oxford: Wiley.

Steffen, L. E., & Smith, B. W. (2013). The influence of between and within-person hope among emergency responders on daily affect in a stress and coping model. *Journal of Research in Personality, 47*, 738–747. doi:10.1016/j.jrp.2013.06.008

Stern, J. M., & Simes, R. J. (1997). Publication bias: Evidence of delayed publication in a cohort study of clinical research projects. *BMJ, 315*, 640–645.

Stoddard, S. A., McMorris, B. J., & Sieving, R. E. (2011). Do social connections and hope matter in predicting early adolescent violence? *American Journal of Community Psychology, 48*, 247–256.

Strom, T. Q., & Kosciulek, J. (2007). Stress, appraisal and coping following mild traumatic brain injury. *Brain Injury, 21*, 1137–1145. doi:10.1080/02699050701687334

Sun, H., Tan, Q., Fan, G., & Tsui, Q. (2014). Different effects of rumination on depression: Key role of hope. *International Journal of Mental Health Systems, 8*, 1–5. doi:10.1186/1752-4458-8-53

Thio, I. M., & Elliott, T. R. (2005). Hope, social support, and postpartum depression: Disentangling the mediating effects of negative affectivity. *Journal of Clinical Psychology in Medical Settings, 12*, 293–299. doi:10.1007/s10880-005-7814-0

Thomas, B. H., Ciliska, D., Dobbins, M., & Micucci, S. (2004). A process for systematically reviewing the literature: Providing the research evidence for public health nursing interventions. *Worldviews on Evidence-Based Nursing, 1*, 176–184.

Truitt, M., Biesecker, B., Capone, G., Bailey, T., & Erby, L. (2012). The role of hope in adaptation to uncertainty: The experience of caregivers of children with Down syndrome. *Patient Education and Counseling, 87*, 233–238. doi:10.1016/j.pec.2011.08.015

Tweed, S. H., & Ryff, C. D. (1991). Adult children of alcoholics: Profiles of wellness amidst distress. *Journal of Studies on Alcohol, 52*, 133–141.

Unwin, J., Kacperek, L., & Clarke, C. (2009). A prospective study of positive adjustment to lower limb amputation. *Clinical Rehabilitation, 23*, 1044–1050. doi:10.1177/0269215509339001

Valle, M. F., Huebner, E. S., & Suldo, S. M. (2006). An analysis of hope as a psychological strength. *Journal of School Psychology, 44*, 393–406. doi:10.1016/j.jsp.2006.03.005

Van Allen, J., & Steele, R. G. (2012). Associations between change in hope and change in physical activity in a pediatric weight management program. *Childrens Health Care, 41*, 344–359. doi:10.1080/02739615.2012.721724

Visser, P. L., Loess, P., Jeglic, E. L., & Hirsch, J. K. (2013). Hope as a moderator of negative life events and depressive symptoms in a diverse sample. *Stress and Health, 29*, 82–88. doi:10.1002/smi.2433

Werner, E. E., & Smith, R. (1982). *Vulnerable but invincible: A study of resilient children*. New York: McGraw-Hill.

Werner, E. E., & Smith, R. S. (1992). *Overcoming the odds: High risk children from birth to adulthood*: Ithaca, NY: Cornell University Press.

Wheeler, A. C., Skinner, D. G., & Bailey, D. B. (2008). Perceived quality of life in mothers of children with fragile X syndrome. *American Journal on Mental Retardation, 113*, 159–177. doi:10.1352/0895-8017(2008)113[159:pqolim]2.0.co;2

Woods, K., Mayes, S., Bartley, E., Fedele, D., & Ryan, J. (2013). An evaluation of psychosocial outcomes for children and adolescents attending a summer camp for youth with chronic illness. *Childrens Health Care, 42*, 85–98. doi:10.1080/02739615.2013.753822

Wright, M. A., Wren, A. A., Somers, T. J., Goetz, M. C., Fras, A. M., Huh, B. K., . . . Keefe, F. J. (2011). Pain acceptance, hope, and optimism: Relationships to pain and adjustment in patients with chronic musculoskeletal pain. *Journal of Pain, 12*, 1155–1162. doi:10.1016/j.jpain.2011.06.002

Wrobleski, K. K., & Snyder, C. R. (2005). Hopeful thinking in older adults: Back to the future. *Experimental Aging Research, 31*, 217–233. doi:10.1080/03610730590915452

Wu, H. C. (2011). The protective effects of resilience and hope on quality of life of the families coping with the criminal traumatisation of one of its members. *Journal of Clinical Nursing, 20*, 1906–1915. doi:10.1111/j.1365-2702.2010.03664.x

Yuen, A. N. Y., Ho, S. M. Y., & Chan, C. K. Y. (2014). The mediating roles of cancer-related rumination in the relationship between dispositional hope and psychological outcomes among childhood cancer survivors. *Psycho-Oncology, 23*, 412–419. doi:10.1002/pon.3433

Zhang, A., Cui, L. J., Iyer, A., Jetten, J., & Hao, Z. (2014). When reality bites: Hopeful thinking mediates the discrimination-life satisfaction relationship. *Analyses of Social Issues and Public Policy, 14*, 379–393. doi:10.1111/asap.12034

PART VI

Hope and Positive Functioning

Hope and Well-Being

Jenny Y. Lee *and* Matthew W. Gallagher

Abstract

Snyder's hope theory defines hope as a cognitively based construct that consists of two components: agency, the willpower to achieve a goal, and pathways, the perceived ability to generate ways to achieve that goal. Hope has been consistently linked to positive outcomes in many life domains, including aspects of positive mental health. This chapter reviews the literature on hope and positive aspects of mental health, including specific findings regarding the impact of hope on subjective, psychological, and social well-being. It also explores findings regarding the potential moderating role of gender, age, race, ethnicity, culture, and other demographic factors on the influence of hope on well-being. Future directions on hope and well-being research are discussed as well.

Key Words: hope, well-being, mental health, subjective well-being, psychological well-being, social well-being, culture

From the myth of Pandora to the words of Dr. Martin Luther King Jr., there is a long tradition in Western culture for the idea that hope may play an importance role in promoting psychological health. Much of the early theorizing and research on hope focused on how hope promoted mental health by impacting mental illness. For example Menninger (1959) and Frank and Frank (1961) both spoke about the importance of hope in the context of promoting recovery from mental illness. In the past decade, there has been increasing recognition that well-being or positive mental health is more than merely the absence of mental illness (e.g., Keyes, 2007) and that it is important to examine predictors of the full range of psychological health. Hope as conceptualized by Snyder (1994, 2002) has now been demonstrated to be a robust predictor of the many different indicators of positive mental health. In this chapter we discuss the theoretical rationale for how hope promotes positive mental health; review the existing literature examining the relationship between hope and indicators of subjective, psychological, and social well-being; discuss

the possible roles of age, gender, race/ethnicity, and cultural factors in moderating the hope and well-being relationship; and identify some important future directions for research.

How Hope Promotes Well-Being

As reviewed in other chapters in this handbook, the theoretical model of hope that was developed over two decades ago by C. R. Snyder has led to a remarkable amount of research demonstrating the benefits of hope in academic achievement, athletics, physical health, and psychological health. A recent meta-analytic review of the hope literature demonstrated that hope is positively associated with improved outcomes across many life domains (Alarcon, Bowling, & Khazon, 2013). Not surprisingly, there is also a rapidly increasing body of research demonstrating the significance and robustness of hope as a predictor of positive mental health (Halama & Dědová, 2007; Lagacé-Séguin & d'Entremont, 2010; Snyder, 2004). There are many different pathways by which hope is believed to ultimately play an important role in promoting well-being.

As articulated in Chapter 3 of this volume, hope is generally conceptualized as an adaptive psychological resource that helps individuals attain their goals, which can have both direct and indirect positive influences of well-being. The most direct influence that hope has on well-being comes from the positive orientation toward the future that is inherent to hope. High-hope individuals pursue their goals with positive thinking (i.e., a focus on success rather than failure), positive emotions, and a sense of invigoration and challenge (Snyder, 1995). They also possess the ability to set goals for themselves and find the pathways to achieve their goals (Ciarrochi, Parker, Kashdan, Heaven, & Barkus, 2015). Hope also allows individuals to effectively manage life's obstacles by acting as a reserve that supports cognitive flexibility in goal-setting and the pursuit of those goals (Folkman, 2010).

Although hope is typically discussed and examined as an individual resource, it can also have a profound impact on social functioning. As articulated by Snyder, Cheavens, and Sympson (1997) and Chapter 24 in this volume, one of the methods by which high-hope individuals pursue their goals is by cultivating and nurturing relationships. Individuals high in hope are capable of identifying pathways and harnessing agency in the pursuit of goals, but they are also more likely to seek support from others and to actively attempt to strengthen their social bonds with others. As a result, high-hope individuals have positive interpersonal relationships and more perceived social support (Snyder et al., 1997). This social and collaborative orientation therefore provides high-hope individuals with another source of more effective coping skills in the face of stressors compared to those with low levels of hope.

In times of hardship, hope is conceptualized as a resource that helps provide individuals a means of coping with seemingly uncontrollable circumstances. There is extensive research now demonstrating that individuals who are high in hope are more likely than those low in hope to use effective coping strategies, particularly when faced with obstacles or challenging situations. For example, individuals high in hope tend to use more adaptive forms of emotion regulation, such as cognitive reappraisal, that have been consistently demonstrated to bolster resilience to mental illness, among other benefits (Aldao et al., 2010; Gross, 2014). Having high hope does not guarantee that individuals will never experience a traumatic event, experience a failed relationship, or develop physical illness, but when individuals with high hope face these challenging circumstances, they are better adjusted to handle life's uncertainties and challenges compared to those low in hope. Hopeful individuals are also more likely than their less hopeful counterparts to be better equipped with and to draw upon their external resources such as social support that promote well-being.

By helping individuals to more effectively cope, hope promotes greater success in the pursuit of goals. Whether an individual is pursuing academic success, healthy relationships, or meaning in life, as reviewed in other chapters in this volume, hope is a consistently robust predictor of greater success in varied domains. Emotional experiences are conceptualized in hope theory to largely occur as the by-products of success or failure in the pursuit of goals. The capacity for hope to help individuals more effectively work toward and achieve goals should therefore lead to the frequent experience of the full range of the components of well-being. Positive psychology researchers have demonstrated that the experience of positive emotions and other forms of well-being can promote a positive spiral by which positive emotions, happiness, and other forms of well-being can positively cascade into the development of greater resources and many other positive outcomes (Fredrickson, 2001; Keyes, 2007; Lyubmirsky, King, & Diener, 2005). By generally improving our ability to achieve success across life domains, hope can therefore play an important role in initiating and sustaining these positive spirals toward flourishing mental health.

Skeptics have sometimes associated hope with naïvete and ignorance, and some question whether hope is beneficial at all in promoting goals that may not be realistic (i.e., false hope syndrome; Polivy & Herman, 2002). However, researchers have shown that individuals with high hope and ambitious goals are no less likely to achieve their goals (Emmons, 1992) and that concerns regarding false hope may be overblown (Snyder & Rand, 2003). Moreover, work by Snyder and others has demonstrated how high-hope individuals tend to describe their goals in vivid and concrete terms, which helps promote a stronger sense of agency and more effective generation of pathways to achieve one's goals and should help individuals be more effective in pursuing their goals.

For all of these reasons, hope is regarded as an inner strength and a positive psychological variable that is often studied as a predictor of positive outcomes (Werner, 2012). It has been associated with a slew of successful outcomes across various domains in life. For instance, high levels of hope predict superior athletic and academic performance as well as better social and psychological adjustment (Curry, Snyder, Cook, Ruby, & Rehm, 1997; Snyder, 2002). Hope is sometimes identified as a component of positive psychological capital and a "strength of the heart" (Avey, Wernsing, & Mhatre, 2011; Park & Peterson, 2006). As such, hope has been found to be consistently and positively associated with well-being (Park, Peterson, & Seligman, 2004). There is also extensive evidence now, however, that hope independently predicts various aspects of well-being, even when controlling for related constructs such as optimism (Gallagher & Lopez, 2009).

Defining Well-Being

Prior to discussing the specific impact that hope has on distinct components of well-being, it is important to briefly discuss current conceptualizations of well-being and positive mental health. Although research examining the components of positive mental health continues to lag behind that examining various forms of mental illness, our understanding of what it means to be mentally healthy and how to best conceptualize well-being has improved dramatically in recent decades as positive-psychology research has increasingly focused on identifying components and correlates of well-being. Current conceptualizations of well-being have distinguished between three broad domains of positive mental health (Keyes, 2005; 2007): subjective well-being, psychological well-being, and social well-being.

Subjective, psychological, and social well-being are related but distinct factors that emerged from and represent distinct philosophical approaches for what it means to have flourishing mental health (Waterman, 1993). Subjective well-being focuses on broad cognitive evaluations of whether individuals are satisfied with their life and the relative balance of positive and negative emotions (Diener, 1984) and follows from expectancy-value theory, which suggests that one's well-being comes from the expectancy to achieve, and ultimately achieving, a goal (e.g., Oishi, Diener, Lucas, & Suh, 1999; Ryan & Deci, 2001). Psychological well-being (Ryff, 1989) stems from the eudaimonic tradition that places greater emphasis on striving to realize one's potential and function fully (Waterman, 1993). The philosophical concept of eudaimonia is rooted in the Aristotelian belief that people's state of well-being comes from living in accordance with their

true self, or daimon (Waterman, 1993). Finally, social well-being (Keyes, 1998) extends the eudaimonic focus of psychological well-being to the interpersonal realm and focuses on how individuals perceive their status within their social groups and communities. Numerous studies have pointed to well-being as a multidimensional phenomenon, such that both happiness and meaningfulness are essential features of the good life (Ryan & Deci, 2001). Although some researchers have questioned whether these domains of well-being are truly distinct (e.g., Biswas-Diener, Kashdan, & King, 2009), empirical examinations of the distinctiveness of these three domains have supported an integrated model containing these three factors of well-being as the best representation of the hierarchical structure of well-being (Gallagher, Lopez, & Preacher, 2009).

Hope and Subjective Well-Being

Subjective well-being, also commonly referred to as hedonic or emotional well-being, consists of three components: life satisfaction, the presence of positive affect, and the absence of negative affect (Diener, Suh, Lucas, & Smith, 1999). Life satisfaction, commonly measured by the Satisfaction With Life Scale (Diener, Emmons, Larsen, & Griffin, 1985), has been described as an individual's cognitive appraisal of his or her life on the whole. Positive and negative affect, commonly measured by the Positive and Negative Affect Schedule (PANAS; Watson, Clark, & Tellegen, 1988), represent the extent to which individuals experience positive and negative emotions. Positive feelings such as joy, pleasure, and contentment are desirable and indicative of a good quality of life. Negative feelings such as anger, contempt, and disgust diminish subjective well-being in that they are related to stress and poor coping (Clark & Watson, 1988). Subjective well-being is based on the individuals' conscious and subjective evaluation of their lives, in terms of how they feel about their life according to personal standards (Diener & Suh, 1997). Although malleable, research has indicated that subjective well-being is relatively stable and that the experience of high levels of subjective well-being throughout adolescence carries into adulthood (Richards & Huppert, 2011).

A formerly widely accepted model of subjective well-being, known as the hedonic treadmill, suggested that individuals return to a neutral affect set point after experiencing an emotionally significant event (Brickman & Campbell, 1971). Thus positive and negative affective states are transient, and individuals will only temporarily deviate from a set point. However, the past few decades of research has shown that most people are not necessarily fixed at neutrality or any set point but rather are generally above neutral. Diener and Diener (1996) found that the most individuals reported their experience of positive emotions as being above neutral, indicating it is likely that individuals have a generally positive rather than neutral set point. The experience of positive emotions is crucial for the flourishing of mental health. For instance, research has shown that frequent positive emotions reduce stress, increase happiness and resilience to adversity, and promote psychological growth (Fredrickson & Losada, 2005). In addition, positive emotions and high life satisfaction work together to reduce the negative effects of stress (Demirli, Türkmen, & Arık, 2015). Subjective well-being and happiness therefore both reflect and promote future well-being (Lyubmirsky et al., 2005).

Snyder's model of hope suggests that hope should have both direct and indirect positive effects on the components of subjective well-being. Hope represents a positive schema that influences how individuals appraise themselves, their circumstances, and their future and therefore helps individuals to generally approach novel situations and the pursuit of goals with more enthusiasm, more positive emotions, and more life satisfaction based on the belief that they previously have been and will continue to be successful in the pursuit of goals. Within hope theory, the experience of positive and negative emotions are thought to occur as the by-product of success or failure, respectively, in the pursuit of goals. Consistent with the broaden and build theory of positive emotions (Fredrickson, 2001), hope should therefore help individuals in the short term maintain greater positive affect and less positive affect as they successfully pursue goals and develop more consistently positive emotional experiences as they effectively and successfully accomplish goals. The ability of hope to promote resilience in the face of adversity or setbacks should also lead to greater positive affect and life satisfaction even in challenging circumstances.

Subjective well-being is the domain of well-being that has most been most widely studied as a potential outcome of hope. This research has demonstrated that hope is consistently a unique and strong predictor of the components of subjective well-being (Bailey, Eng, Frisch, & Snyder, 2007; Park et al., 2004). Multiple studies have indicated that individuals who are hopeful are also generally satisfied with their life, as indicated by the significant correlation between life satisfaction and hope (Bailey & Snyder, 2007; Lagacé-Séguin & d'Entremont, 2010). In a study of older adults, those who had higher hope and were more satisfied with their life were also more confident in goal pursuits (Wrobleski & Snyder, 2005). In addition to the influence of hope on life satisfaction, Demirli et al. (2014) found that high hope was associated with more positive affect and less negative affect. In the experience of stressful life events, hope acts as a psychological buffer that promotes subjective well-being and decreases internalizing behavior problems (Valle, Huebner, & Suldo, 2006).

In a study of injured athletes who were undergoing rehabilitation, researchers found that hope predicted subjective well-being in addition to rehabilitation behavior and beliefs. Thus athletes with high levels of hope have a positive mindset toward their recovery process and are more likely to follow their recovery treatment plans than athletes with low levels of hope (Lu & Hsu, 2013). The influence of hope on subjective well-being has been demonstrated in mental health settings as well. For instance, Irving et al. (2004) conducted a study within a community mental health center and noted that higher hope was linked to increased subjective well-being. Likewise, among persons suffering from serious mental illness, hope played a significant role in predicting subjective well-being and in the overall recovery process for these individuals (Werner, 2012). Proyer, Ruch, and Buschor (2013) conducted a strengths-based intervention examining the effect of hope, among other character strengths, on life satisfaction. Results indicated that the group who participated in the strengths-based intervention showed significant increases in life satisfaction.

Hope consistently and robustly predicts positive affect, negative affect, and life satisfaction above and beyond the effects of optimism (Gallagher & Lopez, 2009). Hope is also a robust predictor of each of the components of subjective well-being above and beyond dimensions of personality (Ciarrocchi & Deneke, 2005). The positive effects of hope on well-being are not limited to cross-sectional examinations. One of the most robust demonstrations of the influence that hope has on the longitudinal course of well-being was a study by Ciarocchi, Parker, Kashdan, Heaven, and Barkus (2015). In a six-year study of nearly a thousand adolescents, hope was found to be a robust predictor of subsequent levels of well-being and to be a better predictor of later well-being than well-being was a predictor of later hope, which supports the idea that hope promotes well-being and does not merely reflect well-being (Ciarocchi et al., 2015). Other longitudinal studies have similarly found that hope is a robust predictor of the longitudinal course of subjective well-being and have demonstrated that perceived emotional control and the use of more adaptive coping strategies may be one mechanism by which hope promotes subjective well-being (Gallagher, 2011). Meta-analytic reviews also clearly demonstrate that hope has a robust influence on the components of subjective well-being (Alarcon et al., 2013).

Hope and Psychological Well-Being

Psychological well-being, also known as eudaimonic well-being, is the second major model of positive mental health and well-being. Whereas subjective well-being emphasizes emotional experiences and general evaluations of satisfaction with life, psychological well-being places greater emphasis on components of mental health such as purpose in life that are not included in subjective well-being (Ryff, 1989). Psychological well-being broadens the focus on what it means to be mentally healthy and is more consistent with Aristotle's concept of eudaimonia and early theories within psychology regarding what it means to be mentally healthy (Jahoda, 1959). Although psychological well-being is related to subjective well-being, the two are empirically distinct (Keyes et al., 2002).

Psychological well-being as currently defined and measured consists of six domains that together promote emotional and physical health: autonomy, personal growth, self-acceptance, purpose in life, environmental mastery, and positive relationships (Ryff & Keyes, 1995). Autonomy suggests self-regulation of behavior, self-determination, and independence. Personal growth involves the continuous strife for individual development. Self-acceptance is regarding the self with a positive attitude toward both personal strengths and weaknesses. Purpose in life encompasses the belief that one's life has meaning and significance. Environmental mastery suggests that individuals have the ability to engage with and actively partake in activities surrounding their environment. Positive relationships are the ability to achieve meaningful and fulfilling interpersonal relations (Ryff, 1989). Empirical examinations of these domains has supported the conceptualization of these six factors as distinct facets that together represent psychological well-being (e.g., Ryff & Keyes, 1995), and there is a robust literature now demonstrating the utility and importance of examining the benefits and contributions of psychological well-being above and beyond other domains of well-being (Ryff, 2013).

The theory and components of psychological well-being place a relatively greater emphasis on the role of personal agency, and how individuals attempt to pursue valued goals can reflect and promote meaning. Given this emphasis, psychological well-being would appear to be the domain of well-being that hope may be most closely related to. Snyder's hope theory suggests that the capacity to effectively identify pathways to achieve one's goals and effectively harness personal agency to pursue those pathways would provide the foundation for pursuing and maintaining each of the six components of psychological well-being.

A robust and statistically significant positive association between hope and psychological well-being has been consistently shown in past studies (Gibson & Parker, 2003; Singh, Singh, & Singh, 2012). For instance, Singh et al. found that hope predicted improved psychological well-being among university students. Hope has been demonstrated to have robust associations with all six components of psychological well-being and to uniquely predict all six components above and beyond optimism (Gallagher and Lopez, 2009). Research suggests that hope is a driving force behind psychological well-being, particularly purpose in life. Purpose represents an intention to pursue a goal that is both meaningful to the self and others, while hope is a means to reaching goals through the will to achieve and the ways to pursue them (Bronk, Hill, Lapsley, Talib, & Finch, 2009; Damon, Menon, & Bronk, 2003). In this regard, it is likely that having a sense of hope encourages individuals to stay committed to their purpose over time despite challenges, thus promoting their psychological well-being (Bronk et al., 2009). Additionally, hope may play an indirect role in promoting longevity. Across young, middle-aged, and older adults in the United States, greater purpose in life was associated with greater longevity (Hill & Turiano, 2014).

The ability to maintain a high level of psychological well-being throughout the course of a lifetime has led researchers to focus on hope as a robust predictor of positive mental health. In a study examining the efficacy of a cognitive-behavioral and solution-based life coaching program for high school students, researchers found that the program was associated with significant increases in level of hope and decreases in depression among the students (Green, Grant, & Rynsaardt, 2007).

The life coaching program provided students with the confidence and the skills to set and attain goals, thus enhancing their psychological well-being in the long term. Moreover, research has shown that older adults tend to exhibit higher levels of psychological well-being compared to younger adults (Jorm et al., 2005). This may be because as adults approach an older age, they tend to reprioritize their goals and lend emphasis to pursuing present goals that are emotionally meaningful (Windsor, Anstey, & Rodgers, 2008). The pursuit of such goals may increase psychological well-being for older adults.

Hope and Social Well-Being

The third major domain of well-being is social well-being. Current theories of social well-being focus on how well individuals navigate their social lives, thus extending the intrapersonal aspects of eudaimonic well-being to the interpersonal realm (Keyes, 1998). Social well-being is a reflection of positive social functioning. Whereas Ryff's (1989) model of psychological well-being maintains a focus on the intrapersonal realm, social well-being extends the focus into the interpersonal realm. The idea that an individual's social well-being is largely dependent on interpersonal relations suggests that it is a primarily public phenomena (Keyes, 1998). Social well-being indicates the ability to successfully navigate one's social environment through relations with people and the community at large. Keyes and others have made a compelling case that although social well-being is related to subjective and psychological well-being, it is empirically and theoretically distinct and worthy of study as a distinct mental health outcome.

Keyes's (1998) model of social well-being consists of five dimensions: social acceptance, social actualization, social contribution, social coherence, and social integration. Individuals demonstrate social acceptance by having positive attitudes toward human differences. Social actualization is the belief that people and society can evolve in a positive manner. Social contribution is having the perception that one's activities are productively contributing toward society. Social coherence suggests that one is interested in society and social life and finds them meaningful. Social integration is the sense of belonging and comfort derived from a community with which the individual interacts.

As mentioned previously, although hope is traditionally discussed and examined as an individual resource, there is clear theory and evidence for why hope should also promote positive social functioning. As articulated by Chapter 24 in this volume, a secure attachment base and positive relationships during development helps to provide the foundation for individuals to develop high hope, and hope has long been conceptualized as a trait that would both reflect and promote positive social dynamics and relationships (Snyder et al., 1997). High-hope individuals do not discount the importance of the influence that others may have in helping to accomplish one's goals, and in fact, actively seek the support of others when pursuing goals or when encountering stress and adversity. High-hope individuals also seek to actively support the goals pursuits of others, which can promote success in others but also serve to develop and strengthen social bonds. Hope should therefore not just be an important predictor of subjective and psychological facets of well-being that place a greater emphasis on the individual but also the interpersonal components of social well-being.

Although there has been less research examining the impact of hope on social facets of well-being, research to date has consistently shown that hope is also an important predictor of social aspects of well-being. Research has shown that engagement in supportive social networks and meaningful social roles can increase mental health (Berkman, Glass, Brissette, & Seeman, 2000). For instance, Son and Wilson (2012) found that volunteer work among midlife adults can increase social well-being in the sense of establishing connections with other people and the greater community. Social connections may be of particular importance for adolescents as well. For example, youth who experience high-quality relationships with their family and peers are less prone to engage in violent behaviors (Brookmeyer, Henrich, & Schwab-Stone, 2005). While it is known that connections to external sources of support reduces risk of adolescent involvement in violence, less is known about how such a protective factor works to promote social well-being. Hope has been explored as a mechanism through which well-being is increased among adolescents. For instance, hope has also been linked to lower levels of aggression and delinquent behavior (Valle, Huebner, & Suldo, 2004). Thus hope may be a channel through which social well-being is enhanced (Stoddard, McMorris, & Sieving, 2011). Indeed, researchers have found that hope is important for maintaining social well-being. Gallagher and Lopez (2009) found that hope was positively associated with each of the components of Keyes' model of social well-being, although the unique effect of hope on social coherence was no longer statistically significant when controlling for the effects of optimism. Further research is needed to examine why hope may have less of an unique effect on social coherence, but research to date appears to generally support the idea that hope promotes social facets of well-being.

Potential Moderators of the Hope and Well-Being Relationship

To date, there is a relative dearth of literature examining hope and well-being in the context of racial and ethnic minorities. The questions that remain to be further researched pertain to potential gender, cultural, and age differences in how hope influences well-being across these demographics. Some researchers argue that an individual's goals can be highly specific to his or her cultural context, thus inviting the question: Does hope enhance well-being through culturally specific goal pursuits? If so, do the pathways to those goals differ?

Gender and Age

Many researchers have been interested in examining the effect of hope on well-being as it pertains to similarities and differences between genders and ages. Past studies have found no discernable difference in hope and life satisfaction between the genders (Bailey & Snyder, 2007). Likewise, researchers have noted that men and women are generally similar in their level of life satisfaction (Diener & Diener, 1995). However, differences have emerged between genders in regard to hope, such that female adolescents exhibited significantly less hope compared to their male counterparts (Heaven & Ciarrochi, 2008). A potential explanation for this finding is that, during the adolescent years, females and males encounter different stereotypes regarding their gender identities and sex-typed behaviors. As such, female adolescents may come to internalize the stereotype that they are less able than males (Heaven & Ciarrochi, 2008). Low hope among female adolescents negatively impacts their adjustment to adversity and ability to effectively cope with challenges in achieving goals, which can be detrimental to their well-being (Cheavens, 2000; Snyder, Rand, & Sigmon, 2002). In a study of middle-aged men and women, Chang (2003) found a small gender difference in agentic thinking but a significant gender difference in pathways thinking. The women in the study tended to report weaker pathways thinking compared to men. The implication of weaker pathways thinking is that mental well-being may decrease for middle-aged women, for they may

experience failures in reaching goals and are less able to find alternative ways to achieve them.

Longitudinal research on trait hope is still relatively limited, though some promising early work has been done. Heaven and Ciarrochi (2008) examined the developmental trajectory of hope among adolescents over the span of four years. They found that although hope tended to decline over the course of the study, those with higher level of hope at baseline showed less decline as time went on. The general pattern of decrease in hope may be reflective of the challenges and stress adolescents must learn to navigate during those years (Steinberg & Morris, 2001). There is also an increasing body of research examining the course and benefits of hope in older adults (see Chapter 12 in this volume), with some research indicating older adults had lower levels of agency and pathways than younger adults (Bailey & Snyder, 2007). These findings have implications for well-being among older adults. Ryff (1989) demonstrated that older adults experience less purpose in life and personal growth than middle-aged and young adults. Findings from two large-scale studies of age trends in positive affect, negative affect, and life satisfaction revealed that at the same time that positive affect declined, negative affect also declined. However, home and work satisfaction increased during this same period in time. This may suggest that there is no fixed level of well-being that remains constant across the lifespan (Heady & Wearing, 1989).

Race and Ethnicity

Research on hope and well-being within racial/ethnic populations is limited, given that European American college students comprise the majority of sampling populations in studies (Chang & Banks, 2007). There are some findings indicating possible racial differences in levels of hope. Minority racial/ethnic groups face significant challenges in daily life and in their goal pursuits (Smith, 1985). Choi and colleagues (2006) found that racial and ethnic minority status was a significant predictor of stress levels and emotional distress among urban adolescents. The threat of racial discrimination is a common reality many minorities encounter in the workplace and in social domains, which may have detrimental effects on mental health (Noh & Kasper, 2003; Okazaki, 2009). Thus, when taking into account particular challenges that racial/ethnic minorities face, it may be possible for the hope to vary across different racial/ethnic groups (Snyder, 1995). Studies show that an individual's mere perception of discrimination based on his or her race/ethnicity can harm well-being (e.g., Sellers, Caldwell, Schmeelk-Cone, & Zimmerman, 2003; Torres & Ong, 2010). Despite these barriers faced by racial and ethnic minorities, Vacek, Coyle, and Vera (2010) found that they tend to be relatively satisfied with their lives. Additionally, the study found hope to be a significant predictor of subjective well-being in minority populations. Chang and Banks (2007) found that hope functions similarly across European Americans, African Americans, Hispanic Americans, and Asian Americans. For instance, agentic thinking was positively correlated with pathways thinking across all four racial/ethnic groups. In addition, Hispanic Americans reported greater agentic and pathways thinking compared to European Americans (Chang & Banks, 2007).

The experience of high hope among racial/ethnic minorities suggests that exposure to adversity may strengthen coping abilities, which is positively linked to hope. It is likely that individuals of a racial/ethnic minority group who experience high levels of hope engage in more adaptive ways of coping that may effectively minimize or eliminate stressors (Roesch, Duangado, Vaughn, Aldridge, & Villodas, 2010). In a study of adolescents from an ethnic minority sample, Roesch et al. found that hope was significantly associated with daily use of effective coping strategies (e.g., direct problem-solving and support for actions). Additionally, ethnic minority adolescents with high agency seek more external sources of support (i.e., social support from family or peers) compared to those with low agency. Therefore, it is possible that effective coping strategies are a mechanism through which hope predicts positive psychological adjustment in racial/ethnic minorities.

Western and Eastern Cultural Differences

Snyder's hope theory revolves around the Western cultural emphasis on goal pursuit and achievement (Snyder & Lopez, 2007). Moreover, the concept of subjective and psychological well-being as we understand it in scientific literature is also partly influenced by Western individualistic ideals. For instance, the focus of subjective well-being is placed on the individual, for it is from the individual's vantage point that his or her life is evaluated (Christopher, 1999). The ability to reflect upon oneself as a separate and independent body from others is highly valued by individualistic cultures. However, many collectivist cultures tend to place less emphasis on individuals' subjective evaluations of themselves. One's view of the self is best

understood in the context of interpersonal relations (Markus & Kitayama, 1991). The concept of self-orientation versus other orientation is relevant to the specific components of psychological well-being (i.e., self-acceptance and autonomy vs. positive relationships). Self-acceptance and autonomy are perhaps more pertinent in individualistic cultures while positive relations with others may hold more significance in interdependent cultural contexts (Ryff, 1995). An examination of a sample of mid-life adults in America and South Korea revealed that Americans reported the highest self-rating on personal growth and Koreans reported the highest self-rating on positive relations with others (Ryff, 1995). In a study of hope and well-being in Americans and Brazilians, Americans were reported to have higher hope and life satisfaction scores than Brazilians. Perhaps this is a consequence of hope being defined on individualistic terms, for hope provides the means to pursue and achieve independent goals, which in turn promotes well-being (Hutz, Midgett, Pacico, Bastianello, & Zanon, 2014).

Moreover, the PANAS, which is the most widely used measure of the positive affect component of subjective well-being, is rooted in Western culture's endorsement of high arousal positive states, such as feelings of excitement. Cultural factors influence which affective states are most desirable to people. For instance, researchers found that European Americans value high arousal positive states significantly more than East Asians. By contrast, East Asians tended to value low arousal positive states such as feelings of peace and calm (Tsai, Knutson, & Fung, 2006). The PANAS, however, does not equally account for low arousal positive states when assessing for positive affect. Numerous factors such as interpersonal communication, peer interactions, religious teachings, the media, magazines, and children's literature all point to the idea that culture influences how well-being is understood (Tsai, 2007). The cultural emphasis placed on subjectively defined positive affect shapes what the people within that culture believe to be desirable states of being.

Given that goal pursuits are prominent in Snyder's (2002) definition of hope, it is also worth examining the types of goals (i.e., influence vs. adjustment goals) that are pursued in individualistic and collectivistic cultures. Research suggests that influence goals are more prominent within American contexts, which are individualistic while adjustment goals are more salient among East Asian cultures, which are collectivistic (e.g., Morling, Kitayama, & Miyamoto, 2002). Tsai, Miao, Seppala, Fung, and

Yeung (2007) found that individuals with influence goals must hold sway over others' thoughts and behaviors in order to have them become consistent with the individual's own desires and needs. The very act of influencing others is associated with increased arousal (Tsai, 2007). It is not surprising, therefore, when individuals who engage in influence behaviors exhibit and learn to value positive high arousal states. Adjustment goals, on the contrary, require one to assess the needs and preferences of others prior to changing one's own behavior to align with those needs and preferences. The act of adjusting entails suppression and suspending action, which involves decreases in physiological arousal. This leads to desirable low arousal states among people who are more likely to have adjustment goals (Tsai et al., 2007). These findings suggest that Western psychology's interpretation of hope and well-being is likely biased in favor of influence goals and high arousal positive states and therefore may not be of equal significance within collectivistic cultures. More research is needed, however, to examine the consistency with which hope predicts various components of well-being in different cultures.

Conclusion

The past 25 years of research has consistently found high-hope individuals to fare better than their low-hope counterparts in various domains, including psychological adjustment (Snyder, 2002). Whether the focus is on the presence of positive emotions, the relative absence of negative emotions, meaning in life, or positive relationships with others, hope is a robust predictor of well-being and consistently predicts higher levels of well-being even when controlling for other powerful predictors of mental health (Gallagher & Lopez, 2009). More than many other positive psychology constructs, hope appears to be a reliable predictor and promoter of positive mental health. As research in this areas continues over the next decade, our knowledge of how hope functions as a positive psychological strength that fosters mental health and drives goal pursuits should continue to develop.

The specific mechanisms through which hope influences well-being is one area that warrants further research. Snyder's model of hope provides clear theoretical predictions for when, why, and how hope should promote well-being, and there is promising research supporting these theoretical predictions. However, more research, particularly longitudinal studies, are needed to examine the specific mechanisms by which hope promotes well-being. Past research has explored factors such as problem-solving, resilience, and coping styles as mechanisms that influence the relationship between hope and well-being (e.g., Chang, 2003), but extending this existing work with longitudinal studies will help us to better understand the mechanisms by which hope promotes well-being.

As with most constructs studied in positive psychology, the field would benefit from a greater consideration and examination of how demographic and cultural variables may moderate the impact of hope on well-being so that we can better understand the consistency of the benefits of hope worldwide. We also need to better understand the impact of hope interventions on well-being and whether fostering well-being via targeting hope is an effective method of promoting recovery in mental illness or positive functioning in individuals with chronic health conditions such as cancer. It is now clear that hope is an important factor in promoting well-being, but by pursuing these topics further we can more fully understand and more effectively target hope as a means of promoting flourishing mental health.

Future Directions

• What are the unique effects of hope on well-being above and beyond other well-established positive psychology constructs that have a positive impact on well-being such as curiosity and gratitude?

• What influence do cultural factors have on the impact of hope on well-being, and does the potential moderating influence of culture vary across the different components of well-being?

• Are hope therapy interventions designed to promote recovery from anxiety and depression equally effective at promoting subjective, psychological, and social well-being?

• What are the mechanisms by which hope promotes well-being, and are the mechanisms consistent across the different domains of well-being?

• Given that hope is a cognitively oriented construct, to what extent and in what ways does the impact of hope on well-being change in individuals with cognitive impairments?

References

Alarcon, G. M., Bowling, N. A., & Khazon, S. (2013). Great expectations: A meta-analytic examination of optimism and hope. *Personality and Individual Differences, 54,* 821–827. doi:10.1016/j.paid.2012.12.004

Aldao, A., Nolen-Hoeksema, S., & Schweizer, S. (2010). Emotion-regulation strategies across psychopathology: A meta-analytic review. *Clinical Psychology Review, 30,* 217–237. doi:10.1016/j.cpr.2009.11.004

Avey, J. B., Wernsing, T. S., & Mhatre, K. H. (2011). A longitudinal analysis of positive psychological constructs and emotions on stress, anxiety, and well-being. *Journal of Leadership & Organizational Studies, 18,* 216–228. doi:10.1177/1548051810397368

Bailey, T. C., Eng, W., Frisch, M. B., & Snyder, C. R. (2007). Hope and optimism as related to life satisfaction. *The Journal of Positive Psychology, 2,* 168–175. doi:10.1080/17439760701409546

Bailey, T. C., & Snyder, C. R. (2007). Satisfaction with life and hope: A look at age and marital status. *The Psychological Record, 57,* 233–240.

Berkman, L., Glass, T., Brissette, I., & Seeman, T. (2000). From social integration to health: Durkheim in the new millennium. *Social Science & Medicine, 51,* 843–857. doi:10.1016/S0277-9536(00)00065-4

Biswas-Diener, R., Kashdan, T. B., & King, L. A. (2009). Two traditions of happiness research, not two distinct types of happiness. *The Journal of Positive Psychology, 4*(3), 208–211.

Brickman, P., & Campbell, D. T. (1971). Hedonic relativism and planning the good society. In M. H. Appley (Ed.), *Adaptation level theory: A symposium* (pp. 287–302). New York: Academic Press.

Bronk, K. C., Hill, P. L., Lapsley, D. K., Talib, T. L., & Finch, H. (2009). Purpose, hope, and life satisfaction in three age groups. *The Journal of Positive Psychology, 4,* 500–510. doi:10.1080/17439760903271439

Brookmeyer, K. A., Henrich, C. C., & Schwab-Stone, M. (2005). Adolescents who witness community violence: Can parent support and pro-social cognitions protect them from committing violence? *Child Development, 76,* 917–929. doi:10.1111/j.1467-8624.2005.00886.x

Ciarrocchi, J. W., & Deneke, E. (2005). Hope, optimism, pessimism, and spirituality as predictors of well-being controlling for personality. *Research in the Social Scientific Study of Religion, 16,* 161–183.

Ciarrochi, J. W., Parker, P., Kashdan, T. B., Heaven, P. H. L., & Barkus, E. (2015). Hope and emotional well-being: A six-year study to distinguish antecedents, correlates, and consequences, *The Journal of Positive Psychology, 10,* 520–532. doi:10.1080/17439760.2015.1015154

Chang, E. C. (2003). A critical appraisal and extension of hope theory in middle-aged men and women: Is it important to distinguish agency and pathways components? *Journal of Social and Clinical Psychology, 22,* 121–143. doi:10.1521/jscp.22.2.121.22876

Chang, E. C., & Banks, K. H. (2007). The color and texture of hope: Some preliminary findings and implications for hope theory and counseling among diverse racial/ethnic groups. *Cultural Diversity and Ethnic Minority Psychology, 13,* 94–103. doi:10.1037/1099-9809.13.2.94

Cheavens, J. (2000). Hope and depression: Light through the shadows. In C. R. Snyder (Ed.), *Handbook of hope: Theory, measures, and applications* (pp. 321–340). San Diego: Academic Press.

Choi, H., Meininger, J. C., & Roberts, R. E. (2006). Ethnic differences in adolescents' mental distress, social stress, and resources. *Adolescence, 41,* 263–283.

Christopher, J. C. (1999). Situating psychological well-being: Exploring the cultural roots of its theory and research. *Journal of Counseling & Development, 77,* 141–152. doi:10.1002/j.1556-6676.1999.tb02434.x

Clark, L. A., & Watson, D. (1988). Mood and the mundane: relations between daily life events and self-reported mood. *Journal of personality and social psychology, 54,* 296–308.

Ciarrochi, J., Parker, P., Kashdan, T. B., Heaven, P. C., & Barkus, E. (2015). Hope and emotional well-being: A six-year study to distinguish antecedents, correlates, and consequences. *The Journal of Positive Psychology, 1–13.* doi:10.1080/17439760.2015.1015154

Curry, L. A., Snyder, C. R., Cook, D. L., Ruby, B. C., & Rehm, M. (1997). Role of hope in academic and sport achievement. *Journal of Personality and Social Psychology, 73,* 1257–1267. doi:10.1037/0022-3514.73.6.1257

Damon, W., Menon, J., & Bronk, K. C. (2003). The development of purpose during adolescence. *Applied Developmental Science, 7,* 119–128. doi:10.1207/S1532480XADS0703_2

Demirli, A., Türkmen, M., & Arık, R. S. (2015). Investigation of dispositional and state hope levels' relations with student subjective well-being. *Social Indicators Research, 120,* 601–613. doi:10.1007/s11205-014-0607-9

Diener, E. (1984). Subjective well-being. *Psychological Bulletin, 95,* 542–575.

Diener, E., & Diener, M. (1995). Cross-cultural correlates of life satisfaction and self-esteem. *Journal of Personality and Social Psychology, 68,* 653–663. doi:10.1037/0022-3514.68.4.653

Diener, E., & Diener, C. (1996). Most people are happy. *Psychological Science, 7,* 181–185. doi:10.1111/j.1467-9280.1996.tb00354.x

Diener, E., Emmons, R. A., Larsen, R. J., & Griffin, S. (1985). The Satisfaction With Life Scale. *Journal of Personality Assessment, 49,* 71–75. doi:10.1207/s15327752jpa4901_13

Diener, E., & Suh, E. (1997). Measuring quality of life: Economic, social, and subjective indicators. *Social Indicators Research, 40,* 189–216. doi:10.1023/A:1006859511756

Diener, E., Suh, E., Lucas, R. E., & Smith, H. L. (1999). Subjective well-being: Three decades of progress. *Psychological Bulletin, 125,* 276–302. doi:10.1037/0033-2909.125.2.276

Emmons, R. A. (1992). Abstract versus concrete goals: Personal striving level, physical illness, and psychological well-being. *Journal of Personality and Social Psychology, 62,* 292–300. doi:10.1037/0022-3514.62.2.292

Frank, J. D., & Frank, J. B. (1961). *Persuasion and healing: A comprehensive study of psychotherapy.* Baltimore: Johns Hopkins University Press.

Folkman, S. (2010). Stress, coping, and hope. *Psycho-Oncology, 19,* 901–908. doi:10.1002/pon.1836

Fredrickson, B. L. (2001). The role of positive emotions in positive psychology: The broaden-and-build theory of positive emotions. *American Psychologist, 56,* 218–226. doi:10.1037/0003-066X.56.3.218

Fredrickson, B. L., & Losada, M. F. (2005). Positive affect and the complex dynamics of human flourishing. *American Psychologist, 60,* 678–686. doi:10.1037/0003-066X.60.7.678

Gallagher, M. W. (2011). Agency, optimism, and the longitudinal course of anxiety and well-being. University of Kansas. ProQuest dissertations and theses. Retrieved from http://search.proquest.com/docview/916606568

Gallagher, M. W., & Lopez, S. J. (2009). Positive expectancies and mental health: Identifying the unique contributions of hope and optimism. *The Journal of Positive Psychology, 4,* 548–556. doi:10.1080/17439760903157166

Gallagher, M. W., Lopez, S. J., & Preacher, K. J. (2009). The hierarchical structure of well-being. *Journal of Personality, 77,* 1025–1050. doi:10.1111/j.1467-6494.2009.00573.x

Gibson, L. M. R., & Parker, V. (2003). Inner resources as predictors of psychological well-being in middle-income African American breast cancer survivors. *Cancer Control, 10,* 52–59.

Green, S., Grant, A., & Rynsaardt, J. (2007). Evidence-based life coaching for senior high school students: Building hardiness and hope. *International Coaching Psychology Review, 2,* 24–32.

Gross J. J. (Ed.). (2014). *Handbook of emotion regulation* (2nd ed.). New York, NY: Guilford Press.

Halama, P., & Dědová, M. (2007). Meaning in life and hope as predictors of positive mental health: Do they explain residual variance not predicted by personality traits? *Studia Psychologica, 49,* 191–200.

Heady, B., & Wearing, A. (1989). Personality, life events, and subjective well-being: Toward a dynamic equilibrium model. *Journal of Personality and Social Psychology, 57,* 731–739. doi:10.1037/0022-3514.57.4.731

Heaven, P., & Ciarrochi, J. (2008). Parental styles, gender and the development of hope and self-esteem. *European Journal of Personality, 22,* 707–724. doi:10.1002/per.699

Hill, P. L., & Turiano, N. A. (2014). Purpose in life as a predictor of mortality across adulthood. *Psychological Science, 25,* 1482–1486. doi:10.1177/0956797614531799

Hutz, C. S., Midgett, A., Pacico, J. C., Bastianello, M. R., & Zanon, C. (2014). The relationship of hope, optimism, self-esteem, subjective well-being, and personality in Brazilians and Americans. *Psychology, 5,* 514–522. doi:10.4236/psych.2014.56061

Jahoda, M. (1959). Conformity and independence: A psychological analysis. *Human Relations, 12,* 99–120. doi: 10.1177/001872675901200201

Jorm, A. F., Windsor, T. D., Dear, K. B. G., Anstey, K. J., Christensen, H., & Rodgers, B. (2005). Age group differences in psychological distress: The role of psychosocial risk factors that vary with age. *Psychological Medicine, 35,* 1253–1263. doi:10.1017/S0033291705004976

Keyes, C. L. M. (1998). Social well-being. *Social Psychology Quarterly, 61,* 121–140.

Keyes, C. L. (2007). Promoting and protecting mental health as flourishing: a complementary strategy for improving national mental health. *American psychologist, 62*(2), 95–108.

Keyes, C. L. M., Shmotkin, D., & Ryff, C. D. (2002). Optimizing well-being: The empirical encounter of two traditions. *Journal of Personality and Social Psychology, 82,* 1007–1022. doi:10.1037/0022-3514.82.6.1007

Lagacé-Séguin, D. G., & d'Entremont, M. L. (2010). A scientific exploration of positive psychology in adolescence: The role of hope as a buffer against the influences of psychosocial negatives. *Internationl Journal of Adolescence and Youth, 16,* 69–95. doi:10.1080/02673843.2010.9748046

Lyubomirsky, S., King, L., & Diener, E. (2005). The benefits of frequent positive affect: Does happiness lead to success?. *Psychological Bulletin, 131*(6), 803.

Lu, F. J. H., & Hsu, Y. (2013). Injured athletes' rehabilitation beliefs and subjective well-being: The contribution of hope and social support. *Journal of Athletic Training, 48,* 92–98. doi:10.4085/1062-6050-48.1.03

Markus, H. R., & Kitayama, S. (1991). Culture and the self: Implications for cognition, emotion, and motivation. *Psychological Review, 98,* 224–253. doi:10.1037/0033-295X.98.2.224

Morling, B., Kitayama, S., & Miyamoto, Y. (2002). Cultural practices emphasize influence in the United States and adjustment in Japan. *Personality and Social Psychology Bulletin, 28,* 311–323. doi:10.1177/0146167202286003

Noh, S., & Kasper, V. (2003). Perceived discrimination and depression: Moderating effects of coping, acculturation, and ethnic support. *American Journal of Public Health, 93,* 232–238. doi:10.2105/AJPH.93.2.232

Oishi, S., Diener, E. F., Lucas, R. E., & Suh, E. M. (1999). Cross-cultural variations in predictors of life satisfaction: Perspectives from needs and values. *Personality and Social Psychology Bulletin, 25,* 980–990. doi:10.1177/01461672992511006

Okazaki, S. (2009). Impact of racism on ethnic minority mental health. *Perspectives on Psychological Science, 4,* 103–107. doi:10.1111/j.1745-6924.2009.01099.x

Park, N., & Peterson, C. (2006). Moral competence and character strengths among adolescents: The development and validation of the Values in Action Inventory of Strengths for Youth. *Journal of Adolescence, 29,* 891–909. doi:10.1016/j.adolescence.2006.04.011

Park, N., Peterson, C., & Seligman, M. E. P. (2004). Strengths of character and well-being. *Journal of Social and Clinical Psychology, 23,* 603–619. doi:10.1521/jscp.23.5.603.50748

Polivy, J., & Herman, C. P. (2002). If at first you don't succeed: False hopes of self-change. *American Psychologist, 57,* 677–689. doi:10.1037/0003-066X.57.9.677

Proyer, R. T., Ruch, W., & Buschor, C. (2013). Testing strengths-based interventions: A preliminary study on the effectiveness of a program targeting curiosity, gratitude, hope, humor, and zest for enhancing life satisfaction. *Journal of Happiness Studies, 14,* 275–292. doi:10.1007/s10902-012-9331-9

Richards, M., & Huppert, F. A. (2011). Do positive children become positive adults? Evidence from a longitudinal birth cohort study. *The Journal of Positive Psychology, 6,* 75–87. doi:10.1080/17439760.2011.536655

Roesch, S. C., Duangado, K. M., Vaughn, A. A., Aldridge, A. A., & Villodas, F. (2010). Dispositional hope and the propensity to cope: A daily diary assessment of minority adolescents. *Cultural Diversity and Ethnic Minority Psychology, 16,* 191–198. doi:10.1037/a0016114

Ryan, R. M., & Deci, E. L. (2001). On happiness and human potentials: A review of research on hedonic and eudaimonic well-being. *Annual Review of Psychology, 52,* 141–166. doi:10.1146/annurev.psych.52.1.141

Ryff, C. D. (1989). Happiness is everything, or is it? Explorations on the meaning of psychological well-being. *Journal of Personality and Social Psychology, 57,* 1069–1081. doi:10.1037/0022-3514.57.6.1069

Ryff, C. D. (1995). Psychological well-being in adult life. *Current Directions in Psychological Science, 4,* 99–104. doi:10.1111/1467-8721.ep10772395

Ryff, C. D., & Keyes, C. L. M. (1995). The structure of psychological well-being revisited. *Journal of Personality and Social Psychology, 69,* 719–727.

Ryff, C. D. (2013). Eudamonic well-being and health: Mapping consequences of self-realization. In A. S. Waterman (Ed.), *The best within us: Positive psychology perspectives on eudaimonia* (pp. 77–98). Washington, DC: American Psychological Association.

Sellers, R. M., Caldwell, C. H., Schmeelk-Cone, K. H., & Zimmerman, M. A. (2003). Racial identity, racial discrimination, perceived stress, and psychological distress among

African America young adults. *Journal of Health and Social Behavior, 44,* 302–317. doi:10.2307/1519781

Singh, A. K., Singh, S., & Singh, A. P. (2012). Does trait predict psychological well-being among students of professional courses? *Journal of the Indian Academy of Applied Psychology, 38,* 234–241.

Smith, E. M. (1985). Ethnic minorities: Life stress, social support, and mental health issues. *The Counseling Psychologist, 13,* 537–579. doi:10.1177/0011000085134002

Snyder, C. R. (1995). Conceptualizing, measuring, and nurturing hope. *Journal of Counseling and Development, 73,* 355–360. doi:10.1002/j.1556-6676.1995.tb01764.x

Snyder, C. R. (2002). Hope theory: Rainbows in the mind. *Psychological Inquiry, 13,* 249–275.

Snyder, C. R. (2004). Hope and the other strengths: Lessons from *Animal Farm. Journal of Social and Clinical Psychology, 23,* 624–627. doi:10.1521/jscp.23.5.624.50751

Snyder, C. R., Cheavens, J., & Sympson, S. C. (1997). Hope: An individual motive for social commerce. *Group Dynamics: Theory, Research, and Practice, 1,* 107–118. doi:10.1037/1089-2699.1.2.107

Snyder, C. R., & Lopez, S. J. (2007). *Positive psychology: The scientific and practical explorations of human strengths.* Thousand Oaks, CA: SAGE.

Snyder, C. R., Rand, K. L., & Sigmon, D. R. (2002). Hope theory. In C. R. Snyder, & S. Lopez (Eds.), *Handbook of positive psychology* (pp. 257–276). Oxford, UK: Oxford University Press.

Snyder, C. R., & Rand, K. L. (2003). The case against false hope. *American Psychologist, 58,* 820–822. doi: 10.1037/0003-066X.58.10.820

Son, J., & Wilson, J. (2012). Volunteer work and hedonic, eudemonic, and social well-being. *Sociological Forum, 27,* 658–681. doi:10.1111/j.1573-7861.2012.01340.x

Steinberg, L., & Morris, A. S. (2001). Adolescent development. *Journal of Cognitive Education and Psychology, 2,* 55–87. doi:10.1891/194589501787383444

Stoddard, S. A., McMorris, B. J., & Sieving, R. E. (2011). Do social connections and hope matter in predicting early adolescent violence? *American Journal of Community Psychology, 48,* 247–256. doi:10.1007/s10464-010-9387-9

Torres, L., & Ong, A. D. (2010). A daily diary investigation of Latino ethnic identity, discrimination, and depression. *Cultural Diversity and Ethnic Minority Psychology, 16,* 561–568. doi:10.1037/a0020652

Tsai, J. L. (2007). Ideal affect: Cultural causes and behavioral consequences. *Perspectives on Psychological Science, 2,* 242–259. doi:10.1111/j.1745-6916.2007.00043.x

Tsai, J. L., Knutson, B. K., & Fung, H. H. (2006). Cultural variation affect valuation. *Journal of Personality and Social Psychology, 90,* 288–307.

Tsai, J. L., Miao, F. F., Seppala, E., Fung, H. H., & Yeung, D. Y. (2007). Influence and adjustment goals: Sources of cultural differences in ideal affect. *Journal of Personality and Social Psychology, 92,* 1102–1117. doi:10.1037/0022-3514.92.6.1102

Vacek, K. R., Coyle, L. D., & Vera, E. M. (2010). Stress, self-esteem, hope, optimism, and well-being in urban ethnic minority adolescents. *Journal of Multicultural Counseling and Development, 38,* 99–111. doi:10.1002/j.2161-1912.2010.tb00118.x

Valle, M. F., Huebner, E. S., & Suldo, S. M. (2004). Further evaluation of the Children's Hope Scale. *Journal of Psychoeducational Assessment, 22,* 320–337. doi:10.1177/073428290402200403

Valle, M. F., Huebner, E. S., & Suldo, S. M. (2006). An analysis of hope as a psychological strength. *Journal of School Psychology, 44,* 393–406. doi:10.1016/j.jsp.2006.03.005

Waterman, A. S. (1993). Two conceptions of happiness: Contrasts of personal expressiveness (eudaimonia) and hedonic enjoyment. *Journal of Personality and Social Psychology, 64,* 678–691. doi:10.1037/0022-3514.64.4.678

Watson, D., Clark, L. A., & Tellegen, A. (1988). Development and validation of brief measures of positive and negative affect: The PANAS scales. *Journal of Personality and Social Psychology, 54,* 1063–1070. doi:10.1037/0022-3514.54.6.1063

Werner, S. (2012). Subjective well-being, hope, and needs of individuals with serious mental illness. *Psychiatry Research, 196,* 214–219. doi:10.1016/j.psychres.2011.10.012

Windsor, T. D., Anstey, K. J., & Rodgers, B. (2008). Volunteering and psychological well-being among young-old adults: How much is too much?. *The Gerontologist, 48,* 59–70. doi:10.1093/geront/48.1.59

Wrobleski, K. K., & Snyder, C. R. (2005). Hopeful thinking in older adults: Back to the future. *Experimental Aging Research, 31,* 217–233. doi:10.80/03610730590915452

Hope and Adolescent Mental Health

Xi Jiang, Kristin L. Otis, Marco Weber, *and* E. Scott Huebner

Abstract

This chapter begins with a description of the tenets of hope theory and then addresses the importance of hope during adolescence from a developmental perspective. Next, two accompanying instruments for measuring hope in adults and adolescents, the Adult Hope Scale and the Children's Hope Scale, are described. Then the chapter summarizes the research findings on the relations between hope and adolescent mental health, focusing on the findings related to emotional, psychological, and social well-being, respectively. In addition, the Making Hope Happen intervention is introduced. Finally, the chapter explores future directions in adolescent hope research, along with implications for use by mental health professionals.

Key Words: hope, adolescent, mental health, well-being, Making Hope Happen, Adult Hope Scale, Children's Hope Scale

Laypersons and scholars have traditionally considered hope to be an affective phenomenon (Snyder, Feldman, Shorey, & Rand, 2002). However, according to the most seminal hope researchers (Snyder et al., 1991), hope is best conceptualized as a cognitive-motivational construct. Specifically, hope has been defined as an underlying goal-directed process that is composed of both a cognitive and motivational component—specifically, agency and pathways thinking (Snyder, Cheavens, & Michael, 1999). When individuals engage in pathways thinking, they actively construct routes or plans for achieving goals. Pathways thinking can be illustrated by internal speech, such as "I'll find a way to get this done" (Snyder, Lapointe, Crowson, & Early, 1998). Agency thinking is the motivational component that ensures a person will be able to begin and sustain the effort necessary to follow a particular pathway. Agency can be characterized by internal speech, such as "I am not going to be stopped" (Snyder et al., 1998). Although pathways and agency thinking are two distinct components of the overall hope construct, they are also functionally

inseparable. More detailed explanations of these two components can be found in Snyder et al. (1991).

Rooted in the positive psychology philosophy, hope has been recognized as an important psychological strength and a correlate of mental health for children and adults (Snyder, 2000; Snyder, McDermott, Cook, & Rapoff, 1997; Valle, Huebner, & Suldo, 2006). The World Health Organization (2014) defines mental health as a "state of well-being in which every individual realizes his or her own potential, can cope with the normal stresses of life, can work productively and fruitfully, and is able to make a contribution to his or her community" (p. 1). Three specific, major domains of mental health have been further identified by the Centers for Disease Control and Prevention (CDC, 2013): emotional well-being, psychological well-being, and social well-being. We review the literature on hope and mental health among adolescents in particular using this broad definition in the next section. In this section, we provide a simple snapshot of the research on individual difference in hope and the mental health of adults. For instance, low levels of hope in adults have consistently been found to be associated with both internalizing and externalizing behaviors (Snyder, Lopez, Shorey, Rand, & Feldman, 2003); whereas higher levels of hope have been associated with higher levels of self-esteem (Curry, Snyder, Cook, Ruby, & Rehm, 1997) and life satisfaction (e.g., Bailey & Snyder, 2007). A more thorough overview of the research on adult hope can be found elsewhere in this book. Most hope studies have focused on adults, with relatively few studies focused on youth in the developmental years, such as during adolescence. In this chapter, we start with the importance of hope during adolescence from a developmental perspective and summarize the research findings on the relations between hope and adolescent mental health. Finally, we explore future directions in adolescent hope research and implications for mental health professionals.

For over a century, research on adolescent development primarily focused on the negative aspects of adolescence. Early findings suggested that the early adolescent years mark the beginning of a downward spiral of storm and stress (Hall, 1904) in adolescence, at least for some individuals. For example, research shows that the rates of depression increase significantly from childhood to adolescence (Costello & Angold, 1988; Rutter, 1986, 1991). Also, a marked decline emerges in some early adolescents' school grades and school engagement as they move into junior high school, and the magnitude of this decline is predictive of subsequent school failure and dropout (Simmons & Blyth, 1987). In addition, one of the most common and significant behavioral changes in adolescence is the sharp increase in risk-taking behaviors (e.g., alcohol and other drug use, risky sexual behavior, and reckless driving), which are associated with increased physical injuries, morbidity, and mortality (CDC, 2014).

Adolescence is characterized by numerous changes, and these changes occur at many different levels, such as pubertal development, emergence of sexuality, cognitive development, self-identity formation, social role redefinitions, school transitions, and more autonomy and responsibility related to making decisions. Exemplary theoretical models (e.g., Brooks-Gunn, 1988; Elkind, 1978; Erikson, 1968), together with the extant empirical research, have contributed to a better understanding of how multifaceted (e.g., cognitive, psychosocial, and biological) changes in development contribute to the overall mental health outcomes of adolescents.

In the areas of cognitive development, adolescents show qualitative changes during the transition from childhood to adolescence (Moshman, 1998). For example, adolescents begin to form more complex cognitive skills, such as abstract and logical thinking ability, in contrast to the concrete operational thought of their childhood years (Montemayor & Flannery, 1990). Consequently, adolescents are more capable of predicting the consequences of actions and understanding the complexity (e.g., ambiguities and uncertainties) of life events (Berndt, 1997; Montemayor & Flannery, 1990). However, some cognitive limitations also occur at this particular developmental stage. For example, research suggests that adolescents are more likely to see themselves as invulnerable to risks (Elkind, 1967) and to more heavily weigh the negative consequences of not engaging in risky behaviors than adults (Beyth-Marom, Austin, Fishhoff, Palmgren, & Quadrel, 1993). Adolescents are also more likely to discount the future and weigh short-term consequences more heavily than long-term consequences, compared to adults (Gardner & Herman, 1991). Based on research in neuroscience, several researchers have advanced the hypothesis that heightened risk-taking in adolescence is the product of an easily aroused reward system and an immature self-regulatory system (e.g., Casey, Getz, & Galvan, 2008; Dahl, 2004; Steinberg, 2008). Readers who are interested in the relations between adolescent brain development and behavioral outcomes should seek out other resources for a detailed description of neuroscience research (e.g., see Steinberg, 2005, 2008).

Changes in motivation also become noticeable and, in many areas, more problematic during adolescence. For instance, early research documented age-related declines during adolescence in terms of interest in school (Elmore & Huebner, 2010; Epstein & McPartland, 1976), intrinsic motivation to learn (Gottfried, Fleming, & Gottfried, 2001; Harter, 1981, 2012) and valuing of school achievement (Eccles et al., 1989; Wigfield, Eccles, Mac Iver, Reuman, & Midgley, 1991). Another consistent finding in this area is that competence-related beliefs decline during early adolescence and adolescence (for reviews, see Anderman & Maehr, 1994; Eccles et al., 1998, Harter, 2012). Specifically, early adolescents' perceptions of their competence for various school subjects and other activities are lower than those of their younger peers (Eccles et al., 1989; Jacobs, Lanza, Osgood, Eccles, & Wigfield, 2002; Wigfield et al., 1991). There are also reports of age-related increases during early adolescence in some negative motivational and behavioral characteristics, such as test anxiety (Hill, 1980) and learned helplessness responses to failure (Rholes, Blackwell, Jordan, & Walters, 1980). In a series of longitudinal studies conducted with large samples of Australian adolescents (Grades 7–12), Ciarrochi, Parker, Kashdan, Heaven, and Barkus (2015) found a significant decline in trait hope during the early years of adolescence (see also Heaven & Ciarrochi, 2008). Consistent with many aforementioned changes in various motivational factors during adolescence, adolescents' decline in hope may be also reflective of the various challenges associated with this period of the lifespan.

The *negative* characteristics and outcomes associated with adolescence are certainly important. However, as Seligman and Csikszentmihalyi argued persuasively in their seminal work, "psychology is not just the study of pathology, weakness, and damage; it is also the study of strength and virtue," (2000, p. 5) it is no less important to recognize and study the *positive* characteristics and resources of adolescents. Hope, as measured by the Children's Hope Scale (CHS; Snyder et al., 1997), has been found to be positively associated with optimal mental health outcomes (e.g., life satisfaction) and negatively associated with adverse mental health outcomes (e.g., psychological distress). More thorough consideration of these studies is provided later. Overall, however, the existing evidence supports that hope, as a cognitive-motivational strength, is among the useful internal resources that foster positive adaptation and promote positive mental health in adolescents. According to some scholars (e.g., Snyder et al., 1991), hope can color one's appraisal of stressors and subsequently facilitate the coping process. More specifically, individuals who have high hope tend to appraise stressors as more challenging (as opposed to more threatening) and thus have the motivation and ability to find solutions to ameliorate stressful feelings and resolve major life stressors (Snyder et al., 1991). This theory is consistent with the transactional model of stress and coping (see Lazarus & Folkman, 1984).

It is also important to understand hope as an iterative cognitive-motivational process composed of agency and pathways thoughts in the service of important goals. For adolescents, the process of hope can serve as a protective mechanism when they encounter some of their stage-salient challenges. For instance, as a goal-directed process, having high hope should help adolescents develop clear goals and direct their behaviors toward achieving specific outcomes, rather than act impulsively, particularly under risky or stressful situations. In addition, although adolescents begin to have the capacity to demonstrate more complex thoughts, including generating alternatives and predicting consequences, some other stage-salient characteristics, such as emotional lability (e.g., Buchanan, Eccles, & Becker, 1992) and excessive self-focused attention (e.g., Ingram & Smith, 1984; Smith & Greenberg, 1981), may limit the level of openness of adolescents' thinking. By having higher levels of hope, particularly pathways thinking, adolescents are more likely to produce workable routes to circumvent possible obstacles to goal accomplishment (Hinton-Nelson, Roberts, & Snyder, 1996). Also, if an adolescent has a higher level of hope, which means he or she is sufficiently motivated to initiate and sustain movement along pathways toward desired ends, it should increase the likelihood that the adolescent is resistant to the developmental declines in motivation that occur commonly at this developmental stage. Keeping the protective function of hope in mind, it should be noted that hope is especially important for those who encounter unpredictable and uncontrollable circumstances (Snyder, 1994), such as neglect or other maltreatment, poverty, bullying, and other significant stress factors (e.g., acculturation, language difficulties).

In accordance with the more recent view of positive youth development (see Lerner, Almerigi, Theokas, & Lerner, 2005) in which adolescents are viewed as resources to develop, rather than problems to be managed (Roth & Brooks-Gunn, 2003; Roth, Brooks-Gunn, Murray, & Foster, 1998), we argue that hope is not only a protective factor that can help adolescents "manage" their problems in adolescence but is also a contributing factor that can promote optimal development and help adolescents reach their full potential. Research has suggested that from preadolescence through late adolescence, impulse control (Steinberg et al., 2008), anticipation of future consequences (Steinberg et al., 2009), strategic planning (Steinberg et al., 2009), and coordination of emotion and cognition (Steinberg, 2008) all increase linearly. Adolescence is also characterized by growing autonomy and increased involvement in one's own development in many aspects. Specifically, young people (particularly those at the later adolescence stage) begin to choose their own environments and make their own decisions that will set trajectories for their future lives (e.g., educational and occupational aspirations, romantic relationships and marriage). According to several development researchers (Erikson, 1968; Gottfredson, 1981; Nurmi, 2004), individual experiences during adolescence also shape expectations regarding future career paths and identity formation. Thus adolescence can also be a "golden age" for individuals to learn and develop hope and other psychological strengths (e.g., optimism, persistence). We assert that it is essential that adolescents establish meaningful goals, perceive themselves as capable of achieving those goals, and are able to identify and implement realistic, specific strategies for attaining those goals. These optimal learning experiences can promote a smoother transition from adolescence to adulthood and will likely benefit adolescents in their future development across their lifespan. As will be seen next, research has shown that not only does higher hope co-occur with important outcomes, but higher hope also predicts *increases* in important outcomes. Thus hope development appears vital for those adolescents who experience or do not experience major barriers to reaching their goals in life.

Review of Hope and Adolescent Mental Health

Prior to reviewing the literature on hope and mental health, we provide a review of the existing assessment measures of hope, based on the seminal definition of Snyder et al. (1991). Because the primary measure for adolescents was derived from a measure for adults, we briefly discuss the Adult Hope Scale (AHS; Snyder et al., 1991) but focus on the measure appropriate for adolescents.

Hope Measurement

Consistent with a positive psychology approach, measures of hope should allow scholars to assess the full range of hope levels from "very low" to "very high." In line with the benefits of possessing higher levels of hope, the tools should provide evidence of reliability and validity with respect to measuring individual differences in hope in adolescents in particular. Furthermore, they should be useful in developing interventions to promote more optimal levels of hope in all adolescents (Snyder, 2005). Thus, in 1991, Snyder and colleagues began the development of several scales to measure levels of hope in children, adolescents, and adults. For the purposes of this chapter, only trait/dispositional scales and scales that correspond with Snyder's hope theory are reviewed.

The first scale developed by Snyder and colleagues (1991) was the AHS, a 12-item scale that measures

hope in individuals above the age of 15 years old. On the AHS, four items measure agency, four items assess pathways, and four items are considered distractors. The eight hope items are averaged together to create a composite hope score that represents each individual's overall hope. Studies have revealed evidence of convergent and discriminant validity of the AHS as well as acceptable levels of internal consistency (.74 to .84) and 3-week to 10-week test-retest reliabilities coefficients of .76 to .85 (Snyder et al., 1991; Snyder, Lopez, & Pedrotti, 2011).

In 1997, Snyder and colleagues adapted items from the AHS to develop the CHS to measure trait hope in children, 7 to 16 years old. The age limit for this scale was set at seven because Snyder argued that in order to express hope, children needed the ability to understand and respond to simple questions (e.g., "When I have a problem, I can come up with lots of ways to solve it"), even though initial hope development is thought to occur at a much earlier age. This instrument consists of six items, three of each measuring the two major facets of hope: agency and pathways. The items are averaged to reach a composite hope score that represents each child's overall hope. Evidence for construct validity (i.e., factor structure) has been provided through exploratory (Snyder et al., 1997) and confirmatory factor analyses (Valle, Huebner, & Suldo, 2004). The CHS has also demonstrated evidence of convergent validity through expected correlations with parent reports (Snyder et al., 1997) and other related self-report measures, such as life satisfaction (Valle et al., 2004) and perceived self-worth (Snyder et al., 1997). Support for discriminant validity was provided by nonsignificant correlations with intelligence test scores (Snyder et al., 1997). Internal consistency estimates have revealed acceptable levels of internal consistency, ranging from.72 to .86 (Snyder et al., 1997). Finally, test–retest coefficients have been reported as .73 for one month (Snyder et al., 1997; Snyder, et al., 2011), .60 for six months (Marques, Pais-Ribeiro, & Lopez, 2011a), as well as .50 and .47 for one year (Marques et al., 2011a; Valle et al., 2004). Although demonstrating moderate levels of stability, hope reports also show sensitivity to changing situations, such as major school transitions (e.g., Ciarrochi, Parker, Kashdan, Heaven, & Barkus, 2015) and planned interventions (Marques et al., 2011). In short, studies conducted across differing samples in different countries have revealed considerable evidence for its reliability and validity with youth. The coefficients of test–retest reliability, along with the findings of the intervention studies reviewed in this chapter, support the notion that individual differences in adolescents' levels of hope reflect moderate degrees of stability but also appear amenable to changes across time and/or circumstances.

Relations with Mental Health

Researchers have demonstrated that there are significant relationships between individuals' hope levels and a wide variety of aspects of their mental health (Dufault & Martocchio, 1985; Kwon, 2002; Snyder, 2000). This finding is true for youth as well as adults (Esteves, Scoloveno, Mahat, Yarcheski, & Scoloveno, 2013; Marques, Lopez, & Mitchell, 2013; Snyder et al., 2003). Consistent with the relatively broad definition of mental health offered by the World Health Organization (2014), we provide an overview of the findings related to emotional, psychological, and social well-being, respectively.

First, with respect to emotional well-being, research on hope has consistently demonstrated statistically significant relations between adolescents' individual differences in hope and their emotional well-being, which is defined by the CDC (2013) as consisting of qualities such as life satisfaction, happiness, cheerfulness, and peacefulness. For example, Valle and colleagues (2006) found that higher hope was correlated with increased life satisfaction in American adolescents concurrently and one year later. Marques and colleagues also observed this relationship among Portuguese adolescents, with hope significantly predicting life satisfaction up to one year (Marques et al., 2013) and two years later (Marques, Pais-Ribeiro, & Lopez, 2011b). These researchers further discovered that by increasing hope through a directed intervention, adolescent students' global life satisfaction was also subsequently increased (Marques et al., 2011b).

Past literature has also consistently illustrated significant inverse relationships, that is, significant associations between lower levels hope and indicators of emotional ill-being (Esteves et al., 2013; Snyder, 2000). For example, researchers found that adolescents and undergraduate students who reported lower levels of hope also reported suffering from both academic and generalized anxiety (Onwuegbuzie, 1998; Snyder, Lapointe, Crowson, & Early, 1998). Similarly, researchers have also revealed a significant negative relationship between hope and negative affect (Burrow, O'Dell, & Hill, 2010; Kwon, 2000; Snyder, 1999). The linkage between hope and depression has also been investigated in several studies, all of which have revealed

strong negative correlations, revealing that adolescents reporting lower levels of hope also report higher levels of depression (Geiger & Kwon, 2010; Simon, Barakat, Patterson, & Dampier, 2009; Swanston, Nunn, Oates, Tebbutt, & O'Toole, 1999; Wong & Lim, 2009).

Second, hope has demonstrated robust positive correlations with psychological-well-being, which is defined by the CDC (2013) to include characteristics such as self-esteem, optimism, self-efficacy, and positive affect (see also Esteves et al., 2013; Peterson & Seligman, 2004; Snyder et al., 1991). Moreover, in a short-term longitudinal study of middle and high school students, Valle and colleagues (2006) found that higher levels of hope predicted higher levels of internalizing behaviors concurrently and one year later. Higher levels of hope also served as a buffer against subsequent increases in internalizing behaviors. Barnum, Snyder, Rapoff, Mani, and Thompson (1998) also found evidence of an inverse association between hope and externalizing behaviors in a sample of adolescents who had experienced burn injuries. Similarly, studies have shown that adolescents displaying lower levels of hope are more likely to engage in risky behaviors, including smoking, substance abuse, and suicidal ideation and suicide attempts (Carvajal, Clair, Nash, & Evans, 1998; Chang, Yu, Jiliani, Fowler, Yu, & Lin, 2015; Wilson, Syme, Boyce, Battistich, & Selvin, 2005). Finally, Visser, Loess, Jeglic, and Hirsch (2013) found that college students who reported low hope and more experiences of stressful life events also reported the highest levels of depressive symptoms. These results suggest that lower levels of hope may elevate the negative effects of stressful life events, leading to more negative outcomes. Valle et al. (2006) speculated that children cannot be sheltered from experiencing stressful life events, such as an unexpected death of a loved one, but by equipping them with a pervasive sense of hope, children will more likely adjust in a more positive manner.

Extending beyond cross-sectional and one-directional analyses of the effects of hope, an impressive six-year longitudinal study of adolescents in Grades 7 through 12 investigated the possibility of reciprocal relations between hope and positive and negative affect (Ciarrochi, Parker, Kashdan, Heaven, & Barkus, 2015). On the one hand, the findings revealed that hope significantly predicted positive affect, while positive affect only weakly predicted hope. On the other hand, hope and negative affect showed reciprocal associations, with hope significantly predicting decreasing negative affect and negative affect predicting decreasing hope. This study thus suggested that hope is an antecedent to positive affect, not simply a consequence or correlate.

Finally, hope has demonstrated robust relations with various aspects of social well-being in adolescents (Barnum et al., 1998; Devlin, 2012; Edwards, Ong, & Lopez, 2007; Mahat & Scoloveno, 2001). The CDC (2013) has defined social well-being to include social relationships, interactions, and satisfaction. For example, researchers have found that youth with higher hope levels report more perceived social support in comparison to lower hope peers. Though studies have varied slightly in the definition and measurement of social support, this positive association has been found across different populations of youth including those from Australia, Nepal, and America, as well as in healthy youth, at-risk adolescents, and adolescent patients who experienced severe burn injuries. Furthermore, individuals with higher hope report higher social competence and experience more positive interpersonal interactions in comparison to lower hope individuals (Barnum et al., 1998; Snyder et al., 1997). This positive perception of social interactions likely encourages an individual to continue to seek out social support as a resource. Researchers have posited that increases in the behavior of seeking social support expand one's resources (i.e., pathways) to reach goals and can increase the quality of future social interactions (Kwon, 2002; Snyder, McDermott, et al., 1997). Thus while higher hope individuals do not necessarily require more support, they perceive that there is more social support available to them in comparison to their lower hope peers (Snyder, Cheavens, et al., 1997).

Hope Interventions

Given the notable relations between hope and mental health, researchers have begun to develop systematic interventions to promote hope in young people, including adolescents. In the following section, we review the literature on hope interventions, especially for adolescents.

McDermott and Snyder (1999) initially developed the Making Hope Happen (MHH) intervention for middle students (Pedrotti, Lopez, & Krieshok, 2000); however the researchers quickly adapted the intervention for elementary and high school students (Bouwkamp & Lopez, 2001; Edwards & Lopez, 2000), as well as for middle school students in special education settings (Buchanan, 2008). Although there was some variation in the intervention materials across the differing groups, the major components (e.g., such as teaching of hope theory, role-playing exercises, peer group activities, and the development "personal hope stories") were included in all the training materials. For example, through peer groups of "hope buddies," students were encouraged to help each other identify personally relevant goals by applying newly learned strategies taught earlier in the program. These interventions consisted of 45- to 70-minute sessions that occurred weekly over a five-week period. The intervention sessions took place during the school day in the classroom, with students in groups of 7 to 20 individuals. The sessions were led by graduate school students. All participating students were administered the CHS before and after the intervention.

Most studies of the MHH intervention have reported significant increases in student's self-report ratings of hope after the five-week intervention (Bouwkamp & Lopez, 2001; Edwards & Lopez, 2000; Pedrotti et al., 2000). One exception was Buchanan's (2008) study of an adapted MHH intervention for middle school students in special education; this study did not demonstrate significant increases in hope. Pedrotti and colleagues conducted a longer follow-up data collection and found that their middle school students maintained increases in hope six months postintervention.

Marques, Lopez, and Pais-Ribeiro (2011) subsequently developed "Building Hope for the Future," a five-week intervention aimed at enhancing middle schoolers' well-being, including their hope, life satisfaction, self-worth, mental health, and academic achievement. During each 60-minute session, students were taught to conceptualize goals, increase pathways, enhance agency, and reframe their hope belief in the face of obstacles (i.e., learning about hope, structuring hope, creating positive and specific goals, practice makes perfect, and review and apply for the future). At the beginning, teachers and guardians of students participated in a one-hour session and were given a reading on hope. After this initial meeting, teachers and guardians did not participate in subsequent sessions. All sessions occurred once a week after school and were led by graduate students. Students were randomly selected for either the intervention group or the control group and were administered a measures of global life satisfaction and global self-worth and a mental health inventory as well as the CHS on four occasions: preintervention, postintervention, 6-month follow-up, and 18-month follow-up. Academic achievement data were collected through obtaining records of students' grades.

Compared to the control group, students in the intervention group demonstrated significantly higher levels of hope, life satisfaction, and self-worth on each of the postintervention occasions. Nonsignificant results were found for the mental health inventory and school grades. These results provided promising further evidence that brief hope interventions can exert significant and lasting effects on important aspects of adolescents' well-being satisfaction and self-worth. Furthermore, Marques et al. (2011) argued that the positive effects of increased life satisfaction and self-worth were indirectly improved by increasing hope.

In summary, the extant research has provided meaningful evidence of robust findings relating hope to a variety of mental health variables in adolescents. Nevertheless, additional empirical research is needed to understand more fully the relations between hope and mental health as well as to provide more specific direction to mental health and other human services professionals in promoting hope, especially in adolescents. We discuss such future directions and implications in the next section.

Implications for Future Research and Implications for Professionals

Empirical research on the role of hope in adolescents' lives has increased considerably over the past decades, leading to a better understanding of the relations between adolescents' hope and their mental health. As shown in the present chapter, hope supports adolescents in dealing with various life stressors and challenges (cf. Snyder et al., 1991); consequently, hope robustly contributes to young people's mental health. As noted in the previous sections, many topics beyond mental health have been examined in relation to adolescents' hope to date. For example, studies have been conducted focusing on the associations between adolescents' levels of hope and their physical health (e.g., frequency of exercising, eating habits, adherence to medication), educational experiences (e.g., academic competence, academic achievement, test anxiety), athletic achievement, interpersonal relationships (e.g., enjoyment of interpersonal interactions, social competence), spirituality, and so forth; all associations were in favor of high (vs. low) levels of hope (for a recent overview, see Marques, Lopez, Rose, & Robinson, 2014).

In this chapter we have provided a summary of the relations between hope and adolescents' mental

health broadly construed. Utilizing mostly cross-sectional and relatively short-term longitudinal designs, higher levels of hope appear to be positively associated with a variety of aspects of mental health, such as self-esteem, optimism, self-efficacy, life satisfaction, well-being, positive affect, adjustment, and social acceptance and competence (e.g., Edwards et al., 2007; Valle et al., 2006). Lower levels of hope appear to be related to depression, anxiety, stress, internalizing and externalizing behaviors, and negative affect (e.g., Barnum et al., 1998; Visser et al., 2013). Furthermore, first attempts to systematically increase individuals' hope have shown that adolescents' levels of hope seem to be malleable through systematic interventions (e.g., Marques et al., 2011). For additional related results, see Chapters 9 and 10 of this handbook. Although there is already a noteworthy body of research on adolescents' hope, and the reported findings appear very promising, future research is needed to further understand the role of hope in adolescents' mental health in a more nuanced way. The nature and boundaries (i.e., nomological network) of the hope construct vis-à-vis other positive psychology constructs (e.g., gratitude, life satisfaction, optimism) should be explored further as well. Although compelling conceptual distinctions have been proposed (see Snyder et al., 1991), the ability of adolescents (and preadolescents) to make such distinctions remains to be demonstrated further.

Another key issue for future research is to address the origins of adolescent hope more deeply. According to Snyder et al. (1991), hope is a disposition of goal-directed thinking and motivation toward achieving different kinds of goals. Measurement tools have been developed to assess overall hope as a moderately stable but malleable psychological construct in youth (e.g., Marques, Pais-Ribeiro, & Lopez, 2009; Marques et al., 2011a; Snyder et al., 1991, 1997). Nevertheless, too little is known about the origins and the development of hope. Because hope appears to be crucial for young people, more research is needed to be able to detect favorable and unfavorable environmental factors, individual difference characteristics, and their possible interactions early in life to prevent mental illness and promote mental health. The role of demographic factors (e.g., gender, ethnicity) also remains unclear given mixed findings across various studies.

Hope is defined as an individual difference that is learned over the course of childhood but also later in life (cf. Snyder, 2002). A possible reason for low levels of hope is that some young people are not taught to think in a *hopeful* way (e.g., Snyder, 2002). Learning hope from watching and imitating significant role models (e.g., parents, teachers) has been postulated as a strategy to learn hope with all its components like creating goals, pathway thinking, and agentic thinking in childhood (e.g., Snyder, Cheavons, & Sympson, 1997). For example, as parents might serve as very influential role models in this stage of life, one could assume that the levels of hope in children systematically relate to the levels of hope in their parents. But empirical results on the relations between children's levels of hope and parents' levels of hope are mixed. In US children, Hoy, Suldo, and Mendez (2013) and Westburg and Martin (2003) found nonsignificant associations between parents' hope and their children's hope. On the other hand, in Portuguese students, a moderate positive association between parents' hope and their children's hope emerged (Marques et al., 2014). Therefore, more research is needed to clarify this postulated influence of role models on the development of hope. However, although research efforts should be devoted to examine further the effects of parents as role models, future efforts should also be devoted to examine the effects of additional significant others, such as teachers, siblings, other close relatives, and so forth.

Such mixed results on the relations between parents' and children's hope also suggest the potential importance of considering a possible genetic contribution to young people's levels of hope. Given that hope demonstrates a significant degree of stability (e.g., Marques et al., 2013; Marques et al., 2011a; Snyder et al., 1991, 1997), like other traits (e.g., personality characteristics), future researchers need to attempt to systematically unravel genetic and environmental influences on hope—also with a special focus on young people. Such investigations should utilize appropriate research designs. For example, the aforementioned studies on the relations between parents' and their children's hope utilized different measures assessing adult (AHS; e.g., Snyder et al., 1991) and youth hope (CHS; e.g., Snyder et al., 1997). It would be useful to design studies that utilize measures that are more comparable to minimize measurement-related biases. Furthermore, adoption studies (e.g., comparing hope levels of adopted children with biological parents vs. adoptive parents), twin studies (i.e., comparing hope levels of monozygotic and dizygotic twins), and other family designs could help us understand the genetic basis and environmental influences on hope. Because

the current results seem to be different across cultures, such designs need to consider a cross-cultural approach as well.

On the other hand, hope can be "lost," according to Snyder (2002). He speculated that youth could lose hope for a number of reasons: neglecting caregivers as role models; physical abuse; loss of a parent; divorce; environments (e.g., families) that lack boundaries, consistency, and support; and so forth. For example, parent attachment has been found to be a significant positive correlate of levels of hope among adolescents (e.g., Jiang, Huebner, & Hills, 2013). Therefore, a disrupted attachment to parents (e.g., caused by low or inconsistent parental support) would likely impact negatively on adolescents' hope. Although all of Snyder's (2002) suggested factors regarding the "loss" of hope appear reasonable, the moderate stability of hope documented in several studies (e.g., Marques et al., 2011a ; Snyder et al., 1997) is not inconsistent with the notion that an adolescent's level of hope may be temporarily lowered when experiencing such traumas (e.g., loss of a parent, lack of support), but the level of hope may typically return to the individual's baseline level (or close to it) in response to many events as has been found for other well-being variables, such as life satisfaction (e.g., Brickman, Coates, & Janoff-Bulman, 1978; Diener, Lucas, & Scollon, 2006). Such a process may occur during transitional stages of schooling, for example, starting high school (Ciarrochi, Parker, Kashdan, Heaven, & Barkus, 2015). Therefore, future research efforts need to uncover such "unlearning" processes in young people as they appear very relevant to understanding if and why systematic decreases in adolescents' hope occur and whether the decreases are temporary or become chronic. Furthermore, gaining more knowledge about such unlearning processes will help to unravel the potential complexities of all variations in levels of hope as well.

Hope is a cognitive-motivational characteristic, and originally Snyder et al. (1991) assumed its consistency across situations (and time). Later, Snyder, Cheavens, et al. (1997) modified their assumption by postulating that although individuals have a general level of hope, it is possible that their experiences of momentary hope vary across situations. Moreover, participants could report different levels of hope in different life domains (e.g., Snyder, 2002). The Domain-Specific Hope Scale (Sympson, 1999) has been developed for the assessment of general *and* domain-specific hope in 15+-year-olds; it covers hope in social relationships, romantic relationships, academics, work life, family life, and leisure life (cf. Lopez, Ciarelli, Coffman, Stone, & Wyatt, 2000). Such a domain-specific approach appears very promising. Why? As an example, research on another cognitive-evaluative characteristic—life satisfaction—is interested in how individuals evaluate their satisfaction with both life as a whole but also in different life domains (e.g., family life, school, friends, etc.; e.g., Huebner, 1994). Such a domain-specific approach offers detailed insights and enables in-depth research. For example, the importance of differentiating reports of global life satisfaction from domain-specific reports of life satisfaction is demonstrated by the fact that although scores on key domains are positively related, they are distinguishable even in children as young as third grade (Huebner, 1994). For example, Weber and Huebner (2015) examined the relations between five broad personality traits (i.e., the Big Five) and five domain-specific satisfaction reports in early adolescents and found that different personality traits were associated with satisfaction in different life domains (e.g., openness to experiences was the strongest predictor of satisfaction with school experiences while extraversion was the strongest predictor of satisfaction with friendships).

Our understanding of the origins and consequences of individual differences in hope may also benefit from such a more nuanced assessment approach. For example, one might assume that family-related hope is more relevant to mastering challenges, tasks, and problems in the family context as opposed to the general hope level, which could be, for example, mainly based on an individuals' sports-related hope. As adolescents' judgments about their general hope level may mask distinctions regarding specific, important domains in their lives (e.g., friends vs. school) the exploration of domain-specific hope is expected to yield more useful information about such an important construct. Furthermore, development of domain-specific assessment tools measuring hope in children und younger adolescents (younger than 15 years) would open the opportunity to extend empirical evidence on domain-specific hope; such research might result in the refinement and extension of hope theory and interventions as well as measurement applications.

With respect to another key issue for future research, we would encourage researchers to design studies that are able to address causal relations between hope and mental health in adolescents. As noted previously in this chapter, a few promising longitudinal studies have investigated the relations between hope and mental health outcomes in adolescents (e.g., Ciarrochi, Parker, Kashdan, Heaven, & Barkus, 2015; Marques et al., 2011b; Marques et al., 2013). However, the studies are sparse in number, and therefore future research should consider conducting short-term and long-term longitudinal research to enlarge the body of evidence on the directionality of relations between hope and important variables. Such studies might also consider incorporating multimethod assessments like parent reports, teacher reports, peer reports, and so forth to provide multimethod assessments that extend beyond the typical self-report methodology typically used in the existing research base.

Also with respect to causality, additional experimental and intervention studies need to be designed for research in samples of children and adolescents. As reported earlier in this chapter, there is already some promising evidence that hope can be increased through systematic interventions with adults (e.g., Cheavens, Feldman, Gum, Michael, & Snyder, 2006, Lapierre, Dubé, Lé Bouffard, & Alain, 2007) and youth (e.g., Feldman & Dreher, 2012; Marques et al., 2011). Nevertheless, more empirical evidence from experimental and intervention studies would bolster the notion that levels of hope, especially in adolescents, are modifiable. Additionally, further delineation of the specific, active ingredients of effective interventions is needed. Such studies should provide refined tools for professionals supporting them in their efforts to enhance adolescents' hope.

Available research has focused on both participants from regularand public schools and on specific pediatric samples (e.g., children with different medical problems, boys with a primary diagnosis of attention deficit hyperactivity disorder, children under treatment for cancer, early adolescents exposed to violence, adolescents with sickle-cell disease, children in treatment for asthma, and children who have survived burn injuries; cf. Snyder, 2002). More research is needed to clarify the role of hope in adolescents who are already suffering from different mental and physical conditions. Such knowledge should inform specific, evidence-based intervention programs for those who are already suffering, prevention programs for those who are at risk, and promotion programs for population-based approaches.

Marques et al. (2014) highlighted that little is known about hope's role in gifted adolescents or in adolescents with learning difficulties. Research has shown that both giftedness (e.g., Neihart, 1999) and learning disabilities (e.g., Smiley,

2005) could be related to mental health problems, but the results are mixed. Hope might be a characteristic that helps prevent mental health problems among gifted students and students with learning difficulties, because hope might serve as a buffer against the development of mental health problems. Although the correlation between hope and intelligence has been found to be close to zero (cf. Snyder, 2002), future research should focus on the role of hope in adolescents stemming from different "extreme" groups (e.g., gifted adolescents) to yield a more nuanced understanding of specific groups that are at risk for mental health problems.

Another key issue for future research should focus on the generalizability of the research findings regarding hope and its impact on adolescents' mental health in different cultures and/or nations. Although there is initial research available examining hope in samples outside the United States (e.g., Marques, Pais-Ribeiro, & Lopez, 2009), the bulk of the research has been conducted in the United States and other Western nations. More cross-cultural/national studies are needed to learn about the generalizability of such findings.

According to Snyder et al. (1991), higher levels of hope are expected to be generally associated with positive outcomes in individuals' lives. Later Snyder (2002) reflected on a possible "false" hope. He categorized false hope into three types: (a) individuals' expectations for their futures could be based on illusions and not on reality, (b) individuals' strategies to attain their goals could be false, and (c) individuals could set goals that are not suitable for them (cf. Snyder, 2002). There is empirical evidence that very high levels of hope remain related to positive aspects in adolescents' lives, like academic achievement (for a review, see Marques et al., 2014). Nevertheless, future research needs to consider the possibilities of "false" hope (cf. Snyder, 2002) as well comprehensively examine adolescents' hope and false hope's consequences for mental health.

Although there is already a strong research base on hope's role in adolescent mental health, and the progress made so far is admirable, future research expanding this evidence within general and specific populations will help to expand our knowledge of the origins and impact of hope in adolescents. High hope appears to be important for both "normal" adolescents and those who are experiencing more challenges in life (i.e., internal or environmental challenging factors). Although hope matters for all individuals, it might be true

that hope is especially crucial for the "challenged" group to ensure positive development in childhood and adolescence. For many adolescents facing major challenges, the provision of supportive educational and mental health services is likely needed to foster strengths like hope, considering that other environmental factors, such as the family or neighborhood, may not be able to support the development of such internal resources without assistance.

Based on this review, the following conclusions seem reasonable:

1. Hope appears to be crucial for adolescents' mental health.

2. Hope can be assessed; consequently, professionals who interact with young people need to learn how to use such measures to detect individuals' levels of hope.

3. Recognizing the differing levels of hope of adolescents should help us understand them in a better way and understand how and why they act in specific ways.

4. When professionals assess unusually low levels of hope among individuals or groups of individuals, they need to consider empirically based treatments to increase the relevant adolescents' hope levels.

5. Hope is a characteristic that significantly contributes to (a) how and if adolescents set goals for their future, (b) if adolescents are able to think of effective ways to reach them, and (c) if adolescents possess the motivation and persistence to reach them.

The levels of the latter aspects of hope vary among individuals, which in turn impact adolescents' mental health significantly. Hence, for optimal advances in promoting hope in adolescents to occur, professionals and scientists may need to work together to facilitate advances in understanding the precise nature of the relations between hope and mental health in adolescents. Forman, Smallwood, and Nagle (2005) provide an excellent discussion of how to operationalize scientist–practitioner interactions to promote evidence-based practices.

Future Directions

• What are the origins of hope? Specifically, what can be explained by genetic effects or other endogenous factors like personality characteristics; and what can be explained by environmental effects like parenting, peer-interactions, schooling, and so forth?

• Hope appears to be relevant for adolescent mental health. What are the causal directions between hope and different mental health indicators in adolescence?

• Will specific domains of adolescent hope (e.g., hope in social relationships, hope in academics) be especially relevant for particular mental health outcomes (e.g., emotional well-being, self-efficacy)?

• Is there a "false" hope in adolescence? What are possible consequences of false hope for mental health?

• What factors foster the positive development of hope, and what factors trigger "unlearning processes" of hope?

• What is the role of hope for mental health of specific adolescent populations (e.g., gifted adolescents, physically ill adolescents, and so forth)?

• Are there cross-cultural/cross-national differences in the relations between hope and adolescent mental health?

• How can hope be enhanced/trained in adolescents suffering from low levels of hope?

References

Anderman, E. M., & Maehr, M. L. (1994). Motivational and schooling in the middle grades. *Review of Educational Research, 64*, 287–309. doi:10.3102/00346543064002287

Bailey, T. C., & Snyder, C. R. (2007). Satisfaction with life and hope: A look at age and marital status. *The Psychology Record, 57*, 233–240. doi:10.1.1.470.4736

Barnum, D. D., Snyder, C. R., Rapoff, M. A., Mani, M. M., & Thompson, R. (1998). Hope and social support in the psychological adjustment of pediatric burn survivors and matched controls. *Children's Health Care, 27*, 15–30. doi:10.1207/s15326888chc2701_2

Berndt, T. J. (1997). *Child development*. Madison, WI: Brown & Benchmark.

Beyth-Marom, R., Austin, L., Fischoff, B., Palmgren, C., & Jacobs-Quadrel, M. (1993). Perceived consequences of risky behaviors: Adults and adolescents. *Developmental Psychology, 29*, 549–563. doi:10.1037/0012-1649.29.3.549

Brickman, P., Coates, D., & Janoff-Bulman, R. (1978). Lottery winners and accident victims: Is happiness relative? *Journal of Personality and Social Psychology, 36*, 917–927. doi:10.1037/0022-3514.36.8.917

Brooks-Gunn, J. (1988). Commentary: Developmental issues in the transition to early adolescence. In M. Gunnar & W. A. Collins (Eds.), *Development during transition to adolescence: Minnesota Symposia on Child Psychology* (Vol. 21, pp. 189–208). Hillsdale, NJ: Lawrence Erlbaum.

Bouwkamp, J., & Lopez, S. J. (2001). *Making Hope Happen: A program for inner-city adolescents*. Unpublished master's thesis, University of Kansas, Lawrence.

Buchanan, C. L. (2008). *Making hope happen for students receiving special education services*. Unpublished doctoral dissertation. University of Kansas, Lawrence.

Buchanan, C. M., Eccles, J. S., & Becker, J. B. (1992). Are adolescents the victims of raging hormones? Evidence for activational effects of hormones on moods and behavior at adolescence. *Psychological Bulletin, 111*, 62–107. doi:10.1037/0033-2909.111.1.62

Burrow, A., O'Dell, A., & Hill, P. (2010). Profiles of a development asset: Youth purpose as a context for hope and well-being. *Journal of Youth and Adolescence, 39*, 1265–1273. doi:10.1007/s10964-009-9481-1

Carvajal, S. C., Clair, S. D., Nash, S. G., & Evans, R. I. (1998). Relating optimism, hope, self-esteem to social influences in deterring substance use in adolescents. *Journal of Social and Clinical Psychology, 17*, 443–465. doi:10.1521/jscp.1998.17.4.443

Casey, B. J., Getz, S., & Galvan, A. (2008). The adolescent brain. *Developmental Review, 28*, 62–77. doi:10.1016/j.dr.2007.08.003

Centers for Disease Control and Prevention. (2013). *Mental health basics*. Retrieved from http:// http://www.cdc.gov/mentalhealth/basics.htm.

Centers for Disease Control and Prevention. (2014). *Morbidity and mortality week report: Youth risk behavior surveillance*. Retrieved from http://www.cdc.gov/mmwr/pdf/ss/ss6304.pdf

Chang, E. C., Yu, T., Jiliani, Z., Fowler, E. E., Yu, E. A., & Lin, J. (2015). Hope under assault: Understanding the impact of sexual assault on the relation between hope and suicidal risk in college students. *Journal of Social and Clinical Psychology, 34*, 221–238. doi:10.1521/jscp.2015.34.3.221

Cheavens, J. S., Feldman, D. B., Gum, A., Michael, S. T., & Snyder, C. R. (2006). Hope therapy in a community sample: A pilot investigation. *Social Indicators Research, 77*, 61–78. doi:10.1007/s11205-005-5553-0

Ciarrochi, J., Parker, P., Kashdan, T.B., Heaven, C. L., & Barkus, E. (2015). Hope and emotional well-being: A six-year study to distinguish antecedents, correlates, and consequences. *The Journal of Positive Psychology, 10*, 520–532. doi:10.1080/17439760.2015.1015154

Costello, E. J., & Angold, A. (1988). Scales to assess child and adolescent depression: checklists, screens, and nets. *Journal of the American Academy of Child & Adolescent Psychiatry, 27*, 726–737. doi:10.1097/00004583-198811000-00011

Curry, L. A., Snyder, C. R., Cook, D. L., Ruby, B. C., & Rehm, M. (1997). Role of hope in academic and sport achievement. *Journal of Personality and Social Psychology, 73*, 1257–1267. doi:10.1037/0022-3514.73.6.1257

Dahl, R. E. (2004). Adolescent brain development: A period of vulnerabilities and opportunities. *Annals of the New York Academy of Sciences, 1021*, 1–22. doi:10.1196/annals.1308.001

Devlin, S. D., (2012). *Hope in at-risk students in relation to life satisfaction and social support*. Unpublished dissertation. Texas A&M University, College Station, TX.

Diener, E., Lucas, R. E., & Scollon, C. N. (2006). Beyond the hedonic treadmill: Revising the adaptation theory of well-being. *American Psychologist, 61*, 305–314. doi:10.1037/0003-066X.61.4.305

Dufault, K., & Martocchio, B. C. (1985). Hope: Its spheres and dimensions. *Nursing Clinics of North America, 20*, 379–391. Retrieved from http://www.ncbi.nlm.nih.gov/pubmed/3846980.

Eccles, J. S., Wigfield, A., Flanagan, C. A., Miller, C., Reuman, D. A., & Yee, D. (1989). Self-concepts, domain values, and self-esteem: Relations and changes at early adolescence. *Journal of Personality*, *57*, 283–310. doi:10.1111/j.1467-6494.1989.tb00484.x

Edwards, L. M., Ong, A. D., & Lopez, S. J. (2007). Hope measurement in Mexican-American youth. *Hispanic Journal of Behavioral Sciences*, *29*, 225–241. doi:10.1177/0739986307299692

Edwards, L. M., & Lopez, S. J. (2000). *Making Hope Happen for Kids*. Unpublished protocol.

Elkind, D. (1967). Egocentrism in adolescence. *Child Development*, *38*, 1025–1034. doi:10.2307/1127100

Elkind, D. (1978). Understanding the young adolescent. *Adolescence*, *13*(49), 127–134. Retrieved from http://eric.ed.gov/?id=EJ182765.

Elmore, G., & Huebner, E.S. (2010). Adolescents' satisfaction with school experiences: Relationships with demographics, attachment relationships, and student engagement. *Psychology in the Schools*, *47*, 55–537. doi:10.1002/pits.20488

Esteves, M., Scoloveno, R. L., Mahat, G., Yarcheski, A., & Scoloveno M. A. (2013). An integrative review of adolescent hope. *Journal of Pediatric Nursing*, *28*, 105–113. doi:10.1016/j.pedn.2012.03.033

Epstein, J. L., & Mcpartland, J. M. (1976). The concept and measurement of the quality of school life. *American Educational Research Journal*, *13*, 15–30. doi:10.3102/00028312013001015

Erikson, E. H. (1968). *Identity, youth, and crisis*. New York: Norton.

Feldman, D. B., & Dreher, D. E. (2012). Can hope be changed in 90 minutes? Testing the efficacy of a single-session goal-pursuit intervention for college students. *Journal of Happiness Studies*, *13*, 745–759. doi:10.1007/s10902-011-9292-4

Forman, S. J., Smallwood, D. J., & Nagle, R. J. (2005). Organizational and individual factors in bridging research and practice: What we know and where we need to go. *Psychology in the Schools*, *42*, 569–576. doi:10.1002/pits.20092

Gardner, W., & Herman, J. (1991, April). *Developmental change in decision-making: Use of multiplicative strategies and sensitivity to losses*. Symposium conducted at the biennial meeting of the Society for Research in Child Development, Seattle, WA.

Geiger, K. A., & Kwon, P. (2010). Rumination and depressive symptoms: Evidence for the moderating role of hope. *Personality and Individual Differences*, *49*, 391–395. doi:10.1016/j.paid.2010.04.004

Gottfredson, L. S. (1981). Circumscription and compromise: A developmental theory of occupational aspirations. *Journal of Counseling Psychology*, *28*, 545–579. doi:10.1037/0022-0167.28.6.545

Gottfried, A. E., Fleming, J. S., & Gottfried, A. W. (2001). Continuity of academic intrinsic motivation from childhood through late adolescence: A longitudinal study. *Journal of Educational Psychology*, *93*, 3–13. doi:10.1037/0022-0663.93.1.3

Hall, G. S. (1904). *Adolescence: Its psychology and its relations to physiology, anthropology, sociology, sex, crime, religion, and education* (Vols. I and II). Englewood Cliffs, NJ: Prentice Hall.

Harter, S. (1981). A new self-report scale of intrinsic versus extrinsic orientation in the classroom: Motivational and informational components. *Developmental Psychology*, *17*, 300–312. doi:10.1037/0012-1649.17.3.300

Harter, S. (2012). *The construction of the self*. (2nd ed.). New York: Guilford Press.

Heaven, P. C. L., & Ciarrochi, J. (2008). Parental styles, gender, and the development of hope and self-esteem. *European Journal of Personality*, *22*, 707–724. doi:10.1002/per.699

Hill, K. T. (1980). Motivation, evaluation and educational testing policy. In L. J. Fyans (Ed.), *Achievement motivation: recent trends in theory and research* (pp. 34–95). New York: Plenum.

Hinton-Nelson, M., Roberts, M., & Snyder, C. R. (1996). Early adolescents exposed to violence: Hope and vulnerability to victimization. *American Journal of Orthopsychiatry*, *66*, 346–353. doi:10.1037/h0080185

Hoy, B. D., Suldo, S. M., & Mendez, L. R. (2013). Links between parents' and children's levels of gratitude, life satisfaction, and hope. *Journal of Happiness Studies*, *14*, 1343–1361. doi:10.1007/s10902-012-9386-7

Huebner, E. S. (1994). Preliminary development and validation of a multidimensional life satisfaction scale for children. *Psychological Assessment*, *6*, 149–158. doi:10.1037/1040-3590.6.2.149

Ingram, R. E., & Smith, T. W. (1984). Depression and internal versus external focus of attention. *Cognitive Therapy and Research*, *8*, 139–151. doi:10.1007/BF01173040

Jacobs, J. E., Lanza, S., Osgood, D. W., Eccles, J. S., & Wigfield, A. (2002). Changes in children's self-competence and values: Gender and domain differences across grades one through twelve. *Child Development*, *73*, 509–527. doi:10.1111/1467-8624.00421

Jiang, X., Huebner, E. S., & Hills, K. J. (2013). Parent attachment and early adolescents' life satisfaction: The mediating effect of hope. *Psychology in the Schools*, *50*, 340–352. doi:10.1002/pits.21680

Kwon, P. (2000). Hope and dysphoria: The moderating role of defense mechanisms. *Journal of Personality*, *68*, 199–223. doi:10.1111/1467-6494.00095

Kwon, P. (2002). Hope, defense mechanisms, and adjustment: Implications for false hope and defensive hopelessness. *Journal of Personality*, *70*, 207–230.

Lazarus, R. S., & Folkman, S. (1984). Coping and adaptation. In W. D. Gentry (Ed.), *The handbook of behavioral medicine* (pp. 282–325). New York: Guilford Press.

Lapierre, S., Dubé, M., Lé Bouffard, L., & Alain, M. (2007). Addressing suicidal ideations through the realization of meaningful personal goals. *Crisis*, *28*, 16–25. doi:10.1027/02275910.28.1.16

Lerner, R. M., Almerigi, J. B., Theokas, C., & Lerner, J. V. (2005). Positive youth development: A view of the issues. *Journal of Early Adolescence*, *25*, 10–16. doi:10.1177/0272431604273211

Lopez, S. J., Ciarlelli, R., Coffman, L., Stone, M., & Wyatt, L. (2000). Diagnosing for strengths: On measuring hope building blocks. In C. R. Snyder (Ed.), *Handbook of hope: Theory, measures and applications* (pp. 57–85). San Diego, CA: Academic Press.

Mahat, G., & Scoloveno, M. A. (2001). Factors influencing health practices of Nepalese adolescent girls. *Journal of Pediatric Health Care*, *15*, 251–255. doi:10.1067/mph.2001.113002

Marques, S. C., Lopez, S. J., & Mitchell, J. (2013). The role of hope, spirituality and religious practice in adolescents' life satisfaction: Longitudinal findings. *Journal of Happiness Studies*, *14*, 251–261. doi:10.1007/s10902-012-9329-3

Marques, S. C., Lopez, S. J., & Pais-Ribeiro, J. L. (2011). "Building Hope for the Future": A program to foster strengths in middle-school students. *Journal of Happiness Studies, 12,* 139–152. doi:10.1007/s10902-009-9180-3

Marques, S. C., Lopez, S. J., Rose, S., & Robinson, C. (2014). Measuring and promoting hope in school children. In M. J. Furlong, R. Gilman, & E. S. Huebner (Eds.), *Handbook of positive psychology in the schools* (2nd ed., pp. 35–50). New York: Routledge.

Marques, S. C., Pais-Ribeiro, J. L., & Lopez, S. J. (2009). Validation of a Portuguese version of the Children's Hope Scale. *School Psychology International, 30,* 538–551. doi:10.1177/0143034309107069

Marques, S.C., Pais-Ribeiro, J., & Lopez, S.J. (2011a). Further evaluation of the test–retest reliability of the Children's Hope Scale and Students' Life Satisfaction Scale. In I. Brdar (Ed.), *The human pursuit of well-being: A cultural approach* (pp. 213–220). Dordrecht: Springer.

Marques, S. C., Pais-Ribeiro, J. L., & Lopez, S. J. (2011b). The role of positive psychology constructs in predicting mental health and academic achievement in children and adolescents: A two-year longitudinal study. *Journal of Happiness Studies, 12,* 1049–1062. doi:10.1007/s10902-010-9244-4

McDermott, D., & Snyder, C. R. (1999). *Making hope happen.* Oakland, CA: New Harbinger.

Moshman, D. (1998). Cognitive development beyond childhood. In W. Damon (Series Ed.) & D. Kuhn & R. Siegler (Vol. Eds.), *Handbook of child psychology: Vol. 2, Cognition, perception, and language* (5th ed., pp. 947–978). New York: Wiley.

Montemayor, R., & Flannery, D. (1990). Making the transition from childhood to early adolescence. In R. Montemayor, G. Adams, & T. Gullotta (Eds.), *Advances in adolescent development: Vol. 2, From childhood to adolescence: A transitional period?* (pp. 291–301). Beverly Hills, CA: SAGE.

Neihart, M. (1999). The impact of giftedness on psychological well-being: What does the empirical literature say? *Roeper Review, 22,* 10–17. doi:10.1080/02783199909553991

Nurmi, J. E. (2004). Socialization and self-development: Channeling, selection, adjustment, and reflection. In R. M. Lerner & L. Steinberg (Eds.), *Handbook of adolescent psychology* (pp. 85–124). New York: Wiley.

Onwuegbuzie, A. J. (1998). Role of hope in predicting anxiety about statistics. *Psychological Reports, 82,* 1315–1320. doi:10.2466/PR0.82.3.1315-1320

Pedrotti, J. T., Lopez, S. J., & Krieshok, T. S. (2000). *Making Hope Happen: A program for fostering strengths in adolescents.* Unpublished master's thesis. University of Kansas, Lawrence.

Peterson, C., & Seligman, M. (2004). *Character strengths and virtues: A handbook and classification.* Oxford: Oxford University Press.

Rholes, W. S., Blackwell, J., Jordan, C., & Walters, C. (1980). A developmental study of learned helplessness. *Developmental Psychology, 16,* 616–624. doi:10.1037/0012-1649.16.6.616

Roth, J. L., & Brooks-Gunn, J. (2003). Youth development programs: Risk, prevention, and policy. *Journal of Adolescent Health, 32,* 170–182. doi:10.1016/S1054-139X(02)00421-4

Roth, J., Brooks-Gunn, J., Murray, L., & Foster, W. (1998). Promoting healthy adolescents: Synthesis of youth development program evaluations. *Journal of Research on Adolescents, 8,* 423–459. doi:10.1207/s15327795jra0804_2

Rutter, M. (1986). Meyerian psychobiology, personality, development, and the role of life experiences. *The American Journal of Psychiatry, 143,* 1077–1087. doi:10.1080/02643949109470747

Rutter, M. (1991). Pathways from childhood to adult life: The role of schooling. *Pastoral Care in Education, 9,* 3–10. doi:10.1080/02643949109470747

Seligman, M. E. P., & Csikszentmihalyi, M. (2000). Positive psychology: An introduction. *American Psychology, 55*(1), 5–14. doi:10.1037/0003-066X.55.1.5

Simon, K., Barakat, L. P., Patterson, C. A., & Dampier, C. (2009). Symptoms of depression and anxiety in adolescents with sickle cell disease: The role of intrapersonal characteristics and stress producing variables. *Child Psychiatry and Human Development, 40,* 317–330. doi:10.1007/s10578-009-0129-x

Simmons, R. G., & Blyth, D. A. (1987). *Moving into adolescence: The impact of pubertal change and school context.* Hawthorne, NY: Aldine.

Smiley, E. (2005). Epidemiology of mental health problems in adults with learning disability: An update. *Advances in Psychiatric Treatment, 11,* 214–222. doi:10.1192/apt.11.3.214

Smith, T., & Greenberg, J. (1981). Depression and self-focused attention. *Motivation and Emotion, 5,* 323–331. doi:10.1007/BF00992551

Snyder, C. R. (1994). *The psychology of hope.* New York: Free Press.

Snyder, C. R. (1999). Hope, goal-blocking thoughts, and test-related anxieties. *Psychological Reports, 84,* 206–208. doi:10.2466/PR0.84.1.206-208

Snyder, C. R. (2000). The past and possible future hopes. *Journal of Social and Clinical Psychology, 19,* 11–28. doi:10.1521/jscp.2000.19.1.11

Snyder, C. R. (2002). Hope theory: Rainbows in the mind. *Psychological Inquiry, 13,* 249–275. doi:10.1207/S15327965PLI1304_01

Snyder, C. R. (2005). Measuring hope in children. In K. A. Moore & L. H. Lippman (Eds.), *What do children need to flourish? Conceptualizing and measuring indicators of positive development* (pp. 61–73). New York: Springer.

Snyder, C. R. (Ed.). (2000). *Handbook of hope: Theory, measures, and applications.* San Diego, CA: Academic Press.

Snyder, C. R., Cheavens, J., & Michael, S. T. (1999). Hoping. In C. R. Snyder (Ed.), *Coping: The psychology of what works* (pp. 205–231). New York: Oxford University Press.

Snyder, C. R., Cheavens, J., & Sympson, S. C. (1997). Hope: An individual motive for social commerce. *Group Dynamics: Theory, Research, and Practice, 1,* 107–118. doi:10.1037/1089-2699.1.2.107

Snyder, C. R., Feldman, D. B., Shorey, H. S., & Rand, K. L. (2002). Hopeful choices: A school counselor's guide to hope theory. *Professional School Counseling, 5*(5), 298–307. Retrieved from http://epublications.marquette.edu/cgi/viewcontent.cgi?article=1082&context=edu_fac

Snyder, C. R., Harris, C., Anderson, J. R., Holleran, S. A., Irving, L. M., Sigmon, S. T., . . . Harney, P. (1991). The will and the ways: Development and validation of an individual-differences measure of hope. *Journal of Personality and Social Psychology, 60,* 570–585. doi:10.1037/0022-3514.60.4.570

Snyder, C. R., Hoza, B., Pelham, W. E., Rapoff, M., Ware, L., Danovsky, M., . . . Stahl, K. J. (1997). The development and validation of the Children's Hope Scale. *Journal of Pediatric Psychology, 22,* 399–421. doi:10.1093/jpepsy/22.3.399

Snyder, C. R., LaPointe, A. B., Crowson, J., & Early, S. (1998). Preferences of high- and low- hope people for self-referential input. *Cognition and Emotion, 12,* 807–823. doi:10.1080/026999398379448

Snyder, C. R., Lopez, S. J., Shorey, H. S., Rand, K. L., & Feldman, D. B. (2003). Hope theory, measurement, and applications to school psychology. *School Psychology Quarterly, 18,* 122–139. doi:10.1521/scpq.18.2.122.21854

Snyder, C.R., Lopez, S. J., & Pedrotti, J. T. (2011). *Positive psychology: The scientific and practical explorations of human strengths, 2nd ed.* Thousand Oaks, CA: Sage Publications, Inc.

Snyder, C. R., McDermott, D., Cook, W., & Rapoff, M. (1997). *Hope for the journey: Helping children through the good times and bad.* Clinton Corners, NY: Percheron Press.

Steinberg, L. (2005). Cognitive and affective development in adolescence. *Trends in Cognitive Sciences, 9,* 69–74. doi:10.1016/j.tics.2004.12.005

Steinberg, L. (2008). A social neuroscience perspective on adolescent risk-taking. *Developmental Review, 28,* 78–106. doi:10.1016/j.dr.2007.08.002

Steinberg, L., Albert, D., Cauffman, E., Banich, M., Graham,S., & Woolard, J. (2008). Age differences in sensation seeking and impulsivity as indexed by behavior and self-report: Evidence for a dual systems model. *Developmental Psychology, 44,* 764–1778. doi:10.1037/a0012955

Steinberg, L., Graham, S., O'Brien, L., Woolard, J., Cauffman, E., & Banich, M. (2009). Age differences in future orientation and delay discounting. *Child Development, 80,* 28–44. doi:10.1111/j.1467-8624.2008.01244.x

Sympson, S. (1999). *Validation of the domain-specific hope scale: Exploring hope in life domains.* Unpublished doctoral dissertation, University of Kansas, Lawrence.

Swanston, H. Y., Nunn, K. P., Oates, R. K., Tebbutt, J. S., & O'Toole, B. I. (1999). Hoping and coping in young people who have been sexually abused. *European Child & Adolescent Psychiatry, 8,* 134–142. doi:10.1007/s007870050094

Valle, M. F., Huebner, E. S., & Suldo, S. M. (2004). Further validation of the Children's Hope Scale. *Journal of Psychoeducational Assessment, 22,* 320–337. doi:10.1177/073428290402200403

Valle, M. F., Huebner, E. S., & Suldo, S. M. (2006). An analysis of hope as a psychological strength. *Journal of School Psychology, 44,* 393–406. doi:10.1016/j.jsp.2006.03.005

Visser, P. L., Loess, P., Jeglic, E. L., & Hirsch, J. K. (2013). Hope as a moderator of negative life events and depressive symptoms in a diverse sample. *Stress and Health: Journal of the International Society for the Investigation of Stress, 29,* 82–88. doi:10.1002/smi.2433

Weber, M., & Huebner, E. S. (2015). Early adolescents' personality and life satisfaction: A closer look at global vs. domain-specific satisfaction. *Personality and Individual Differences, 83,* 31–36. doi:10.1016/j.paid.2015.03.042

Westburg, N. G., & Martin, D. (2003). The relationship between a child's hope, a parent's hope, and student-directed, goal-oriented academic instruction. *Journal of Humanistic Counseling, Education and Development, 42,* 152–164. doi:10.1002/j.2164-490X.2003.tb00003.x

Wigfield, A., Eccles, J. S., Mac Iver, D., Reuman, D. A., & Midgley, C. (1991). Transitions during early adolescence: Changes in children's domain-specific self-perceptions and general self-esteem across the transition to junior high school. *Developmental Psychology, 24*(4), 552–565. doi:10.1037/0012-1649.27.4.552

Wilson, N., Syme, L., Boyce, W. T., Battistich, V. A., & Selvin, S. (2005). Adolescent alcohol, tobacco, and marijuana use: The influence of neighborhood disorder and hope. *American Journal of Health Promotion, 20,* 11–19. doi:10.4278/0890-1171-20.1.11

Wong, S. S., & Lim, T. (2009). Hope versus optimism in Singaporean adolescents: Contributions to depression and life satisfaction. *Personality and Individual Differences, 46,* 648–652. doi:10.1016/j.paid.2009.01.009

World Health Organization. (2014). *Mental health: A state of well being.* Retrieved from http://www.who.int/features/factfiles/mental_health/en.

Attachment Processes and the Social/Developmental Bases of Hope

Hal S. Shorey, Steve Bisgaier, *and* Scott R. Thien

Abstract

Theory and research support a developmental model of hope, wherein hope is formed in the context of secure attachment to supportive parents in childhood. This chapter reviews the literature and articulates the many biopsychosocial processes involved in instilling a secure attachment style and the hopeful cognitive processes that go with it. In so doing, it highlights the critical balance between exploratory and attachment systems, with the need for approach-oriented goal pursuits on the one side and having a secure base to retreat to on the other. It demonstrates how both functions (exploration and attachment/proximity-seeking) are needed for hope to flourish and highlights key elements needed for use in resiliency and intervention efforts as well as for research on developmental positive psychology.

Key Words: Hope, attachment, exploration, positive development, resiliency, well-being

As highlighted in the many chapters of the present volume, hope is a positive motivational construct that has strong implications for functioning across a range of social, achievement, and mental health outcomes that span the childhood and adult years. Hope was originally defined by Snyder, Harris, et al. (1991) as "a cognitive set that is based on a reciprocally derived sense of successful (a) agency (goal-directed determination) and (b) pathways (planning of ways to meet goals)" (p. 571). Snyder's definition was built on the work of earlier scholars who placed the attainment of goals as the driving force in the hope construct. In this respect, goals can be conceived as the "what" and agency and pathways can be conceived as the "how" of hopeful thinking.

Given hope's theoretical and research-based importance in the human experience, it is reasonable to conclude that developing and fostering hope should be a societal priority (Shorey, Snyder, Yang & Lewin, 2003). Of course, if we want to develop programs and conduct research on the development of hope, it makes sense to first look at how hope develops naturally. In this respect, Snyder (1994) posited that hope develops in the context of secure

attachments to supportive adults in childhood (Snyder, 1994). Snyder linked this conceptualization to Erik Erikson's (1963; Erikson & Erikson, 1982) notion of hope, which results when the child develops a sense of trust in the continuity and predictability of his or her environment through having quality relationships with primary caregivers during the first two years of life.

Moving beyond Erikson's stage theory, however, Snyder (1994) suggested a longitudinal course in that "secure early attachments contribute to an adult mindset of empowerment and goal-directed behavior" (p. 87). This assertion is consonant with Bowlby's (1969) idea that attachment processes operate across the life course and continue to influence personality development "from the cradle to the grave" (Bowlby, 1988, p. 163). As such, when viewed from the lenses of these theorists, it is important to understand both the means of internalizing a hopeful disposition in childhood and how that disposition is transmitted across time into adulthood.

With the development of the Trait Hope Scale (Snyder, Harris, et al., 1991), researchers have supported many of Snyder's (1994, 2002) theoretical propositions including those relating to attachment processes (Jankowski & Sandage, 2011; Jiang, Huebner, & Hills, 2013; Shorey et al., 2003; Simmons, Gooty, Nelson, & Little, 2009; Simmons, Nelson, & Quick, 2003). It is the goal of this chapter to review this research and elaborate on the empirical and theoretical connections between hope and attachment. In so doing, we aim to explore the many developmental processes through which a hopeful mindset can be instilled. Distilling the specific psychological processes involved should promote more exact testing of hope-related concepts and provide guidance for those developing programs that either directly or indirectly target the development of hopeful thinking and related positive psychological and achievement-related outcomes. But first we must look to attachment theory and the natural course of positive human development.

Attachment Theory

In opposition to the psychoanalytic context in which he was trained, Bowlby (1969, 1988) proposed that factors present in the child's real external environment (i.e., interactions with parents), as opposed to sexual and aggressive drives and fantasies, were the primary forces in personality development and psychopathology (see Bretherton, 1992). Drawing on works of ethologists and others in the natural sciences, Bowlby (1969) proposed that young humans, similar to other animals, are biologically predisposed to maintain attachment to groups and more powerful others because maintaining proximity to attachment figures has direct survival value. The primary force driving the maintenance of proximity in relation to an attachment figure is anxiety. In this respect, the attachment system can be viewed as a homeostatic control mechanism (in contrast to drives) that uses anxiety to keep child exploration and proximity-seeking systems in balance (Mikulincer & Shaver 2003).

Initially, attachment theory focused almost exclusively on the maintenance of proximity and the parent acting as a "safe haven" in times of need. These aspects of functioning collectively are known as the "attachment system." Contemporary theorists, however, view the attachment system as being inextricably linked to a corresponding "exploratory system" (Elliot & Reis, 2003). When a child strays too far from the caregiver in exploring the environment, anxiety becomes intolerably high and impels him or her to re-establish proximity. This is where attachment-related psychodynamics

come into play. How the parent responds to the child upon his or her return and how well the parent regulates (or exacerbates) the child's distress will determine whether the child develops a secure attachment style or one of the three insecure attachment styles (avoidant/dismissing, anxious/preoccupied, or disorganized/fearful). Parenting and resultant attachment styles will have a profound impact on the child's subsequent exploratory and goal-directed behavior; not to mention his or her developing brain, social perception, self-other-environment schema, emotion regulation, and hope (Lemche et al, 2006, Mikulincer & Shaver, 2003; Schore, 2001).

Attachment patterns, commonly known as styles, are relatively stable personality traits with concordance rates in the 60% range for retaining an original attachment style classification from childhood (at age 18 months) to early adulthood (approximately 70% if simply looking at retaining secure vs. insecure classification; Shorey & Snyder, 2006). In childhood, styles are typically assessed with the strange situation paradigm (Ainsworth & Wittig, 1969) that classifies children as secure, avoidant, anxious-ambivalent, or disorganized (Main & Solomon, 1990). In adulthood, these styles correspond with classifications on the Adult Attachment Interview (AAI; George, Kaplan, & Main, 1985) and any one of several self-report measures. The AAI labels are "autonomous" for secure, "dismissing" for avoidant, "preoccupied" for anxious ambivalent, and "unresolved" for disorganized. Self-report methodologies typically retain the secure classification for adulthood and label the adult version of child disorganized style as "fearful" (Brennan, Clark & Shaver, 1998). For the remainder of this chapter, we use the self-report labels because, to our knowledge, no research has been conducted on the relationship between hope and attachment using the AAI. We return to the insecure attachment styles later after first describing secure attachment and the processes involved in instilling a coherent, organized, and autonomous sense of self.

Whipple, Bernier, and Mageau (2009) used self-determination theory (SDT; Deci & Ryan, 2000, 2008) to articulate how secure attachment can be defined in terms of an attachment/exploration balance. Self-determination theory has many overlaps with hope theory and views children as active agents who are innately drawn to explore and master their internal and external environments. Children strive to develop competence through acquiring new skills and seeking novel challenges. Deci and Ryan (2000, 2008) referred to this ongoing process as intrinsic motivation, and, in their natural states, children can be viewed as agentic beings who develop pathways to goals. In other words, the natural state of the healthy child is to explore and be hopeful.

The goals of exploration according to Wilcock (1993) are to (a) satisfy basic needs for food and shelter; (b) develop skills, relationships, and strategies needed to guarantee safety; and (c) develop the capacity for continued growth and development. The child's natural propensity toward healthy exploration and intrinsic motivation, however, is shaped through interactions with "social agents" (i.e., parents) who can support or inhibit the development of these natural tendencies (Deci & Ryan, 2000). This notion of social agents who support or inhibit exploration is consistent with how parents shape attachment styles.

The role of parents in promoting healthy exploration has been well documented. In this respect, Baumrind's (1967, 1991) conceptualization of the authoritative parent who provides autonomy support through being warm and available while also maintaining high standards and encouraging independent achievement strivings is the hope-inspiring prototype. Whipple et al. (2009) assessed parenting behaviors that they hypothesized would support both the attachment system and the exploratory system among 71 upper-middle-class mother–infant dyads. During home visits, the mother was rated on sensitivity (using the maternal sensitivity Q-sort; Pederson & Moran, 1995) as she attempted to divide her attention between the research tasks (completing questionnaires and engaging in the interview) and attending to her infant. Mother–infant dyads were then asked to complete a challenging problem-solving task (puzzle) together, and videotaped recordings of these interactions were used to code maternal support for autonomy. Coding of autonomy support was based on

> the extent to which the mother (1) intervenes according to the infant's needs and adapts the task to create an optimal challenge for the child; (2) encourages her child in the pursuit of the task, gives useful hints and suggestions, and uses a tone of voice that communicates to the child that she is there to help; (3) takes her child's perspective and demonstrates flexibility in her attempts to keep her child on task; (4) follows her child's pace, provides the child with the opportunity to make choices, and ensures that the child plays an active role in the completion of the task. (Whipple et al., 2009; p. 23)

Infants attachment security in Whipple et al.'s (2009) study was assessed with the attachment behavior Q-set (Waters & Deane, 1985). Results indicated that whereas maternal sensitivity and autonomy support were not correlated ($r = .17$), both maternal sensitivity ($r = .33$) and autonomy/support ($r = .32$) correlated positively with infant attachment security. After controlling for sensitivity, which predicted 10.8% of the variance, autonomy support predicted an additional 7.2% of the variance in secure attachment. These results suggest that authoritative parents are maximally positioned to provide the sensitivity needed to support their infants emotionally as well as the ability to coach their infants in exploring the environment, with both sensitivity and autonomy support needed to maximize secure attachment.

Parenting and the "Goal Corrected Partnership"

Parental sensitivity and autonomy support can both be seen to underlie the development of hope through a process that Bowlby (1969/1982) called the "goal corrected partnership." In discussing this material, we propose that sensitivity is the basis of hope agency and autonomy support is the basis of hope pathways. As with the development of a secure attachment style, both are needed to instill hopeful thinking.

The target of the attachment exploratory system, and the first component of hopeful thinking, is goals. If the baby reaches for a piece of food the goal may be to eliminate hunger. If the toddler chases after a butterfly, the goal may be to learn about her environment. If the school-age child wants designer clothes, the goal may be to explore the possibility of greater social inclusion. In each of these examples, the underlying goal (eliminating hunger, learning, social inclusion) could be satisfied in many ways. One job of the healthy parent, therefore, is to propose to the child various goal targets that, if achieved, will fulfill the deeper goal. Hope theory (Snyder, 2002; Shorey, Snyder, Rand, Hockemeyer, & Feldman, 2002) holds that adaptive goals will be (a) satisfying (moderately high valence) and therefore personally meaningful, (b) well defined and therefore amenable to being communicated to others, (c) challenging and therefore exciting and stimulating, and (d) achievable, therefore increasing the probability of success and mastery experiences.

In the context of the goal-corrected partnership (Bowlby, 1969), we argue that the hopeful self is formed through a cyclical process wherein the child uses the parent as a "secure base" from which to venture out and pursue goals (Ainsworth, Blehar, Waters, & Wall, 1978). When the child inevitably faces goal blockages and experiences resultant negative emotions, he or she then retreats to the parental "safe haven" for anxiety reduction and comfort (Bowlby, 1969). The "empathically attuned" parent then uses mirroring to validate the child's feelings and perceptions before upregulating emotions by expressing and modeling more positive emotions and hopeful thoughts about the future.

Empathic attunement is similar to metacognitive monitoring and is important for exploration. This corresponds with Snyder's (1994) notion that metacognitive processes are needed to rationally support and evaluates one's goal pursuits. Empathically attuned parents will have a theory of mind that enables them to understand the experiences of their child and, by extension, be tuned in to the child's skill level and tolerance for challenges and frustration. Hope-instilling parents will tend to give the child goals that are challenging but achievable and within the child's zone of proximal development. Moss, Gosselin, Parent, Rousseau, and Dumont (1997), for example, found that mothers of secure children focused their problem-solving guidance to be well within the child's zone of proximal development whereas mothers of insecure children either suggested strategies that were too simple or too difficult.

Once the child's emotions are regulated, and a feeling of agency reinstilled, the parent can help the child strategize and consider new pathways to success in subsequent goal pursuits. And, in our view, such is the genesis of hope: .goals, agency, and pathways. Securely attached children grow up believing that they are lovable, that other people are available and willing to provide support when needed, and that the world is a safe and predictable place where their efforts and goal strivings are likely to be rewarded (Bowlby, 1988). In the goal-corrected partnership, the parent, acting as a secure base, is focused on supportive behaviors that encourage exploration, mastery, and related satisfaction and pleasure in the goal-pursuit activity. The secure-base role according to Bowlby (1988) is

> one of being available, ready to respond when called upon to encourage and perhaps assist, but to intervene actively only when clearly necessary. In these respects, it is a role similar to that of the officer commanding a military base from which

an expeditionary force sets out and to which it can retreat, should it meet with a setback. Much of the time the role of the base is a waiting one, but it is none the less vital for that. For it is only when the officer commanding the expeditionary force is confident his base is secure that he dare press forward and take risks. (p. 11)

Bowlby (1988) was referring to the secure base in terms of children's relationships to their parents. Across the past decade, however, scholars have increasingly viewed attachment processes and the secure-base function as being operative through adulthood in interpersonal relationships and even in relationships with bosses at work.

Feeney (2004) conducted research on the secure-base function in adulthood by looking at how people provide responsive or unresponsive support for a relationship partner's goal pursuits, personal grown, and exploration. Couples were observed first as they discussed their personal future-oriented goals and then as they engaged in an experimentally manipulated goal activity. Results demonstrated that nonintrusive/responsive support of the relationship partner's goal pursuit and exploration had a strong impact on that person's happiness, self-esteem, and self-perceived likelihood of achieving specific goals.

Feeney and Thrush (2010) similarly investigated secure-base behaviors among married couples engaged in a novel problem-solving task. One partner was engaged in the problem activity in the presence of the other partner who would by default serve as the "base." Feeney and Thrush operationalized secure-base behaviors based on the aforementioned descriptions of the secure base in childhood. Findings indicated that when the exploring partner perceived the base partner as being responsive to his or her needs and sensitive to his or her distress cues, that person experienced greater independence and self-efficacy, engaged more in independent exploration, and was more successful in achieving goals. In the context of discussing goals for the future, one partner's acceptance (expressing future availability, sensitive/responsive, and willingness to provide support) of the other partner's dependence corresponded with the latter partner functioning more autonomously in terms of confidently exploring independent goals. Moreover, these effects lasted over six months and resulted in greater likelihood of the partner having accomplished important personal goals outside of the study context.

Feeney (2007) described this relationship between healthy dependency and autonomous functioning as a "dependency paradox," which stipulates that a responsive attachment figure remains the source of security across the lifespan and that only when a person experiences this security, will he or she be able to explore confidently and autonomously.

While acceptance of an exploring person's dependency needs may promote independence and hope, controlling and interfering behaviors on the part of the person occupying the "base" position is likely to have the effect of undermining one's confidence, concentration, and abilities to achieve goals (Feeney, 2007). In other words, controlling or offering support that is not needed or desired will have the effect of diminishing hope and impeding goal pursuits.

The Secure Base and Hope Agency

As presented in the preceding section, the process of using a secure base from which to venture forth, explore, and develop hope begins in infancy and continues throughout the developmental years. A key point is that parental behaviors aimed at providing support and challenge to the child are just as important for instilling hope as attachment sensitivity is in instilling secure attachment (Grossmann et al., 2002). Controlling and intrusive behaviors, in contrast, should be expected to thwart exploration and the development of hope. Drawing on Baumrind's definition of authoritative parenting, Grolnick, Frodi, and Bridges (1984) examined how mothers autonomy-supportive versus controlling behaviors affected the child's motivation to explore. They found that mothers who engaged in more autonomy-supportive behaviors had children who were more persistent (an indicator of hope agency) during play activities. Similarly, Deci, Driver, Hotchkiss, Robbins, and McDougal-Wilson (1993) assessed mothers and their six- to seven-year-old children in a laboratory play activity. Results indicated that when mothers were more controlling in their vocalizations, their children reported liking the target play activity less and persisting in the activity for shorter durations of time relative to children whose mothers were less controlling in their vocalizations. These findings suggest that controlling parents inhibit the development of hope and autonomy in their children.

Koestner, Ryan, Bemieri and Holt (1984) similarly engaged six- and seven-year old children in a painting task and found that when instructions were given in a controlling manner, the children displayed less intrinsic motivation relative to children who were given instructions in an autonomy-supportive manner or children who were given no instructions at all. These findings all support Bowlby's (1988) contention that interfering and intrusive behaviors are diametrically opposed to providing sensitive and responsive support and are a prime inhibitor of exploratory behaviors.

Whereas low-hope people tend to denigrate their own abilities, high-hope people regularly engage in a stream of positive self-talk (Snyder, 1994). Snyder was fond of drawing an analogy to Wally Pipers childrens' book in which the little blue engine keeps saying to herself "I think I can. I think I can. . . ." Obviously this is an analogy to the agency component of hopeful thinking and an "I can do it" attitude. One should not surmise, however, that this positive achievement-oriented attitude comes just from success experiences. On the contrary: limited failure experiences and related anxiety provide the fuel to put the attachment system, exploratory system, and hope into motion in the formation of a health personality (Snyder, Cheavens, & Sympson, 1997).

After a failure experience, for example, the well-adjusted parent will first validate the child's distress and feeling of disappointment. In terms of reflective functioning (Fonagy & Target, 1997), this parent does not gloss over the loss with a general upbeat and cheerful disposition but, rather, initially reflects in his or her mood and facial expression an empathic understanding of what the child is feeling. The reflected affect is not exaggerated; nor is it minimized. Accuracy and validation of the child's feelings and perceptions helps the child calibrate his or her emotional response. This type of dynamic is seen between clients and their therapists (McCluskey, Hooper, & Miller, 1999) where the therapist helps the client to develop emotional responses that are equal in intensity and quality to the situations that are encountered. As such, the developing person will come to trust in his or her own emotions and be able to use them as data to inform decision-making. He or she will also be able to use emotions intentionally to keep going when times get tough.

Having validated his or her child's emotional experience, the secure parent proceeds to upregulate the child's emotions. Consider, for example, a child who returns to his father distraught over not making the school sports team. Having validated the child's experience ("This is a tough thing to handle. I know how disappointed and angry you must be"), the father's ensuing upregulation ("You know what buddy? It's going to be okay. Bad things happen, but we can figure it out and help you do better next time. You're going to have a lot of successes in life and a great future") transitions the child from a troubled and dysphoric mood to a more positive mood and hopeful outlook on the future.

Across innumerable iterations of proximity-seeking, validation, upregulation, and subsequent reengagement, the developing person learns how to engage in this process internally without the need for an external "coach." This person will develop the ability to maintain positive emotions in the face of failure and keep agency thinking alive as he or she continues to strive for meaningful personal goals (Snyder, Shorey, Cheavens, Pulvers, Adams, & Wiklund, 2002).

Exploration and Pathways Thinking

As the exploration and proximity-seeking cycle is repeated in innumerable iterations and increasingly complex patterns across the developmental years, the young person internalizes the goal-corrected partnership and starts to perform each of the functions him- or herself (i.e., obtaining an internal or external secure base; goaling, actively pursuing the goals, validating subjective experience, upregulating emotions and maintaining agency, and strategizing new pathways to goals). The internalized patterns, in attachment theory terms, are known as "working models" (Bowlby, 1969). The working models of securely attached individuals typically involve views of the self as worthy of love and support, others as willing and available to provide that support when needed, the worlds as safe and predictable place, and the self as highly efficacious and able to achieve personally meaningful goals (high hope).

In his writings, Snyder often referred to the parent as a hope-inspiring coach. This coach function can be seen in the goal corrected partnership. After emotionally regulating the child, the parent fosters instrumental problem-solving by helping the child re-goal. Re-goaling involves evaluating the feasibility of implementing strategies to the goals, exploring goal difficulty, and identifying necessary subgoals and needed resources (Snyder, 2002; Shorey et al., 2002). These functions also can be viewed under the rubric of hope pathways. In this respect, pathways thinking can be seen to be part of the attachment exploratory system. Backed by a parental secure base, the secure child is free to venture forward to pursue goals, explore the implementation of various pathways, evaluate the relative success or failure of each pathway, obtain parental

feedback, and use that feedback to identify and implement new pathways (see McClelland, 1973). Knowing that goals can always be modified and new pathways developed also enables people to persevere in the face of failure (Shorey, 2003). When high-hope people fail in their goal pursuits, they do not denigrate their abilities. Rather, they simply infer that the right strategies have not been found or that they failed to put forth the requisite motivation to succeed (Snyder, 2002; Snyder et al., 1997).

Moving Hope and Attachment into Adulthood

Attachment theory proposes that the development of attachment security in childhood will generally result in positive adjustment, competence, and mental health in adulthood. Snyder (1994) also posited that secure attachment to parents in childhood should impart a hopeful disposition that will be carried forward into adulthood and be responsible for positive mental health outcomes. Shorey, Snyder, Lewin, and Yang (2003) tested these propositions among 267 college students who completed retrospective reports of the types of parenting experienced in childhood, as well as measures of adult attachment, hope, and mental health. Parenting was assessed using the Parental Authority Questionnaire (Buri, 1991), which assesses three parenting styles identified by Baumrind (authoritative, authoritarian, and permissive) and the Parental Bonding Instrument (Parker, Tupling, & Brown, 1979) to assess parental rejection. Attachment was assessed using the Experiences in Close Relationships Scale (ECR; Brennan et al., 1998). Findings using structural equation modeling indicated that the type of parenting experienced in childhood (more authoritative and less rejecting or authoritarian) led to more secure attachment in early adulthood and, through secure attachment, to adult levels of dispositional hope. Hope, in turn, partially mediated the relationship between secure attachment and adult mental health (less anxiety, depression, and loss of behavioral control and more general positive affect) in a model that accounted for 53% of the variance in adult mental health outcomes.

More specifically, Shorey et al. (2003) found that the mother's parenting was primary, and the father's parenting was secondary, in the development of attachment styles. The effect of father's parenting on attachment was fully mediated by the parenting provided by the mother. This does not detract from the importance of fathers, but it does fit with Bowlby's (1969) original view of the mother as the primary parent. Bowlby called the mother the "psychic organizer" who, through providing both the ego and super ego functions (see Bretherton, 1992) provided the building blocks for an organized and coherent personality. In later years, and in light of a growing body of research, Bowlby (1988) moderated his position in stating that attachment related more to who the primary caregiver was, as opposed to any secondary sex characteristic of the parent.

More recently, researchers have conceptualized mothers and fathers as both contributing to the development of secure attachment but through different mechanisms. Even when fathers have primary caregiver responsibilities, they still evidence lower caregiver sensitivity (Grossman et al., 2002). Fathers appear to exert their primary influence through providing knowledge and advice and challenging the child's ability to adapt to new environments (Grossman et al. 2002). In other words, mothers may be more relevant to the safe-haven function and hope agency, and fathers may be more relevant to the exploration function and hope pathways. In Grossman et al's (2002) study, fathers' sensitivity in how they provided emotional support and gentle challenging to their playing toddlers was the greatest predictor of latter attachment classifications. For mothers, attachment quality, but not play sensitivity, predicted latter attachment classifications. This finding that fathers sensitivity in play related to attachment can perhaps be seen in the Shorey et al. (2003) model in which we see a direct effect of father's parenting on hopeful thought that bypassed internalized attachment schema and related primarily to hope pathways as opposed to agency thinking. But perhaps the greatest contribution of the Shorey et al. (2003) study was to support the continued interaction of attachment and hope in later adolescence and adulthood.

Jankowski and Sandage (2011) tested the hypothesis that hope and adult attachment would mediate the relationship between meditative prayer and interpersonal forgiveness among 209 protestant, master's-level students. Attachment dimensions of avoidance and anxiety were assessed with the ECR (Brennan et al., 1998), and hope was assessed with the Trait Hope Scale. A direct effect was found between hope and adult attachment with hope pathways correlating with both attachment anxiety ($r = -.31$) and avoidance ($r = -.19$) and hope agency correlating with both attachment anxiety ($r = -.37$) and avoidance ($r = -.19$). Structural equation modeling indicated that hope and adult attachment together mediated the relationship between meditative prayer and forgiveness.

Simmons, Nelson, and Quick (2003) assessed the relationships between adult attachment, hope, and health perceptions among 175 mostly female home healthcare nurses. They used Joplin, Nelson, and Quick's (1999) Self-Reliance Inventory to assess how people form and maintain supportive attachments with others in adulthood based on interdependence (secure attachment), counterdependence (avoidant attachment), and overdependence (anxious attachment). Hope was assessed with the State Hope Scale (Snyder et al., 1996). Health perceptions were assessed using four items from the Health Perceptions Questionnaire (Ware, Davies-Avery, & Donald, 1978). Results indicated that hope correlated with interdependence ($r = .42$), counterdependence ($r = -36$), and overdependence ($r = -.38$), and hope fully mediated the relationship between interdependence and overdependence and self-reported health.

Jiang et al. (2013) similarly found that hope partially mediated the relationship between attachment and a measure of life satisfaction in a large sample of racially diverse adolescents. A caution relating to the definition of attachment, however, is in order in interpreting this latter study. This is an important point that may help the consumer of this line of research make better sense of the findings. Jiang et al. used the Inventory of Parent and Peer Attachment (IPPA; Armsden & Greenberg, 1987), which in our view does not map onto Bowlby or Ainsworth's conceptualization of attachment styles as being internalized "working models" or self-other schema. Rather, examination of IPPA item content reveals that it relates more to the quality of parent or peer relationships (in relation to trust, communication, and alienation) as opposed to commonly recognized attachment styles or dimensions. This is not to say that IPPA research is not greatly valuable and informative. It merely points out that just because a construct uses the word "attachment" (or "hope," for that matter) does not mean that it is assessing the same construct.

The foregoing studies all conceptualized hope as an important variable that mediates the relationships between attachment and important adult outcomes. Although some of these studies assessed insecure attachment styles, for the most part, all hypotheses and conceptualizations were made in relation to secure attachment. This should not be taken to mean, however, that all securely attached individuals are high in hope or that all insecurely attached individuals are low in hope.

Insecure Attachment and Domains of Hope

The foregoing descriptions of attachment security and the genesis of hope assume that parents consistently provide a safe-haven and secure-base function and that the child will develop a corresponding secure attachment style. In actuality, however, this represents only about 55% of the parents in Western societies (see Shorey & Snyder, 2006). The other 45% of people are likely to have one of three "insecure attachment styles." As previously described, the parents of securely attached children promote a balance between social- and achievement-area goals (corresponding with healthy dependence and autonomy, respectively). These parents are socially invested, consistently warm, available, and responsive for their children while at the same time maintaining high achievement expectations. By extension, their children are free to use proximity seeking as their primary emotion-regulation strategy and are able to make full use of the goal-corrected partnership to achieve their social and achievement-area goals (Bowlby, 1988).

The parents of avoidant/dismissing individuals, in contrast, are consistent but they are not typically warm or responsive. They characteristically (a) reject the child's negative emotions (e.g., "little boys don't cry" and "don't be a sissy"), (b) are not empathically attuned ("you're not really hurt"), (c) provide skewed mirroring (the parent smiles while the child is feeling sad), (d) force the child to regulate emotions though a secondary affect regulation strategy termed "deactivation" (of the attachment system; see Mikulincer & Shaver, 2003), and (e) encourage autonomy and achievement goals over social goals and close relationships (Connors, 1997).

When the parent fails to validate the child's negative emotions, the child, over time, will be forced to ignore or deny (i.e., suppress) negative feelings. If this process begins when the child is very young, it will affect the development not only of his or her schema but of his or her right brain social perception, stress, and regulatory functions (Schore, 2001). This child is likely to grow into an adult who selectively ignores negative social cues, has little awareness of his or her own negative emotional experiences, and has little emotional perspective-taking or empathy in relation to others (Connors, 1997). Snyder (1994) thought that perspective-taking was an important process that provides greater access to pathways and helps in the anticipation of goal blockages. Failures in reflective functioning and perspective-taking may lead parents to upregulate emotions too quickly and divert the child's attention

away from social problem in order to derive positive self-esteem from achievement areas such as sports, school, or work. Shorey (2008), for example, found that when dismissing college students were exposed subliminally to negative social cues, they automatically turned their attention away for social goals and onto achievement goals.

This latter finding is consistent with Ainsworth et al.'s (1973) research, where they found that although secure infants were the most likely to explore, avoidant infants also engaged in high levels of exploration, but the motive appeared to be to gain distance from the parent as opposed to enjoying exploration for its own sake. Just as avoidant children engage in premature self-reliance, dismissing adults strive for emotional and psychological independence from significant others in order to suppress threat-related thoughts and emotions (Mikulincer, Gillath, & Shaver, 2002). Martin, Paetzold, and Rholes (2010) similarly found that dismissing adults engage in exploration primarily for independence motives and as a means of distancing from close relationships as opposed to dependence motives or being intrinsically drawn to explore.

Because dismissing adults tend to be focus on high achievement in areas such as school, sports, or work while also turning away from social domains of functioning, they may be assessed as high in hope when using a general trait measure such as the Hope Scale (Snyder et al., 1991). The present lead author's research using the Domain Specific Hope Scale (Sympson, 1999) for example, demonstrates that dismissing adults report high hope in achievement domains and relatively low hope in social domains. At the same time, they score similar to secure individuals on trait hope. This indicates that trait hope scores may reflect an individual's goals in his or her areas of attentional focus and not reflect functioning in areas that are not held in the forefront of consciousness. When self-reporting on hope, for example, one person may be thinking about his social prowess even though he is a low academic achiever; another person may be thinking about his academic prowess even though he is a low social achiever. Given these different domain targets, however, both of these exemplar individuals may assess as equal in trait hope. Thus although higher levels of hope are correlated with more secure attachment and by extension less insecure attachment, it cannot be said that all insecurely attached individuals are low in hope.

A stronger low-hope connection can be made for preoccupied attachment. The parents of anxious/

preoccupied individuals tend to focus overly on social domains and tend to be inconsistent in how they respond to their children. Sometimes they are warm and accepting. Sometimes they are cold and rejecting. When the parent responds inconsistently to the child who returns to the safe haven for emotion regulation, the child's negative affect may or may not be regulated. Thus proximity seeking may not work consistently for this child, who may have to rely on a secondary affect regulation strategy know as "hyperactivation" (of the attachment system; see Mikulincer & Shaver, 2003).

In hyperactivation, the child's attachment system is stuck in the "on position" (Mikulincer & Shaver, 2003). Because the parental system is unreliable, this child will do his or her utmost to closely monitor the parent to stay in close proximity and is likely to become hypervigilant for threat cues that could signal rejection. In this respect, parental inconsistency in rewarding dependency bids can be seen to put in place a variable ratio reinforcement schedule that will further promote proximity seeking and approach behaviors in times of emotional activation. By extension, the anxious/preoccupied person is likely to regulate emotions by obtaining reassurance from others. In this case, the person does not develop a belief that he or she can control or upregulate his or her own emotions, with obvious implications for exploration. Ainsworth (1973), for example, found that anxious infants tend to be clingy and do not explore far from their attachment figures. Difficulty upregulating emotions internally without the need for external other should have the effect of inhibiting agency thinking. Maintaining a hypervigilant stance toward the social environment along with high base levels of anxiety will also interfere with instrumental problem-solving and pathways thinking. By extension, anxious/preoccupied attachment is generally associated with lower hope levels (Jankowski & Sandage, 2011; Jiang, Huebner, & Hills, 2013; Shorey et al., 2003; Simmons, Gooty, Nelson, & Little, 2009; Simmons, Nelson, & Quick, 2003).

Whereas people high in attachment avoidance are motivated to explore and achieve out of independence motives, those high in attachment anxiety prefer to work with others and are motivated by a need for approval (Hazan & Shaver, 1990). Carnelley and Ruscher (2000) researched leisure activities and found that higher levels of attachment anxiety predicted engaging in leisure activities for social reasons and to regulate negative emotions about relationships. Martin et al. (2010)

similarly found that people high in attachment anxiety engage in exploration as a means of obtaining approval from others. High attachment anxiety in Martin et al.'s study also predicted enjoying exploration less and perceiving less support or encouragement for their exploration from relationship partners. Less support and lower confidence in the ability to explore should result in lower hope in both social and achievement life areas.

Unresolved/fearful attachment is also associated with low hope levels. The parents in this instance are often characterized as "frightening or frightened" (Cassidy & Mohr, 2001). The parent may be abusive, may be a victim or otherwise traumatized, or may have severe mental health issues. The most important aspects to consider here are that the child's negative emotions are not ameliorated through the primary affect regulation strategy of proximity seeking. Because the parent is often a source of fear, the secondary deactivation or hyperactivation strategies also do not work. By extension, the child is left with no viable coping mechanisms and develops a disorganized perception of self, the world, and the cause and effect linkages necessary for adequately conceptualizing or effectively pursuing goals (see Mikulincer & Shaver, 2003). These individuals are highly anxious in terms of attachment, but they are also behaviorally avoidant (Brennan et al, 1998). By extension, of all the attachment styles, they may be most in need of support but least able or willing to ask for it. Resultant difficulty finding a safe haven or secure base from which to explore should result in paucity of hope and, relative to people with other attachment styles, the worst mental health and achievement-related outcomes (see Shorey & Snyder, 2006).

Expanding the Notion of Goals and the Secure Base

Snyder et al. (1997) suggested that hope is an "individual motive for social commerce" (p. 107). These authors suggest that high-hope people choose goals that are socially sanctioned. This social goal focus is consistent with Baumeister and Leary (1995), who suggested that goals lead to positive mental health outcomes only to the extent that they are supported by the important people in one's life. But because cultures and social support systems differ, whether goals are adaptive or maladaptive is not an objective question. Pursuing goals that are valued by the attachment figure and one's primary social groups should promote in-group identification and social inclusion (i.e., make it easier to maintain proximity). By extension, acceptance and in-group identification should assure provision of the safe-haven and secure-base functions. In this respect, an emotional connection to a group can be seen as an attachment bond (Mikulincer & Shaver, 2007).

Smith and Tonigan (2009) conducted a survey of 158 participants who had attended at least 30 Alcoholics Anonymous (AA) meetings (and more than any other type of 12-step meeting). Participants rated their present and retrospective (before going to AA meetings) perceptions of the degree to which Hazan and Shaver's (1984) attachment style descriptions (secure, avoidant, anxious) fit them at both time points. Results indicated that meaningfully engaging with the sponsors and group members, but not the number of AA meetings attended, predicted increased ratings of secure attachment and decreased ratings of avoidant attachment across their group participation. This research should be considered preliminary given the retrospective assessment of attachment, but it does support Mikulincer and Shaver's (2007) propositions that attachment to a group and group leaders promotes secure attachment and a hopeful and pro-social orientation to the future.

But what happens when the values of the attachment figure and the group are not socially sanctioned by the larger society (or even the world community)? Hope and optimism have often been characterized in the literature as virtues (Peterson & Seligman, 2004). But in conflict situations, hope is a virtue only when it is supporting "your" position. Street gangs, for example, are organized groups that can provide a secure base and hope for their members (see Vigil, 1988). Research suggests that gangs can function as families and secure bases by providing members with support and safety, especially when the individual's family is not able to do so (Ruble & Turner, 2000). Nevertheless, the benefits of gangs to the individual members is likely to be far outweighed by their negative impacts on the larger society (Ruble & Turner, 2000; Sharkey, Shekhtmeyster, Chavez-Lopez, Norris, & Sass, 2011). This may not matter to the individual gang member, however, because the larger society does not provide him or her with security in the form of a safe haven or secure base and falls short of providing strategies to achieve his or her basic goals.

We can similarly make the case that terrorist groups provide some attachment functions, such as the safe haven, secure base, and goal-corrected partnership. By extension, they may impart high levels of hope to their members. They also promote goals that are socially sanctioned in their localized groups and even by some segments of their host cultures. Their goals may be well defined, high in valence, and achievable. They also appear to be highly motivated. When they lack resources and their pathways are blocked, they may even resort to blowing themselves up to achieve their goals. One should appreciate that if the goal is to hurt the "enemy" and obtain martyrdom, then dying while carrying out a suicide attack may be an ultimate high-hope expression.

The aforementioned examples of gangs and terrorist groups are provided to demonstrate that the attachment and hope systems are value neutral when considered from a cross-culture perspective. The only values that we see operating universally from an attachment theory framework are (a) warmth, care, and acceptance for the individual by an attachment figure or group; (b) acceptance and validation by the group of the individual's experience; (c) the group serving an anxiety reducing/affect regulation function; (d) group membership promoting positive emotions; and (e) goaling and pathways provision. Attachments to others and to groups also are not the only sources of hope. New research on attachment to God also shows a high-hope connection.

Hope and Attachment to God

Because God often is turned to by believers in times of need, Kirkpatrick (1992) proposed that God, just as a human parent, can be conceived as an attachment figure. God may fulfill the two essential roles of a primary caregiver (Kirkpatrick, 1992, 1998). As a safe haven, God can offer sanctuary for worshipers during times of distress or increased anxiety. God also may serve as a secure base by offering a sense of security, courage, and reassurance to people as they explore and perform their daily activities. This secure base function may explain why secure attachment to God, similar to secure attachments to parents (Bowlby, 1969) and attachment to romantic partners (Hazan & Shaver, 1987), has been found to yield positive mental health benefits (Kirkpatrick, 1992). For example, higher levels of secure attachment to God have associated with less loneliness (Kirkpatrick, Shillito, & Kellas, 1999), more positive affect (Rowatt & Kirkpatrick, 2002), and higher levels of optimism (Sim & Loh, 2003).

If, as Kilpatrick (1992, 1998) suggested, attachment to God operates similarly to attachment to parents and significant others, then attachment to God also should lead to positive benefits through its influence on instilling higher levels of hope. Those with secure attachments to God show reduced suicide risk, lower substance abuse, and overall greater hope levels (Koenig, 2004).

Research shows that parent–child relationships can substantially influence one's perception of attachment to God (Allen, 2013; Beck & McDonald, 2004; Hall, Fujikawa, Halcrow, Hill, & Delaney, 2009; McDonald, Beck, Allison, & Norsworthy, 2005). Secure adult attachment correlates with perceptions of God as more loving, less distant, and less controlling (Beck & McDonald, 2004; Hall et al., 2009). Referring back to our discussion of support: a controlling god should have the effect of inhibiting exploration and hope. The compensatory hypothesis suggest that insecurely attached individuals use God and religion for affect regulation more than secure individuals use God and religion or affect regulation. Securely attached individuals are better able to regulate emotions, better able to self-sooth, and are likely to use religion for its own sake (Schore, 2003). The compensatory hypothesis thus suggests that attachment to God could correlate with lower levels of secure and higher levels of insecure attachment. Of course, this is a question that only future research will be able to answer.

Conclusions and Suggestions for Future Research

The empirical research we have reviewed and the theoretical integration we have put forth in relation to the attachment based genesis of hope suggests that the role of hope is primarily that of a mediator that translates developmentally based personality dispositions into an adult exploratory and goal-directed mindset with corresponding implications for positive adjustment and achievement outcomes.

The secure base propositions from attachment theory are ripe for empirical investigation. In this respect, we are highly interested in finding out if autonomy/support versus controlling/support behaviors in adulthood will lower hope just as it thwarted exploration and pleasure in the goal-directed activity in the research by Deci et al. (1994), Grolnick et al. (1983), and Koestner et al. (1984). Both sensitivity and autonomy support should be needed to instill hope that is truly a motive for social commerce. On the flip side of the equation, false hope may be that which is not social in nature. If the parent provides autonomy support without providing sensitivity, then a dismissing attachment style may result. In this case, the child may become overly achievement oriented to the detriment of being socially oriented. By extension, the

child's primary goals, and hope, may not be social in nature. This is problematic because achievement goals and hope, without social support, may not yield expected mental health related outcomes (Baumeister and Leary, 1995; Shorey, 2008).

We also would like to see research on whether attachment sensitivity promotes hope agency and autonomy support promotes hope pathways similar to how these two attachment theory variables (sensitivity and autonomy support) support the attachment system and the exploratory system, respectively. This research is important because it suggests a secondary avenue for interventions that target the development of hopeful thinking. To date, hope has been viewed primarily as a trait-like thought process that can be taught (Snyder, Shorey, & Rand, 2005). While this may be true, we believe that the present work makes the case that hope may be more deeply instilled at the dispositional level of working models and emotion-regulation systems that underlie the effective operation of the exploratory system. If this is the case, then the safe haven and secure base processes, including the goal-corrected partnership, can be harnessed and provide a roadmap for instilling hope experientially even in later adolescents and adulthood.

References

Ainsworth, M. D. S. (1973). The development of infant-mother attachment. In B. M. Caldwell & H. N. Ricciuti (Eds.), *Review of child development research* (Vol. 3, pp. 1–94). Chicago:University of Chicago Press.

Ainsworth, M. D. S., Blehar, M. C., Waters, E., & Wall, S. (1978). *Patterns of attachment: A psychological study of the Strange Situation.* New York: Basic Books.

Ainsworth, M. D. S., & Wittig, B. A. (1969). Attachment and exploratory behavior of one-year-olds in a strange situation. In B. M. Foss (Ed.), *Determinants of infant behavior* (Vol. 4, pp. 111–136). London: Methuen.

Allen, J. (2013). Hope in human attachment and spiritual connection. *Bulletin of the Menninger Clinic. Special Issue: The Spirituality of Hope and Healing, 77*(4), 302–331.

Armsden, G. C., & Greenberg, M. T. (1987). The Inventory of Parent and Peer Attachment: Individual differences and their relationship to psychological well-being in adolescence. *Journal of Youth and Adolescence, 16,* 427–454.

Baumeister, R. F., & Leary, M. R. (1995). The need to belong: Desire for interpersonal attachments as a fundamental human motivation. *Psychological Bulletin, 117*(3), 497–529. doi:10.1037/0033-2909.117.3.497

Baumrind, D. (1967). Child care practices anteceding three patterns of preschool behavior. *Genetic Psychology Monographs, 75,* 43–88.

Baumrind, D. (1991). The influence of parenting style on adolescent competence and substance use. *Journal of Early Adolescence, 11,* 56–95.

Beck, R. & McDonald, A. (2004). Attachment to God: The Attachment to God Inventory, tests of working model

correspondence, and an exploration of faith group differences. *Journal of Psychology and Theology, 32*(2), 92–103.

Bowlby, J. (1969/1982). *Attachment and loss: Vol. 1, Attachment.*
New York: Basic Books.

Bowlby, J. (1988). *A secure base: Clinical applications of attachment theory.* London: Routledge.

Brennan, K. A., Clark, C. L., & Shaver, P. R. (1998). Self-report
measurement of adult attachment. In J. A. Simpson & W. S.
Rholes (Eds.). *Attachment theory and close relationships* (pp.
46–76). New York: Guilford Press.

Bretherton, I. (1992). The origins of attachment theory: John
Bowlby and Mary Ainsworth. *Developmental Psychology,
28*(5), 759–775. doi:10.1037/0012-1649.28.5.759

Buri, J. R. (1991). Parental Authority Questionnaire. *Journal of
Personality Assessment, 57*(1), 110–119.

Cassidy, J., & Mohr, J. J. (2001). Unsolvable fear, trauma, and
psychopathology: Theory, research, and clinical considerations related to disorganized attachment across the life span.
Clinical Psychology: Science and Practice, 8(3), 275–298.
doi:10.1093/clipsy/8.3.275

Connors, M. E. (1997). The renunciation of love: Dismissive
attachment and its treatment. *Psychoanalytic Psychology, 14*,
475–493.

Deci, E. L., Driver, R. E., Hotchkiss, L., Robbins, J., &
McDougal Wilson, I. (1993). The relation of mothers'
controlling vocalizations to children's intrinsic motivation.
Journal of Experimental Child Psychology, 55, 151–162.

Deci, E. L., & Ryan, R. M. (2000). The "what" and "why" of
goal pursuits: Human needs and the self-determination of
behavior. *Psychological Inquiry, 11*, 227–268.

Deci, E. L., & Ryan, R. M. (2008). Self-determination theory: A macrotheory of human motivation, development and
health. *Canadian Psychology, 49*, 182–185. doi:10.1037/
a0012801

Elliot, A. J., & Reis, H. T. (2003). Attachment and exploration
in adulthood. *Journal of Personality and Social Psychology,
85*(2), 317–331. doi:10.1037/0022-3514.85.2.317

Erickson, E. H. (1963). *Childhood and society* (2nd ed.).
New York: Norton.

Erikson, E. H., & Erikson, J. M. (1982). *The life cycle completed.*
New York: Norton

Feeney, B. C. (2004). A secure base: Responsive support of goal
strivings and exploration in adult intimate relationships.
Journal of Personality and Social Psychology, 87, 631–648.

Feeney, B. C. (2007). The dependency paradox in close relationships: Accepting dependence promotes independence.
Journal of Personality and Social Psychology, 92(2), 268–285.
doi:10.1037/0022-3514.92.2.268

Feeney, B. C., & Thrush, R. L. (2010). Relationship influences on exploration in adulthood: The characteristics and
function of a secure base. *Journal of Personality and Social
Psychology, 98*(1), 57–76. doi:10.1037/a0016961

Fonagy, P., & Target, M. (1997). Attachment and reflective
function: Their role in self- organization. *Development and
Psychopathology, 9*(4), 679–700.

George, C., Kaplan, N., & Main, M. (1985). *An adult attachment interview: Interview protocol.* Unpublished manuscript.
University of California, Berkeley.

Grolnick, W., Frodi, A., & Bridges, L. (1984). Maternal control style and the mastery motivation of one-year-olds. *Infant
Mental Health Journal, 5*, 72–82.

Grossmann, K., Grossmann, K. E., Fremmer-Bombik, E.,
Kindler, H., Scheuerer-Englisch, H., & Zimmermann, P.
(2002). The uniqueness of the child–father attachment relationship: Fathers' sensitive and challenging play as a pivotal
variable in a 16-year longitudinal study. *Social Development,
11*, 307–331.

Hall, T. W., Fujikawa, A., Halcrow, S. R., Hill, P. C., & Delaney,
H. (2009). Attachment to God and implicit spiritual-
ity: Clarifying correspondence and compensation models.
Journal of Psychology and Theology, 37(4), 227–242.

Hazan, C., & Shaver, P. R. (1990). Love and work: An
attachment-theoretical perspective. *Journal of Personality
and Social Psychology, 59*(2), 270–280. doi:10.1037/
0022-3514.59.2.270

Jankowski, P. & Sandage, S. (2011). Meditative prayer, hope,
adult attachment, and forgiveness: A proposed model.
Psychology of Religion and Spirituality, 3(2), 115–131.

Jiang, X., Huebner, E. S., & Hills, K. J. (2013). Parent attachment and early adolescents' life satisfaction: The mediating
effect of hope. *Psychology in the Schools, 50*, 340–352. http://
dx.doi.org/10.1002/pits.21680

Joplin, J. R, Nelson, D. L., & Quick, J. C. (1999). Attachment
behavior and health: Relationships at work and home.
Journal of Organizational Behavior, 20, 783–796.

Kirkpatrick, L. A. (1992). An attachment-theory approach to the
psychology of religion. *International Journal for the Psychology
of Religion, 2*(1), 3–28.

Kirkpatrick, L. A. (1998). God as a substitute attachment figure: A longitudinal study of adult attachment style and
religious change in college students. *Personality and Social
Psychology Bulletin, 24*, 961–973.

Kirkpatrick, L. A., Shillito, D. J., & Kellas, S. L. (1999).
Loneliness, social support, and perceived relationships
with God. *Journal of Social and Personal Relationships, 16*,
513–522.

Koenig, H. (2004). Religion, spirituality, and medicine: Research
findings and implications for clinical practice. *Southern
Medical Journal, 97*(12), 1194–1200.

Koestner, R., Ryan, R. M., Bernieri, F., & Holt, K. (1984).
Setting limits on children's behavior: The differential effects of
controlling versus informational styles on children's intrinsic
motivation and creativity. *Journal of Personality, 54*, 233–248.

Lemche, E., Giampietro, V. P., Surguladze, S. A., Amaro, E. J.,
Andrew, C. M., Williams, S. C., . . . Phillips, M. L. (2006).
Human attachment security is mediated by the amyg-
dala: Evidence from combined fMRI and psychophysiologi-
cal measures. *Human Brain Mapping, 27*, 623–635.

Main, M., & Solomon, J. (1990). Procedures for identifying
infants as disorganized/disoriented during the Ainsworth
Strange Situation. In M. T. Greenberg, D. Cicchetti, & E.
M. Cummings (Eds.), *Attachment in the preschool years* (pp.
121–160). Chicago: University of Chicago Press.

McClelland, D. C. (1973). Testing for competence rather than
for intelligence. *American Psychologist, 28*, 1–14.

McCluskey, U., Hooper, C., & Miller, L. B. (1999). Goal-
corrected empathic attunement: Developing and rating the concept within an attachment perspective.
Psychotherapy: Theory, Research, Practice, Training, 36(1), 80–
90. doi:10.1037/h0087684

McDonald, A., Beck, R., Allison, S., & Norsworthy, L. (2005).
Attachment to God and parents: Testing the correspond-
ence vs. compensation hypotheses. *Journal of Psychology and
Christianity, 24*(1), 21–28.

Mikulincer, M., Gillath, O., & Shaver, P. R. (2002). Activation
of the attachment system in adulthood: Threat-related primes

increase the accessibility of mental representations of attachment figures. *Journal of Personality and Social Psychology, 83*(4), 881–895. doi:10.1037/0022-3514.83.4.881

Mikulincer, M., & Shaver, P. R. (2003). The attachment behavioral system in adulthood: Activation, psychodynamics, and interpersonal processes. In M. Zenna (Ed.), *Advances in experimental social psychology* (Vol. 35, pp. 53–152). Amsterdam: Elsevier Academic Press.

Mikulincer, M., & Shaver, P. R. (2007). Boosting attachment security to promote mental health, prosocial values, and inter-group tolerance, *Psychological Inquiry, 18*(3), 139–156.

Moss, E., Gosselin, C., Parent, S., Rousseau, D., & Dumont, M. (1997). Attachment and joint problem-solving experiences during the preschool period. *Social Development, 6*(1), 1–17. doi:10.1111/1467-9507.ep11631667

Parker, G., Tupling, H., & Brown, L. B. (1979). A parental bonding instrument. *British Journal of Medical Psychology, 52*, 1–10.

Pederson, D. R., & Moran, G. (1995). A categorical description of infant-mother relationships in the home and its relation to the Q-sort measures of infant-mother interaction. *Monographs of the Society for Research in Child Development, 60* (2–3), 111–132.

Peterson, C., & Seligman, M. (2004). *Character strengths and virtues: A handbook and classification.* Oxford: Oxford University Press.

Rowatt, W. C., & Kirkpatrick, L. A. (2002). Two dimensions of attachment to God and their relation to affect, religiosity, and personality constructs. *Journal for the Scientific Study of Religion, 41*, 637–651.

Ruble, N. M., & Turner, W. L. (2000). A systematic analysis of the dynamics and organization of urban street gangs. *The American Journal of Family Therapy, 28*, 117–132.

Schore, A. N. (2001). The effects of early relational trauma on right brain development, affect regulation, and infant mental health. *Infant Mental Health Journal, 22*(1–2), 201–269.

Schore, A. N. (2003). *Affect dysregulation and disorders of the self.* New York: Norton.

Sharkey, J. D., Shekhtmeyster, Z., Chavez-Lopez, L., Norris, E., & Sass, L. (2011). The protective influence of gangs: Can schools compensate? *Aggression and Violent Behavior, 16*, 45–54.

Shorey, H. S. (2003). *Theories of intelligence, academic hope, and persistence after a failure experience.* Unpublished master's thesis. University of Kansas, Lawrence.

Shorey, H. S. (2008). The interactions of hope and attachment styles in a social-cognitive- motivational model of depressive vulnerability. *Dissertation Abstracts International, 69*, 699.

Shorey, H. S., & Snyder, C. R. (2006). The role of adult attachment styles in psychopathology and psychotherapy outcomes. *Review of General Psychology, 10*(1), 1–20.

Shorey, H. S., Snyder, C. R., Rand, K. L., Hockemeyer, J. R., & Feldman, D. B. (2002). Authors' response: Somewhere over the rainbow: Hope theory weathers its first decade. *Psychological Inquiry, 13*(4), 322–331.

Shorey, H. S., Snyder, C. R., Yang, X., & Lewin, M. (2003). The role of hope as a mediator in recollected parenting, adult attachment, and mental health. *Journal of Social and Clinical Psychology, 22*(6), 685–715.

Sim, T. N., & Loh, B. S. M. (2003). Attachment to God: Measurement and dynamics. *Journal of Social and Personal Relationships, 20*, 373–389.

Simmons, B. L., Gooty, J, Nelson, D. L., & Little, L. M. (2009). Secure attachments: Implications for trust, hope, burnout, and performance. *Journal of Organizational Behavior, 30*, 233–247.

Simmons, B. L., Nelson, D. L., & Quick, J. C. (2003). Health for the hopeful: A study of attachment behavior in home health care nurses. *International Journal of Stress Management, 10*(4), 361–375. doi:10.1037/1072-5245.10.4.361

Smith, B. W. & Tonigan, J. (2009). Alcoholics Anonymous benefit and social attachment. *Alcoholism Treatment Quarterly, 27*(2), 164–173.

Snyder, C. R. (1994). *The psychology of hope: You can get there from here.* New York: Free Press.

Snyder, C. R. (2002). Hope theory: Rainbows in the mind. *Psychological Inquiry, 13*(4), 249–275.

Snyder, C. R., Cheavens, J., & Sympson, S. C. (1997). Hope: An individual motive for social commerce. *Group Dynamics: Theory, Research, and Practice, 1*, 107–118.

Snyder, C. R., Harris, C., Anderson, J. R., Holleran, S. A., Irving, L. M., Sigmon, S. T. . . . Harney, P. (1991). The will and the ways: Development and validation of an individual-differences measure of hope. *Journal of Personality and Social Psychology, 60*, 570–585.

Snyder, C. R., Hoza, B., Pelham, W. E., Rapoff, M., Ware, L., Danovsky, M., . . . Stahl, K. J. (1997). The development and validation of the Children's Hope Scale. *Journal of Pediatric Psychology, 22*, 399–421.

Snyder, C. R., Shorey, H. S., Cheavens, J., Pulvers, K. M., Adams, V. I., & Wiklund, C. (2002). Hope and academic success in college. *Journal of Educational Psychology, 94*(4), 820–826. doi:10.1037/0022-0663.94.4.820

Snyder, C. R., Shorey, H. S., & Rand, K. L. (2005). Applying hope theory to teach and mentor academically at-risk students. In B. Buskist & S. Davis (Eds.), *The handbook of the teaching of psychology* (pp. 170–174). Malden, MA: Blackwell

Sympson, S. (1999). *Validation of the Domain Specific Hope Scale.* Unpublished doctoral dissertation. Department of Psychology, University of Kansas, Lawrence.

Vigil, J. D. (1988). Group processes and street identity: Adolescent Chicano Gang members. *Ethos, 16*(4), 421–445.

Ware, J. E., Davies-Avery, A., & Donald, C. A. (1978). *Conceptualization and measurement of health for adults in the health insurance study: Vol. 5, General health perceptions.* Santa Monica, CA: Rand Corporation.

Waters, E., & Deane, K. (1985). Defining and assessing individual differences in attachment relationships: Q-methodology and the organization of behavior in infancy and early childhood. In I. Bretherton & E. Waters (Eds.), *Growing points of attachment theory and research* (pp. 41–65). (Monographs of the Society for Research in Child Development 50). Chicago: Uninversity of Chicago Press.

Whipple, N., Bernier, A., & Mageau, G. A. (2009). Attending to the exploration side of infant attachment: Contributions from self-determination theory. *Canadian Psychology/Psychologie Canadienne, 50*(4), 219–229. doi:10.1037/a0016322

Wilcock, A. (1993). A theory of the human need for occupation. *Journal of Occupational Science: Australia, 1*(1), 17–24.

Hope and Work

Angela R. Mouton *and* Monica N. Montijo

Abstract

The world has an employee engagement crisis. Low employee engagement has a detrimental impact not only on employee performance and well-being but also on organizational outcomes, including revenue and profitability. This chapter sets out the argument that a key predictor of employee engagement (and therefore performance and well-being) is hope. The relationship between these variables is unpacked from a theoretical and empirical perspective. While the literature has tended to focus on the agency and pathways components of hope theory, this chapter argues that much more attention should given to the fact that hope rests on the pursuit of positively valenced, personally valued, meaningful goals. The chapter offers suggestions on how organizations and employees might amplify hope, engagement, and positive outcomes in the workplace by focusing on goals that matter not only to the organization but to employees also.

Key Words: engagement, goals, hope, positive outcomes, work, employee engagement

Today's workplace is dynamic and subject to a number of challenges, including the aftermath of the global financial crisis of 2008, downsizing, mergers and acquisitions, new trade agreements, cyber terrorism, hypercompetitive business practices, and unrelenting advances in technology, to name a few. The related disciplines of positive organizational behavior (Luthans, 2002), positive organizational scholarship (Cameron, Dutton, & Quinn, 2003), positive organizational psychology (Bakker, 2013; Ko & Donaldson, 2011), and positive leadership (Cameron, 2008) have taken a lead in suggesting how to harness the best in employees, and mitigate the effects of these challenges. However, there is a worldwide employee engagement crisis (Gallup, 2016). As of January 2016, 68% of US employees were actively or passively disengaged at work, a statistic that has remained stable for 15 years. The situation is even worse when we consider the global picture, where a staggering 87% of employees worldwide are actively or passively disengaged (Gallup, 2016).

Engagement has been variously defined in the psychology literature (see Mills, Fleck, & Kozikowski [2013] for a review), including as the "harnessing of organization members' selves to their work roles" (Kahn 1990, p. 694), and when "individuals are emotionally connected and cognitively vigilant" (Harter & Schmidt, 2008, p. 37). Schaufeli, Salanova, Gonzalez-Roma, and Bakker (2002) defined engagement as "a positive, fulfilling, work-related state of mind that is characterized by vigor, dedication, and absorption" (p. 74). In this definition "vigor" refers to high levels of energy, persistence, and resilience. "Dedication" involves deep psychological identification with work in which one takes pride and which provides a sense of significance, inspiration, and challenge. "Absorption" refers to being fully focused and engrossed in one's work and is related but not identical to the concept of flow (Csikszentmihalyi, 1990). Gallup operationalizes "engagement" as an employee's enthusiasm for and emotional commitment to his or her work, which promotes discretionary effort (i.e., being willing to go the extra mile for the organization; Gallup, 2013). Whichever definition we choose to adopt, Gallup's engagement statistics are a concern. A large body of evidence has linked employee engagement with favorable workplace outcomes, including employee performance, productivity, discretionary effort, creativity, organizational commitment, and well-being, as well as customer satisfaction, profitability, and financial return (Gallup, 2016; Mills et al., 2013). Gallup (2013) reports that companies with highly engaged workforces perform better than their competitors, with 147% more in earnings per share, 41% fewer quality defects, 48% fewer safety incidents, 65% less turnover in low turnover organizations, 25% less turnover in high turn-over organizations, and 37% less absenteeism. Similar differences are evident between high and low engagement work units (Harter, Schmidt, Agrawal, & Plowman, 2013). It is estimated that active disengagement costs the United States $450 billion to $550 billion, Germany $151 billion to $186 billion, and the UK $83 billion to $112 billion each year (Gallup, 2013).

Many researchers and practitioners have offered suggestions for increasing workplace engagement. Gallup (2013), for example, suggests that employees need to understand what is expected of them, have the support and resources to do their work, have an opportunity to use their strengths each day, receive recognition and appreciation, have a sense of purpose, have close relationships at work, obtain feedback regarding progress, believe that their opinions count, and have opportunities to learn and grow. This chapter sets out the argument that a key predictor of engagement, performance, and well-being at work is hope (Snyder, 1994). The relationship between these variables is unpacked from a theoretical and empirical perspective, concluding with suggestions for amplifying hope, engagement, and positive outcomes in the workplace.

Hope in the Workplace
Hope Theory
In colloquial terms, "hope" is usually described as a belief or expectation that the future will be better than the present (Reichard, Avey, Lopez, & Dollwet, 2013; Synder, Lopez, & Pedrotti, 2011). Various constructs of hope have been suggested in the scientific literature (see Reichard et al. [2013] and Snyder, Lopez, & Pedrotti [2011] for reviews). The most widely accepted (and investigated) theory of hope in the psychology literature is Snyder's hope theory (Snyder, 1994; Snyder et al., 1991). Snyder

defined hope as goal-directed thinking, coupled with agency (or motivation) to begin and continue striving towards a goal (willpower), and the ability to create multiple pathways to reach that goal by identifying potential obstacles and engaging in contingency thinking (waypower). Both agency and pathways thinking are required for hope to be present, and these components are additive and reciprocal, such that when one increases so does the other (Reichard et al., 2013; Snyder et al., 2011).

Positive Outcomes of Hope at Work
Hope, like engagement, is associated with a host of positive workplace outcomes, from the perspective of both the organization and the employee. A recent meta-analysis explored the impact of hope at work, examining 133 effect sizes in 45 studies comprising 11,139 employees. The meta-analysis found a statistically significant, moderate, positive aggregate correlation between hope and employee performance based on self-report measures, third-party assessments, and objective measures such as financial performance and commission earned. Hopeful employees were 28% more likely than low-hope employees to achieve high performance at work, a stronger result than findings reported in meta-analyses exploring the effect of goal-setting, feedback, and behavior modification on work performance (Reichard et al., 2013). Hopeful employees have been shown to be high in conscientiousness, helping attitudes, and courteousness, and they set clear goals, find multiple paths to their goals, and are able to stay motivated even during trying circumstances (see Snyder et al. [2011] for a review). Hopeful leaders have been shown to have positive impacts on profitability as well as their direct reports (Norman, Luthans, & Luthans, 2005; Peterson & Luthans, 2003). High-hope organizations have been shown to exhibit a number of positive characteristics, including high profitability, a respectful and supportive working environment, open communication between employees and managers, delegation of responsibility to employees, inclusion of employees in setting company goals, and enduring relationships with customers (Peterson & Byron, 2008; see Snyder et al. [2011] for a review).

Hope has also been examined as a component of psychological capital (PsyCap), a higher order construct comprised of hope, self-efficacy, resilience, and optimism (Luthans, Avolio, Avey, & Norman, 2007). PsyCap has been positively associated with a number of desirable outcomes in the workplace, including performance, organizational commitment, and organizational citizenship behaviors (Avey, Reichard, Luthans, & Mhatre, 2011; Luthans et al., 2007). Finally, in terms of desirable outcomes from the employee's perspective, statistically significant, moderate, positive relationships have been reported between hope and job satisfaction, health, and well-being, along with statistically significant, moderate, negative relationships between hope, burnout, and stress (Reichard et al., 2013).

How and Why Does Hope Predict Positive Outcomes at Work?

A number of explanations for how and why hope promotes positive outcome at work are offered in the literature. First, it has been suggested that hopeful employees show higher levels of performance and well-being because they are motivated to pursue goals with energy, and they create multiple pathways to these goals. When encountering difficulties or impediments, hopeful employees are creative problem-solvers, using if-then contingency thinking to find ways around obstacles, persisting with their goals rather than giving up (Lopez & Calderon, 2011; Peterson & Byron, 2008; Reichard et al., 2013). In other words, it has been argued that hope promotes positive work outcomes primarily because of the interaction of agency and pathways thinking.

Second, it has been suggested that hope elicits positive emotions, which in turn promote optimal outcomes at the organizational as well as the individual level (Fredrickson, 2001, 2009; Reichard et al., 2013). The broaden-and-build theory of positive emotions suggests that positive emotions broaden one's thought-action repertoire by freeing up attention, encouraging approach behaviors, and promoting creativity. Furthermore, positive emotions undo the negative physical and psychological impacts of negative emotions and bolster our resilience by building personal and social resources (Fredrickson, 2001, 2009). These theoretical suggestions are supported by a growing body of empirical evidence (see Fredrickson [2009] for a review). Positive emotions have been linked to performance (Lyubomirsky, King, & Diener, 2005), effective problem-solving (Erez & Isen, 2002), job satisfaction, affective commitment, health, and psychological well-being (Fredrickson, 2009; Reichard et al., 2013).

Third, hope is related to engagement (Malinowski & Lim, 2015; Ouweneel, Le Blanc, Schaufeli, & van Wijhe, 2012), which is related to positive workplace outcomes as discussed previously. A recent study examined hope (as per Snyder et al., 1991) and engagement (as per Schaufeli, Bakker, & Salanova, 2006) in frontline hotel employees (Karatepe, 2014). The data revealed a positive and significant relationship between hope and work engagement, which in turn was positively related to various third-party measures of performance, including extra-mile discretionary behaviors. In fact, the results indicated that the relationship between hope and performance was fully mediated by work engagement. This study suggests that engagement is the pivotal motivational construct that links hope with performance at work. Similarly, a recent study of nurses found that both hope (as defined by Snyder) and personal growth initiative predicted engagement (as defined by Schaufeli and colleagues), with hope being the stronger predictor of the two (Vaksalla & Hashimah, 2015). The authors noted that engagement is crucial in nursing since it impacts patient care outcomes.

Finally, hope involves creating an optimistic vision of the future and then acting in accordance with this vision (Lopez, 2013a, 2013b; Snyder et al., 2011). It has recently been suggested that human beings are not solely driven by the past but are also drawn by future possibilities, as we engage in conditional thinking, evaluations of possible outcomes, and Bayesian updating and then act in accordance with these evaluations and expectations (Seligman, Railton, Baumeister, & Sripada, 2013). This concept of prospection can be applied to the process of hope. Arguably, hope is a prospective process whereby a hopeful person is drawn by a positively envisioned future. More specifically, hope involves the freedom to create a positive vision of the future unfettered by the past, generating and weighing multiple paths to that desired future, engaging in conditional thinking and evaluating possible outcomes, adjusting these evaluations when new information becomes available via Bayesian updating, and acting in accordance with these evaluations by pursuing the best available options for obtaining the desired goal (Mouton, 2015).

All of these explanations for how and why hope predicts positive work outcomes are insightful. However, we suggest that there is another crucial reason that hope predicts desirable outcomes, a reason that has received relatively little emphasis in the literature to date.

The Importance of Positively Valenced, Personally Valued, Meaningful Goals

Much of the literature on hope and work has tended to focus on the importance of agency and pathways thinking (e.g., Luthans & Jensen, 2002; Peterson & Byron, 2008; Reichard et al., 2013). Previous researchers have suggested that hope can be increased by encouraging employees to set stretch goals, use positive self-talk and mental imagery, and engage in contingency planning, strategies that primarily focus on optimizing the "willpower" and "waypower" components of hope (Avey, Avolio, & Luthans, 2011; Luthans, Avey, Avolio, Norman, & Combs, 2006). However, focusing on agency and pathways thinking alone fails to adequately address actively and passively disengaged employees—that is, those who show little interest in pursuing work goals, let alone with enthusiasm via multiple pathways. Why are some employees willing to work on their willpower and waypower while many others are not?

We suggest that the answer lies in the quality of goals being set and pursued in the workplace. Although agency and pathways thinking have received more attention in the literature, hope theory is underpinned by goal pursuit. Indeed, "goal thoughts are the foundation on which hope theory is built" (Rand & Cheavens, 2009, p. 324). We suggest that hope at work depends on employees pursuing positively valenced, personally valued, meaningful goals.

Positively Valenced Goals

Snyder's (2002) early articulation of hope theory referred to the pursuit of "positive" goals (p. 249; see also Snyder et al., 1991). Snyder emphasized that hope is both cognitive (in that it is based on goal-oriented thinking) and affective. Hope theory suggests that those who have succeeded in attaining their goals in the past tend to attach positive emotion sets to similar goal pursuits, and these positive emotion sets positively reinforce the continued pursuit of goals. Those who have failed to achieve their goals in the past experience passive and negative emotions when pursuing similar goals, emotions that undermine continued goal pursuit (Rand & Cheavens, 2009; Snyder et al., 2011). The theory of emerging goals, a cornerstone of flow theory, is also illustrative here (Csikszentmihalyi, 1990; Csikszentmihalyi & Nakamura, 1999). Emerging goal theory suggests that when we experience an event, we become aware of the experience and its emotional valence, which we compare to previous experiences. If the comparison is favorable, our goal is to maintain the present state. If the comparison is not favorable, our goal is to change our experience. This feedback loop brings about a dynamic emergence of goals. Positive emotions reinforce the pursuit of goals that bring about these positive emotions, negative emotions promote the search for new goals, and an individual may experience positive emotions from avoiding so-called anti-goals. As such, emotions determine goals, and achieving our goals promotes positive emotions (Csikszentmihalyi & Nakamura, 1999).

It is noted that some authors have criticized the hope scales for failing to tap the affective aspects of hope adequately. For example, Bullough and Hall-Kenyon (2012) examined hope, calling, and commitment in exemplary teachers. Surprisingly, they found no relationship between hope and calling, notwithstanding that their qualitative interviews suggested strong connections between hope, calling, and teacher commitment. The authors argue that rather than reduce hope to cognitive components of willpower and waypower, hope should include the mix of emotions that typically accompany it. The authors state, "It is, we believe, this broader conception of hope, as an emotion and as a virtue, that best captures what is at stake in teaching and with our 'hopeful' teachers" (Bullough & Hall-Kenyon, 2012, p. 20).

Whether or not the hope scales could be improved, it is clear that hope theory was intended to refer to the pursuit of positively valenced goals.

Valued Goals

Hope also rests firmly on the pursuit of valued goals. In the early days of hope theory, Snyder (2002) described hope in terms of the pursuit of "desired" goals "of sufficient value to warrant sustained conscious thought about them" (p. 250; see also Lopez, Snyder, & Pedrotti, 2003). Snyder et al. (2011) emphasized that "[o]nly those goals with considerable value to the individual are considered applicable to hope . . . sufficient value must be attached to a goal pursuit before the individual will continue the hoping process" (p. 185). In fact, hope theory was borne out of Snyder's desire to understand the process by which people move toward the things that they want (Rand & Cheavens, 2009; Snyder, 2002).

Valued goals are also implicit in the Adult Hope Scale (Snyder et al., 1991). While the instrument primarily taps the agency and pathways components of hope, some scale items refer to goals that are personally valued (e.g. "I can think of many ways to get the things in life that are important to me"; "I meet

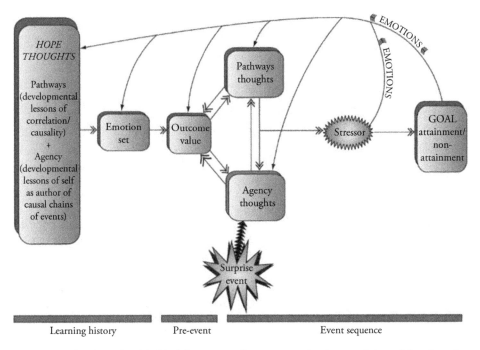

HOPE
THOUGHTS

Pathways
(developmental
lessons of
correlation/
causality)
+
Agency
(developmental
lessons of self
as author of
causal chains
of events)

Emotion
set

Outcome
value

Pathways
thoughts

Agency
thoughts

Stressor

EMOTIONS

EMOTIONS

GOAL
attainment/
non-
attainment

Surprise
event

Learning history   Pre-event   Event sequence

Fig. 25.1. Schematic of feed-forward and feed-back functions involving agency and pathways goal-directed thoughts and emotions in hope theory.

the goals that I set for myself"). The same is true of the shorter State Hope Scale (Snyder, Sympson, Ybasco, Borders, Babyak, & Higgins, 1996).

Values have been described as an enduring belief that some goals are preferable to others (Rokeach, 1973). It has, therefore, been suggested that our values or value assessments precede our goals (Feldman & Snyder, 2005; Grant, 2012). As indicated in Figure 25.1, hope theory suggests that individuals assess potential goals in terms of their outcome value (Lopez et al., 2003; Rand & Cheavens, 2009). Sufficiently valued goals will elicit continued attention and goal pursuit. It is at this point that agency and pathways thinking kicks in. Individuals continuously assess the outcome value of their goals, in the context of the pathways that they identify, and their motivation to adopt these pathways. If the outcome value is assessed as "not being important enough to merit continued effort," then the individual is likely to abort goal pursuit (Rand & Cheavens, 2009, p. 325).

Feldman, Rand, and Kahle-Wrobleski (2009) have reported a positive relationship between goal importance and the agency component of hope, which in turn is positively related to goal attainment.

Hope's Relationship to Flow and Passion

Related to the subject of valued goals is the positive relationships between hope, flow, and passion

(Mouton, 2015). Flow is an intrinsically motivated psychological state of complete absorption in a task, predicated upon clear and proximate goals, immediate feedback, and a perceived balance of challenge and skill (Csikszentmihalyi, 1990). Passion has been defined as "a strong inclination towards a self-defining activity that people love, that they consider important, and in which they devote significant amounts of time and energy" (Vallerand, Salvy, Mageau, Elliot, Denis, Grouzet, & Blanchard, 2007, p. 124). Harmonious (as opposed to obsessive) passion involves flexible engagement in the passion activity, leaving room for other important aspects of life (Vallerand, Blanchard, Mageau, Koestner, Ratelle, Léonard, Gagné, & Marsolais, 2003). Both flow and harmonious passion have been associated with positive outcomes at work, including performance, engagement, and well-being (see Engeser [2012] and Landhäußer & Keller [2012] for reviews on the relationship between flow and positive outcomes; see Vallerand [2015] for a recent review on the relationship between passion and positive outcomes).

The first author recently explored which positive psychology constructs predict performance, including in an employee sample comprised of 40 managers of a publicly held North American entertainment and dining company. As indicated in

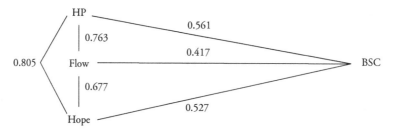

Fig. 25.2. Correlations between harmonious passion (HP), flow, hope, and employee performance against a balanced scorecard (BSC) as rated by their managers (Mouton, 2015).

Figure 25.2, the results indicated that harmonious passion, flow, and hope were significant predictors of employee performance against a balanced scorecard (as rated by their managers). After controlling for self-reported level of expertise, harmonious passion, flow, and hope explained an additional 32.3% of the variance in performance against the balanced scorecard. In addition, the three variables were moderately to strongly related to each other.

As far as the first author is aware, this is the first study to report a positive and significant relationship between hope and harmonious passion and between hope and flow. Leading researchers on hope, passion, and flow recently confirmed that they too are not aware of these relationships having been reported elsewhere (Drs. Reichard, Vallerand, and Csikszentmihalyi, personal communications, March 12, 2015). The first author offered three potential explanations for the positive relationships between hope, flow, and passion, and between these variables and performance in the previous study, namely that all three constructs require investment of attention, time, and energy; all three are action-oriented; and all three require a degree of flexibility in pursuit of goals (see Mouton [2015] for details).

Another possible link between hope, flow, and passion is the pursuit of valued goals. As we have seen, hope rests on the pursuit of goals that are valued by the individual. Similarly, flow is predicated (in part) on clear and proximate goals and is an intrinsically motivated experience of complete absorption in a task for its own sake (Csikszentmihalyi, 1990). Passion, by definition, involves a self-defining activity that a person likes or even loves, and in which he or she invests heavily (Vallerand et al., 2007). We therefore suggest that a common underlying feature of hope, flow, and passion is the pursuit of goals that are valued by the individual. Hope theory, therefore, requires the pursuit of valued goals, which may be aligned with one's passions and flow activities (although they are not required to be).

Meaningful Goals

It has also been suggested that hope depends on the pursuit of personally meaningful goals (Feldman & Snyder, 2005; Lopez, 2013a; 2013b). Feldman and Snyder demonstrated that hope and meaning in life are related, since both are predicated upon meaningful goal pursuit. They argue that

[i]n . . . theories of life meaning, then, goals become repositories of meaning whereby their achievement brings purpose to one's life. This goal-dependent nature of meaning places Snyder's (1994) hope construct at the very heart of [life meaning] theories. (Feldman & Snyder, 2005, p. 406)

The authors suggested that when people are both hopeful and focused on goals that they find meaningful, they perceive that they can achieve their meaningful goals and, therefore, that they can construct a meaningful life. Further, if they take immediate steps toward their meaningful goals, they are able to create a sense of meaning in the present. Other studies have supported the relationship between hope and meaning in life (e.g., Vela, Lerma, Lenz, Hinojosa, Hernandez-Duque, & Gonzalez, 2014; Yalçın & Malkoç, 2015).

Pursuing Positively Valenced, Personally Valued, Meaningful Goals At Work

Based on this analysis, hope theory rests on agency and pathways thinking but in the context of pursuing positively valenced, personally valued goals (that may be aligned with one's passions and flow activities) that the person considers to be meaningful. This raises two important questions for the workplace. First, what proportion of employees feel that they are pursuing these types of goals at work? Second, how can organizations and employees increase the opportunities for pursuing these types of goals at work? Gallup's (2016) finding that 87% of employees worldwide are actively or passively disengaged suggests that very few employees feel that they are pursuing positively valenced, personally valued, meaningful goals at work. Some may feel that their work goals are unrelated to their personal goals. Others may feel that their work goals are misaligned with their personal goals. In the worst cases, employees may feel that work goals are in direct conflict with their personal goals and values (Gardner, Csikszentmihalyi, & Damon, 2001). This brings us to the second question: How can opportunities be increased for employees to pursue positive, personally valued, meaningful goals at work?

The Role of the Organization

We agree with early suggestions by Snyder and colleagues (2003) that organizations should foster hope in their employees by focusing on the *development* of valued goals (alongside agency and pathways thinking; see also Snyder, Feldman, Shorey, & Rand, 2002). We also suggest that much more attention needs to be paid to *alignment* of organizational goals with the goals that employees regard as positive, valued, and meaningful. Hope, engagement, and positive outcomes at work can be amplified when work goals are aligned with an employee's interests, strengths, and values and are balanced with non-work-related goals (Snyder, Lopez, Shorey, Rand, & Feldman, 2003). This requires managers to know their employees, to ascertain and understand what they are good at, and to inquire as to what their interests and aspirations are.

Without alignment of work-related and personal goals, employees may find it difficult to remain engaged, build a sense of meaning at work, excel, and thrive. More than 15 years ago, Howard Gardner and colleagues (2001) discussed the difficulty of doing good work (defined as work high in excellence, ethics, and engagement) when organizational and personal (or societal) goals and values are misaligned. These authors pointed to the profession of journalism as a case in point at the time. We suggest that many examples of misalignment might be found today across a variety of professions, given that worldwide engagement levels have remained low (and in some countries stagnant) for more than a decade (Gallup, 2016). Some have suggested that organizations should proactively engage employees in the establishment of organizational and personal goals, as well as in the generation of pathways to these goals (Luthans & Jensen, 2002). As Peterson and Byron (2008) note, "For hope to affect job performance, employees likely need to have some autonomy in determining what their goals are and how they might accomplish them . . . employees

must want to achieve the goals that constitute job performance (pp. 798–799). This suggests that organizations must provide employees with a degree of autonomy to set and pursue goals that matter not only to the organization but to the employee as well.

The Role of the Employee

We also suggest that employees should take responsibility for setting, requesting, and pursuing goals at work that they find positive, valuable, and meaningful (and here we prefer to frame "responsibility" as the ability to respond). As Tims, Derks, and Bakker (2016) recently noted:

> Changes in the way work is structured and performed nowadays call for workers who take agency in influencing their work characteristics. . . . Generally speaking, proactive person–environment fit behaviors . . . may be key for individual workers to match their needs and abilities with the opportunities and demands of the work environment. (p. 44)

We agree that good jobs are made, not found (Lopez, 2013b). While only 13% of people worldwide are actively engaged in their work, the fact is that engaged employees are located in a wide variety of industries. In their recent meta-analysis, Reichard and colleagues (2013) found no moderating effect of industry on the relationships between hope and workplace outcomes. Employees can amplify their engagement by understanding their own interests, strengths, passions, values, and what they find meaningful, and shaping their jobs to align their work-related and personal goals to the extent possible. It is not the organization or industry that matters per se but rather whether employees are able to set and pursue goals that matter to them as well as the organization.

Job crafting is a process whereby an employee shapes, molds, redefines, and crafts his or her job in a personally meaningful way (Wrzesniewski, LoBuglio, Dutton, & Berg, 2013). The process might involve changes to what employees do, how they do it, how they interact with their colleagues, how much challenge they have, the number of obstacles they encounter, or the resources that are available to them (Tims, Bakker, & Derks, 2012; Wrzesniewski et al., 2013). Job crafting has been linked to a number of positive work outcomes, including employee satisfaction, engagement, and performance (Bakker, Tims, & Derks, 2012; Lyons, 2008; Petrou, Demerouti, Peeters, Schaufeli, &

Hetland, 2012), meaningful work experiences (Tims et al., 2016; Wrzesniewski, 2003), and the creation of a sense of identity (see Berg, Dutton, & Wrzesniewski [2013] and Wrzesniewski et al. [2013] for reviews). While a search of the peer-reviewed literature failed to uncover any studies linking hope and job crafting directly, Shane Lopez (2013b) has referred to the work of Wrzesniewski and colleagues in suggesting how employees can mold their jobs into ones that they love. We agree that employees who wish to amplify their work experiences should take the initiative in redesigning their working lives, rather than relying on organizations or bosses to do it for them. Indeed, hopeful employees are likely to be proactive as they envision the working life they desire, generate multiple pathways to their goal, and energetically pursue these pathways.

That said, we acknowledge the possibility that some professions or working environments may provide more opportunities for job crafting and/or goal alignment than others. In a recent qualitative study, we explored love, passion, and peak experience in 22 countries on six continents (Mouton & Montijo, 2017). We found that substantially more participants who were working in helping professions reported being passionate about their work than did participants in other professions (45% compared to 14%). In that study, helping professions included medicine, nursing, teaching, and community work. As such, it may be that individuals in helping professions, for example, have greater opportunities to job craft or to align their work and personal goals. Further research is needed to test this possibility, However, we suggest that, except in the most dire of working environments, most employees have some opportunity to create an engaging, meaningful, hopeful working life by reshaping their jobs and aligning their work goals with what they value.

Paying Attention to Universal and Widely Valued Goals

Is it not impractical to suggest that every employee can pursue goals that he or she perceives as positive, personally valued, and meaningful while still ensuring that organizations meet their goals? Perhaps not, if organizations and employees focus their attention on goals that are universal or widely valued.

There is, of course, evidence that goals and values vary amongst people and by culture. For example, values may vary along spectra relating to traditional/secular rational values and survival/self-expression values (World Values Survey, n.d.) or conservation/openness to change and self-enhancement/self-transcedence (Schwartz, 1992; Schwartz, Cieciuch, Vecchione, Davidov, Fischer, Beierlein, & ... Konty, 2012). It has also been argued that so-called Western cultures tend to be more individualistic, privileging the individual over the group and valuing competition, personal freedom, achievement, and autonomy. By contrast, it is argued that so-called Eastern cultures are more collectivist, privileging the group over the individual and valuing cooperation, harmony, duty, sharing, and interdependence (see Snyder et al. [2011] in the context of positive psychology). Westerners might tend to seek out external rewards and adopt a linear path to their goals, while Easterners might tend to seek transcendence and "move with the cycle of life" (Snyder et al., 2011, p. 20).

However, there is also evidence that some goals and values are universal or at the very least widely held. Maslow (1943, 1954) suggested that all human beings are motivated to fulfill a hierarchy of needs beginning with basic biological needs, progressing to safety, belongingness, and esteem, and culminating in self-actualization, the realization of one's full potential. Csikszentmihalyi (1990) suggests that all human beings are driven to achieve psychological complexity, "the ability to develop and use the full range of potentialities open to human beings," achieved through the complimentary processes of integration with and differentiation from one's environment (Csikszentmihalyi & Rathunde, 1998, p. 677). Psychological complexity is related to the flow state and is associated with optimal functioning, eudaimonic well-being, and cultural evolution (Delle Fave, Massimini, & Bassi, 2011; Inghilleri & Bartoli, 1999). Similarly, Ryan and Deci (2000) suggest that human beings have three universal needs required for flourishing, namely autonomy, competence, and relatedness, which together comprise self-determination (see also Deci, Ryan, & Guay, 2013). Although Maslow's self-actualization concept does not form part of self-determination theory per se, Deci and Ryan (2013) acknowledge that their theory is consistent with Maslow's idea of self-actualization.

All of these theories relate to the need to connect to others, learn and grow, and fulfill one's potential, and the literature typically supports the universality of these goals. For example, Tay and Diener (2011) explored universal needs in 123 countries. Based on previous work by Maslow (1954), Ryff and Keyes (1995), Ryan and Deci (2000), Csikszentmihalyi

(1988), and the Gallup World Survey, the authors focused on the following universal needs: basic needs for food and shelter, social support and love, feeling respected and pride in activities, mastery, self-direction, and autonomy. The authors coded responses to the Gallup World Survey between 2005 and 2010, which included 60,865 people representing 66% of the world's population, with an average of 494 respondents in each country, for the universal needs mentioned, as well as levels of subjective well-being. The authors compared results across eight regions, namely Africa, East and South Asia, former Soviet Union nations (including Eastern Europe), Latin America, the Middle East, Northern Europe and Anglo nations, Southeast Asia, and Southern Europe. The results supported the notion that some needs are more universal than others, particularly those associated with autonomy, competence, and relatedness (i.e., self-determination: Ryan & Deci, 2000). In addition, the results indicated that, as suggested by Maslow (1954), people tend to satisfy basic needs (e.g., biological and safety needs) before higher order needs (e.g., belonging, esteem, and self-actualization) but that a person can achieve subjective well-being via fulfillment of higher order needs even if lower order needs have not been met. Finally, the data indicated that the society in which a person lives has a strong influence on satisfaction of lower order needs but only a modest impact on whether higher order needs are met.

Schwartz and colleagues (2012) have developed an impressive body of literature on human values and how they are (and are not) influenced by culture. Fischer and Schwartz (2011) used three data sets comprised of 41,968 participants from 67 countries, 42,359 participants from 19 countries, and 84,887 participants from 62 countries, respectively, to explore the influence of culture on value priorities. The authors found more similarities than differences in value priorities across countries and evidence that values associated with autonomy, relatedness, and competence tend to be universally valued (Fischer & Schwartz, 2011). Similarly, Church and colleagues (2013) investigated the universality of autonomy, competence, and relatedness, as well as self-actualization and pleasure stimulation, in the United States, Australia, Mexico, Venezuela, the Philippines, Malaysia, China, and Japan (Church, Katigbak, Locke, Zhang, Shen, de Jesús Vargas-Flores, & ... Ching, 2013). In line with much (but not all) previous research, the results supported the universality of the three self-determination needs:

Consistent with SDT, we found that perceived satisfaction of SDT needs—as well as needs for self-actualization and pleasure-stimulation—was moderately related to most aspects of well-being in all cultures. Indeed . . . satisfaction of each need predicted overall well-being equally well in each culture. Thus, although some researchers have questioned whether SDT needs are cultural universals . . . [o]ur findings are consistent with the proposition that SDT needs represent "part of the common architecture of human nature" (Deci & Ryan, 2000, p. 252) (p. 527).

Finally, we recently undertook a qualitative study, asking 150 diverse people in 22 countries on six continents, "What do you love?", "What is a great passion in your life?", and "What has been a peak experience in your life?" (Mouton & Montijo, 2017). The data revealed that the top two themes for all three questions were *other people* (including but not limited to family and friends) and *learning and growing* (including learning a new subject or craft, traveling, and leaving home). In addition, more similarities than differences were found between continents, suggesting a degree of ubiquity if not universality in participants' responses. We suggested that the top themes of *other people* and *learning and growing* may reflect the universal human motivation to achieve psychological complexity by balancing integration with and differention from one's environment. We noted that psychological complexity echoes self-determination theory, which depends on achieving relatedness (integration), autonomy, and competence (differentiation). While further research is required to ascertain whether the findings in this qualitative study are generalizable to wider populations, the findings and suggestions made are in line with the findings of previous researchers.

In summary, there is a strong body of evidence that some goals are universal, or at the very least widely valued, particularly goals related to autonomy, competence, and relatedness. In other words, all or most people are driven to learn and grow but also to connect to other people. A balance of these needs allows an individual to self-determine, self-actualize, become more complex, and flourish. We suggest that organizations and employees should focus on the pursuit of work-related goals that are aligned with these universal needs. For example, goals aligned with the need for competency might include learning a new skill, focusing on strengths, or being recognized as an industry expert. Goals aligned with the need for autonomy might include working from home, working in virtual and/or self-managing teams, or increasing delegated authority. Goals aligned with the need for relatedness might include coaching and mentoring others, deepening client relationships, or undertaking company outreach or pro bono programs. The specifics will vary by work unit, organization, and industry. However, it is suggested that organizations and employees have much to gain in terms of engagement, performance, and well-being by considering how work responsibilities can be aligned with positively valenced, personally valued goals that employees perceive to be meaningful.

Conclusion

The world is facing an employee engagement crisis, with a slew of detrimental outcomes and opportunity costs. This chapter has argued that, by elevating employee hope, employee engagement, performance, and well-being can be increased also. However, little is known about how hope operates to bring about positive work outcomes. There has been a call for researchers to "determine which changes in workplace conditions, training, or management lead to increases in hope and corresponding improvement in outcomes" and to undertake further research on "contextual and employee moderating and mediating factors" that may be at play (Reichard et al., 2013, p. 302). Previous research has tended to focus on the agency and pathways components of hope. This chapter has argued that much more attention needs to paid to the fact that hope theory rests on the pursuit of positively valenced, personally valued goals that hold meaning for the individual. As such, in order to optimize employee hope, engagement, and positive work outcomes, an alignment of organizational and personal goals is crucial. The fact that some human needs and values are universal, or at least widely valued, is of great practical importance. In particular, the literature points to the universality of autonomy, competence, and relatedness needs, which together comprise self-determination. In other words, human beings, including employees, appear to universally value the opportunity to learn and grow as individuals and to connect with other people. If organizations and employees are able to structure work so that employees are able pursue goals that are related to these universal needs, we will stand a far better chance of optimizing hope, engagement, and positive outcomes in the workplace.

Future Directions

• How can organizations create conditions that allow employees to set and pursue positively

valenced, personally valued, meaningful goals at work?

• What can employees do to set and pursue positive valenced, personally valued, meaningful goals at work?

• What obstacles do you see for aligning personal and work-related goals, and how might these obstacles be overcome?

• Which other values do you think might be universally valued by employees? How can these be accommodated?

• What new, innovative interventions could be designed to increase employee hope, engagement, performance, and well-being at work?

References

Avey, J. B., Avolio, B. J., & Luthans, F. (2011). Experimentally analyzing the impact of leader positivity on follower positivity and performance. *The Leadership Quarterly, 22*(2), 282–294. doi:10.1016/j.leaqua.2011.02.004

Avey, J. B., Reichard, R. J., Luthans, F., & Mhatre, K. H. (2011). Meta-analysis of the impact of positive psychological capital on employee attitudes, behaviors, and performance. *Human Resource Development Quarterly, 22*(2), 127–152. doi:10.1002/hrdq.20070

Bakker, A. B. (2013). *Advances in positive organizational psychology.* Bingley, UK: Emerald Group.

Bakker, A. B., Tims, M., & Derks, D. (2012). Proactive personality and job performance: The role of job crafting and work engagement. *Human Relations, 65*(10), 1359–1378. doi:10.1177/0018726712453471

Berg, J. M., Dutton, J. E., & Wrzesniewski, A. (2013). Job crafting and meaningful work. In B. J. Dik, Z. S. Byrne, & M. F. Steger (Eds.), *Purpose and meaning in the workplace* (pp. 81–104). Washington, DC: American Psychological Association. doi:10.1037/14183-005

Bullough, R. V., & Hall-Kenyon, K. M. (2012). On teacher hope, sense of calling, and commitment to teaching. *Teacher Education Quarterly, 39*(2), 7–27.

Cameron, K. S. (2008). *Positive leadership.* San Francisco, CA: Berrett Koehler.

Cameron, K. S., Dutton, J., & Quinn, R. (Eds.).(2003). *Positive organizational scholarship.* San Francisco, CA: Berrett-Koehler.

Church, A. T., Katigbak, M. S., Locke, K. D., Zhang, H., Shen, J., de Jesús Vargas-Flores, J., . . . Ching, C. M. (2013). Need satisfaction and well-being: Testing self-determination theory in eight cultures. *Journal of Cross-Cultural Psychology, 44*(4), 507–534. doi:10.1177/0022022121124665

Csikszentmihalyi, M. (1988). *Optimal experience.* New York: Cambridge University Press.

Csikszentmihalyi, M. (1990). *Flow: The psychology of optimal experience.* New York: HarperCollins.

Csikszentmihalyi, M., & Nakamura, J. (1999). Emerging goals and the self-regulation of behavior. In R. J. Wyer (Ed.), *Perspectives on behavioral self-regulation: Advances in social cognition* (Vol. XII, pp. 107–118). Mahwah, NJ: Lawrence Erlbaum.

Csikszentmihalyi, M., & Rathunde, K. (1998). The development of the person: An experiential perspective on the ontogenesis of psychological complexity. In W. Damon & R. M. Lerner

(Eds.), *Handbook of child psychology: Vol. 1, Theoretical models of human development* (5th ed., pp. 635–684). Hoboken, NJ: Wiley.

Deci, E. L., & Ryan, R. M. (2000). The "what" and "why" of goal pursuits: Human needs and the self-determination of behavior. *Psychological Inquiry, 11*, 227–268.

Deci, E. L., Ryan, R. M., & Guay, F. (2013). Self-determination theory and actualization of human potential. In D. M. McInerney, H. W. Marsh, R. G. Craven, & F. Guay (Eds.), *Theory driving research: New wave perspectives on self-processes and human development* (pp. 109–133). Charlotte, NC: Information Age.

Delle Fave, A., Massimini, F., & Bassi, M. (2011). *Psychological selection and optimal experience across cultures: Social empowerment through personal growth.* New York: Springer Science + Business Media. doi:10.1007/978-90-481-9876-4

Engeser, S. (2012). *Advances in flow research.* New York: Springer Science + Business Media. doi:10.1007/978-1-4614-2359-1

Erez, A., & Isen, A.M. (2002). The influence of positive affect on the components of expectancy motivation. *The Journal of Applied Psychology, 87*, 1055–1067.

Feldman, D. B., Rand, K. L., & Kahle-Wrobleski, K. (2009). Hope and goal attainment: Testing a basic prediction of hope theory. *Journal of Social and Clinical Psychology, 28*(4), 479–497. doi:10.1521/jscp.2009.28.4.479

Feldman, D. B., & Snyder, C. R. (2005). Hope and the meaningful life: Theoretical and empirical associations between goal-directed thinking and life meaning. *Journal of Social and Clinical Psychology, 24*(3), 401–421. doi:10.1521/jscp.24.3.401.65616

Fischer, R., & Schwartz, S. (2011). Whence differences in value priorities? Individual, cultural, or artifactual sources. *Journal of Cross-Cultural Psychology, 42*(7), 1127–1144. doi:10.1177/0022022110381429

Fredrickson, B. (2001). The role of positive emotions in positive psychology: The broaden-and-build theory of positive emotions. *American Psychologist, 56*(3), 218–226.

Fredrickson, B. (2009). *Positivity: Groundbreaking research reveals how to embrace the hidden strength of positive emotions, overcome negativity, and thrive.* New York: Crown Publishers/Random House.

Gallup. (2013). *State of the global workplace: Employee engagement insights for business leaders worldwide.* Omaha, NE: Author. Retrieved from www.gallup.com/services/178517/state-global-workplace.aspx.

Gallup. (2016). *The employee engagement crisis.* Omaha, NE: Author. Retrieved from www.gallup.com/businessjournal/188033/worldwide-employee-engagement-crisis.aspx.

Gardner, H., Csikszentmihalyi, M., & Damon, W. (2001). *Good work: When excellence and ethics meet.* New York: Basic Books.

Grant, A. M. (2012). An integrated model of goal-focused coaching: An evidence-based framework for teaching and practice. *International Coaching Psychology Review, 7*(2), 146–165.

Harter, J. K., & Schmidt, F. L. (2008). Conceptual versus empirical distinctions among constructs: Implications for discriminant validity. *Industrial and Organizational Psychology: Perspectives on Science and Practice, 1*(1), 36–39. doi:10.1111/j.1754-9434.2007.00004.x

Harter, J. K., Schmidt, F. L., Agrawal, S., & Plowman, S. K. (2013, February). *The relationship between engagement at work and organizational outcomes: 2012 Q12® meta-analysis.* Omaha, NE: Gallup. Retrieved from www.gallup.com/services/177047/q12-meta-analysis.aspx.

Inghilleri, P., & Bartoli, E. (1999). *From subjective experience to cultural change.* New York: Cambridge University Press. doi:10.1017/CBO9780511571343.

Kahn, W. A. (1990). Psychological conditions of personal engagement and disengagement at work. *Academy of Management Journal, 33*(4), 692–724. doi:10.2307/256287

Karatepe, O. M. (2014). Hope, work engagement, and organizationally valued performance outcomes: An empirical study in the hotel industry. *Journal of Hospitality Marketing & Management, 23*(6), 678–698.

Ko, I., & Donaldson, S. (2011). Applied positive organizational psychology: The state of the science and practice. In S. I. Donaldson, M. Csikszentmihalyi, & J. Nakamura (Eds.), *Applied positive psychology: Improving everyday life, health, schools, work, and society* (pp. 137–154). New York: Routledge/Taylor & Francis.

Landhäußer, A., & Keller, J. (2012). Flow and its affective, cognitive, and performance-related consequences. In S. Engeser (Ed.), *Advances in flow research* (pp. 65–85). New York: Springer Science.

Lopez, S. (2013a, May 25). Hone the job you have into one you love. *The New York Times.* Retrieved from www.nytimes.com/2013/05/26/jobs/honing-the-job-you-have-into-one-you-love.html?_r=0

Lopez, S. J. (2013b). *Making hope happen: Create the future you want for yourself and others.* New York: Atria Books.

Lopez, S. J., & Calderon, V. J. (2011). Gallup student poll: Measuring and promoting what is right with students. In S. I. Donaldson, M. Csikszentmihalyi, & J. Nakamura, (Eds.), *Applied positive psychology: Improving everyday life, health, schools, work, and society* (pp. 117–133). New York: Routledge/Taylor & Francis.

Lopez, S. J., Snyder, C. R., & Pedrotti, J. T. (2003). Hope: Many definitions, many measures. In S. J. Lopez & C. R. Snyder (Eds.), *Positive psychological assessment: A handbook of models and measures* (pp. 91–106). Washington, DC: American Psychological Association. doi:10.1037/10612-006.

Luthans F. (2002). The need for and meaning of positive organizational behavior. *Journal of Organizational Behavior, 23*, 695–706.

Luthans, F., Avey, J. B., Avolio, B. J., Norman, S. M., & Combs, G. M. (2006). Psychological capital development: Toward a micro-intervention. *Journal of Organizational Behavior, 27*(3), 387–393. doi:10.1002/job.373.

Luthans, F., Avolio, B., Avey, J., & Norman, S. M. (2007). Positive psychological capital: Measurement and relationship with performance and satisfaction. *Personnel Psychology, 60*, 541–572.

Luthans, F., & Jensen, S. M. (2002). Hope: A new positive strength for human resource development. *Human Resource Development Review, 1*(3), 304–322. doi:10.1177/1534484302013003

Lyons, P. (2008). The crafting of jobs and individual differences. *Journal of Business and Psychology, 23*(1–2), 25–36. doi:10.1007/s10869-008-9080-2

Lyubomirsky, S., King, L., & Diener, E. (2005). The benefits of frequent positive affect: Does happiness lead to success? *Psychological Bulletin, 131*, 803–855.

Malinowski, P., & Lim, H. J. (2015). Mindfulness at work: Positive affect, hope, and optimism mediate the relationship between dispositional mindfulness, work engagement, and well-being. *Mindfulness, 6*(6), 1250–1262. doi:10.1007/s12671-015-0388-5

Maslow, A. H. (1943). A theory of human motivation. *Psychological Review, 50*(4), 370–396.

Maslow, A. (1954). *Motivation and personality.* New York: Harper & Row.

Mills, M. J., Fleck, C. R., & Kozikowski, A. (2013). Positive psychology at work: A conceptual review, state-of-practice assessment, and a look ahead. *The Journal of Positive Psychology, 8*(2), 153–164. doi:10.1080/17439760.2013.776622

Mouton, A. R. (2015). *Positive psychology predictors of performance in academics, athletics and the workplace.* Doctoral dissertation. Retrieved from ProQuest.

Mouton, A. R., & Montijo, M. N. (2017). Love, passion, and peak experience: A qualitative study on six continents. *Journal of Positive Psychology, 12*(3), 263–280. doi:10.1080/17439760.2016.1225117

Norman, S., Luthans, B., & Luthans, K. (2005). The proposed contagion effect of hopeful leaders on the resiliency of employees and organizations. *Journal of Leadership & Organizational Studies, 12*(2), 55–64. doi:10.1177/107179190501200205

Ouweneel, E., Le Blanc, P. M., Schaufeli, W. B., & van Wijhe, C. I. (2012). Good morning, good day: A diary study on positive emotions, hope, and work engagement. *Human Relations, 65*(9), 1129–1154. doi:10.1177/0018726711429382

Peterson, S. J., & Byron, K. (2008). Exploring the role of hope in job performance: Results from four studies. *Journal of Organizational Behavior, 29*(6), 785–803. doi:10.1002/job.492

Peterson, S. J., & Luthans, F. (2003). The positive impact and development of hopeful leaders. *Leadership & Organization Development Journal, 24*(1), 26–31. doi:10.1108/01437730310457302

Petrou, P., Demerouti, E., Peeters, M. W., Schaufeli, W. B., & Hetland, J. (2012). Crafting a job on a daily basis: Contextual correlates and the link to work engagement. *Journal of Organizational Behavior, 33*(8), 1120–1141. doi:10.1002/job.1783

Rand, K. L., & Cheavens, J. S. (2009). Hope theory. In S. J. Lopez & C. R. Snyder (Eds.), *Oxford handbook of positive psychology* (2nd ed., pp. 323–333). New York: Oxford University Press.

Reichard, R. J., Avey, J. B., Lopez, S., & Dollwet, M. (2013). Having the will and finding the way: A review and meta-analysis of hope at work. *The Journal of Positive Psychology, 8*(4), 292–304. doi:10.1080/17439760.2013.800903

Rokeach, M. (1973). *The nature of human values.* New York: Free Press.

Ryan, R. M., & Deci, E. L. (2000). Self-determination theory and the facilitation of intrinsic motivation, social development and well-being. *American Psychologist, 55,* 68–78.

Ryff, C. D., & Keyes, C. L. M. (1995). The structure of psychological well-being revisited. *Journal of Personality and Social Psychology, 69,* 719–727. doi:10.1037/0022-3514.69.4.719

Schaufeli, W. B., Bakker, A. B., & Salanova, M. (2006). The measurement of work engagement with a short questionnaire: A cross-national study. *Educational & Psychological Measurement, 66*(4), 701–716.

Schaufeli, W. B., Salanova, M., González-Romá, V., & Bakker, A. B. (2002). The measurement of engagement and burnout: A two sample confirmatory factor analytic approach. *Journal of Happiness Studies, 3*(1), 71–92. doi:10.1023/A:1015630930326

Schwartz, S. H. (1992). Universals in the content and structure of values: Theory and empirical tests in 20 countries. In M.

Zanna (Ed.), *Advances in experimental social psychology* (Vol. 25, pp. 1–65). New York: Academic Press.

Schwartz, S. H., Cieciuch, J., Vecchione, M., Davidov, E., Fischer, R., Beierlein, C., . . . Konty, M. (2012). Refining the theory of basic individual values. *Journal of Personality and Social Psychology, 103*(4), 663–688. doi:10.1037/a0029393

Seligman, M. P., Railton, P., Baumeister, R. F., & Sripada, C. (2013). Navigating into the future or driven by the past. *Perspectives on Psychological Science, 8*(2), 119–141. doi:10.1177/1745691612474317

Snyder, C. R. (1994). The psychology of hope: *You can get there from here.* New York: Free Press.

Snyder, C. R. (2002). Hope theory: Rainbows in the mind. *Psychological Inquiry, 13,* 249–275.

Snyder, C. R., Feldman, D. B., Shorey, H. S., & Rand, K. L. (2002). Hopeful choices: A school counselor's guide to hope theory. *Professional School Counseling, 5*(5), 298–307.

Snyder, C. R., Harris, C., Anderson, J. R., Holleran, S. A., Irving, L. M., Sigmon, S. T., . . . Harney, P. (1991). The will and the ways: Development and validation of an individual-differences measure of hope. *Journal of Personality and Social Psychology, 60*(4), 570–585. doi:10.1037/0022-3514.60.4.570

Snyder, C. R., Lopez, S. J., & Pedrotti, J. T. (2011). *Positive psychology: The scientific and practical explorations of human strengths* (2nd ed.). Thousand Oaks, CA: SAGE.

Snyder, C. R., Lopez, S. J., Shorey, H. S., Rand, K. L., & Feldman, D. B. (2003). Hope theory, measurements, and applications to school psychology. *School Psychology Quarterly, 18*(2), 122–139. doi:10.1521/scpq.18.2.122.21854

Snyder, C. R., Sympson, S. C., Ybasco, F. C., Borders, T. F., Babyak, M. A., & Higgins, R. L. (1996). Development and validation of the State Hope Scale. *Journal of Personality and Social Psychology, 70*(2), 321–335. doi:10.1037/0022-3514.70.2.321

Tay, L., & Diener, E. (2011). Needs and subjective well-being around the world. *Journal of Personality and Social Psychology, 101*(2), 354–365. doi:10.1037/a0023779

Tims, M., Bakker, A. B., & Derks, D. (2012). Development and validation of the job crafting scale. *Journal of Vocational Behavior, 80*(1), 173–186. doi:10.1016/j.jvb.2011.05.009

Tims, M., Derks, D., & Bakker, A. B. (2016). Job crafting and its relationships with person–job fit and meaningfulness: A three-wave study. *Journal of Vocational Behavior, 9244*–53. doi:10.1016/j.jvb.2015.11.007

Vallerand, R. J. (2015). *The psychology of passion: A dualistic model.* New York: Oxford University Press. doi:10.1093/acprof:oso/9780199777600.001.0001

Vallerand, R. J., Blanchard, C. M., Mageau, G. A., Koestner, R., Ratelle, C., Léonard, M., Gagné, M., & Marsolais, J. (2003). Les passions de l'âme: On obsessive and harmonious passion. *Journal of Personality and Social Psychology, 85,* 756–767.

Vallerand, R. J., Salvy, S.-J., Mageau, G. A., Elliot, A. J., Denis, P. L., Grouzet, F. M. E., & Blanchard, C. (2007). On the role of passion in performance. *Journal of Personality, 75,* 505–534.

Vaksalla, A., & Hashimah, I. (2015). How hope, personal growth initiative and meaning in life predict work engagement among nurses in Malaysia private hospitals. *International Journal of Arts & Sciences, 8*(2), 321.

Vela, J. C., Lerma, E., Lenz, A. S., Hinojosa, K., Hernandez-Duque, O., & Gonzalez, S. L. (2014). Positive psychology and familial factors as predictors of Latina/o students' hope and college performance. *Hispanic Journal of Behavioral Sciences*, *36*(4), 452–469. doi:10.1177/0739986314550790

Yalçın, İ., & Malkoç, A. (2015). The relationship between meaning in life and subjective well-being: Forgiveness and hope as mediators. *Journal of Happiness Studies*, *16*(4), 915–929. doi:10.1007/s10902-014-9540-5.

Wrzesniewski, A. (2003). Finding positive meaning in work. In K. S. Cameron, J. E. Dutton, & R. E. Quinn (Eds.), *Positive organizational scholarship: Foundations of a new discipline* (pp. 298–308). San Francisco, CA: Berrett-Koehler.

Wrzesniewski, A., LoBuglio, N., Dutton, J. E., & Berg, J. M. (2013). Job crafting and cultivating positive meaning and identity in work. In A. B. Bakker (Ed.), *Advances in positive organizational psychology* (pp. 281–302). Bingley, UK: Emerald Group Publishing. doi:10.1108/S2046-410X(2013)0000001015

World Values Survey. (n.d.). World values survey. Retrieved from www.worldvaluessurvey.org

Hope and Meaning-in-Life: Points of Contact Between Hope Theory and Existentialism

David B. Feldman, Meenakshi Balaraman, *and* Craig Anderson

Abstract

Freidrich Nietzsche famously said, "He who has a why to live for can bear almost any how," a quote that pioneering existential psychiatrist Viktor Frankl cited often. This chapter argues that it is through the *whys* in people's lives—their goals—that they establish a sense of meaning. The chapter makes both an empirical and a theoretical case that, linked by an emphasis on goals, hope and meaning in life are closely connected. It begins by defining the meaning-in-life construct, continues with a discussion of the empirical relationships between hope and meaning, and concludes with a theoretical exploration of hope in the context of existential philosophical systems.

Key Words: meaning in life, hope, goals, existentialism, empirical relationship, meaning.

Philosopher Freidrich Nietzsche famously said, "He who has a why to live for can bear almost any how." Pioneering existential psychiatrist Viktor Frankl cited this line often, in part to explain how he and others endured life in concentration camps during the Holocaust. Decades later, this simple phrase probably best summarizes the robust relationship between hope and the construct of life meaning.

In this chapter, we argue that it is through the *whys* in our lives—our goals—that we establish a sense that life is meaningful. We make both an empirical and a theoretical case that, linked by an emphasis on goals, hope and meaning are close cousins, influencing and contributing to one another.

We begin by defining the meaning-in-life construct and discussing various ways in which it has been measured, continue with a discussion of the empirical relationships between hope and meaning, and conclude with a theoretical exploration of hope in the context of existential philosophical systems.

Defining and Measuring Meaning in Life

Given that scholarship on life meaning spans centuries, the field of psychology is a relative newcomer to the issue, tracing back only several decades. Most psychological theorists have reframed the age-old question "What is the meaning of life?" to reflect a more contemporary perspective—"How do people arrive at their own senses of meaning?" To echo this distinction, researchers tend to use the term "meaning *in* life" rather than "meaning *of* life."

It is worth noting that the words "meaning" and "purpose" are often used synonymously, though they have somewhat different connotations. In recent years, it has become common to view the two as distinct parts of a broader conceptual framework. According to Yalom (1980), meaning refers to "sense or coherence," whereas purpose refers to "intention, aim, function" (p. 423). Meaning includes people's ability to make sense of, and find patterns and significance in, life events. Purpose includes a set of related aspirations and life objectives.

Theorists have proposed a number of models of meaning and purpose in life. Due to space limitations, however, we briefly review only the approaches of Frankl (logotherapy), Greenberg, Pyszczynski, and Solomon (terror management theory), Antonovsky (sense of coherence [SOC]), and Baumeister (four needs for meaning) here. We also review common measures of each of these related, yet distinct, meaning constructs.

Viktor Frankl and Logotherapy

Viktor Frankl (1972, 1992) was one of the first to translate existential philosophy into psychological terms. His theory, known as logotherapy, begins with the notion that contemporary society faces an unprecedented crisis of meaning known as the "existential vacuum," a sense that life is without inherent purpose or significance. People meet this vacuum, however, with an equally strong "will to meaning," the universal drive to find meaning in life. Although this drive can help lead to inner fulfillment (Hillmann, 2004), if we fail to find meaning, we risk experiencing mental illness (Dyck, 1987; Feldman & Snyder, 2005).

Frankl believed that people find meaning through acting on three types of values: creative, experiential, and attitudinal. When an individual creates or produces something, a creative value has been actualized (Feldman & Snyder, 2005). When a musician composes a symphony or a builder constructs a house, he or she is acting on creative values. Experiential values are actualized when an individual sees, touches, tastes, or in another way experiences something (Feldman & Snyder, 2005). Indulging in a meal, watching a movie, or enjoying the touch of a cool cloth on a hot day are emblematic of experiential values. Attitudinal values are actualized through the attitude one takes toward one's life (Feldman, 2011). Frankl (1965) observed that this final value can be a source of meaning even when one may no longer easily be able to create or experience anew, as in debilitating illness. Individuals at the end of life, for instance, may actualize attitudinal values in the stance they take toward their fate.

Crumbaugh and Maholick (1964) created the Purpose in Life Test (PIL) to the measure Frankl's meaning-in-life construct. The PIL comprises 20 items that respondents rate on 7-point scales. A typical item is, "In thinking of my life I . . . ," which is rated on a scale ranging from 1 (*often wonder why I exist*) to 7 (*always see a reason for my being here*). Despite the widespread use of the PIL in research, it has been criticized on psychometric grounds. In particular, some items may tap other constructs such as depression or boredom (Schulenberg, Schnetzer, & Buchanan, 2010; Schulenberg & Melton, 2010).

Terror Management Theory

Terror management theory (Greenberg, Pyszczynski, & Solomon, 1986, 1991) was developed from the work of cultural anthropologist Ernest Becker (1962, 1964, 1973, 1975). According to this theory, when people contemplate their lives, they are naturally confronted with the fact that they will eventually die. The self manages the anxiety or terror associated with this realization through the use of two constructs that operate in sync: culture and self-esteem (Landau & Sullivan, 2015). Culture prevents the terror of our inevitable demise by creating a sense of order, structure, and meaning, all of which possess the power to symbolically eclipse death (Landau & Sullivan, 2015). In Christian culture, for instance, individuals are promised immorality provided that they adhere to certain precept and laws. In secular culture, individuals are promised "symbolic immortality" though the accumulation of accolades, accomplishments, and histories that last beyond their lifespan. When people believe that they have lived up to the standards of their particular cultures, they are buffered from the terror associated with mortality. Terror management theorists believe that the psychological mechanism serving in this buffering role is self-esteem, which is bolstered when people fulfill culturally valued roles.

Battista and Almond (1973) developed the Life Regard Index, which assesses a meaning construct similar to terror management theory. This 28-item scale contains two subscales: Framework and Fulfillment. Framework items assess the perception that one has a structure or philosophy from which to derive life goals, whereas Fulfillment items assess the perception that one is conforming to or satisfying that framework. Typical items include "I have really come to terms with what's important for me in my life," and "I feel that I'm really going to attain what I want in life," which respondents rate on scales ranging from 1 (*totally disagree*) to 5 (*totally agree*). A slightly revised version of the Life Regard Index has also been developed (e.g., Debats, 1998).

Sense of Coherence

Antonovsky (1979, 1987) proposed a construct called the sense of coherence, which is theorized to reduce the negative effects of stress on mental and physical health. The SOC consists of three components: meaningfulness, comprehensibility, and manageability. Accordingly, people are theorized to enjoy greater well-being to the extent that they are pursuing personally *meaningful* activities. In order to effectively pursue those activities, people must *comprehend* their environments and believe that they can effectively *manage* or control them.

To measure the SOC construct, Antonovsky (1987) developed the 29-item Sense of Coherence Scale, which consists of subscales to assess meaningfulness, comprehensibility, and manageability. A sample comprehensibility item is "Do you have the feeling that you are in an unfamiliar situation and don't know what to do?" with a scale of 1 (*very often*) to 7 (*very seldom or never*). A sample meaningfulness item is "How often do you have the feeling's that there's little meaning in the things you do in your daily life?" with a scale of 1 (*very often*) to 7 (*very seldom or never*). Finally, a sample manageability item is "How often do you have feelings that you're not sure you can keep under control?" with a scale of 1 (*very often*) to 7 (*very seldom or never*).

The Four Needs for Meaning

Baumeister and Wilson (1996) concur with McAdams (1996) that individuals construct identities partially by constructing stories. Through these narratives, people attempt to answer the question "Who am I?" by organizing the past, present, and future, as well as assimilating their diverse roles, values, and skills into meaningful patterns. These patterns center around four basic needs for meaning (Baumeister, 1991).

The first need is for purpose (Stillman & Baumeister, 2009). That is, people have a need to believe that their current actions will lead to the future achievement of goals. The second need is for efficacy or a sense of control over possible outcomes in one's life (Stillman & Baumeister, 2009). The third need is for value; that is, people desire to see their actions as right, good, or justifiable (Stillman & Baumeister, 2009). The final need is for self-worth, to see oneself as having positive value.

There is no single widely used self-report measure of the four needs for meaning. However, in research studies, Baumeister has developed strategies for coding elements of meaning in participants' life stories (e.g., Baumeister & Wilson, 1996).

A Commonality among Theories of Life Meaning

Though, at first blush, the four theories of meaning just discussed appear dissimilar, they share

an important commonality. Namely, all of them contain an underlying focus on goals (Feldman, 2011; Feldman & Snyder, 2005). Frankl's (1992) three value categories—creative, experiential, and attitudinal—can be conceptualized as varieties of goals that, when accomplished, provide meaning to one's life. Goals also play an important role in terror management theory (Greenberg et al., 1986). Specifically, self-esteem is strengthened and people are buffered against the terror associated with mortality to the degree that they endorse a cultural framework through which to derive and meet goals. Antonovsky's SOC (1979, 1987) likewise makes use of goals. That is, meaning in life arises when people perceive that they can effectively comprehend and manage their environments to accomplish their goals. Baumeister's (1991; Stillman & Baumeister, 2009) four needs for meaning are also goal-oriented. The need for purpose, in particular, refers directly to goals. The need for efficacy further concerns the ability to act so as to obtain valuable outcomes, or goals, in one's life.

Because hope is the cognitive process through which individuals pursue goals, it is at the heart of all of these conceptualizations of meaning in life (Feldman, 2011; Snyder, 1994). Hope theory (Snyder, 1994) conceptualizes hope as the combination of two interrelated types of goal-directed cognition: pathways thinking and agency thinking. Pathways are routes to or strategies for reaching goals. Thus people engage in pathways thinking when they plan ways to reach their goals. Agency thinking consists of thoughts that enable people to begin and maintain movement on selected pathways (Snyder, Michael, & Cheavens, 1999, p. 180). As in Watty Piper's (1978) children's book, *The Little Engine That Could*, agency thoughts such as "I think I can" provide people the motivation to pursue goals (Snyder, LaPointe, Crowson, & Early, 1998). As such, hope theory details the cognitive process through which goals are pursued, and the pursuit of goals is the process through which life meaning is established.

Perhaps a metaphor would be helpful here. If we equate seeking life meaning with the process of constructing a house, goals would be the bricks (i.e., the units of meaning) and hope would be the bricklayer (Feldman & Snyder, 2005). Goals do not pursue themselves any more than bricks assemble themselves; the process requires planning and motivation. In short, it requires hope. Hope theory offers a coherent account of the process of assembling one's goals into a meaningful life.

Following this bricklayer metaphor, one might ask how the bricks are made—that is, how people form goals. There is evidence that goals are related to, and perhaps derived, from one's values (Oishi, Schimmack, Diener, & Suh, 1998). Sheldon and colleagues (Sheldon, 2001; Sheldon & Elliot, 1999) have shown that values-concordant goals are more motivating and lead to greater increases in well-being than nonconcordant goals. Thus a well-articulated set of values may contribute to one's ability to form goals from which to construct a meaningful life. Feldman (2013) has thus proposed that the construction of a meaningful life can be divided into two processes: (a) the selection of personally meaningful goals based on one's values and (b) the pursuit of those goals. The second of these processes is most directly governed by the tenets of hope theory.

Empirical Relationships

Various studies demonstrate empirical relationships between higher hope and greater meaning in life. This has been shown in both longitudinal (Mascaro & Rosen, 2005) as well as cross-sectional studies (Cheavens, Feldman, Gum, Michael, & Snyder, 2006; Feldman & Snyder, 2005; Kim, Lee, Yu, Lee, & Puig, 2005; Mascaro & Rosen, 2005, 2006;). In cross-sectional studies, meaning has been measured using a variety of scales (many detailed previously in this chapter). Regardless of the instruments used, meaning and hope appear to correlate strongly, with an impressive average correlation of .67. The aforementioned studies all involved American samples. A recent study on college students in Iran (Hedayati & Khazaei, 2014), however, is consistent with these results, showing a strong positive correlation of .62 between hope and life meaning.

In a longitudinal study on the topic, Mascaro and Rosen (2005) demonstrated robust relationships between hope and meaning in life. These researchers measured meaning and hope in college students at two time-points, three months apart. An intriguing feature of this study was that both implicit and explicit meaning were assessed. A revised version of the Life Regard Index (Debats, 1998) was used to measure explicit meaning (i.e., participants' subjective evaluations that life has meaning), and the Personal Meaning Profile (Wong; 1998) was used to measure implicit meaning (i.e., characteristics that people from the outside would consider gives meaning to participants' lives). Despite statistically controlling for personality traits and social desirability,

there remained a significant relationship between life meaning at Time 1 and hope at Time 2. The authors also found that both implicit and explicit meaning were correlated with lower depressive symptoms as well as higher levels of both trait and state hope.

Hope and meaning in life account for a large amount of shared variance in positive indicators of mental health such as self-esteem and life satisfaction (Halama, 2003; Halama & Dedova, 2007). In another longitudinal study, Braun-Lewensohn and Sagy (2010) measured life meaning (SOC) and levels of hope in adolescents living in southern Israel at two time-points, spaced three years apart. Results indicated that both hope and SOC correlated with one another and predicted well-being.

Hope and meaning in life also appear to share a large amount of variance in accounting for negative mental health indicators such as depression and anxiety. In a study by Feldman and Snyder (2005), 33% to 34% of the variance in scores on the Beck Depression Inventory (Beck, Ward, Mendelson, Mock, & Erbaugh, 1961) and 41% to 42% of the variance in trait anxiety scores on the State-Trait Anxiety Inventory (Spielberger, Gorsuch, & Luchene, 1970) were accounted for redundantly by meaning and hope.

Though most research on the topic is correlational, a number of experimental studies have cast light on causal connections between hope and meaning. In particular, controlled studies show that hope-based therapeutic interventions seem to enhance meaning in life. Cheavens and colleagues (2006) found that, in a community sample of adults diagnosed with various disorders, an eight-session hope intervention increased life meaning in comparison with a wait-list control. Additional studies show similar results. Lapierre, Dubé, Bouffard, and Alain (2007) offered a 12-week goal-skills intervention to groups of newly retired individuals with suicidal ideation; results indicated that the treatment group experienced increases in state hope as well as purpose in life relative to a control group. Moreover, Feldman and Dreher (2012) found that a single-session, 90-minute hope intervention resulted in increases in scores on measures of life meaning in college students as compared to a no-treatment control group and a relaxation training comparison group.

Hope and Existentialism

Modern scholarship on the issue of life's meaning began in the 19th and early 20th centuries with existential philosophers such as Kierkegaard, Nietzsche, Heidegger, and Sartre. Although meaning was only one of the many concepts in their respective philosophical systems, it was arguably the most important. For Kierkegaard and Nietzsche, for example, society's (as well as their own) encroaching sense of nihilism—the belief that life has no intrinsic meaning, purpose, or value—brought urgency to their philosophizing (Guignon & Pereboom, 1995a). The purpose of existential philosophy has been in part to show that, despite the inability of human beings to prove absolutes such as God and objective morality, life still can be meaningful.

But the great existential philosophers hardly agreed on much. In fact, their philosophical systems varied greatly, differing in arguments, vocabulary, and sometimes conclusions. Nonetheless, most existential systems of thought share certain concepts in common. In this section, we discuss these commonalities and show how, even beyond the concept of life meaning itself, hope theory appears to be at the heart of them. The intension of this section is not to reduce existentialism to hope theory; we do not believe this is possible. Rather, we wish to show that the relationship between hope and existential themes runs deeper than contemporary research might easily demonstrate.

Existence, Essence, and Responsibility

A central proposition in existentialism is that *existence precedes essence*. As observed most directly by Sartre (1957/2000), human beings are conscious actors, capable of and responsible for selecting who they will be. In its simplest terms, this phrase means that "man turns up, appears on the scene, and, only afterwards, defines himself" (Sartre, 1957/2000, p. 15). Human beings "exist" as entities before their "essence" takes form. A common difficulty is that elements of society attempt to define this essence for the individual on the basis of labels, stereotypes, and other expectations. The individual ultimately is responsible, however, for choosing whether to take agency upon him- or herself, on the one hand, or to cede that agency to others. Put differently, human beings, through their own actions, determine the meaning of their lives.

According to hpe theory, hope drives such goal-pursuit actions. In a three-month longitudinal study, for instance, Feldman, Rand, and Kahle-Wrobleski (2009), found that higher hope individuals tended to make greater progress toward attaining self-nominated goals than their lower hope counterparts. In particular, the relationship between hope and goal progress appeared to be driven by the agency component of hope.

On a related note, hope is similar to optimism. But Snyder (1995, 2002) has observed an important distinction: Optimism is an expectancy that positive outcomes will occur *regardless of personal action*. In contrast, hope is explicitly concerned with the attainment of positive outcomes through one's own planning (pathways) and motivation (agency). Responsibility—the ability to *act* so as to pursue one's goals and thus define who one is—is therefore integral to hope theory, as it is to existentialism.

Authenticity

Closely related to responsibility is the concept of authenticity. In existentialism, authenticity is the degree to which one adheres to one's own values, goals, or character, despite the external pressures noted previously (Guignon & Pereboom, 1995b). As mentioned, human beings define their essence through action in the context of responsibility. When an individual acts out of a responsible, self-determined choice, he or she is acting authentically. When acting solely on the basis of outside forces (e.g., to meet others' expectations, to garner praise, to avoid criticism, etc.), particularly when these run counter to one's own values, a person is said to be acting in "bad faith."

Recall that we have argued that two processes are involved in the establishment of a meaningful life—(a) the selection of intrinsic, value-consonant goals and (b) the active pursuit of those goals. It is important to note that these two processes are theoretically and practically separable from one another. The goal-directed thinking present in the second process may be utilized to pursue both intrinsic goals that flow from personal values as well as extrinsic goals that are unrelated (or even opposed) to personal values. In the context of hope theory, this is one way to understand the distinction between living authentically versus living in bad faith. That is, an authentic existence involves the use of both processes in tandem, whereas bad faith involves only the second process in isolation.

Thrownness/Facticity

Existentialists generally acknowledge that human beings' ability to choose responsibly and authentically is challenged by the practical circumstances of their lives. Largely synonyms, the terms *thrownness* (Heidegger, 1953/2010) and *facticity* (Sartre, 1956/1992) refer to the givens of one's life. Quite literally, thrownness is the set of circumstances into which the individual is "thrown" at any particular moment. Much of one's thrownness consists of things one did not have the power to choose, such as place and family of birth, genetic endowment, and so on. Someone who is born into a wealthy family, for instance, will likely have more opportunities available to him or her than someone born into an impoverished one. Human beings are said to be a hybrid of facticity, on the one hand, and *transcendence*, on the other. That is, though one's facticity/thrownness can be set by outside forces, people have the ability to transcend that facticity. In other words, though we do not always have control over what life throws at us, we do have control over what we *do* with that set of circumstances.

Facticity or thrownness often consists of circumstances that can block the way to achieving goals. When a goal is blocked, the individual is faced with the choice of how to approach such a circumstance. In this regard, Snyder, Lopez, Shorey, Rand, and Feldman (2003) have written that high-hope people "do not denigrate their abilities when they 'fail', and they do not let such failures affect their self-worth in the long run" (p. 125). According to hope theory, high-hope people tend to interpret most blockages as temporary obstacles to their goals rather than as permanent failures. They also tend to produce many pathways to their goals in order to circumvent such obstacles, should they arise. Indeed, studies show that higher scores on the pathways component of the Hope Scale (Snyder et al., 1991) predict the generation of greater numbers of actual plans for accomplishing particular goals (Irving, Snyder, & Crowson, 1998; Snyder et al., 1991). At least in this context, it may be said that high levels of hope help people transcend obstacles, setbacks, and seeming "failures."

In a similar vein, high-hope individuals tend to use more problem-focused coping. Eggum, Sallquist, and Eisenberg (2010) interviewed 52 adolescents who lived in rural areas near Tororo, Uganda, to investigate the connection between hopeful thinking and coping with adversity. At an average age of 13, 21% of participants had lost a parent, 63% did not have enough food to eat, and 56% had witnessed violence. According to the results, higher hope children tended to practice higher levels of a variety of coping strategies in comparison to their lower hope counterparts, but, most relevantly, they reported engaging in greater levels of problem-focused coping. That is, they reported *doing* things to comfort themselves and improve their lives. It is precisely this orientation toward doing, as long as it occurs in the context of authenticity, that characterizes existential transcendence.

Despair

In existentialism, despair is viewed as the polar opposite of hope. More specifically, it is a loss of hope in reaction to the impeding of defining qualities of one's identity—one's goals and projects.

This perspective is directly compatible with hope theory, in which goal-pursuits are conceptualized as the major sources of emotions (Feldman & Bach, 2015; Snyder, 2002). Feelings of despair are thus the result of long-term movement away from goals. In hope theory, virtually everything that human beings do is directed toward achieving goals, whether large or small (Snyder, 1994; Snyder, Michael, & Cheavens, 1999). According to Shorey, Snyder, Rand, Hockemeyer, and Feldman (2002), the role of emotions "is to serve as an indicator of whether given goal-pursuit thought-to-action chains are perceived as successful or unsuccessful" (p. 327). People feel positive emotions when they achieve goals or move toward achieving them and negative emotions when they fail in this regard. In addition, Snyder (2002; Snyder et al., 1991) theorized that hope and goal progress (or lack thereof) reciprocally influence one another. That is, not only does hope lead to goal progress and attainment, but hope then is readjusted to bring it into line with level of goal success. Thus, according to hope theory, long-term goal blockage leads to a lack of hope, which, in the language of existentialism, would be called despair.

Hope and Meaning in Psychotherapy

To summarize, we have argued that life meaning is established through two processes: (a) setting intrinsic, values-concordant goals and (b) actively pursuing those goals. The empirical relationship between hope and meaning-in-life is likely driven by the latter of these two processes. It is worth noting, however, that some people may have particular difficulty with one of these processes versus the other. This brings us to the topic of therapeutic interventions.

Traditionally, existential therapy has been viewed as the appropriate treatment for issues of life meaning and purpose. Indeed, for those with issues related to the first process, existential interventions that help identify important values and values-consistent goals may be helpful. Nonetheless, those with issues related to the second process may be better served by hope-based therapy. For those who already have identified a set of values-concordant goals, learning hope theory-based, goal-directed thinking skills may be more beneficial for the construction of a meaningful life.

As mentioned previously, a number of therapeutic interventions based on hope theory have been developed (e.g., Cheavens et al., 2006; Feldman & Dreher, 2012; Lapierre et al., 2007). For instance, Cheavens and colleagues randomly assigned adults with a variety of mental illness diagnoses to either eight sessions of hope-based group therapy or an eight-week wait list. Each two-hour hope session consisted of psychoeducation regarding a skill related to one of the components of hope theory (e.g., pathways mapping, generating alternative pathways around goal blockages, high-agency self-talk) as well as less structured periods in which participants helped one another to apply these skills to their particular life situations. Skills-based homework was also provided. Relative to control participants, hope-therapy participants showed greater increases in agency thinking and marginally significantly greater increases in both overall hope and pathways thinking. Most important for the present discussion, however, hope-therapy participants showed significant increases in their sense of life meaning, demonstrating that hope-based skills can impact what is traditionally considered an existential issue.

Conclusion

In this chapter, we have reviewed hope's relationship to both contemporary psychological theories of life meaning as well as classical existential philosophical approaches. Both theoretically and empirically, it appears that hopeful goal-directed thinking plays an important role in the construction of a meaningful life. Perhaps if Nietzsche and Frankl were alive today, they would agree to a slight rewording of their famous phrase. "He who has a why to live for can bear almost any how" could very well read "He who has a why to *hope* for can bear almost any how."

Future Directions:

• What additional psychotherapeutic and/or psychoeducational techniques increase both hope and life meaning?

• Do particular interventions increase levels either only of hope or only of meaning in life, or are both constructs always affected in tandem? For instance, in this chapter we refer to hope-based interventions that increase levels of life meaning,

but do more traditional existential interventions also increase hope? This knowledge may help to further tease apart these two constructs.

• What characteristics of goals contribute most to meaning in life? In this chapter, we indicate that one such characteristic appears to be the degree to which a goal is concordant with one's personal values. Are there additional factors that render a goal particularly likely to contribute to one's sense of life meaning?

• What is the longitudinal relationship between hope and life meaning? Most studies to date are cross-sectional in nature. Further longitudinal studies may elucidate how these two constructs are related to one another over time.

References

Antonovsky, A. (1979). *Health, stress, and coping.* San Francisco, CA: Jossey-Bass.

Antonovsky, A. (1987). *Unraveling the mystery of health.* San Francisco, CA: Jossey-Bass.

Battista, J., & Almond, R. (1973). The development of meaning in life. *Psychiatry, 36,* 409–427. doi:10.1521/00332747.1973.11023774

Baumeister, R. F. (1991). *Meanings of life.* New York: Guilford Press.

Baumeister, R. F., & Wilson, B. (1996). Life stories and the four needs for meaning. *Psychological Inquiry, 7,* 322–325. doi:10.1207/s15327965pli0704_2

Beck, A. T., Ward, C. H., Mendelson, M., Mock, J., & Erbaugh, J. (1961). An inventory for measuring depression. *Archives of General Psychiatry, 4,* 53–63. http://dx.doi.org.libproxy.scu.edu/10.1001/archpsyc.1961.01710120031004

Braun-Lewensohn, O., & Sagy, S. (2010). Sense of coherence, hope and values among adolescents under missile attacks: A longitudinal study. *International Journal of Children's Spirituality, 15,* 247–260. doi:10.1080/1364436X.2010.520305

Cheavens, J. S., Feldman, D. B., Gum, A., Michael, S. T., & Snyder, C. R. (2006). Hope therapy in a community sample: A pilot investigation. *Social Indicators Research, 77,* 61–78. http://dx.doi.org/10.1007/s11205-005-5553-0

Crumbaugh, J. C., & Maholick, L. T. (1964). An experimental study in existentialism: The psychometric approach to Frankl's concept of noogenic neurosis. *Journal of Clinical Psychology, 20,* 200–207. http://dx.doi.org/10.1002/1097-4679(196404)20:2<200:AID-JCLP2270200203>3.0.CO;2-U

Debats, D. L. (1998). Measurement of personal meaning: The psychometric properties of the life regard index. In P. T. P. Wong & P. S. Fry (Eds.), *The human quest for meaning: A handbook of psychological research and clinical applications* (pp. 237–260). Mahwah, NJ: Lawrence Erlbaum.

Dyck, M. J. (1987). Assessing logotherapeutic constructs: Conceptual and psychometric status of the purpose in life and seeking of noetic goals tests. *Clinical Psychology Review, 7,* 439–447. doi:10.1016/0272-7358(87)90021-3

Eggum, N. D., Sallquist, J., & Eisenberg, N. (2010). "Then it will be good": Negative life events and resilience in Ugandan youth. *Journal of Adolescent Research, 32,* 8–22. doi: 10.1177/0743558410391259

Feldman, D. B. (2011). The meaning of hope and vice versa: Goal-directed thinking and the construction of a meaningful life. In J. Hicks & C. Routledge (Ed.), *The experience of meaning in life: Perspectives from the psychological sciences.* New York: Springer. doi:10.1007/978-94-007-6527-6_11

Feldman, D. B., & Bach, J. (2015). Hope. In H. Friedman (Ed.), *Encyclopedia of mental health* (2nd ed.) New York: Elsevier.

Feldman, D. B., & Dreher, D. E. (2012). Can hope be changed in 90 minutes? Testing the efficacy of a single-session goal-pursuit intervention for college students. *Journal of Happiness Studies, 13,* 745–759. doi:10.1007/s10902-011-9292-4

Feldman, D. B., Rand, K. L., & Kahle-Wrobleski, K. (2009). Hope and goal attainment: Testing a basic prediction of hope theory. *Journal of Social and Clinical Psychology, 28,* 479–497. doi:10.1521/jscp.2009.28.4.479

Feldman, D. B., & Snyder, C. R. (2005). Hope and the meaningful life: Theoretical and empirical associations between goal-directed thinking and life meaning. *Journal of Social and Clinical Psychology, 24,* 401–421. doi:10.1521/jscp.24.3.401.65616

Frankl, V. (1965). *The doctor and the soul: From psychotherapy to logotherapy.* Translated by R. Winston & C. Winston. New York: Knopf.

Frankl, V. (1972). The feeling of meaninglessness: A challenge to psychotherapy. *American Journal of Psychoanalysis, 32,* 85–89. http://dx.doi.org/10.1007/BF01872487

Frankl, V. (1992). *Man's search for meaning: An introduction to logotherapy.* Translated by I. Lasch. Boston: Beacon Press. (Original work published in 1959).

Greenberg, J., Pyszczynski, T., & Soloman, S. (1986). The causes and consequences of the need for self-esteem: A terror management theory. In R. F. Baumeister (Ed.), *Public self and private self.* New York: Springer-Verlag.

Guignon, C., & Pereboom, D. (1995a). *Existentialism: Basic writings.* Indianapolis, IN: Hacket.

Guignon, C., & Pereboom, D. (1995b). Sartre. In C. Guignon & D. Pereboom (Eds.), *Existentialism: Basic writings* (pp. 247–267). Indianapolis, IN: Hacket.

Halama, P. (2003). Meaning and hope—Two factors of positive psychological functioning in late adulthood. *Studia Psychologica, 45,* 103–110. https://www.infona.pl/resource/bwmeta1.element.d747ef3f-f979-39a9-bfa8-dc0bf5b6cb61

Halama, P., & Dedova, M. (2007). Meaning in life and hope as predictors of positive mental health: Do they explain residual variance not predicted by personality traits? *Studia Psychologica, 49,* 191–200. https://www.infona.pl/resource/ bwmeta1.element.0fddf64e-14ed-3e4b-ad46-58b1b65564f7

Heidegger, M. (1953/2010). Being and time. Translated by J. Stambaugh. Albany, NY: SUNY Press.

Hedayati, M., & Khazaei, M. (2014). An investigation of the relationship between depression, meaning in life and adult hope. *Procedia—Social and Behavioral Sciences, 114,* 598–601. doi:10.1016/j.sbspro.2013.12.753

Hillmann, M. (2004). Viktor E. Frankl's existential analysis and logotherapy. In M. W. Cox & E. Klinger (Eds), *Handbook of motivational counseling: Concepts, approaches, and assessment* (pp. 357–372). New York: Wiley.

Irving, L. M., Snyder, C. R., & Crowson, J. J. Jr (1998). Hope and coping with cancer by college women. *Journal of personality, 66,* 195–214. http://dx.doi.org/10.1111/1467-6494.00009

Kim, T., Lee, S. M., Yu, K., Lee, S., & Puig, A. (2005). Hope and the meaning of life as influences on Korean adolescents' resilience: Implications for counselors. *Asia Pacific Education Review, 6,* 143–152. doi:10.1007/BF03026782

Landau, M. J., & Sullivan, D. (2015). Terror management motivation at the core of personality. In M. Mikulincer, P. R. Shaver, L. M. Cooper, & R. J. Larsen (Eds.), *APA handbook of personality and social psychology: Vol .4, Personality processes and individual differences* (pp. 209–230). Washington, DC: American Psychological Association. http://dx.doi.org/10.1037/14343-010

Lapierre, S., Dubé, M., Bouffard, L. & Alain, M. (2007). Addressing suicidal ideations through the realization of meaningful personal goals. *Crisis, 28,* 16–25. http://dx.doi.org/10.1027/0227-5910.28.1.16

Mascaro, N., & Rosen, D. H. (2005). Existential meaning's role in the enhancement of hope and prevention of depressive symptoms. *Journal of Personality, 73,* 985–1014. doi:10.1111/j.1467-6494.2005.00336.x

Mascaro, N., & Rosen, D. H. (2006). The role of existential meaning as a buffer against stress. *Journal of Humanistic Psychology, 46,* 168–190. doi:10.1177/0022167805283779

Oishi, S., Schimmack, U., Diener, E., & Suh, E. M. (1998). The measurement of values and individualism-collectivism. *Personality and Social Psychology Bulletin, 24,* 1177–1189. doi:10.1177/01461672982411005

Piper, W. (1978). *The little engine that could.* New York: Grosset & Dunlap.

Sartre, J. P. (1992). *Being and nothingness: A phenomenological essay on ontology.* Translated by H. E. Barnes. New York: Washington Square Press. (Original work published 1956)

Sartre, J. P. (2000). *Existentialism and human emotions.* New York: Citadel Press. (Original work published 1957)

Schulenberg, S. E., & Melton, A. M. A. (2010). A confirmatory factor-analytic evaluation of the Purpose in Life Test: Preliminary psychometric support for a replicable two-factor model. *Journal of Happiness Studies, 11,* 95–111. doi:10.1007/s10902-008-9124-3

Schulenberg, S. E., Schnetzer, L. W., & Buchanan, E. M. (2010). The Purpose in Life Test–Short Form: Development and psychometric support. *Journal of Happiness Studies, 12,* 861–876. doi:10.1007/s10902-010-9231-9

Sheldon, K. M. (2001). The self-concordance model of healthy goal striving: When personal goals correctly represent the person. In P. Schmuck & K. Sheldon (Eds.), *Life goals and well-being: Towards a positive psychology of human striving* (pp. 18–36). Ashland, OH: Hogrefe & Huber.

Sheldon, K. M., & Elliot, A. J. (1999). Goal striving, need satisfaction, and longitudinal well-being: The self-concordance model. *Journal of Personality and Social Psychology, 76,* 482–497. http://dx.doi.org/10.1037/0022-3514.76.3.482

Shorey, H. S., Snyder, C. R., Rand, K. L., Hockemeyer, J. R., & Feldman, D. B. (2002). Somewhere over the rainbow: Hope theory weathers its first decade. *Psychological Inquiry, 13,* 322–331. doi:10.1207/S15327965PLI1304_03

Snyder, C. R. (1994). *The psychology of hope.* New York: Free Press.

Snyder, C. R. (1995). Conceptualizing, measuring, and nurturing hope. *Journal of Counseling & Development, 73,* 355–360. doi:10.1002/j.1556-6676.1995.tb01764.x

Snyder, C. R. (2002). Hope theory: Rainbows in the mind. *Psychological Inquiry, 13,* 249–275. doi:10.1207/S15327965PLI1304_01

Snyder, C. R., Harris, C., Anderson, J. R., Holleran, S. A., Irving, L. M., Sigmon, S. T., . . . Harney, P. (1991). The will and the ways: Development and validation of an individual–differences measure of hope. *Journal of Personality and Social Psychology*, *60*, 570–585. http://dx.doi.org/10.1037/0022-3514.60.4.570

Snyder, C. R., LaPointe, A. B., Crowson., J. J. Jr., & Early, S. (1998). Preference of high-and low-hope people for self-referential input. *Coginition and Emotion*, *12*, 807–823. doi:10.1080/026999398379448

Snyder, C. R., Lopez, S. J., Shorey, H. S., Rand, K. L., & Feldman, D. B. (2003). Hope theory, measurements, and applications to school psychology. *School Psychology Quarterly*, *18*, 122–139. http://dx.doi.org/10.1521/scpq.18.2.122.21854

Snyder, C. R., Michael, S. T., & Cheavens, J. S. (1999). Hope as a psychotherapeutic foundation of nonspecific factors, placebos, and expectancies. In M. A. Huble, B. Duncan, & S. Miller (Eds.), *Heart and soul of change* (pp. 205–230). Washington, DC: American Psychological Association. http://dx.doi.org/10.1037/11132-005

Spielberger, C. D., Gorsuch, R. L., & Luchene, R. (1970). *Test manual for the State-Trait Anxiety Inventory*. Palo Alto, CA: Consulting Psychologists Press.

Stillman, T. F., & Baumeister, R. F. (2009). Uncertainty, belongingness, and four needs for meaning. *Psychological Inquiry*, *20*, 249–251. http://dx.doi.org.libproxy.scu.edu/10.1080/10478400903333544

Wong, P. T. (1998). Implicit theories of meaningful life and the development of the personal meaning profile. In P. T. P Wong & P. S. Fry (Eds.), *The human quest for meaning: A handbook of psychological research and clinical applications* (pp. 111–140). Mahwah, NJ: Lawrence Erlbaum.

Yalom, I. (1980). *Existential psychotherapy*. New York: Basic Books.

PART VII

The Future of Hope

Future Directions in the Science of Hope

Matthew W. Gallagher, Jennifer S. Cheavens, Lisa M. Edwards, David B. Feldman, Amber M. Gum, Susana C. Marques, Kevin L. Rand, Lorie A. Ritschel, Jennifer Teramoto Pedrotti, *and* Hal S. Shorey

Abstract

The scientific study of hope has progressed rapidly since Rick Snyder first published his theoretical model of hope and developed assessments for quantifying individual differences in hope, but much work remains to more fully understand when, how, and why hope promotes resilience and human flourishing. The field has lost the titans of hope in Rick Snyder and Shane Lopez and is now led by the second generation of hope scientists. In this chapter, a collection of prominent hope researchers share their thoughts on future directions in studying hope. These topics include improving the understanding of how to promote hope; identifying the influence of hope on both positive outcomes such as meaning, healthy coping, and healthy relationships and negative outcomes such as depression; and more generally how hope can help promote flourishing communities. These topics and the researchers studying them represent the future of hope, which has never been brighter.

Key Words: hope, coping, flourishing, resilience, hope researchers

The scientific study of hope will soon enter its fourth decade. What Rick Snyder started in Fraser Hall at the top of Mount Oread in Lawrence, Kansas, has flourished into a worldwide research endeavor focusing on how the will and the ways of hope can help individuals of all backgrounds achieve their goals. Unfortunately, the field has now lost both Rick Snyder and Shane Lopez, but their legacy is being carried on by former students, colleagues, and friends of both Shane and Rick as well as many other researchers and practitioners around the world.

As Snyder (2002) outlined in his review of the first dozen years of the study of hope, hope theory was initially an expansion of his work on how people make excuses for and make sense of negative outcomes through the process of reality negotiation (Snyder, 1989; Snyder & Higgins, 1988). Hope theory and research has now blossomed into one of the most productive and promising fields of research in positive psychology. Hope is a topic that has long fascinated both practitioners and lay persons, but it

was not until Snyder developed his theory and measures that the scientific study of hope took flight, and we began to more fully understand when, how, and why hope played such a crucial role in promoting flourishing. Snyder's initial definition of hope as a "positive motivational state that is based on an interactively derived sense of successful (a) agency (goal-directed energy), and (b) pathways (planning to meet goals)" (Snyder, Irving, & Anderson, 1991, p. 287) continues to be a remarkably useful and robust conceptualization of hope. As highlighted in the chapters of this handbook, a remarkable amount of knowledge has been amassed highlighting the myriad ways and contexts in which hope impacts positive functioning. Nevertheless, much remains to be done to fully understand the impact of hope.

Prior to his unexpected passing in July of 2016, Shane Lopez was planning to write this chapter on the future of hope research. As all who knew Shane were aware, he had a unique ability to identify big-picture ideas, whether on the specific topic of hope research or broader topics such as how to advance the field of positive psychology or change the educational system to better support students to identify and achieve their goals. Shane was fond of framing these plans as "three big ideas" for the future, and he had a special capacity to not only articulate these ideas in an approachable manner but to identify clever and feasible pathways for achieving those ideas, and he had the energy and agency to make those ideas a reality. He was one of the most hopeful people I have ever known.

In deliberating about how to best approach this chapter in the aftermath of Shane's passing, it seemed most appropriate to honor both Shane and Rick's legacy of spreading hope and fostering collaboration by making the future directions chapter a collaborative work by scholars whose work has and continues to be inspired by Rick and Shane. I therefore asked nine other former colleagues, mentees, and friends of both Rick and Shane to share their ideas about future directions in the scientific study of hope. Each of these individuals also contributed a separate chapter to this handbook and are leaders in the field of hope.

Jen Cheavens and Lisa Edwards highlight the need to expand our understanding of how to promote hope specifically within therapeutic settings but also what we can do as researchers and practitioners to more generally give hope away by spreading ripples of hope. Susana Marques and Amber Gum discuss the importance of examining hope across the lifespan so that we can understand how to measure and promote hope whether we are examining children in school or older adults during retirement and to better understand both the developmental trajectories of hope and how the influence of hope may vary across the lifespan. Jennifer Teramoto Pedrotti echoes the words of the Reverend Dr. Martin Luther King Jr. in highlighting the potential impact hope can have on communities by helping to promote social justice. Kevin Rand identifies key future directions in the study of how hope promotes adaptive coping, which has long been one of the most productive and promising areas of research in hope theory. Lorie Ritschel discusses the importance of hope in promoting resilience to and recovery from mental illness and specifically highlights how hope can influence depression in youth. Hal Shorey identifies how hope functions in interpersonal contexts and the ways in which it can play a crucial role in promoting supportive and healthy relationships. Finally, Dave Feldman shares his thoughts about the role of hope in promoting meaning in life, which

for centuries has been identified as one of the fundamental goals that we all seek (e.g., Aristotle, 1925). This is not an exhaustive list of the future directions in the study of hope but represents many of the most pivotal, and it represents a collaborative vision about the future directions in the scientific study of hope.

Hope in Psychotherapy
Jennifer S. Cheavens

In moving forward with the study of hope, it is not enough to focus on the ways in which those with high hope excel. An unacceptably large proportion of adults suffer from psychological conditions associated with low hope, including depression, anxiety, suicidality, loneliness, and existential angst. There is reason to believe that hope-based interventions may result in increases in hope and decreases in symptoms of psychopathology (see Chapter 11 in this volume). Further, hopeful thought may improve response to evidence-based treatments such as cognitive-behavioral therapy. Given the scope of the problem and the promising evidence for the role of hope in treatment, it is imperative that future hope research focus on ways to harness the beneficial effects of hope for those most in need.

The future directions for hope intervention research can be organized into three overarching questions. First, what *is* hope therapy? Research on hope interventions is in its infancy, and the trials that have been done vary significantly in their definitions of hope interventions (e.g., essential components, dosage) and measured outcomes (e.g., hope, psychological symptoms, goal-setting behaviors). Thus, although several small trials of various hope interventions have been conducted, to date none of these trials have been replicated. Before moving to understanding mechanisms, facilitative conditions of treatment, or dissemination efforts, we must first come to consensus on the prescriptive and proscriptive components of hope therapy and demonstrate that hope therapy produces reliable and strong effects on outcomes that matter.

Second, are particular provider behaviors associated with increases in hope? To date, we have primarily conceptualized hope as an individual difference construct; there has been much less attention to the interpersonal aspects of hope. As we move forward with efforts to understand how to best enhance hope and incorporate hope interventions into existing treatments, we will likely benefit from efforts to understand the ways in which providers impact clients' hopeful thought. For example, do providers who are particularly hopeful (or have high levels of hope for a particular client) have better outcomes than their less hopeful counterparts? Similarly, attending to particular provider behaviors (e.g., specificity in goal-setting, highlighting the congruence between goals and values) in explaining improvements in hope will aid in efforts to standardize and disseminate hope interventions.

Third, how can we deliver hope-based interventions to those who might most benefit? Presently, only approximately 30% of those with a diagnosable disorder seek prompt, professional care (e.g., Zachrisson, Rodje, & Mykletun, 2006). Even when people do seek treatment, our systems are overwhelmed with appointment wait-times often lasting for months. If we want to use hope interventions to reduce suffering for as many people as possible, we need to start studying ways in which these interventions can be delivered quickly and in settings that are easily accessible to those in need. Specifically, research that points to the minimal effective dose and/or can be delivered in primary care settings, via telehealth portals, or in work places or schools is likely to help reach the greatest number of individuals who would potentially benefit from these interventions.

Giving Hope Away
Lisa M. Edwards

"I can imagine nothing we could do that would be more relevant to human welfare, and nothing that could pose a greater challenge to the next generation of psychologists than to discover how best to give psychology away" (Miller, 1969, p. 1074). The words of George Miller in his 1969 address to the American Psychological Association are still relevant today and could be argued about hope as well. With over 25 years of research about the power of hope for the well-being of youth and adults, we must ask ourselves if we are doing enough to share and give hope to others, and we must creatively consider the ways in which we can do more.

While it has taken some time for the field of psychology to move toward applying theories and research toward making a difference in the daily lives of the general public, great progress has been made (Zimbardo, 2004). Positive psychology, the subfield in which hope is most prominently situated, has also taken this charge to make a difference, and authors have argued that positive psychology is an applied science poised to be "a force for social change" (Biswas-Diener, Linley, Govindji, & Woolston, 2011, p. 412).

Similarly, hope also has the potential to transform lives and our world. In fact, the earliest writings by Snyder and colleagues (Snyder, 1994; Snyder, McDermott, Cook & Rapoff, 1997) focused a great deal on how to promote hope. Most recently, Lopez (2013) argued in *Making Hope Happen* that leaders need to lead with hope, that hope should be taught to the next generation, and that we can "network" hope to others through our support and modeling. The epilogue in Lopez's book asks the reader to consider the "tiny ripple of hope" that can be set in motion by each of us to change the path of someone's life and make the future better.

So we must ask ourselves: What can we do to start a ripple of hope? Can we give a talk about hope at a school, church, or parenting group? Can we be active on Twitter or other forms of social media to promote hope? Can we become a hope mentor? Can we be a guest blogger for a mental health or wellness website? All of these are possible, and much more. As Lopez (2013) reminds us: "You can start small. You merely need to create momentum where there was none" (p. 217).

Hope across Developmental Stages
Susana C. Marques

Dozens of studies have examined hope in adolescence, adulthood, and old age, but this research has not yet produced a comprehensive model of the developmental trajectory of hope. The lack of knowledge regarding age differences across developmental stages, as well as limited information concerning hope stability, indicates the need for more research in which participants from all age groups complete the same hope measure and are then followed longitudinally. Connected to this tractable issue, the literature on hope development would benefit from refining our theoretical framework for when, how, and why hope changes across the lifespan. Most past theoretical work has focused on particular developmental periods (e.g., the transition to old age) and particular life domains (e.g., school). Consequently, although the literature has generated many possible reasons why hope might change during old age, questions remain regarding how the various proposed processes work together to shape hope development. Given the complexity of hope development, such a model would necessarily incorporate biological, social, and psychological factors; account for reciprocal and dynamic causal influences; and include mechanisms of continuity as well as change (e.g., various forms of person–environment interaction). Our hope is that, by examining patterns of findings across developmental contexts (childhood to old age) and across life domains (work, school, relationships, health), the field will move toward an overarching theory of the life-course trajectory of hope.

Additionally, research is needed on the mediating mechanisms underlying hope change. On this link, lifespan research should draw on experimental work to develop hypotheses about long-term change in hope. Finally, genetically informed designs are needed to explore the mutual influence of nature and nurture on hope development. Researchers have yet to fully explore the profound implications of the finding that hope, like most traits, may have a genetic basis.

Hope and Healthy Aging
Amber M. Gum

To radically advance the study and promotion of hope for older adults, it is not enough to study and intervene with older adults—we must take a lifespan approach to hope. We could obtain a wealth of information by measuring hope in large-scale, longitudinal epidemiological studies of children and adults across ages. This approach would help us better understand factors that impact hope and are impacted by hope across the lifespan, expanding upon what is being done in epidemiological studies of older adults (see Chapter 12 in this volume). Questions to be explored further include: How stable is hope across ages? What factors lead to stable changes in hope (increases or declines)? How does childhood and early-adult hope contribute to goal achievements in midlife and later life in important domains like physical and mental health, social relationships, financial security, and civic participation? Which factors earlier in life predict an older adult's ability to remain hopeful?

It will be vital to not overlook a very important aspect of aging that begins in childhood—ageism. Variables related to ageism and perceptions of aging will be essential in future longitudinal epidemiological research. Why? Ageism harms and even kills older adults. Older adults are treated unfairly in many institutions in society, including in healthcare settings. Many older adults themselves believe the negative ideas about later life; as a result, they slow down, engage less, and deteriorate, in a tragic self-fulfilling prophecy. What does this have to do with children and younger adults? Ageist attitudes are so subtly ingrained in society that even young children harbor negative attitudes and beliefs about older adults. Experts often point out that old age is the only prejudiced category that most of us will one day join—long after we have learned and

internalized ageist beliefs and actions. From a hope perspective, it seems that we are being taught that later life is a time in which goal blockages become insurmountable and in which a person will no longer have the requisite pathways and agency to achieve meaningful goals.

Studying ageism and perceptions of aging in children and younger adults would allow us to understand how beliefs about older adults develop, how they impact relationships (especially across generations), and how they impact people's adjustment to midlife and preparation for later life (e.g., investing in health-promoting behaviors, investing in retirement). The ultimate goal, of course, would be to intervene at a societal level to eliminate ageism and to replace it with more hopeful beliefs that later life can be a time to achieve meaningful goals, and with more hope-promoting actions, such as ensuring that older adults more consistently have equal access to opportunities (e.g., where to live, physical accessibility, being welcomed in all social settings, high-quality healthcare).

While we await results from lifespan research on hope and perceptions of aging, undoubtedly we must continue to advance hope research with current middle-aged and older adults. It seems clear that the basic facets of hope theory operate similarly later in life as compared to earlier in life. We do not know how to intervene to improve hope and other outcomes for less hopeful older adults, however. Only one study of a hope intervention has been conducted with older adults, a small pilot study completed almost 20 years ago. Although older adults certainly achieve many goals, we should not take an unrealistically rosy view of later life. As with all ages, novel challenges become more common, many of which have never been confronted earlier in life, such as retirement, widowhood, chronic health problems, and death. Thus an important component for this research and intervention work will be greater study into the role of values and meta-regulation—how older adults choose goals in which to engage, and how they decide when to disengage from goals.

The ultimate vision is that this research would result in a lifetime of hope—older adults who have lived hopeful lives as children and younger adults, pursuing and achieving many goals that they chose for themselves and managing goal losses and blockages. As children and younger adults, they also would perceive older generations as valuable and able to achieve goals, and they would anticipate and prepare for their own later years as a time of continued goal pursuits. When they reach later life, they would continue to achieve personally meaningful goals, carefully consider which goals to pursue or set aside, and even prepare for a dying process and legacy to carry on their values and goals.

Hope and Social Justice: "Keep on Keeping On"

Jennifer Teramoto Pedrotti

"We must accept finite disappointment, but never lose infinite hope."

These words, spoken by Reverend Dr. Martin Luther King, Jr., stay with us today because of the call they make toward staying with a cause despite losses. Though today many remember Dr. King as a man who succeeded in championing change for African Americans and other racial, ethnic, and socioeconomic minority groups, he experienced loss and faced significant obstacles many times along the way. Dr. King and his followers were beaten, imprisoned, threatened, and blacklisted. In addition to these more obvious obstacles, their pathways were often quietly thwarted with moves executed by those with more power, more money, more control over the country and by apathetic groups who did not understand the need for this fight. The civil rights movement did not occur overnight but was fraught with the need to change strategies and plans (i.e., work around obstacles) and discover sustained motivation (i.e., agency) and new routes (i.e., pathways) toward the admirable goal of equality in the United States. Hope is at the center of this fight and continues to be an important factor in social justice work today.

Biswas and colleagues (2011) state that positive psychology can be a "force for social change" (p. 412), and they discuss several areas in which the use of strengths can help society become a better place both emotionally and physically. Hope in particular is central to the idea of change. Goals often emerge due to some dissonance or dissatisfaction with a current state. When one is feeling stuck, new personal goals may emerge to change the goal maker's current emotional or physical landscape. That said, Rodriguez-Hanley and Snyder (2000) also wrote specifically about the death of hope sometimes occurring as a result of constant thwarting of a particular goal. When one looks at the lives of social justice activists, it is common to see more thwarting than success throughout the movement. Goal success appears infrequent and long sought after, yet activists persist. Perhaps there is something unique in the fight for social justice and equality that spurs a more resilient hope. Or is it primarily those with particularly high hope who are drawn to this type of

fight? Though some researchers have begun inquiry into this area (see Sandage, Crabree, & Scheweer, 2014), these are largely unanswered questions at present and offer a new area of hope study.

The following questions are areas that might be interesting and fruitful in studying hope as a construct relevant to the work of social justice. How do social justice movements and their followers sustain agency despite multiple obstacles? In what ways is agency contagious, and how is it imparted from leaders of social justice movements to their followers? How are new pathways developed in the face of multiple thwarting of older pathways? Some research (e.g., Mattis et al., 2009) seems to suggest that certain strengths may be stronger in some groups with shared experiences. Is the construct of hope stronger in some members of disenfranchised or disempowered groups? If so, how does this occur? What causes social justice workers to continue to give so much personally, though they may be aware that the length of such campaigns often precludes their personal benefit from their efforts? In an era where some claim that activism is scant, these are perhaps questions that will help us to develop new understandings of the role of hope in the continued and necessary pursuit of social justice.

The Future of Hope and Coping

Kevin L. Rand

Hope is clearly associated with better performance and well-being (Alarcon, Bowling, & Khazon, 2013). As we continue to study the role of hope in people's lives, we need to clarify the mechanisms by which hope exerts its influence. An obvious candidate is coping. Within the hope framework, coping can be conceptualized as efforts to manage barriers to goals. There are some clear hypotheses about how hope should influence coping with these barriers. Hope should predict greater efforts to overcome them. Indeed, higher hope correlates with greater use of problem-focused coping (Holleran & Snyder, 1990). A hypothesis that needs further study is that hope should not be a strong predictor of emotion-focused coping. According to hope theory, emotions function as feedback about goal pursuits. Consequently, hopeful people should cope with emotions indirectly by focusing on their causative stressors. This hypothesis can readily be tested. The bigger challenge, however, is examining the inconspicuous ways hope might affect coping. I briefly discuss three.

First, we must examine the differential influences of pathways and agency on coping. Pathways should drive the use of a broader array of coping strategies in pursuing goals. This would be particularly important when one coping strategy proves ineffective. Agency, hope's motivational dimension, should drive greater persistence at a particular coping strategy, even during adversity. This is consistent with the finding that greater hope predicts greater pain tolerance (Snyder et al., 2005). But these two processes seem to work in opposition. What is the net result of agency and pathways on goal-directed coping? What conditions determine when someone sticks with a coping strategy versus switches to another one?

Second, we need to examine the differential influence of hope on coping in the presence of other personality traits. For example, research has shown that both hope and optimism predict well-being, but only hope predicts goal-directed performance (Rand, Martin, & Shea, 2011). Also, Gallagher and Lopez (2009) found that hope and optimism differentially relate to various dimensions of well-being. Do hope and optimism work through different coping mechanisms? I have argued that they do (Rand, 2009)—that hope influences coping with controllable stressors, whereas optimism influences coping with uncontrollable ones. However, this hypothesis needs to be tested.

Third, it is unclear how hope affects coping with unattainable goals. How, exactly, does a hopeful person decide a goal is impossible? According to hope theory, higher hope people should diversify their goals across several life domains, and hope should correlate with goal flexibility. However, some goals may have no alternative. When people develop a life-limiting illness, how does hope influence their coping? Perhaps a lifetime of successful goal pursuits renders them unable to cope effectively with such a stressor. Hope may explain why advanced cancer patients sometimes cope by continuing to pursue aggressive treatment when the disadvantages potentially outweigh any benefits. If so, this represents a maladaptive effect of hope (Snyder, Rand, King, Feldman, & Taylor, 2002). Rick Snyder viewed coping as the most important asset for navigating life (Snyder & Dinoff, 1999), and it is time to understand hope's role in this process.

Hope and Depression in Youth
Lorie A. Ritschel

As discussed earlier in this volume, major depression is a serious public health problem and a leading cause of disability worldwide. On average, first episodes of depression occur between ages 14 and 24 (Kessler, Avenevoli, & Merikangas, 2001), and

earlier ages of onset are associated with a greater number of depressive episodes over the lifetime, as well as longer illness duration within each episode (Rohde, Lewinsohn, Klein, Seeley, & Gau, 2013). Adolescent depression is strongly linked to attempted and completed suicide, which is currently the second leading cause of death in 15- to 19-year-old adolescents, behind only motor vehicle accidents (World Health Organization & UNICEF, 2008). Depression in youth is associated with a host of deleterious psychosocial outcomes in adulthood; depressed adolescents are less likely to graduate from college and are more likely to engage in substance use, become unwed parents, and report stressful events in their lives (Klein, Torpev, & Bufferd, 2008; Lewinsohn & Clarke, 1999). As such, there is a great need for prevention and intervention efforts to reduce the frequency and duration of depressive episodes in youth.

Part of the beauty of hope theory is that it can be broken down into simple lessons that offer concrete steps that people can take to improve their lives. Moreover, the concept of hope is sufficiently simple and elegant such that hopeful lessons can easily be taught to children and adolescents without making major alterations to the central construct, which is sometimes the case in modifying psychological treatments or interventions for younger samples. Teaching hope offers a viable route for building psychological strength and resilience in youth, particularly given that hope can be taught in schools—the very environment where kids spend most of their time and where they encounter most of their stressors. The tenets of hopeful thinking—setting achievable and worthwhile goals, finding pathways to those goals, and engaging in the positive self-talk necessary for goal attainment—can be taught in classroom settings and in ways that are easily accessible to youth. In addition to being associated with better academic and athletic performance, higher hope may offer just what is needed to mitigate the impact of the social stressors that so often contribute to first episodes of depression in youth. For example, peer victimization is an unfortunately common problem for young students; approximately 10% to 20% of school-aged youth report victimization experiences (Craig et al., 2009). Peer victimization is associated with depression, and this link is particularly strong when the victimized child makes critical self-referent attributions about the victimization (Prinstein, Cheah, & Guyer, 2005), has poor emotion regulation skills (McLaughlin, Hatzenbuehler, & Hilt, 2009), or is chronically victimized (Bogart et al., 2014; Bowes et al., 2013; Haltigan & Vaillancourt, 2014; Rueger, Malecki, & Demaray, 2011). Moreover, results from one study showed that hope moderates the relationship between peer victimization and depression (Cooley & Ritschel, 2012); specifically, victimized youth with higher levels of hope were less likely to become depressed than their low-hope counterparts. As such, hope appears to be a protective factor against the development of depression in youth faced with psychosocial stressors. By extension, improving hopeful thinking by teaching it directly in schools—and particularly with at-risk youth—could offer a cornerstone of resilience for vulnerable children and adolescents.

Hope and Healthy Relationships

Hal S. Shorey

From the beginning, Snyder and his colleagues viewed hope as a social construct; "an individual motive for social commerce" (Snyder, Cheavens, & Sympson, 1997, p. 107). Erikson (1963) believed that hope resulted from the interplay of the individual and the social environment during the first years of life. Baumeister and Leary (1995) believed that goal attainment only leads to positive mental health outcomes to the degree that goals are supported by meaningful others. Shorey et al. (2003) found evidence to support Snyder's theory that hope develops in the context of secure attachments to parents in childhood. In addition, I have found that goals in social domains are more predictive of mental health outcome than goals in performance domains.

Theory and research thus support the notion that hope is a socially situated construct. What remains to be seen, however, is the extent to which hope operates as a predictor, outcome, or both in various realms of social functioning. The research on attachment theory and hope, for example, suggests that developing hope requires a secure base to return to when one is exploring the environment and developing an agentic sense of self (Shorey, Snyder, Yang, & Lewin, 2003). The job of the secure base provider is to help regulate distressed emotions (provide a holding environment), normalize failures and help adjust goals, assist in new pathways development (strategizing), encourage and motivate the person to go out and try again (agency), and provide ongoing coaching. Future research is needed to determine the relative contribution of each of these secure base factors to the development of hope.

Using this secure base formulation, attachment researchers already have extended the applications of attachment theory to functioning in dyadic adult relationships (Martin, Paetzold, & Rholes, 2010). In their research on romantic couples, Fenney and Thrush (2010) found that nonintrusive coaching by a partner resulted in more enjoyment and higher levels of achievement on a laboratory problem-solving task by the exploring partner. Future research looking into the functioning of romantic couples and hope, however, will need to determine the directionality of the relationship; is hope needed to sustain a healthy relationship, or is having a healthy relationship needed to sustain hope? Are there bidirectional influences? Carefully controlled research that goes beyond cross-sectional designs is needed to establish the causal relationships in such models. The field is moving beyond the stage of making inferences from cross-sectional data to more laboratory and longitudinal direct research.

Other important questions that have impacts on hope-based interventions are whether fostering hope, attitudinally, in the absence of secure base provision, will lead to positive outcomes. Also, will increasing social support, in the absence of a specific secure base provider, increase hope? In other words, is it a global positive social support perception that drives hopeful thinking, or is repeated experiential exploration in the context of having a secure base needed to truly establish hope?

Moving beyond close relationships, it also will be important to investigate hope's role in larger social and group processes. What role, for example, does hope play in people's decisions about who to vote for in presidential elections? I suspect that hope's role in reducing anxiety has much to do with who one supports to be their leader. Similarly, research is needed to determine the role that hope plays in the relationships within hierarchical work structures. For example, can someone have high hope in the domain of work if that person does not have a supportive relationship with his or her boss?

Hope and Meaning in Life

David B. Feldman

As detailed in Chapter 26 of this volume, hope boasts stronger empirical relationships with measures of meaning in life than with any other construct (Feldman & Snyder, 2005). Moreover, hope-based interventions have been shown to increase meaning in life (Cheavens, Feldman, Gum, Michael, & Snyder, 2006; Feldman & Dreher, 2012). I argue that these robust connections are due to the fact that a meaningful life is established through two interrelated processes—(a) the setting of meaningful goals and (b) the active pursuit of those goals—and that the empirical relationship between hope and life meaning is likely driven by the latter. These findings open up a number of additional research questions.

First, if a meaningful life is founded on the active pursuit of meaningful goals, what exactly makes a goal "meaningful"? There is some research, for instance, that values-concordant goals are more motivating than nonconcordant goals and are more satisfying when accomplished (Sheldon, 2001; Sheldon & Elliot, 1999), but it is not clear whether this translates into greater contributions to life meaning. Other goal characteristics worth investigating may include goal motivation (e.g., intrinsic vs. extrinsic, achievement vs. mastery), the degree to which goals are interpersonal (e.g., serving others, requiring the collaboration of others to complete), and the degree to which goals are abstract versus concrete.

Second, one implication of the two-process approach to life meaning detailed in Chapter 26 is that any effect of the second process (i.e., actively pursuing goals) upon one's global evaluation of meaning in life should be moderated by the first process (i.e., setting meaningful goals). That is, if one has not identified a set of meaningful/values-concordant goals, the goal-pursuit process should not yield an increased sense of life meaning. Future research could further delineate these processes by distinguishing between individuals who have and have not identified a set of meaningful goals. For those who have been unable to identify such goals, measures of hope should not as strongly relate to measures of life meaning as for those who have identified such goals.

Third, we know that hope and meaning in life are highly correlated. Given the cross-sectional nature of much of the research, however, it would be useful to further investigate in what ways these two constructs causally influence one another. We know that some interventions designed to increase hope also increase life meaning (Cheavens et al., 2006; Feldman & Dreher, 2012). But do all interventions targeting hope increase meaning in life? Does the causal arrow also run in the opposite direction? That is, it may be that interventions targeting life meaning—such as existential therapy—also increase hope?

Traditionally, existential therapy has been viewed as the appropriate treatment for issues of life meaning. It is an exciting prospect to add hope-based interventions to therapists' arsenal of tools intended to increase meaning in life, particularly given the practical and well-defined nature of Snyder's (1994) hope construct. We hope that with continued investigation, the relationship between hope and life meaning will be further understood, ultimately leading to a proliferation of such tools.

Conclusion

The scientific study of hope has dramatically expanded in the decades since Rick Snyder first published the dispositional hope scale (Snyder et al., 1991). As discussed previously throughout this handbook, Snyder was not the first person to propose that hope may be beneficial and worthy of study (e.g., Menninger, 1959), but Snyder and colleagues' foundational work in many ways represents the developmental origin of the field of hope that is now flourishing and that now consists of more than 25 years of investigation into the ways in which hope helps individuals and communities lead lives worth living.

An initial question that was sometimes raised after Snyder first proposed his model and measures of hope was whether hope was too fuzzy a concept to be studied empirically, or whether hope as a construct was meaningfully distinct from related constructs such as optimism (Scheier & Carver; 1985) and self-efficacy (Bandura, 1997). This has now been definitively answered. The theoretical distinctions between hope and related positive psychology constructs have been clearly articulated (Snyder, 2002; also see Chapter 4 in this volume). Decades of empirical findings have now also clearly demonstrated that, although hope is related to these other constructs, hope represents a distinct latent construct and uniquely contributes to outcomes across many settings. The robust nature of these relationships has been synthesized in meta-analytic reviews that demonstrate the impact of hope on indicators of well-being, personality traits, superior outcomes in academic and professional settings, and many other important outcomes (e.g., Alarcon et al., 2013; Reichard, Avey, Lopez, & Dollwet, 2013; Weis & Speridakos, 2011). There has been increased awareness in the field of psychology in recent years of the crucial need to replicate and reproduce findings (Open Science Collaboration, 2015), so the consistency with which empirical findings regarding the benefits of hope have been demonstrated are encouraging. This effort to replicate and extend empirical findings must continue, and this and other chapters in this handbook highlight many of the directions that this research may take in the next decade of study.

Another common theme highlighted in this chapter and in other chapters of this handbook is the need to continue to use more rigorous and creative methodology to examine the benefits of hope in different circumstances. For example, by increasing the use of longitudinal methods, we will be better able to identify the lasting effects of hope; the extent to which demographics, cultural factors, or other variables moderate the effects of hope; and the mechanisms by which hope promotes positive outcomes. It will also be important to more precisely determine the situations and circumstances when the effects of hope may be less pronounced so that we can identify the boundaries of the benefits of hope. Finally, increasing the examination of hope as a predictor of outcomes simultaneously with other strengths or relevant predictors of resilience will help to improve our understanding of the unique effects of hope and the circumstances in which hope interacts with other factors to promote well-being and other outcomes.

Shane Lopez was fond of speaking about the importance of spreading ripples of hope. A fundamental premise behind hope theory is that we have the ability to exert personal agency so as to help ourselves and those around us achieve the goals that we set. In many ways, the contributors and contents of both this chapter and this volume represent the past, present, and future ripples of hope promoted by Rick and Shane. Hope is not a panacea, but the capacity for hope and the belief in a more positive future represents one of the most common character strengths worldwide (Gallagher, Lopez, & Pressman, 2013; Park, Peterson, & Seligman, 2006). We must continue this mission to spread the science and practice of hope to maximize the impact of hope theory and research. In doing so, as a field we can help achieve the goals of positive psychology by both maximizing our understanding of the myriad ways in which hope is beneficial and increasing the real-world impact of the science of hope by helping to cultivate hope across all corners of the world.

References

Alarcon, G. M., Bowling, N. A., & Khazon, S. (2013). Great expectations: A meta-analytic examination of optimism and hope. *Personality and Individual Differences, 54*, 821–827.

Aristotle. (1925). *The Nicomachean ethics.* New York: Oxford University Press.

Bandura, A. (1977). Self-efficacy: Toward a unifying theory of behavioral change. *Psychological Review, 84*(2), 191–215.

Baumeister, R. F., & Leary, M. R. (1995). The need to belong: Desire for interpersonal attachments as a fundamental human motivation. *Psychological Bulletin, 117*, 497–529.

Biswas-Diener, R., Linley, P. A., Govindji, R., & Woolston, L. (2011). Positive psychology as a force for social change. In K. M. Sheldon, T. B. Kashdan, & M. F. Steger (Eds.), *Designing positive psychology: Taking stock and moving forward* (pp. 410–418). Oxford: Oxford University Press.

Bogart, L. M., Elliot, M. N., Klein, D. J., Tortolero, S. R., Mrug, S., Peskin, M. F., Schuster, M. A. (2014). Peer victimization in fifth grade and health in tenth grade. *Pediatrics, 133*(3), 440–447. doi:10.1542/peds.2013-3510

Bowes, L., Maughan, B., Ball, H., Shakoor, S., Ouellet-Morin, I., Caspi, A., . . . Arseneault, L. (2013). Chronic bullying victimization across school transitions: The role of genetic and environmental influences. *Development and Psychopathology, 25*(2), 333–346. doi:10.1017/S0954579412001095

Cheavens, J. S., Feldman, D. B., Gum, A., Michael, S. T., & Snyder, C. R. (2006). Hope therapy in a community sample: A pilot investigation. *Social Indicators Research, 77*, 61–78. doi:10.1007/s11205-005-5553-0

Cooley, J. L., & Ritschel, L. A. (2012, August). *Hope as a protective factor against the effects of peer victimization.* Poster presented at the 2012 annual meeting of the American Psychological Association Convention, Orlando, FL.

Craig, W., Harel-Fisch, Y., Fogel-Grinvald, H., Dostaler, S., Hetland, J., Simons-Morton, B., . . . HBSC Bullying Writing Group. (2009). A cross-national profile of bullying and victimization among adolescents in 40 countries. *International Journal of Public Health, 54*, 216–224. doi:10.1007/s00038-009-5413-9

Erikson, E. H. (1963). *Childhood and society.* New York: Norton.

Feldman, D. B., & Dreher, D. E. (2012). Can hope be changed in 90 minutes? Testing the efficacy of a single-session goal-pursuit intervention for college students. *Journal of Happiness Studies, 13*, 745–759. doi:10.1007/s10902-011-9292-4

Feldman, D. B., & Snyder, C. R. (2005). Hope and the meaningful life: Theoretical and empirical associations between goal-directed thinking and life meaning. *Journal of Social and Clinical Psychology, 24*, 401–421. doi:10.1521/jscp.24.3.401.65616

Fenney, B. C., & Thrush, R. L. (2010). Relationship influences on exploration in adulthood: The characteristics and function of a secure base. *Journal of Personality and Social Psychology, 98*, 57–76. doi:10.1037/a0016961

Gallagher, M. W., & Lopez, S. J. (2009). Positive expectancies and mental health: Identifying the unique contributions of hope and optimism. *The Journal of Positive Psychology, 4*(6), 548–556. doi:10.1080/17439760903157166

Gallagher, M. W., Lopez, S. J., & Pressman, S. D. (2013). Optimism is universal: Exploring the presence and benefits of optimism in a representative sample of the world. *Journal of Personality, 81*(5), 429–440. doi:10.1111/jopy.12026

Haltigan, J. D., & Vaillancourt, T. (2014). Joint trajectories of bullying and peer victimization across elementary and middle school and associations with symptoms of psychopathology. *Developmental Psychology, 50*(11), 2426–2436. doi:10.1037/a0038030

Holleran, S., & Snyder, C. R. (1990). *Discriminant and convergent validation of the Hope Scale.* Unpublished manuscript. University of Kansas, Lawrence.

Kessler, R. C., Avenevoli, S., & Merikangas, K. R. (2001). Mood disorders in children and adolescents: An epidemiologic perspective. *Social Biology and Psychiatry, 49*, 1002–1014. doi:10.1016/S0006-3223(01)01129-5

Klein, D. N., Torpey, D. C., & Bufferd, S. J. (2008). Depressive disorders. In T. P. Beauchaine & S. P. Hinshaw (Eds.), *Child and adolescent psychopathology* (pp. 477–509). Hoboken, NJ: Wiley.

Lewinsohn, P. M., & Clarke, G. N. (1999). Psychosocial treatments for adolescent depression. *Clinical Psychology Review, 19*, 329–342. doi:10.1016/S0272-7358(99)00055-5.

Lopez, S. J. (2013). *Making hope happen: Create the future you want for yourself and others.* New York: Simon & Schuster.

Martin, A. M., Paetzold, R. L., & Rholes, W. S. (2010). Adult attachment and exploration: Linking attachment style to motivation and perceptions of support in adult exploration. *Basic & Applied Social Psychology, 32*(2), 196–205. doi:10.1080/01973531003738452

Mattis, J. S., Powell Hammond, W., Grayman, N., Cowie, S., Bonacci, M., Brennan, W., . . . Hilt, L. M. (2009). Emotion dysregulation as a mechanism linking peer victimization to internalizing symptoms in adolescents. *Journal of Consulting and Clinical Psychology, 77*(5), 894. doi:10.1037/a0015760

McLaughlin, K. A., Hatzenbuehler, M. L., & Hilt, L. M. (2009). Emotion dysregulation as a mechanism linking peer victimization to internalizing symptoms in adolescents. *Journal of Consulting and Clinical Psychology, 77*, 894–904. http://dx.doi.org/10.1037/a0015760

Menninger, K. (1959) The Academic Lecture: Hope. *American Journal of Psychiatry, 116*, 481–491.

Miller, G. (1969). Psychology as a means of promoting human welfare. *American Psychologist, 24*, 1063–1075.

Open Science Collaboration. (2015). Estimating the reproducibility of psychological science. *Science, 349*(6251), aac4716.

Park, N., Peterson, C., & Seligman, M. E. (2006). Character strengths in fifty-four nations and the fifty US states. *The Journal of Positive Psychology, 1*(3), 118–129.

Prinstein, M. J., Cheah, C. S., & Guyer, A. E. (2005). Peer victimization, cue interpretation, and internalizing symptoms: Preliminary concurrent and longitudinal findings for children and adolescents. *Journal of Clinical Child and Adolescent Psychology, 34*(1), 11–24. doi:10.1207/s15374424jccp3401_2

Rand, K. L. (2009). Hope and optimism: Latent structures and influences on grade expectancy and academic performance. *Journal of Personality, 77*(1), 231–260.

Rand, K. L., Martin, A. D., & Shea, A. M. (2011). Hope, but not optimism, predicts academic performance of law students beyond previous academic achievement. *Journal of Research in Personality, 45*(6), 683–686.

Reichard, R. J., Avey, J. B., Lopez, S., & Dollwet, M. (2013). Having the will and finding the way: A review and meta-analysis of hope at work. *The Journal of Positive Psychology, 8*(4), 292–304.

Rodriguez-Hanley, A. S., & Snyder, C. R. (2000). The demise of hope: On losing positive thinking. In C. R. Snyder (Ed.), *Handbook of hope* (pp. 39–54). San Diego, CA: Academic Press.

Rohde, P., Lewinsohn, P. M., Klein, D. N., Seeley, J. R., & Gau, J. M. (2013). Key characteristics of major depressive disorder occurring in childhood, adolescence, emerging adulthood, and adulthood. *Clinical Psychological Science, 1*(1), 41–53. doi:10.1177/2167702612457599

Rueger, S. Y., Malecki, C., & Demaray, M. K. (2011). Stability of peer victimization in early adolescence: Effects of timing and duration. *Journal of School Psychology, 49*, 443–464. doi:10.1016/j.jsp.2011.04.005

Sandage, S. J., Crabree, S., & Schweer, M. (2014). Differentiation of self and social justice commitment mediated by hope. *Journal of Counseling & Development, 92*, 67–74. doi:10.1002/j.1556-6676.2014.00131.x

Scheier, M. F., & Carver, C. S. (1985). Optimism, coping, and health: Assessment and implications of generalized outcome expectancies. *Health Psychology, 4*(3), 219–247.

Sheldon, K. M. (2001). The self-concordance model of healthy goal striving: When personal goals correctly represent the person. In P. Schmuck & K. Sheldon (Eds.), *Life goals and well-being: Towards a positive psychology of human striving* (pp. 18–36). Ashland, OH: Hogrefe & Huber.

Sheldon, K. M., & Elliot, A. J. (1999). Goal striving, need satisfaction, and longitudinal well-being: The self-concordance model. *Journal of Personality and Social Psychology, 76*, 482–497. http://dx.doi.org/10.1037/0022-3514.76.3.482

Shorey, H. S., Snyder, C. R., Yang, X., & Lewin, M. R. (2003). The role of hope as a mediator in recollected parenting, adult attachment, and mental health. *Journal of Social and Clinical Psychology, 22*, 685–715.

Snyder, C. R. (1989). Reality negotiation: From excuses to hope and beyond. *Journal of Social and Clinical Psychology, 8*, 130–157.

Snyder, C. R. (1994). *The psychology of hope: You can get there from here.* New York: Simon & Schuster.

Snyder, C. R. (2002). Hope theory: Rainbows in the mind. *Psychological Inquiry, 13*, 249–275.

Snyder, C. R., Irving, L., & Anderson, J. R. (1991). Hope and Health: Measuring the will and the ways. In C. R. Snyder & D. R. Forsyth (Eds.), *Handbook of social and clinical psychology: The health perspective* (pp. 285–305). Elmsford, New York: Pergamon Press.

Snyder, C. R., Berg, C., Woodward, J. T., Gum, A., Rand, K. L., Wrobleski, K. K., . . . Hackman, A. (2005). Hope against the cold: Individual differences in trait hope and acute pain tolerance on the cold pressor task. *Journal of Personality, 73*(2), 287–312.

Snyder, C. R., Cheavens, J., & Sympson, S. C. (1997). Hope: An individual motive for social commerce. *Group Dynamics: Theory, Research, and Practice, 1*(2), 107–118. doi:10.1037/1089-2699.1.2.107

Snyder, C. R., & Dinoff, B. L. (1999). Coping: Where have you been? In C. R. Snyder (Ed.), *Coping: The psychology of what works* (pp. 3–19). New York: Oxford University Press.

Snyder, C. R., Harris, C., Anderson, J. R., Holleran, S. A., Irving, L. M., Sigmon, S. T., . . . Harney, P. (1991). The will and the ways: Development and validation of an individual-differences measure of hope. *Journal of Personality and Social Psychology, 60*(4), 570–585.

Snyder, C. R., & Higgins, R. L. (1988). Excuses: Their effective role in the negotiation of reality. *Psychological Bulletin, 104*(1), 23–35.

Snyder, C. R., McDermott, D., Cook, W., & Rapoff, M. (1997). *Hope for the journey: Helping children through the good times and the bad.* Boulder, CO: Westview.

Snyder, C. R., Rand, K. L., King, E. A., Feldman, D. B., & Taylor, J. D. (2002). "False" hope. *Journal of Clinical Psychology, 58*, 1003–1022.

Weis, R., & Speridakos, E. C. (2011). A meta-analysis of hope enhancement strategies in clinical and community settings. *Psychology of Well-Being: Theory, Research and Practice, 1*, 1–16.

World Health Organization, & UNICEF. (2008, December 9). World report on child injury prevention. Retrieved from http://whqlibdoc.who.int.libproxy.lib.unc.edu/publications/2008/9789241563574_eng.pdf

Zachrisson, H. D., Rodje, K., & Mykletun, A. (2006). Utilization of health services in relation to mental health problems in adolescents: Population based survey. *BMC Public Health, 6*, 1–7.

Zimbardo, P. G. (2004). Does psychology make a significant difference in our lives?. *American Psychologist, 59*(5), 339–351.

INDEX

Page references for figures are indicated by *f,* for tables by *t,* and for boxes by *b*